CHUCK NOLL

CHUCK NOLL
HIS LIFE'S WORK

✦　　✦　　✦

MICHAEL MacCAMBRIDGE

University of Pittsburgh Press

Published by the University of Pittsburgh Press, Pittsburgh, Pa., 15260

Copyright © 2016, University of Pittsburgh Press

All rights reserved

Manufactured in the United States of America

Printed on acid-free paper

10 9 8 7 6 5 4 3

ISBN 13: 978-0-8229-4468-3

ISBN 10: 0-8229-4468-5

Cataloging-in-Publication data is available from the Library of Congress

Cover design by Joel W. Coggins

Cover photo by Walter Iooss Jr. / *Sports Illustrated* / Getty Images

For my sister,
Angie MacCambridge Szentgyorgyi

CONTENTS

✦   ✦   ✦

And in a world we understood early to be characterized by venality and doubt and paralyzing ambiguities, he suggested another world, one which may or may not have existed ever but in any case existed no more: a place where a man could move free, could make his own code and live by it; a world in which, if a man did what he had to do, he could one day take the girl and go riding through the draw and find himself home free.

JOAN DIDION

PROLOGUE

✦ ✦ ✦

From the sidelines, through the maze of bodies, he could see it developing—the initial misdirection, Harris taking a step to his left, turning completely around and now heading right; Mullins setting back in a pass-blocking stance, then releasing to lead interference; Harris accepting the ball from Bradshaw and sliding into the vacated outside hole, beginning to rumble as his blockers cleared the way. By the time the exhausted Vikings, defenders dragged him down, he'd gained 15 yards, the Steelers had another first down, and the final result was no longer remotely in doubt.

As the lights cast an ethereal glow through the frigid gloom of the New Orleans twilight, and the scoreboard clock worked its way toward :00 in the heavy Louisiana air, Super Bowl IX neared its conclusion, and the Pittsburgh Steelers stood on the verge of becoming world champions. The season's work was nearly complete.

It was in these moments, with the end of the quest imminent, when Chuck Noll often would feel the emptiest.

All the shared effort and focus that Noll had mustered throughout the long season was bound up in that moment and then, after the inevitable diminution of time, it was all over. He was left then with nothing but the formalities—the handshakes and mere words that could never do justice to the things he felt. For a time, he held the melancholy and hollowness at bay, in the negative space where the sense of purpose had thrived for months. It all remained on the inside, where he kept his deepest feelings —unshared, unremarked upon, often unexamined.

On the outside, where his football players were whooping and hollering, there was only a sublime, sincere expression of joy in that moment of complete triumph. Noll often seemed impervious to these common sentiments, but in this case he too was swept up in the tide, grinning as his players hoisted him on their shoulders.

Yet even in this instant of complete victory, the head coach of the Pittsburgh Steelers enjoyed but did not exult. Five years earlier in the same stadium, Hank Stram had triumphantly waved the rolled-up sheets of his game plan while being carried off the field by his Chiefs; two years earlier, following Super Bowl VII in Los Angeles, Don Shula had rejoiced on the shoulders of his Miami Dolphins, raising a pair of fists skyward at the completion of a perfect season.

But on January 12, 1975, there would be no such indelible image. Noll, ever the pragmatist, simply used his arms to steady himself on the shoulders of Franco Harris and the helmetless, beaming Joe Greene as they carried him across the field on his brief victory ride. He appeared delighted but composed, keenly aware that the trip he was taking was a fleeting one.

He was back on his feet by the time they reached the tunnel, heading to the bowels of the decrepit Tulane Stadium. Inside the visitors' dressing room, with its long wooden benches and low-slung ceilings, there was a cacophony of noise and sweat and deadline journalism, with a mob of cameramen, reporters, league executives, team employees, and interlopers standing amid the oversized men reveling in the greatest moment of their sporting lives.

In sports, all championships carry an air of redemption. But this one went beyond that. More than forty years after they'd entered the league, the Steelers had finally won their first NFL title. There was a deep, primal release from decades of frustration for the city of Pittsburgh and the team. Players were crying tears of joy, coaches were hugging, others in the room were shouting exhortations.

In the midst of all that revelry, Chuck Noll, the head coach of the Steelers, did none of those things. He smiled, exchanged congratulations, and shook hands.

Grasping Terry Bradshaw's hand, he said, "Congratulations, we did it."

"Congratulations, Andy," he told the veteran linebacker Andy Russell, shaking his hand. "This is why we do the hard work."

Then he shook Frenchy Fuqua's hand, and said, "Congratulations, we did it."

NFL Commissioner Pete Rozelle entered, and then everyone in the room focused on the owner and team patriarch, the white-haired Art Rooney, "The Chief," he of the thick glasses, jaunty Ascot, and outsized cigars. It was only after Rozelle presented the Lombardi Trophy to Rooney, and after Franco Harris was awarded the game's most valuable player award, that Noll was cornered in the locker room by NBC broadcaster Charlie Jones and asked on national television about his thoughts on the occasion of finally attaining the greatest goal in professional football. How, asked Jones, were Noll and his players going to celebrate this achievement?

"I think we're going to enjoy it for just a short time, and then get on to next year."

It took Jones another instant to realize that Noll's brief answer was complete.

"And then be ready for next season . . . already?," Jones prompted.

"That's right, it comes around fast."

Even then—perhaps most especially then—Chuck Noll was cognizant that success was not a fixed point but an ongoing state of mind, a series of habits and commitments. He'd made a life out of setting them and honoring them. He wouldn't stop now.

More than two hours later, after he'd extended dozens more congratulations to players and staff, and faced the gauntlet of television, radio and print interviews, he made his way back to his suite at the Fontainebleau Hotel.

His wife Marianne, wearing her lucky Steelers' bracelet, had been sitting on the sofa, still reveling in the thrill—thinking about how much it meant to Chuck, the assistants and the players, and how this game would change all of their lives—when she heard the key in the door. She stood up, beaming broadly and held her arms out as he walked in the room.

And as he approached her, he extended his right hand, shook hers firmly and said, "Congratulations. We did it."

Years later, Noll's detractors would cite this scene—a coach celebrating the culmination of his greatest victory by offering a perfunctory, congratulatory handshake to his own wife—as proof of his bloodless personality and his inability to relate to the people nearest to him.

And, just as forcefully, Marianne Noll would maintain that the proffered handshake from her soul mate was just one more inside joke—"We both were laughing at the time," she said—as well as further proof, perhaps, that you had to know Chuck.

Then again, perhaps no one else did.

✦   ✦   ✦

Vince Lombardi's name is on the Super Bowl trophy that is presented to the National Football League champion each year, and he remains the standard by which all football coaches are judged.

Chuck Noll won twice as many Super Bowls as Lombardi and presided over arguably the greatest dynasty in football history. But he never found the place in the public imagination that Lombardi and others did. No one was making Broadway plays about the life of Chuck Noll. He didn't wear a trademark fedora, and his statue was not outside any stadiums. He didn't open a chain of steakhouses upon retiring or wind up as the centerpiece of a recurring *Saturday Night Live* sketch. In the pantheon of great coaches whose names might be invoked by writers or announcers, he was infrequently mentioned.

Part of it was that Noll didn't strive to be known, didn't give much of himself away. The writer Roy Blount Jr., who spent the entire 1973 season with the Steelers and produced numerous intimate portraits in his classic *About Three Bricks Shy of a Load*, concluded at the end of six months spent in close quarters with Noll that the man was "opaque." Others wondered how the leader of such a diverse group of men could be so ostensibly bland himself. "No burning zeal is evident," wrote Dave Brady of the *Washington Post*. "There is hardly an identifying mannerism."

This was not solely the impression of outsiders.

"I worked there thirteen years, and I know nothing about him," said the defensive end L. C. Greenwood. "The only time I went into his office was when he cut me."

But the measure of his impact on his team and pro football was simple and ineluctable: In the nearly four decades of the team's existence before Noll was hired, the Pittsburgh Steelers were the least successful franchise in professional football, never winning so much as a division title; in the nearly five decades since his arrival in Pittsburgh, they became the most successful franchise in the sport, winning six Super Bowls, eight American Football Conference championships, twenty-one division titles, and twenty-nine playoff berths.

Noll surely didn't do it alone, but he was the catalyst, the man who drew a line under everything that had gone before and set the tone—over his twenty-three seasons as head coach of the Steelers and beyond—for everything that would follow.

"Losing," he said on his first day on the job, "has nothing to do with geography." Yet in Noll's era, the people of Pittsburgh came to believe that winning *did*. The success the Steelers enjoyed became a vital part of the city's history and sense of itself. Undoubtedly, the combination of his reserved nature and the dissonant circumstances of the Steelers' rise—the team became dominant at the very point at which the steel economy in western Pennsylvania began to crumble—added a measure of poignancy. One could not tell the story of the Pittsburgh renaissance that came after without discussing what Noll's teams meant to the people of the region. The man Pittsburghers could never fully know helped them see themselves better. They weren't victims. They were resilient. They were, in a real sense, a reflection of the football team.

That Steelers dynasty of the '70s—with its thick, rollicking mix of black players and white, street smart and country strong, devout and profane—was molded into a cohesive unit by the will of one man. Along the way, every one of the team's players, in one way or another, subjugated themselves for the greater good of the team.

Jack Ham, the Steelers' Hall of Fame linebacker, was once asked how such a diverse, seemingly disconsonant group of people could set aside their considerable differences and find common cause.

"Chuck Noll," he said. "We all became clones of Chuck Noll."

✦ ✦ ✦

Noll was "square" in every respect of the word. Physically, he possessed a resolute, formidable blockiness, a solid foundation that seemed to extend from his feet all the way up to his neck. Socially, he was a straight arrow, a regular communicant who never experimented with drugs, rarely drank anything stronger than beer or wine, kept his hair trimmed short, wore his clothes conservatively, and remained—by every account—scrupulously faithful to his wife during their fifty-seven years of marriage. In sensibilities, he was square: He preferred nonfiction over fiction, facts over interpretation, knowledge over philosophy. Finally, he was square in a behavioral sense—strict, honest, with a clearly defined sense of right and wrong, and a demeanor that remained calm in the face of adversity. "We never saw him crack," Joe Greene once said. "He was a solid block."

On the sidelines, Noll cut a stolid, mostly nondescript figure. Burly without being stout, he had brownish-blond hair and a handsome, chiseled face that softened over the years. His countenance betrayed little information beyond seriousness of purpose.

At a time when many football coaches were sartorially daring, wearing suits and ties, snap-brim hats and tailored vests, Noll preferred a fashion statement that seemed to make no statement at all: black windbreakers, collared sports polos, off-the-rack slacks. It was tempting to look at the understated personality, the underwhelming clothes, and determine that Noll *himself* was colorless and humorless. And he was secure enough with himself to not be troubled by people reaching such a conclusion.

His press conferences were notoriously uninformative, not because he wasn't articulate or had little to say but because he viewed all information about his team as potentially damaging, a subtle edge for opponents. "Chuck Noll was at the top of his game yesterday," wrote a beat writer in 1974. "He held an informal meeting with a handful of sports writers and his answers to four of the first six questions were 'I don't know.'" The week of one of the Super Bowls, a sheet was distributed in the media room titled "Highlights of Chuck Noll Press Conference." The rest of the page was left blank.

Yet he possessed confidence in his abilities and a calm assurance that he knew what he needed to know. This sense of certainty often alienated writers, who were intimidated by it, and players who were intimidated by Noll himself.

For Noll, the game was not a metaphor or a mystery or a test of manhood. It was a matter of simple execution, of blocking and tackling and an adherence to the fundamentals of the game. There were few of the loud exhortations of other coaches, no fiery inspirational speeches before taking the field. "I am not a motivator," he said. "I do not holler or pound on the table. We [he and his assistants] are just choosers and teachers. We try to choose self-motivators and then teach them." These techniques were instilled, refined, and emphasized tirelessly to his team. Roy Blount Jr. joked about it, "I can just see the movie ads for *The Chuck Noll Story* now: 'He came out of Cleveland, well schooled in techniques!'"

The view then became common that Noll was merely a facilitator, a basic coach who lucked into one of the greatest assemblages of talent in pro football history. The players from that team are still recalled in romantic detail—Joe Greene and Franco Harris, Terry Bradshaw and the Steel Curtain, Lynn Swann and John Stallworth all became part of pro football lore. Noll, in turn, was not forgotten, exactly. But neither was he celebrated. As his friend and University of Dayton teammate Pat Maloney once put it, "Well, I guess Chuck is famous, but not *real* famous. You know what I mean? And just to his area. You know what I mean? Right around Pittsburgh. And Dayton."

✦　　✦　　✦

So it was by equal parts design and circumstance that one of the most successful coaches in football history was so little known.

Part of the challenge was the degree to which Noll seemed removed from the monomaniacal rhetoric of football coaching. At a time when one of his contemporaries, George Allen, was famous for statements such as, "I demand of my men that they give 110 percent," Noll was pointedly rational. Football was a love but not his lodestar. He had adopted from Paul Brown, his own coach in the pros, the belief that football was something for a man to play before he found "his life's work." He repeated that mantra to his players hundreds of times during his tenure in Pittsburgh.

He also had a wealth of interests outside the game. No Super Bowl–winning coach had as many dimensions; at various times during his twenty-three years coaching the Steelers, it became known that Noll had earned a pilot's license to fly small aircraft, could skipper a forty-two-foot yacht, was a connoisseur of wines who'd experimented with homemade vintages, was an audiophile and a gourmet chef, and an aficionado of classical music who once enjoyed a stint as a guest conductor of the Pittsburgh Symphony Orchestra. Yet he could be maddeningly obtuse when questioned about any of these outside interests. When the writer Peter King first interviewed Noll, in 1984, he asked about the coach's well-known regard for wines. Noll stared back at him and said, "I have no idea what you're talking about."

There were, in the end, no easy paths to get to precisely who Chuck Noll was, though he himself suggested the most obvious approach during his retirement press conference in 1991, after completing his final season coaching the Steelers. "Obviously, you'd like everything to be smooth, but termination is not easy," he said. "It's not usually smooth. I heard somebody tell me poet Ralph Waldo Emerson probably put it best when he said, 'Your actions speak so loudly, I can't hear what you're saying,' and I'd like to keep it that way."

And through his retirement, he succeeded in doing just that. He disappeared like Johnny Carson, courting no attention following his celebrated career, rarely appearing in public. Through the 1990s and 2000s, he'd occasionally show up at a dedication or a Steelers' game or a card signing, but even then he remained a cordial, largely distant figure.

Because of this, Noll remains an elusive enigma. Though his players' lives were profoundly shaped by their time with him, and while their gratitude ran deep, they couldn't escape the fact that they didn't really *know* their coach nor fully understand how he'd gotten that way. Hall of Famer John Stallworth spoke often of Noll being a father figure, but he also conceded that in the four decades of their association, they never had a conversation that lasted longer than five minutes.

"The bottom line on Chaz," said running back Frenchy Fuqua, evoking the nickname that many players used, "Chuck Noll, if he's in the room, no one, I think, from the Steelers really got to know him, nor truly understand anything but his teaching."

"I was very uncomfortable talking with him," said trainer Ralph Berlin, who worked side by side with Noll for more than two decades. "If you said what a beautiful day it is, you better be ready to defend *why* it is a beautiful day, or if you want to say you went to dinner at some restaurant, and had this for dinner, and how great it was, you better be able to tell him why. So, from that standpoint, I don't know that I ever really was entirely comfortable with him."

The distance created a mystique, and Noll's sometimes imperious manner—combined with his success and the complete authority he held over football operations for nearly the entirety of his tenure—created the image of someone who was infallible and omnicompetent. To many of those who played for him, the myth became the fact.

"I heard this story once," said Ron Johnson, cornerback on Noll's last two Super Bowl teams. "I heard that his wife had prepared some kind of meal for him, and Chuck looked at it, and it wasn't how he wanted, and he cooked his own dinner—he cooked the same thing all over again! He cooked his own dinner his own way, and I said to myself, you know— *I can see Chuck doing that.*"

✦ ✦ ✦

Back home, however, there was no mystery, no myth, no mystique. The intensely private man in the relentlessly public job took refuge in his family. He didn't merely have a loyal wife; he also had a best friend. And the timeless, abiding relationship between Chuck and Marianne Noll offered the best clues to who he truly was.

The dutiful, self-serious scholar, handsome but too shy to date regularly in high school, and bashful into his college days, found a life partner with whom he had a deep, unspoken connection. The man who'd fought hardship, poverty, and formidable health obstacles earlier in his life found sanctuary in the arms of a woman who saw him for exactly who he was.

With her manner of sweet steel, she protected him through the decades, cherished the strength and shelter he gave her, and stood by him when he grew ill. And he repaid her with his devotion, his companionship, and one last solemn promise, made on a tearful afternoon in 2005.

Even those closest to Chuck Noll maintained that Marianne was the only one who truly knew him. So, in the end, his life—and perhaps his life's work—made the most sense as a love story.

CHUCK NOLL

one

"WE WERE A VERY CLOSE FAMILY"

✦ ✦ ✦

On the morning of June 27, 1917, William Noll and Kate Steigerwald, along with their numerous friends and seemingly innumerable relations, gathered where they always gathered, at the Holy Trinity Catholic Church on Cleveland's East Side. The wedding mass had been short, and the emotions banked, as was the custom of both families—though some were sure they saw one or two of Kate's twelve younger siblings with brimming eyes upon hearing her declare her vows. The union was blessed, and then, as William and Kate emerged from the dark solemnity of the sanctuary, out into the brilliant light of the Cleveland morning, they were greeted with cheers and applause and a shower of rice.

Kate was beautiful and self-conscious, still not entirely comfortable in the fine heels she was wearing for the occasion. Out in the light, seeing the swirl of faces, she lifted her hand to wave—and stumbled, nearly tumbling awkwardly down the cement stairs. William, deft and casually gallant, caught her by her slender waist and helped her back to her feet, and everyone laughed. He smiled, they embraced again, and the wedding party all applauded.

1

It was only years later, after all that would follow, that anyone wondered if those first minutes of married life for William and Katherine Noll had carried some kind of omen. By the time their youngest son, Charles Henry Noll, arrived fifteen years later, so many things had gone wrong.

✦   ✦   ✦

It wasn't easy being an American of German descent in 1917, as the United States was entering the Great War, and it wouldn't get easier in the decades ahead. But William Noll belonged to a family of strivers possessed of an indefatigable work ethic and an unsentimental resolve. The Nolls had made their way across the Atlantic from Frankfurt in 1880, and they soon settled in Cleveland.

William's parents, Carl "Charles" Damasus Noll and Katherina Odenwald, married in 1881, and set about finding a place in the dense ethnic polyglot of nineteenth-century Cleveland. Charles Noll found work quickly as a mason laborer and discovered early that working harder and longer solved most language barriers.

By 1883, working as an independent contractor, he'd fashioned a life on the pillars of faith, family, and unremitting hard work. A Catholic with a bushy mustache and a zest for churches, he'd built the Holy Trinity Parish in Avon, twenty miles west of Cleveland. For two years during the construction, Charles rode a horse and wagon into Avon and worked ten hours a day, six days a week to finish the church in 1900. He kept up that pace for most of his life, until 1925; working on a job through a driving rainstorm, ignoring his own hacking coughs and increasingly short breaths, he contracted pneumonia and died.

By then, his son William Valentine Noll, the fifth of his eight children, was happily married and already the father of two. He was cheerful and industrious, with a long, elastic face and a broad smile, beaming eyes setting off his fair complexion and blond hair. The Nolls were a musical family, and William grew up singing with his brothers, often around a keg at the spirited family gatherings. William had quit school after sixth grade to help his father finish another project.

But it was at the other Holy Trinity, the church at 72nd and Woodland Avenue in Cleveland, where William's social life was centered. It was here at a church social where he first encountered the comely, self-possessed Kate Steigerwald—she had a soft smile, her chestnut hair up in a delicate bun. He courted her with the same air of determination his family brought to all its enterprises.

The Steigerwalds had a similar story of assimilation. Kate's own father, Henry Steigerwald, was just thirteen when he came to America from Aschaffenburg, Germany, along with his brother and father, in 1880. They eventually settled in a house at 7215 Montgomery on the East Side of Cleveland, in an area thick with factories, just a few blocks from Holy Trinity, a magnet for the growing German American community, especially the working-class immigrants who hadn't yet been able to afford a house in Shaker Heights (known as "Mortgage Hill" by the locals) where the more affluent citizens attended the Our Lady of Peace parish.

Over the long months supervising the building of the house on Montgomery, Henry Steigerwald took a liking to the demure maid who worked for the family in the handsome house across the street. Her name was Mary Fox, and she had been born in Cleveland to German immigrants (they'd changed their name from Fuchs shortly after they became familiar with American vernacular profanity). Mary's father, like many newcomers to the American land, was adamant about loyalties. "Nobody speaks German!," he declared to his children. "We are in America, and we're American!"

Henry and Mary wed in 1891. He would spend much of his professional career on the maintenance staff of the Cleveland Railroad Company and its successor, the Cleveland Transit System. The Steigerwalds' first child, Katherine, was born on a spring day in 1892. By the time she finished grammar school, after sixth grade in 1904, she already had six younger siblings. There would be six more born by 1915, when baby Coletta came. By then, everyone called her Kate.

William Noll was smitten with Kate Steigerwald. While courting her, he loved gathering friends around and serenading her with "K-K-Katy," the Billy Murray hit written by Geoffrey O'Hara.

> K-K-K-Katy, beautiful Katy,
> You're the only g-g-g-girl that I adore;
> When the m-m-m-moon shines,
> Over the cowshed,
> I'll be waiting at the k-k-k-kitchen door

She blushed and thought it all foolishness. But she was keen on him, found his calm manner a nice counterpart to her more temperamental personality, and was ready to dispense with the burden of being the oldest of the thirteen Steigerwald children. When he proposed, she said she'd devote her life to him.

✦   ✦   ✦

William had registered for the draft the same month he was married and entered service a year later, in May 1918. It pained him to leave, especially in the bloom of early matrimony. He was stationed at Camp Gordon, outside of Atlanta, but spent the balance of the war there, never assigned to a unit that would see action. He was honorably discharged on New Year's Day in 1919.

They didn't have money to buy, so they rented, lived with relatives, and prepared to start a family. Their first son, Robert, was born in 1920. William had worked at a butcher shop before the war, but he became convinced he needed to pursue different work in the changing world of 1920s Cleveland. He bought an automobile repair manual, read it cover to cover, spent some time working on a relative's car, and went out applying for jobs. By the time their second child, Rita, was born in June 1924, William was working as the head mechanic at the National Oil Refinery Company.

Kate had been present at several of her mother's deliveries, had burped babies, changed diapers, helped pull out teeth and given haircuts, and cooked and cleaned and ironed and canned. So she knew all about child-rearing.

"She was strict and she flew off the handle easy," said Rita. "But she was always loving afterwards. I mean, we got punished immediately and then it was forgotten; she never held anything over us."

As the homemaker, Kate did her wash on Monday, her ironing on Tuesday, her trips to the market on Wednesday. Active around the home, she was often prone to fits of redecoration—moving furniture around to suit her whims, from the family dinner table to the handmade desk that Bill had made before the war. Saturday mornings were spent baking, and the kitchen was filled with the smell of fruit-filled German kuchen cakes that were her specialty.

But the love that Kate held for their children was never articulated.

"You knew it because of the things she did for you," said Rita. "I don't think the vocal part."

In the spring of 1928, William and Kate had their third baby, Beatrice. As with the others, she delivered at home. But the birth was breach, with gruesome complications, exacerbated by a nervous young doctor performing the delivery. Beatrice broke both arms and her skull during the delivery. A day later, William lifted young Rita up to the edge of the crib, to look at the baby's dark eyes and hair.

Two days after her birth, Beatrice Noll was dead. Money was tight, so they buried her with Kate's aunt Franny, who had died the same week. Quiet grief compacted into a single ceremony, and then barely another word ever about Beatrice. This was, already, the Noll family way.

"No, I mean, she never talked about it, my mother," said Rita.

William and Kate were still grieving the loss of baby Beatrice a year later, when the stock market crashed. He didn't immediately understand the implications, but he would soon enough. The effects of the Depression were felt throughout the family. Houses were lost, businesses shuttered, families that had been on their own moving in with relatives, heading back to the farm, or simply vanishing for months at a time. Soon his mother, the widowed Katherine, moved in with William and Kate. They soldiered on.

When Kate found out she was pregnant again, in the late summer of 1931, she vowed to have the child in a hospital this time. She was just a few months shy of her fortieth birthday when she delivered the healthy baby boy, Charles Henry Noll, on January 5, 1932, at St. Ann's, a maternity hospital close to their home. He weighed 11 pounds, 11 ounces and was surprisingly strong—laying on his stomach when he received his first shot, the baby lifted his head up toward the doctor administering the inoculation.

But despite the joy of the healthy addition, and sister Rita's mooning over baby Charles, the litany of losses continued. William's mother died of cancer in 1933. After bouncing around to different rental homes, they moved in with Kate's parents, the Steigerwalds, back in the house that Henry Steigerwald had built on Montgomery Avenue, a broad, deep unit with two stories and plenty of room, with a garage in the back.

From there, they had a front-row view of the Depression. Heavy industry was taking a hit, and many of the shift workers lost hours or jobs altogether. To make money, one of William's in-laws would buy a dozen eggs, then go door-to-door selling individual eggs, since many people in the neighborhood couldn't afford an entire carton. Rita would recall her father coming home on more than one night and telling Kate, "I still have my job—but I had to take another pay cut."

✦ ✦ ✦

This was the world in which William and Kate's youngest child grew up.

He was bright, willful, energetic, strong, and precocious. He had the same light hair and blue eyes as his sister, Rita, both of them favoring their father.

From a very early age, he was known as Chuck. "Don't call me Charlie!," he'd shout whenever addressed by that name. "That's the name of a horse!"

He spent most of his free time out of doors, playing stickball or football in the streets—a friend remembered him running into a car while trying to catch a pass, and dashing home in tears, only to emerge a few minutes later, eyes dried, ready to continue. Inside, he was intent, even studious, concentrating for extended periods on maps, books, and the sports pages of Cleveland newspapers.

Kate had been fetching in her teens, but the rigors of raising three children and losing another in infancy had worn on her, as both her body and her dreams settled into middle age. She was not one to dote, but it was clear she fancied her youngest son. He was speaking more quickly than his siblings had and possessed an innate fearlessness. At age three or four, he befriended a pair of twins who lived across the street. After playing on the sidewalk in front of the house one day, the three of them disappeared. A frantic Kate organized a neighborhood search before the boys reappeared, about an hour later. "The three of them came walking home and were like, 'What were you worried about?'" said Rita. "They took a walk around all these blocks without telling anybody."

For the Catholic German Americans on the East Side of Cleveland, all roads led to Holy Trinity. The parish had been a part of William and Kate's life even before they knew each other. Established in the spring of 1880 for the burgeoning population of German Catholics who'd come to Cleveland, it was the institution that bound people not only religiously but also socially. The Nolls began attending almost as soon as they arrived in the city. The Steigerwalds also gravitated to the church, where the Ursuline Sisters had been teaching at the grammar school since the early 1890s.

The church was dramatic in appearance, with its three arched doorways beneath two forbidding towers and the long expanse of fourteen cement steps that set the building back from the bustle of streetcars and horses and automobiles on Woodland Avenue. It was in that building that Rita was baptized and the funeral mass was given four years later for Beatrice.

Chuck was five years old in the summer of 1937 when, greeting Father Joseph Trapp outside after mass, he implored the priest to let him enter the first grade that fall. Trapp pondered the idea for a moment and then told Kate Noll, "Oh, bring him in. If we have to, we'll keep him back a year." That September, Chuck—nearly a year younger than many of his classmates—began his first-grade studies at Holy Trinity. Discussing it later, he would say, "I couldn't wait any longer."

The boxy school next door to the church was much more functional, with a vacant lot on the side where the children played during recesses. Chuck's preternatural maturity and gift for recall soon became apparent. The family doctor had been alarmed at first by his natural left-handedness, but Kate told the nuns to let him write whichever way he wanted to. Eventually, he started writing with both hands.

It was an athletic family. The Nolls played baseball; many of the Steigerwalds—even the women—were adept at basketball. The family would often spend weekend Saturdays at Lewis Park, where William and his brothers played baseball in a recreational league. He was also an avid bowler, who recruited Rita for his mixed league because Kate disliked the sport. What Chuck's cousins would remember was his older brother Bob being the athlete of the family. "We would have family reunions, and we'd play the single guys against the married guys, and Bobby just dominated the thing," said cousin Ed Steigerwald. "So as I grew up, I didn't realize Chuck was the athlete."

There were signs. Chuck was preternaturally strong, wrestling against his cousins at family gatherings, showing surprising speed for someone his size, and excelling at an early age at football, basketball, and baseball.

The Nolls celebrated St. Nicholas day each December 9, with fruit and nuts on the tree, and typically exchanged gifts at the Steigerwald house on Christmas Eve. The children would have to sing a song or recite a poem to receive a single, token gift—the boys often got a ball, the girls would sometimes receive paper dolls.

By 1940, they'd grown accustomed to the Steigerwald house. Looking back on this time in his life, Chuck once said, "It wasn't like we didn't have food on the table. But we had to live with our grandparents."

At the time, there was little talk about the Germans and what was happening in Germany. "Nobody talked about the old country," said a family friend. "See, a lot of these people were born in America." Even less of it went on at the Noll dinner table. "My parents weren't that political," said Rita. "So we didn't discuss it much." This was the family way, observed over deaths, illnesses, conflicts, and anything else unseemly or unpleasant.

As the war in Europe expanded and American debated whether to get involved, William Noll's ordeal began. By 1941, he was transferred to the National Oil Refinery's plant 120 miles west of Cleveland in Findlay, Ohio. The family joined him, though Bob stayed back, working at a pickle factory (though shortly after the Pearl Harbor invasion he would find himself in the military). In Findlay, Chuck enrolled in a Catholic school, but the family never did get settled. Within months, National folded part of its operations, and William took a job with the Findlay-based Ohio Oil Company, only to be transferred again, to one of the Ohio Oil Company's plants in Robinson, Illinois.

Robinson in 1941 was a forbidding city for outsiders, which meant virtually anyone other than white Anglo-Saxon Protestants. At the edge of the city limits, there was a sign advising any Negroes who were driving into town to keep driving and not stop.

In the first weeks there, Kate struck up a conversation with a citizen who asked her how she liked the town and where she was attending church. When Kate explained that she was Catholic, the woman turned on her heels and rapidly walked away. A single small parish served all of Crawford County and the thirty or so Catholic families therein. The parish priest, when he paid a visit to the Nolls' rental home in Robinson, apologized for not wearing a Roman collar. He explained that when he'd done so in public in the past, he'd been shot at.

The family and community ties that had been so much a part of their lives in Cleveland were nowhere to be found. Kate would come home from almost every marketing trip with a new indignity to report. Once, she asked a Robinson grocer if his store carried sour cream. "Certainly not," huffed the clerk. "All our cream is fresh!"

But most worrisome of all was William. His health had been declining —in recent years, a fluttering in the eyes had plagued him, and at times he suffered from uncontrollable blinking. By now, he was no longer fixing cars but working as a dispatcher.

Away from their family and community in Cleveland, the Nolls felt isolated, inert. They saw their way through a chilly spring of 1942, before Rita headed back to Cleveland the week following her high school graduation. There were no jobs in Robinson, and she knew she wouldn't want any even if there were. By August, with William's condition worsening, he gave his notice to the Ohio Oil Company, and they packed up and returned to Cleveland.

They moved back in with Henry and Mary Steigerwald for a couple of weeks before they found a rental home at 2521 East 81st Street. It was their fourth residence in less than a year. But after all the moving, and after never living in any place for more than three years, this would be the home in which Chuck would reside for the rest of his childhood.

The duplex was on the end of 81st Street, less than a block off of Woodland Avenue. The first-floor dwelling was tiny, wedged into a small corner lot next to Austrian Court, which ran between 79th and 82nd streets. There were three bedrooms, one for Bill and Kate, a smaller one for Chuck, and another, toward the front, for Rita. At night, Rita could hear the military representatives' dress shoes clicking up the walkway to drop off cables at 1 or 2 in the morning. As a mechanic in the Air Force, Bob was never in combat, but he had to fly in any plane he worked on.

The home was nestled in the midst of a dense cluster of German-Austrian immigrants, with an Italian neighborhood up Woodhill Road to the north, on the other side of Quincy Avenue; a Hungarian-Slovenian area to the east, straddling Buckeye Road; and plenty of Irish to the south and west, who gravitated to St. Edward's parish, on Woodland Avenue and 69th Street.

◆　◆　◆

Back in Cleveland, Chuck returned to Holy Trinity, beginning sixth grade in the fall of 1942. In the mornings, he walked to school, walking down to the corner of 81st Street and Woodland, where the newsboys were hawking papers on the corner—the *Plain Dealer*, the *News*, even the *Call & Post*, which served the growing African American community. There were two Greek beer joints on that block, and St. Joseph's Cemetery across the street. He would walk under the bridge that carried the B&O Rail Line, all the way down Woodland Avenue to 72nd street, gathering with his classmates on the two flights of cement steps that led up to the three arched doorways of Holy Trinity, below the statue of Jesus on the facade of the building's imposing stone exterior.

It was still a town of heavy industry. Chuck walked to school hearing factories hard at work, though many still waited until night to discreetly spew their most toxic exhaust; it wasn't uncommon to see a fine layer of soot on the cars he passed on his way to Holy Trinity each morning.

The school day began with 8 a.m. mass at the church, the students sitting together. What was inculcated in these years for Chuck was a thirst for knowledge—his test scores earned more approval from teachers and parents than his athletic achievements—and a respect for authority. The Ursuline nuns drilled the students daily in the rigorous application of penmanship and grammar, math and science, and Chuck proved particularly gifted. His memory was sharp and facile—he could hear a concept once and remember it. His mind was orderly, and he took a satisfaction from accruing facts.

But he was no one's idea of a bookworm. Football was his sporting love. He read about it in the pages of the *Cleveland Press* and *Cleveland Plain Dealer*. On Saturday mornings, he walked down to the Knickerbocker Theater on 65th Street for sports newsreels, cartoons, and serials. For first-run movies, he would go to the Sun, the Regent, or the Moreland Theater. It was one of those places where he and his friends had watched *Knute Rockne: All American* in 1940.

He played football every chance he could get. During the recesses at Holy Trinity, while the boys would throw around the football or play stickball and the girls mostly hung back and watched from near the side door to the school, Chuck developed a reputation as a clean player but spirited tackler.

"Chuck only wanted to do two things," said classmate Joe Devera. "He wanted to play football. And he wanted to play football for Notre Dame."

✦ ✦ ✦

One of Chuck's best friends was his classmate Ralph Yanky, a sweet-tempered, soft-spoken boy who'd gravitated to the same park and play areas where Chuck went. They had known each other before all the moves of 1941 and 1942, but now they lived about a hundred steps from each other, as Ralph's family lived on East 80th Street, a quick jaunt down Austrian Court between the two houses.

There was a matter-of-factness to Chuck that Ralph soon learned to appreciate. He was confident in knowledge, had the courage of his convictions. "He was a quiet individual, not rowdy," said Yanky. "He had good manners. Once he was your buddy, we were close, and he would do anything for you."

Once a basketball rim was mounted to the brick wall of the school, the boys would play even in the snow. From the playground, they occasionally could see the boxers from the Savoy Gym shadowboxing and jogging around the Woodland Cemetery across the street. Jimmy Bivins, who'd fought Jersey Joe Walcott, would sometimes acknowledge the boys when they called his name.

At lunchtime on school days, Chuck and Ralph would, along with most of the class, head quickly home. On the trips to and from school, Chuck would pass one of the Fisher Brothers Meat markets ("It's Fresher at Fishers!"), where, in the fall, the freshly killed deer would be hanging on a hook outside the store, waiting to be processed.

At Holy Trinity, school let out at 3:00. The boys would walk back to their homes, and in that afternoon light—from the end of school until about 6 p.m—they were almost always outside. "We would pal around, play tag, play football in the street and baseball," said Yanky. "And we were busy. We were trying to cram everything into a couple of hours."

Chuck and Ralph and the other neighbor boys played stickball on the red-brick streets of 81st Street, hitting mostly grounders, taking care not to put anyone's car window out.

On weekends, they often rode the streetcar to Shaker Heights. They would go fishing in one of the twin lakes. In the winter, they often went with friends to go ice fishing. One day, the snow was on the banks and Chuck was confident the ice was thick enough. But when he started chipping away at it, to cut a hole to fish through, the ice broke and he fell in. Sputtering and clawing at the slippery surface, he reached up for help.

Another boy held Ralph by his ankles as he laid out on the ice toward the crevice where Chuck had fallen in. After they extricated him from the icy water, they bundled him in their coats and trudged back to the streetcar and home. But he'd already learned his lesson years earlier, the day he'd come running into the house in tears after playing street football. Chuck simply went into his room and changed, and never mentioned to his family what had happened.

While the ethnic enclaves largely defined the neighborhoods of Cleveland's East Side, there was another reality impinging on those housing patterns by the early 1940s. The neighborhood was changing, as the coded euphemism of the era put it. By the '30s, the number of black people moving from the Mississippi Delta up to the industrial belt cities of the Midwest had grown significantly. There had been 10,000 African Americans in Cleveland at the beginning of the First World War, but the number had grown to 85,000 by the start of the Second World War. In many of the ethnic communities, they found a harsh bigotry, different from the rural South but, in some cases, no less toxic.

For Chuck and his friends, though, the situation was more complex. Shortly after the Nolls moved to 81st Street, the homeowners they rented from sold to an African American family named the Louises, who moved in upstairs. "My mother and Mrs. Louis used to get together with recipes and stuff like that," said Rita.

The white flight to the suburbs that would be seen decades later wasn't really an option for many of the factory workers and wage laborers on the East Side. But for many of the African Americans in Cleveland, they were in the community but not of it. Black people were essentially excluded from the Catholic schools; most in the neighborhood went to East Technical High School.

One day, Chuck and Ralph were out in the neighborhood when they met an African American boy whom they recognized. "We're looking for players for a football team," he told them. "We got a real good coach, and they're going to get us uniforms."

He told them to meet up by the coach's house, and on that day in 1942, Chuck and Ralph walked up to 83rd Street. On a trim, tidy porch, a black man with neatly cropped hair, a broad nose, and an even broader smile introduced himself to Chuck and Ralph. He was Russ Alexander, about thirty years old, active in the Cleveland youth sports field. (Alexander would later become the first black coach in the Cleveland School District, taking over as track and field and football coach at Central High.)

Alexander asked the boys if they'd be able to get free for practices once a week and play games on the weekend. They eagerly responded that they could, and Alexander tousled Ralph's hair and said, "We will teach you guys how to play football."

The team was known as the Clippers, and the one picture that remains shows a team of twenty-four players in which twelve of the boys are black and twelve are white. (Among Chuck's teammates was Burrell Shields, who would later attend East Technical High School and go on to a career in the NFL.)

Farther up Woodland, there was a Nabisco factory next to a field. The Clippers practiced and played their games there. Alexander would line them up before practices and have them walk across the field, picking up any rocks or stray pieces of glass they spied.

The boys were disparate in size and aptitude but unified in their love of the rituals of the game. Chuck's first pair of shoulder pads were bulky, his leather helmet ill-fitting. But as he buckled the strap and learned the rudiments of the three-point stance, he soon developed an ability to take off quickly at the snap of the ball.

Alexander taught him the first lesson of line play—the fundamental piece of wisdom about leverage that could be distilled to "low man wins." Chuck soon realized that if he sprung from his stance at a lower angle, and engaged his opponent underneath the other boy's shoulder pads, driving into him with the power of his sturdy legs, he could often hold his own or even outmuscle larger, stronger boys.

The integrated nature of the team was obvious, but Alexander and his assistant, a white coach, said nothing about it specifically. Alexander did tell his team before one practice, "I play no favorites, and you progress as you show me you can, and do the best you can." Among the boys, too young to have absorbed the most virulent strains of racism, there was only the shared purpose of a sporting achievement.

At home, Chuck practiced his stances, mimicking the calisthenics that the Clippers performed before practices. There weren't many games, but they took on an outsized importance in his life.

"We were lucky we had any helmets," Yanky said. "I don't know where

Coach Alexander got these. Our thigh pads were like down on your knees. But we loved it. And Coach Alexander was one of the nicest people that I think I ever met."

The Clippers ran out of a single wing, with a back named Richard Floyd leading the way, and teammate Harold Owens (reputed to be a nephew of the Olympic hero Jesse Owens) also a frequent ballcarrier. The crowds were not large: kids from the neighborhood would stop by, along with a smattering of parents.

Chuck and Ralph would play for the team for just that one year, but it would leave an impression on Chuck for the rest of his life. And he would not soon forget the lessons of that first team. As an adult, in an office adorned with hardly any personal mementos, he saved the team picture of the Clippers in his desk drawer for decades.

✦　✦　✦

Kate Noll worried. At times, her statue of St. Joseph, which usually faced inward to oversee the family, was pointed toward the corner, facing outside of the house to the daunting world at war. "Whenever St. Joseph was pointed to the corner," said one of Chuck's cousins, "we knew something was wrong."

She fretted about the neighborhood, she worried about money, but mostly Kate Noll worried about the illness of her husband. William had possessed an almost boundless zest when she'd met him, both goofy and sweet, but she'd seen him weakened when he returned from the military.

At first he thought it was nerves and the stress of trying to provide for his family, but there was a physical component to his anxiety. His hands, once strong and steady, were now tentative and shaky. His eyes bedeviled him. He couldn't control his blinking, and doctors were at a loss to find a treatment (one suggested a surgery pulling his eyelids up so that his eyes would remain permanently open).

He wondered occasionally about his experience during the war. Though he hadn't seen any action, he had taken part in some Army medical testing. And he complained often since then that he—and some of the other vets he knew—didn't feel quite right. Back in Cleveland, he tried to go back to work at a butcher shop but the knife work was too hazardous, his hands and eyes unsteady. He came home to recuperate and spent most of his time lying on the couch in the parlor, listening to Indians' baseball games on WBK radio. Rita was the only one in the family working, until Kate went back and started working part time at a florist's shop.

By 1944, William had stopped playing baseball and didn't sing as much as he used to. He was able to do less and less and then, for a time, nothing at all. He would ask Kate or the children to draw the drapes and turn off the lights. The tight grimace remained and, eventually, seemed to freeze into a mask of impenetrability. He often came home, mutely distraught and exhausted—the only thing more tiring than the tremors was the effort required to conceal them over the course of a workday.

The final realization that something was wrong with William Noll came when he was driving one day and the eyelid fluttering began. He lost control and drove the car into a telephone pole.

"I remember Chuck's father," said Yanky. "In fact, that is one of the reasons I didn't like going there when I knew his dad was home. He would be on the couch, and they tried to take good care of him the best they could. But Chuck mentioned a couple of times that he is having trouble seeing. I remember that, so I figured I didn't want to be here making noise or whatever, when the guy is laying there needing peace and quiet."

"He had no expression," said Rita. "He had no expression in his face." It would be years before his illness was properly diagnosed. For now, all his family knew was that William shook and tried to stop, that he couldn't reliably see, and that his visage had warped into a static mask.

With no work to be found for much of the period, things grew even tighter. Pictures from the era show Chuck on an Easter Sunday with a hand-me-down sport coat and dungarees. But the difficulties were never discussed, rarely even mentioned. In the face of those deprivations, there was little room for grumbling.

"My favorite dish that my mother cooked was whatever was in front of me," Chuck said. "Because I was taught, 'Eat what's in front of you, and like it.'"

"My mother never said, 'I don't have the money,'" said Rita. "When we would ask for something, she would say, 'What do you think, I've got a money tree in the backyard?' Then we knew she couldn't buy it, and that was that. So that is the way she would say no."

By the time he was an adult, Chuck had gained some perspective on his circumstances. But even then, he drew strength from it.

"I wouldn't say we were poor," he once said. "I'd say lower-income.

There's a difference. I'd see other people with a little more than we had, and maybe I'd envy them a bit, but in the long run it ended up being the best thing that could have happened to me. You knew that if you wanted something you'd have to get it yourself. No one was going to give it to you. You became a realist very early in life. Lack of material things is not as important as lack of emotional things. We were a very close family. A lot of people are loaded with material stuff, but they're poor from an emotional standpoint. They're the ones who are deprived."

Chuck sang with the boys choir, and he also took part in some plays. Coffee and Kuchen nights, put on by Holy Trinity, featured the students acting out playlets, often updates of *Grimm's Fairy Tales*. One Noll family picture showed Chuck in a black coat with a top hat, wearing a sinister moustache and carrying a magic wand.

On June 3, 1945, Chuck stood on the front steps of the church, as part of the graduating class of Holy Trinity School. He had finished eighth grade, received strong marks, and was as eager to go to high school as he'd been to go to grammar school.

The public school for the area was East Tech, but Chuck wanted to go to Benedictine High, the Catholic school up on East Boulevard. The all-boys Catholic school, off of Buckeye Road, seemed impossibly elusive. Tuition was $125 per year.

Kate gave the refrain about there not being a money tree in the backyard. But Chuck, just as he'd been eight years earlier, was steadfast.

"I'll work for it," he said.

two

"AS LIFE CAME ALONG"

✦ ✦ ✦

Throughout that summer of 1945, in a city and nation elated by victory in Europe and the promise of similar triumph in Japan, Chuck worked intently on earning the $125 he would need for tuition. Remembering the years later, he said, "It was drilled into me very young, that if I wanted to do anything, it was up to me. If I wanted to accomplish anything, it was up to me. Anything I wanted to do, it was up to me."

Chuck began his Benedictine career on Tuesday, September 4, 1945, as the morning radio broadcasts were detailing the news that the last 2,000 Japanese soldiers on Wake Island had finally surrendered, weeks after the Japanese government had formally capitulated. He and Ralph Yanky took the streetcar from Woodland that morning, getting off at the corner of Buckeye Road and East Boulevard, then walked the long half-block past St. Benedict's Parish and the abbey. Beyond that was the long, stately rectangular building, with its three vaulted awnings, and neatly cut shrubs outlining the perimeter.

Benedictine was not one of the more celebrated of the Catholic schools in the city—Holy Name was older and more established, Cathedral Latin had a more successful athletic program—but among the contingent of German Catholics on the East Side it had a loyal following, and its athletic programs were growing.

The school had been founded as part of the mission of Benedictine monks, originally located on the grounds of the St. Andrew Abby in Cleveland in 1927. By the end of the '20s, it had moved to the spot on East Avenue, just off a busy stretch of Buckeye Road. In the '30s, it developed into a more traditional all-boys high school, adding football and other extracurricular activities.

The previous March, while still a student at Holy Trinity, Chuck had taken Benedictine's standardized entry test, and scored 100 on it. He was put on the normal college-preparatory course track, taking classes in English, biology, algebra, and religion, but also beginning two years of intensive Latin (he already knew some, having served as an altar boy at Holy Trinity) with Father Placid Pientek, a tough, crisp cleric who also taught English classes and was the business manager in the athletic department.

Chuck didn't go out for any sports his freshman year. "He was busy," said Fr. Placid. "I started a freshman basketball team, and we practiced one hour before school started. Chuck couldn't make it: paper route."

For a time, Chuck delivered papers in the morning, later it was the afternoon, with a route for the *Cleveland Press*. When Chuck sprained his ankle, he recruited Ralph to help him distribute the papers, pulling a wagon up and down the streets around Woodland. One time, while he was making the rounds collecting subscription fees, a woman in an apartment told him she'd already paid to another neighborhood teen, "a boy in a green shirt." Chuck and Ralph knew exactly who it was, a neighborhood kid named Russ. Chuck proceeded to find him and confront him. Eventually, the boy paid him.

"Chuck was never one to start a fight," said Yanky. "But he could finish them when he had to."

There were other jobs that Chuck tried that first year. For a while, he was a pinsetter at a nearby bowling alley, but soon enough he grew weary of getting nicked by the ricocheting pins. In the spring of 1946, he started working at the Fisher Brothers Market on Cedar Road after school, earning fifty-five cents an hour toward his annual tuition. The job had been arranged by Chuck's uncle, Leonard Schreiber. Chuck was alarmed, when his first check arrived, to see so much of his wages going to union dues.

He soon looked for a different job and, in the summer of 1946, began digging graves in the Calvary Cemetery. He was strong enough for the labor and determined enough to weather the drudgery.

"How do you know when you've dug the hole six feet deep?," asked Rita.

"I stand in it and I go like this," said Chuck, moving his hand level with the top of his head. "And if it's level with the ground then I know I got my six feet."

There would be a lot of six feets.

At other times in the summer of '46, he took the streetcar out to the eastern edge of the line, then walked a couple of more miles to the Beachmont Country Club. There, he would sit with the other boys in the caddy shack, playing cards and waiting for a round. Chuck and fellow Benedictine student Rudy Lawrenchik soon became favorites among the female golfers. Caddymaster Eli Ross would sometimes duck his head into the shack and call out, "Give me the Golden Twins!" That meant Chuck and Lawrenchik had been drafted for a foursome of women. "Chuck was mostly quiet," said Lawrenchik. "The only time I can remember him saying something really important is, one day we were out with this foursome of women, each of us carrying two bags apiece, and he leaned over to me and said, 'I hope I look as good when I'm 50 as these ladies do.'" After the day's work looping, Chuck and Rudy would start back toward Cleveland, hoping to hitch a ride into the city.

The conditions that made it necessary for Chuck to work for tuition were not discussed. Ralph Yanky remembered coming over to Chuck's and being fed jelly sandwiches. "But Chuck was never undernourished," said Yanky. "He was well taken care of." Chuck was growing into his sturdy, thick legs. His hair, brownish during football season, with a cowlick over the right temple, would turn a sandy blond during his work outside in the summer.

During the Benedictine years, William was mostly dormant. Bob, back from the military, was living elsewhere in Cleveland. William and Kate did not ask him for help. Rita, still living at home, working for Cleveland Trust bank, gave part of each check to her mother. Kate added that to the wages she earned in her part-time florist's job. Chuck offered to pitch in, but Kate told him, "You made that money for school—you put it toward school."

By the fall of 1946, Chuck had saved up enough money from his jobs to give up the paper route and go out for the football team, where he made the junior varsity as a fullback. The team's facilities were not up to par—they practiced on a rock-strewn field behind the high school ("You wouldn't even want to get tackled there," said Joe Hornack, two years behind Chuck at Benedictine)—and played their home games at John Adams Public School Field nearby.

In Cleveland that fall, the talk was of the new football team in town. The NFL champion Cleveland Rams had moved out to Los Angeles after winning the title in 1945, because they didn't want to go head-to-head with the Cleveland Browns of the new All-America Football Conference. The former Ohio State coach Paul Brown had decided to join the new league after the war, rather than return to Columbus, and his announced purpose was to build the new Browns into a model of professional efficiency.

Brown made a good start. On Friday evening, September 6, Chuck joined some friends and Benedictine teammates, taking the streetcar down to the Public Square, and then walking to Cleveland Municipal Stadium for the Browns' first league game. They paid twenty-five cents for a seat in the bleachers to watch the opener; as Chuck surveyed the crowd of 60,135 (at the time, the largest crowd for a league game in professional football history), he noticed the excitement, the filled stands, and the large number of black patrons. He knew his old Clippers' coach, Russ Alexander, was going to be at the game, but he didn't see him. The whole neighborhood, black and white, had been buzzing about the Browns breaking the color barrier by signing the gifted Ohio State lineman Bill "Duke" Willis and the legendary former Canton McKinley fullback Marion Motley.

The Browns' first opponent, a team called the Miami Seahawks, had no chance against Paul Brown's new machine. The score was 27–0 at halftime, 44–0 when it was over. Chuck loved the way the Browns seemed so well-drilled. But there was more to it than that. The night presented football not merely as a game but as a spectacle; George "Red" Bird and his Musical Majorettes played at halftime, and there was a door prize of a new car for one patron.

Back at Benedictine, Chuck grew even more fascinated with the sport. He was well-muscled enough and mastered the plays easily. But his hands were a problem. He'd often exert himself so much attempting to break tackles that he'd fumble.

In 1936, the Cleveland Athletic Senate had opened itself to parochial schools, allowing private and public high schools to compete side by side. That meant they were eligible for the Charity Game, a part of Cleveland's Thanksgiving festivities since 1931, pitting the champions of the East and West Senate on the Friday or Saturday after Thanksgiving, at Municipal Stadium. Benedictine had never played in one of these games, but Chuck and his friends were among the 70,000 in attendance to watch Cathedral Latin defeat Holy Name for the city championship in November 1946.

By the fall of 1947, having moved to the line on offense and linebacker on defense, Chuck made the varsity team. His coach was Joe Rufus, a rumpled, rotund man who taught three major sports at Benedictine. Forever in khaki pants and a long-sleeved sweatshirt, a whistle around his neck, Rufus possessed the inclusionary zeal of a prophet. Though the Bengals had never beaten their big rivals, Holy Name and Cathedral Latin, they showed distinct promise under Rufus, ending the season on a positive note. Studious, mindful, and intelligent, Chuck stood out as among the most mature players on the team.

At home, Chuck's already quiet father was even more difficult to decipher. His expression was frozen into a noncommittal half-smile. People would walk through, say their greetings, and William remained on the couch.

"What's wrong with your dad?," Ralph asked once, after they were back outside.

"He is having trouble with his eyes," explained Chuck. "He can't see very well."

This was an understatement. William Noll's tremors had expanded from his eyes—which he now couldn't control at all—to his hands, which shook steadily, despite his effort (exhausting in itself) to try to steady them. Already quiet, his condition made it almost impossible to tell whether he was happy or sad.

"You couldn't," said Rita. "You didn't know. It is like you have a stone face. Your expression doesn't change."

More time was spent with William laying on the couch, in the darkness. "I never went to their home that the father was not laying down," said Ralph Yanky.

More than once, Chuck or Rita would hear him snoring and turn off the radio broadcast of the Indians' game.

"No! Don't turn that off!," William would say, instantly.

"You're sleeping," said Rita. "You were snoring."

"No I wasn't."

"Well, what's the score?"

And William Noll would always tell his children what the score was.

Because of his father's condition, and his mother's stoic resolve, the Noll household wasn't gloomy so much as subdued. And with William so often out of commission, it fell to Kate to effectively run the household, though William would still intercede occasionally.

"I remember one night my father had the radio on, and he was sleeping on the davenport, or at least we thought he was sleeping," said Rita. "My mother and I were in the living room. Chuck, being a teenager, he was going back and forth about something with my mother, and Chuck got real sassy with her, and all of a sudden, my father jumps up and says, 'Don't you dare talk to your mother like that!' He didn't hit him or anything, but it was real sudden. We all just stood there and looked at him."

✦   ✦   ✦

By then, Chuck had his own mysterious physical ailment with which to contend.

In his junior year, he was in math class, sitting in a desk near Ralph Yanky when his line of vision shifted and then went black. He began to quiver, then fell to the floor, shaking violently. "I heard this scuffling," said Yanky, "and I looked around and here is Chuck falling off his chair. I realized what was happening to him, so I put my hand under his head so he wouldn't hurt himself, and someone hollered out, and the head coach, Joe Rufus, and another coach came running in. They tried to free his mouth open—he tried to shove his wallet, I think it was, into Chuck's mouth, so he could bite on his wallet."

The men carried Chuck out of the classroom, past his classmates. "There were at least two times I was sitting in the office, and he had a fit in the classroom," said Fr. Placid. "They would grab one of our coaches and they went up to the classroom—they'd be looking for the medical bag, 'get the tongue depressor,' it was scary."

He'd had a seizure once before, at age eleven, while sleeping at home, but the family passed it off as an anomaly. Now, with the event occurring in public, they took it more seriously, but there were no obvious causes or answers. "It's not epilepsy," concluded the family doctor. "He's too bright of a boy to have epilepsy." Kate and Chuck came home on the streetcar, unsatisfied with the lack of an explanation. Kate reassured her son that he would be fine. And then she dropped the subject.

But the episodes continued, and eventually the diagnosis became clear: Chuck had epilepsy. Later, another doctor told him that he might grow out of it one day. He also was told that the best treatment for it was taking medication every day.

The stigma of the condition, combined with the family's limited resources, meant that sometimes there were weeks when the family couldn't afford the remedies that Chuck used to prevent seizures. At times Chuck would take them every other day. At times, he would feel like he'd be okay without. But sooner or later, it would happen again.

How do you live with an open secret that everyone knows about? You ignore it. After his first seizure at school, Chuck found Ralph Yanky later in the day and asked, "What happened?"

Ralph told him.

"Was everybody there?," asked Chuck.

"Well, yeah . . . they were."

Chuck didn't ask again.

In this, even at this young age, he was observing a family custom. Once a calamity was encountered—whether it was a financial setback due to the Depression, the loss of baby Beatrice at two days old, or the health problems of Chuck and his father—it was at first tersely acknowledged and then simply ignored.

Within the family, such topics were never broached. "He probably was trying to hide it," said Rita. "He never said anything, he never talked about it. I mean, he was very quiet about it."

When dealing with the outside world, the Nolls chose the most benign possible euphemisms. When Chuck had to discuss his father's tremors, he would refer to it simply as "a tic." Later, when mentioning his own seizures, and the epilepsy that caused them, Chuck distanced himself even further; when he referred to it at all to his family, he would say that he had "a spell."

"We didn't talk about sicknesses," said Rita. "We would just accept it, my father's doings, and went along with it. I think my mother's whole family, being from a large family and everything . . . I mean, we just took it as life came along."

Though embarrassed by his seizures, Chuck found refuge, solace, and confidence in sports. Starting in the summer of 1945, he went out for junior baseball with the Cleveland Baseball Federation. Third base was his specialty. "Wherever they needed me," Chuck once said. "Every place but pitcher."

Chuck was an unabashed fan. Back home on East 81st Street, the glue for the Noll family was the Cleveland Indians. William would wait patiently for each game to start and lay listening to every broadcast. Kate was a fan as well, and she'd started attending Bill Veeck's Ladies Day promotions when they began after the war. They liked Jack Graney's new partner, the young announcer Jimmy Dudley, who shared the broadcasts with Graney on WJW radio, and greeted listeners with the bright welcome, "Hello, baseball fans everywhere."

On their junior baseball team, Chuck and Ralph were coached by an African American neighbor, Hunchy Johnson, who worked at Alcoa and played for the company's industrial league team—the boys would go down and watch him play during "Amateur Day" at the Cleveland Municipal Stadium.

Yanky's family moved to Garfield Heights, but the boys still got together frequently. Their classmate Louis Podesta, among the first to own a car, was a frequent running buddy as well, as was football teammate and lineman Ed Powell, with whom Chuck shared a fascination for Notre Dame football.

The summer and fall of 1948 was a vivid, magical time, and sports played a central role. Chuck was still working—at both the cemetery and the golf course—and playing baseball. Walking around town in those summer months, almost every home's windows were open to let in the air. And most of the houses seemed to have radios on, tuned into the Indians' games.

Whenever they could, Chuck and Ralph would take a streetcar downtown, each with a sandwich in their pocket, and watch an Indians game from the bleachers. Chuck looked up to the Indians' third baseman Ken Keltner—whom he'd admired since the day in 1941 when Keltner's fielding had helped end Joe DiMaggio's fifty-six–game hitting streak—even requesting Keltner's number for his youth league teams.

"Chuck was a very, very good third baseman and a good hitter," said Ralph Yanky. "But he had this football in him, and when football season came, that's all he wanted to do."

✦ ✦ ✦

By the start of his senior year, Chuck had become one of the more popular boys at Benedictine. And the team had a sense of promise. Rufus had coached his team to city titles in both basketball and baseball earlier in the calendar year. Now, convinced that he had a team that could finally challenge powers Cathedral Latin and Holy Name, he persuaded the track star Yanky to rejoin the team his senior year. He also brought in a key assistant—an itinerant football zealot named Ab Strosnider, who had been an assistant at Cathedral Latin—to be the new line coach.

Strosnider had been around, forged in the competitive crucible of Cleveland high school football. "Sort of a gruff guy," said fellow Benedictine alum Ed Steigerwald, Chuck's cousin. "Very plainspoken. Obsessed with this winning business." All coaches wanted to win, but Strosnider, through his own experience playing college football at the University of Dayton and coaching underprivileged kids around Cleveland, had seen how the games could transform lives, opening young boys to entirely new possibilities.

"He was a good coach, not a good head coach," said one Benedictine administrator. "Not the right guy for head coach." Strosnider was teaching classes during the day, coaching in the afternoons, taking a short nap after dinner, and driving a cab through the night.

Strosnider placed Chuck at right tackle and did more than drill him. He broke down the intricacies of the blocking game into component parts, speaking not only in terms of leverage and mass but also the subtle mechanics of "fitting" into a block. Chuck had known football, and was taking physics that senior year, but before then he'd never considered the two to be of a piece.

There was a resigned kindness to Strosnider. It was only later that the boys would hear the priests' whispers about Strosnider's personal life, and the opinion that he drank too much. For Chuck and his linemates, Strosnider invested practices with an urgent energy, addressed them with what sounded to Chuck like a friendly bark.

For his part, Strosnider took to Chuck's deep commitment to the game. "He was really outstanding," said Strosnider of Chuck years later.

"He was class—in every way—and there's not many boys you say that about."

On October 3 of that year, Benedictine won its third straight game, to remain undefeated. The next day, Chuck and his family gathered around the radio as Keltner's three-run homer in the fourth lifted the Indians to victory in the one-game playoff with the Boston Red Sox, giving Cleveland the American League pennant. The next afternoon, they were by the radio again, hearing the Browns move to 5–0 with a win at Baltimore over the Colts. Two weeks later, Chuck was one of 200,000 Clevelanders to line Euclid Avenue for the Indians' World Series victory parade, and he continued closely monitoring the Browns' undefeated run to their third straight All-American Conference championship.

And as the Indians and Browns kept marching forward, Benedictine High kept winning football games. They had defeated Holy Name, 23–0, in the opener, powered by the line and quarterback Gil Verderber. Later in the year, they'd knocked off Cathedral Latin for the first time ever, in a rainy Cleveland Stadium on the first Friday night in November, with a 15–0 win that clinched a spot in the prestigious Charity Game, where they would play Cleveland South High.

The 1948 Charity Game was played two days after Thanksgiving, November 27, with 45,117 in attendance at Municipal Stadium. The Bengals had played a regular-season game at the stadium just three weeks earlier, but playing in their first Charity Game brought attention of a different order of magnitude. The Benedictine marching band had even practiced on Thanksgiving Day. At the pep rally earlier that week, the usually bashful Rufus had spoken about the team giving it their all, and Eddie Powell promised that the Bengals would do everything they could to bring a city championship back to Benedictine.

The teams fought to a scoreless tie for nearly the entire game, before Benedictine scored with a touchdown pass in the final minute, from Verderber to fullback Jimmy McNeeley, sending Benedictine home to a 7–0 win. In the game, Chuck had performed marvelously, neutralizing the bigger South High linemen. Walking off the field, he saw Rita in the stands. She'd attended virtually all his games that year, reporting the details back to their parents.

After the win, the team clattered on the bus, nearly everyone singing the Benedictine fight song as they headed to the school. Back at Benedictine, the players went to the locker room and showered, then changed into their street clothes to meet their family and friends in the Benedictine gymnasium, with live music and refreshments. This was the time to bask in the glow of victory, but for Chuck it was a muted celebration.

"I learned very early in my football career," said Chuck, "you play a game, it's a very emotional thing, you get all up for it, you work like hell, you get keyed up. Then when it's over, you take a shower and go out and sit down on the bus, and it's like someone stuck a pin in you. For me. What I'm saying is the doing is the pleasure, not the rejoicing therein."

Happy, tired, he engaged in little rejoicing, instead remaining composed and particularly appreciative of Strosnider, who was still indignant over Chuck not winning the game's outstanding lineman award.

The spring of 1949 found Chuck growing more confident and self-assured. He'd gone out for wrestling, on something of a whim, and held his own against a heavyweight state champ. "After that match, the other coach came to our coach," said Ed Steigerwald, Chuck's cousin and classmate. "He said, 'Boy, your heavyweight is really something else.' Because nobody really trained Chuck. He just went out and started wrestling. He was a tremendously strong, quick guy."

He had always been beefy, but by his senior year in high school, he'd lost the baby fat of his youth, and grown out of the awkwardness of his middle teens. His pronounced jaw, and lightening hair, along with his clean-cut manner, made him not only attractive to girls but disarmingly safe. "He was never a loud guy," said Yanky. "He is the kind of guy that, if you wanted someone to date your sister, that is who you picked."

Chuck was still shy, often skipping the Benedictine dances, and rarely taking dates out on his own (years later, Ralph would suspect this was because Chuck was afraid that he'd have a seizure). But he was becoming, in many ways, more self-assured. Chuck was more active socially, often accompanying Ralph and his girlfriend Joan Bulger on double dates, along with one of Joan's high school classmates (she attended the all-girls school of Cleveland Notre Dame), for movies downtown at the State or the Palace Theater. "Chuck was a lot like Ralph," Joan remembered. "Very well-mannered, didn't get into much trouble, but still a lot of fun. And *good-looking.*"

By that spring, anything seemed possible. Chuck had grown ambitious about his college plans; he'd applied to just one school, Notre Dame. Though the Irish didn't offer either him or teammate Eddie Powell a scholarship, they did encourage them to attend.

Benedictine would send Chuck's transcript to Notre Dame in December 1948, and again the following June, once he'd graduated. He would report with the other non-scholarship freshmen, but there were no guarantees for him at Notre Dame—to earn a scholarship, he would have to make the team of the most powerful football squad in the country. It was audacious to say the least. Chuck had earned all-*Catholic Universe Bulletin* honors in the fall of '48, but Rufus would say later "Chuck was a fine football player; but he was maybe the sixth or seventh best player on that team."

"To be honest with you, at first I was surprised he was going to Notre Dame," said Yanky. "That was the school at the time. Everybody was crazy about Notre Dame. They had some great players there. Chuck didn't seem to fit."

But he'd developed self-belief, built on his high school successes. There was no Benedictine yearbook in 1949, but there was a compendium of school newspapers, which featured class pictures. Under Chuck's it read: "CHARLES NOLL, 'All-American,' Football, Track, Bengal A. C." He graduated twenty-eighth in the class of 252 students.

That summer, he trained for football, faithfully took his epilepsy medication, worked at Calvary Cemetery, and caddied again out at Beachmont Country Club.

At every other stop in his development, when Chuck had put himself to the test, he'd found that he was the equal of other, more celebrated athletes. Now he'd get a chance to do so for the Fighting Irish. He didn't dwell on it, never boasted about it, but the ones who knew him best recognized that, in going to Notre Dame, he was fulfilling a longtime dream.

"I think it meant everything to him," said Yanky.

three

GOLDEN DREAMS

✦ ✦ ✦

When Chuck arrived in South Bend with the other walk-on freshmen in late August, he must have felt like he had touched down at the mecca of college football. The iconic gilded golden dome atop the university's main building, with its nineteen-foot-tall statue of St. Mary, was splendid, shimmering in the distance on a clear summer day. On a corner of Cartier Field, the practice field, freshman coach Bennie Sheridan led the group of more than fifty freshman aspirants through their first calisthenics.

The Fighting Irish, under head coach Frank Leahy's strict regimen—full contact practices on Thursday and Friday, before Leahy determined the squad that would suit up Saturday—had been invincible. Since Leahy returned after a two-year stint in the Navy during the Second World War, the Irish had gone undefeated for three straight seasons.

All Chuck had to do was prove that he could compete with the best college football players in the country. He may have wanted that so much that he held off on his epilepsy medications (he sometimes complained that the pills left him feeling logy). Whatever the case, he began with strong, productive workouts, holding his own against the other freshman. Then one day in early September, it all went wrong. He felt the dreaded light-headedness, the unsteady balance, and his world strobing to black-and-white. And then nothing. As the seizures went, it wasn't severe. But it left him flat on his back, regaining consciousness with that horribly familiar cottony grogginess, while looking up at strange faces.

And in a matter of hours, his Notre Dame career was over.

In years later, he'd confide to one friend that he'd had a seizure at practice, and another friend overheard that there had been an incident in the dining hall. Whether it had been just one seizure or two, it had been one too many for Frank Leahy. He dispatched an assistant to impart the news. The university thought it best if Chuck went home. Coach Leahy didn't want to take the risk.

Less than two weeks after arriving at Notre Dame, Chuck trudged back to his dormitory, packed up his few belongings, and went down to the depot, waiting for the next bus to Cleveland.

There was little notice taken even among the team. "I remember him being there," said fellow Notre Dame freshman Charles Dodd. "And then I remember he had that happen. And then I remember he was gone." The incident didn't even register for many of the other freshmen. Kids came from all over the country. Most of them didn't make it.

Chuck officially withdrew from the university on September 14, 1949, one day before classes were scheduled to begin. Late that night, he got home—he'd taken a streetcar from the Cleveland station—and opened the door.

"Chuck!," said his alarmed mother, dressed in her nightgown, blinking in the dark. "What happened?"

He was glum, his lips drawn inward in a tight line. "I had another spell."

After that, they didn't talk about it. Chuck walked back into his bedroom. There was nothing left to do or say that night. He would get up the next day and figure out what to do next.

But Rita, watching her brother heading for his room, knew what it meant to him.

"I think he was crushed," she said.

✦ ✦ ✦

There were no heart-to-heart discussions at the breakfast table the next morning. Instead, Chuck got up, showered and dressed, and did what he'd done most days the previous four years: he walked up to Woodland Avenue to grab the streetcar heading out to Benedictine.

The semester had just begun, and the school was in the early stages of earnest fall activity. Chuck went straight to the athletic department and found who he was looking for—Ab Strosnider.

With his eyes fixed on his shoes, Chuck told Strosnider what had happened. They talked for a few moments, and Strosnider asked him what his plan was now. Chuck didn't have one.

But very soon, Strosnider did. He told Chuck to give him a few hours.

Strosnider had played, with distinction, at the University of Dayton, about 215 miles downstate, in southwestern Ohio. Soon, he got on the phone with Joe Gavin, the head football coach at Dayton and also, as it happened, a college roommate of Frank Leahy.

It made perfect sense. Leahy and Gavin were still close friends, and at times Leahy would call Gavin on the phone and have him try a new wrinkle with his team that Leahy couldn't risk trying in practice—because of all the attention on Notre Dame—with his own team. Surely Gavin would take on Chuck Noll.

Gavin called Leahy, to find out the story on the Noll kid. There wasn't much information: Leahy knew the kid had a seizure, and Notre Dame hadn't become Notre Dame by taking on problems. Whatever Leahy said wasn't enough to convince Gavin to take Chuck. But then, after Gavin called Strosnider back and politely declined, he'd found the old Dayton alum unwavering in his insistence on Chuck's worthiness. Strosnider wouldn't take no for an answer.

He was speaking quietly at first, but soon he raised his voice, loudly enough for Fr. Placid, sitting in another corner of the Benedictine athletic department office, to hear one side of the conversation.

"Look," Strosnider continued, more emphatic. "Joe, I tell you he's a good kid! You *got* to take him. If you don't, you won't get another guy from Benedictine, I swear to God."

As threats went, it was not an idle one: Strosnider had been around, and he knew virtually everyone in Cleveland football. After a few more moments on the phone, Gavin relented. Strosnider signed off with a relieved affirmation—"You'll see"—and then a quick good-bye.

He put the phone back in its cradle and eased back into the chair. The next call was to Chuck, to tell him that he should keep his bags packed; he would be enrolling at the University of Dayton.

✦ ✦ ✦

It had already been a brilliant recruiting campaign for Joe Gavin, well before he took the call from the adamant Strosnider. Beginning his third year as head coach at Dayton, Gavin reached the realization that most coaches arrive at sooner or later: It didn't matter how well he applied Xs and Os, how clever his game plan was, or how rousing his pregame speeches were. He needed talent first to contend with Miami University, Xavier, and Cincinnati, the perennial powers that dotted Dayton's schedule.

This was a particular challenge for him. Gavin had lost out on dozens of recruits, he realized, solely because of his own perpetual stutter. And so he'd worked harder than his competition and did everything within the rules to find talented athletes to come to the school. The previous January, on a recruiting trip to Cincinnati, he'd buttonholed Jim Currin, a talented end out of Elder High, who'd sat out a semester recovering from eye surgery. Talking to Currin and his friend, quarterback Jerry Kiley, in the gym that day, he casually invited them to watch some Dayton game films with him. After they did so, he went a step further. "You should really come visit the campus," he said, and invited them up for the next day.

The two boys took the Greyhound up to Dayton the next morning, and when they reported to the athletic department, the secretary asked, "Where's your bags?"

The boys looked at each other, and Currin asked, "What do you mean?"

"Classes start tomorrow," said the man. "Go back, get your bags, we'll cover the ticket." That's how the strapping, agile end Currin was recruited into the fold. Within two weeks of reporting that January, well before any official spring practices were scheduled for the football team, "They had us over in the women's gym; we had shoulder pads and helmets on, and we were learning the different blocking styles."

Many of the rest came through conventional means. Gavin still had a broad network of friends and fellow coaches in Cleveland. He'd brought in a fast lineman from Cleveland Holy Name named Len Kestner. He'd lured a bruising center named Ed Clemens, who'd originally gone to Clemson, only to grow weary of the freshman hazing (Clemens' hair was just starting to grow back when he arrived on the UD campus). There was an all-state quarterback named Jim Raiff, already getting too big to play the position, who had turned down scholarship offers from Michigan and Southern Cal to stay in town. His teammate at Chaminade High was a genial, jug-eared center named Pat Maloney, whose father was an executive at AT&T. Others came from farther away. There was a talented young quarterback from New York named Frank Siggins, who'd also had a brief glimpse at Notre Dame before winding up in Dayton.

Then, after fall practices had already begun, Strosnider called and pleaded Chuck's case, and Gavin relented. There was, after all, room in the dorm. And it was already a truism in football that you couldn't have too many decent linemen.

Gavin called his de facto trainer, his old friend from Cleveland, Hank Ferrazza. The soft-spoken, cerebral Ferrazza, working on his master's at John Carroll, but also helping with the Dayton training staff, said he'd get his brother, Dan, then a student at Dayton, to meet the boy at the Dayton train station.

So, on September 18, 1949, Chuck Noll went to Terminal Tower and got on a train, bound for Dayton. He was met at the station by Dan Ferrazza who drove him to campus so he could watch the practice. One of the other freshman recognized him. It was Len Kestner, who was on the *Catholic Universe Bulletin's* All-Catholic team with Chuck in '48.

"Hey, Chuck!," said Kestner. "What you doing here? I thought you were at Notre Dame."

"It's a long story," Chuck said.

After the practice, Chuck asked Kestner whom he was rooming with and if he might convince his roommate to find a different dorm mate so that Chuck and Len could room together. After the switch was made, Chuck moved his duffel into the third-floor dorm room at St. Joseph's Hall, which overlooked the football field.

Dayton, which sat just south of the National Road in southwestern Ohio, had been a hub to a growing business and industrial community for years. By 1949, the hometown of Orville and Wilbur Wright was a small-time city with big-time aspirations. National Cash Register, founded in 1884 and thriving in the postwar economy, was right across the street from the campus, and there were several General Motors subsidiaries—Delco and Frigidaire plants among them—that were paying well for manual labor. Against this growing industrial metropolis, the University of Dayton stood out as a redoubt of Catholic learning. Unlike most of the prominent private colleges that excelled in sports—Marquette, St. Louis University, the University of San Francisco, Xavier, Holy Cross, and others—Dayton wasn't a Jesuit university but, instead, Marianist. While not as single-mindedly devoted to teaching as the Jesuits, they shared many of the same assumptions.

The wave of GI Bill attendees had swelled enrollment, and the school was racing to try to catch up, building Quonset huts to complement the handful of permanent buildings on campus. In 1949, there were 2,500 students enrolled, less than 500 of them women. The compound on which Dayton had grown was focused on Emmanuel Hall, the main administration building; St. Mary's Hall, which held most of the classes; Chaminade Hall, which included the college dining room; and St. Joseph's Hall, whose top three floors were occupied solely by scholarship athletes in football and basketball.

It lacked the bustle of Cleveland or the mystique of Notre Dame, but it was welcoming, approachable, and Catholic. It didn't take long before Chuck felt at home.

Before they'd even met him, some of his teammates saw Chuck one afternoon, a solitary figure out on the practice field, relentlessly ramming out at a blocking sled. Later that day, Maloney became the first to make his acquaintance. They sat together in the narrow corridor outside the athletic office and struck up a conversation. "We must have talked for about 20–25 minutes before Gavin got there," said Maloney. "I remember afterwards that I said, 'Boy, what a nice guy; I really like this guy. I'm glad I came to UD because it is going to be good.'"

Out on the practice field, Chuck's credentials were clear. "Right away, you knew he was a player," Currin said. "There was no question he could play the game, and he knew it. He was smarter than all the rest of us, had blocking techniques we didn't have yet. You could just tell."

✦　✦　✦

Sometimes the freshman team was relegated to a far corner of the practice field. On other instances, they ran patterns in a nearby parking lot, with a coach coming over to summon one or more players to the main field. Under freshman coach John Marschall, the freshman team was designated cannon fodder. "We just got the shit kicked out of us by the varsity," said Maloney. "That was it. No ifs, ands, or buts about it."

Eventually, though, by the end of that first season, something changed. In 1949, many of Dayton's starters were nearing their mid-twenties, Second World War veterans who attended on the GI bill. But for the veterans like team captain Bill Gutbrod and others, football meant something less—or at least something different—than it did to Chuck and his classmates. Gutbrod had been wounded in the war; he'd returned to the States, enrolled at Dayton, and played football because he'd always loved it. At first, Gavin thought the older, hardened athletes would be the key to Dayton's rise. But there was something missing in the GI Bill vets—a degree of abandon characteristic of the best players. Gavin found it hard to convince someone who'd survived the Battle of the Bulge to whip themselves into an emotional fervor for the sake of beating St. Bonaventure.

By the end of the season, as the freshmen grew physically and in confidence, the tide turned in their scrimmaging against the varsity. "Some of them were married, so football wasn't a big thing," said Jim Currin. "So when we came in, we were all recruits, ready to go, and we would have a scrimmage, and by the end of that year we would just knock the snot out of them."

Chuck's life centered around the rambunctious and, at times, juvenile group of scholarship athletes at St. Joe's. The second, third, and fourth floors had about ten rooms per floor and two students to a room. There were a couple larger rooms that were shared by four freshmen, and a single that usually went to the basketball team's tallest player.

St. Joseph's Hall overlooked UD Stadium, and on game-day Saturdays, the friends and family of the players could sneak beers up to the dorm rooms and watch the games from the window. While Chuck roomed with Kestner, he soon fell in with two other freshman: the end Currin, a cantankerous, mischievous figure who shared many of Chuck's sensibilities, and Maloney, the amiable center from Cleveland.

The thin walls and fiberboard bed frames didn't give much privacy. The athletes called them the Cardboard Flats. The accommodations were sparse, the cockroaches in the shower sizable. "There was one lavatory," said Don Donoher, who'd played basketball from 1950 to 1954. "Two showers, one bowl in there. That is where everyone shaved because you only had cold water in the room. It was kind of sparse. But I tell you there weren't any of us that would have traded it for the Taj Mahal."

Another frequent member of the group was a paraplegic Second World

War vet named Jerry Von Mohr. He'd climbed on Currin's shoulders one day when he needed to get up to a third-floor classroom and would become a quasi-mascot/supporter of the football team, traveling with the team and sitting on the sidelines during games. The football players took to carrying Von Mohr and his wheelchair up the stairs to his classes.

In a room across the hall from Chuck and Len, a Hawaiian named Jimmy Akau and his roommate Pat Bennington were often heard playing Akau's Hawaiian ukulele. Soon, Chuck was spending his free time sitting with Akau, learning how to play the simple chords on the instrument. By the end of the fall semester, he'd mastered several songs.

Kestner, Chuck's roommate, left school before the spring semester, returning to his family and girlfriend in Cleveland. That second semester of freshman year, Chuck took a heavy academic load—eighteen-and-a-half credit hours, including Inorganic Chemistry, English Composition, Military Science, and Introduction to Psychology. He still found time, in the margins, to comply when UD basketball coach Tom Blackburn asked him to occasionally fill a spot in basketball practice.

That summer, Chuck went with Currin to the Fort Scott camp for Catholic boys in New Baltimore, Ohio. There they served as counselors tending to the hundreds of boys, aged eight and up, on a daily basis. There was horse riding, athletics, and songs around the campfire (*"We are a bunch of boys / Made out of fun and noise . . ."*).

"We rode horses, played softball, did all the things that young guys do," said Currin. One night, they went to a Cincinnati nightclub called Castle Farm, and Chuck wound up sitting on the bar, playing a ukulele. But these moments of spontaneity were never yoked to any moments of self-confession or even, it seemed, self-awareness. Chuck didn't talk about these things, didn't seem to spend a lot of time dwelling on the music. He just got up and played.

Chuck and Currin were down at Fort Scott early, before camp opened, painting the floorboards of the cottage porches. "We were talking back and forth," said Currin, "and all of a sudden I heard *bonk bonk bonk* and I look over and there's Chuck laying on the ground, beating his head down in the paint. That kind of scared me, and I went up and I remembered hearing them say you've got to get the tongue. So I helped him up. I walked him back over to the counselor's cottage and we got some rags. He never said a thing. He never said a word about it, and I never asked him a question. I figured if he wanted to tell me what the problem is . . . but he never did."

The condition wouldn't go away, and Chuck—for all of his expertise and discipline—continued to struggle with managing it. Faced with that reality, he stuck close to friends, went out in groups, and rarely put himself in a situation where he was alone a long way from home or UD.

As sophomores, Chuck and the Dayton football class of '53 moved en masse up to the varsity, where Gavin waited, whistle in hand, broad slab of a face fixed in concentration. His dimpled, prominent chin and slicked-back hair gave him the aspect of a somewhat intimidating, authoritarian figure—he could have been a gangster or the bouncer at a speakeasy.

But this formidable presence was undercut by Gavin's voice and stutter. "Now this week, we are going to play Chat-Chat-Chat-Chat-Chat-anooga," he'd say—and the stutter grew worse in times of pressure. During training camp once, a freshman named Bernie Hoage raised his hand and, in response to a Gavin comment, stuttered out his own question. The assistant Joe Quinn cuffed Hoage for his impertinence, before realizing the boy had a stuttering condition as well.

Gavin's authority was unquestioned, but he was never close to his players. "He wasn't overly friendly, and he wasn't really a good communicator," said Pat Maloney. "He wasn't a good teacher, as far as what he had to teach and what he wanted to be played. Very rarely did he ever praise anybody—once in a while, but not often."

On the field that sophomore year, Chuck found a new influence. He was Ralph McGehee, an All-American under Leahy at Notre Dame, who was rehabbing an injured knee on his way to trying out for the pros. If Russ Alexander had taught Chuck the principles of leverage, and Strosnider helped him with the nuances of using his arms to shed and control opponents, McGehee gave Chuck a master class in the initial explosion off the line of scrimmage.

"He had the most powerful lunge out of the three-point stance that I had ever seen or have seen since," said Currin. "And he watched Chuck, because Chuck had a good lunge from three-point stance, and worked with Chuck. Between the two of them, they would break those sliding machines." The facility Chuck had exhibited in the classroom—hear or read something once and he retained much of it—translated to the football field as well, and by his sophomore year, Chuck was already coaching his teammates.

"Charlie ate up everything," said tackle Tom Carroll. "He would pick me out to go one-on-one," said Carroll, "and he would say, 'You're getting off too slow. You've got to get off faster, you've got to follow through better, you've got to stay lower.'"

Chuck's initial burst often featured a powerful right arm to his opponent's chest, at the point of contact he would raise both hands up under his foe's shoulder pads and then—in a technique that McGehee added—would wrench the defender right or left, clearing the hole for the Dayton ballcarrier to run through.

Even that first year on the varsity, Chuck was beginning to stand out. "The philosophy, what was taught, was to hit, turn, and raise," said Pat Maloney. "Chuck did that to perfection. He really was a good blocker."

But it wasn't all physics and brute force. Gavin's Precision-T offense used aspects of the Michigan Spin, with the quarterback, necessarily nimble and expert at ball-handling, executing a series of well-timed fakes. One Dayton signal-caller said he felt like he was on a merry-go-round. The running game was built on traps and influence plays. "Part of it is what you can do," Chuck once explained. "When you have undersized people, you're not just going to go out there and straight block." The key action on the play was the play-side guard leaving his defensive tackle unblocked to reach the linebacker a few yards behind him. The defensive tackle would then burst into the vacated hole to make the tackle, only to be trapped by the pulling guard from the other side crossing behind the center to take him out of the play. When it worked to perfection, it had a kind of inevitability about it—cleverness taking advantage of human nature.

Chuck's roommate sophomore year was Frank Siggins, the Long Island quarterback still serving as an understudy to upperclassman Joe Zaleski. Siggins had served two years in the Marines, and he was both older and more mature than most of his teammates. That also made him an ideal candidate to room with Chuck.

"When you'd walk through the halls, most of the rooms were open and there was no one sitting at the desks," said Tom Carroll. "But Chuck and Frank would be at their desks."

Both were strong willed. "Frank was a stern guy and a no-nonsense guy," said Don Donoher. "He had some convictions, too. He could get into a discussion and have the last word also. I don't know how he and Chuck would ever conclude a discussion."

Chuck had briefly changed his major to science, but he'd switched it back to secondary education in the fall of 1950. He also became even more dedicated to his studies. After each class, he'd return to his classroom and recite his notes into a reel-to-reel tape recorder, then play those back to himself throughout the week.

"We would go to Kramer's or by the Heidelberg or one of these places," said Currin. "He would sit and have a beer or two and a sandwich, or whatever, and you would look around—and he was gone. His sense of urgency to get back to the books was always greater than most of the rest of us. He was different from most of the guys because he had that desire, always, to learn. He studied. We all got by, but Chuck applied himself."

Money was still tight. Some of the players would give blood at St. Elizabeth Hospital not far from the school. Eventually, Chuck and Currin found work, along with a few other players, at a supper club called the Hungarian Village, where they'd park cars on Friday and Saturday nights. Chuck occasionally worked, along some other teammates, as pallbearers for hire, when the Harris Funeral Home needed able bodies.

But for the athletes at St. Joe's, the surest source of income, besides reselling the pair of tickets they received for each of their games, was working at the games of the other sport. The basketball players would sell programs at the football games (each arguing over who got the best sections, where the alumni and other boosters bought the most programs), and the football players would make $6 serving as ushers at the basketball games, a more lucrative proposition simply because there were more games.

At St. Joe's Hall, the friendships were often forged across sports. Basketball player Chris Harris and Chuck had become friendly by the time Harris received a one-game suspension for arguing with a teacher, on a night that the UD basketball team was visiting Baldwin-Wallace in Cleveland. By then, Chuck had his own car (he'd purchased a humble, faded-green junker from his older brother for $25, over their mother's protestations). Harris invited himself along on the ride in the old Ford they'd all dubbed the Green Hornet.

"We're going back, and it started snowing like you can't believe," said

Harris. "And Chuck's lights went out. It was an old, beat-up car and the lights went out, and there we were, on these backroads in a snowstorm. We still had an hour or so to go, and Chuck said, 'What are we going to do, guys? I've got a big flashlight.' And someone said, 'Let's put the roundballer on the hood of the car, and tie him there with the flashlight, and we will drive slow.' And I said, 'What!?!' I thought they were kidding, and Chuck said, 'Come on, roundballer—get out. You are going up.' And they kind of tied me so I wouldn't fall, and there I am on the hood of Chuck's car, driving with this big flashlight in the snow."

✦   ✦   ✦

Chuck's first meaningful action came in the second game of his sophomore season. On the road against star quarterback Ted Marchibroda and St. Bonaventure, Gavin tried Chuck as a defensive halfback and to field punts. He fumbled one of the earlier ones (echoing the problem holding the football that he'd had as a fullback in high school). "And that was the end of Chuck, as a defensive halfback," said Maloney. "He was an offensive lineman." A week later, they lost 40–0 to Bear Bryant's Kentucky team, ranked number six nationally.

Yet even as a sophomore, Chuck's preternatural feel for the fundamentals of the game were clear. When Dayton's starting fullback was injured against Quantico Marines, Gavin barked at Chuck on the sideline. "Nollie, you be ready if we need you as a fullback." Chuck replied in the affirmative.

That fall, Chuck got his only family visitors during his time at Dayton, as Rita drove down with her new beau. She had met Clarence Deininger at a dance at St. Cecilia's one night in 1950. He'd asked her to dance because she was tall. It was only after a few dances that they realized that Rita's mother's sister was married to Clare's father's brother, making them distant cousins.

Rita was drawn to Clarence's eminent decency ("He's the best Catholic I know," she once said). He had been drafted in the Second World War, but he couldn't pass the physical due to an irregular heartbeat. He'd gone to work for the Cleveland Water Co. A fan of sports and a lover of statistics, he was particularly interested in Chuck, and they hit it off immediately.

Chuck played, albeit sparingly in that game, a 24–12 loss to John Carroll. (One of Carroll's players was an avid, tough halfback named Don Shula, who remembered that day as the time "I first heard of Chuck Noll.")

Rita and Clarence were married that spring of 1951. Chuck was a groomsman.

At the church, he was in high spirits. "You better think twice," he told his sister. "After this, it's official."

Rita, nervous, shrill, fiddling with her hair and her veil, was not in the mood for hijinks.

But Chuck was undeterred. "It's not too late," he said.

Rita turned to their mother. "Mom, if you don't tell him to stop . . ."

Back in Dayton, the absence of family by this time had become a topic of conversation among his teammates. "It was bantered between the guys once in a while," said Currin. "'Have you ever met Chuck's dad?' 'No,' and then it was dropped. We knew none of his family." His old freshman roommate Kestner did recall Chuck talking a lot about his older sister.

At the end of the 1950–1951 school year, Currin was looking forward to spending another summer with Chuck in Fort Scott. "He was going to come back down to the camp," said Currin, "but he had to cancel, because he had to go home and work. He had to get some money. Now looking back on it, I can see why."

Chuck had to go home because he was needed. His parents had moved from the East Side to the West Side, renting another small home. With Rita having married and moved out, William and Kate were alone for the first time in thirty years.

William had finally found work again, though it was menial. Rita had a friend whose father owned a parking lot downtown, a large lot just off Lake Erie, within blocks of Cleveland Municipal Stadium. William Noll gladly accepted the job, taking a streetcar downtown; he bore up without complaint, but he could no longer drive. When he was in town, Chuck would often pick up his father from work.

One day, Chuck and Maloney applied for jobs at the Cleveland Zoo, located at the bottom of a hill. Leaving after the job application, Chuck wasn't able to get the Green Hornet up the hill. "So he rolls it back down," said Maloney, "and we go up in reverse. That's how we got out of that damn zoo down there."

Chuck finally landed a job with Cleveland Illumination, working changing out street lights on a cherry picker. That summer, Maloney became the rare college friend of Chuck's to spend time with his family. Maloney found Chuck's mother warm ("She always had a smile so nice, and wanted to feed you and everything"), while Bill's condition was clearly declining. "His father, he seemed older," said Maloney. "I don't know how old he actually would have been at that time, and I figured that, somewhere, he might have had a stroke or something."

But Maloney, like all the rest of Chuck's friends, had long ago learned an ineluctable fact: If there was something difficult or painful or embarrassing or emotional, Chuck probably didn't want to talk about it.

four

"THE POPE"

✦ ✦ ✦

By the time he returned for training camp in the late summer of 1951, Chuck might have felt he was coming home to his second family. The connections between those Dayton players ran deeper than mere teammates. They lived together, studied together (those that studied), went out together, and drank together. In that midcentury American moment, they were all big men on campus, enjoying status and privilege, getting a sense of their emerging place in the world.

They had spent much of the previous two years giving each other nicknames: Chuck had dubbed Currin "Dennis the Menace" for his mischievous ways. Maloney, a fan of Damon Runyon, was called "Big Nig" after the craps shooter from one of Runyon's stories, "Life in the Roaring Forties," and others followed in the same vein—carousing lineman Paul Cassidy was "Harry the Horse," and Tom Carroll was known as "the Silver Duke"; the ever-expanding Raiff was "Fat Herman," his father's name. Frank Siggins was "Siggs," Ed Clemens was "Doozie," John Chaney was "Dingbat," Akau was simply "Sneeze." Even the team's legless mascot/spirit leader Jerry Von Mohr had a nickname—everyone called him "Snatcher," though no one could remember exactly why.

Chuck's nickname was definitively bestowed during the spring intrasquad game in 1951. He was playing at tackle, next to Currin at end. In Gavin's offense, the line calls at scrimmage were not the responsibility of the center but each of the tackles, who called out adjustments for themselves and the guard and end flanking them. Before one play, Chuck made a line audible that would send him wide to block the end and have Currin moving inside to catch the linebacker coming through the vacated hole. The call was made but the play broke down from the start, Chuck not getting a good shot on the end and Currin missing the linebacker entirely.

Walking back to the huddle, both Chuck and Currin were adamant that the other man had failed.

"That's your fault!" Chuck said.

"You called it!," said Currin. "He was too far over!" Then, perturbed, he added, "You think you're always right—you think you're *the Pope!*"

Teammate Joe Molloy, walking back to the huddle with them, overheard and echoed the sentiment. "Yeah, you're the Pope!"

"The Pope." It stuck. In later years Len Kestner would remember calling Chuck by that name a year earlier, when they were rooming together in the fall of 1949. Others would claim it as well, but Currin knew him best, and witnesses remembered the instance in '51 most specifically. If it wasn't the first time Chuck had been called by the nickname, it was the first time that many of his contemporaries recalled it. And from that day on, nearly everyone in St. Joe's Hall referred to him by that name or some variation.

The nickname poked fun at Chuck's certitude, but there was also a sense in which it was a descriptive of the authority of his opinions. "If there was ever a discussion, whatever his conclusion was, end of discussion," said Don Donoher. "Chuck's was the last word, so it just became *he is infallible.*"

"They built a million-dollar library next door," said teammate Chuck Spatafore. "But if we had a bet, nobody would think to go look it up. 'Ask Chuck—ask the Pope.' And you'd tell him what the argument was, and he'd say, 'You're wrong. You owe him $5,' or whatever it was."

"He was incredible," said the basketball player Chris Harris. "He was just brilliant. Whatever Chuck said, that was it; it was dogma."

For the rest of his time at Dayton, and beyond, Chuck remained the Pope or Pius. He didn't openly court the name, but he also didn't avoid it. (A few years later, before Currin's marriage, when Chuck sent his sizes for a tuxedo rental to Currin's fiancee, Judy, he signed the note "Pius.")

And so it developed that Chuck became the go-to source for the athletes in St. Joe's Hall. To help with homework. To settle bets. To iron a shirt. On the eve of a surprise ROTC inspection, Spatafore realized his hair had grown longer than military protocol would allow.

"My hair was really bushy," said Spatafore. "I went to put the hat on and it sat on [there] like I was working in a Dairy Queen or something, and I said, 'What am I gonna do? I need a haircut.' We had a tough officer; he was from Korea. Everybody said, 'See the Pope.' So I knocked, said, 'Chuck, can you help me?' He said, 'What?' I said, 'I've got an inspection tomorrow. The hat doesn't even fit me.' And he says—now, he is a year and a half or something older than me—he says, 'Are you willing to sacrifice?' I mean, I'm eighteen years old. I said, 'I have no choice, Chuck.' He said, 'I will cut your hair, but I can't do it tonight. I'm studying, but if you can get up around 5:30 or 6:00 tomorrow morning, I will do it and it will cost you fifty cents.' I said, 'Deal.' So I go in the morning, he put the hat there, he trimmed around it, and inspection passed, and everything was fine. I mean, that is the kind of guy he was."

During one season, Maloney saw Chuck removing a teammate's stitches with a pocket knife and some tweezers. When Maloney visited the team physician, Dr. Pete Rau, later in the day, he was asked about the teammate and explained that he'd seen Chuck taking care of it.

"Chuck Noll better not!," said Rau. "Where did he get his medical degree from?"

One day that spring, Chuck was working in the parking lot on the old Ford he'd bought from his older brother Bob. Tom Carroll saw Chuck, in an auto mechanic's jumpsuit, underneath the Green Hornet, replacing the brakes.

"How in the hell are you doing that?" asked Carroll, frankly amazed.

"Well, you dumb bunny, all you got to do is buy the book," said Chuck. "Get the Ford manual that shows you where the stuff is and you do it."

It was not merely teammates to whom Chuck shared his expertise. One morning, at a diner to eat breakfast with Carroll, Chuck asked to have his eggs basted, and the fry cook looked at him with a quizzical expression. Chuck volunteered to show him, promptly jumping over the counter into the kitchen area, then demonstrating how one could get the yolk cooked by basting it in the oil and butter it was being cooked in. He then jumped back over the counter and ate his egg. For the rest of their time together, whenever Chuck would order a meal, an ice cream cone or even a beer, Carroll would pipe in, deadpan: "Do you want that basted, Chuck?"

Throughout the time, a pattern became clear—Chuck was with the group, but in many ways not of the group. "He used to like jazz, and after practice, he would have his shorts on, and he would stand on the bench," said Jim Currin. "He would do some jazz, some kind of bebop, whatever." What he was actually doing was scatting, like one of his musical heroes, Mel Torme. (Some nights, he'd take his teammate Chuck Spatafore, a drummer from Pittsburgh, and the earnest Ohioan Tom Carroll down to East Third Street to the "black and tan clubs," where black jazz musicians would play for integrated audiences.)

It was during the nights out on the town that Chuck's teammates first became aware of their friend's facility for attracting women. Chuck was not worldly nor was he particularly adept at talking up women. Among the guys around the dorm, he did not speak with any particular authority about his experience with women. But in mixed company, something curious happened: Chuck, clean-cut, well-mannered, possessed of a kind of brawny wholesomeness, drew women without particularly trying. (Maloney was the first to notice that the lack of obvious effort might have been one of the key attributes of Chuck's appeal.)

One day on campus, a coed walked up to Maloney and said, smiling, "Pat, your friend Chuck asks some really intelligent questions. He's got a really good mind on his shoulders."

Chuck didn't date much during these early years of college, but he was noticed. "I know that girls were very attracted to his good looks," said Carroll. "Because we would be some place, and someone would say, 'Hey, who's that guy over there?' Chuck was blonde, and he had that All-American look at the time, he had a crew cut. Just perfect for the time."

Dayton's 1951 training camp was particularly intense, as Gavin sensed he had the makings of a special team. On more than one occasion, when players started grumbling about the endless wind sprints in the muggy Ohio heat, Chuck would speak up, "Gentlemen, we are here on scholarship," he said. "You are getting room, books, tuition, laundry, fees. Why are you complaining?" This would often prompt the grumbling to be redirected at Chuck, but it was good-natured.

Others noticed that Chuck was becoming a team leader, setting the bar of expectations for his teammates. In one-on-one drills, linemen Tom Carroll and John Chaney had a tacit understanding—"We would kind of lean on one another and go through the motions," said Carroll, "and that used to irritate the hell out of Chuck. He would say, 'You know, if you are going to get better . . .' And how true it is. You never got better dancing around the other guy. You've got to *do* it."

With Siggins as the new quarterback, and much of Chuck's class now entrenched as starters, Dayton began the '51 season with verve, beating the Quantico Marines, 21–14, then routing St. Bonaventure (the same team they'd lost to by a 40–14 score the previous season), 35–14. His apprenticeship completed, Siggins was now assured in the pocket. "He was accurate," said Currin. "I think the first game I caught seven passes, and two touchdowns. None of them were very long. Twenty yards would be about the furthest, but he was accurate with them." By mid-season, Currin's receiving exploits were earning national attention. "The King of All Small Colleges," said one newspaper story, which went on to describe Siggins's authority in the huddle, and "The Stare" that his teammates spoke about.

Chuck was anchoring a fast, strong line, adept in the techniques of blocking instilled by McGehee, who by the start of the season had moved on to another tryout with the NFL. By then, Chuck had become the player most willing to coach his teammates. "The coaches told you to get off on the *T* of 'Hut,'" said Tom Carroll. "Chuck would always say to me, 'Get off on the *H*. When you hear that *H*, go.' And I swear to God, that really helped."

For time immemorial, the battle at the line of scrimmage had been about leverage. "Root hog or die!" shouted line coaches at all levels. The concept was drilled into the Dayton players, who heard dozens of times a season that they needed to "strike a rising blow" against their opponent.

In one practice, Chuck attempted to break the action down to its component parts. Watching Carroll try to get in position for an open-field block, he brought him back over and put an arm on his shoulder. "Now you're Catholic," Chuck said. "You genuflect before you get in the pew, don't you?"

"Yeah."

"When you're pulling, just before you hit the guy, think about genu-flecting—and coming up under him."

"What?" asked Carroll.

"You drop your knee," Chuck explained, illustrating the move. "That will get you a little bit lower, but you don't put your knee on the ground."

The rest of the season, before the point of contact in a block, Carroll would think to himself, *genuflect.*

On the morning of Dayton's game against their rival Xavier, Siggins showed up injured, with a bandage on his hand (he had lanced a boil himself). Gavin, perhaps outsmarting himself, had experimented that week with a surprise, an unbalanced line that sent the left end Currin in pre-snap motion to the right side, leaving Chuck, at tackle, exposed as an eligible receiver on the left. But the plays out of that set lacked the fine-honed execution of Dayton's staples in the Precision-T. And when Currin broke his foot in the second half of that game, Dayton couldn't rally. They suffered their first loss of the year, 21–0.

They regrouped with an easy 36–0 win in Cleveland over John Carroll, with Rita and Clarence and many of Chuck's high school friends on hand. Chuck had a strong season, though his Achilles tendon occasionally gave him trouble, knocking him out of the second half of the Miami game. That loss particularly stung—the Flyers led 20–7 well into the fourth quarter, when Miami's diminutive Johnny Pont ran for a touchdown. The usually reliable Akau fumbled deep in Miami territory, and Miami then drove down for the winning score, a last-minute touchdown run by Pont.

The regular season ended on a positive note, a 34–13 win over Mar-shall. In the locker room, after the game, Gavin gathered his players and announced that they had received an invitation from the Salad Bowl, played in Glendale, Arizona.

There were real questions within the administration over the cost. One day, dean of students Father Charles Collins and athletic director Harry Baujan were sitting in Brother Paul's Cafeteria, discussing the expense. Currin, self-appointed team spokesman, walked up to the administrators and offered his own solution.

"Look, the team would love to go," he said. "If you would just take a freight car, throw straw in it and a barrel of beer in each corner, we would be glad to go that way."

"The hay and the train car is fine," said Collins. "But we wouldn't put the beer in there." (Currin wouldn't endear himself to the university administration later on when he started a rumor that the school hadn't accepted the invitation yet because all the priests wanted new suits.) Dayton finally accepted.

It would be the greatest moment in Dayton's major-college football history. They took a chartered train from Dayton, with eleven newspapermen and two train cars full of boosters along for the ride. At a stop in Albuquerque, Gavin had the entire team don sweats and tennis shoes and brought them out to the train platform for calisthenics.

The game itself, played on January 1, 1952, drew a crowd estimated at 17,000. But Gavin's defense, again, let him down. Houston ripped off 488 yards of total offense, and even though Siggins threw for 188 yards, and star back Bobby Recker ran for two touchdowns, Dayton couldn't catch up. Chuck, bedeviled again by a dodgy Achilles tendon, sat out part of the second half, as Dayton fell, 26–21.

They still returned to acclaim, the ambassadors from the small school having played in an exciting New Year's Day game. In December, it was announced that Chuck and lineman Ed Clemens would be team co-captains in 1952. He and Clemens appeared on the cover of the 1952 Dayton football media guide, walking through campus, sporting their letter sweaters with patches noting the previous season's Salad Bowl appearance.

✦ ✦ ✦

Training camp for the 1952 season began not on the campus of UD but out at Mount St. John's, the seminary near campus. The season was to open with a game against the University of Cincinnati, coached by Sid Gillman. Gavin and Gillman had developed a rivalry over recruits, and Gillman carried a reputation as a coach who was not above espionage. So the Flyers took a long bus ride every day. "We got out of our routines," said Maloney. "Instead of staying in the campus, we would be bussed out to Mount St. John's. Gavin didn't want people to come and see what we were doing."

The ruse didn't help. Gillman's Cincinnati team thumped the Flyers, 25–0, to begin the '52 season. Though UD recovered to win their next three games, it was soon apparent the feeling wasn't the same. Some questioned Siggins's commitment. "Frank went off and fell in love and got married," said Maloney, "and it really wasn't the same team our senior year."

"I don't want to put the blame on Frank," said Currin, "but he didn't want to be there, and he openly admitted that he didn't want it." What vexed Currin and some of the other teammates was that Ted Marchibroda, the standout St. Bonaventure quarterback, could have come to Dayton when the Bonnies gave up football in 1951. But Gavin was reluctant to invite Marchibroda, because he already had Siggins.

Through the up-and-down season, Chuck helped hold the pieces together, not with speeches but, as he had throughout his Dayton career, by example. "He was a leader, in his own way," said Currin. "He took no guff. He was not aggressive, other than on the football field."

Chuck absorbed as much punishment as anyone. While he was a stickler for technique, he'd also internalized the idea of getting the job done. "Chuck was a big one for sticking the crown of his helmet into the other guy's chest," said Currin. The hitting took its toll on all of them. Chuck's hands, at twenty-one, were already grizzled from the infighting of line play, and he suffered back pain from McGehee's follow-through technique of wrenching defenders one way or another at the end of his blocks.

The players understood the toughness that came with the game, though not the long-term effects of the hits they endured. So they lived by a code of stoicism and often made light of what they didn't understand. Maloney was knocked out in the Cincinnati game. When trainer Hank Ferrazza rushed out to tend to him, he knelt over Maloney and said, "Pat, how are you doing?"

Groggy, Maloney looked up at him and said, "I think I'm okay. But . . . how's the crowd taking it?"

The '52 season also featured a rare home-and-home series with Xavier. Dayton lost their home game, 14–13, but came back three weeks later to win on the road, 13–0, the first win over their rivals since 1948. The game was immortalized with a picture of Chuck, next to Ed Clemens, holding on to the President's Cup (presented to the captains of the winning team after each game in the rivalry), Chuck's face and his sky-blue jersey both caked with mud.

Four days later, on Thanksgiving, they went down to Chattanooga for their last game and were blown out, 40–7, to end a disappointing 6–5 season.

As they took off their sweaty football gear in the Chattanooga locker room, they each knew, to a man, it was probably the last time they'd play the sport. Though Chuck was named All-Ohio, he was undersized for a lineman and was already focused on looking for teaching jobs after graduation. The co-captain Clemens and the star running back, Recker, were also considered too small for the pros. Only Currin, who'd earned national attention with his receptions, was given a chance. For everyone else, it seemed, the ride was over.

So when a man called the dorm one day in January 1953 to inform Chuck he'd been drafted, he at first assumed it was the Army and was perplexed; he'd already been declared 4-F due to his epilepsy.

"No, the Browns—the Cleveland Browns," said the reporter. The confirmation came later from Howard Brinker, one of the Browns' assistant coaches, who told Chuck he'd be receiving a contract in the mail. The Browns kept close tabs on Ohio schools, and Gavin had recommended Noll as the sort of brainy football player that Paul Brown loved; Cleveland drafted him in the twentieth round. When Brinker learned Chuck would be coming to Cleveland to visit his parents over Easter, he told him to stop in to the Browns' offices in the Leader Building and visit with Paul Brown.

After William Noll heard the news, he was unusually demonstrative. "My father was *very* happy," said Rita Deininger.

The standard contract for rookies was $5,000. Among the teaching opportunities that had been offered Chuck, one was at Holy Name High School in Cleveland, for a pay of $2,700.

Of course, the odds were stacked against Chuck making the team. NFL rosters had thirty-three players. From one year to the next, there might be twenty-eight or twenty-nine holdovers, even more on a perennial contender like the Browns. But Brown had been told about Chuck's technical skills.

"Well, you're big enough," said Brown to Chuck when he visited Cleveland that spring. "Let's see if you're brave enough."

In his meeting with Paul Brown, Chuck chose not to mention the seizures. They had dissipated in frequency, but had not gone away. "He had one in the field house one day," said teammate John Vukelich. "I think from that he really started watching himself. When he would go out, he was a sipper. He would make you think he was drinking big but he wasn't."

"He said if he took his medicine he never had a problem," said Pat Maloney. The medicines—Dilantin and phenobarbital—were effective, but Chuck disliked the side effects.

"I remember we went down to the athletic office to pick up our grades," said Carroll. "And he got his grades and he turned around and he said, 'Can you believe this? That guy gave me a D.' And I said, 'In what?' And he said, 'In that stinking PE class.' And then the next thing he said to me was, 'Don't let my head hit the floor.' I looked at him like, 'What the hell are you talking about?' And then I looked and I could see him starting to go. And I stuck my hand out and I got it stuck, you know where you bend your elbow? I got it stuck on his bicep and I couldn't let go if I wanted to. So I eased him down and I started yelling for help. I tried to cradle his head, and one of the trainers came out and they did something, and we helped him down to the training room, and then the trainer said, 'Go on, and get out of here. Go on up to the hall.' I saw him that night up in bed, and he said, 'Yeah, I am awful tired.' He said, 'They take all my energy.' And then he was fine."

Despite the sporadic seizures, Chuck's social life became more active. He and his friends often went to the Sigma Theater for movies; on Friday nights, everyone went down to a tavern called the Double K, to watch boxing on *Gillette's Cavalcade of Sports* on NBC—the club being one of the only places in town with a television set.

By the end of senior year, most of the players were hanging out at Kramer's Party Supply, just a few minutes from the campus. They were drawn to its rustic furnishings, low-slung refrigerator behind the bar, and utter lack of pretension. Teammates Tony Kramer (no relation to the proprietor) and John Vukelich had both started working there. But even when they were off work, they liked the humble, comfortable atmosphere. "The Heidelberg was a little small," said Vukelich. "Kramer's was bigger. You got to sit down at tables." In the summer, they would swim in the quarry down by the hill behind the restaurant.

At Kramer's, they would listen to the crooners and the jump blues working their way through the airwaves and the jukebox in the days before rock 'n' roll. Chuck was particularly attuned to the sounds. "He would always be right on top of all the things that were going on," said Tom Carroll. "And he always said that, if he was ever a disc jockey, he had a little saying—something like, 'Hello to all you chicks and Chucks out there,' and he had a regular spiel. He said, 'This is the way I would start my show.'"

For many of the seniors, whose college careers were winding down, relationships with women moved to the fore. Siggins was already married. Akau had grown serious about his girlfriend Iris, a Greek American dancer whom everyone called "The Greek." Jim Currin had begun to date a coed named Judy, whom he'd met at the Democratic Club in Dayton. And throughout that spring semester, Chuck was dating a vivacious brunette coed named Shirley Stemley.

"They were really involved," said Maloney. Chuck was not one to parade dates around to his friends, but he enjoyed the relaxed evenings double-dating with Akau. "He called his car his 'mobile,'" Shirley Stemley remembered. "'I'll pick you up in my mobile.'" That spring, when the frost broke, and the fresh fruit started coming to the stores, they'd buy a watermelon on their way over to Shirley's, take a hypodermic needle (Shirley had a friend in nurses' training), and inject it with vodka. They'd go out with Sneeze and The Greek who would, with enough alcohol and a little encouragement, get up and dance on the tables. With a few drinks, Chuck loved to dance the Charleston.

That spring, the *Cleveland Plain Dealer* ran a story on Chuck and interviewed Joe Gavin, who had offered Chuck a job working as his line coach after graduation. "Waitin' to see what Chuck Noll intends to do," said Gavin. "The Cleveland Browns drafted him, you know, but Chuck hasn't decided whether he will play pro football. If he signs a contract, I'll start looking for a line coach because he'll make the team. If he doesn't—and I hope he decides to pass up the chance—he'll have a job with me."

Chuck had known for years he wanted to be a teacher, but now with the Browns drafting him, he had to decide whether to give football a shot.

Decades later, Chuck would admit to his doubts. "I was concerned, when I graduated, about losing the security of going to school and having to earn a living," he said. "That was a very traumatic time."

With Stemley, Chuck was unusually open in discussing his future. "He did ask me," said Stemley, "if I thought he would be able to make the Cleveland Browns team. I told him, 'They want you. They are after you. Go! What have you got to lose?'"

"Maybe I'll go," Chuck said.

That summer of 1953, Chuck, Currin, Maloney, and Carroll, along with basketball player Chris Harris, wound up renting space in the attic of an apartment on Grafton Avenue, behind the Dayton Art Institute, and within easy walking distance of McKinley Park. They each paid the owner $5 a week for a mattress in the attic. Someone brought up a fan, and they shared the one bathroom and shower. At night, mattresses soaked with sweat, they'd try to sleep. (Maloney and Carroll finally retreated to the cooler basement, where they slept on two cots next to a washing machine.) Eventually, Chris Harris was joined by his brother Ted, just back from Korea. The boys reveled in a final summer of camaraderie, before heading off to begin their adult lives.

They'd found work for a squat, gray-haired man named Shorty Wetzel, the proprietor of Dayton Asphalt, laying tar and working nearly dawn to dusk every weekday. It was hot, dirty work, and only the money and the friendship made it worthwhile. "They called it 'the ass company,'" said Shirley Stemley. "Then we would do these things on Saturday night, after they finished their asses."

When they returned to the apartment, most of them would collapse. Not Chuck. Each day, he would change into his Dayton athletic shorts, grab his stopwatch and implore Maloney or Carroll to join him at McKinley Park a few blocks away.

"Chuck, I'm tired—you go," Carroll would protest.

"You don't have to *do* anything!," Chuck said. "Just come along and sit down and time me."

There, in the gathering dusk, Chuck would run 40-yard sprints, and then have Carroll time the intervals—first sixty seconds, then fifty seconds, then forty seconds, down to ten-second breaks. Chuck would run until he collapsed from exhaustion. Carroll, stopwatch in hand, would sit with his back against a tree and time his friend.

The sight of the other tired young men sprawled in the stifling heat of their threadbare apartment while Chuck changed into sweatpants and tennis shoes became one of the recurring motifs of that summer.

"Pius, slow down, man," said Chris Harris one hot evening.

"Gotta do it," Chuck replied. "Gotta make this team."

Friday, July 3. Chuck and the crew were laying asphalt on one of Dayton's hottest days, temperatures hovering around 100 degrees. After cleaning off the machinery, they discussed what they'd do that night. "We can go to the country club," said Jim Raiff, whose parents belonged to Miami Valley Country Club.

So that night, Chuck and Raiff, Maloney and Currin, Chris Harris and his brother Ted, just weeks back from military duty, snuck into the pool area—passing through the clubhouse, as Raiff had learned to do.

It didn't take long before the horseplay started. Maloney was doing cannonballs and splashing water, and others were doing their dives. And then Ted Harris went up on the high dive with Maloney and executed an arcing dive off the board. Maloney was still up on the board, looking down, when he saw Ted's splash, and the water turning inky with blood right afterward. Ted had not accounted for the pool floor's sharp ascent, and he cracked his head on the floor. Chuck and the others dove down and tried as best they could to carry him gingerly to safety. The ambulance came later, but Ted Harris was clearly hurt. As Chuck and Pat and Chris and Jim waited outside the emergency room at Good Samaritan Hospital, shocked and afraid and still wet, there was little to say.

Six days later, on July 9, Ted Harris died. Chuck was one of the pallbearers. All of the boys who turned to men that summer suffered with the second-guessing and the memory of the horrific moment. Maloney would for the rest of his days remember the billowing cloud of blood rising up through the water after Ted's landing. After the funeral, they met over at the Heidelberg for a somber lunch.

Each of them were marked by the tragedy, and each of them struggled to articulate their loss and regret. Chuck articulated the least of all.

"I don't think he really ever got over that," said Shirley Stemley.

It was only days later that Chuck left for Cleveland, still shocked and saddened by the tragedy. He had said good-bye to Shirley a night earlier. On a hot morning in late July, he put his belongings in the backseat and trunk of the Green Hornet, shook Maloney's hand, and headed north. He'd stop for a while in Cleveland, unload his things, check in with his parents, and meet Clare and Rita's baby boy, Rick.

Then he would try to shift his mind back toward the goal that had driven him through the spring and summer. The next few weeks would determine whether he was going to be a schoolteacher or a professional football player.

five

MESSENGER

✦   ✦   ✦

Rookies did not try out for the Cleveland Browns so much as they were indoctrinated into the environment that Paul Brown had created. The Browns did things differently from other NFL franchises and prided themselves on this distinctiveness.

The conditioning began with "The Speech," which had remained largely unchanged since Brown gave it the first time, in the basement lounge of the Alpha Xi Delta sorority house on the campus of Bowling Green University in 1946.

On the first day of training camp in 1953, on the campus of Hiram College, Chuck was sitting in a small student desk, with the flip-top writing surface, along with eighty other players. The veterans strolled in a little later than the rookies, and seemed more relaxed, but everyone was in his seat minutes ahead of the start time.

At a few moments before 9 a.m., the man appeared. Dressed in khaki pants and a white T-shirt, sporting a ball cap, he greeted a few of his veterans with a thin smile. Brown began speaking at the stroke of 9.

"I am Paul," he said. "I want you to call me Paul. I give this speech every year, in fact, I consider this our most important meeting of the year. Some of you have heard it a few times. That's okay, I want you to familiarize yourself with it, to know it better each year."

There were a few more opening procedural points, Brown introduced assistants and club executives before he articulated the sort of relationship he wanted. He expanded on the methods of address. "I want us all to be on a first-name basis," he said. "We are friends."

Brown repeatedly asked players to "be a man about it." They were asked to "pay the price." Brown sang the praises of smart players and cited numerous examples of dim-witted players. "We weed them out. The veterans know what I'm talking about."

Throughout the two-hour presentation, separated by a ten-minute break, there were no asides or murmuring among the players, the stillness in the big hall punctuated only by the sound of muffled coughs and large men shifting uncomfortably in their chairs. Brown never told a joke, and no one laughed.

He warned against "dissipation," by which he meant the dangers of having sex the night before a game. Finally, Brown told the players to enjoy themselves during training camp, to be sure to dress and talk appropriately, to not fraternize with any of the coeds at Hiram or any of the townsfolk. He even told them to be sure to not slurp their soup at the cafeteria.

Among Chuck's previous coaches, neither Joe Rufus nor Joe Gavin had been overly demonstrative. But Paul Brown was a breed apart—his emotion remaining on a flat plane of businesslike cordiality, laced with impatience with anyone who deviated from his chosen methods. Not many did. What Chuck found, seven years after he had sat in the stands for the Browns' first-ever regular season game at Cleveland Stadium, was a tone and setting completely consistent with the academic work he'd done the previous four years at Dayton.

Each player received a green notebook, into which he was expected to copy down each and every play diagram and coaching point that he heard. Chuck went back to his dorm room and studied. The physical part of preparing for camp had been a months-long slog. But now, the game reduced to its component parts, it was as though school was back in session. It was a setting in which he knew he could excel.

By 1953, Paul Brown had been a coaching legend for years. He'd built a high school powerhouse at Masillon High, then coached Ohio State to a national championship in 1941, left to coach at Great Lakes Naval Academy during the war, decided that Ohio State did not want him back with sufficient enthusiasm, and agreed to coach with the new Cleveland franchise in the upstart All-America Football Conference.

There he'd brought about the biggest revolution in the sport in decades, integrating the professional game with the signing of Marion Motley and Bill Willis, leading the Browns to four AAFC titles, dominating the league so completely that fans in other cities (and, eventually, even in Cleveland) lost interest. At the end of the 1949 season, Cleveland agreed to join the NFL, along with two other AAFC franchises, and proceeded to win the NFL title in 1950, before losing the title games in 1951 and 1952. In seven years of pro football, Brown's Browns had been to seven championship games, winning five.

Along the way, he had been credited with rescuing the often brutal game of football, helping to turn it into a profession. The Browns' players were held to a higher standard. They were viewed, just as Brown had envisioned before his first season coaching the team, as "the New York Yankees of pro football."

Brown wasn't outwardly boastful, but there was a self-consciousness, even a self-righteousness, that could seep into his public comments. After the team's inaugural championship, in 1946, he pronounced himself happy, then added, "For the players' sake, too, I'm tickled with that victory. But my satisfaction is in proving my principles, proving that the same ideas and ideals that won in high school and college can win, too, in pro ball."

Compared to the rest of pro football, the Browns were more organized and, in Brown's view, more humane. Brown ran the team with a pronounced didacticism; there were intelligence tests, weekly quizzes of comprehension, and a rigorous college scouting process that was more detailed and comprehensive than any other team in the league, save the scouting pioneers the Los Angeles Rams.

Unlike the Rams, the Browns did not yet employ a full-time scout. On January 22, 1953, the NFL Draft—the "annual selection meeting," as it was officially known—was held at the Bellevue-Stratford Hotel in Philadelphia. While Brown had constructed his first pro team based largely on former players and opponents, he'd recognized that, in the unified NFL, the only real way to maintain a powerful club was through the draft. While assistant Blanton Collier was charged with overseeing the minutiae of grading every single Browns' player on every single play from the previous season, the scouting of college players was coordinated by another assistant, Wilbur "Weeb" Ewbank, the diminutive Ohioan who'd signed with the Browns in 1949 after two successful seasons as the head coach of Washington University in St. Louis.

The drafts were still largely informal affairs for most teams, coaches calling a network of friends to discuss a particular player's prospects, while some teams literally arrived with copies of the *Street & Smith's College Football Annual* from the previous August. After the first two years of the drafts in the NFL, Brown concluded that Washington's George Preston Marshall wasn't stopping by the Browns' table just to chat with his colleague, but also was hoping to peek at names on the Browns' draft list, which was significantly better researched than the Redskins' own list. In response, Brown developed an oversized three-faced master list that showed the Browns overall top-rated players, as well as designations of best players by position. It could quickly be folded up like a restaurant menu when another owner would walk over to fraternize. "He felt Marshall was the one that would come over," said his son, Mike Brown. "They were working off of *Sport* magazine, so he would want to see what was up—or at least that was the concern."

At the '53 draft, with guard Lin Houston having announced his retirement, a new guard was one of the needs for the Browns. They made it a priority, selecting three guards from major colleges—Gene Donaldson of Kentucky in the third round, Elmer Willhoite of USC in the twelfth, and Tom Cain of Colorado in the nineteenth—before announcing their twentieth-round selection, Charles H. Noll of the University of Dayton. Chuck's friend Jim Currin had gone four rounds earlier, selected by the Baltimore Colts, while fellow co-captain Ed Clemens was selected five rounds later, by the San Francisco 49ers.

✦   ✦   ✦

The son of a railroad man, Paul Brown prided himself on his precision. His habitual punctuality was most obvious at training camps. "We would go to practice," said Don Colo, the big lineman who'd been involved in the fifteen-player trade with Baltimore (in which young defensive back Don Shula went to the Colts), "and he would say we are going to be on the field for one hour and fifteen minutes, and we were on one hour and fifteen minutes, never deviated a minute one way or the other. So there was no standing around. Everything was functional, it was organized and that was the biggest thing."

Within the dormitory halls at Hiram, the age-old guessing game proceeded as usual. Veterans relaxing, focusing on getting fit, secure in their positions. The Browns engaged in very little rookie hazing, save for veteran defensive lineman Bob Gain's calling card, of striking up a friendly chat with rookies in the showers and maintaining a pleasant smile and eye contact with the rookie, even as he was urinating on him.

For fringe players like Chuck, every day was a chance to prove one's self or to affirm the doubts of the coaching staff. Chuck had reported in excellent condition and was easily integrating Brown's methodical teaching into his routine. He knew the playbook. Then one day, early in camp, he felt the loss of equilibrium coming on and collapsed onto the field and began quivering. It was a grand mal seizure, that left the other players backing away with concern and trainer Leo Murphy rushing onto the field to assist Chuck.

"If you ever see a grand mal, it is kind of awe-inspiring," said Colo. "And all I said to myself is, 'He is gone.' Not anything derogatory; I was just thinking, *That's it*. But he survived. After that, I noticed him more, and it went from there."

Chuck had not previously notified the Browns of his condition, and while he never talked to his teammates about it, he finally confided in Currin, whom he saw in Akron a few days later, when the Browns played their third exhibition game. "Paul Brown was ready to cut him," said Currin, "and Chuck went to him and told him his story, that he has had them before, and that he held off his medicine. He said, 'Would you call Joe Gavin and Dr. Pete Rau at Dayton and find out?' And he did, and Paul Brown made him promise that he would take the medicine every day. If he would do that, he would let him continue in the camp."

The Browns' team physician, Dr. Vic Ippilito, knew the Dayton trainer Hank Ferrazza, as both men frequented a restaurant in Cleveland's Shaker Square called the Wagon Wheel. Soon, Ferrazza had briefed Ippilito, and Ippilito explained the condition to Paul Brown.

Through training camp, Chuck was outplaying every other rookie guard on the team. Then on August 7, Lin Houston, the retired starting right guard who'd alternated with Joe Skibiniski in 1952, announced he was coming out of retirement. With Houston back in camp, Chuck would not only have to beat out the other draftees but also the holdover Skibinski.

But Chuck remained in the forefront, one of the most pleasant surprises in camp. Every Sunday afternoon, following lunch, the players would report to one of the classrooms at Hiram and answer a series of questions based on the material they covered that week. Chuck scored consistently high.

Over the years, the tests changed little—a sheet, but rarely more, of mimeographed questions. They weren't multiple choice ("I don't want you guessing," Brown said) but simple situational queries. If the defense overloads on the weak side, how does the blocking change? How do we best attack the deep zone? Chuck was frequently among the first to turn in his quizzes. The questions weren't tricky or surprising or particularly complex.

"We used to call Willie Davis 'Univac,'" said Colo. "Because on the test, the coaches would have to stay there until the last guy finished. And Willie kept Weeb Ewbank there until 5 o'clock because he was taking it seriously."

Brown had long placed speed and intelligence over raw physical brawn in building his football teams (prior to his first season coaching the Browns, he told one reporter, "I think too much stress has been placed on weight in professional football. I always believed—and I still do—that a light, fast team can beat a heavy squad"). He liked the agility and speed Chuck showed from the guard position and recognized that Chuck was already adept in the crucial techniques needed for any undersized lineman to succeed at the pro level. But it went beyond that. Simply put, Chuck exuded the sort of clean-cut, no-nonsense Midwestern sensibility that Brown valued, and he demonstrated the trademark zeal ("I want players who run on their own gas") that he'd always prized.

By the middle of August, Brown was publicly complimenting Chuck. "He ranks pretty high among the rookies trying out as offensive guards," Brown said on August 12. "He's an intelligent boy and learns fast. It's refreshing working with someone like that again."

The offensive line coach Fritz Heisler found Chuck a quick study. "He was the type who went all out even doing exercises," said Heisler. "I couldn't believe it."

On August 23, the Browns played their first preseason game, in San Francisco against the 49ers, winning 20-7. "I'll never forget the first game I played with the Browns," Chuck said decades later, "and I realized I could play in the National Football League."

When the final cuts were made, the veteran Skibinski was released in favor of Chuck. The rookie had earned the right to alternate with Houston. When he realized he'd made the team, he didn't celebrate. He merely returned to his parents' home and shared the good news. He also called Shirley Stemley and thanked her for urging him to stick with football.

"You were right," he said. "I'm glad I did it."

Teaching could wait. He was now a professional football player.

✦   ✦   ✦

After the relative freedom and autonomy the athletes enjoyed at Dayton, Chuck had to adjust to the degree to which Brown ran the lives of his players. The veteran lineman John Sandusky spoke for much of the team when he said, "We didn't necessarily like Paul Brown all the time and we definitely didn't love him most of the time. But we all had such reverence and respect for his genius, his intelligence, his forward thinking. We all knew we were around something really special."

The area where the Brown philosophy most affected Chuck was in play calling. In 1949, after Graham had won Brown three AAFC championships, the coach stripped quarterback Otto Graham of play-calling duties and began a shuttle system with messenger guards Houston and Bob Gaudio.

At training camp, Chuck had a humble start with Brown's system. "He gave me a play," Chuck said, "and I dashed onto the field for the huddle. As soon as I got there, I forgot it. It was really very embarrassing, but Paul just laughed."

Another time in camp, Brown sent him in with a play for George Ratterman, Graham's backup.

"I-22," said Chuck.

Ratterman looked nonplussed and replied, "Nah, I don't want to run that one. Go back and tell him I want another." Chuck was just starting to turn back toward the bench when Ratterman grabbed him by the shoulder and said, "Get back here."

Many of the Browns' players resented the messenger guard system, few more than Otto Graham. To Chuck, the Browns' huddles felt different; after Siggins's regal stare and the way he ran the huddle at Dayton, Chuck had to adjust to the Browns' players standing around waiting for the messenger guard to give the play to Otto Graham or Ratterman and then have the quarterback repeat the play to the rest of the offense. "It emasculates the quarterback," Chuck would observe later.

It was also not easy for the messenger guards themselves. While each messenger guard ran only half the team's offensive plays, both guards ran a 30- to 40-yard sprint after each play, either to the bench to confer with Brown or back to the huddle to bring in the play call.

For his part, Chuck only knew that the game was much tougher at the pro level. "There's a big difference between the pros and college football," he told one newspaper reporter that fall. "In college, you hit the guy opposite you a few times and he decides, 'This is too tough.' But in the pros, they belt you right back."

Two old Dayton teammates, Jim Currin and Paul Cassidy, joined Chuck for a drink following a win over Washington in October. "After the game was over, we all met with Chuck, and he was obviously still suffering from a bang in the head—it was obvious he had taken a couple of hits," said Cassidy. "The impression was he was a little dazed. In those days, the way they treated the concussion was smelling salts and a tap on the ass, and told them to get going again. But Chuck was playing linebacker and special teams, and Chuck was about, I don't know, 200 pounds?"

But he was playing, and the Browns were winning. On Thanksgiving Day of 1953, the *Cleveland Press* had run a human-interest feature on Chuck, with the headline, "Sorry, Gals! Handsome Chuck Noll's Heart Belongs to Cleveland Browns." Hal Leibovitz noted that Chuck's father was a parking lot attendant and that "his mother, thoughtfully, lets Chuck sleep 'til noon the day after each game. 'That running on and off the field is fatiguing,' he says."

Leibovitz's story didn't focus on the beating Chuck was taking on a weekly basis, the pain in his legs on the morning after games, or the multiple bruises he inherited from trying to block players who outweighed him by as much as sixty pounds. But it did note that his clean-cut air and polite manner, combined with the strong jaw and blue eyes, made for a winning combination.

Chuck had broken it off with Shirley Stemley at the end of the summer. "Let's just cool it for now," he told her. "I've gotta go do this." She saw him at a couple of Browns' games, but they drifted apart.

The Saturday after Thanksgiving, Ralph Yanky was marrying his longtime girlfriend, Joan Bulger, with whom he'd double-dated back in high school. Yanky was just returning on military leave and had asked Chuck to be the best man at his wedding. Chuck had to decline, because Brown wouldn't agree to let Chuck stay out after the appointed time he was supposed to report to the Carter Hotel, where the Browns stayed on the eve of home games. Chuck and his mother attended the wedding mass on Saturday morning, then Chuck returned to the hotel, the day before the team won its tenth consecutive game, 27–16, over the Chicago Cardinals. They won again the following week, routing the Giants, 62–14, to clinch a spot in yet another title game, before losing their regular-season finale, 42–27, at Philadelphia.

The championship game was a rematch of 1952's title contest, with the Browns traveling to Detroit's Tigers Stadium to face the Lions again. The '53 title game got off to a poor start when Lin Houston, pulling from his right guard position to pick up the Lions' Joe Schmidt on an outside blitz, failed to deter him, allowing Schmidt to strip Otto Graham of the football. The Lions scored a few plays later to make it 7–0.

Throughout the game, Chuck found himself matched up against the Lions' mammoth nose guard Les Bingaman, who outweighed him by at least sixty pounds. He couldn't drive Bingaman anywhere, but he consistently got underneath the bigger man, stood him up at the line of scrimmage, and slowed his pursuit.

There was little to separate the teams, and Cleveland led 16–10 deep into the fourth quarter, before the Lions' Bobby Layne found Jim Doran for a touchdown pass in the closing minutes, beating defensive back Warren Lahr. Doak Walker's extra point gave the Lions a 17–16 lead and prompted a flurry of hats and paper down on the field.

After the ensuing kickoff, Brown sent Chuck in with a pass play for Otto Graham, but the Browns' catalyst had been off all day. Two fumbles had led to 10 Lions' points, and Graham (who complained later of chapped hands that prevented him from gripping the football well) threw a wounded pass that was intercepted, giving the Lions their second straight NFL title game win over Cleveland.

Including 1951's loss to the Rams, it was Cleveland's third straight championship game loss, and left Brown quietly simmering. The team took a long, funereal train ride home—"longest train ride I ever took," said Lou Groza—after which a crestfallen Lahr was in tears, as he and Heisler carpooled to their homes in suburban Aurora.

While the ending was shocking, Chuck had acquitted himself well in his first season. Now, he was faced with his first off-season as a professional. It didn't take him long to find a new outlet. On January 4, 1954, he drove downtown to the Hanna Building, where he joined the staff of the Manufacturers Life Insurance Company.

He'd found the connection to work at the job through Groza, who'd been working for the firm for years. The company sent out a mailing that winter, noting "With Great Pleasure, the Manufacturers Life Insurance Company Announces that Charles H. Noll Is Now Representing This Company. Mr. Noll graduated from Benedictine High School and the University of Dayton, where he was an outstanding football player. Last year he was a member of the Cleveland Browns Professional Football Team. Mr. Noll is well known to the residents of Cleveland and we are sure that his many friends will welcome this announcement of his appointment as a Representative of the Manufacturers Life." That same week, Chuck sold his first policy to Ralph and Joan Yanky.

There was still something that felt surreal about making his living playing football. When Chuck was listed in the 1954 Cleveland City directory, the listing read "agt Manufacturers Life Insurance Co" and made no mention of the Browns. William V. Noll, listed at the same address of 1362 W. 114th St, was listed as "atndnt."

In his free time, Chuck found work as a substitute teacher at Holy Name High School, where John Spezzaferro, the former Dayton assistant, was now the head football coach.

While many of the Browns' players went back to their hometowns in the off-season, a few lived in Cleveland full time. A handful like Chuck had been born and raised there. Others, like Dante Lavelli and Lou Groza, had found steady work and bought homes in the area.

With many of his teammates gone, his Dayton teammates increasingly scattered around the country, and Ralph Yanky now a newlywed, Chuck began spending more time with Hank and Dan Ferrazza. The brothers, both veterans of the Second World War, had been confidantes of Chuck's at Dayton, and while Dan had moved back to Cleveland upon his graduation in 1951, Hank commuted to Cleveland frequently (he'd earned his master's degree from Case Western Reserve). Hank was older, more muted, and serious, and Dan, the younger brother, was still steadfast but with a wry sense of humor. Chuck trusted and enjoyed the company of both—they hewed to the eternal verities.

Now they were part of a tight amalgam of people who gathered regularly at the rustic Shaker Square tavern known as The Wagon Wheel, situated next door to a burger joint and across the street from a piano bar. Through the front door and down a spiral wrought-iron staircase was Etienne's French Cuisine, owned by two brothers. "Ladies in furs, perfectly tailored gentlemen," Chuck recalled. "The guy who owned the bar, Doc Mangine, knew the two brothers who owned the restaurant. When they had tenderloin or tournedos or something left over, he'd get them to grind it up into hamburger for us. They'd mix a sauce in with it and it was delicious. We never could have afforded it, not at the $5,000 a year Paul Brown was paying us."

The group was close-knit—Mangine; Mike Bordinaro, whose family worked in produce; the Ferrazza brothers; and Chuck. As in the Dayton days, he was not the wild carouser. But he didn't mind spending time with some who were.

Chuck had also begun dating again, though only casually.

"Chuck came in town and I fixed him up with someone," said Maloney, remembering a double-date in the spring of 1954. "Anyway, the girl I was with fell all in love with Chuck. She was all over him the whole freaking night, and I was way out in left field. Chuck was one hell of a good-looking guy. He was not a hound. He wasn't out chasing girls or anything like that. Just, if he met somebody he liked, they seemed to end up liking him a lot more than he liked them."

There was a green-eyed, dark-haired Italian beauty named Mary Jo. Shirley Stemley, back in Dayton, heard Chuck's friends exclaiming about how beautiful she was. "Chuck's friends used to refer to her as 'Sex on a Stick,'" she said.

"She was a 10!," said Pat Maloney. And yet, through all of these courtships, Chuck seemed curiously uninvolved. He retained a seriousness of purpose that was resistant to the imperatives of carousing. A few beers, a couple nights out, then it was back to work—selling insurance, substitute teaching, helping his parents, fixing things around the house.

At the beginning of the 1954 season, there was a directive from Brown that all players needed to wear the new face masks that Riddell had fashioned for the team (Brown had devised them in the wake of the gruesome facial injury Graham had suffered the previous season against the 49ers). Chuck didn't care for the face mask and beefed with trainer Leo Murphy.

"Paul Brown says everybody wears them," said Murphy. "If you don't want to wear it, that's *your* prerogative."

So before the season, Chuck took off his mask and played without one until the December 5, 1954, game at Washington.

"They called an end-around," said Murphy. "Well, Abe Gibron and Chuck pulled, and they ran right back of Otto, and they both got knocked down. Chuck didn't have a mask on, he had taken his off. He comes running out of the game and says, 'I need a mask.' I said, 'Chuck, you don't need it anymore. Your two front teeth are gone.'"

Chuck's tenacious style earned him the appreciation of his teammates but not always his opponents. One player he persistently tangled with was Chuck Bednarik, the Eagles' cantankerous two-way lineman. Early in his career, Chuck laid a good shot on Bednarik at the line of scrimmage on a punt. After the game, still peeved, Bednarik took a swing at Chuck with his helmet, striking him and knocking him to his knees. Chuck was hurt, angry, and also venting a moral rage. According to Lou Groza, what Chuck shouted to Bednarik after the two men were separated was, "May your soul burn in the fires of hell!"

NFL Commissioner Bert Bell was watching the game on television with his son, Upton Bell, and was incensed both by Bednarik's unprovoked violence and the fact that TV cameras showed the skirmish at the end of the game. That week, he called Bednarik into his office, disciplining him with a fine and orders to apologize to Chuck when the two teams played in Philadelphia later in the season.

Before the next Browns-Eagles game, Bednarik walked up to Chuck during warm-ups, and said, "I want to apologize for what happened."

"Bullshit!," said Chuck. The feud would continue for years.

The 1954 regular season ended with the Browns losing for the fourth straight time to the Lions. But a week later, in the 1954 NFL Championship Game in Cleveland, the scene was much different. Cleveland rolled to a 56–10 win over Detroit, with Chuck and the offensive line protecting Otto Graham expertly (he completed 9 of 12 passes for 163 yards), to gain a measure of revenge from losses to the Lions in the previous two title games. In the jubilant locker room, teammates embraced Graham, who announced during the postgame celebration that he was retiring. At the end of his second season as a pro, Chuck was a world champion.

With Chuck making extra money selling insurance and substitute teaching at Holy Name, plus the championship share—$2,478.57, nearly half his annual salary—for winning the 1954 NFL title, he was in a position to sit down with Clarence and Rita and talk about buying a home, where William and Kate would also live. His father still had his job at the parking lot downtown, but his health was poor, and other than going to work, he rarely left the house. His mother was picking up occasional hours at a florist's shop but was less active and struggling with her weight.

Over at Clarence and Rita's, there were two children—two-year-old Rick and one-year-old Margie—and another baby on the way. Chuck and Clare found a trim, two-unit home on East 141st Street, just a few doors down from St. Mary's of Czestachowa, the parish Clare and Rita already attended, and one that featured a school for their growing family.

That January, Chuck and Clare helped move both families into the new dwelling. It was convenient for both to get downtown—about a twenty-minute drive for Chuck to League Park, where the Browns practiced—and also close to the bus line for William's trips to work at his parking lot job. For the first time in their adult lives, William and Kate would be homeowners.

Chuck had wanted his parents to have their own place. Clarence, Rita, and their children would be downstairs. Their third child, Bill, arrived in April (with Ken to follow in 1957 and Joanne in 1959). William and Kate took the upstairs, and Chuck used one of the rooms on the top level. There was no big celebration or tearful thank yous, only a profound sense of appreciation. "My parents weren't very emotional," said Rita. "But you could still tell how they felt."

Throughout the first year of being a homeowner, Chuck continued to cast about for some idea of his ultimate goal. Brown's admonitions that his players should find "their life's work" was a frequent refrain. Chuck never mustered the passion for selling insurance—after selling some policies to his friends, he found that potential clients were more interested in talking about the Browns than about their own plans. The substitute teaching was enjoyable—he remained on call to teach math and science classes at Holy Name—but he knew he couldn't get a full appointment during his playing career. More than one of his friends had told Chuck he ought to study law, and so out of curiosity as much as determination, he enrolled in the Cleveland-Marshall College of Law on Euclid Avenue. The school offered night classes for those considering career changes, and he began attending classes that fall.

To make some extra money in the off-season, Chuck also latched on to a spot with Dante Lavelli's basketball team, the Lavellis. Dante himself had won two titles as a high school player, and his cousin, Tony, played in the NBA. Occasionally, the Lavelli All-Stars would play the Harlem Globetrotters. Even against the barnstorming stars in these exhibitions, Chuck was resolutely hard-nosed. "Curly Neal was dribbling away and Chuck wouldn't bite on it," said Don Colo. "He wasn't going along with the show; he was trying to get the damn ball. I said, 'Hey, Chuck, relax.' That is how competitive he was. He had some hot-headed German in him, and that was part of it."

By the beginning of his third season, Chuck had earned Paul Brown's trust. "After a while," Brown would say later, "Chuck could have called the plays himself, without any help from the bench. He was that kind of football student."

Going into training camp in 1955, Brown told Chuck that he wanted to move him over to defense to play linebacker. The reasons were clear: left linebacker Tom Catlin had been called up for Air Force duty (flying missions in Korea), and the team's number one draft choice, Kurt Burris, had signed with the Canadian Football League. Chuck was the one player who could be counted on to immediately master the technical aspects of changing not merely positions but units. In the words of linemate John Sandusky, Chuck possessed a "quiet confidence"; his teammates knew he'd be up to the task.

"He's big enough, he's fast enough, and he's smart enough," said Brown in training camp. "I'm not worried."

It was another charmed year, graced by Otto Graham belatedly coming out of retirement to play a tenth and final season. The regular season ended with a 35–24 win over the Cardinals, with Chuck's key interception fueling a 21-point rally. Cleveland had qualified for its tenth straight championship game, and sixth straight NFL title game, setting up a championship game matchup with the Rams—and their first-year coach Sid Gillman—out in Los Angeles.

On the flight out to L.A. for the title game, Chuck was in the back of the plane, playing gin rummy with Curly Morrison, when it happened again.

"All of a sudden, Chuck set his cards down on the table and put both arms straight out," said Morrison, "Like he was stretching, but then this terrible shrieking scream came out of his mouth. And I looked, and then I could see his panic in his face and he just sort of slumped over." At the sound of Chuck's scream, trainer Leo Murphy grabbed his bag from a luggage compartment and hurried back to the last row, with his tongue depressor out.

A few moments later, when the commotion had subsided, and the plane was deathly quiet, Brown pulled Morrison aside.

"Curly, listen," Brown said. "We know about this with Chuck. He's an epileptic. Let me tell you what I think has happened. He thinks that the medication that he takes affects his play and, every once in a while, he will swear off and not take this medication, and that is probably what he has done in preparation of this game and it has caught up with him. We've already talked to the captain. They are phoning ahead. There'll be an ambulance on the tarmac the minute we hit L.A."

Chuck spent a day in the hospital but did return in time for the game. He lasted one play before injuring himself. In Graham's finale, the Browns stormed to a 35–14 victory. Chuck would get another big check, but he felt as though he'd let his teammates down.

In fact, it was the kinship he'd already established with his teammates that would transform his life. There was a sizable group of Browns' players —about a third of the roster, maybe a dozen players in all—who regularly gathered at a downtown restaurant for a casual sit-down banquet the Sunday evening following home games. They would regularly invite trainer Leo Murphy and equipment manager Morrie Komo. Each player could bring a date or a friend or both. In addition to allowing the players to unwind from the game, it was also a way to sidestep the blue laws, which forbade the selling of beer or alcohol by the glass on Sundays. With a "private dinner," the Browns' players could drink.

"They always had a party, and Morrie and I were always invited, and I went because they were great people," said Leo Murphy. "And you throw in maybe $10. But then you could have a meal and drinks and that and dancing. Always the camaraderie with the guys."

"We had two groups on our team," said Don Colo. "We had the Coke drinkers and the non-Coke drinkers, and we had two busses. The Coke drinkers and the rookies rode in the first bus with Paul Brown. So it was the guys in the second bus that mainly had the parties. The Coke drinkers didn't come to the parties. Chuck was in the second bus."

On December 11, 1955, the Browns had celebrated the regular-season ending comeback win over the Chicago Cardinals. They had clinched the title with a 30–7 mauling of Pittsburgh a week earlier, but they didn't want to go into the playoffs on a loss.

It was just another dinner that night. Down at a restaurant in the city, just a few blocks from Municipal Stadium. Chuck was there with Mary Jo, the striking woman he'd been dating for some months. Herschel Forester, the courtly SMU grad who was a guard for the Browns, was also there, with a woman he'd been set up with, a sociable, pony-tailed school-teacher named Marilyn Hall. At the dinner, Hall sat between Forester and Chuck, and found herself impressed with Chuck's understated intellect.

Hall had a soft spot for athletes. Before Forester, she'd dated the baseball player Rudy Regalado, for whom she still carried a torch. She had long ago recognized that football players could be polite—Forester himself had impeccable manners—but she'd never met one quite so interesting and earnest as Chuck. The Browns spoke very little about the game itself, but soon enough, Chuck was talking with her about his nasturtiums in the yard, about attending law school, and about his parents.

It was late by the time Forester dropped off Hall at the apartment she rented with three other women in Shaker Square. She hung up her coat and headed upstairs to the room she shared with one of her flatmates.

Marianne Hanes, Marilyn's close friend and roommate, was already in bed when Marilyn arrived. Hall quickly briefed her on her evening and then she looked at her friend evenly and said, "So, Marianne, you're always saying there aren't any intelligent men out there. Well, I found the guy for you—his name is Chuck Noll; he's handsome and nice."

Marianne Hanes put down the book that she'd been reading and looked at her friend with a mixture of skepticism and bemusement.

"What does he do?," she asked.

"He's a defensive linebacker," explained Marilyn, "for the Browns."

Marianne laughed ruefully.

"Oh, God, he plays *football*?" she said, wincing. "For a living?"

Marianne laid back down and sighed. Then she placed the pillow over her head.

six

MARIANNE

✦ ✦ ✦

By that point in her life, Marianne Hanes had been following her own muse for more than a decade.

She had blanched, as far back as the eighth grade, in Portsmouth, Ohio, at the different set of standards she was expected to observe because she was a female. She'd been sent to the principal's office, more than once, and told that to be argumentative or opinionated was acceptable for boys but not girls.

The pretty, willful daughter of peripatetic grocery executive father and a schoolteacher mother, Marianne had grown up, creative and observant, in a number of small southern Ohio towns, mostly in and around Portsmouth, on the southern edge of the state, at the confluence of the Ohio and Scioto rivers. Bright, questioning, vibrant, she grew up wondering about the social norms that existed in southern Ohio in the '40s. Her mother, a sophisticated woman with a keen fashion sense, still lapsed into the old Southern lady roles. Marianne used to think to herself, *Why do you do that? You don't have to do that.*

At Portsmouth High, Marianne joined the cheerleading squad, dated a football player or two, and quickly learned the value of a knowing smile and a pleated skirt. There was still resistance to her carefree attitude—people taking pains to explain to her that girls shouldn't be hanging banners from a ladder or organizing other students in class.

After a couple of brief, unhappy spells at college, she had arrived at Terminal Station in Cleveland in 1953, aged twenty years with a suitcase, $50, and the stubborn belief that she had the poise and wherewithal to succeed in the big city. In this respect, she was correct.

In the three years since, she'd found both steady work and a full social life working in the physical medicine department of the Cleveland Clinic. She had alert, wise eyes, supple lips, and the soft cadences of southern Ohioans cut with a with a dollop of worldliness.

Like her three roommates, Marianne Hanes had found her way to the single life in Cleveland through a circuitous path, requiring smarts, persistence, and a kind of self-reliance that was not commonly associated with single women in the 1950s. In time, she would meet Chuck Noll. And she would be unlike any of the other women he had ever known.

✦ ✦ ✦

Rollie William Hanes and Elizabeth Muriel Henson had met in the late '20s in Portsmouth, when he was working for the A&P grocery chain, moving from city to city in southern Ohio towns where the company was opening a new supermarket. Bill was authoritative without being domineering. He'd played football, but hadn't lettered, at Ohio State and remained a staunch fan. He would move to a town where A&P was opening a new supermarket and help the enterprise get off the ground. When it was up and running, he would move on.

It was in Portsmouth in 1929 that he'd become enamored of the graceful schoolteacher Elizabeth "Bets" Henson. It was a whirlwind courtship; they eloped six weeks later. Even after their wedding, on May 3, 1930, he had to climb furtively into her bedroom window—teachers just didn't get married during the schoolyear.

Marianne was born May 19, 1933, in Portsmouth, her younger brother John two years later, and the family spent much of her first eight years moving from town to town. In 1941, they were in Arcanum, living with Bill's father, Joseph Hanes, one of the richest men in Darke County. Bets was not fond of living under her father-in-law's shadow, nor of the humble farmhouse that lacked indoor plumbing. Before the year was out, they moved back to the outskirts of Portsmouth. Then came December 7, 1941, and Bill Hanes decided it was his duty to go into the military. He joined the Navy and was stationed in New Orleans, while Bets and the children moved back to Portsmouth.

At the end of the war, there was a position for Bill Hanes in the Navy, but he'd had his fill of military regimen. ("I can't take any more of this bullshit," he told Bets.) When he returned to Ohio, he was intent on making it with his own business. He purchased a landscaping business and bought a working farm.

All the while, Marianne was emerging as a teenager with a mind all her own. In her sophomore year at Portsmouth High, she started going steady with the earnest senior basketball star D. E. Newman, whom she'd known for years. He was over the moon about her. They continued dating throughout high school and when he started college at Ohio Wesleyan. His mash notes back to Portsmouth were sweetly vacant—she sure was a swell girl, and he was thinking about her a lot—and pregnant with what was unstated, implicitly pressing a question he was afraid to ask out loud. "He was a nice man," said Marianne. "I can remember my mother sort of saying they thought I was going to marry him. I can remember thinking, *Are you kidding?!*"

In the fall of 1951, she broke it off with D. E. and started college at Miami University in Oxford. She came to resent much about college life; the rote learning methods contradicted her instinctive and at times mercurial intelligence. She spent long hours in science labs thinking to herself that this was exactly what she'd hated about high school. That summer of 1952, she'd worked part time in Portsmouth and steeled herself to return to college. As the date drew nearer, Marianne drew more resistant.

"I can't do this," she finally told her parents. "I absolutely cannot do this. I hate it."

Her father fretted—working as a teacher seemed to him an ideal job for a young woman—and her mother struggled to understand. "I was so wired and so emotional about it," Marianne said. "They just said okay. But I couldn't get a job because I couldn't do anything. I'd been a telephone operator, and I sure as hell was not gonna go back and be a telephone operator."

She agreed to go to Miami-Jacobs Career College in Dayton to learn some office skills, to make herself more employable. In Dayton, she stayed with her aunt and uncle, who was a doctor, helping out in the office and, much of the time, making the necessary computations for his horse-handicapping system. In the winter of 1952–1953, she even went onto the Dayton campus and attended a few basketball games. She returned home to Portsmouth in May 1953, eager to set out in the world.

"I looked around and said, 'I can't stay here,'" she said. "Because all of my friends were still in college. So I said, 'I think I'll go to California.' My father said, 'You are *not* going to California.' I said, 'Well, then I think I'll go to Cleveland.' Cleveland was the only big city I knew. I had never been there, obviously. So they finally said all right. They gave me $50 and put me on the train."

Cleveland, 1953. Marianne's mother had insisted she get in touch with a woman who owned the Kenilworth Club, a boarding house for single ladies in the city. Victorian in both design and sensibility, the three-level building, on 97th Street, was in a dicey neighborhood.

Close by, though, Marianne was hired on at the Cleveland Clinic, the group practice begun in the 1920s by four physicians. The clinic had become nationally renowned by the '50s, especially for its innovative treatment of heart disease.

That summer, at the Kenilworth, Marianne became friends with the teachers Marilyn Hall and Alice Bowman, both of whom taught at South Euclid Lyndhurst Elementary. There was a couple, and another elderly woman, who managed the building, meeting gentlemen callers at the door, admonishing the women to turn off the lights when they left the room, frowning at all the Jewish boys who seemed to trail after young teachers.

To the other women, Marianne was young and irrepressible. "She was a very, very interesting girl but also very . . . let's say chic," said Alice Bowman. "Marianne enjoyed what she was doing."

"I remember her telling us that her parents really wanted her— especially her mother—to go to college," said Marilyn Hall. "She seemed to want to just get away from home like we all do." Because of the neighborhood, the girls would always go out in groups of three or four, often going shopping downtown to the Higbee's department store.

One evening, in the fall of 1953, they saw *How to Marry a Millionaire*, with Lauren Bacall, Marilyn Monroe, and Betty Grable, and came home captivated with the idea of getting their own place. "We came back," said Marilyn Hall, "and we were all sitting around, going, 'You know, why *couldn't* we?'" Alice was intrigued, and soon Marianne pledged for the cause as well.

"We just decided it would be fun to live someplace else," said Alice. Marianne and Marilyn and Alice and another teacher decided to set out. They soon found an apartment they liked, in a handsome brick building, called the Park East, just above Shaker Square, the highbrow metropolitan hub of the East Side and a magnet for shoppers and diners. Then there was the matter of placating the manager; four women renting an apartment just wasn't *done* in Cleveland in 1953.

The building was filled with older Jewish residents, many of whom wanted to set up the women with their sons or grandsons or nephews. Marianne, Marilyn, and Alice lived there from the start. The other teacher moved out and eventually they were joined by Geri Shevlin, Marianne's friend, an occupational therapist at Cleveland Clinic. There were plenty of interesting, eligible bachelors about, and the women occasionally saw Dr. Benjamin Spock, who lived in a nearby building, heading to and from work.

Marianne, young and carefree, self-possessed and attractive, had her share of suitors. She began dating a chief resident of surgery, a Mormon intent on moving to Utah, before the relationship dissipated. Another doctor, who lived on the West Side, began taking her out regularly, and one night at dinner he asked her intentions. "Because I think it's time I got married, and if you're not interested, then I'm not making this drive anymore."

"I think that's a wise choice," she said.

Marianne's combination of looks and poise helped her stand out. Marilyn Hall, who'd started dating the Indians' third baseman Rudy Regalado, took Marianne with her to the airport to pick up Rudy one evening. "We are standing there and I remember Bobby Avila got off the plane and his eyes just came out of his head," said Marilyn. "Because you know, she was 5-foot-8, very slim and looked like a model. A lot of the guys said, 'Who is *that*, Rudy?'"

There were other doctors, most of them five or ten years older than her, but she wasn't serious about any of them the night that Marilyn came home and told her about Chuck Noll. Marianne listened with interest for a moment, until Marilyn told her that he was a football player. A few moments later, Marianne peeked back out from under the pillow, looked up at her friend and asked, "How tall is he?"

Marilyn smiled.

"He's tall enough for you."

✦   ✦   ✦

So Marilyn Hall called Hershchel Forester and suggested the match, and Forester called Chuck, and the men agreed to visit the women at the apartment on Moreland.

It was not love at first sight. Perhaps Chuck was being flippant, perhaps he was nervous for the blind date. For whatever reason, he showed up with Herschel and two other teammates at the appointed time, knocked on the door, and, as he waited, removed his dental bridge. So when Marilyn Hall opened the door, Marianne demurely standing a few steps behind her, there was Chuck, brandishing a huge gap where his front teeth used to be, smiling manically and lisping, "Is this the place?! I'm ready for my date!"

In the midst of the nervous laughter, he quickly returned the bridge and regained his polite manner. But the first impression had been made.

"They came up and I had worked really late because sometimes it was such a madhouse," said Marianne. "I don't think I had even changed my clothes, and they all came in, and I'm thinking, 'Oh, God.' So eventually, Chuck asked me out, and I said, 'I don't think so,' and I went to bed. I was not interested. And I was probably rude to him. I just got up and left, and then I was sorry that I had said no."

Forester continued courting Marilyn Hall. A month or so later in the winter, when Chuck and a group of bachelors held a Las Vegas night at a local house, the women from the Park East were invited. It was that night, under different circumstances, with Chuck playing the part of the assured, urbane host, that Marianne got a better sense of him. She struck up a couple of conversations with him that evening. Later in the night, when Chuck left to get more drinks, Marianne looked at Marilyn, smiled, and said, "You know, you *could* go find something to do." That was the first night Chuck drove Marianne home.

Two evenings later he called her on the phone and asked, "Can we try this again?"

"All right—when?"

"How about now?"

"Okay," Marianne said. "Where are you?"

"I'm downstairs—in the lobby."

She came downstairs. It was a short walk from there to the Wagon Wheel.

From that opening hiccup, they soon became inseparable. He was drawn to her native intelligence, alluring manner, and comfort around men. She was drawn to his obvious intellect, strong demeanor, and the formidable moral rectitude that set him apart from most men, not to mention most football players.

"I think that was very early on," Marianne said. "I think we both knew."

Maybe it was a coincidence and maybe it wasn't. But from that day on, Chuck Noll never suffered another epileptic seizure.

✦ ✦ ✦

They often began and ended nights as Chuck had before, at the Wagon Wheel, enjoying the clubby atmosphere, as well as the contrast—and occasional interplay—between the workaday patrons upstairs and the elegantly dressed diners downstairs at Etienne's. "It really was a neighborhood bar," Marianne said. "The guys sat and played cards at the table, and if you came in there and you didn't really belong, they would make you so uncomfortable you would leave."

In those early months of dating, both their schedules were crowded. Chuck was getting out of his law school classes at Cleveland-Marshall at 10, racing over to Shaker Square to pick up Marianne for a drink or late dinner, usually at the Wagon Wheel or Shaker Tavern across the street. The handsome young couple caught the eye of piano player Tony Vale, and he would play "I've Got the World on a String" for Marianne and "Pomp and Circumstance" for Chuck when they arrived.

For the regulars at Doc Mangine's spot, the change in Chuck was clear. He was showing up with Marianne more frequently and stopping by alone less often. And he was doing things he didn't frequently do: They went to see chamber music performances and to the Cleveland Symphony. He'd been intrigued with these pursuits before but had never had a partner with whom he could regularly enjoy the arts. As in Dayton, he continued to be fond of jazz music, and he and Marianne would frequent music clubs in and around Cleveland.

When Marianne mentioned to her father that she was dating a Browns' player named Chuck Noll, she was impressed that he knew the name— "Oh, the kid from Dayton!"

Earlier, Chuck brought Marianne and Marilyn Hall to meet his parents. "His mother was very German," said Marilyn. "She was a strong woman, strong character, but also physically strong. But Chuck's dad I think was ill and he didn't do much. I remember Chuck saying that he won't get up because bowling is on, and he is going to sit there and watch bowling. But then I realized that physically he wasn't *able* to do too much."

After the second time Marianne met Chuck's parents, she asked him about his father's tremors and what his doctors were doing about it.

"Well, I take him to the family doctor," Chuck said.

"Please let me take him to the Clinic," she asked. Marianne made an appointment, and the doctor at the Cleveland Clinic finally gave William Noll a definitive diagnosis of Parkinson's, prescribing medications to lessen the tremor.

Chuck was slower introducing his rambunctious Dayton friends to Marianne, but Maloney spent part of a weekend with the couple. "Chuck had bought a kayak, it was a Saturday afternoon, and Marianne, Chuck, and this other girl [it was Marilyn Hall] show up at my parents' house in Fairview Park. We went out to a beach on the other side of Rocky River State Park. I could see the way, the attention that Chuck was paying to her, which was . . . not typical. I do remember that, that there was something really pretty serious for Chuck."

At the Wagon Wheel, the loose affiliation of friends figured out very quickly that Chuck was serious. "I kind of thought that when Marianne came on board, I figured, *That's it*," said Dan Ferrazza. "She is going to lock him up."

Marianne's friends knew it as well. "It is so nice when you are young and you are looking for prospective mates, to *find* somebody," said Marilyn Hall.

✦ ✦ ✦

When he left for Hiram and training camp in July 1956, Chuck kept up a steady correspondence with Marianne. Grousing about the schedule and the routine, he evinced some annoyance with Paul Brown's dictatorial approach. "There is a chance that our lord and master might free us after supper Sat., this is not, however, a certainty," wrote Chuck. "It all hinges on how we look Sat. afternoon when we knock heads."

The Browns had lost on average less than two games per year for the first decade of the franchise's existence. But in '56, with Otto Graham having retired, they were an aging side bound for a letdown. The hint came in preseason, when after beating the College All-Stars, they lost five straight preseason games, then lost four of their first five games to start the season. Chuck had adapted to the left linebacker position and started all twelve games (he returned a fumble 39 yards for a touchdown early in the Browns' 24–7 win over Green Bay). But it was the Browns' worst season yet, ending in a 5–7 record, the first time they'd ended a season in anything short of a league championship game.

There was less social time during the season. But Chuck and Marianne still found a way to get together almost nightly. It was obvious, to her friends at least, that the couple was falling in love. Early that December, Chuck came over to help trim the tree at the Park East, and one difference became apparent: Chuck carefully hung each individual strand of tinsel on the tree, while Marianne had always delighted in tossing the shiny icicles over the branches.

On Christmas Eve, 1956, Marianne was working at the Cleveland Clinic and had a train to catch back home to Portsmouth. Chuck had arranged to pick her up and drive her to the station, but he was out drinking with some of his old Dayton friends that afternoon. He arrived late to pick her up that afternoon and found Marianne angry and in tears. ("And I don't cry very often," she said.) She missed her train. Chuck, hoping to set things right, told her he'd simply drive her down to Portsmouth himself. He did so and met Marianne's parents, and another hurdle was cleared.

By early 1957, Marilyn Hall had fully rekindled her romance with the baseball player Rudy Regalado, and the four of them frequently double-dated when Rudy was in town with the Indians. When Rudy and Marilyn and Chuck and Marianne went out, the two athletes shared a natural affinity that transcended sports. "Marianne and I tried to teach the boys bridge," Marilyn remembered. "But Chuck has the mathematical mind, and in like two minutes he was one of these people who knew exactly where the cards are."

They made the most of weekends, spending more than one bleary Sunday at family dinner with the Nolls after they'd been out with friends well past midnight the previous night. They'd even begun talking about marriage, and Marianne had started attending Catholic conversion classes.

Then, in April 1957, the discussion became more urgent. Marianne was pregnant.

When she told him, Chuck didn't waver. "Well," he said, "then we'll get married right now."

The build-up was quick. Marianne sat down with her roommates at the Park East one evening and explained that she was going to be married at the end of the May. Hall remembered her sharing the news, the friends congratulating her, then Marianne leaving. After she was gone, Marilyn looked at Alice, and Alice looked at Geri, and Geri shook her head. "I don't want to know," she said, "and I *don't* want to talk about it."

It was a bit of a shock to Chuck's friends as well.

"I didn't know Marianne too well," said groomsman and teammate Don Colo. "So I would say I knew it was serious then—when he got her pregnant and told us he was getting married."

But Chuck's family understood. "He brought her over," said Rita, "and they came in and we talked, and they said they were going to get married. Fine, great. [Our parents] just accepted it. They didn't get upset about it or anything."

There was little time for deliberation. "I was working and he wasn't," said Marianne. "So he took care of the wedding—I just showed up—including the cake." Chuck decided his brother Bob should be the best man, since he had been Bob's best man. He invited Colo and Mike Bordinaro, from the Wagon Wheel, to be groomsmen. (He'd originally asked Dan Ferrazza, but he would be away on his own honeymoon and couldn't make it.) Rita was due to have her fourth child in October, and the custom was that pregnant women didn't stand for a wedding. In lieu of Rita, and because a non-Catholic could not be a matron or maid of honor, Marianne agreed to have Bob's somewhat high-strung wife, Stella, be her matron of honor. Stella had quarreled with Chuck's mother earlier, and in the weeks leading up to the wedding, she expressed disapproval over Marianne's wedding dress.

"Stella told me it wouldn't do," said Marianne. "I loved my dress."

Paul Brown, friendly with several doctors at the Cleveland Clinic, made inquiries about Marianne's character, which made her furious until she learned that some of the doctors she knew had been asking Brown about Chuck's character. Everyone checked out.

The ceremony was held May 25 at Our Lady of Peace (where Marianne had taken Catholic conversion classes), with a reception that afternoon at the Carter Hotel. They had each purchased simple wedding bands, at $6 each. (Two years later, she had his engraved. It read, "M to C, my life.")

For Chuck's old Dayton teammates, the marriage was a sign that their time with Chuck would change. "A very intelligent young lady who probably had the same mind makeup that he did," said Jim Currin. "Very strong-willed and very nice, but we didn't know her well prior to then. She told me before they were married, 'The only time Chuck is ever late is when you guys come to town.'"

As the wedding let out, and Chuck and Marianne walked outside into the sunlight, a few of his Browns' teammates were jauntily showering the couple with pebbles rather than rice. Geri Shevlin and Marilyn Hall had been attendants. Chuck and Marianne stayed at the DeLuxe Motel in Mentor on their wedding night, then drove east, eventually getting to Wilmington and the coast of Delaware.

Upon their return, Marianne moved out of the Park East, and Chuck packed up the room in his parents' house. They found a home in Maple Heights, on a street full of white frame houses. Chuck was already paying his portion of the note at the home on 141st Street, but he agreed to let Marianne borrow money from her parents so they could make the down payment on a newlywed home.

"We borrowed $3,000 from my dad," said Marianne. "We took a second mortgage on his parents' house, and then a mortgage on this one, so I had three house payments a month, plus the money that he was adamant about paying back to my dad as soon as possible." Their first dining room table was a folding card table. After a lifetime spent worrying about money, Chuck was eager to let Marianne handle all the finances and let him know what he would be able to spend each month.

"I learned to cook really cheap," said Marianne. "And, you know, we did it. I am very obsessive about, 'If you can't pay for something, you can't afford it.' So we never did. Debt as debt was never, ever in our lives an issue."

With only secondhand furniture and very little money, Marianne was hoping to get a new living-room set for their honeymoon, but Chuck had been pining for a boat. They purchased a small, hand-me-down metal fishing boat on a trailer. On Independence Day weekend, they took it out onto Lake Erie. That afternoon, after their fishing expedition, Chuck backed up the car and trailer, to load the boat back onto the trailer. It proved to be something of a calamity, with his uncertain docking skills leaving the boat askew, lodged partly on the trailer, much of their fishing gear sliding to the back and into the water. Chuck took off his shoes, rolled up his pants legs, and removed his Browns' 1954 championship ring and 1955 Browns' championship watch. "Here," he said, handing the jewelry to Marianne. "Hold my watch and ring." He then went in the water after it.

The phrase became a touchstone for them. In the decades ahead, more than once, when he was facing a crisis or stern test or difficult moment, he would look in his wife's eyes and say, "Here—hold my watch and ring."

In those early months of marriage, Marianne learned what she'd long suspected: Chuck was never idle. In the bathroom on the ground floor in Maple Heights, he improvised a darkroom. Chuck not only cared about photographic technique but also was a buff for equipment. He was inclusive about his pursuits, inviting Marianne along. "I mean, we developed our own stuff," she said. "He read magazines. He read books constantly. He never read novels. He read for information. If he gets interested in something, he knows everything there is to know about it."

There were adjustments. The first night she cooked at their home, he ate everything, asked for second helpings of everything and ate all that. The next night, it was the same. Finally, she realized that he was simply hard-wired to eat everything that was put in front of him.

They communicated well, but they rarely talked about feelings, and Chuck seemed allergic to discussing his emotions. A few weeks after they were married, she asked him about it.

"Chuck, is everything okay? You haven't said you loved me since we were married."

Chuck straightened up. "I told you I loved you once," he said. "If that ever changes, you'll be the first to know."

✦ ✦ ✦

Coming off the first losing record in his career, Paul Brown was determined to make his team tougher for the 1957 season. Lineman Frank Gatski announced early in a training camp scrimmage that he was renaming the line of scrimmage "The Gaza Strip," and the intramurals took on a tougher tone.

On the plane for the Browns' annual preseason trip out to California, Brown asked Chuck if the woman waving to him at the airport was his wife. When Chuck confirmed it was, and mentioned that they were expecting their first child in December, Brown seemed pleased.

A week later, at the Hotel Green in Pasadena, when the team was eating a meal, Chuck was paged over the loudspeaker. He got up to get the call when Brown rose to cut him off walking out to the lobby. "Remember, be smart," Brown said gravely. "It's different now—you're married." The words were said so quickly and with such seriousness, that Chuck had to restrain himself from laughing. (He was going to meet an old friend, the lawyer Dudley Gray.) When he mentioned it later, in a letter to Marianne, he speculated "his doctor friends at the clinic must have really sold you to him."

On the trip, Chuck continued corresponding regularly. After he missed part of the game with an injured hand, he wrote her a note of explanation. "Some joker stomped on my hand, and made it larger and more ugly than usual. I had it X-rayed and got to look at the pictures. All they showed were a few extra calcium deposits, mostly on my crushed finger. The real sorrow in it all is that I can't wear my ring. The third finger left hand is enlarged."

For Marianne, the revelation of the season would be the physical toll. She had known Chuck to move slowly on the Mondays after games but now, sharing a home and a bed, she saw the aftermath of a football game in much greater detail. Chuck slept deeply and often awoke in pain, his body betraying deep cuts and vivid bruises that had been barely visible the previous night. There were times when it took an immense effort even to get out of bed.

She knew he was fit and strong. But the nature of the game, and the oversized opponents he was facing on a regular basis, meant that even when Chuck played well and didn't suffer any serious injuries, he often felt the effects for days. Tuesdays were sometimes worse than Mondays. By Wednesdays, he would be moving toward a reasonable approximation of his morning routine. But the following Monday, the signs of the battering returned. It wasn't even a question of specific injuries. It was the overarching physical cost, exacerbated by the fact that Chuck was smaller than most of the players he was squaring off against.

One day, as they were laying in bed the morning after a game, Chuck mentioned a veteran teammate whose body had deteriorated noticeably over a long career, and said, "I'm not going to do it that long. I don't want to be that way when I walk away from this."

On October 27, the Browns were playing the Chicago Cardinals at Comiskey Park when Chuck moved in to make a stop on the fleet, long-striding Ollie Matson, whose blend of speed and power made him notoriously hard to tackle. Chuck dove into the runner, his right arm caught flush by Matson's driving thigh. Chuck crumpled on the field instantly and knew his arm was broken.

When he arrived back in Cleveland and went to have the break set, the doctor explained that it was too swollen to X-ray. They told him to return the next day. The following morning, Chuck took Marianne to her regular appointment with her obstetrician, and it wasn't until later in the day that he was able to get the break X-rayed. Chuck would miss the remainder of the season. The arm was set in a cast that Monday, and he returned to League Park a day later, offering to help in any way he could. He soon learned the feeling of helplessness that engulfed injured football players.

Unable to practice or play, Chuck spent more time preparing for their child's arrival. He had to relearn the basics of daily life (getting dressed, bathing, driving a car) without the use of his right arm. One night, they had a laughing fit after straining—Marianne eight months pregnant, Chuck in a full arm cast—to move a box spring and mattress up a narrow stairway to the attic, which was being converted to a guest room (the next year, Marianne's brother John came to live with them for a while).

After Chuck drove them through the slick, snow-filled streets to Marymount Hospital, Marianne gave birth to their baby boy, Christopher, on December 22, 1957. As Marianne delivered, Chuck paced in the waiting room. After he met their child, he didn't even try to find the words. "He just smiled a lot," said Marianne. (They had agreed, if it was a boy, to call him Christopher William Noll, the middle name an homage to their respective fathers. But on the birth certificate, Marianne gave the name Christopher Charles Noll.)

In 1957 Cleveland, everyone did the math—they'd only been married for six months when Chris was born—and nobody said a word.

"Nobody knew I was pregnant when we got married," said Marianne. "We didn't tell anybody, and I think when Chris was born, I think my parents were more shocked than his parents. But I think they knew how much we loved each other, so . . ."

On Christmas Day, Chuck went back to the house on 141st Street, and introduced Kate and William to their new grandchild. Chuck also spent some time with his growing brood of nieces and nephews. Rita had been in the hospital, giving birth to her fourth child, Ken, on the same weekend that Chuck had broken his arm. She and Clare were harried but happy, with plenty of advice and supplies for the new parents.

During the week before New Year's, back at the home in Maple Heights, a procession of regulars visited from the Wagon Wheel, led by Dan Ferrazza, whom Chuck had asked to be Chris's godfather. On the day his son came home, Chuck managed to give him a bath with his one free arm; he'd read books on infants and soon mastered diaper changing and burping, a frequent necessity as young Chris often spit up his formula.

✦　✦　✦

Against the backdrop of his lost season and his new baby, Chuck was still struggling to find what Paul Brown frequently referred to as "his life's work." He had decided to give up law school when they got married. The evening classes often left him peeved at the entire thrust of legal logic. "I can remember him saying that he was disappointed," said Marianne, "because he thought their sole game was to go around the law, and he was offended morally, I think."

Dissatisfied with selling insurance, he tried his hand working as a salesman for a trucking firm. Early in 1958, Chuck left for a week in Dayton, where he began training as a salesman with the Trojan Trucking Co., a short-line hauler with routes predominantly between Dayton and Cleveland. The work was mostly drudgery, but Chuck found it marginally less stifling than selling insurance. Like insurance, Chuck worked on commission. He and Marianne assiduously saved from the twelve checks he received during the football season, and he continued to let her manage the money.

"We just had to be careful how we lived," said Marianne. "We did not live like a lot of the other players did because we had responsibilities. Milk cost like 10 cents a quart then. Chris's formula cost $1. And the constant medication. I learned to handle money."

Over the summer, the added responsibility of Chris had caused Chuck to again reconsider his future career path. In August 1958, on the Browns' annual West Coast preseason swing, he wrote to Marianne, who had offered to check with Case Western Reserve about getting him into medical school. "If you'll call W.R.U. and scope me in, I would appreciate it," he wrote. "The more I think about it, the more I'm sure. I've always wanted that, but didn't think I could make it financially, and then I became fascinated by this football stuff—a fascination which is slowly waning. I like to think of it or rationalize that it's a growth and change thing—what was important last year isn't important this year. What I'm trying to say is football is a goal reached about which I can't get too excited about. Medicine is for now." He signed it "Love, Chuck," and added a postscript for Marianne to give Chris a smooch. He'd come a long way in expressing his feelings, though it remained easier for him to do so in print. A day or two later, he wrote Marianne again—recommending the book *Auntie Mame* and updating her on his progress.

He was a man who seemed caught between a life in football—the urgency, the camaraderie, the gravity of the game—and the commitment to his wife. Writing from Los Angeles, he noted, "I haven't set my watch for this time. I look at it and get a picture of what you usually are doing at about that time. I feel much closer that way."

Their biggest challenge continued to be Chris's health. The first year of his life would be marked by allergies and eczema all over his body. Then trying to find a formula that he could keep down. He'd weighed 8 pounds and 8 ounces when he was born, and at nine months, weighed just 16 pounds. No matter what medications used, what variations on formulas were attempted, he remained sickly. While Chuck was in California on the Browns' preseason swing, Marianne brought Chris to the doctor for what was originally diagnosed as a throat infection, giving him a shot.

"Marilyn came out to the house that night," said Marianne. "So we were sitting in the living room talking for a really long time, having a couple of drinks, and I would just go in and check him. So the next morning, at 6 o'clock, I went in, and the soft spot looked like he had a golf ball on top of his head. So I took him to the emergency room and they kept insisting I had dropped him. I said, 'I did NOT drop him!' So they did spinal taps and then they had to do subdurals and then it finally dissipated, but they really were on me about, 'How did you drop him?'"

The allergies became life threatening. The only four foods he could eat as a toddler were summer squash, mashed potatoes, beef heart, and beef liver. After trying dozens of different formulas, they settled on liquified beef hearts. "That's the only thing they could give him that he could drink," said Marianne. "He loved it. It looked like chocolate milk, see. So a kid would come to the house, and they would say, 'I want what he has!' I would say, 'No, you don't.' So I would let them taste it, and they would all go, 'Yuk!'"

✦　　✦　　✦

In the second game of the '58 season, Brown moved Chuck back over to the offense, to fill in for injured Gene Hickerson, who'd had his leg gashed in a win over the Cardinals, leaving him in the hospital. "He's a fellow who could do a competent job at almost any spot on the team," Paul Brown said. But if Chuck was adaptable to any position, it was also true that he was essential to none.

The '58 season emphasized something that had been festering for years. The Browns had grown increasingly alienated from their coach. There was a sharper edge to Paul Brown by now. His critiques in film sessions were more pointed.

"Stop the film," Paul Brown would say, then he would have an assistant rewind the tape, and play back, in slow motion, a player missing an assignment.

"Whose man was that?," he'd ask.

"Mine," said Jim Brown.

"Well if you can't block, you can't play for me."

There may have been a time when this was true, but the players knew it patently wasn't for Jim Brown, the most talented football player of his generation.

And the arbitrariness of Brown's treatment of Jim Brown showed the fissures that were developing in the Paul Brown mystique.

When Ratterman, fading in the pocket to pass, lost his footing and fell on his butt on a third down, it was embarrassing. When the quarterback got to the sidelines, he could hear his coach asking the trainer to "check him for a concussion."

The team's strong record covered up many of the internal fissures. The Browns jumped out to a 9–2 record and needed a win or tie to qualify for the NFL title game going into their season finale at the Giants. Leading by a touchdown, they were on the verge of kicking a field goal to go up 13–3, when Brown called for a fake field goal, which the Giants stopped. New York won the game, 13–10. "From that point on, Paul never had quite the same respect from the players," said *Cleveland Press* beat writer Bob August.

A week later, in the Eastern Conference playoff game, the Giants beat the Browns again, for the third time that season. Teammates and fans were furious that Jim Brown carried just seven times (for eight yards) in the game. The Giants' defensive coach Tom Landry had clearly found a key to stopping the Browns, and Paul Brown's play calling had become predictable.

During the 1959 off-season, Chuck continued to consider a career as a doctor. "I knew a lot of doctors on a social basis, and so did he," said Marianne. "They talked to him about going to med school." He applied to Case Western Reserve and was provisionally accepted, pending taking another year of classes in biological sciences. "They didn't formally accept him, but it was pretty much understood," said Marianne. "I could see he wasn't really enjoying those classes, and he was working [at the trucking company] and playing ball."

Given a free day off on the annual preseason jaunt to California in 1959, Chuck and a group of other Browns went to visit Republic Studios and take a tour. But he didn't stop there, urging a group of teammates to Venice Beach, where they wanted to witness firsthand the counterculture. He saw a pair of women walking hand in hand and, out of genuine curiosity, followed them to the door of a gay club, then moved farther down the boardwalk to see a beatnik coffee shop. Chuck was not impressed with the quality of the art—"Poetry to the Beat is anything he sees fit to call poetry," he wrote to Marianne. "It need not (and never does) have meter, rhyme, or any form of restrictions whatsoever. It is any expression period. We were shown one poem that has been preserved, written by a beat who thought Charlie 'Bird' Parker was the most." But his intellectual curiosity continued to be piqued. "I don't think I'd make a very good beatnik," he wrote in conclusion. "The only poetry I know—'I love Marianne!' This however is not acceptable to them."

By the time the '59 season began, Chuck was growing more perturbed with his head coach. He came home furious one day, after Cleveland cut its fifth-round draft choice, Dick LeBeau (who would go on to a thirteen-year Hall of Fame career with the Lions).

By the end of the preseason Chuck was back to the guard position. "Chuck is our handyman," Brown told the *Press*. "He can play six positions and is very quick at adapting himself."

Clare always came to his brother-in-law's games, often bringing along Chuck's parents, when they were up to attending. Rita had her fifth child, Joanne, in January of 1959, and by the time the '59 season started, she was pregnant again (her sixth, Jerry, would be born in March 1960).

At the end of that season, Chuck engaged in one of a relative few unabashedly romantic moments.

He told Marianne that now, in a better financial state, he wanted her to have a proper wedding ring. Marianne insisted that it wasn't important, but Chuck was adamant about wanting to give her the gift. Dante Lavelli referred them to a jeweler who specialized in opals, which Marianne wanted—and he made the purchase. "It's a beautiful ring," she said. "But he's funny. He came home one day and he brought in golf clubs. He said, 'Here. I want you to learn how to play golf.' That is about as romantic as he usually got."

Through it all, Chuck seemed intent on his various tasks but oddly untethered about his future. He was fighting for time as a starter and losing his thirst for the physical grind of the game. He wanted to get on with his life's work, but he didn't know what that was. In football, the end seemed, if not imminent, then inevitable. And his off-season work simply didn't compel.

"I had a horrible, horrible fear of him ending up selling time on a truck line forever," Marianne said. "And I wanted him to have a passion."

Chuck's old roommate Jim Currin called near the end of the 1959 season, to pass on a message. Dayton was about to hire a new football coach, and the former assistant coach Joe Quinn was among those in the alumni club who thought that Chuck would be a good candidate. He hadn't spoken about that as a profession, but he wasn't closing any doors, and he agreed to drive down and talk with the athletic director. He explained to Marianne, "I could hang on for a couple more years, but I really don't want to. I need to make a decision."

He called Paul Brown and explained Dayton's interest. Brown was complimentary and supportive and told him that if he didn't take the job, there would still be a place for him with the Browns in 1960. If he did get the job, Brown hinted, he'd likely be willing to extend his greatest compliment—giving Chuck a copy of his playbook.

Chuck drove down through the slush of a snow-filled winter to two days of meetings at Dayton. After an in-depth interview the second day, he returned home, pulling into the driveway in pure darkness.

Marianne was waiting, with dinner and a bottle of wine. "Do you think you'll get it?," she asked.

"No," he said. "If they were going to give me the job, they would've asked me today."

There was something else.

"But I do know one thing now: This is what I want to do. I really want to coach."

He said it with the sort of authority that Marianne knew that he had finally decided. But he added a note of caution.

"He just said, 'You have to understand about insecurity, about moving around, that that is what it would be,'" said Marianne. "I was like, 'So— whatever.' I wanted him to be happy."

Chuck Noll was twenty-seven years old. He'd spent time in myriad jobs: delivering newspapers, digging cemetery plots, setting up bowling pins, substitute teaching, selling insurance, selling trucking services, playing football. He'd studied law and had considered going to medical school. Now, after all of that, he'd come back to where he started, to his first love. He wanted to be a football coach.

He'd found his life's work.

seven

A FOOTBALL LABORATORY

✦ ✦ ✦

Chuck had made his decision at the moment when the staid landscape of professional football was in the midst of convulsive change. Attendance at NFL games was booming, having increased every year during the 1950s. In December 1958, forty-five million Americans had watched the classic NFL Championship Game, with the Colts defeating the Giants in overtime. Seven months later, a twenty-six-year-old Texan named Lamar Hunt had announced the formation of the American Football League, directly challenging the NFL by launching eight new franchises that would begin play in fall 1960.

So Chuck reached out to the names he knew in the new league. He called Dick Gallagher, the longtime Browns' scout who'd taken the job as general manager of the new Buffalo Bills franchise. He called down to Houston, where former Brown Lou Rymkus had hired a staff that included former teammate Mac Speedie. And he called out to Los Angeles, where Sid Gillman, the onetime University of Cincinnati coach, had just been fired after five seasons with the Los Angeles Rams and immediately hired as the head coach of the new AFL entry, the Los Angeles Chargers.

Gillman was a different breed from the football coaches Chuck had known before. The son of a Minneapolis movie theater operator, he'd played college football at Ohio State under Francis "Close the Gates of Mercy" Schmidt, where he became increasingly fascinated with the myriad intricacies of offensive tactics and strategy. Later serving as an assistant under Schmidt, Gillman was one of the first coaches to exploit the value of film study. Through his family and network of motion picture exhibitors, he often pinched football newsreels to study the standout players of the day. Gillman spent his honeymoon with his bride, Esther, watching the College All-Stars practice in Chicago and, later that fall, spent $15 of their limited funds on a used 35-millimeter projector that would allow him to watch game films at home. He had intended to go into law school but fell under the spell of Schmidt and the game of football. "I went back and I haven't seen a law school yet," he said. "I wasn't interested in anything else after that."

The Sunday morning the Japanese bombed Pearl Harbor, Gillman was in his office at West Point, already looking at game films to prepare for the 1942 season ahead. After West Point, he landed head-coaching jobs at Miami University and Cincinnati. While at Cincinnati, Gillman developed his reputation for gamesmanship and chicanery. The Dayton coaches were convinced that Gillman had someone spying on their preseason practices in 1952; earlier, Paul Brown was certain Gillman had snuck off with one of the coveted Browns' playbook during one of Brown's coaching clinics. But the classic instance of Gillman's quest for a competitive edge was seen in 1949. Preparing to play a deep Nevada team in the season opener, he dispatched young assistant Jack Faulkner (who'd played for Gillman earlier at Miami University) to assume an alias and walk-on at Nevada as a country recruit. The guise worked, and Faulkner made the team, drilling much of the preseason with the Wolfpack, then sticking around just long enough to receive the game plan for the season opener with Cincinnati, before pleading homesickness and dropping out of school. When the Nevada assistants noticed Faulkner in the Cincinnati coaches' booth prior to the opener, they were apoplectic.

Gillman had a manner of dismissing many of the allegations without denying them, exactly. It was clear that in his world view, the ends might occasionally justify the means. Cosmopolitan in disposition and appearance, Gillman had by this point in his career adopted some of the same vaguely tweedy affectations as Schmidt, favoring bow ties and a pipe. He looked like a kindly, erudite uncle. But this was an illusion. What Gillman was, most of all, was a football obsessive.

After the phone interview, Gillman called Harry Baujan, the athletic director at Dayton for a reference, then called Chuck back and offered him the job—as a defensive assistant, primarily in charge of the linemen, for $10,000 a year. Chuck accepted.

✦   ✦   ✦

Paul Brown wasn't pleased with the news. Back when the Dayton job came open, he'd given Chuck his blessing. But the news that Chuck was going to work for Gillman was greeted differently. "They had a good relationship," said Marianne. "Not too many players did with Paul, I don't think, but they did. But when he went to the Chargers, he didn't get the playbook."

To his players, Brown dismissed the new league out of hand. "I remember Paul Brown had us convinced it was bad for football," said Len Dawson, who'd been drafted by the Steelers in '57, but came to the Browns in 1960. "I can remember sitting in a meeting and he said, 'The league is not going to last. It's a bunch of sons of rich guys. It's a hobby with them. They don't know anything about football. The people playing there are not capable of playing in the National Football League. They'll be nothing but castoffs and they won't last more than a year or two.'" It was a risk Chuck was willing to take to break into coaching.

The friends who'd known him were not surprised by Chuck's career decision. "I knew he had the ability," said Don Colo. "He followed the game and knew it exactly. He would not necessarily argue with coaches but he would have strong discussions with coaches about this way and that way to do something."

Neither Chuck nor Marianne had ever lived outside of the state of Ohio. But they'd have friends nearby. Rudy Regalado was already headed to San Diego, to play with the Padres in the Pacific Coast League. And Marilyn Hall had decided to follow him there, "to settle this once and for all." She stopped by the Nolls' house in Maple Heights one day to share the news that she'd signed a teaching contract in California. "Before I had a chance to tell her," said Marilyn, "she said, 'Chuck and I are moving to L.A.' I went, 'What!? I'm moving to San Diego!'"

Chuck's old friend and Dayton teammate, John Vukelich, was living with his wife Rose, a former UD cheerleader, out in Los Angeles, and coaching at Chaminade High School, when he received a call from Chuck asking if he could stay with them for a while. Marianne and Chris would remain in Cleveland until the house in Maple Heights was sold.

The no-nonsense teammate that Vukelich remembered from the early '50s had changed in the intervening years and had grown more worldly. Chuck was becoming a connoisseur of wines, was eager to sample Rose's forays into Mexican cuisine, and was drawn to the relaxed, elegant atmosphere of the torch singers in L.A.'s supper clubs. "Chuck loved this one real fancy place we went to," said Vukelich. "They used to have a lot of the singers from Hollywood come into this little bar and put on solos. We had a good time running around looking for places like that. When he lived with us, he was kind of into going to listen to those singers. The movie stars would come in there. They would just get up and tell the piano player to play this, and then they would sing a song. I bet we spent about one night a week down there after he moved in with us."

Back in Cleveland, Marianne was trying to sell a house in the midst of one of Cleveland's toughest winters—for a time, people couldn't even get up the street to look at the house.

They were both wounded by the time apart. Chuck wrote long letters, bemoaning how much he missed her. She wrote back, equally distraught. "Now that I've had a taste of what it would be like to be without you, perhaps it will help me to be a better wife," she wrote in January. "You are my life, my very existence. Thank God for Chris. Sometimes I think I could not endure were it not for this much of you."

As they waited for the house to sell, Chuck's letters grew more and more lonely. On March 8, he wrote, "The only thing that is pounding in my mind is that I miss you. That most of my present problem is that I miss you. That this will be resolved when finally we are one."

Three days later, he'd reached his limit. He wrote her that he was coming to get them, and return with them to Los Angeles, "and the house and Maple Hts. and Cleveland and the realtor and the prospective buyers and the money and everything else can take a flying leap. This is ridiculous and crazy and all that. We belong together."

He found a cozy apartment in Van Nuys, on the ground floor of a long but busy residential stretch of Hazeltine Avenue, though he was concerned that there wouldn't be a place for the Ironrite automatic ironing machine that Marianne used on all their clothes.

Chuck had a new two-tone Pontiac—sky blue body, white top—though he would be the only driver. By this time, both he and Marianne had concluded that she shouldn't be driving. For such a confident, self-reliant woman, she was curiously lacking in this central skill. She had an inner ear malady that affected her sense of spatial relations, and though she drove for a time in Ohio, the experience never felt truly comfortable. Their son sensed this as well; even as a toddler, Chris was scared to have her drive. So by the time she got to California, Marianne had given up driving. She and Chris stayed at the apartment. Marianne learned to love Mexican food and grew less shocked, as time went on, to see women grocery shopping in bikinis.

"L.A. was such a culture shock to us," said Marianne. "Two pretty naive Midwestern kids. It was just like a whirlwind. We had a good time there, but I knew I did not want to raise my family there." As it turned out, they wouldn't have to.

✦ ✦ ✦

Down at the Chargers' offices on South La Brea Avenue, Chuck was reunited with a name from his past. The general manager of the Chargers was Frank Leahy, the former Notre Dame coach who'd sent him home from South Bend in the summer of '49. If Chuck felt any measure of pride by having completed a seven-year pro career after the coach of Notre Dame refused to give him a shot in college, he didn't show it. (Leahy wouldn't last long—quitting in July 1960, due to declining health.)

In the months ahead, Chuck would become a key component in a laboratory of football. Two of his fellow assistant coaches had crossed paths with him before. The rough-hewn but amiable Jack Faulkner had coached against Chuck in both the colleges and pros, as an assistant under Gillman. The slender, acerbic Brooklynite Al Davis, all jaw-clenching, gum-popping nervous energy and Machiavellian proclamations, had visited with Chuck and roommate Curly Morrison at a Browns' training camp a few years earlier, sitting in their dorm room with them and talking football until late in the night. Joe Madro, the other assistant, was a squat firecracker of irascible energy.

But Chuck made an impression on them. "He was a very bright guy with no experience," said Faulkner. "He was not very outward. Maybe coming from Paul Brown's system rubbed off. With Paul, everything was a mystery."

With eight teams starting fresh, the franchises of the AFL had to balance box-office concerns (teams in Dallas and Houston stocked their franchises heavily with recognized names from Southwest Conference schools) with pure competition. It meant that the old prejudices against having too many black players—still quietly observed in much of the NFL—would begin to disappear.

Chuck's friend Vukelich visited several Chargers practices. "I used to ask Joe Madro questions when I was down there, about offense and stuff," said Vukelich. "He would say, 'John, all you need to win is a *black-field*.'" Though this kind of casual racism was common in pro football at the beginning of the decade, the Chargers were mostly a departure. Gillman, sensitive about the bias he faced because he was Jewish, was a social progressive. Chuck and Al Davis had grown up in racially integrated settings.

The first Chargers' training camp was held on the campus of Chapman College in Orange. Gillman and his staff had staged an open audition in April (later featured in *Life* magazine), working out more than three hundred would-be players. But there were genuine finds, including one ringer: former college star Paul Lowe, who had been working in the mail room for the Hilton hotel chain, impressed enough to get a call to training camp, along with dozens of underrated former college standouts, and all manner of semipro and Canadian football league castoffs. Gillman couldn't remember Lowe's name and kept referring to him as "Luther" (running back Luther Carr was also trying to make the team) until Lowe ran back the opening kickoff in the Chargers' first preseason game 105 yards for a touchdown.

Chuck found Gillman's system less structured than Paul Brown's, befitting Gillman's restless intelligence. But there were new and illuminating discoveries. The Browns would watch films, with both sideline and end zone views, but Gillman dug deeper. He was a resolute deconstructionist. Not content to watch offensive and defensive reels, he'd cut them up and splice together all the post patterns that a team would run or all their plays in third-and-long situations.

What Chuck got from watching Gillman was a methodology that allowed for a more granular dissection of the game and, if the right person was watching, a deeper understanding of how the elements related. In Cleveland, Brown's treasured assistant, Blanton Collier, had spent his off-season grading every player on every play of the previous Browns' season. But with Gillman's system, a coach could take that analysis a step further, if he was willing to take the time, by lining up all of a player's similar plays and discern why a player was having trouble with a particular aspect of his game. Gillman was willing to take the time, and soon Chuck realized that the same obsessive attention to detail on the defensive side of the ball could be fertile ground for breakthroughs.

Stung by constant fan and media criticism, Gillman had grown more conservative during his final years coaching the Rams. But reinvigorated with the Chargers, he vowed to open up his attack and more completely carry on the tradition that Francis Schmidt had laid down.

The Gillman passing tree was a marvel of economical nomenclature. Each pass pattern included a three-digit code to indicate the different routes run by the split end, tight end, and flanker, with the tight end always the middle digit. Those numbers then corresponded to a specific route, with odd-numbered routes cutting toward the boundary, and even-numbered ones going to the center of the field.

What Chuck learned, in that first season, was that Gillman cared little about defense—his obsessions were almost entirely with the attack, with the intricate pass patterns that he drew up, many of them designed to spread out the defense. He left the defensive game plan to Faulkner and Chuck.

Among the assistants, Faulkner established a teasing relationship with some of his players, Al Davis asked them about their lives and backgrounds, and Madro was adept at bawling them out with explicit language and humor. Chuck, alone among the assistants, remained almost entirely businesslike.

"A meeting was a meeting," said Paul Maguire. "You went in the meeting, and you didn't go in there jacking around. I mean you went in, and 'We're going to look at film, and we're going to do this; here's the game plan, and here's what we're going to do, and here's what we're going to practice.' He was a hard-ass. He was just so intense about *everything*. He never smiled, he had no sense of humor whatsoever at that time. Or, he probably did, but not with the players."

✦   ✦   ✦

The Chargers' opening game, against league founder Lamar Hunt's Dallas Texans, drew just 17,724 to the cavernous 97,500-seat Los Angeles Memorial Coliseum, but the Chargers rallied to win. Though they lost three of their next four games, the team eventually came together and won the Western Division title. But even as they were closing the season out with four home wins, they were averaging barely 12,000 fans per game during the final month. While owner Barron Hilton spoke bravely in public about plans to stay in Los Angeles, the team had actually already started negotiating for a move to San Diego.

In the 1960 AFL Championship Game, the Chargers visited the Houston Oilers—with whom they'd split two regular-season games—at the small Jeppeson Stadium (a high school football stadium where the Oilers played their home games) on New Year's Day 1961. With the Oilers leading 17–16 and facing third and nine on their own 12-yard line, George Blanda found Billy Cannon for an 88-yard touchdown pass that provided the final margin, 24–16. The Chargers drove down to the 22-yard line near the end of the game, but turned the ball over on downs.

Four days later, Barron Hilton and Gillman were down in San Diego, examining the city's humble 24,000-seat Balboa Stadium and negotiating with city officials. Within three weeks, the city of San Diego had promised to spend $700,000 on stadium renovations, and Hilton had announced that the franchise would move to San Diego.

They packed up their apartment. Chuck—convinced his hunting days were over—sold his Winchester 12-gauge to Vukelich. They eventually found a house not far from San Diego State University, on Landa Drive, dotted with palm trees and homes with long, dramatic roof pitches covering two-car garages.

William and Kate had visited in Los Angeles, and now came out again and stayed for six weeks in San Diego, though they felt guilty about leaving Clare and Rita and their growing family (their seventh child, Marilyn, was born in March 1961). William sat outside in the temperate clime. Kate, nursing a lingering cold, still insisted on planting a bed of roses.

In San Diego, the Chargers' offices were located on the second floor of the Lafayette Hotel, purchased by Conrad Hilton in the '50s. When Barron Hilton moved his team there, the Lafayette was a natural. Chuck and some of the other assistants used to meet at the Red Fox Room steakhouse and supper club in the hotel. While the hotel was upscale, the practice facility—at the Marine Corps Recruit Depot—was not.

But in San Diego, Chuck and Marianne would find an idyllic setting. Even more than the Browns in Cleveland, the Chargers became the focal point of the city. Chuck and Marianne found the city open and livable. The picturesque Embarcadero Beach was perfect for Chuck's forays into photography.

The off-seasons were busier now, full of player recruitment and scouting and still more film study. Gillman would finish a long siege and magnanimously tell his coaches to take the rest of the week off. Then, a day or two later, absorbed with a new discovery, he'd call everyone back in.

"We learned that what you had to do is leave town," said Marianne. "Chuck would call me and say, 'I have three days off. Get ready.'"

It was thirty minutes down Interstate 5, and across the border to Tijuana in Chuck's car.

"My only memory is sitting in the back seat with my sugar cane," said Chris Noll. "And when we got to the border, they took it away from me. I was devastated, screaming and crying. I was sucking on the sugar cane and they wouldn't let me go through the border with it."

There were not many days off, even during the off-season, because the war between the leagues was changing the nature of football coaching. Instead of taking months off at a time during the winter and spring, Chuck spent from the end of the season throughout much of the spring trying to sign players. For their player personnel director, the Chargers hired the magnetic Don Klosterman, an insinuating, debonair presence who had played college football at St. Mary's before a skiing accident ended his playing career.

At the earliest opportunity after the drafts (held in November of the previous season), and sometimes even *before* the draft, teams would fly in prospective draftees, and one of the assistants would take the player around the city and make the pitch for the new league.

Bob Petrich, the West Texas A&M defensive lineman, visited the

NFL's Giants before his visit to San Diego. When Chuck picked him up at the airport, he made a point of taking Petrich for a scenic drive into the city. "It was like a jungle," said Petrich. "And coming from New York where it was so cold, and coming from West Texas, and being there for a couple of years with no greenery or anything like that, it was kind of like, 'Wow, I'm home.'"

A tougher sell was John Brown (drafted by Cleveland in the NFL), the formidable, soft-spoken offensive lineman from Syracuse, who'd opened many holes for 1960 Heisman winner Ernie Davis.

After flying Brown in on a redeye from Philadelphia, Chuck showed him around and then took him out to dinner.

"John, you don't want to go to Cleveland to play," said Chuck.

"Why?"

Chuck understood the recruiting game, and he'd seen both Davis and Gillman say exorbitant things to convince players to sign with the AFL, but he couldn't criticize his former coach.

"You just don't want to go to Cleveland to play," said Chuck. "This is a better situation for you."

The visit went well. John Brown was drawn to Chuck's quiet confidence. Before getting back on the plane, Chuck gave him a handsome watch. "This is for your coming to sign with San Diego," he said.

Though he didn't sign a contract before leaving, Brown was set to go to the new league, but then upon returning to Syracuse, he spoke with Ernie Davis. "I asked him where he was going, and he said he was going to Cleveland, because Washington had traded him," said Brown. "So I said, 'Well, I'm going to Cleveland also.'"

Brown, ridden with guilt over accepting the watch from Chuck, packed it up into a box and returned it to Chuck, with a note of explanation.

Back in San Diego, the news was greeted with derision. "Goddamnit, Chuck!," said Al Davis. "See, you give the watch to *them*, not the other way around! You've got to get these guys when they're here."

But Chuck, through Davis's hectoring and Gillman's frustration, was steadfast that there were certain things he wouldn't say and wouldn't do. It would be neither the first nor last of Chuck and Al's philosophical differences.

The 1961 draft brought two fierce defensive linemen, the 6-foot-5, 260-pound Indiana end Earl Faison, and the 6-foot-9, 315-pound Grambling tackle Ernie Ladd. Along with second-year middle linebacker Chuck Allen, who won the starting job in training camp, they helped to solidify the defense.

Allen was a smart, fundamentally sound player who was very much in the mold of his coach. Chuck had him spending extra time in film study, and his conscientious adherence to Chuck's tenets set the tone for the Chargers' defense. On the field, Allen was the extension of Chuck, the man responsible for calling the team's fronts and coverages. He was not a punishing tackler or overly fast, but he was a cerebral football player, a quick study, and a perfect expression of Chuck's philosophy that if everyone did their own job, the parts would fit together marvelously. "He was so much like him, it was scary," said Petrich. "Both clean-cut, that type of guy."

By 1961, the Chargers' defense began to come together. Instead of allowing 336 points, as they had in 1960, they gave up just 219 points (less than 16 points per game) and intercepted a pro football record 49 passes during the season. The Chargers marched to a 12–1 record, before a blowout loss to Boston in a meaningless regular-season finale during which Gillman rested most of his defensive regulars.

In the 1961 AFL Championship, a rematch against the defending champion Oilers—played in San Diego—the Chargers' defense rose to the occasion. San Diego forced seven turnovers and gave up just 10 points to an Oilers' offense that had set a pro scoring record that season, averaging more than 36 points a game. But it wasn't enough, as the Chargers' offense turned the ball over six times, and Houston won 10–3. Chuck was vexed with the result, but in just two seasons, he and Jack Faulkner had built a menacing, cohesive defensive unit.

✦　✦　✦

The 1962 season began with Chuck taking charge of the defense. Faulkner had left the Chargers for the head-coaching job with the Denver Broncos. Chuck found it disloyal that his colleague had taken a head coaching job in the same division, but the exit allowed Chuck to be promoted to the overall defensive coordinator.

"Sid was a great offensive mind," said Chuck later. "He was offensively oriented, that's what he liked. I went out there as a defense coach. He let me handle the defense. I was on my own there."

They had lost the '62 opener to the Broncos, Gillman steaming that his old assistant Faulkner seemed to know everything they were doing. Matters got worse a week later—Jack Kemp had thrown two touchdown passes in a 40–14 win over the Titans but broke a thumb. With just the young John Hadl backing him up, Gillman feared the worst. After the Chargers lost their next game, 42–17 to the Oilers, Gillman attempted to sneak Kemp through the league's waiver system, so the injured quarterback wouldn't count against the team's thirty-three-player roster limit. But Buffalo alertly claimed him, and suddenly the quarterback who had led the team to two straight league championship games was the property of the Bills. Despite the dispiriting loss, the Chargers won their next two games, and stood at 3–2 before heading on a three-game road trip.

It was a disappointing jaunt. After losing to the Bills and Patriots, they went to the Polo Grounds to play the shambolic New York Titans, a team struggling to make its payroll each week. Yet the Titans roundly defeated San Diego, 23–3, as Chuck was confounded that none of his defensive backs seemed to be able to keep up with Don Maynard, who caught six passes for 157 yards and two touchdowns.

A gloom pervaded the team on its return to the West Coast. They stood 3–5 now, a full three games behind both Faulkner's Broncos and Hank Stram's high-scoring Texans, running rampant behind new quarterback Len Dawson. Chuck was frustrated, experiencing the lowest moment of his three-season coaching career.

It would get worse.

On Saturday evening, October 27, while Chuck was preparing for the Titans game in New York, his sister Rita was back at home in Cleveland, waiting for her husband to arrive and commence with their son Ken's fifth birthday celebration.

Clarence had worked half a day that Saturday, putting in another shift as a plumber for the City of Cleveland. It had snowed the night before, so when he got home that afternoon, he told Rita he would shovel the small driveway leading back to the garage and clear the front sidewalk so the postman could get through. Afterward, Clare sat in his chair in the living room for a moment, his coat still on. Ken and Joanne were playing cards in front of the chair where Clare was sitting. Suddenly, he slumped in the chair; Rita, in the other room, heard a gurgling noise and ran in to see her husband keeled over. She yelled up to her mother, then ran to the telephone to call the family physician. Kate crossed herself, rushed downstairs, and hurried down the street to St. Mary's of Czestachowa, to get the parish priest.

"I remember my mom came running in and at that time calling the police," said Ken. "He had passed out. Basically, my grandparents came down and you know, back then, they all had the crucifixes with the holy water and the candles. Immediately, all that came out. They light the holy candles and sprinkled some holy water, but then they scooted the kids out of there. We all went upstairs."

While Rita rushed with Clare to the hospital, the Deininger children worried, and eventually ate Ken's birthday cake. Clare had suffered from a rheumatic heart from having strep throat when he was younger. He ignored Rita's many pleas to see a doctor but what happened on that Saturday was similar to a severe stroke. The ambulance rushed him to Marymount Hospital where he was comatose.

When Chuck and the Chargers got back to the West Coast late that Sunday night, after another loss, Marianne related the whole story.

Three days later, on Halloween evening, they got the call from Kate: Clarence Deininger was dead. Chuck's sister, now thirty-eight years old, was quite suddenly a widowed housewife—with seven children, all under the age of ten.

And without the words even being said, Chuck also knew that her seven children were now, in some way, his responsibility, just as his parents had become.

Chuck's parents, Kate Steigerwald Noll and William Valentine Noll, shortly after their wedding in 1917. *Courtesy of the Noll Family.*

The Nolls before Chuck was born, circa 1926 or 1927: Kate, Robert (born 1920), Rita (born 1924), and William. *Courtesy of the Noll Family.*

One of Chuck's first school pictures, taken while he was attending Holy Trinity School on the East Side of Cleveland. *Courtesy of the Noll Family.*

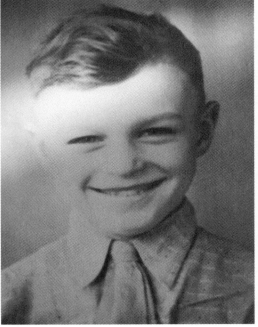

Chuck's first football team, the Clippers, an interracial sandlot team coached by Russ Alexander, far left. Chuck is next to him, wearing number 21 in the picture. *Courtesy of the Noll Family.*

The graduating class of Holy Trinity Grammar School, June 1945. Chuck is in the top row on the far left. *Courtesy of Ralph Yanky.*

Chuck and his sister Rita. Their bond was deep—a college roommate remembered Chuck raving about his big sister—and would remain so throughout their lives. *Courtesy of the Noll Family.*

Chuck and his childhood friend Ralph Yanky, in the old neighborhood, on the East Side of Cleveland. At left, Yanky is in the foreground, Chuck is in the background. At right, Chuck mock-fighting with Ralph. *Courtesy of the Noll Family.*

Benedictine High won the Cleveland city championship in 1948. Chuck is in the front row, wearing number 32. Assistant coach Ab Strosnider is in the third row, second from right. *Courtesy of Ralph Yanky.*

Chuck's senior portrait. The school newspaper captioned it, "CHARLES NOLL, 'All-American,' Football, Track, Bengal A.C. [Athletic Club]." He graduated 28th of 252 students in the Class of '49. *Courtesy of the Noll Family.*

In the fall of 1949, after a brief spell at Notre Dame, Chuck enrolled at University of Dayton. His dorm, St. Joseph's Hall, center, overlooked the football stadium, right. *Courtesy of University of Dayton.*

At Dayton, Chuck came into his own on the football field and off, establishing himself as someone who looked at life beyond the game. "He would always be right on top of all the things that were going on," said teammate Tom Carroll. *Courtesy of University of Dayton.*

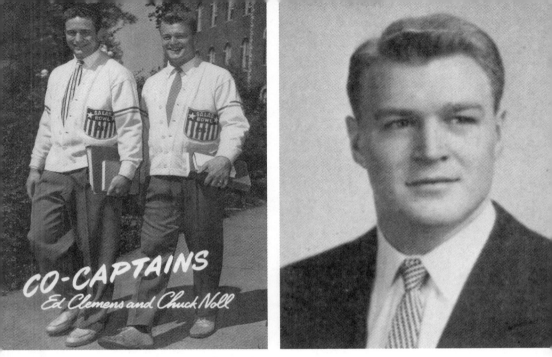

CO-CAPTAINS
Ed Clemens and Chuck Noll

After the Salad Bowl appearance as juniors, Chuck and fellow lineman Ed Clemens were named co-captains, appearing on the cover of the 1952 Dayton football media guide. By the time of his senior portrait, at right, he was considering offers for teaching jobs. Then the Browns drafted him in the twentieth round of the 1953 NFL Draft. *Courtesy of University of Dayton.*

One of the high points of the Dayton years, winning the Governor's Cup back from Xavier near the end of the 1952 season. Chuck, with fellow co-captain Ed Clemens, at the trophy ceremony. *Courtesy of University of Dayton.*

Impressing with his discipline and technique, Chuck earned a job as one of the Browns' two "messenger guards" in his rookie season of 1953. *Courtesy of the Cleveland Browns.*

Chuck at the Browns' training camp, in Hiram, Ohio, with his brother-in-law Clarence "Clare" Deininger and his nephew Bill. *Courtesy of the Noll Family.*

Chuck on the sidelines next to Paul Brown. During his seven years in Cleveland, Chuck encountered a different coaching style and absorbed the philosophy of a leader who expected his players "to run on their own gas." *Courtesy of the Cleveland Browns.*

The woman who would change Chuck's life was Marianne Hanes, who'd come up from Portsmouth to Cleveland and found work at the Cleveland Clinic. When her friend told her about Chuck, she said, "Oh, God, he plays football? For a living?" *Courtesy of the Noll Family.*

Chuck and Marianne were wed May 25, 1957. "[Our parents] just accepted it," said Chuck's sister, Rita. "They didn't get upset about it or anything." *Courtesy of the Noll Family.*

Chris Noll was born December 22, 1957, and spent the first year of his life fighting allergies, with eczema all over his body. *Courtesy of the Noll Family.*

The legendary Chargers' coaching staff of 1960–1961, Sid Gillman (top) with, from left, Joe Madro, Chuck, Al Davis, and Jack Faulkner. *Courtesy of the San Diego Chargers.*

By the early '60s, Chuck had become a photography buff and took this portrait of Marianne and Chris. *Courtesy of the Noll Family.*

William and Kate Noll visited Chuck in San Diego in 1962. Later that year, Clarence Deininger would die suddenly, altering the lives and fortunes of everyone in the family. *Courtesy of the Noll Family.*

Responsibility grew quickly in Chuck's first coaching job; after Faulkner left to join the Broncos in 1962, Chuck became the Chargers' defensive coordinator. *Courtesy of the Noll Family.*

The Baltimore Colts coaching staff in 1967. Colts' head coach Don Shula is flanked by Bill Arnsparger and Chuck in the front row. *Courtesy of the Indianapolis Colts.*

eight

OBLIGATIONS

✦   ✦   ✦

In the midst of the shock, there was an overwhelming sense of helplessness. It was unthinkable for him to go to the funeral, with the Chargers in the middle of their season—and he could not begin to find the words that would comfort his sister. It was another setback, another thing to get through, like the epileptic seizures or his father's condition or the tragedy in Dayton.

In a sense, the death would shape the rest of Chuck and Marianne's life as surely as it did Rita's. Marianne had learned earlier she couldn't have any more children, and while she and Chuck had spoken extensively about adopting, those conversations were shelved in the face of Clarence's death.

Just weeks later, Rita was driving the family's old Chevy when it broke down on Center Ridge Road in Cleveland. Chuck bought her another car and would continue, over the years, being the resource when something unexpected happened in the family.

What Rita's children witnessed, in the months and years ahead, was

Chuck becoming the focal part of the family, not just for Rita and her children but for William and Kate as well. In Margie's eyes, her grandmother "idolized" Chuck. "When he finally came home after my dad died that [next] summer, she had baked him a pie. He walks in and she is just so excited that he is here. She goes to get the pie, and she is like, 'Chuck, look what I made for you!' And it slid out of her hands and fell onto the floor. And, I mean, we're kids, we just think this is the funniest thing in the world. And she's like, 'Oooooh, my pie!,' and she has a fit because she always was a little drastic about things like that. I remember him going up to her and hugging her and he's like, 'Mom, believe me the pies are just as good whether they're on the floor or in my mouth.' And he hugs her and calmed her down."

It wasn't all Chuck and Marianne, of course. Clare's oldest sister, Agnes, would stop by with bagfuls of clothes from Higbee's department store. "Here, Rita, these are for the kids—see who fits into what." Bob Noll, Rita and Chuck's older brother, was in Cleveland as well, but less involved. "Bob's wedding ring was a little tight, let's put it that way," said Rick Deininger. But the primary onus was on Chuck. Family was the defining belief system in his life. Family was where he was from and what he was made of. More than ever, everyone was looking to him.

By then, William Noll was largely housebound. "I still remember him, as a little kid," said Rick. "He would be standing at the top of the stairs with a cane, saying something. I would be like, 'God, is he going to fall down these steps?' The most physical thing he did was cut the grass with a push lawnmower, and that was every Saturday. That was it as far as physical activity. That was all he could do. I mean, if you are the man of the house and you pay the bills, you know—that whole part of it just wasn't working. I know that affected things, and not in a good way. But, you know, you cope. People go on and deal with things."

Rita persevered, with help from Kate. But the most severe and expensive problems, whether it be plumbing or the roof, appliances or the garage, were left to Chuck. What Rita's seven children would experience, in the years ahead, was their indefatigable mother carrying on day by day and their Uncle Chuck helping in ways big and small. "She didn't let us use it as an excuse," said Ken. "It was like, *Keep going.* I give her credit. She is a saint. Well, that is the family, that's Uncle Chuck all the way. Whatever happens, happens. Keep going. Keep moving forward."

✦　✦　✦

Back in San Diego, Chuck and Marianne carried on. From their home in Del Cerro, where Chris could walk to the school across the street, the Nolls were close to St. Therese Parish, a spacious, quintessentially California Catholic Church, with stucco buildings and an open sanctuary, on the lazily winding strip of Camino Rico, just up the road from the fire station.

A few times a year, the Nolls would be invited out to Sid and Esther's handsome ranch house, and Chris would be allowed to pick apricots off their trees in the spacious backyard.

In these social situations, Marianne's gracious manner transcended Chuck's natural reticence. "I think my wife learned more about Chuck through Marianne, because they sat next to each other in the stands," said Paul Maguire. "She's just the loveliest person, she really is. And everybody kept thinking, 'How did he get her?'"

"We always thought his wife looked like Ali MacGraw, and beautiful, and too good-looking for him," said Bob Petrich.

The connection between Chuck and Marianne continued to deepen. They found each other attractive, respected one another's mind, had similar philosophies on raising their child. They were, in short, best friends.

They were also co-conspirators; despite Chuck's schedule, they'd find a way to steal away. In the regular season, game film didn't arrive until 2 p.m. Mondays. Chuck and Marianne would drop Chris off at school and drive to Tijuana for lunch and shopping, then return in time for him to be at the office before the game film would arrive Monday afternoon. When they would take trips, Marianne would sit in the front seat and read out loud to Chuck—often historical fiction, from a period of shared interest. "We never got any other time off during the season," said Marianne.

Though he never shirked his coaching duties, he retained his eclectic sensibilities and interests. By now, Chuck was spending more time with photography, converting a closet in their home into a darkroom. (When Rudy Regalado and Marilyn Hall got married, Chuck was their photographer.)

In the summer of 1963, Chuck and Marianne took a tour of the California wineries and began developing a more nuanced appreciation for wines, which had became a staple of their nightly dinners. There were pictures taken of Chris when he was five, sitting on the steps outside of a winery, where Chuck and Marianne had gone for a wine tasting.

"If you said something that Chuck didn't know about, I guarantee you the next time you talk to him, he knew every single thing about that subject," said Maguire. "It had to have happened that he either went to dinner with someone, and they said, 'We'll have this wine,' or 'This is one of the best wines I've ever had.' I guarantee you that's why he became a connoisseur of wines. I'm serious; I really mean that. Because when anybody ever said something and he didn't know about, he was quiet—he just shut up. And then, the next time you bring that subject up? Good God—it goes back to Noah."

On a trip to Kalamazoo, Michigan, to scout a lineman named John Lomakoski, Chuck bought the album *Telemann Trio Sonata for Recorder, Viola da Gamba and Continuo*. He and Marianne had been enamored of chamber music in Cleveland in the '50s and he continued pursuing the passion, eventually buying a recorder himself, though his friends routinely had no idea what he was talking about. "I started playing the recorder myself," he said, "and when I'd tell someone, they'd say, 'Oh, you play the recorder? What speed, 33 rpm?'"

While they relished San Diego, Chuck was taken aback by the extremities of the political conservatism of the area. "One thing I remember is my father being distressed by the John Birch Society," said Chris. "I can remember hearing them talk about that." The racial egalitarianism that he'd grown up with in integrated Cleveland was nowhere to be found in the upper-middle-class enclaves of southern California in the early '60s. In its absence, he found elements of the movement nativist and exclusionary. Or as Chuck once said to Marianne, "I thought I was a Republican —until I moved to California."

✦　✦　✦

There was a heightened urgency to the off-season work following 1962's lost season, in which the Chargers finished with a 4–10 record. In February, the coaches meticulously went through every play of every game's film footage. Each working with a portable viewer, they'd cut up the film, and then note the down, distance, and outcome of each play. Around the coach's office there were dozens of bags, each with a different play listed—Gillman's staples of the 405 and the 866 were front and center.

On a sheet, the assistants would write down the play, the defensive front it was run against, and the result. After filling a sheet and cutting the twenty-five corresponding plays, the coach would cut up the sheet of paper into twenty-five small strips and then affix each strip to corresponding play with a paper clip, roll up the combination, and throw it in the appropriate bag. In so doing, the staff would divide nearly a thousand plays of a season. (Back in L.A. in 1960, they'd divided the strips of film into numerous wastebaskets, until the Chargers' janitorial service emptied the wastebaskets one night; from then on, Gillman decreed that they would use paper bags, clearly marked "Do Not Throw Away.")

Chuck would help out with the offensive plays, then do a variation on the same thing with defense, though this would be done without Gillman's participation. Chuck would come home and marvel to Marianne, "Sid doesn't care anything about defense."

After the title-game losses in '60 and '61, and the debacle of '62, Gillman was seething. He knew there was too much talent—among players and coaches alike—for the team to fail.

One solution for focusing the team's efforts had hatched in Gillman's mind in January 1963, when doing a postmortem on the '62 season. He felt the Chargers were too soft, too comfortable in their training camp environs on the campus of the University of San Diego. They needed to suffer, to endure, to come together in a crucible of heat and competition and discomfort.

The solution, as Gillman saw it, was to hold the 1963 training camp on a patch of forbidding land called Rough Acres, located seventy miles east of San Diego. The ranch-style main building housed the team meetings and meals, while the tiny, flat-roofed "ponderosas" were where the players and coaches spent their nights and free time. There were snakes and industrial-sized bugs. Sam DeLuca, a city boy from Brooklyn, was so frightened of the latter that he made his roommate, George Blair, check for invaders before he'd walk in the room.

"Sometimes you ate dirt," said Paul Lowe. "There was dirt on your plate. There were flies you had to slap off when you eat. You would go in there and sometimes the cook didn't have the food ready."

"I'd never been on a football field that didn't have grass," said Petrich. "It was curlicues from wood shavings from a lumber mill, and they wet it down. It was hard ground but they watered it a lot."

There were two bars in the area, one in the basement of the main complex, called the Gopher Hole, and another one, just up the desolate road, named the Oak Knoll. The players would drink there, but Chuck kept a bottle of wine on ice in his room.

The heat and the humble conditions left many of the players with a nasty disposition, as did Gillman's insistence that his coaches push the players hard. During a preseason scrimmage, Chuck split the defensive players into two squads, one led by Ernie Ladd and the other by second-year linebacker Chuck Allen. Each had a defensive unit that was to play seven consecutive plays, then cycle out. The immense, 6-foot-9, 325-pound Ladd had been discontent from the beginning of the camp, agitating for a new contract. After his unit's second set of downs, Chuck Allen called for Ladd's unit to come in. Ladd, winded and still getting into playing shape, pulled Petrich by the shoulder and said, "Stay here, rookie."

Ladd's unit sat out a couple of more plays before going out on the field. After five plays, not seven, Ladd took them off again. From the far sideline, supervising the defensive scrimmage, Chuck shouted, "Ladd, if your team doesn't come in on seven plays, you're going to take a lap."

Ladd, peeved and exhausted, yelled back, "You can lap my *dick* head!"

"And Chuck Noll's face," said Petrich, "I have never seen somebody so red in the face. And the whole field blew up laughing except for one man, and he turned around and even Sid Gillman was laughing. And when Chuck looked at him, Sid's face went, *zoop.* He just tensed up. And Chuck made Ernie get up and take a lap, and I tell you what—it was the longest, slowest lap I have ever seen in my life. He could have walked faster. That was the end of it; he never confronted Chuck again."

From the location, and his edgy manner, Gillman had made the urgency of the season clear. He also had hired a charismatic Louisiana bodybuilder named Alvin Roy to lead the Chargers through weight training. For all the portrayals of football players as muscle-bound lunkheads, there'd been a long bias against weight training in the sport. Roy brought thousands of pounds of weights out to the desert, along with his vast experience as a coach on the USA's 1952 Olympic weightlifting team—and thousands of pills as well. The "nutritional supplements" that he gave the players with each meal were actually 5 mg doses of the steroid Dianabol.

"I learned a secret from those Rooskies," is how Roy put it to Ron Mix and his teammates. The players were trusting and, at first, impressed—the Dianabol pills given with meals increased their strength. Steroids had been taken in pro football before, but never in such a widespread, systematic fashion, and never with such a dedicated combination of monitored programs of weight training. (While the debilitating effects of steroids would eventually become clear, in 1963—and for more than a decade after—there was nothing in either the AFL or NFL to make them illegal.) Chuck wasn't completely convinced on the utility of weight training and soon became dubious of the scientific basis for their use. But he did concede that the combination of both made the Chargers stronger heading into the new season.

By that second year as the Chargers' defensive coordinator, Chuck's coaching philosophy had crystallized. While remaining mindful of the big picture, he continued to be absorbed in the fine-grained details of technique. It wasn't merely the secondary, where Chuck specialized. He'd also interceded with Ernie Ladd and convinced him to refine his basic tactic for warding off an offensive lineman. For years, Ladd had dealt with opposing lineman by swinging his forearm up toward the head of his opponent.

Chuck wanted Ladd to vary his technique and use his full arm to sweep the blocker aside.

"If you deal with it for two weeks, just don't use your forearm at all, let me teach you one move," said Chuck. "Use it for two weeks. If you don't like it, then go back to the forearm."

In the first week of the effort, Ladd loathed the awkward swipes he was taking, but by the middle of the second week, he'd realized why Chuck had changed it.

"Best move that ever happened," said Ladd. "Chuck had a way of reaching out and touching his players. If you brought something to the table, Chuck would develop it for you."

The players noticed, as well, Chuck's scrupulous fairness. "He would never play a favorite," said Maguire. "And he would never hesitate to yank your ass out of a ballgame."

Chuck didn't resort to emotional pleas. It was, rather, a system of different players performing different roles in unison. "If somebody got beat physically, okay, we can live with that," said Petrich. "Figure out a way to beat them the next time. But mental errors were not tolerated, and Chuck Noll, of all people, would not tolerate a mental error. Getting beat? That happens."

"I will tell you the most important thing he taught me and taught all of us," said Maguire. "And he kept stressing it every time we either had a scrimmage or if we had a game. You only do your job. Just let everybody else take care of whatever the hell they're supposed to do. You do what you're supposed to do, and everything is going to be fine. It's a team thing, but it is individuals doing their own jobs. Once you do that, the whole team is successful with it."

The Chargers' secondary included the Dick Westmoreland, a rookie free agent from North Carolina College whom Chuck saw as having the speed and raw man-to-man coverage skills to handle the league's best wide receivers, like Lionel Taylor of Denver and Don Maynard of New York. While Westmoreland made plenty of mistakes, and began to doubt himself, Chuck consistently encouraged him.

"He would tell me, 'Don't get your dauber down,'" said Westmoreland. "And I appreciated that, though I had no idea what a dauber even was."

"None of us did!," said Maguire. "Well, everybody was so afraid of Chuck they wouldn't ask him! I mean, if he said it, that's good. I like it, we'll use it. You know, whatever the hell a dauber is."

Yet Chuck also had to learn, during this period, how to deal with different types of players. Not everyone absorbed instruction as quickly as he had as a player. And, clearly, not everyone was as dedicated to honing his craft. The other main cornerback in 1963 was edgy, free-spirited Dick Harris, with whom Chuck would occasionally clash. "Dick Harris used to drive him absolutely crazy, and I'll tell you why," said Maguire. "Because Dick Harris was a clown. They called him Chuckles. And he didn't give a shit. But I'll tell you what, he could cover and he could play and he was smart. He used to drive Chuck nuts because when guys do things kind of naturally and they're kind of self-taught, and they do things like that, it really bugs the shit out of someone because as you have observed Chuck wanted to break it down into its parts. And when a guy just goes out there and says, 'I got it. I can cover this.' Dick was that kind of guy. Drove Chuck *nuts.*"

One day, after practice, Chuck was walking off the field at Sunset Park in La Mesa and heard a familiar voice, calling out softly, "Chuck." He turned, and there was Paul Brown.

Brown had been fired by the new Browns owner Art Modell after the 1962 season and was by now exiled in La Jolla. "He did not go to Chargers' football games," said his son, Mike Brown. "He wouldn't watch football games on television because it bothered him so. He would spend his day playing golf or trying to divorce himself. He felt abandoned. He felt rejected. It was just the way it was."

But Brown also couldn't resist stopping by to visit one of his former players. He and Gillman mostly ignored one another. But Chuck and Brown shared a few moments quietly catching up. Later, Chuck confided to Marianne how desperately lonely Brown seemed.

Paul Brown wasn't the only one stopping by. The Chargers' system and the team's coaches were generating attention. Young college and high school coaches from throughout southern California and beyond came around to watch the Chargers practice.

"The Chargers' practice field was a favorite place for young coaches to run up to," said Joe Gibbs, who started monitoring the Chargers while serving as a line coach at San Diego State. "I'd follow their line coach, Joe Madro, around wherever he went. They'd share everything with you. The techniques were what I wanted to copy. I'd think, *Hey man, those guys are great!*"

Throughout the '63 season, as the Chargers' offense made headlines—Canadian Football League refugee Tobin Rote capably taking the reins at quarterback—the defense continued to play solid football. It reached its apex in a four-game stretch in November and December, giving up just 26 points over four games.

Chuck had developed a defense that could rush the passer with just the front four—Ladd and Faison used to joke that they would "race you to the quarterback" after breaking the huddle—leaving the still talented but less dominating back seven to patrol the pass. During the year, Patriots' coach Mike Holovak described the Chargers' zone defense as "probably the best in the league."

Over the course of the season, as the Chargers dominated opponents, one could frequently hear the yells of "Oskie!" in the Chargers' secondary. That was the code word that Chuck had implemented, shouted by defensive players to let their teammates know the ball had been intercepted, and it was time to find an offensive player to block. (The term had been popularized in Ohio football and had roots going at least as far back as General Robert Neyland at Tennessee.)

The season's jarring interruption came on November 22, 1963, while the Chargers were preparing to play host to the Denver Broncos, with the news that President Kennedy had been shot. Chuck had taken Chris and some neighborhood boys to see the president's motorcade the previous summer. A distraught Marianne went to Chris's school to take him home as the nation began to grieve (the AFL postponed its games that weekend, and made them up on December 22). "I remember my mother crying," said Chris Noll. "I think it was more just the horror of the president being killed—one that we liked—than any particular Catholic connection."

The Chargers went 11–3 on the season, losing once to Faulkner, their former assistant, in Denver, and twice to Al Davis, who'd taken over the struggling Raiders and led them to respectability. It was after one of the losses to the Raiders that Gillman, who'd been relentless with the team since July, let off a bit and told his team, "Boys, it's a long, hard haul from the shithouse to the penthouse, but it is one quick drop from the penthouse to the shithouse."

The next week, the Chargers clinched the Western Division title with a 58–20 bombing of the Broncos.

That set up an AFL Championship Game with the Boston Patriots, at Balboa Stadium, on Chuck's birthday, January 5, 1964, a week after the Bears had edged the Giants, 14–10, in the NFL Championship Game.

On the day, the Chargers' defense neutralized the Patriots' attack—intercepting two passes and allowing just fourteen first downs—and San Diego won the AFL title, 51–10. It was an epic offensive performance, but lost in the headlines was the way the Chargers dominated on defense.

Gillman was boldly confident afterward. "We're the champions of the world," he said. "If anyone wants to debate it, let them play us."

Chuck felt somewhat deflated that day, just as he had after the title game wins with the Browns, and after the President's Cup win over Xavier in college, and after the big win over South High in the Charity Game in high school. His players were jubilant, but no one later would remember any meaningful words from Chuck.

"With Chuck, I think the true intensity was translated without a lot of words," said Petrich. "When you walked around him, you stood a little bit more erect and a little straighter."

✦ ✦ ✦

But 1963 was a zenith that wouldn't be repeated. The Chargers remained a perennial power, but in both 1964 and 1965, they lost to the Buffalo Bills—and former teammate Jack Kemp—in AFL title games.

The Chargers' personnel superiority had diminished—after 1962, the vital Klosterman joined Lamar Hunt's Kansas City Chiefs—and Hilton couldn't afford to compete for college stars with some of the wealthier owners in the AFL.

"It was all so costly," said Sid Gillman. "There were very few men who could stand the losses the owners absorbed in those years. At the draft, we'd have two blackboards, one with the names of players who would cost big money to sign, the other with those who didn't figure to come high. We always drafted from the second board."

While the personnel was not as strong as it had been, the film study under Gillman, as refined by Chuck and defensive assistant Walt Hackett and others, reached its apex in game planning. Against the Jets in 1965, Chuck and Hackett determined that the Jets' Matt Snell was tipping a play when he came to the line of scrimmage, going immediately into a three-point stance if they were going to quick-snap the ball, but keeping his hands on his knees if they were going to count it out. With that as a cue, the Chargers demolished the Jets, 34–9.

But they couldn't stop Kemp and the Bills in successive championship games—or, more to the point, the Chargers' offense couldn't move the ball, generating only 10 points in two games.

By the end of the 1965 season, Chuck felt trapped. He'd seen the money draining out of the Chargers' coffers. Faison had been traded prior to the 1965 season; Ladd would be gone before the '66 campaign started. There was little hope—given the nature of contracts being offered to rookies—that they'd be able to replace those players or compete with the rising Chiefs and Raiders in the AFL Western Division.

Chuck had seen the loss of personnel to richer teams, seen the team often avoid drafting the best available players because they couldn't sign them. They'd lost two championship games in a row to a team quarterbacked by an old teammate, who'd been lost only because of Gillman's hubris. He knew the time had come to make the move back to the NFL.

✦   ✦   ✦

A couple of weeks later, early in 1966, Chuck heard from Don Shula, the young coach of the Colts, who was looking to hire an assistant. The opening in Baltimore came when assistant coach Charlie Winner left his job as a defensive assistant to coach the St. Louis Cardinals. Chuck was recommended for the job by his old teammate on the Browns, John Sandusky, who was an assistant to Shula.

Chuck took a flight to Baltimore's Friendship Airport, where he was greeted by Upton Bell, son of the late NFL commissioner Bert Bell and the personnel man for the Colts.

Bell was youngish for his job but doubly ambitious to prove that he wasn't in his position just because of his last name. As he drove Chuck downtown toward the Colts' offices, he engaged him about the attractiveness of Baltimore as a place to live and the Colts as a team to coach for.

"It will be great, Chuck," Bell said. "You'll love it here. We've got the greatest quarterback in football, and a terrific offense. We've Lenny Moore and Raymond Ber—"

"Upton remember something," said Chuck, interrupting. "Defense wins championships."

Shula's offer came a few days later. It was a job back in the NFL, it was closer to home, and it was for more money.

The only problem, upon his return to San Diego, was explaining the move to the eight-year-old Chris.

"I told them I wasn't leaving," Chris said. "They could go ahead and move to Baltimore, but I was going to stay here because I loved California. I unpacked my suitcases and said, 'Go ahead; I am staying with friends.'"

The news was greeted more happily back in Cleveland. "I remember grandma yelling down the stairs, 'Chuck just got a job with the Baltimore Colts!,'" said Margie. "She was ecstatic, because he was going to be closer. I was like, 'Is that good?' 'Yes! That's good! Come here, let me hug everybody!,' or something like that. She didn't yell down the stairs very often, so that was big time."

After six seasons in a new league, Chuck was coming back to the NFL. And back to work with another protégé of Paul Brown.

nine

"KNUTE KNOWLEDGE"

✦   ✦   ✦

The parallels in the careers of Chuck Noll and Don Shula were likely apparent to both men. Shula was two years older, born January 4 rather than Chuck's January 5. Both began the first grade as precocious, headstrong five-year-olds, both were the children of working-class parents, both attended Catholic grammar schools in northeastern Ohio. Both had successful football careers in high school, then went to a private Catholic college in Ohio (in Shula's case, it was John Carroll University in suburban Cleveland). Both were drafted by the Browns and inculcated in Paul Brown's philosophy of football. (Shula was traded by the Browns the same off-season that Chuck was drafted by Cleveland, so the two were never teammates.) Both built seven-year pro careers by being smart and consistently intense about football as a vocation rather than being more physically talented than other players. Both went directly from their playing career into coaching and soon revealed themselves to be among the brightest and most respected minds in the game.

So it was not a surprise that they hit it off immediately.

"I knew the minute I sat down with him that I wanted to hire him," said Shula. "Chuck was that impressive. He was the complete package, total—exactly what you would want in an assistant coach."

Where they differed was in demeanor. Shula was an intense extrovert, headstrong and combustible; Chuck remained cooler, calmer, and more cerebral. Their mutual respect and complementary styles would define their time together in Baltimore.

It is hard to overstate how separate the two leagues were in the first half of the 1960s. While Chuck had remained in pro football, he was returning from six seasons in an entirely different world. Not only were the players different and the philosophies different, the rules were different as well. In a sense, he was returning to the more traditional approach to football. "Don was so much like Paul Brown, which I was used to," said Chuck. "And Sid was not, so it was like coming home in a sense."

"I hired him from Sid Gillman, and that was a completely different style of football, philosophy, everything," said Shula. "It was completely different from what Paul Brown or what I was doing, so Chuck had to just come back and get back into the Paul Brown style of football. Get that Al Davis out of his mind." Of course, Davis had been gone from the Chargers for three seasons by the time Chuck left San Diego, but Shula's point still stood. The slashing, open-ended passing offenses of the AFL, and the innovative zone defenses of the younger league had not filtered into the National Football League yet.

In 1966, the NFL was a league thoroughly dominated, both on the field and in the collective mind-set, by Vince Lombardi. His Packers (who'd been to the title game in 1960, and won the NFL title in 1961, 1962, and 1965) were the standard against which the rest of the league judged its progress. Baltimore was perhaps the most recognized perennial rival, led by the redoubtable presence of quarterback Johnny Unitas, already a legend in the game after a decade in the pros. So the mission was clear: Chuck was hired to help the Colts get past Green Bay. He knew that if he succeeded in doing so, a head-coaching job offer was likely to follow.

Chuck and Marianne packed up the house in San Diego, put it up for sale, and then Chuck drove the car across the country while Marianne and Chris flew to Baltimore to look for housing. They found a tidy home in suburban Towson, on a street dotted with pine trees, across from a creek, and just down the street from Riderwood Elementary School.

But even before Chuck's first training camp with the Colts, the world of pro football changed again. On June 8, 1966, the war between the leagues ended, Tex Schramm and Pete Rozelle having brokered a truce with AFL founder Lamar Hunt. The most immediate impact was that the era of recruiting college players ceased—the two leagues agreed to a common draft beginning in 1967, and a championship game between the winners of each league (Hunt dubbed it the Super Bowl; though the league wouldn't officially adopt the term for another two years) that would be played following the 1966 season. The merger would become complete in 1970.

✦   ✦   ✦

Earlier that spring, Chuck had stopped into Cleveland. While William Noll's physical health was deteriorating—the tremors remained and dementia began to set in—Kate took extra work when she could but usually stayed home, so she could feed the grandchildren lunch and watch over them after school. For William Noll, the world constricted. He sat in a rocking chair and watched television much of the day, waiting for the children to come home from school.

When Chuck appeared, he felt compelled to rally his parents from their malaise. He would get out the ukulele or the guitar and lead his nieces and nephews in a sing-along. There were magic tricks—pulling a quarter out of a nephew's ear, then making it disappear—and jokes and pointed questions about how their school was going.

On the same trip in the spring of '66, Chuck spent time with Rita's oldest son, Rick, who was thirteen years old and had entered a car in the Pinewood Derby of his local Boy Scout troop. The local scout leader asked Rick if his uncle would come to speak to the boys, and Chuck agreed to do so. He was still not comfortable with public speaking, and he didn't give a formal talk. Afterward, a Boy Scout raised his hand and asked, "What do you have to do to be a pro football player?"

"Go to school, do your homework, get good grades," said Chuck. "And study, because we don't want any dumb kids. We want smart kids."

"The kid's face just fell," said Rita. "That wasn't the answer he was looking for."

On one of Chuck's visits to Cleveland, Margie was upstairs at her grandparents.

"How's school?," he asked.

"Um, okay," she said, unconvincingly.

"What do you mean 'okay'? You should be doing real well."

"I don't get algebra."

"What do you mean you don't get algebra? Go get your book."

What transpired was an intense session, in which Chuck conveyed the concepts in a way his niece understood.

"He went over every problem with me," said Margie. "I don't know what it was, if it was the attention, or that he explained it right, but it clicked. From that day on, math was my best subject."

The Nolls' move to Baltimore precipitated the Deininger family's first vacation out of state. In late June of that summer, Rita had put her children in the station wagon, with her billy club under the front seat, and drove them to Baltimore. Chuck had come back to help ferry supplies to Baltimore. The seven Deiningers could all fit in the station wagon but not their luggage. So Rita had five, and two more were in Chuck's car with all the bags. That first night in Towson, Margie, Joanne, and Marilyn were assigned the fold-out sofa in the living room.

"I remember we were just all excited being there on our first vacation, and we couldn't go to sleep," said Margie. "I remember he came down to the room. The three of us were on the sofa couch, and he's like, 'Pretend you're floating on clouds.' He literally calmed us to sleep."

Befitting Chuck's nature, the itinerary of the visit was crammed with activities and culture. They went to a frontier town in Virginia. They went to the Capital Mall. They stopped in Gettysburg on the way home, and Chuck spoke to his nieces and nephews about the history of the place.

Early in their visit, he came back from the Colts' offices one day to find Rita's entire family still indoors.

"What's everybody doing in the house?," Chuck asked. "Why aren't they out playing?"

"Because of the air conditioning," explained Rita. Her children had never spent time in an air-conditioned home before.

✦　✦　✦

The Colts began 1966 still stinging from their 1965 playoff loss to Green Bay, when they were convinced (and game films seemed to confirm) that the Packers' tying field goal at the end of regulation had actually sailed wide.

On defense, Chuck sat down at a desk next to Bill Arnsparger, who'd coached with Shula under Brown protégé Blanton Collier's staff at the University of Kentucky. Avuncular and unassuming, Arnsparger was in many ways a perfect match for Chuck.

At the Colts' training camp in Westminster, Maryland, Chuck began inculcating the linebackers and secondary in his coverage principles (Arnsparger was in charge of the defensive linemen). "Chuck made sure that everything was outlined step by step," said Shula. "You learned by listening, writing, seeing, and practice on the field—four steps of the learning process."

It was the Browns' method, modernized. "When I first went into coaching," Chuck once said, "I heard it one time and I knew it, and I thought everybody functioned that way. It didn't work, until I learned you had to go over it and over it and over it and over it and over it, and when you think you've gone over it enough, you go over it some more, and then finally, in another year, somebody is going to learn it."

And that change was soon instilled. While Arnsparger varied the fronts to employ the Colts' superior defensive line, Chuck began to emphasize a cohesive structure for his linebackers and defensive backs.

"When I first joined the Colts, I knew my assignments and I didn't really understand where all the linebackers were and where the other defensive backs were," said Jerry Logan, the crafty fourth-year safety from West Texas A&M. "I understood after a little while with Chuck Noll that defense was a team game. Everybody has to know what everybody else is doing. And that makes you a better player."

Arnsparger and Chuck's collaboration on the defensive game plan was seamless. Chuck had absorbed Gillman's fanatical devotion to film study, and Arnsparger had earned the nickname "One More Reel" for his indefatigable devotion to inquiry through game film.

During games, Chuck, often wearing a pin-collar shirt, a narrow black tie, and the Colts' blue satin warm-up jacket, prowled the sidelines with a headset, communicating with Arnsparger up in the booth. The Colts players noticed Chuck's composed demeanor. He in turn understood, from his career as a pro, that there were times almost any player was going to be physically manhandled.

"If you got beat physically, that wasn't a problem," said Dennis Gaubatz, the middle linebacker in 1966. "But you better not get beat mentally —wrong coverage, pick up the wrong man, that was a no-no with him."

In 1966, the Colts' defense showed marked improvement over the course of the year, giving up more than 20 points only once in the last ten weeks of the season. The season came down to a showdown with the Packers, who'd routed them in the season opener in Green Bay. Back at Baltimore in December, the defensive game plan devised by Arnsparger and Chuck neutralized the Packers' offensive thrusts, though they ultimately fell, 14–10, and were eliminated from playoff contention.

The Colts finished in second place in the Western Conference, qualifying for the dreaded end-of-the-season contest called the Playoff Bowl, which was really neither. The game was a matchup between the two runners-up in each conference, played on a neutral field in Miami, with the ticket proceeds going to benefit the players' pension fund. Lombardi called it "the Shit Bowl," according to Bob Skorinski ("He said it was a losers' bowl for losers"), and Shula's opinion of the game wasn't much different. Still, it was a game, and they all wanted to win it—and they did, as the Colts edged the Eagles, 20–14, to end the season on a winning note, however extraneous it may have seemed at the time.

✦   ✦   ✦

Chuck's two biggest fans remained his parents. William Noll watched the games in hopes of seeing a glimpse of Chuck on the sidelines. Kate Noll, still temperamental, still steadfast in her devotion to her family, kept her daily routine. The focus on frugality never left. Kate still saved her dimes to take weekly bus trips downtown to the Cleveland Trust. Helping his grandmother up the stairs with groceries one time, Ken dropped a bag and crushed some of the eggs. "Looks like we're having scrambled eggs today," she said.

But mostly William and Kate were marooned upstairs. He wasn't healthy enough to get around much, though he'd unsteadily make his way downstairs on occasion. Kate's sister, Toot, would come over with her husband Stewart, and the two couples would play gin or cribbage.

"My grandmother was so severe," said Rick Deininger. "She was the sort of typical German, you know: 'Do it this way.' You did not cross grandma. She was a tough woman, but I think a lot of that was a result of things not working out. Chuck had loads of that, too: Suck it up, deal with it, and get on with life."

It was difficult for Chuck to see his father. The frozen rictus of a smile on his face was there, but there was also a hint of a haunted countenance. The pack-a-day habit of unfiltered cigarettes didn't help either. By the '60s, with the Parkinson's tremors, emphysema, and the beginnings of dementia, William Noll was a wreck. At the Noll family reunions, the emphysema prevented him from singing along with his siblings.

By 1967, he was finally on disability, and the extra $40 a month helped Rita make ends meet. The grandchildren would come upstairs to keep him company. He played gin rummy with them, and the kids would cheat, slipping the cards to each other under the table. "I thought I was the best card player ever," said Joanne. "I always beat my grandfather."

Rita had gone back to work around the time Marilyn started elementary school, working part time for Adams Spices in Cleveland. Beyond that, Chuck helped out whenever possible, paying the school tuition for some of the children, helping out with the house note, covering any extraordinary expenses.

Rita, hewing to family practices, refused self-pity or second thoughts or any conjecture about her life had Clare lived. "It's over with," she'd say. "It's done with. I've gotta get on with my life. Let's go on."

But she remained true to Clare for the rest of her days. Still attractive and fun-loving, she nonetheless rejected her children's suggestions to start dating again. "What man," she'd ask, "is gonna want a woman with *seven* kids?"

From Baltimore, it was easy for Chuck and Marianne and Chris to visit each summer. "It was such a different world for me when we went to visit," Chris said. "It was an old house, the doilies on the back of the furniture, and the food was different. [My grandma] was big at making the different nut rolls and German stuff. So I loved going for the food. I was an only child and those were my cousins, and my closest relatives, so for me it was time to go play with people my age."

The visit in 1967 had an added significance. Chuck and Marianne and Chris drove back to Cleveland for his parents' fiftieth wedding anniversary, and they arrived to a family quarrel.

The strained relationship between Bob's wife, Stella, and the Noll family became a breach that summer. William and Kate didn't want to make a fuss but agreed to a large sit-down dinner at the church. Stella had wanted a smaller, fancier affair.

"His wife wanted a sit-down dinner for adults," remembered Margie. "And my mom wanted all the kids to be there. All I know is Aunt Stella walked out mad and, from that point on, that was it."

"It was very tense," said Marilyn, "and then we just never saw them again." With Bob almost completely out of the picture, and Rita already working a full-time job, the responsibility continued to fall on Chuck. "Stella kept him in his place," Rick said. "Bob was never around to help."

The fiftieth wedding anniversary went as planned. Chuck and Marianne and Chris were there, as were all seven of his cousins. Bob showed up, somewhat sheepishly, and Stella did not.

"We didn't talk about it," said Joanne. "We really didn't. I just knew they stopped coming around, and my mom and my grandparents didn't talk about it. That is what a lot of the family does—we didn't talk about a lot of things."

The Deininger family visit to Baltimore in '66 launched a tradition that would affect all of Rita Deininger's children. For each of the next fifteen years, at least one Deininger niece or nephew would spend some or all of the summer with the Nolls. In the summer of '67, Ken came to Baltimore to spend a few weeks. He was about the same age as Chris, the closest thing to a brother, and eager for time with his uncle.

"I absolutely loved it," said Ken. "When I got there in June, Uncle Chuck was there, and they took a vacation, and I would be with them. I remember them saying, 'What do you guys want to do for vacation?' Well, I wanted to go to amusement parks. Uncle Chuck is like, 'No, no, we are going to go someplace good. We are going to go to Gettysburg and Williamsburg,' all the historical stuff that he loved. It was absolutely cool. Everything was an adventure. Even eating—when they would cook, they just wouldn't cook. He would have the grill, and it had to be charcoal or mesquite. Everything was a lesson or an adventure, and I loved that. We decided to get into badminton one day. So, do you get the store badminton with the dinky nets? Uncle Chuck had nothing to do with that. He went out and bought a full-sized net and lined the backyard for the court. The whole neighborhood was over. It was the coolest thing."

✦ ✦ ✦

With the 1967 season, the NFL added a sixteenth franchise, New Orleans, and realigned to four four-team divisions, adding an extra tier of playoffs. The Colts, oddly, were placed in the Coastal Division of the Western Conference, with the Rams, 49ers, and expansion Atlanta Falcons. The defense was even better, as two talented rookies—defensive lineman Bubba Smith and safety Rick Volk—earned starting jobs. The Colts were still unbeaten when Chuck went into the hospital for an emergency appendectomy on Friday, October 27. He was in the hospital for the Colts' 17–13 win at Washington that Sunday, but he returned to work the next day. "I was afraid to stay out of work any longer," he told the *Baltimore Sun*. "I was afraid they'd find out they could get along without me."

Six days after Chuck's return, Baltimore's defense sacked Bart Starr six times in edging the world champion Packers, 13–10, before a deafening din in Memorial Stadium. After seven games, the Colts were undefeated, at 6–0–2, caught in a breakneck race with George Allen's Los Angeles Rams, at 5–1–2. The win over the Packers marked the first of four straight weeks the Colts gave up 10 points or less. While the players in Chuck's secondary were slow-footed, they were exceedingly well trained.

The Colts were still unbeaten, at 11–0–2, heading into the regular-season finale against the 10–1–2 Rams. But on that day, the Colts' offense broke down miserably, and the Colts' defense couldn't hold out against a gifted Rams' offense and a raucous Los Angeles Memorial Coliseum crowd. After the 35–10 loss, their first of the season, the Colts' campaign was over. In that single stroke they were eliminated from it all—no playoffs, not even a spot in the loathed Playoff Bowl.

The following spring, Chuck crossed paths with a young Morgan State running back named John "Frenchy" Fuqua, a garrulous, irrepressible Detroit native who'd come to Baltimore on a football scholarship. The Morgan State team played its games at Memorial Stadium as well and shared some workout facilities with the Colts. "The guy that I was trying to impress at the time was Don Shula," said Fuqua. "He didn't have time for it. But Noll sat down and talked to us."

"What position do you play?," Chuck asked Fuqua.

"Running back," he said. "I played guard in high school—I was an all-city guard for my last two years in Detroit."

"I played the line," said Chuck. "That's good; you ought to be a good blocker."

It was a quiet conversation but left a mark on Fuqua. He would notice what other African American players already had. Chuck was undemonstrative; he didn't presume to be hip, nor did he condescend to black players the way so many coaches of the era did. Yet among the staffs he worked on, Chuck seemed to be the coach most attuned to black athletes. "Chuck is probably the least color-conscious person I know," said Marianne. "His coaches used to tease him because couldn't remember if some of his players were black or white. He couldn't remember their names and he couldn't remember their color. Those weren't important things to him."

Early evening, April 4, 1968, Marianne was ironing when the news came over the radio that Dr. Martin Luther King Jr. had been assassinated in Memphis. Baltimore, like so many American cities, was inflamed by the incident. Chuck was out of town on a scouting trip; Chris and Marianne watched the National Guard trucks rolling over the freeway bridge just a block away from their Towson home.

The summer of racial unrest was felt in Cleveland as well. On the streets of 141st and Harvard, there was the same kind of urban change going on that had marked Chuck's childhood. The white families were moving out to the suburbs. Attendance at the school and the church was declining. St. Mary of Czestochowa was the last white Catholic enclave in that area of the city. After some flare-ups with public school children, the parochial school began letting their students out a half hour earlier. The children would walk down the street from the school each day, a little more isolated in the neighborhood. "It got integrated pretty bad," was how Rita put it. The classes were smaller, the parish was smaller, and through the summer of discord in 1967, black and white youth in Cleveland seemed to find less common ground.

✦ ✦ ✦

By the beginning of the 1968 season, the template had been set for the Colts' coaching staff. Shula, the energetic firebrand, was at the top, demanding and enthusiastic, more than willing to call out players as he perceived the need. In contrast, the assistants were more low-key. On offense, John Sandusky had a loud bark and a barrel chest, but his critiques poked rather than bit. On defense, the studious Arnsparger and Chuck devised cerebral, sound defensive game plans employing more zone defenses than was the norm in the NFL.

Among the staff, Chuck's nickname was "Knowledge" (or, a little more sharply, "Knute Knowledge," bestowed on him by Upton Bell), and he and Marianne gravitated to John and Ruth Sandusky and Bill and B. J. Arnsparger.

In the off-seasons, they remained close—the Nolls, the Arnspargers, and the Sanduskys. Some days, they'd all get sitters and go out on the town. "In hindsight I see why because the assistant coaches didn't make much money back then," said Gerry Sandusky, John's son. "They still worked crazy hours. They were all Catholics, so they all had kids. There was this connectedness of nobody else understood their lives. They had these low-paying, high-pressure jobs. You had to beat the Packers on Sunday or you might not be around to pay the tuition at Catholic school for your five kids. It was a crazy degree of pressure. My dad was a South Philly guy. He put ice in his red wine. He wasn't a fancy-schmancy guy. Chuck was that rare guy who was very well educated and became very refined in life and could relate to anybody at any point of the spectrum. As different guys get higher up on the coaching food chain they tend to lose a little bit of connection with the guys who are doing the work. I think my dad identified Chuck early on as someone who was going to be fabulously successful but never lose sight of his friends."

Some on the Colts and elsewhere in the NFL were already noticing Chuck as a potential head coach. "Arnsparger was extremely smart," said Upton Bell. "He was good at spotting weaknesses and suggesting what we should be doing. Chuck was quiet, too, but he had a real command. I thought even then that he would be the better head coach."

The Colts' defense possessed an array of seasoned old pros like Billy Ray Smith and Odell Braase, interspersed with some game-changing young stars, including Bubba Smith, the imposing defensive lineman who was moved to end prior to the '68 season, hyperemotional linebacker Mike Curtis, a converted fullback whose personality perfectly suited the marauding mind-set of the defense, and the athletic safety Rick Volk, in just his second season, who covered more ground and seemed more attuned to Chuck's philosophy than the previous safety, Alvin Haymond.

The late '60s was a time of social unrest, but Baltimore on Sundays was still the province of Nixon's silent majority, shift workers and middle managers for whom the Colts were the center of their social life. The Colts' crowd—Cooper Rollow of the *Chicago Tribune* had dubbed the stadium "The World's Largest Outdoor Insane Asylum"—carried a fervent, collegiate air. The big, round stadium bordered by 33rd and 36th streets just north of downtown, was a shambling, inviting structure. The Colts' late kickoff times (2 p.m.), combined with the fog coming in from the Chesapeake Bay, gave the second halves of their home games an eerie, noirish quality, and the clamor of the fans was heightened by the percussive, blaring accompaniment of the Baltimore Colts Marching Band.

Marianne and Chris sat together, high in the stands, in front of a group of loud, often abusive fans who'd figured out they were the family of one of the coaches. "There were these people who would sit behind us and always heckle us, a mother, daughter, and son," said Chris Noll. "They would just give us the hardest time and be really nasty to us. One time, we came up and there were two drunks in our seats, and these people effectively threw them out—they defended us; they were like our best friends."

There were worrisome portents in the '68 preseason, when Unitas suffered an arm injury that would sideline him for much of the season. Weeks earlier, Shula had cannily traded for the journeyman veteran Earl Morrall, who'd lost any hope of starting for the New York Giants with their acquisition of the dynamic scrambler Fran Tarkenton. Morrall's first-quarter pass in the season opener against San Francisco was intercepted and returned for a touchdown, but the Colts quickly righted themselves and marched to a 27–10 win. Two weeks later, against the Steelers, the Colts' defense tied an NFL record with three interceptions returned for touchdowns in a 41–7 rout. Watching the stampede on TV with Dorothy Shula at the Shula's house, and aware that Baltimore's success would only increase Chuck's chances of getting a head-coaching offer, and that the hapless Steelers might be in the market for a new coach, Marianne had a premonition. "I just had this sudden thought," she said. "*My God, we're going to be in Pittsburgh next year.*"

On the field, the Colts were adept at mounting a pass rush with just four men, but Chuck had taken to blitzing part of the time, usually with the maniacal Mike Curtis coming in from the outside. After an October loss to the Browns, Baltimore righted itself with a 27–10 rout of the Rams, a measure of vengeance for the previous year's season-ending loss, marked by a host of big plays (including one in which Curtis tackled the Rams' quarterback Roman Gabriel by the head, which would be replayed on NFL Films' productions ad infinitum for decades to come). From that point, through the rest of the season, the Colts' defense was irrepressible. It was the first of seven games in which the Colts held their opponents to 10 points or less. They'd already clinched their division title ahead of the final regular-season game against the Rams.

The playoffs began on December 22, a cold, rainy day in Baltimore, as the Colts fought a young and rising Vikings team to a 7–0 halftime lead, then broke the game open in the third quarter, when Curtis again made a game-changing play, ranging in from the side to snatch a Joe Kapp pass out of the air and return it for a touchdown and a 21–0 lead.

The next week, the NFL Championship Game, was Chuck's first return to Cleveland Stadium as a coach. Chuck hadn't been in Baltimore when the Colts were steamrolled by the Browns in the 1964 NFL title game, but Shula still bridled at any mention of the game. The Browns had remade themselves in the wake of Jim Brown's retirement, and Blanton Collier's well-coached team had found itself behind Bill Nelsen, another in a long line of quarterbacks who'd disappointed in Pittsburgh only to succeed elsewhere. Leroy Kelly had been the league's leading rusher, scoring twenty touchdowns in all, and wide receiver Paul Warfield had scored another dozen.

In the week before the game, Chuck and Arnsparger watched film of the Browns' 31–20 playoff win over the Dallas Cowboys, as well as Cleveland's 30–20 win over the Colts, the only game Baltimore lost in the regular season. Chuck devised a defense that keyed on tight end Milt Morin, frequently used by the Browns to aid blocking for Kelly. "We didn't change our defense in any basic way," said lineman Odell Braase. "We simply read their offense better." The Browns were stymied, their deepest penetration of the day was to the Baltimore 33-yard line. The game was 24–0 by the end of the third quarter, and Shula kept piling it on, just as he'd felt the Browns did in 1964. Writing in *Sports Illustrated*, the gravely serious writer Tex Maule intoned "seldom in the long history of NFL championship games has one team so thoroughly dominated the other."

After the win, the Colts returned to Baltimore for a New Year's celebration. The next weekend saw a Saturday and Sunday in which Shula and then Chuck celebrated their birthdays, before the team flew to Miami on the Sunday before the game.

By the time the postseason began, it was clear that Chuck was going to be considered for some of the vacant head-coaching jobs. He told suitors he wouldn't talk to anyone until after the Super Bowl. Shula, who'd been contacted about Chuck by some teams, appreciated the focus. The first two interviews—with the Steelers and the Bills—were scheduled for the days following Super Bowl III.

The Colts were installed as 17-point favorites, reflecting the lopsided outcome of the first two Super Bowls, the Colts' ransacking run through the NFL, and the fact that the AFL representative wasn't the Raiders but instead the lightly regarded New York Jets, seen as little more than a group of supporting players surrounding celebrated bachelor quarterback Joe Namath.

"I remember clearly that it was like, 'The Jets? Pfft,' going into it," said Chris Noll. "The expectation was we were going to wipe them out. There wasn't even a doubt." This exaggerated sense of confidence wasn't exclusive to the Colts' camp. After the Packers' decisive pair of victories in the first two Super Bowls, conventional wisdom held that it could be another decade or more before the AFL caught up with the talent level of the NFL.

"We certainly were aware that we had dominated and we were 17-point favorites," said Don Shula. "Anytime you are 17-point favorites, you know, you're very guarded, and you have to make sure that your players don't think you are 17-point favorites. That was discussed, and we tried to do the same things preparation-wise that we had done to get there, and be in that position. But it didn't happen."

By the weekend before the game, the betting line had gotten up to 19 points. There was, after two lopsided Super Bowls, an air of anticlimax about this one. NFL Commissioner Pete Rozelle addressed this concern in his annual press conference the Friday before the game, announcing that the league would consider altering the structure of the postseason tournament after the merger in 1970, so that two NFL teams (presumably more evenly matched) might meet in the final game. The *New York Times* headline the following day read, "Rozelle Indicates Tomorrow's Super Bowl Contest Could Be Next to Last."

There was no feeling of overconfidence in the coaching staff. Shula and his assistants understood well that Weeb Ewbank—still a revered figure around Baltimore for having guided the Colts to their first two world championships—was a coach to be reckoned with. But Chuck knew, better than anyone, what the new league was capable of. He hadn't spent much time coaching against Namath, but he understood the power of the Jets' offensive line, and the deceptively fast Don Maynard, who'd given Chargers' defensive backs fits over the years.

By kickoff, the Colts had been down in Miami for seven days, practicing, lounging in the sun, entertaining all media requests, and losing their edge. "I think Coach Shula could have been a little more disciplined with the guys," said Preston Pearson. "The media could come and go right up to your hotel room. And the guys really didn't send anybody away. Guys, as guys will, had women going in and out the front door, out the back door. I can't tell you how many possibilities that Bubba Smith may have had with his entourage of people going in and out. And the rules allowed that."

Back at the hotel that week, Chuck was more tense than usual. He'd talked to the team, but he sensed that they were—like an overconfident teenager—tuning him out. "Everyone was loose that week but Chuck," said Marianne. "All week long, he was really worried about the game."

The Colts were bored and restless and growing increasingly annoyed with Namath, whose comments were generating more headlines each day. On Thursday night, at the Miami Touchdown Club dinner, he'd guaranteed the Jets would win. "Football players who are real good don't have to talk," said Bubba Smith in response.

Chuck's concern, as it happened, proved well-founded. Throughout the season, Chuck and Arnsparger had kept the Colts' defense simple, focusing on a four-man rush, occasional blitzes, and mostly vanilla coverages, rarely veering far from the base strong-side combination zone that served the team well. But during Super Bowl III Namath, weaned on the complex defensive looks and strategies of the AFL, audibled the Jets out of trouble and was able to run on linebacker Don Shinnick. (By halftime, Gaubatz was asking Shula and Chuck to put in the faster outside linebacker, Ron Porter, in place of Shinnick, to help with containing the Jets' running game. "Shinnick was better on pass coverage," said Gaubatz. "But that run around my right side, they were just eating us up.")

In truth, the Colts' defense played well. The Colts' offense, however, committed a raft of mistakes—not just the five turnovers but numerous missed opportunities, ranging from Earl Morrall missing wide open receivers to dropped passes to missed assignments. Shula eventually brought in the sore-armed Unitas, who drove the Colts to a touchdown, but it wasn't enough to avert a 16–7 upset win for the Jets, which cemented

Namath's position as an iconic figure in the sport, as well as the Colts as an overconfident team that had let down the NFL.

And when it was over, Chuck trudged off the field, not shocked so much as despondent. In the locker room, there was more shock than disappointment. The Colts showered quietly. Unitas, hard-bitten as ever, walked up to owner Carroll Rosenbloom and apologized. So complete was the Colts' apparent dominance, some players never got over the feeling. (Forty-five years after Super Bowl III, Gaubatz said, "The only way they could beat us is if that game was rigged; and it was rigged.")

When the team bus returned to the hotel, Chuck glumly greeted Marianne. "He was obviously devastated," she said. "I have never seen him quite so."

As they were laying on the bed, Marianne gently pointed out, "We really have to go to this party." For players and coaches alike, attendance at Carroll Rosenbloom's postgame party was mandatory. Chuck sighed, resignedly. But moments later, they heard a loud commotion down the hall. Marianne went out to investigate and came back moments later. "It's Rick!," she said. "Something's wrong!"

Volk, Chuck's prized safety (and young Chris's favorite Colt) had suffered two concussions during the game and willed himself back out onto the field after each one. But by that evening in the hotel, he'd gone into convulsions in the bathtub. Chuck went with the ambulance that raced him to the hospital, where Volk's condition stabilized.

Later, Chuck made his way back to the hotel, and he and Marianne forced themselves to join the second bus heading out to Rosenbloom's predictably funereal postgame party. "I remember Chuck getting on the bus," said Upton Bell, "and he had a terrible look on his face, just talking about Volk, and the shock of it." At the "party," the Cowboys' Tex Schramm would later remember, the usually magnanimous Rosenbloom spent much of the party pouting behind a potted plant.

They got back to the hotel after midnight. It had been the worst day of Chuck's professional life. With a team that was heavily favored, the Colts had failed to carry the standard of the National Football League. As disappointed as Chuck was, he didn't dwell on the defeat. Instead, he did what he always had done. He got over it and got ready for what was next.

ten

A GOOD MAN IS HARD TO FIND
(PITTSBURGH)

✦　✦　✦

In 1933, the Pennsylvania state legislature relaxed their blue laws, effectively legalizing professional sports on Sundays. The news was greeted with delight by the sly, rumpled horseplayer named Art Rooney. The son of a saloon owner, Rooney bought an NFL franchise for $2,500 that summer and named his team the Pirates—there were, after all, New York Giants in both baseball and pro football. (After seven seasons of dismal results, he would change the team's nickname to the Steelers.)

The franchise's first home game was played on September 20, 1933, in front of a crowd estimated at 15,000 people, and the home team was routed, 23–2, by the New York football Giants. Rooney's notation after the game was succinct and apt: "Our team looked terrible. Our fans didn't get their money's worth." He could have used the same words to describe a lot of Sundays to follow.

By the time the Steelers completed the 1968 campaign with a 2–11–1 record, they had gone thirty-six consecutive seasons without so much as a division or conference title. In twenty-eight of those years, they'd had a losing record. The history of ignobility was ingrained at the outset. As early as 1941, when Rooney showed up to training camp with his team wearing new uniforms, he was asked what he thought of the team that year. "The only thing different is the uniforms," he said. "It's the same old Steelers."

For the first quarter century of the league's existence, most NFL teams were run with a kind of slangy collegiality, as though the owners couldn't quite believe that they were expected to treat this game played by thick-legged hicks and hard-bitten factory workers as an actual business. That barnstorming spirit receded through the league by the '50s and '60s, but it lasted longer in Pittsburgh than anywhere else. Player-coach Johnny "Blood" McNally once showed up to watch a Green Bay game, unaware that his own team was playing elsewhere that same day.

The lovable loser lore built up around the Steelers in large part because Art Rooney, "The Chief," was soft-hearted and impish, credulous and loyal to a fault.

During the manpower shortages of the Second World War—when more than six hundred NFL players were fighting overseas—the Steelers and Eagles merged for a season in 1943. "Had to do it," explained Bert Bell, then owner of the Eagles. "Pittsburgh had no backs left, and Philadelphia had no linemen." The "Steagles" went 5–4–1, and, a year later, with Philadelphia back on its own, the Steelers merged with the Chicago Cardinals. "Card-Pitt," or the Carpets, as they became known throughout the league, went 0–10.

In 1946, the Steelers hired Pitt coaching legend Jock Sutherland, and a year later, they managed to tie for the 1947 Eastern Division title with the Philadelphia Eagles, only to lose the playoff, 21–0. Sutherland died the following spring on a scouting trip in Kentucky, and it would be eleven years before the Steelers won more than six games in any single season.

The team seemed perpetually behind the times. They were the last NFL team to move from the single-wing to the T formation, in 1951. To Chuck, playing in Paul Brown's state-of-the-art system in Cleveland, the Steelers of the era looked like haphazard misfits. "They didn't seem to wear the same helmets all the time," he said.

The team's first full-time scout was an undertaker. In 1955, with the very first pick in the NFL draft, the Steelers selected a defensive back from Colorado A&M named Gary Glick, based solely on a letter of recommendation sent to the Steelers' head coach, Walt Kiesling.

Weeks later, after the young Dan Rooney had called the school and received a reel of film on Glick, he invited his father up to the Steelers' scouting office to watch it. "But my father wouldn't go," said Dan. "He said, 'I'm busy.' So we go off to the eighth floor, where we've got our personnel office, and we put the film on. And it's, like, the smallest college that you could imagine, dogs running out on the field. So we come back down into my dad's office, and nobody says anything. And I remember my father saying, 'He didn't look very good, right?'"

Even when they found good players, they often didn't know what to do with them. In the 1950s and 1960s, the Steelers would release or trade away five different quarterbacks—two of whom would later be inducted into the Pro Football Hall of Fame—who would go on to start a total of twenty-one league championship games or Super Bowls over the following fifteen seasons. None was more famous than Pittsburgh's own Johnny Unitas. Drafted in the ninth round of the '55 draft (the Browns had been eyeing him as well, as a possible replacement to Otto Graham), he reported to the Steelers' training camp in Olean, New York, and found that he was soon ostracized by the veterans (who started referring to him as "Clem," in honor of comedian Red Skelton's country rube Clem Kadiddlehopper). Though he looked sharp in practices, Walt Kiesling preferred veterans. In five exhibition games, Unitas never took a snap. He was released before the season.

"Unitas was totally ignored," said Dan Rooney. "They never did anything with him. It wasn't a question of misjudging him. They would have had to judge him first. But they never did a thing with him." In February 1956, the Colts signed him. By 1958, Unitas and the Colts won the first of back-to-back NFL championships.

He wasn't the only one. Jack Kemp, who would play in five championship games in the AFL, was released in the preseason of 1959. Future Hall of Famer Len Dawson, who would become one of the most accurate passers in league history, was drafted first overall in 1957, but he never really got a chance to prove himself. It was Parker's first year, and he traded instead for veteran Earl Morrall.

"I got very little work," said Dawson. "I would work like as a receiver and that because there weren't that many bodies out there."

In 1958, the Steelers lost their first two games behind Morrall.

"You guys are too tight," Parker told his players. "Go out and get drunk and come back in here on Tuesday. We will have this problem solved."

That Tuesday, at the weekly quarterback meeting to watch game films, Morrall was gone. Shortly into the meeting, in the dark, someone walked into the meeting room and sat down next to Dawson.

"Hi, partner—how ya' doing?," he asked.

It was Bobby Layne. Parker had traded Morrall and two draft choices (a number two in 1959, and a number four in 1960) for Layne, a legendary carouser—"I want to run out of money and breath at the same time," he once said—whose lifestyle was not conducive to the finer points of football. Layne's family didn't move to Pittsburgh during the seasons, so he would often convene to Parker's home after games.

There were further problems with Parker's reign. But the biggest may have been his fondness for veterans at the expense of draft choices. Under Parker in 1959, the Steelers traded away their top seven choice; in 1960, they drafted Jack Spikes of TCU in the first round (but lost him to the Dallas Texans of the AFL) and traded away their next six choices. In both 1961 and 1962, they traded five of their first six draft choices. In 1963, they dealt each of their first seven choices. "That was his downfall," said Steelers' running back Dick Hoak. "What he did, he traded all of our draft choices. I mean, if you were from Texas, he was going to trade for you."

Parker's last season was 1964, but he'd already dealt Pittsburgh's first rounder in the 1965 draft, which the Chicago Bears used to select Hall of Famer Dick Butkus. By that time, Dan Rooney was taking a more active role in the management of the Steelers. He revered his father, but he also had a business background and a strong desire not to be part of any more Runyonesque tales of buffoonery on the part of lovable losers.

Inevitably, he would clash with Parker. "I just felt we had to have structure that was sound, and you had to know what you are doing," Dan Rooney said. "A lot of people thought that Buddy was just a plain drunk, but that is not true. Buddy only really drank to excess on two occasions. One, after a game, win, lose, or draw, he drank. Two, if he was making a speech, which was the worst time, because now he is going to get up. He was so nervous making a speech, he would end up drinking and then get up and maybe say something crazy or be slurring and things like that. But, I mean, that was unfortunate because he did get that reputation and it wasn't really factual."

Rooney made clear to Parker that he had to consult with him before making a trade. One night, on the eve of the 1965 season, disgusted with his quarterbacking play, Parker set up a deal to send defensive end Ben McGee to the Philadelphia Eagles for King Hill.

"No trades tonight," said Dan.

The next morning, Parker resigned and was replaced by assistant coach Mike Nixon, who went 2–12 and was fired at the end of his one season.

"This time," Dan Rooney suggested to his father, "what if we hire somebody we don't know?"

They made the rounds at the league meetings, and Art Rooney's good friend, Vince Lombardi, gave a glowing recommendation for his own assistant, Bill Austin.

That was all the Chief needed to hear. "Call him back," said Art. "We'll take him right now."

"I said to wait," said Dan. "Let's get him home and we can talk to him again. But once Vince said what he said, it was too late." Austin was introduced as the next coach of the Pittsburgh Steelers. This seemed to make perfect sense at the time. Lombardi had just won his third NFL title in five years, with two Super Bowls to immediately follow. Austin had been operating in Lombardi's shadow as the offensive line coach for six seasons in Green Bay (before serving on the Rams staff a single year before the hire). "He wanted to be Vince Lombardi, and he wasn't Vince Lombardi," said Dan Rooney. The Steelers players went even further. "Bill Austin wanted to be Vince Lombardi and Steve McQueen rolled into one," said John Brown, who came to the Steelers in 1967.

Austin's attempts to instill toughness came through a series of punishing grass drills—the timeworn custom of having players run in place, then jump onto their bellies on the ground, then leap up and run in place again, almost literally ad nauseam. "We would come out there at the beginning of practice, and we would do all of these up-and-downs, up-and-downs," said Dick Hoak. "[After those,] you couldn't stand up, you couldn't practice! You were worn out by the time you started to practice. And then, if somebody did something wrong, you've got to roll 20 yards on the ground and get up and sprint back, and stuff like that."

One day at the Steelers' training camp, Austin conducted a full-contact goal-line drill, and numerous players were injured. "About six guys got hurt, some serious," said Dan Rooney. "They didn't make the season. So that sort of set the tone for the rest of the players." By the end of the 1968 training camp, Austin was already a gaunt figure, barking loudly to his assistants and his players, carrying a haunted look when he would come down to equipment manager Tony Parisi's area during the unit meetings to inhale a couple of cigarettes.

The team was a shambles. John Brown, who'd played under Paul Brown and his model of professionalism at Cleveland, came to Pittsburgh and remembered an assistant coach asking him to borrow money.

Nowhere was the second-class perception felt more acutely than at the Steelers' practice facilities, South Park. "When we came out of training camp, I had never seen South Park," said Ralph Berlin, who began as the team's trainer in 1968. "When I got there I couldn't believe it was this little house. And on one side was the coaches' dressing room, and it had nails in the wall where they hung their stuff up, and the other side was the office, there was a telephone there. And then in the back there was one Universal gym setup. That was the weight training—a Universal gym machine. Off of that was a smaller room, and that was the training room supposedly. Upstairs there were two large bedrooms, and that became the offensive meeting room and the defensive meeting room. Then down in the basement was the locker room, and there were stalls but they had nails on the wall. They didn't have hangers or anything. They just had nails where they hung their stuff up. The shower was atrocious."

One day, upstairs at the little house in South Park, the offense emerged from their meeting room only to hear a persistent sound coming from the other room. "We're leaving our meeting and the defense is still in the other room," said Dick Hoak. "And you could hear this flip flip flip. Their game film was flipping around. Everybody in there was asleep: Players, coaches, everybody. What we used to do a lot of times was practice in the morning and then go out to lunch, and the only place to go to lunch, there were two bars, so the guys would go there—they'd drink a beer and eat a sandwich."

By 1968, Bill Austin's facade of Lombardi-esque control was crumbling, and he himself was losing his bearings. "He had no control of the team; he had no respect from the players," said Rocky Bleier, who played his rookie year under Austin in 1968, before being drafted into the Army. "Bill had arguments with players questioning him, not doing what they wanted to. Roy Jefferson was a guy like that, but it only takes one, and then it just gives everybody else the ability to either question or talk back."

Jefferson, the fluid, powerful wide receiver from Utah, was clearly the Steelers' best player during Austin's years, an All-Pro caliber performer who served as the Steelers' lone true offensive weapon. He was also part of a wave of African American athletes who were growing more outspoken about racism in both society and pro football. The '68 season had been a watershed anyway, galvanized by *Sports Illustrated*'s five-part series that summer on "The Black Athlete," which included a section entirely dedicated to the patriarchal mind-set of many professional football coaches. This was a particular problem in Pittsburgh, where many of the black players—and some of their white teammates—felt that Austin was prejudiced against the black athletes.

Bill Nunn, the highly respected columnist for the *Pittsburgh Courier*, which still had a national audience in the black community, had been recruited by Dan to help the Steelers scout the historically black colleges and universities of the South. In his dealings with Austin, Nunn saw what the players saw. "That was one of the things that I had learned from the gal that was going with Bill Austin," said Nunn. "She was a nurse. A white lady who had been around blacks, and it just so happened that I knew her. And the way I found out about it was, I went into a restaurant one time and they were together. So [later] I said, 'Find out what he thinks about blacks.' And she did it for me and she came back and said, 'He can deal with them, but he has a tough time.'"

As the losses mounted, Austin grew more tense, and the players grew bolder in their dissent. "Roy was doing everything he could to screw the thing up," said trainer Ralph Berlin. "Bill was still trying to be Lombardi, and he wasn't going to be Lombardi, and the fact that we were losing and weren't getting any better. I think maybe if we had won, but we weren't going to win because Jefferson had turned the team against him."

During one meeting in '68, watching game film, Austin upbraided Jefferson for running a wrong route. Jefferson, taking umbrage at the pettiness of the critique, glared back at his head coach and slowly bellowed, "You're about a dumb motherfucker." It escalated from there. The two men nearly came to blows.

Pittsburgh lost its first six games in 1968, won two, tied one, then lost five more to end the season. As the season deteriorated, Austin grew more irritable and more nervous. When stressed, he had a nervous tic of scratching his chest.

"It was like he was repeating Lombardi's speeches," said Andy Russell, "and it wasn't necessarily true to what his own nature was. He couldn't really pull it off because he wasn't Lombardi, and we knew that. Guys who had been traded from Green Bay said, 'That's the exact same speech Lombardi gave.' So we got cynical, in a way."

Austin and Dan Rooney had Monday morning postmortems over breakfast at a small deli next to the Roosevelt. The meetings were often curt and combative, with Austin taking a defensive stance while a frustrated Dan at times lost his temper. "I was actually out of line, because I would be yelling at him," said Rooney. "And I did it every week. Finally, the restaurant was getting wise to it, and people were coming in, so we ended up going in the hotel."

Dan Rooney's wife, Pat, had seen her husband struggle to reconcile his respect for his father with the revulsion at how shabbily the Steelers had been run during much of their history. "I think Dan could see that he had a whole different vision of how he wanted the Steelers to go," she said. "He wanted a better kind of office structure, and wanted to change the way things worked in each department. And, of course, football wise— he would never say an awful lot, but he was clearly not pleased with the direction that things were going."

"Definitely, the third year," said Dan, "I knew he was gone. I was nice to him, and things like that. But I knew he was gone."

Dan was always stoic in the face of Sunday defeats, but his late-night calls with his closest confidantes sounded graver and graver. Before the season was over, he got off the phone one night and confided in Pat, "Something's got to happen."

✦　✦　✦

By the time Dan Rooney called Chuck for the first time, he'd already been turned down by the Penn State coach Joe Paterno, who'd just led the Nittany Lions to their first unbeaten and untied season in school history. Paterno had been intrigued with the job, had visited Dan and Pat Rooney in Pittsburgh, but ultimately turned it down.

That had prompted Dan Rooney to call Chuck, after soliciting a recommendation from Don Shula (and receiving an unsolicited one from Upton Bell). So on that Monday morning, January 13, 1969, Chuck and Dan met in Rooney's suite in Miami Beach to talk. Over the next two hours, Chuck remained composed, reasonable, and—what intrigued

Dan the most—extremely knowledgeable about the Steelers' personnel and their shortcomings. Save for the veteran end McGee, he saw a lack of quality along the defensive line. He recognized Jefferson's superior skills, as well as the fact that Pittsburgh didn't really have a quarterback good enough to consistently get him the ball.

Chuck and Dan had different personalities but compatible sensibilities. They were both young for their line of work, bright, respectful, and impatient. Chuck balked at the casual racism of many of his coaching peers and at the indiscriminate expression of testosterone—the maniacal yelling and the furious love of hitting that he felt bordered on sadism. Dan Rooney revered his father, but he'd seen too often how Art's casual oversight and presumption of competence on the part of all those who worked for him had gotten the Steelers in trouble. Dan was ready to try another way.

The Rooneys had brought in both Chuck and the Browns' assistant Nick Skorich for second interviews and to meet the rest of the staff. But while Art Sr. was still the nominal man in charge, and was consulted, it was, ultimately, Dan's decision. On the morning of January 27, 1969, Dan woke up at 7 a.m., clear that Chuck was the choice. He called him up in Baltimore.

"We want you to be our coach," said Dan.

"I want that, too," said Chuck. He got on the next plane to Pittsburgh, and the Steelers scheduled a midday press conference.

The press conference at the Roosevelt had the air of an inquisition. Chuck would be the Steelers' fourth coach in six years. One reporter asked him how he felt coming to a city of losers.

"A city of losers?" said Chuck. "That's a lot of nonsense. Geography has nothing to do with winning. Winning is a product of work and attitude."

Later that day, Sid Gillman sent a telegram to Art Rooney, which read, "Congratulations on your choice of Chuck Noll stop He's the future coach of the year."

There was initially a question about whether Shula would release Noll in time to take part in the NFL Draft, which began a day later. Fifteen years earlier, Paul Brown had effectively prevented longtime assistant Weeb Ewbank from communicating with the team that just hired him, not letting him join the Baltimore Colts until the draft was completed. But Shula relented.

With the draft twenty-four hours away, there was little time for formalities. Marianne was left to sort out the selling of one house and buying of another. Chris would be taken out of one school and enroll in Pittsburgh as soon as possible.

Chuck would handle the draft without a coaching staff; he hadn't had time to even interview anyone yet. He got a room at the Roosevelt and huddled with Dan, Art, Dan's brother, Art Rooney Jr.—known throughout the family and organization as "Artie"—and Bill Nunn, who by now was working as a full-time scout in the Steelers' organization.

Nunn, hoping to avoid a repeat of the prejudice of Bill Austin, was pleased when he asked around about Chuck. "They said he was an upfront guy, intellectual, but a straightforward guy who believed in The Best Man Wins," said Nunn.

In Pittsburgh, among the loyal and informed football fans, there was a clear sentimental favorite for the Steelers' first-round draft choice. Quarterback Terry Hanratty, who'd led Notre Dame to a share of a national championship as a sophomore in 1966, was from nearby Butler, Pennsylvania. He was seen as the hometown boy who could lead the Steelers to greatness, and a surer thing than either of the two "project" quarterbacks, the University of Cincinnati's Greg Cook and Marty Domres, who'd played Ivy League football at Columbia.

O. J. Simpson was the foregone conclusion as the first pick, as the Heisman Trophy winner from USC was snatched by the Buffalo Bills. Atlanta took Notre Dame tackle George Kunz, and Philadelphia drafted the Purdue running back Leroy Keyes. Pittsburgh was up next, with the fourth pick.

In the draft room, on the second floor of the old Roosevelt Hotel, where Artie had written a list of the top players at each position on chalkboards that spanned one wall, Chuck walked in that day and said, "I know who I am drafting." Artie asked him who, and Chuck pointed to the name of Joe Greene, the raw, gifted defensive tackle from North Texas State.

"Joe was rated high, don't get me wrong," said Bill Nunn. "But the way Chuck insisted on taking Joe is a day I'll always remember."

The Steelers were a favored member of the BLESTO (Bears, Lions, Eagles, and Steelers Talent Organization) scouting group, which had as its leader the former Steelers standout defensive back Jack Butler. Artie Rooney would remember that the Steelers' and BLESTO scouts had other players rated more highly. "But there was no argument." (And the Steelers still got the hometown favorite Hanratty in the second round.)

Pitt coach Carl DePasqua had made a scouting trip for the Steelers the previous spring, and his report on Joe Greene was glowing: "Great skill. Best kid I saw on my tour. Has quickness, strength, and speed." That same spring, Chuck himself had also been down to Denton, Texas, to scout Greene in his work for the Colts. What Chuck saw was a football player with a rare blend of speed and strength and a deep wellspring of competitiveness. Greene was physically massive (6-foot-3, 275 pounds) but also fast. He had modeled his game on the Cowboys' Bob Lilly and had developed an absurdly quick first step to control opposing linemen.

Greene, prideful and motivated, was distressed when he got the news he'd been drafted. "My heart sank," he said. He knew much about the Steelers' history but nothing of Chuck Noll.

✦   ✦   ✦

After the draft, when Marianne and Chris got to Pittsburgh, they started looking for a home. They went to several places but settled on the first house they looked at, a handsome brown two-story on 81 Warwick Drive in suburban Upper St. Clair, about a half hour south of the city and slightly to the west, off of Route 19. After the purchase, Chuck and Marianne brought Chris to see their new home. From the front yard, the three looked at it, and Chuck and Marianne mused on what color they wanted to paint it. Finally they settled on a shade of gold with black trim.

Chris looked up at them and beamed. "That's so cool!," he said. "Steelers' colors!"

Chuck and Marianne looked at each other, aghast. The connection hadn't even occurred to them.

They wound up painting the house green.

Across the street was Eisenhower Elementary, where Chris would attend school. The junior high, Fort Couch Middle School, was less than a half mile up the road. At the bottom of the hill, across Route 19, was a big new shopping mall, South Hills Village, anchored by a Gimbels department store.

With the head-coaching job secured and the house acquired, Chuck agreed to two previously elusive luxuries. Marianne could now schedule a regular visit to the beauty parlor (previously, Chuck had cut her hair himself). And he told her she could now hire someone to mow the lawn while he was away to training camp.

Marianne was sold immediately. Coming into town, she had the same reaction as all first-timers: the overwhelmingly gorgeous vista upon emerging from the Fort Pitt tunnel and coming across the bridge and into the city. That night, the Rooneys took the Nolls out to dinner at the tony LeMont Restaurant on Mount Washington. Suitably impressed, enjoying the company, Marianne looked out the window to the city lights below and allowed herself to wish: "I hope this is forever," she said. And the Rooneys and Nolls drank to that.

Back in Cleveland, Kate Noll was thrilled that her son had finally gotten a head-coaching job but even more so that Chuck and Marianne would be closer (Pittsburgh was only a two-hour drive from Cleveland).

Saturday evenings, she and William would turn on the console and listen to Mass on the Catholic radio station. The grandkids would come up and sit with them while they said the Rosary.

When Marianne spoke to her mother-in-law on the phone on March 15, just days before a planned visit, Kate seemed noticeably happy to talk with her and content.

Two days later, on St. Patrick's Day, Kate Noll died of a heart attack. Bill Deininger had come home from school during lunch and heard his grandfather calling his name from upstairs. He rushed up to find his grandmother slumped in the bathroom, dead. William had been on the couch, unable to get up and move.

The death came only months after Marianne had lost her own mother to cancer after a long illness. That following weekend, they drove to the funeral in Cleveland, Chuck mostly mute about his mother, Chris scared in the backseat. Holy Trinity was nearly full for Kate Noll's ceremony, and Chuck struggled to get through it without succumbing to tears.

By now, William Noll was an invalid. His tremors were worse than ever. Even getting downstairs for the nightly supper could be an ordeal. His preference was to sit and watch the television. At the end of the weekend, Chuck and Marianne sat down with Rita. "We will take Dad," Chuck said, "and you sell the house."

Cleveland Trust, the bank where Rita had worked for much of the '40s, would not give her a loan ("They said they wouldn't give loans to widows with dependent children," said Rita) to buy a bigger house, so she and Chuck cosigned for the loan, then put the whole house in his name, and he and Marianne made the down payment on the new home.

Rita found a home in Lakewood, on the west side of Cleveland, a new enclave of white flight out of the city. The same week that the Deiningers were moving to Lakewood, Chuck hugged Chris and kissed Marianne goodbye and drove the forty miles east, amid the hills of rural Pennsylvania, to St. Vincent College. The Steelers' training camp site was a new place that felt curiously familiar to Chuck. St. Vincent had been the first Benedictine monastery in the United States.

✦   ✦   ✦

Coaching pro football in the 1960s was a little like medicine before the invention of the microscope. Statistical analysis was rudimentary. The practitioners of the craft clung to what they'd observed or experimented with hunches.

Lombardi, who'd come out of retirement to coach the Washington Redskins, remained the defining coach of the era. Every other coach in the NFL seemed to be imitating him or responding in contrast. But even those who chose different methods—the hyperemotional George Allen, the imperious Tom Landry—still hewed to one of the central assumptions. Football coaching in the '60s seemed infused by a cult of personality.

Lombardi's approach was autocratic, but at its heart was the belief that football mattered above all else. In the course of a pregame speech, he would even draw on biblical themes, once invoking St. Paul's epistles as proof that teams needed to run to win. "Vince has a knack for making all the saints sound like they would have been great football coaches," said Jerry Kramer.

Chuck pointedly avoided the Lombardi ethos, both the notion that he was responsible for the players' motivation or that repeated physical punishment would toughen them. Chuck rejected these assumptions.

Many made note of his impeccable coaching influences—the inveterate horse player Art Rooney said around the time of the hire, "His pedigree is super: He was by Paul Brown, out of Sid Gillman, by Don Shula." He naturally drew from the influences of all three men, but he also consciously avoided some of each man's style. In sum, Chuck's sensibilities were decidedly more rational and less grandiose than Lombardi. This became apparent to the Steelers very early in that first training camp.

Before that first team meeting, some of the veterans—who'd become accustomed to their own collective discontent—joked among themselves that they had been here before the new coach arrived and would be here after he left. They'd watched Bill Austin lose control of the team and seen him flounder over the final months of the awful 1968 season. Over time, the team had grown somewhat resigned to its own futility, not comfortable in defeat, exactly, but used to it.

But now, as the new man walked before them, the low murmur in the room evaporated into an attentive stillness. Chuck did not look distinct or particularly commanding. There would be no yelling on this day, virtually no profanity, nothing to get a real grip on. Unlike so many of his peers at the time, he wasn't projecting anything. He appeared confident, though not arrogant; calm but hardly meek; wholly sure of himself and his message.

He would never get entirely comfortable with public speaking. But talking to a football team in private had become second nature. In front of eighty football players, he introduced himself and calmly explained to the Pittsburgh Steelers players why they hadn't been successful. "I've watched the game films," he said, "and I can tell you guys why you've been losing. It's not because you're not trying hard enough. This isn't a good football team, and most of you aren't going to be here when this *is* a good football team."

The players were struck by the indisputable facts of the rational argument he presented. He went on to explain that winning was about mastering the right techniques and then having the discipline to carry those out in a game. It was a long way from "Win One for the Gipper," and it left them off-balance, unsure of what would come next.

An hour later that morning, out on the field at St. Vincent College, as a bus drove away with four players cut before the first practice, the holdovers gathered around and commenced with the ritual, obligatory whoops and yells that marked the beginning of every football practice everywhere.

And then the whistle blew, and Chuck raised his voice slightly.

"Quiet," he snapped. "You don't win football games with noise—cut the false chatter."

Some veterans exchanged sidelong glances, but they responded, and soon enough, as he began the painstaking process of rebuilding each of them from the most fundamental elements—stance, spacing, alignment, and the form to be used for the most basic elements in the sport, blocking and tackling—the professionals of the Pittsburgh Steelers began to learn the game all over again. In the process, the empty bravado of the Austin years—and the cynicism that accompanied it—instantly disappeared.

"There was no being late," said the veteran running back Dick Hoak. "If the meeting was at 9 o'clock, the door closed at 9 o'clock and you couldn't come in. I mean, that stuff was all done. And that is what a lot of those guys were used to, all of this kind of lax things going on. And then there was just none of that anymore."

It was more than a week before the prized rookie, Joe Greene, showed up. He'd held out, finally signed his contact, and arrived, still out of shape, struggling to run the sideline-to-sideline gassers with which the Steelers began their conditioning drills.

Chuck introduced him to the team that evening, and then Greene looked around and uttered a brief "Hi, fellas," his voice cracking as he said the words, in what he would recall as "a tenor higher than I had been hoping for."

But that wasn't what stuck with Greene that week. Chuck's speeches to the team during the evenings at Bonaventure Hall were not long, but they were very clear. One night, he explained to the club that "our ultimate goal is simple: to win the Super Bowl." From the back of the room, the third-year running back Don Shy let forth with an audible laugh.

"I remember Don Shy laughing," Greene said. "And I also remember, a couple of days later, Don Shy was gone." He had been traded to New Orleans, for a player and two draft choices.

Greene soon realized something else. The veterans, whom he'd been so anxious about, had lost some of their cocksure arrogance. It was as though everyone in camp was a rookie. No one seemed sure of themselves, no one seemed comfortable under Chuck's watch. Many of the conventions they'd grown up with had changed. He didn't yell at them, he reasoned with them. "I'd had good coaching," said the veteran All-Pro linebacker Andy Russell. "But I'd never seen anyone like Chuck."

"I knew what you had to do to win," Chuck would say later. "Number one, you had to not lose. And that means you have to play good defense. And you wanted an offense that didn't get your defense in trouble. That was our first thought, we had to improve our defense. We have to play good defense and we have to not make mistakes on offense—even if we have to run the ball on every down and punt. Don't get turnovers. Don't get yourself in trouble giving the ball up at the 20-yard line where they need only 20 yards to score or they're in field-goal range already. You don't want to do that. That's a prescription to lose."

The team was as bad as advertised. Neither quarterback, Dick Shiner or Kent Nix, had the arm or the leadership skills to be consistent winners in the NFL. Beyond Jefferson, the offense was populated with aging overachievers, like the tenacious running back Hoak, who'd extended his career through smarts and grit.

Before the end of July, Chuck traded the veteran linebacker Bill Saul, a team leader and popular player, to the Dallas Cowboys. Saul, the first player ever to wear a live microphone during a game (for an NFL Films segment), was one of the team's best-known players. But Chuck was convinced he lacked either the instincts or intelligence necessary for a middle linebacker. He showed Dan Rooney footage of Saul playing in 1968, making tackles 10 and 15 yards down the field, because he was overpursuing and taking poor angles to the ball carrier.

Among the players, there was curiosity to see if Jefferson, notoriously divisive during his time under Austin, would change with Chuck. They got their answer during the team's preseason game in Montreal, when Jefferson—listening to a jazz combo in a downtown club—missed curfew by hours rather than minutes.

When Jefferson finally arrived at the team hotel, Chuck called Dan Rooney.

"Roy was not a carousing guy that was out all night," said Dan. "But he was a tester. He was testing Chuck Noll to see what was going to happen. So Chuck calls me on the phone and says, 'Could you come down here? I've gotta talk to you and we've gotta do something.'"

When Rooney arrived, Chuck presented the situation.

"Jefferson missed curfew," said Chuck.

"Okay."

"I can't let that happen."

"Okay. What are you going to do?"

"I want to send him home and not play him."

"All right."

Next, Chuck called Jefferson down to his room. When Jefferson walked in, he saw Dan and smiled. "He sees me," said Dan, "and he thinks he's gonna win this one."

Jefferson apologized to Chuck, but Chuck explained that he was sending him home. Shocked, Jefferson protested, first to Chuck then to Dan, who remained firm. Before the discussion was over, Jeffeson was in tears and Rooney said, "We're gonna do what Chuck said."

"Go home," Chuck told Jefferson. "We will talk about it on Monday."

Each of the moves—disciplining Jefferson and trading Shy and then Saul—was defensible in purely football terms, but taken together, they set the tone for what was to follow. It was Chuck's team now. And they would play his way.

A day or two before the first preseason game, Chuck drove home to the new house on Warwick Drive. Chris and some friends were out playing basketball in the driveway. Marianne was tending to the garden.

He seemed atypically grim when he got out of the car. "Come inside for a minute," he told her.

When she was inside, Chuck gave her notice: "We have a very bad football team. It's going to be a long season. Just be prepared."

For another year, until the gleaming new bowl that was Three Rivers Stadium—to be shared by the Steelers and Pirates—opened in 1970, the Steelers would play their games at Pitt Stadium, would have their offices at the Roosevelt, and would practice at South Park. Collectively, they had the worst facilities in the NFL.

"The offices were in a rundown hotel," said Chuck. "They were just horrible. The practice facilities were bad. But the Steelers were going to move into Three Rivers Stadium the next year, so it was a situation that was going to be corrected. These things are important. You can't win a championship from a rundown office. Not these days anyway."

The Steelers won their opener, a 16–13 win over what would turn out to be a good Detroit Lions team. An ebullient Chris cheered his father's new team on to victory. "We were elated," Chris said. "I thought, 'This is going to be easy.' The next thirteen, it was not so easy."

Chuck's training camp analysis had been correct. The Steelers simply didn't have enough good football players, and in the course of those next thirteen games—all losses—that fact would be exposed, in numerous ways. The year was perhaps remembered most vividly for the time that Joe Greene, in a fit of competitive rage during a 52–14 blowout loss to the Minnesota Vikings, grabbed a pair of scissors from Tony Parisi's trunk on the sidelines and went after the Vikings Carl Eller and Alan Page in the bench area at Metropolitan Stadium in Bloomington, where both teams' benches were on the same side of the field.

Russell, one of the most respected veterans on the team by '69, would remember that Chuck never lost the team. He would come in each week and explain what they'd done wrong and then strive to get better.

Against the Cardinals, when Russell guessed wrong on a play and gave up a touchdown, Chuck was waiting for him on the sidelines. He neither screamed nor cursed but evenly asked, "What were you thinking there?"

Russell had studied the Cardinals' tendencies and knew that they rarely passed from the formation he'd seen. It had been an educated guess.

"Stop guessing," said Chuck.

The key, in many players' estimation, was that Chuck kept the team focused. "I think you lose people when you start blaming everyone," Chuck said. "Instead of coming in and saying, 'This is your fault, it's your fault, it's your fault,' we came in and said, 'This is what we've got to do to get better.' And that was the approach. And 'We have to learn how to do this better. It's we, not you.' You got that message across and made progress, and you found the players who couldn't or didn't want to, all they were interested in was collecting a paycheck. Those were the guys we would get rid of."

The Steelers' 1–13 record tied the Bears for the worst in the league— and the Bears routed Pittsburgh when the two teams played head to head.

At the end-of-the-season press conference, Chuck raised a vigorous defense in the press. "We made progress, although it doesn't reflect in the win-loss column," he said. "It was progress in areas that are not convertible to win-loss. Our ultimate goal is the championship. There is talk, 'If we can just be respectable,' but we'll not be satisfied with that. Our goal is the championship, but I don't know when we'll realize it. It's hard to put a time schedule on it."

At home, he remained taciturn, even-tempered. For Chris Noll, the season was marked by a fan's anguish. "I remember the stress that we had lost so many in a row, were we ever going to win again," he said. "I had a lot of the same emotions as a typical fan did. And part of it I think is because he never brought that stuff home. It wasn't like he came home and we talked about it. He come home and it was home. I lived through the papers—I learned more from the papers than I did from him."

The afternoon of the season-ending press conference, Dan Rooney came to Chuck's office in the Roosevelt and put an envelope on his desk.

"What's this?," asked Chuck.

"It's a bonus. For a job well done."

Chuck blanched. "We're 1–13. You can't give me a bonus for that." They went back and forth, and Chuck finally accepted the envelope. He put it in his desk.

He told Marianne about it that evening. "How much was it for?"

"I'm not going to tell you," he said, "because you'll tell me we should take it."

The check was for $10,000. It remained in his desk drawer for weeks before Dan returned. He'd heard from bookkeeping that it had never been cashed.

"Chuck," Dan said. "My father will be hurt if you don't accept the check."

Chuck eventually relented, bringing the check home to Marianne and placing it on the kitchen counter.

"Put it in a separate account," he told her. "We're not going to touch it until we've earned it."

eleven

GROWING PAINS

✦　✦　✦

On January 9, 1970, the Friday before Super Bowl IV, at the Fairmont Hotel in New Orleans, Pete Rozelle hosted a gathering that included his aide Jim Kensil; the Bears' Ed McCaskey, son-in-law of George Halas; and Dan Rooney. The occasion was a coin flip to break the tie in draft order between Chicago and Pittsburgh, since both teams finished the 1969 season at 1–13.

Dan Rooney offered to let McCaskey call the coin in the air. McCaskey called heads, and it landed tails. With that, Chuck and the Steelers received the first overall selection in the 1970 NFL draft. At dinner that night, when the Rooneys were joined by the Nolls, Dan gave Chuck the 1921 silver dollar, with Lady Liberty on the face, that had been flipped for the first choice. "This is the start of something big for us," Dan declared.

There was no question about the identity of the first player who would be selected. With narrow eyes, golden hair, and the jutting jaw of a TV Western star, Louisiana Tech's Terry Bradshaw looked like a star quarterback. Chuck's offensive assistant, John Bridgers, had written the breathless scouting report on Bradshaw in the fall of 1969: "He has the physique, strength, quickness, arm strength, and mechanics for playing QB as you will seldom see. Sets up fast, throws on balance, can really 'hum' the ball. Has had good training. Would be the kind of QB who would try to do what you wanted him to do. The biggest drawback or question mark would be just how he could stack up mentally and perform strategically or read the defenses. We may never have a chance at a QB who has better physical assets."

The offers came in. At one point, the St. Louis Cardinals were offering seven players, including All-Pro defensive back Roger Wehrli, for the first pick in the draft. Chuck held firm. "All those guys are going to do is get us closer to mediocrity," he told Dan Rooney. "Our objective is to win the championship." On January 27, they drafted Bradshaw.

In the second round, they chose Joe Greene's former North Texas State teammate, wide receiver Ron Shanklin, and in the third round, they drafted Mel Blount, a 6-foot-3, 205-pound defensive back from Southern, long and wiry. While Bill Nunn was sure he could be a terrific safety, Chuck still held out hope that Blount could be a very physical cornerback.

Like many of his African American teammates, Blount was a product of the Jim Crow South. Chuck would be his first white coach, Pittsburgh would be the first big city he'd ever lived in. When Blount visited Pittsburgh the first time, days after the draft, the Steelers were still on the eighth floor of the Roosevelt Hotel. Looking out of his office window onto the city, Chuck asked Blount, "What do you see out there?"

The country-bred Blount replied, "Well, I see a lot of tall buildings, and I can sort of see the barges on the river out there . . ."

"I'll tell you what I see," said Chuck. "I see . . . *championships.*" It would be as close as Chuck would get to motivational oratory.

Bradshaw was, in his own way, equally provincial. After a physical exam, the team doctor John Best recommended an operation to remove calcium deposits from Bradshaw's hamstring. The surgery, performed at Divine Providence Hospital in Pittsburgh shortly after the draft, was routine.

"Where's my mama? I want my mama!" said Bradshaw when he came out of anesthesia. Bradshaw's maturity and emotional stability would remain an issue for years. But with the coin flip, the Steelers had received a necessary ingredient to any football dynasty: a potential franchise quarterback.

✦   ✦   ✦

It wasn't the only reason for hope and promise. The Steelers would change leagues with the new season. In the spring of 1969, Art Rooney had agreed, along with the Browns' Art Modell and Colts' Carroll Rosenbloom, to move over to join the ten existing AFL teams (with each NFL franchise receiving $3 million for the move). In doing so, the sixteen-team NFL and ten-team AFL were finally fully merged and balanced into two thirteen-team conferences, the NFC and the AFC, with the start of the 1970 season.

In the AFC Central, Pittsburgh would be grouped with their old rival the Browns, as well as the Cincinnati Bengals (both coached and co-owned by Paul Brown, who'd returned to pro football with the AFL expansion team in 1968) and the Houston Oilers, whose Astrodome was viewed as a luxury stadium in 1970. When Dan Rooney called Chuck with the news, he was pleased. Knowing the talent level of the AFL from his years with the Chargers, he didn't feel the stigma that some NFL loyalists did. (Dan found a less receptive audience from his son, Art Rooney II, who was in high school at the time. Reared on the superiority of the NFL, he initially felt as though his father and grandfather had made a mistake in accepting the money to move to join the newer group of teams.)

That August, the Steelers moved into the gleaming multipurpose Three Rivers Stadium, which they'd share with the Pirates. Rather than having their offices in the Roosevelt, and practicing out at South Park, and playing their home games at Pitt Stadium, they would now be entirely based inside Three Rivers, located just off the banks of the city's North Shore, right above the Golden Triangle, the confluence where the Monongahela and Allegheny Rivers joined to form the Ohio River. The circular $55 million edifice conformed to all the generic state-of-the-art requisites of the day, featuring Tartan Turf and offices around the perimeter of the stadium.

After years as boarders in Forbes Field and Pitt Stadium, and the low-rent atmospherics of practices at South Park, it felt regal. "It had as much of an effect on the football team as anything we did," said Chuck of the move.

In the off-season, John Bridgers had left—returning to the college ranks as an assistant at South Carolina—and Chuck had decided to take over the offensive coordinator's role. To fill the spot on the staff, he hired Lionel Taylor as his receivers coach. Taylor, one of the very first black assistant coaches in the pro game, had just ended a sterling pro career with the Denver Broncos. Chuck knew of Taylor's receiving skills from game-planning against him in San Diego, but he also admired his confidence. Far from being deferential, Taylor was a voluble coach, a shouter on the field (or as he would put it, "I believe in correcting real loud, so that if you made a mistake the [receiver] on the other side of the field could hear it as well"). Taylor felt free to tell Chuck that his offense wasn't spread out enough; Chuck, in turn, felt comfortable enough both with Taylor's manner and the input that he chose to room with him on the road.

Chuck also hired Lou Riecke, a strength coach from Louisiana, for training camp. A disciple of the legendary and notorious strength coach Alvin Roy, who brought weight training—and anabolic steroids—into the game with the Chargers in 1963, Riecke was part of Chuck's attempt at making the team stronger.

While the golden rookie Bradshaw earned most of the headlines, the main discussion among Chuck and his coaches at camp was what to do with Roy Jefferson, the Steelers' player rep who'd announced he was unhappy with the terms of the settlement between the league and the NFL Players Association that was hammered out as teams were reporting for camp.

By turns brilliant and sullen, Jefferson had exerted an outsized influence on his teammates, especially Joe Greene. One day that summer, Jefferson advised Greene to spit on *Pittsburgh Press* columnist Pat Livingston, and Greene had done so, to his lasting regret.

At St. Vincent, Jefferson had lapsed into more expressions of attitude and petulance. He'd parked in a faculty area, rather than in one of the spaces designated for the Steelers. Another day, he'd showed up to the field without his helmet. When Bradshaw underthrew one pass low and at his feet, a frustrated Jefferson grabbed the ball, and theatrically threw it back at Bradshaw's feet. Another day, Jefferson ran 15 yards and cut in on what was designated as a 20-yard down-and-in pattern. As mess-ups go, it wasn't the worst sin committed, but it also wasn't Jefferson's first, and Chuck knew Jefferson well enough to know it wasn't an accident.

Chuck burst onto the field, yelling, "That's exactly what we don't want! That is exactly what will kill us. We needed a first down. You're six fucking yards short!"

"What you hollering about?!," countered Jefferson. "I caught the ball, didn't I?"

The whole team grew quiet and waited for the outcome. Chuck had already decided. Talking to Dan Rooney that evening, he said, "We've had enough of him. If we're building, we've got to build with people."

Two days later, the Steelers traded Jefferson to the Colts for Willie Richardson, who'd played well in '67 and '68 but was already on the down side of his career, and a fourth-round draft choice.

"You haven't reached your potential yet," Chuck told Jefferson. "And I don't think you ever will."

For Jefferson's former teammates, the exit was not surprising. "He was a hell of a player," said Frenchy Fuqua. "But yes, you could see that something was gonna come to a head there between Chaz and Roy."

Meanwhile, Chuck was trying to find out what he had in Bradshaw, who'd arrived in Pittsburgh convinced that what a young quarterback needed to do was command a team from his arrival. When the veterans returned from their four-day strike at the beginning of training camp, Bradshaw audaciously tried to sit with them in their reserved area in the St. Vincent cafeteria.

The first football game at Three Rivers, a preseason match with the New York Giants, was on August 25, 1970, broadcast on national television by ABC. It was the first broadcast of the *Monday Night Football* crew, and in the pregame opening, Don Meredith mentioned that Bradshaw had told him, "Pittsburgh needs a leader, and I can lead 'em!"

That afternoon, Chuck (dressed, as he had for games the previous year, in a shirt and tie, stylish variations on chocolate and tan) walked into the new carpeted locker room—which seemed a world removed from the faded benches and tiny quarters at Pitt Stadium—and saw center Ray Mansfield euphoric. "When we went into that stadium for the first game," Chuck said, "I couldn't contain those guys. They were smiling, looking around. Pregame, they went after it so hard, we had to bring them in and try to settle them down. Or we would have shot our wad before the game. Everybody was so excited."

Bradshaw threw an interception but also a perfectly weighted corner route to Ron Shanklin in the end zone for a touchdown, and Pittsburgh won its preseason debut at its new home. And yet there was something unsettling about Bradshaw's demeanor. In an era when the premier quarterbacks exuded a steely resolve—Unitas, Dawson, Bart Starr all seemed unflappable—Bradshaw radiated a kind of manic hyperactivity, along with a deep insecurity. Following the touchdown pass, he came to the sidelines and paced around, with primal whooping after every few steps. After the game, an ecstatic Bradshaw walked into the locker room, strode up to the chalkboard where Chuck had written the pregame schedule, and scrawled "WINNERS" in large letters across the board.

"Terry always revved a little high," was how one teammate put it.

Even with Bradshaw in the fold, the heart and soul of the team remained Joe Greene. Other players had larger biceps or bench-pressed more weight, but during games Greene exerted a kind of timeless, country strength, from some deep wellspring that other players could not access. Like many of his young African American teammates from the South, it took him time to adapt to life in the industrial northeast. But he also possessed a maturity off the field that many of the others didn't share. Greene and his wife, Agnes, had married while they were still in college.

That maturity didn't always extend to the field. During the break between morning and afternoon practices at Latrobe, while players were in the cafeteria and resting, equipment manager Tony Parisi routinely locked the dressing room, where the players kept their shoulder pads and helmet. For those coming down for the afternoon practice, it meant an additional detour to suit up again after lunch. One day, when a tired Greene decided he didn't want to make that extra trip, he confronted the locked door and simply kicked it in, collecting his pads and helmet and bringing them with him to the dorm.

Word got out quickly, and there was little question whom the culprit was, since Greene volunteered himself that he'd done it. That evening, after the last meetings, Chuck came by Greene's dorm room and ducked his head in. "Joe," he said. "That'll be $500 for the door." Then he left. But it was lost on no one that from the next day forward, the equipment room was never locked during the lunch break at training camp.

"That is one of the many things he changed to accommodate players," said Greene. "That was just his way. He didn't have his head in the sand;

he wasn't so rigid that he couldn't be flexible to change things according to what was needed."

At a time when many teams had a strict dress code—the Kansas City Chiefs traveled to the stadium in tailored blazers and pants, with neckties required—Chuck was more relaxed. The three rules for dress on the road were: "No shorts. No tank-tops. No slippers." That left a lot of room for personal expression. Frenchy Fuqua wearing his cape and, at least once, stack heels with goldfish swimming in the heel. "You could switch it anyway you wanted to," said Greene, "whether it was the high point or the low point. But we went from Frenchy to everything in between, to Jon Kolb wearing boots and jeans and a plaid shirt."

The 1970 season, to a great extent, was a laboratory for the rookie Bradshaw. On the field, for all the raves about his powerful arm, he could strike an ungainly pose. Eschewing a chin strap, he pulled the helmet tightly onto his head. His throwing motion was unlike anyone else in the game—he bent forward at the waist on his release, and he held the football in an unusual fashion, with his index finger on the tip of the ball to direct the throw. Chuck puzzled for weeks in training camp about whether to intercede but ultimately decided to leave well enough alone.

The Steelers opened at home, with a loss to the Oilers, in which Bradshaw ran out of the end zone for a safety, part of a day in which he completed just 4 out of 16 passes for 40 yards. In the third quarter, Chuck brought in Terry Hanratty to try to spark the offense, two drives after Bradshaw's safety left Pittsburgh down, 16–0. After the game, Bradshaw shrugged off radio play-by-play man Myron Cope's interview request, headed out to the parking lot and sat in his new car and cried. The next two weeks, the Steelers would lose again (to the Broncos and Browns), and Bradshaw would be tackled for a safety in each game. At that point, the Steelers' losing streak was at sixteen games.

In the second game, at Denver, Bradshaw recalled, "I got my first look at Chuck Noll when he was angry. I don't mean displeased. I mean flat-out mad. A group of guys were goofing off in the half-time locker room meeting, not paying attention, and he jumped on them like a chicken on a june bug. Man, the coaches never talked that way at Louisiana Tech. It made an impression on me—scared me to death—and you'd better believe I've listened to every word he has ever said to me since."

Opinions varied on that statement, but the Steelers broke through in week four at home against the Bills and proceeded to win four of their next five games (including a win over Paul Brown and the Bengals), leaving them at 4–4 and tied for first place in the AFC Central with the Browns. From there, things deteriorated, based largely on turnovers (the Steelers gave the ball up twenty-eight times in losing five of their last six games). Neither the erratic Bradshaw (who threw six touchdowns to twenty-four interceptions on the year) nor the weak-armed Hanratty could complete even 40 percent of their passes.

Over the course of the long season, Bradshaw's confidence collapsed under the weight of expectations, media attention (he wound up on the cover of *Newsweek* in the fall), harsh public criticism, and his own callow bluster.

"Bradshaw needed help and he wanted help," said trainer Ralph Berlin. "Chuck wanted him to do it, and at that time from a mental standpoint and from a knowledge standpoint, Bradshaw couldn't do it."

After the Steelers beat Houston, 7–3 in the Astrodome on October 18, Bradshaw went back to Shreveport with his parents. But that Tuesday morning, on an early connection back to Pittsburgh, he was fogged in at the St. Louis airport. "All I missed was a film session and some light running," said Bradshaw in his memoir, *Looking Deep*. "I arrived later that day but the following day, [Chuck] made me stand up in a team meeting and announced that he was going to fine me. Unloaded on me. We had won our game, beaten Houston, and instead of coming back as a hero, I felt I was being scolded like a child."

By the middle of the season, Bradshaw had grown withdrawn and moody. Teammate Preston Pearson (acquired in a preseason trade from Baltimore) became convinced the quarterback was not thinking about football away from the building. "Terry really got frustrated with Chuck's style," said Pearson. "I even went over to Terry's apartment at the time with game film. I recognized he wasn't studying, wasn't doing what was necessary to get better. He had no idea what he was talking about. He was just a young guy from Shreveport, Louisiana, that really didn't know himself. He didn't know who he was. He wasn't grounded."

Of his rookie season, Bradshaw once remarked, "I tried to learn how to read defensive formations, but the other team intentionally made it difficult for me."

Bradshaw wasn't the only one still maturing; there were adjustments throughout the young team. Against the Dolphins, Mel Blount allowed three touchdown passes to Paul Warfield. The headlines would be about the green cornerback, but Chuck knew the fuller story (on at least one of the routes, a safety was supposed to help Blount and missed his assignment).

On the bus out to the airport following the game, Steelers' radio man Myron Cope asked Chuck about his rookie corner.

"Don't worry about Blount," Chuck said. "He'll be just fine."

The last game of the season found the Steelers visiting a poor, aging Philadelphia Eagles squad, which would finish the season with a 3–10–1 record. The game, the last the Eagles would ever play at Franklin Field, was a physical contest, marked by Frenchy Fuqua having a career day, carrying 20 times for 218 yards and two touchdowns. Bradshaw, who had played himself out of the starting quarterback job, was called on to spell injured punter Bobby Walden (nervous, Bradshaw punted three times for a 17-yard average). But the game would be remembered for Greene, still competing fiercely, objecting to being repeatedly held by Eagles' offensive linemen. Greene was tangling with the Eagles' starting guard Jim Skaggs who, it quickly became apparent, was not going to be able to handle him without holding him.

"Joe was not going to accept a possible loss," said Andy Russell. "So they are about maybe at our 20-yard line or something like that, and I hear him say to the guy who is blocking him, 'If you hold me again, I'm gonna have to hurt you.' And the guy can't block him. I mean, there is no way he can block him, so he has to hold him. So he holds him, and you hear this *thump*, and they had to carry the guy off."

Later, with the Eagles about to score to clinch the game, Greene boiled over. He snatched the football as the Eagles were coming up to the line of scrimmage, turned toward the crowd behind the end zone, and launched the ball into a majestic arc; it carried high into the crowd. Greene was walking off the field even as players from both sides were squabbling—Mel Blount of the Steelers and Steve Zabel of the Eagles both were ejected.

After the game, with the season ended, Chuck could be seen saying a brief word or two to many of the players. But as he frequently did, he spent more time with Greene. Sitting down in front of Greene, he squared up and said to him, softly, "Joe, I don't think those officials like the names you're calling them. You might want to think about that next time."

✦ ✦ ✦

On January 21, a week before the 1971 draft, Chuck was called out of the offices at Three Rivers by an urgent phone call from Marianne, bearing the news that Chuck's father had just died.

Chuck returned to the draft room, stunned, and gave Art Rooney Jr. the news, adding that he was going to have to run the draft room for a few days. Chuck, ashen, walked out. He didn't say when he'd return. Artie had never seen Chuck so shaken—and that left him tearful and rattled.

The funeral a few days later in Cleveland was less well-attended than Kate's had been. William Noll lay in the casket, a smile forced onto his face. "That's not Grandpa," said Ken Deininger.

"They put a smile on because he is in heaven," Rita explained.

Chuck was quiet at the funeral, predictably somber, but also pained by the continued family rift that still remained. Though Chuck's older brother Bob attended, his wife Stella didn't come.

The loss of both of his parents may have absolved some of Chuck's responsibilities but not all of them. For the seven children of Rita and Clare, Uncle Chuck had become a lifeline of sorts.

"He bought the house, he bought the car, I mean—he owned everything," said Ken Deininger. "My understanding was he and his parents owned the house and we lived there for free. I am not sure of the financial setup at the time, but that is what they talked about. He always said, 'You have to go to college.' I can remember my mom saying, 'Look, you've got to think about this; I don't care what you study, but you've got to go.' But I don't think my mom knew how to get us there. Because she didn't have a college education, she was only high school. And, of course, Uncle Chuck did."

"When he came, he was just Uncle Chuck," said his niece Marilyn. "He comes up to me and lifts up my ponytail and says, 'You know what is under a pony's tail?' It was just jokes like that. Nothing that ever separated him from being the uncle."

It would be a trying off-season. In April, Chuck received a call that assistant Walt Hackett—out at Long Beach State during a two-week stretch of scouting spring practices—had suffered a heart attack and died. Hackett had been the first coach Chuck hired and, like Chuck, lived in Upper St. Clair.

That necessitated another change in the coaching staff. Chuck hired Dan Radakovich, a former Penn State assistant who'd just spent a year on the staff at the University of Cincinnati, to replace Hackett. Radakovich's demeanor was less Marine drill sergeant than eccentric professor. He lacked much experience on the defensive line but showed a keen mind. Noll liked Radakovich enough to tell him he could attend law school at night while he was coaching with the Steelers.

Chuck had already petitioned for and been granted the opportunity to hire an extra coach just for the team's quarterbacks. He had reached out to his old Browns teammate, the recently retired quarterback Babe Parilli (who'd backed up Joe Namath in the Jets' Super Bowl III upset of the Colts), and asked him if he would come in and work with Bradshaw not only on techniques and fundamentals but also confidence. "You be the good cop," Chuck said. "I'll be the bad cop."

The coach remained a mystery to the men who played for him. Running back Rocky Bleier was rooming with Warren Bankston that year, and one night they were in their room, talking with Terry Hanratty and Bob Adams.

"So we were sitting there and we were bullshitting, and Chuck walks in," said Bleier. "I think it was Warren who had the guitar. And Chuck's manner was, well, he tries, but he can't be one of the guys. He is just not comfortable. So he sits down and picks up the guitar, and he starts playing the guitar. And he *can play.* So, it's like, you're thinking, *Maybe he knows a couple of chords.* But he's playing, and it wasn't as if there was a lot of picking, but it was good. And you go, *Oh, fuck!* Then he puts it down, and he goes, 'Whose camera is this?' 'It's my camera,' and then he would explain all about the camera—it's got a 120-yard scope, you can take these kind of pictures with it . . . " After a while, Chuck left, and the players paused for a moment, looked at each other, and broke out laughing. What else could be said?

The humor was limited, and it was almost always dry, but it could be found. Another night at training camp, Warren Bankston and Bob Adams were out at a local tavern, when they realized they had less than ten minutes before curfew. Racing to their car, they peeled out of the parking lot and back toward the campus. With the configuration of the buildings, cars had to be parked nearly 100 yards away from the dorm. In the dark of night, wanting to hurry but also not make excessive noise, Bankston pulled his shoes off and sprinted stealthily across the newly watered grass up to the front door of the dorm. He and Adams got into their room with seconds to spare and quickly dove into their beds, pulling the covers over their clothes. A moment later, there was a knock at the door, and Chuck walked in.

"How you doing, guys?"

"Great," said Bankston. "We've just been studying the playbook. Quiet night in."

Chuck looked bemused, but didn't bite. He exchanged a couple more remarks, then turned to leave. Almost at the door, he looked back.

"Warren?"

"Yes, sir?"

"Your feet are all wet."

Another morning at St. Vincent, near the end of training camp, one of the ball boys knocked on guard Jon Kolb's door and asked him to go down and see Chuck Noll. The weightlifting-obsessed Kolb, by then in his third year, thought he was having his best camp as a Steeler. Now, having received the universal summons to be cut, three years of effort welled up in him. Eyeing the brick wall in the back of his dorm room, he recalled that the assistant had neglected to ask him to bring his playbook. Kolb lifted the thick binder in his hands and threw it against the brick wall, where it exploded, loose papers scattering everywhere.

Kolb then walked down the hallway, waves of despair flooding over him, and as he was about to knock on Chuck's door, he felt a tear on his cheek. He stepped back, gathered himself, wiped the tear away, and knocked on the door.

When he walked in, Chuck had his back turned to him and a handful of 8 × 10 photographs in his hand. "Oh, Jon, come in," he said. "I took my vacation in Florida this year, and I heard you like outdoors and wildlife and stuff. I wanted to show you some of my wildlife pictures." Handing a glossy to Kolb, he said, "This is a pileated woodpecker."

Chuck started talking about the other pictures, explaining to Kolb the difference between alligators and crocodiles.

Kolb, still convinced he was about to be cut, was growing impatient. Finally, he flipped through the last few.

"I'm sorry to bother you," said Chuck. "I just thought you'd like to look at those."

Finally, Kolb couldn't stand the suspense and blurted out, "You mean . . . I'm not cut?"

Chuck looked surprised. "Oh, no—you're having a really good camp. Why would I want to cut you?" He thanked Kolb for coming by and told him he should probably get ready for practice.

"And so I walk out and I am *not* cut," said Kolb. "And so then I go down the hallway and as I am going down the hallway I am thinking, 'I'm not cut!,' and as I turn into the room there is the playbook with two hundred pages all over the place. That was my first conversation with Chuck Noll."

By this point, with two years together, Chuck and Artie and the scouting staff had developed a profile of the sort of players they were seeking, best articulated by Dan Rooney. "We didn't want big fat guys who just leaned against somebody and that was the only thing they could do," said Dan. "We wanted to be able to move the football outside, inside, trap, and do all the things you had to do, and still be able to pass-protect." In short, they wanted smart, agile, slightly undersized linemen—linemen exactly like Chuck Noll was when he played.

But it went beyond that. As soon as he arrived, Chuck told Artie, "We have to improve the team speed and quickness." A year later, prepping for the 1970 draft, he emphasized the need to improve the collective team intelligence. "I'm not saying we have a bunch of Phi Beta Kappas," said Artie. "But I do think we have a bunch that can comprehend."

It was very early in the '71 season that the Steelers realized they had a remarkable draft class. Frank Lewis, the wide receiver from Grambling, was a natural with good hands and speed. Second-rounder Jack Ham, the linebacker from Penn State, moved almost immediately into a starting role. Gerry Mullins, a tight end at Southern Cal, was moved onto the offensive line as a prototype of the Steelers' smart, mobile guard. Dwight White and Ernie Holmes, two projects from small schools in Texas, provided additional speed and strength in the defensive line. Even Mike Wagner, an eleventh-round pick from Western Illinois, provided competition at the safety position.

Bradshaw was back in the starting role in 1971, and in the opener at Chicago, the Steelers had a 15–3 lead late in the fourth quarter before fumbling on two consecutive possessions, leading to a surreal 17–15 loss, at the end of which a furious Joe Greene threw his helmet. In a stroke of luck, it hit the crossbar and shattered, rather than flying into the stands and hitting a spectator.

"I thought, I hate that cliche about hating to lose," said Ham, recalling his first pro game. "But this guy actually gets *violent* when you lose a game. This guy's a competitor. This guy's a helluva player for us. And I'm sure he felt there was no way in the world we should be losing to the Bears."

In the third game of the season, they made a stand at the goal line, stopping the Chargers. "It's a sign we're coming of age," said Andy Russell. "Two years ago, we would have lost this game." *Sports Illustrated* put Greene on its cover, accompanied by a story on the emerging Steelers, with the magazine's pro football writer, Tex Maule, observing Chuck's coaching bloodlines: "He has some of the reserve and dignity of Brown, some of Gillman's flair, and all of Shula's ability to identify with the players."

They hadn't entirely come of age. Two weeks later, in front of a national television audience on *Monday Night Football* in Kansas City's Municipal Stadium, the Steelers were holding their own against the Chiefs, one of the best teams in football. Bradshaw found wide receiver Dave Smith in a seam in the secondary and he sliced between the cornerback and safety to glide in for a touchdown. As he triumphantly raised the football in his right hand around the 5-yard line, the ball slipped out of Smith's grasp and out of the back of the end zone for a touchback. So instead of a Steelers' touchdown, the Chiefs got the ball on the 20. At Municipal Stadium, both benches were on the same side of the field, and Smith had to trot by the Kansas City bench. "So he is coming by our guys," said the Chiefs' Len Dawson, "and they were giving him all kinds of stuff. And he stops to take it—because Chuck Noll was waiting for him."

Back home in Pittsburgh, Marianne watched aghast. "I think she swore," said Chris. "She is the swearer in the family. You knew not to ask him about it."

"Now that, in itself, would not spur Chuck to get rid of a player," said Rocky Bleier. "It was *everything* else that would lead up to it. Dave, specifically, was a locker-room lawyer. We like to say Dave talked himself into the league and out of the league."

It would take another full year, and the maturation of Shanklin and Lewis, before Smith was gone, dealt to Houston in 1972 for a mid-round draft choice. (In the weeks following the game, though, Smith was inundated with hate mail from Steelers fans, though the touchdown would have changed little in the Chiefs' 38–16 win.)

Pittsburgh won two of its next three games, including a victory over the Browns, 26–9, to move into a first-place tie with Cleveland on November 7.

The team was beginning to get a sense of its potential. The new defensive line coach Radakovich had prevailed upon Chuck to overhaul the defensive line. The anchor Greene was joined by slow-footed veterans Lloyd Voss, Chuck Hinton, and Ben McGee. Radakovich moved both Voss and McGee from defensive end into defensive tackle, where they shared time, and he put the slender, 6-foot-6, 230-pound L. C. Greenwood at one defensive end and the rookie Dwight White at the other.

There was some spirited debate over the subject. "You know what Butkus did to L. C. Greenwood?," asked defensive assistant Charlie Sumner. "Butkus hit him and knocked him out—they had to carry him off the field."

"That's nothing," said Radakovich. "Fuck, I saw him play in college. He does that to everybody."

White was sensitive and took umbrage at Radakovich grading him in film study, eventually complaining to Lionel Taylor, who immediately stood in Radakovich's defense. "Hey, Dwight," he said. "How many other rookie defensive ends are playing first string in the league? Only one, Dwight. *You.* And that 'racist' took a starting white end, Lloyd Voss, and put him at tackle so you could fucking start. You're calling him a racist. Get the fuck out of here."

While Bradshaw was improving (throwing thirteen touchdowns and for over 2,200 yards), he still made crucial mistakes, including twenty-two interceptions. In the next two games, Bradshaw passed for 67 yards against Denver and 59 yards against Houston, both losses to subpar teams. The season ended with a 23–14 loss to the Los Angeles Rams. It was the franchise's eighth straight losing season, and Chuck's third. He had gone 12–30 in his first three seasons. Another Christmas Day came with the football season already over.

✦   ✦   ✦

By the time of the 1972 draft, Chuck and Artie Rooney had grown to respect one another. Artie, consumed with his job and a desire to prove to his father that he was worthy—and to everyone else that he wasn't merely a product of nepotism—worked indefatigably, traveling the country for much of the year. He was both stubborn and socially insecure, which meant that when he formed opinions, he would defend them so strongly he would often grow truculent if Chuck didn't agree with him.

Ahead of the '72 draft, both Chuck and Artie viewed an explosive running back as a first-round priority, but they differed on which player might be the best fit. Chuck had his eye on Robert Newhouse, a diminutive, dynamic back (his nickname was "The Human Bowling Ball") whose outsized effort and wide range of skills made him the key player in the heart of Bill Yeoman's prolific veer offense at the University of Houston.

Artie, though, was convinced that the player the Steelers wanted was Franco Harris, the 6-foot-2, 225-pound fullback who was splitting carries with the faster, more explosive Lydell Mitchell at Penn State. Though some questioned Harris's attitude, Artie's report was glowing: "The type kid we are looking for. . . . Outstanding body-control. Has the strength to brake [sic] tackles and the movement and speed to be a big threat outside or in the open field. Hands look ok on the short stuff. Only a fair blocker but he has the tools to develop into a good blocker as a pro. Hit into the line a bit inconsistent on goal line but later smacked in real tough. Good lateral movement and quickness. Feet are quick. Not a straight line runner. Lots of movement and wiggle. Would give us a big gun in the backfield."

Chuck ran his draft meetings with the same philosophy that John F. Kennedy ran his cabinet meetings—encouraging debate and open dissent, expecting all parties to be willing to fight for their point of view.

"Artie did not want any of those things to happen," said Dan Rooney. "He frowned on it, even when you would do things that would be to his favor. He put the best guys out there; the problem was he would not let the debate happen."

So Chuck and Artie would go back and forth. In the weeks ahead of the draft, Artie made reel-to-reel tape recordings of each of the scouts who had seen both Harris and Newhouse. He offered to play it one day for Chuck, but Chuck blanched. When Artie persisted, Chuck said, "I studied law, and you ask all of these leading questions."

Through BLESTO, the Steelers also hired the shrewd personnel man Dick Haley (another former Steeler, who'd played college at Pitt), who'd worked for four years as BLESTO's southeastern scout. "It wasn't even close," said Haley. "Chuck had this thing—he went for the overachiever. Robert Newhouse was a good player. But you have to look forward, at what a player is *going* to be."

In the days leading up to the draft, Artie was commiserating with the Colts' George Young, who knew Chuck well from his days in Baltimore.

"Tell Chuck that was settled 2,000 years ago," said Young, "when Alexander the Great used elephants to take Babylon. A good big man is better than a good little man any day."

Artie passed the line on to Chuck, who simply said, "Of course—that smart ass . . ."

One of Chuck's concerns was whether Harris was a good character. But the reports were clear—though he could seem moody and stand-offish, he was in fact a conscientious worker and a good teammate. Both running backs were still on the board when the Chicago Bears, drafting immediately before Pittsburgh, bypassed running backs to take safety Craig Clemons from Iowa.

There was quiet in the room—an extended, pregnant pause.

Then Chuck exhaled and said, "Well. Let's take the Penn Stater." And with that, Franco Harris became a Pittsburgh Steeler.

As the '72 draft moved to the middle rounds, the top names on the Steelers' positional board were crossed off at each position. At the end of the first day, one name stood out—the only player left on the board with a rating in the top four rounds. He was Tennessee State quarterback Joe Gilliam, "Jefferson Street Joe," already a legend at his school, where he'd played for his father and set numerous school passing records. Bill Nunn, genial and easy-going as a matter of course, had learned to be firm about matters of principle. He sat at the table, at the end of the first day, pointed to the board and said, "That's what's wrong with pro football."

That night, Nunn left, along with most of the scouts and assistants, spanning the country to be close to the undrafted free agents they'd contact soon after the draft ended. The next day, during the final rounds of the draft, he kept calling the Steelers' offices. After the tenth round, Nunn phoned Dan Rooney again and was more insistent. "He's not drafted," Nunn said of Gilliam. "What are you gonna do?"

"He's gonna be drafted on the next round or we will take him," said Rooney. In the eleventh round, the selection came up. Pittsburgh hardly "needed" a quarterback. In an era of forty-man rosters, most teams had just two. The Steelers already had Bradshaw and Hanratty. But Chuck also valued Nunn's input and was sensitive to the plight of black quarterbacks—who during the era were routinely projected as wide receivers or defensive backs in the pros. Chuck thought Gilliam was perhaps too slight to be a durable quarterback, but there was no doubt he had a world-class throwing arm. (For his part, Gilliam had intentionally run slower times in the 40-yard dash in order to dissuade pro scouts from seeing him as wide-receiver or defensive-back material.) The Steelers took Gilliam.

After the draft, Chuck and the coaches went over the playbook and analyzed film. It left him encouraged. "That was a season where we were 6–8, but could have been 9–5 with very little change in our play," he said.

He had been on the job three years. He'd felt the owner's support. He had a sense that he was building a good football team. But he also knew that it was a results-oriented business. And he sensed that, one way or the other, the 1972 season would prove decisive.

"Chuck said he didn't think the team realized how good it was yet," said Marianne.

That would have to change.

twelve

ARRIVAL

✦ ✦ ✦

Chuck's fourth season as head coach of the Steelers began as the others had, on a hot July day on the campus of St. Vincent. There was a slight difference. Driving into camp for the first time that summer, he drove down to Tony Parisi's equipment shed and dropped off the fifteen-year-old Chris Noll, who was going to be a ball boy.

Even at this early age, Chris was his father's son. Stoic and quiet to begin with, he grew more guarded in his years in Pittsburgh, recognizing quickly which people approached him because of his father and which people might truly be friends.

At Eisenhower Middle School, he'd learned to weather the remarks. The ones whose opening salvo was a request for autographs or free tickets never got close. After a loss in 1970, a boy shoved him and razzed, "Your dad can't coach." Chris lashed out, cuffing the boy about the ear until he relented. No principal was called. Chris understood that some things he would have to settle himself.

Before training camp in 1972, without belaboring the point, Chuck made it clear to Chris that he was going to be treated like any other ball boy. He warned his son about language—"You're going to learn some new words"—but beyond that he told him he would be on his own. Jackie Hart, the irascible field manager, was down on the fields at St. Vincent when Chuck drove up. "Here he is," Chuck said to Hart, and before turning to drive off, he told his son, "Have fun."

Hart glanced in the general direction of Chris, satisfied that the formalities had been dispensed with, then began pointing and ordering him around. "*Get that fucking thing over there and bring it here! . . .*"

In Latrobe, it was inevitable that Chris would be initiated, and in this case, the ordeal came quickly. He was staying on the first floor of Bonaventure Hall, with the other ball boys. The first night, while he was sleeping, someone snuck into his room in the dark and dumped an entire garbage can full of cold water on his bed, before dashing away.

Chris didn't complain, didn't cry, didn't report the incident. Instead, he got up, changed into dry clothes, turned over the mattress, and went back to sleep. He never told his father about it. (Though he strongly suspected that the culprits were the veteran ball boys Bob McCartney and Bill Nunn Jr.) "I knew they were testing me," said Chris.

At Baltimore, Chris's favorite player was Rick Volk. In Pittsburgh, it was the Steelers' young safety Mike Wagner. But he befriended several players. He walked down to Joe Greene's dorm and listened to some of Greene's music, and played a Boz Scaggs album for Greene. Chris drew the line when players tried to use him as a conduit to his father. "One of my memories is somebody asked me, 'Go ask your dad this,' in training camp," Chris said. "I said, 'You go ask him. Why am I going to ask him? I don't want to know that.'"

The ball boys would routinely warm up the quarterbacks prior to drills. One day, with Chris catching his passes, Bradshaw rifled one in with such velocity that it went through Chris's hands and hit him in the face, breaking his glasses. "He was terrified," said Chris, "and I started laughing. He was like, 'Oh, my God!' He had the prettiest throw I have ever seen, the tightest spiral."

✦ ✦ ✦

The biggest change heading into the 1972 season wasn't in the players but the coaches. Chuck had heard good things about the brooding, intense

Bud Carson, who'd recently been fired from the thankless job of succeeding the legendary Bobby Dodd at Georgia Tech.

The interview, conducted in January 1972 in Chuck's office at Three Rivers, went on for much of the day. The conversation was less animated than intensely focused—an exchange of fundamental concepts between two coaches equally convinced that coaching was ultimately about teaching. Carson's seriousness of purpose and deep focus matched Chuck's own. They agreed on the danger of too much blitzing, that it was unsound fundamentally—and Chuck spoke about the crucial need for a defense to get a rush with four men. They shared an openness to zone defenses, as a way to defuse the modern passing game. "We really hit it off," Carson said. "He seemed very intelligent compared to other football coaches I had known."

Carson had another interview scheduled later in the week with the Bears, but Chuck persuaded him not to make the trip and offered him the job that day. In doing so, Chuck showed a continued preference for coaches who'd had college rather than pro experience.

During his last season at Georgia Tech, Carson had proposed to his fiancée Linda, an Atlanta newscaster, and now he convinced her to come to Pittsburgh with him.

"The day of their interview, they talked the entire day at the chalkboard," said Linda Carson. "They never stopped talking. Bud said he would be at the board outlining a play, and Chuck would finish the play for him. He said he had never met anybody that thought like he did so very, very much. So he came back and got his things that weekend and went back to Pittsburgh." She noticed that Bud, gloomy since his firing at Tech, seemed to have acquired a spark of optimism. "Noll can do it," he told her. "I know he can do it." (The headline in one Atlanta paper noted Pittsburgh's dire history: "Carson goes to Purgatory U.")

Chuck also hired George Perles, recommended by some of Chuck's old colleagues on the Colts' staff. The gruff, garrulous Perles was a fleshy, boisterous line coach with an easy rapport with players and a respite from the moody introspection of the intense Carson. The displaced Charlie Sumner had coached the secondary in 1971, but now took over responsibility for coaching the linebackers, while Carson handled the secondary. No defensive coordinator was named, but Sumner—the only one with pro experience—was put in charge of calling the signals for the defensive unit.

But in making the hires—he also brought in former Steelers running back Dick Hoak, who'd spent a year coaching high school football, to handle the running backs—Chuck emphasized teaching and technique over personality. (The only remaining assistant from Chuck's original staff was the veteran offensive line coach Bob Fry, whose repeated arguments with Chuck over blocking technique were one of the defining characteristics of the early years.)

"All I know is, everything we did, the whole staff, he taught us," said Perles. "He wanted things done his way. He taught me what he wanted out of the pass rush, how he wanted the technique done. It was all technique. He wanted it done his way, and he wanted teachers. He had somewhat of a feeling that it was difficult for great pro players to understand why other people couldn't do the job like they did. He wanted teachers."

"College coaches were teachers," said Chuck, "and a lot of the pro coaches that I knew were players and only wanted to administer, and we wanted a teaching staff. You can't assume your players know everything. We thought it was very important that you taught your football and sold it. That's a big part of teaching, the selling part."

Franco Harris, whom Chuck had reluctantly taken with the Steelers' first-round pick, skipped part of the spring rookie orientation at the behest of his agent, Tony Rossano. When the deal was signed and he finally reported to training camp, the broad physicality that the scouts saw was there, along with a strikingly serious countenance—the Roman nose, the deep-set eyes—but there was something clearly isolated about Harris. At times, he seemed vaguely miffed, distant, neither friendly nor fully engaged, yet neither clearly disruptive nor disobedient.

That preseason, Chuck seemed nonplussed, reserving judgment even in the staff meetings. "So [Franco] gets there late and he's behind, and I'm spending time with him and, boy, he doesn't look very good those first few weeks," said the new running backs coach, Dick Hoak. "And we're all wondering, *What the heck?*"

The revelation came against the Falcons in a preseason game. Bradshaw gave him the ball on an outside pitch, Harris got a glimpse of daylight past the line, and he was gone for a 75-yard touchdown run.

The next week, Chuck sidled up to Hoak before a practice and counseled, "Don't over-coach him." There was little danger of that. Harris was a man of singular self-possession anyway. He held the opinion, which he would share if prompted, that the skills of a running back were at some level uncoachable anyway. His own improvisational genius would be revealed over the course of his first pro season.

The 1972 campaign began with a 2–2 start. The team that Chuck had carefully built over three full seasons was beginning to gain a sense of confidence, that it could compete on equal footing with any team in football. In the first half of a game at St. Louis, Bradshaw was injured ("He had a flare for the theatrics," said Ham, "because it looked like, you know, we were going to have to bury him after the game"), but came back in the second half for a 25–19 win. There was a frustratingly narrow loss to the defending world champion Cowboys in Dallas in week four, with the Steelers' defense tricked on an option pass from Calvin Hill to Ron Sellers.

The next week, Pittsburgh put Harris in a more central role in the offense, and he carried 19 times for 115 yards. It was the first of five consecutive wins, during which the trapping game repeatedly sprung Harris and Fuqua for big gains. Bradshaw was still shaky in his third pro season, completing less than 50 percent of his passes. But he'd reined in his impulses and, for the first time in his career, threw as many touchdowns as interceptions on the season (twelve of each).

From the sidelines, Joe Greene began to see Chuck's offense coming together. "They didn't change what they were doing," said Greene. "The offensive line, the only thing that changed is they were [Chuck's] type of guys, smaller, quicker, and could run. But in terms of the type of plays that we were running, everything was the same. What we did on defense, everything was the same. We got better players. We didn't change anything."

The statement victory came at home against a veteran Kansas City Chiefs team that had pounded the Steelers in Kansas City a year earlier. "In that game, we gave the ball to Franco at about the 20, and I don't think we blocked one person," said Dick Hoak. "Wilbur Young had him, and he broke free from Wilbur Young, and runs into the end zone. It was just a great run, and then I heard the next day about how good our offensive line was."

"If you get a great back," Chuck said the next day, "all of a sudden you've got a good line."

But there was something else that both men had noticed by then. Harris had an on-field awareness that seemed equal parts alertness and instinct. In the Vikings game, Bradshaw fumbled the ball, but Harris was in the area and caught the fumble on the bounce, sprinting nearly 80 yards, before being brought down inside the Vikings' 5-yard line. The play was called back for a Steelers' penalty, but the scene remained in the memory. "He had a knack," said Hoak. "He was always around the ball. He always ran to the ball."

After a narrow loss at Cleveland, Pittsburgh came home and beat the powerful Vikings, 23–10, with Harris again the lead rusher. For a big man, Harris was terrifically adept at changing speed and direction. "He'd start up the hole and he'd be off in another direction in a flash," said Chuck. "He had the ability to do that, and there aren't too many who can, especially when you get long striders. Franco would lengthen his stride in the open field, but inside he'd make the choppy steps and make cuts tremendously."

As the Steelers progressed toward a playoff berth, Andy Russell and Ray Mansfield, the two senior veterans on the team, rode to the stadium together each week in mounting wonder. "We'd say, 'Can we possibly win this? Are we this good? These guys, how can they be this good?,'" said Russell. "And we couldn't convince ourselves that we were that good, but we kept winning and winning . . . and pretty soon you start believing it. And you just see so much talent around you. Guys making plays everywhere. It was astounding."

They routed Cleveland, 30–0, and then struggled to beat a bad Oilers team, 9–3, in a game dominated by the relentless Greene. Chuck did not often dwell on how well a single player did his job in a game, but Greene's playing that day was an exception. "Just an incredible performance," he'd say later. "I've watched it a dozen times on film, and I still can't believe it." It would not be the first or the last time that the one man carried thirty-nine teammates, refusing to let the Steelers lose.

The Steelers needed a win at San Diego or a Cleveland loss on the final day of the season to clinch their first ever division title.

During the mostly quiet pregame warm-ups, players kept looking up to the Jack Murphy Stadium scoreboard, only to be updated on the Browns beating the Giants. The Steelers would have to win. Chuck didn't mention it, remained matter of fact in the moments before they took the field.

"I've never seen a locker room so quiet," said Ray Mansfield. "There wasn't a sound."

They went out and dominated the Chargers, winning 24–2, with San Diego's only points coming when Bradshaw was tackled in the end zone. At the end of the game, Mansfield and Jim Clack lifted Chuck up on their shoulders and carried him a short way across the field. He looked happy and vaguely embarrassed, using his arms to balance himself, before coming down.

There was elation in the locker room, but very little of it emanating from Chuck. "One thing I learned very early, you never have it made," he'd later say of that day. "You never relax, never rejoice very long. What happened then, that day was great. Coming back on the plane was great. But the next day, I just got to work on Oakland. There's no such thing as coasting." The next day's *Pittsburgh Post-Gazette* included a six-column headline at the top of its front page, "Steelers Win 1st Title in 40 Years."

✦　✦　✦

Pittsburgh entered the playoffs having won nine of its last ten games. The defense had surrendered nothing but a field goal in the final three games. The team was in uncharted territory. In 1947, they'd played and lost the playoff to break a tie for first place and the East Division title; in 1963, they played in the Playoff Bowl, a consolation game for runners-up in the NFL's two divisions. But this, the first real postseason game in franchise history, found the city electrified.

It would take place on December 23, 1972, against the Oakland Raiders and Al Davis, who'd made some coy advances toward hiring Chuck for the Raiders' head-coaching job in 1969 but wound up hiring John Madden, who used to regularly watch the Chargers' practices when Chuck was on Sid Gillman's staff in the sixties.

On the field, about an hour before kickoff, Ben McGee came up beside Chuck and said, "Coach, I just wanted you to know that I am going to retire at the end of this season." Chuck, still looking out at the rest of the team going through calisthenics, didn't respond, and McGee figured that he hadn't heard. He would bring it up later, perhaps.

The two teams had played the season opener, with the Steelers winning a 34–28 shootout. But this was a far different game. There was a manic intensity in the Three Rivers crowd that day, fueled by Christmas cheer, hope, alcohol, and forty years of frustration, not necessarily in that order.

The two defenses dominated the first half, warding off every offensive thrust. Scoreless at halftime, the Steelers broke through in the chill with an 18-yard Gerela field goal in the third quarter. After they widened the lead with another field goal in the fourth quarter, Madden lifted starter Daryle Lamonica for Ken Stabler. In the final two minutes he drove them across midfield, but the Raiders faced a third-and-eight at the Steelers' 30. On the next play, Stabler escaped Craig Hanneman's rush from the left and ran 30 yards for a touchdown, to take a 7–6 lead. Andy Russell was furious after the play. "If we hold contain, it's an 8-yard loss," he said. "You talk about being beaten on a mental mistake on a play, and then ends up with no containment."

There was one minute and thirteen seconds left, and the Raiders— who'd gotten one step from the Super Bowl in 1968, 1969, and 1970— were still celebrating when they kicked off. Bradshaw threw a couple of short passes and drove the ball up to the Steelers' 40, but three straight incomplete passes left them at fourth-and-ten, the season hanging in the balance, and twenty-two seconds left on the clock.

Among the Steelers' bench, accounts vary on the mood. "I was telling the guys on the sideline," said Glen Edwards, "I said, 'Man, the game ain't over until the last second off the clock.'"

"I remember standing there with Glen Edwards, and Glen was bitching about our offense being so bad that day, we'd only scored a few points," said Andy Russell. "I always tried to be positive, pull [for] the offense. So I'm like, 'Something can happen.' Because the game seemed like it was over."

Terry Hanratty, standing close to Chuck in the frantic final minute, noticed something. "Chuck seldom gets emotional," he said. "But you can look at his face and tell if everything's all right. When I looked, I saw he still thought we'd win. He called those final pass patterns very calmly. He knew something would break. It was weird."

Chuck sent in the play, a variation on 66 Basic, called "half right, split opposite, 66 out end in," a route in which the primary receiver was sure-handed alternate Barry Pearson (playing his first game of the season, fill-ing in for the injured Frank Lewis) for enough yards for a first down.

Bradshaw faded back but was flushed out of the pocket as the pass rush came from the right. Running away from where an open Pearson was standing just beyond the first-down marker, Bradshaw found his safety valve, Fuqua, near the middle of the field and rifled the ball 20 yards downfield. Coming from behind was the Raiders' defensive enforcer Jack Tatum, who arrived at the same time the ball did, converging with Fuqua and deflecting it back toward midfield.

Chris Noll was on the sidelines, even with Fuqua. "The ball came in, he got hit," said Chris. "I remember just turning my back to the play—and then all of a sudden the noise was overwhelming. So I turned around to see Franco running into the end zone. And it was deafening; I mean it was physically painful, it was so loud. It was just unbelievable, the emotion."

Having leaked out of the backfield to give Bradshaw another option, Harris sprung into action when Tatum (or perhaps it was Fuqua) deflected Bradshaw's pass, picked it up in stride a few inches off the Tartan Turf surface, and raced untouched 50 yards for the touchdown. The city of Pittsburgh experienced that rare collective emotion of shocked jubilation.

Afterward, other Steelers recalled their coach's reservoir of calmness in those final moments. "Chuck seemed to have some confidence that it was going to get done," said John Dockery, the journeyman defensive back who had signed with the Steelers in '72. "Then I remember this mad rush to the field, and the excitement and everything else, and then was it going to stand? Was it not going to stand? Did we get the ball? Did they get the ball?"

Who touched the ball before Harris was vital. If it was Fuqua, the pass would have been ruled incomplete, owing to an archaic NFL rule forbidding two players from the same team consecutively touching a forward pass. If it was Tatum, there was no foul and the touchdown had to stand. It took more than ten minutes after the play before referee Fred Swearingen confirmed that it was a touchdown.

(The NFL remained somewhat vague on how much assistance Swearingen received on the call, but Bill Chastain's *Steel Dynasty* noted that when NFL Director of Officials Art McNally, speaking to Swearingen by phone from the press box, asked the referee his call, Swearingen said "Touchdown," and McNally replied, "Right.")

In the locker room bedlam afterward, Chuck was puckish but calm. "We're putting in the play tomorrow," he said. After speaking with the press, he returned to the locker room, walked over to Ben McGee, and said, "Ben, I'm sorry you're retiring." McGee looked up in wonder. Chuck *had* heard him in the pregame. McGee also realized that, in his coach's mind, what he had said before the game was merely a distraction until the game was over.

The win set the Steelers up for the AFC Championship Game with the Miami Dolphins, who were 15–0 and attempting to become the first NFL team of the championship era to finish a season with a perfect record. The NFL, still rotating home playoff assignments rather than seeding by regular-season record, faced much criticism for forcing the undefeated Dolphins to go on the road.

Pittsburgh was in an exalted state. A group of supporters hired a small plane to drop two thousand leaflets near the William Penn Hotel downtown, where the Dolphins were staying, with the handbills reading, "This leaflet will guarantee safe passage out of town to any member of the Miami Dolphins."

As the game neared, Bradshaw had regained some of the old hyperactive confidence. "It's been a good week for me," he said. "I got all my learning down, and I'm throwing the ball well. I've been in high spirits all week. Before San Diego and Oakland and now again, I've had this feeling. It's kind of like ESP and it's that we can't lose."

Pittsburgh went up early, when Bradshaw, racing for the end zone, fumbled after being tackled by Jake Scott, before Gerry Mullins fell on the loose ball in the end zone. In the second quarter, the score was still 7–0, and the Dolphins were lining up to punt, when the momentum swung decisively. Punter Larry Seiple spotted an opening in the Steelers' punt return alignment and ran 37 yards for a first down, keeping alive a drive that eventually tied the score.

Less a product of Shula outsmarting Noll, it was a player with the autonomy to freelance going for the big play and making it. "It was all Seiple," said Shula. "He was in there to punt and as he caught the ball and took the first step up, he noticed nobody was looking at him and then he took the next step and they were still not looking at him, so he just tucked it in and ran behind them along the sideline. I said, *You better make it.* I always said about that—he had a great life as long as he made it."

"That fake punt," said Edwards. "I'm the only one that saw it, because I was the punt returner. All of my men were coming back toward me and I'm yelling at them, 'Stay! Stay! They're running the ball!' But they tricked us pretty good."

Pittsburgh went ahead, 10–7, in the third quarter, but the Dolphins responded with a pair of touchdowns to go up 21–10. Bradshaw, injured again in the first half, came back in the second half to cut the deficit to 21–17, but that ended the scoring. The Dolphins also exposed the weaknesses in the Steelers' stack over defensive alignment, which left the relatively undersized Russell or Ham taking on a bigger guard in the Dolphins' running game.

Afterward, the Steelers, almost to a man, felt that the better team had lost.

"We made too many mistakes, or maybe we didn't make enough big plays," said Chuck.

"Walking off that field," said Ham, "I think we felt like we now understood what it was all about to win playoff games and to be in pressure situations and what it takes to be a championship football team. And even though we lost that game, I think we drew a lot from that game."

But over the course of the season, the team had gained a greater appreciation of Chuck's overarching philosophy and the method to the program he was installing. There was an accumulation of details that had begun to reach critical mass. "Defense, give up three yards or less on first down," said Joe Greene. "Wide receivers, block down the field. Offensive linemen, protect the quarterback. It was a list of things. If we do these things, we are going to win, and if we don't, we probably won't win. And he would call off these things every week in our film review. I didn't chart them, but they started to become ingrained in my head—if we do these things, we are going to win—and by 1972, it all started to make sense."

✦ ✦ ✦

A few days before the 1973 draft, Art Rooney Jr. and some of the other scouts and assistant coaches were watching film on Chuck Foreman, the University of Miami's big, deceptively fast runner.

Chuck expressed some doubts about his maneuverability, but Artie held firm on his belief that Foreman could be a successful pro.

"I don't know," said Chuck, skeptically. "But I am probably wrong about this guy, the same way I was wrong about that Penn Stater last year."

And then he walked away.

Artie smiled and looked at an assistant coach, who turned off the projector and said, "That right there? That is as close as you are ever going to get in your life to Chuck Noll saying 'I was wrong and you were right.'"

It was six weeks after the draft, mid-March 1973, and Chuck was still in his office, working with the staff on the coming season's playbook, when the call came in that Ernie Holmes was in trouble.

The 6-foot-3, 260-pounder was an expansive, conflicted man-child, alternately bubbly and turbulent. Many players had financial problems, domestic disputes, relatives asking for money. Holmes had all of these things and seemed to take them to heart, unable to compartmentalize the distractions. The deprivation he'd known as a child fueled his desire to succeed. But in the off-season he lacked an outlet.

A notoriously poor manager of money, he led all Steelers in visits to Dan Rooney's office to negotiate advances and raises. At times, Rooney sent him to accountant Dennis Thimons to advance him some cash. Other times, Rooney flashed the tough Irish exterior and told him there was nothing the Steelers could do. On one occasion that led to a furious Holmes walking out and kicking a large metal trashcan, which rattled off the walls and startled several of the women in the secretarial area.

But in this instance—stuck in traffic and unable to reach the Steelers' offices before closing on a Friday—Holmes snapped. He turned back around and headed west, shooting at trucks on the highway and, eventually, evading officers in a high-speed chase. At one point, he fired shots at a Highway Patrol police helicopter before surrendering to police in Goshen Township, Ohio. Chuck and Dan visited him that evening in jail, and later they made a case on his behalf that he needed psychiatric counseling (he was diagnosed with acute paranoid psychosis), rather than prison time.

Holmes was put in an inpatient psychiatric facility in western Pennsylvania. Back at the Steelers' offices, there was concern about whether he would be psychologically stable enough to continue his career, as well as some anxiety about whether Chuck would allow that to continue with the Steelers. "I just remember how protective Chuck was," said Marianne. "Because he knew how troubled Ernie was."

Chuck had shown less tolerance for more established players. Roy Jefferson had the capacity to be divisive, but he was never unstable. Dave

Smith was occasionally combative, but he never became unhinged. And yet Chuck chose to stand by Holmes. He saw a player whom teammates liked and respected, someone who both practiced and played with an implacable fire and, surely, a key component to an increasingly potent defensive line that would be very hard to replace.

Chuck had begun doing a television show the year before, being interviewed live by Sam Nover of WPXI Channel 11 in Pittsburgh. Chuck soon stopped doing the show, at least in part, some assistants said, because Nover pressed him on the air about Holmes' status after Chuck had said he didn't want to discuss it.

"You know, what I really respected," said John Brown, who made the trip to Youngstown to see Holmes, "is that Chuck went with and went down [there]. He was in that group that went to the jailhouse to see Ernie. Because Paul Brown would have just said, 'That's it.'"

As the complex mix of personalities on the Steelers continued to evolve, some key ones demanded more nurturing. Terry Bradshaw, in the early 1970s, was still sorting out who he was. There was a scene at the end of the Immaculate Reception game, the '72 playoff win over the Raiders, that was captured on NFL Films and remained indelibly in the memory. After the Steelers' victory, fans poured onto the field in an expression of bedlam tinged with disbelief. Bradshaw, grinning, is walking on the field and is joined by a fan who embraces him. Bradshaw hugs the fan back and starts to let go, but the fan won't let go. Bradshaw keeps smiling and hugs the fan again, hoping for release. But the fan remains glued to him, as the quarterback's smile turns to a perturbed grimace. It would be like that for Terry Bradshaw in Pittsburgh. He was bewildered by what they wanted; the fans still held him too close. He could not shake them off—nor work through his own neediness—during his time in Pittsburgh. His rough, uneven maturation would mark Chuck's tenure as well.

By the third year of Babe Parilli's time as the quarterbacks coach, cracks were starting to show in his relationship with Chuck. "Babe Parilli and Chuck Noll were oil and water," said John Dockery. "Babe was a friendly, easy-going nice guy who had a great career. Was he going to be a hard-nosed coach who was able to teach and impart information to quarterbacks in the way that Chuck would want? No, it was just a different style, and it was destined not to work."

Parilli still loved the physical aspects of football. He would demonstrate fakes to start drills two or three times, carry them out with a purposefulness that seemed to go beyond teaching. "I think he wanted to play a little more than he wanted to teach," said Hoak.

The good cop–bad cop plan was fine in theory. But Bradshaw recognized who the ultimate authority was. At times, Parilli would tell his quarterback to stand up to the head coach, "Terry, just tell him to go to hell." But Bradshaw wasn't prepared to do that. And self-conscious about his upbringing, defensive about his intelligence and ability to read defenses, he took any criticism from Chuck to heart.

"You could just see Terry's head sometimes, just shrinking down between his shoulders as Chuck was talking to him," said Mike Wagner.

"I don't think Terry's personality was ready for the amount of pressure on him to perform," said Gerry Mullins, one of Bradshaw's closest friends on the team.

One of Chuck's other methods was to stare Bradshaw straight in the face to emphasize a point, with a hand on each of Bradshaw's shoulder pads. At other times, as Bradshaw was prepared to run onto the field, Chuck would grab his jersey and tug him back to add a reminder. Bradshaw, in one of his memoirs, would recall Chuck's hands: "he always seemed to have them strategically locked onto a jersey or an arm or a face mask, just to make his point. You could feel the anger in his grip. I got to where I couldn't stand for Chuck to put his hands on me. When I was a rookie, Chuck jerked me around on the sidelines during the games. Against the Giants my second year, he grabbed me by the face mask in front of teammates, dragged me around like an animal, and screamed at me. It was humiliating." (Several other teammates, asked about the incident, didn't recall the event.)

Others viewed it differently. "I always felt that he tended to be a little bit more lenient with Terry on issues versus anybody else," said Jack Ham, "where if it was me or Andy Russell, I think it would have been cut and dry. I just think Chuck was trying to deflect a lot of that stuff away from him and maybe, in turn, don't throw all of this pressure on Terry."

In practices, when Chuck wanted precision and repetition, Bradshaw could seem flighty and inconsistent. On a simple rollout that called for a short pass to a fullback in the flat, he rocketed passes that were too hot for Rocky Bleier or Preston Pearson to handle.

"Terry, why do you do that?" Andy Russell asked one day as they were walking off the field. "Why don't you loft it a little bit and let him catch it?"

"I don't want Noll to think I'm good at those kind of passes," said Bradshaw. "I want to go deep."

Receivers would have nicks on their finger tips from the intense revolutions of Bradshaw's passes. "We used to call them cancer shots," said Chuck, "bruises on your chest because they couldn't catch it with their hands so they had to catch it with their chest and it would leave them black and blue."

Bradshaw knew Chuck wanted him to study, so he'd ask for reels of game film and bring them home with him. The reels often remained in Bradshaw's trunk, unwatched. At home, Bradshaw's first marriage was dissolving. On the field, his confidence was shot. Publicly, he remained devoted to his coach. "He's so gawl-dang smart he'll make a believer out of you," Bradshaw told Skip Myslenski of the *Philadelphia Inquirer* in 1973. "He teaches and teaches and teaches so much, when you go to bed you feel, *oh-oh, I don't want to go to sleep. I want to get better.* I tell you, I don't want to play for anyone else. That's how much I respect him. I think I have a great future and I want to end it right here."

Privately, he often seemed demoralized and petulant over the lack of praise for which he clearly thirsted. "Terry needs reinforcement," said Mike Wagner, who'd roomed with Bradshaw in 1971. "He is insecure or he wasn't tough and was being piled on by the media, by the fans, and Terry doesn't take to criticism well, okay? Terry needs you to say, 'Don't worry about it, you're the best. We'll get it next time.' And whether Chuck was frustrated with him, or whatever the reason—he talked to Joe gently and stuff like that. But not with Terry."

Greene, as pivotal a player on the defense as Bradshaw was on the offense, had matured more quickly than Bradshaw and had become one of the most formidable players in the game by 1972.

"He put up with Joe Greene's sometimes childish reactions to things," said Andy Russell. "And it was clear to all of us that that was a smart thing to do. Joe Greene was probably the most significant player of the decade."

Greene was, in English soccer parlance, "unplayable," a force that other teams couldn't reckon with by any conventional means. His first move at the snap of the ball was the quickest in football, and his ability to knife through the gaps in the line and control the line of scrimmage was already legendary. So was his temper. On at least three occasions in his first three seasons—at Minnesota in '69, Philadelphia in '70, and Chicago in '71—he'd become so apoplectic that Chuck was concerned for his well-being.

"Chuck was carrot-and-stick with most players," said Wagner. "It was all carrot with Joe."

Still obsessively competitive and filled with rage when the team lost, he had become the team's leader.

"Joe was the boss in the locker room," said trainer Ralph Berlin. "If there was a problem, Joe took care of it."

The most surprising new face in camp at 1973 belonged to the gifted *Sports Illustrated* writer Roy Blount Jr., who had been granted permission to spend the season with the team, with full access to locker rooms, practices, and team trips.

"Chuck was against it; there was no question about it," said Dan Rooney. "And I said that it will be all right. We won't let him do certain things. He was not allowed in meetings." Blount wasn't merely a good sportswriter; he was an acutely observant, empathic soul, raised in Decatur, Georgia, who'd selected the Steelers because he liked Pittsburgh and felt the Steelers' team chemistry was somewhat reminiscent of baseball's '71 world champion Pittsburgh Pirates. In the heady stew of the locker room, and the cacophonous mixture of personalities, races, and styles, Blount felt at home.

Chuck had opposed the idea from the beginning. He made a case to the Rooneys that any shred of information within the team's brain trust—the Steelers' scouting philosophy, how Chuck talked about opponents, the techniques they used in their trapping game—could be used by someone else to beat the team later. But the Chief and Dan wanted it; after so long spent as the butt of jokes, they valued the national attention and respect. So they agreed to Chuck's one stipulation, that Blount not be allowed to sit in on team meetings. Having been granted that, Chuck treated Blount's presence as he would any other distraction, which meant he ignored it.

"I never heard Chuck say anything about it," said John Dockery. "We knew he was around. Blount was invisible to Chuck. Chuck was not going to say anything that he could use."

It wasn't merely with the players that Chuck didn't speak about Blount. "It was completely avoided," said Woody Widenhofer. "He never even talked about. It was never brought up at a meeting. It was like it never happened."

Some other writers might have been abashed by the strong personalities; Blount gamely worked his way in, glomming on to Ray Mansfield from the early days of training camp. "God, he went *everywhere*," said Jack Ham. "He went to every saloon in Greensburg with Ray. I thought they were joined at the hip."

For Blount, who naturally gravitated to the players, Chuck was a source of bland authority. In the book he compared the colorful players to the buttoned-down Chuck thusly: "Being around the day's previous people and then bumping into Noll was like poking around in a woods full of interesting new trees, bushes, creatures, shadows, and noises and then bumping into one of those modern aluminum light poles you see along the Interstate. Noll had every right to be a pole; it was *interesting* to encounter a pole in the middle of the woods. But it was unsettling."

During the writing of the book, Blount developed a distant respect for Noll. "He was not forthcoming," Blount said. "But that was okay with me. There were plenty of other forthcoming people around so that was my main interest. I found out early on that he had epilepsy, and I was trying to think about how to bring that up to him, when a friend—I have forgotten who it was—said that her ex-husband was epileptic, and was so ashamed of it that he never wanted anybody to know about it, and that he was afraid he wouldn't get a driver's license if it became known. And I thought, 'I don't want to put Noll in that position.' I thought about going to him and saying, 'Listen, if you don't want me to write about it, I won't write about it, but I thought you might want to make some kind of statement about it for other people who suffer from it,' but I heard myself saying that to Noll and I just didn't want to do it. I didn't want him to think I was holding it over his head. And I didn't want to *say*, 'I'm not holding it over your head.' You know what I mean? Because he was allowing me all of the access I needed and he wasn't the kind of person you wanted to disconcert. I mean, I *liked* the fact that he was sort of impermeable or something, the fact that he was opaque."

✦   ✦   ✦

The season began with talk of the Steelers as a Super Bowl contender. The mind-set going into the season was that the Steelers had arrived. "We're a team of confidence," said Joe Greene. "From a team which figured it was futile to a team of confidence."

Bradshaw was even bolder. "Shoot, I don't care what other people say, I think I read defenses as well as anybody," he said. "I may be bragging, but I'm not going to take a back seat to anyone. I've been around, this is my fourth year now, and I know there's a key to give away every defense. And I think I can read them. Shoot, I'm going to start exhuberating [*sic*] some confidence in myself."

The season began with four straight wins; while that matched the franchise's best start ever, Chuck was unconvinced. The running game was not in synch, and Bradshaw, again, seemed to take a step back. A 19–7 loss to Paul Brown and the Bengals broke the winning streak. After a win over the Jets, they had a rematch against Cincinnati at Three Rivers.

Throwing against the Bengals, Bradshaw was hit by Steve Chomyszak, and he walked off the field, hunched over, his left hand over his right collarbone, wincing in pain. His teammates, who'd seen Bradshaw gesticulate over many hits, knew this one was bad. And in this acrid atmosphere, a cheer went up in the crowd. When the Three Rivers scoreboard flashed the update, "Terry Bradshaw has a broken right collarbone," there was more scattered applause. (The injury was later diagnosed as a shoulder separation.) Hanratty came in and took over, and the Steelers prevailed. But the cheering by Steelers fans over Bradshaw's injury was objectionable to many of the players. "That was vicious," said Greene after the game. "They don't know what it's like to bust your ass out there and take all that, and then hear people cheering when a guy has been hurt."

Over the next month, the Steelers survived without Bradshaw, though Hanratty himself got knocked out of two of the games, the second with a sprained wrist. That left the third-stringer Joe Gilliam as the starter for another Monday night game, this time a rematch of the '72 AFC Championship Game, with the Steelers visiting Miami.

But the Dolphins, coming off their perfect season, jumped out to a 30–3 lead at halftime, their defense having harried the callow Gilliam into 0 for 7 passing and three interceptions. At halftime, Bradshaw insisted to Chuck that he could go in. He did throw two touchdown passes, but it was Carson's splenetic rage at halftime that roused the Steelers' defense, which shut out Miami in the second half, ultimately losing 30–26.

"It took getting the shit kicked out of us to wake us up," said Greene after the game.

There was a sense by then that none of the quarterbacks were giving Chuck what he wanted. Hanratty, arm ravaged by injuries, couldn't throw with Bradshaw and Gilliam, but he was well-liked by teammates. Bradshaw, who had been through the wringer, was convinced that Chuck took pains to single him out for abuse and was just as convinced that Chuck was soft on Gilliam.

The dynamic in the quarterback meetings was complex. Gilliam, eager, avid, the coach's son better able to read defenses; Hanratty, with the Yosemite Sam mustache and his sardonic sense of humor; Bradshaw, always chewing Red Man, spitting into a cup or can, trying to calm himself and focus. Hanratty used to delight in needling Chuck about Cleveland. One day, watching film of the Browns' defense, Hanratty intoned, at the beginning of the film, "Another beautiful day in Cleveland."

"The weather's no better in Butler," Chuck replied.

"It was funny watching the three quarterbacks come out of the quarterback meetings," said Tom Keating. "Bradshaw looked whipped, Gilliam would look mad, and Hanratty would just be smiling and shaking his head. I'd come from Oakland, and when John Madden would yell at Lamonica or Blanda, they'd yell right back. But with Noll—never."

The Steelers rolled to easy wins in their last two regular-season games, but they lost the divisional tiebreaker to Cincinnati, winding up as a wild-card playoff qualifier, necessitating a trip to Oakland. They spent the week in Palm Springs, acclimating to the weather. Counting 1972's playoff win, they'd beaten the Raiders three straight times. Blount described them as keyed up heading into the game, and he recounted Bradshaw putting an arm around the writer's shoulder and singing the opening lines of the Buck Owens's hit "Hello Trouble" while taking the field. Oakland dominated, 33–14; Bradshaw threw three interceptions and left the game without talking to the press, returning home to Louisiana. Within months, his marriage had dissolved.

Throughout the team, there was a sense that the Steelers were good, but something was missing. Greene was ruminative following the playoff loss. "We're one of the best teams in the country with one of the best coaching staffs," he said. "But something was missing. We didn't have that kind of frenzy that Miami put on us [earlier in the regular season]. That's the way Pittsburgh plays football. . . . But today, that special ingredient was missing."

Some players would blame Bradshaw and his inability to maintain the best of his '72 form (he'd again completed less than half his passes and threw ten touchdowns to fifteen interceptions). But the real problem was in the running game. The Steelers, as a team, had averaged more than 5 yards per attempt in 1972. Now, with the injuries to Harris, the team averaged less than 4 yards per carry in 1973.

"We're too good a team to be losing," said Chuck to his players in the locker room at the Oakland Alameda County Coliseum after the game. "We're going to take a long concentrated look at the season. We're going to find out where the mistakes came and why. All I can say is Merry Christmas. Merry Christmas."

thirteen

WHATEVER IT TAKES

✦ ✦ ✦

As they prepared for the 1974 draft in late January, Chuck and Art Rooney Jr. had been working together—sometimes testily—for five years. Chuck valued Artie's input, but they were not temperamentally suited to one another. Artie was intimidated by Chuck's demeanor and was also insecure and defensive, eager to prove to any doubters that he deserved the job he'd been given. Chuck was not going to provide Artie with the reassurance he wanted.

So they argued, and Artie sometimes became peevish; he felt that he should have more influence, perhaps even the final word, on the draft decisions for which he would ultimately take responsibility. On his better days, Chuck accepted the oppositional nature of the relationship. "The upper molars and lower molars grinding together makes the teeth stronger," he once explained to Artie. "That's what we do."

But other times, the men could make each other furious. The first draft meeting after the 1973 playoff loss to Oakland began with a rhetorical slap. "I never thought I'd see a team of yours embarrassed like that," Artie told Chuck as they sat down. Chuck remained stolid, focused, but his assistants could tell he was incensed.

For a team that had been to the playoffs for two straight years, the Steelers still had holes to fill. Center Ray Mansfield was aging, as was middle linebacker Henry Davis. While Ron Shanklin and Frank Lewis were good receivers, neither was a game breaker.

There were two wide receivers in the draft that both Chuck and the scouting department particularly admired. One was Lynn Swann, a key part of USC's 1972 national champions, and a consensus All-American in 1973. Handsome, witty, a peacock with a gliding stride and a tough demeanor, he was generally regarded as the best receiver in the draft. But Chuck had become enamored of a lesser-known player, a strong, supple, 6-foot-4 receiver from Alabama A&M named John Stallworth. Stallworth's 40-yard dash time was worryingly slow, but Bill Nunn emphasized that the times run by Stallworth, in inferior equipment, on the rougher surface and longer grass of the Alabama A&M field, would not directly compare with the times posted by other receivers on the manicured lawns of major universities.

Nunn had gotten a reel of Stallworth's game film, the only one in the country, and Chuck had asked to watch it on numerous occasions. Nunn dawdled about returning the film to A&M in the weeks leading up to the draft.

With the twenty-first pick in the first round, the Steelers waited while several teams that might have taken wide receivers went for running backs or linebackers instead. It was common knowledge in personnel circles that the Cowboys, drafting right behind Pittsburgh at number 22, saw Swann as the best available player on the board. When the Steelers' turn came, Chuck wavered; he preferred Stallworth, but both Rooney and Dick Haley argued he would be available later. Swann had to be taken right away.

Chuck was churlish about it, predicting that Stallworth wouldn't be available in the fourth round (they had other positional needs in the second round, and had traded away their third-round pick to Oakland). But he agreed to select Swann.

In so doing, Chuck once again had acceded to the wishes of his scouting staff. The decision remained ultimately Chuck's, and yet in this situation—as with the choice of Harris in the '72 draft—he responded to the impassioned plea of his scouts. While the end result was usually in the best interests of the team, it could leave both Chuck and Artie feeling aggrieved.

"Chuck was pissed," said Artie. "He was *really* pissed."

In the second round, there was another close call between two linebackers, Iowa State's Matt Blair, a 6-foot-5, 230-pound prototype linebacker and the worryingly slender Jack Lambert, from Kent State, who had impressed Artie and linebackers coach Woody Widenhofer with his unstinting drive. During the time allotted to make the selection, both the staff and the scouting department weighed in on the relative merits of the two players.

With less than a minute left to decide, Chuck turned to second-year linebackers coach Widenhofer. "Woody, how do you feel about this?," he asked.

"I want Lambert."

"Lambert it is."

Then the Steelers waited, through the rest of the second round, and all of the third, in hopes that Stallworth would last until the fourth round. Pittsburgh had the Chicago Bears' pick, the fourth pick in the fourth round. The San Diego Chargers, drafting directly in front of them, were also looking at a receiver.

The entire room sat in a hush until the Chargers' pick was announced. They had gone for a receiver—but it was Harrison Davis out of Virginia. With that, Chuck's face opened into a broad grin, and the Steelers chose Stallworth. Later, with their own pick in the fourth round, they selected the squat, slightly undersized Wisconsin center Mike Webster, who had impressed both scouts and coaches alike with his bulldog tenacity. By the time the draft ended the next day, Nunn was already on the road, signing a free agent defensive back named Donnie Shell from South Carolina State.

Before the staff was done with the second day of the draft, Lambert had phoned Woody Widenhofer.

"Coach, I'm taking some time off from school," he said. "I want to be able to come down there and learn all of those defenses before we come in during the spring."

Widenhofer—hoping for some time off after the grind of his first pro season and the overtime of draft preparation—asked Lambert when he wanted to come in, and Lambert told him he could come three days a week starting immediately. Rangy and lithe, Lambert also exhibited a distinctive playing style; his lateral movement was exceptional, and his missing front teeth gave him a look of menace. Artie's scouting report had noted that Lambert needed to gain weight, but his statement of intent served notice to the staff that he was a serious football player.

Chuck and his assistants didn't, and couldn't, have known it as they were leaving Three Rivers following that 1974 draft. But finally, after five seasons, the pieces were in place.

✦ ✦ ✦

As the new season approached, the industry that gave the Steelers their nickname was falling into seriously troubled times. Steel had been in heavy demand during the Second World War and the generation of widespread growth and expansion that followed it. But by the time of the 1973 oil crisis, with other nations developing the means of production, there were widespread layoffs, and many other mills were simply shutting down. The changes had come quickly and without prior warning. U.S. Steel had opened a new skyscraper, the sixty-four-story U.S. Steel Tower, in 1970. But after a generation of postwar boom, the American economy contracted. In 1974 alone, wages fell by 2.1 percent, and income shrunk by $1,500. Manufacturing jobs, which accounted for more than 30 percent of the American workforce in the years after the Second World War, would drop to 20 percent by the end of the seventies. And among all sectors of American society, the steel industry felt the contractions most acutely. Building was down, and union membership began to fall.

Generations of families that had grown up in and around the steel industry were finding their livelihoods suddenly extinguished. The industry was down to 521,000 jobs in 1974 (and would continue to contract dramatically in the coming years, falling to 204,000 jobs by 1990). The decline would hit even harder in Pittsburgh. U.S. Steel's massive Homestead Works, which employed 15,000 workers during the Second World War, closed down forty years later. In the 1970s, one out of ten workers in Pittsburgh were employed in the steel industry. As that industry deteriorated, it played on the insecurity of the populace.

"People—including a good many in Pittsburgh—tend to look upon Pittsburgh as a Loser town," wrote Blount. "Perhaps it is the 'Pitts' in the name, suggesting depression. Perhaps it is the immigrant millworker image of the population. Perhaps it is the fact that Pittsburgh has never been westerly enough to imply sophisticates, or middle enough to imply stolid prosperity."

In the face of all that, there was the emergence of the Steelers, a long-time staple of the city, now newly robust and potent. The city had fallen in love with its football team. Steeler Fever was rampant, but it went beyond an identification with the team or even the four stalwarts on the defensive line, dubbed "The Steel Curtain." Almost every player of consequence had developed his own rabid band of followers. Ham's fans were the members of Dobre Shunka (Polish for "good ham"); placekicker Roy Gerela inspired a group of Ukrainians who called themselves Gerela's Gorillas. In 1972, there was Franco's Italian Army, in honor of the mixed heritage of the rookie star (Frank Sinatra even posed for a picture during the '72 playoff run). Then came Preston's Soul Patrol (Pearson), Wagner's Wild Bunch (Wagner), Bruce's Mooses (for Bruce "Moose" Van Dyke), Frenchy's Friends (Fuqua), and Rocky's Flying Squirrels (Bleier). Yet the one player whom the city hadn't quite fully embraced was Bradshaw. It may have been in part because, while most of the team's stars had moved to Pittsburgh, Bradshaw got out of town almost the moment each season was over.

So the city suffered, families split apart, factories closed down. Through it all, the bond between the people of Pittsburgh and the Steelers grew even stronger. The team was providing something that it hadn't before: hope, at a time when that was a rare and precious commodity in the region.

✦   ✦   ✦

By 1974, Chuck's hair was worn longer, a relaxed departure from his well-trimmed crew cuts and flattops of the '50s and the Brylcreemed, close-cropped haircuts of the '60s. He'd even allowed his sideburns to grow a bit, down to even with the top of his earlobe. There were emerging flecks of gray developing, but he had grown distinguished looking in his forties, only the single mole on his right cheek blemishing his frequent expression of quiet self-assuredness. The stylistic flourishes of coat and tie on the sidelines had been abandoned after 1971, in favor of athletic shirts and coaches' double-knit slacks. He frequently wore a windbreaker on the sidelines, even on cold days.

The mantra that he repeated most often was "Whatever it takes." It was declarative and definitive. In Chuck's version, it meant something far different than when the Raiders' Al Davis used the same phrase. There were lines Chuck wouldn't cross, and his use of the phrase was a subtle indication that he wouldn't even *think* about crossing them. But it was meant as a counter thrust to excuses, injuries, distractions, internal debate. What do you do when your quarterback goes down? When the veterans are on strike? When the media is on your back.

Whatever it takes.

"We heard that so often we always said he had it embroidered on his shorts," said Ray Mansfield.

They would hear it a lot in 1974.

The 1973 season had brought an end to the ongoing tension between Chuck and two of his assistants, Babe Parilli and Bob Fry. The latter was a football lifer, who'd played in the NFL and was the only coach on Chuck's staff who'd had previous pro coaching experience. "He was sort of laid-back and disorganized," said John Brown. "I wondered why Chuck hired him."

The NFL rulebook in 1974 still prohibited offensive lineman from using their hands to ward off defenders. In keeping with that, Fry taught many of the old methods, instructing his linemen to keep their hands at the center of their chest. But Chuck was sharply attuned to the way the rules were evolving. More linemen were using their open hands to ward off the blows of the defender. That was the style Chuck wanted taught, and he and Fry would regularly argue about the fine points of blocking technique.

After Fry's exit, Chuck rehired Dan Radakovich, who'd left after 1971 to be the defensive coordinator at Colorado. Radakovich returned as offensive line coach with an explicit mission, from Chuck, to be more aggressive than Fry and teach everything within (and perhaps on the edge of) the letter of the league rules.

"Elvin Bethea of Houston, he used to take a couple of knee pads, and he had this big thing taped to his hands, and he would bring that head slap and *Boom!*," said Jon Kolb. "So if you're keeping your hands in, you had no chance. So the thing we learned was that if I see that coming, I can hit you in the chin underneath your headgear and pop your neck back.

Before you can do *this*, I can do *that*. And so Rad brought at that time radical offense, that punch thing. And a lot of that was when to pull the trigger. We just did so many reps. I can't pull the trigger on you now because you are too far, and if I wait 'till you get up to me, then you're too close."

The coaching staff had developed into a blend of complementary styles. On offense, Radakovich's eccentric exhortations and Lionel Taylor's loud protestations were countered by the circumspect, low-key toughness of Chuck and running backs coach Dick Hoak. On defense, the often wild gesticulations and jocular nature of George Perles and Woody Widenhofer were tempered by the more subdued (though no less intense) Carson.

Perles's weekly review of the defensive line, with grades, was one of the focal points of the week for Greene, Greenwood, Holmes, and White. "Plusses and minuses," said Greene. "And, oh gee, 'loaf.' Loaf was a big one. He would say, 'Number 78, loaf!' Dwight would get so pissed. 'Number 75, loaf!' The way he would call the grade out. And you were sitting there looking at it on paper."

While the Major League Baseball Players Association was fighting for free agency, the National Football League Players Association (NFLPA) was still trying to bargain for equitable pay for preseason games and some measure of guarantees on player contracts. As a former player, Chuck sympathized with players on some of these issues, but he was deeply distrustful of NFLPA leader Ed Garvey and the threatened '74 strike. An earlier player walkout, in 1970, had fizzled after a couple of days. But in 1974, the players were more unified, and training camp opened with many of the Steelers veterans picketing the main entrance to St. Vincent.

Preston Pearson, who'd been elected player rep, had called Chuck in July and asked if he could stop by and meet with him before training camp. The pair already had a tense relationship—Pearson felt Chuck didn't give him enough playing time—and nothing that happened during the meeting would bridge that gap.

When Pearson entered his office and sat down, Chuck's opening salvo was, "What are you doing with my football team?"

Pearson argued that he was doing everything he could to keep the team together, and that it was in the best interests of both men if the Steelers remain unified. But there was a complex series of forces pulling the team in different directions. The strike, officially declared July 1, was hard to ignore in a strong union town like Pittsburgh. On the other hand, many Steelers felt close to the paternal Art Rooney Sr. and the rest of the Rooney family.

The rookies reported on July 15, crossing picket lines. Two days later, on the morning that the veterans were to report, someone asked Chuck if he wished they would ignore the strike and cross the picket line. "That's like asking if you'd rather die by machine gun or fire," he said. "I just want this thing to get over with and see everyone in camp."

Some players broke with the union stance. Joe Gilliam, still the third quarterback on the depth chart, crossed the picket lines in the first week of camp. NFL roster limits being what they were, he felt expendable and wanted to make his best case for his position on the roster. Perhaps it was because of the experience he'd gained the previous season, perhaps it was because there were few veterans around. But the occasional uncertainty and inconsistency that Gilliam had displayed the previous season had vanished; he possessed a slangy authority and exhibited a complete mastery of the playbook. Without Parilli as a buffer, Gilliam could more closely interact with Chuck. And Chuck liked the young quarterback's mixture of confidence and deference. As the son of a coach, he understood and was comfortable with the teacher-student relationship—one that Bradshaw, with his history of adoration and his own insecurity, had trouble with.

As a rule, Gilliam was not lacking in self-assurance. But his excellent training camp gave him even more. Gilliam would joke with the rookies Swann and Stallworth when working on the particulars of delivering the ball on the break of pass routes: "How you want it there—laces up or laces down?" He had the ball boys—Chris Noll and Bill Nunn Jr.— running out patterns and could hit them in stride, throwing the ball 30 and 40 yards in the air *behind his back.*

The strike wasn't called off until August 11, though several Steelers veterans had reported before then. Through training camp, as Gilliam, the 273rd player taken in the 1972 draft, was clearly outplaying Bradshaw, the first player selected in the 1970 draft, there was a growing sense of excitement around the team that Gilliam was making a strong case to be named the Steelers' starting quarterback.

Chuck didn't blink, announcing the week before the season that Gilliam had locked down the starting job.

Bradshaw, hurt, petulant, and angry over the decision—though he couldn't argue with the consensus that Gilliam had looked the better, more effective, more confident quarterback in preseason—asked to be traded.

Chuck was calm but firm.

"You're going to be a great quarterback someday," he said. "It takes time."

The decision reverberated. "The black guys were elated," said J. T. Thomas. "That was a year that there was a lot of racial tension in the city here. The world is going upside down. So you look at that role again: The head coach and the quarterback have a father-son relationship. Suddenly, you know—Chuck Noll got a black child."

✦ ✦ ✦

The season opened with Gilliam looking sharp, dominating the Colts in a 30–0 win. Hanratty was tabbed for mop-up duty, over the sullen, disconsolate Bradshaw. Gilliam completed 17 of 31 passes for 257 yards and two touchdowns, throwing to a cast of receivers—Shanklin and Lewis in the first and third quarters, the rookies Swann and Stallworth in the second and fourth. The performance—and the milestone of a black quarterback starting for a playoff contender—landed Gilliam on the cover of *Sports Illustrated*, under the headline "Pittsburgh's Black Quarterback."

A week later, against Denver, Gilliam was in his element, throwing for 358 yards and rallying the Steelers from a 21–7 first-half deficit. But leading 35–28 with about eight minutes to play, and driving down near the Broncos' goal line, he threw a costly interception, and Denver tied it at the end of regulation. In the first year of sudden-death overtime for regular-season games, the two teams played fifteen more minutes without scoring and the game finished at 35–35.

But Gilliam was dealing. The confidence was noticed by opponents and teammates alike.

The Steelers occasionally felt as though they were participating in Gilliam's own stream-of-consciousness monologue. "Rock steady" was his mantra, an incantation spoken both in preparation, before kneeling in the huddle, and exclamation, as after a completed pass. The phrase was in the air—Aretha Franklin had enjoyed a hit single by that name, and it had later been co-opted by the basketball star and style maven Walt Frazier as the title of his book *Rockin' Steady: A Guide to Basketball and Cool*. In Gilliam's lexicon, the expression connoted not only the experience of "being in the zone" in athletics but also achieving that state with an accompanying sense of style.

As he was approaching the line of scrimmage before a play, Gilliam might see a player on the opposing team whom he'd played against in college and say, "I see you—you know what happened at Grambling."

"Most quarterbacks are very studious, looking around, analyzing," said J. T. Thomas. "Joe'd walk up there like one leg longer than the other, he's got his pimp walk on, he's cool. Looking around, talking smack, making audibles. Dwight White would say, 'That sucker is bad!' And Chuck was wondering what in the hell is Joe talking to. 'Why is he talking to those people?'"

But the offense was completely flummoxed the next week, in a 17–0 loss to Oakland. Pittsburgh then won three straight games, a tense win at Houston, a shootout win over an aging Kansas City team, and a 20–16 home win over Cleveland in which the defense forced three turnovers.

On defense, Carson found that Lambert—who'd been named the starter at middle linebacker when Henry Davis was injured in the pre-season—was the perfect complement to the Steel Curtain up front. Though he remained inordinately light for his position, the presence of the formidable line in front of him meant that he had to shed fewer blockers than most middle linebackers.

But the larger change that had been implemented in 1972 and was still being perfected in 1974 was Carson's insistence that "we will always be in the right defense." Other teams lined up in specific defenses, but when presented with pre-snap shifts and men in motion, would default into a more standard vanilla or "safety" zones.

"Most teams, if they see something they didn't expect, they'd just shift out of it," said Rocky Bleier. "But Bud goes, 'Well, fuck no; if we got a man defense, we are not going to a safety.' We will adapt and make sure the best defense is on the field.' So *that* means you now have to study."

All through '72 and much of '73, the Steelers' defensive meetings often ended with players looking overwhelmed. But by 1974, with the Carson system heading into its third year, they were ready to assert themselves.

Yet even as the Steelers were getting off to a successful 4–1–1 start, there were inklings that something was amiss. By the time of the win over Cleveland, Gilliam had lost some of his swagger, completing just 5 of 18 passes for 78 yards.

He had been late for meetings, and more than one, during the previous weeks. Chuck's players were rarely late, and the quarterbacks virtually never were. His teammates noticed.

"It wasn't until the season started that I started to see some of Joe's habits," said John Stallworth, the rookie wide receiver who'd been Gilliam's favorite target in the preseason. "Not that I was around him a whole lot, but enough to see that some of that was going on, and I honestly did not know what my place was in that. What should I be doing? I know that is not something that I personally wanted to be involved with, but as a player should I be doing something other than acknowledging that is not something I want to do?"

"So the stories were, people would find him in the Hill District, you know?," said Bleier. "I mean, kids knew. They would see him up in the Hill District, and they knew he was buying coke as a football player. And the players knew that Joe was taking drugs. Even during that period of time when he was starting, he would come in feeling *real* good. You know, not crazy—but just feeling good, high. Not necessarily high off the charts, but . . . pumped up."

With the Steelers standing at 4–1–1, Chuck began polling his assistants. Radakovich was strongly in favor of elevating Bradshaw to starter. Lionel Taylor preferred Gilliam for another start, for at least a quarter. On October 28, Chuck announced that Bradshaw would start. The reaction was mixed—some teammates were still loyal to Gilliam—but there was never any dissension around it.

"I don't think any of us thought it was a racial thing," said John Stallworth. "And I think it was because we knew Joe's habits, but I think partly because we knew Chuck. I mean, I think it was a big move to even start Joe in the beginning, to put him in there."

With Bradshaw, Pittsburgh beat Atlanta, 24–17. Another change in that game was also significant. After rotating five running backs for much of the season, Chuck put Harris and Bleier in the same backfield for the first time, and Pittsburgh ran for 235 yards on the Falcons.

Afterward, Chuck was typically oblique about the reasons he'd benched Gilliam for Bradshaw. "It was based on the facts," he said. "I don't always disclose those facts."

A week later, Pittsburgh beat Philadelphia, but then Bradshaw looked mostly awful in a 17–10 loss to Cincinnati, completing 13 of 35 passes for 140 yards and an interception. It was always painful for Chuck to lose to Paul Brown, but it was particularly galling when Brown's quarterback, Ken Anderson, went 20 for 22. Bradshaw seemed flummoxed after the game. "We'd have a receiver open and I'd miss him bad," said Bradshaw. "That frustrates me. It has to."

Amid speculation over who would start in the wake of another poor Bradshaw performance—Cleveland coach Nick Skorich said his team was preparing for both Bradshaw and Gilliam—Chuck instead tabbed Hanratty, the one quarterback who stayed out for the entire strike during the preseason. It was, at first, a popular choice in Pittsburgh. That week, 120,000 coal workers went on strike across the country, and U.S. Steel laid off 13,700 workers, nearly 3,000 of whom lived in the Pittsburgh area.

It was a daring ploy on Chuck's part but also a severe miscalculation. The game itself was an agonizing exercise in ineptitude, with the Steelers' offense turning the ball over six times. Hanratty went 2 of 15 for just 63 yards and three interceptions. Gilliam, brought in in the second half, completed just 1 of 4 passes.

But Cleveland was worse. The Steelers' defense intercepted three passes and recovered four fumbles, one claimed by J. T. Thomas, who raced 14 yards with the go-ahead touchdown in a 26–16 win.

Pittsburgh was 7–2–1, but its quarterback situation was a shambles. The *Pittsburgh Post-Gazette* began a readers' poll that week, asking readers to rate their favorite Steelers' quarterback. (The three quarterbacks, in turn, took out a small ad in the *Post-Gazette* asking readers to rate their favorite *Post-Gazette* sportswriter.)

Chuck refused to divulge what he'd decided to do, but another important vote came in that week. Joe Greene weighed in, to both Chuck and Dan Rooney, that he "liked Bradshaw and favored Bradshaw."

With the team's leader having made his wishes clear, Chuck's decision making was further simplified. Hanratty's arm was shot, and his spells in the lineup were ineffective. Gilliam had been erratic in games, often late to team meetings, and there were ominous rumors swirling around his off-field activities.

"If we are going to the Super Bowl," Chuck concluded, "it is going to be Bradshaw to take us." Later that day, he spoke to Bradshaw, and told him he'd start for the rest of the season.

To the press, Chuck continued to be maddeningly oblique. "I've made up my mind," he said, though he declined to share his conclusions. "Have

I told them who's starting? Well, yes and no." He said he'd told one player the news, but he declined to elaborate on the rest.

On *Monday Night Football*, in New Orleans, Bradshaw was unexceptional—8 of 18 passing for just 80 yards and two interceptions—but he also threw two touchdown passes and ran for 99 yards, as the Steelers rolled, 28–7.

While the quarterback situation was seemingly settled, things would get worse before they got better. On December 1, the Steelers played host to the Houston Oilers, coached by Sid Gillman. The Oilers' stout 3–4 defense, anchored by All-Pro Curley Culp, gave Pittsburgh fits. Bradshaw was again mostly awful—completing 6 of 20 passes for 60 yards and throwing an interception, before being knocked out of the game in the third quarter with bruised ribs. Hanratty came in and was even worse, going 0 for 5. After Skip Butler's field goal put the Oilers ahead, 13–10, with 2:32 left, Houston intercepted Hanratty twice before running out the clock. "They beat the hell out of our offense," said Chuck after the game.

Dan Radakovich recalled "the defense was about ready to take all three quarterbacks on a long, long ride like the Mafia was known to do."

No one was more frustrated than the immensely prideful Greene. The next night, the two-time defending world champion Dolphins trounced the Cincinnati Bengals on *Monday Night Football*. Greene, sitting at home with Agnes, grew increasingly irate while watching the game, seeing the Dolphins' offense gain yardage with brutal efficiency, and the defense—not as talented as the Steelers but every bit as disciplined—rendering helpless Cincinnati's short passing game.

The frustration had been building in Greene all season, and after the meeting with Bud Carson and George Perles the next morning, it crested. Greene grabbed his things from his locker and walked out to his car. "I could have mumbled something," he said. "I just wasn't one to hide my emotions very well. If I didn't say anything, I might have voiced it really well in my body language."

Word traveled fast among the coaching staff.

"The first thing I thought," said Lionel Taylor, "was, Oh shit!—if Joe walks out, we are *all* fired. That is for damn sure, because that is our ballplayer."

Taylor hurried out to the car and sat with Greene for a while, patiently discussing his frustration and his options. "I couldn't tell him not to go home," said Taylor. Eventually, Greene relented and returned. "I was really, really happy that Lionel came out to the car," he said.

"He said, 'I'm going home and I'm not coming back,'" said Andy Russell. "And we had to convince him. We've got another game next week. But he was so upset with our offense. My point was, Coach Noll really handled him differently than he would have handled, I think, almost anybody else on that team."

The crucial moment often seems obvious only in retrospect. But that moment would remain fixed in the mind of many Steelers. "I remember Joe went to tripping," said Glen Edwards. "But we got it together after that. See, Joe was the spokesman. I don't know who made him the spokesman, but he was the spokesman. Any problem that occurred, Joe would go in and address it and stuff."

The stuff had been addressed—and as all this was happening, Blount's superb book, *About Three Bricks Shy of a Load*, was published to rapturous reviews. Chuck didn't read it, though Marianne, of course, did.

The next week, the Steelers faced the New England Patriots. After falling behind 7–0, Bradshaw steadied himself and completed 10 of 16 passes (though for just 86 yards) in a 21–17 win. True to his word, Chuck stuck with him. The following week, at Three Rivers, in front of a crowd of just 42,878, the Steelers dominated Cincinnati, and Bradshaw had one of his best statistical days of the year, completing 8 of 13 passes for 132 yards and two touchdowns. Pittsburgh wound up 10–3–1 on the year, and clinched its third straight playoff trip, this time as Central Division champions. They were not viewed as a popular favorite going into the postseason—in *Sports Illustrated,* Dan Jenkins joked that the Steelers were "the only team to reach the playoffs without a quarterback."

But something had come together during the season. Some would feel that the team had finally internalized Chuck's messages. Others would cite subtler nuances. Bleier remembered the point that Chuck had made after the win over the Chiefs. In the team meeting, Chuck had told the team that Kansas City lost to Pittsburgh largely because the Chiefs' perennial All-Pro tackle Ed Budde had slipped in his technique, cheating back in the second and third quarters to prepare for the rush.

Chuck spent some time zeroing in on the deficiency. "When you practice against Buck Buchanan every day, it's easy to tell yourself, 'I'll let you go through. It's not gonna happen in the game, but I will let you go through.'"

"For me, that was my buy-in," said Bleier. "I go, 'Oh, *fuck.*' If he can take this, everything we did and everything we accomplished and boil it down to the lack of preparation or lack of habits by one good player in one position, and the reasons why, because you didn't do things in practice that you need to do consistently, I'm going, 'Ugh—he knows his stuff.'"

Realizing how erratic the quarterbacks could be, and recognizing that the strength of the team was in the running game, Chuck leaned heavily on the offensive line and the new backfield pairing of Harris and Bleier. The staple for short-yardage was a play called "15 Lead C," which found the center blocking back on the opposing tackle, while the guard next to him folded behind and into the vacated space to pick up the middle linebacker. Pittsburgh would run it, again and again and again, in the weeks ahead.

The playoffs began in Pittsburgh on Sunday, December 23, 1974, when the Steelers played host to O. J. Simpson and the Buffalo Bills. Simpson was a year past his electrifying 2,003-yard season. But he was still the engine of the Bills' run-dominated offense.

What Pittsburgh unveiled on the day was a slight wrinkle that would play an increasingly large role as the playoffs wore on. It was a variation on the 4–3 defense which the team called the "Stunt 4–3," an alignment in which Joe Greene took a different stance, cocked diagonally on the nose of the center from his left tackle position. In the geometric jujitsu of line play, a force like Greene at that point in the line play could wreak havoc. Ernie Holmes was lined up shaded inside the other guard. If the Bills' center moved to block Holmes, Greene had a clear path to the quarterback. If the center double-teamed Greene with the right guard, Holmes was in perfect position to demolish the play. Simpson was held to 49 yards rushing. "It started out as a pass technique," Chuck later explained, "but we found it really screws up the offensive blocking. It's an aggressive defensive play because our front four isn't sitting and reading the offense. Instead, they're the ones making things happen."

From one perspective, installing a new base defensive alignment at the start of the playoffs was folly. But then, so was changing your starting quarterback three times during the regular season. It was that kind of season.

Pittsburgh scored 26 points in the second quarter en route to a 32–14 win. It was Bradshaw's best performance of the season (12 of 19 passing for 203 yards and no interceptions, plus 48 yards rushing on 5 carries).

With the Raiders knocking off the two-time defending champion Dolphins the day before, Pittsburgh would go on the road, back to Oakland, for the 1974 AFC title game.

"We're happy to have the opportunity to play them again," said Chuck. He also announced that the team wouldn't spend the week in Palm Springs, as they had before the playoff game in 1973. Bradshaw, for one, was happy: "It's too warm out there," he said. "We get too soft."

By Monday morning, Chuck was well aware of Raider coach John Madden's quote, amid the postgame jubilation after Oakland knocked off the two-time defending champion Dolphins, "When the two best teams in football get together, anything can happen."

The two best teams. Chuck cared very little about pregame talks, but the assumption grated. He said nothing to his assistant coaches that day, nor to Dan, nor to the PR man Joe Gordon.

But Tuesday morning, Chuck strode in to the team meeting—held at the large conference room in Three Rivers Stadium—and did something he had rarely done before. He quoted Madden again, in full, and raised his voice slightly for the first part of the quote—*When the two best teams in football get together*—before slowing down, an octave lower, to complete it. *Anything can happen.*

Chuck's jaw was set, and he'd clenched his fists at his side, the telltale sign that he was agitated. "I'll tell you what *anything* is," Chuck said. "*Anything* is that Oakland isn't getting to the Super Bowl. The Super Bowl is three weeks from now. And the best team in football is right here in this room."

It was the closest thing to a full-fledged inspirational speech that Chuck's team would ever receive, and it was greeted with more than the usual affirmations. Greene launched out of his college desk chair, and several other players whooped in affirmation.

"It wasn't long," said Jack Ham of the talk. "It wasn't one of these running speeches kind of thing and, to a man, I've got to admit, this one hit a nerve. It hit a nerve for me, and whether we were going to play that way no matter what, maybe we would have, but that did set a tone for the intensity of the week. Not that you needed much. You are playing an AFC Championship Game. You are playing the Raiders. But Chuck set the tone of what this was going to be about."

On Christmas Day, the Tuesday prior to the game, Marianne and Chris joined Chuck in the basement. She had decorated Chuck's film projector with a wreath and a red ribbon and surrounded the area with red and green candles. With holiday decorations in place, Chris and Marianne sat down with Chuck while he watched game films of the Raiders.

In the build-up to the game, Chuck was asked about the spotty weather forecast for the game, and how it might affect the Raiders' often-sloppy field. He said the league office had promised to put a tarpaulin on the field. "I can't do anything about it," he added. "Al Davis is in charge of the weather."

He was even more deadpan when a reporter for the *New York Times* mentioned the Raiders' Davis-coined motto, "Pride and Poise," and asked if the Steelers had pride and poise as well. Chuck's answer: "Not on our stationery."

That Sunday afternoon, in Oakland-Alameda County Coliseum, the Steelers played the game in an angry state. Before the Raiders' first play from scrimmage, Ernie Holmes was bellowing to the Raiders' Gene Upshaw that Pittsburgh was "going to kick your ass!" In football terms, that's what they did. The stunt 4–3 proved particularly lethal as it matched up Greene and Holmes on Oakland's aging, bruised, undersized veteran center Jim Otto. After the first series—which Greene concluded by beating a double-team block to sack Ken Stabler—the Raiders' offensive line was on the sidelines with a chalkboard, trying to draw up a suitable response. It never came; the Raiders ran for just 29 yards on the day.

Oakland went ahead in the third quarter, when Cliff Branch beat Mel Blount on a 38-yard touchdown pass from Stabler. The Steelers still trailed 10–3 heading into the fourth quarter, when Harris ran for the game-tying touchdown. From there, the Steelers took over. Two interceptions in the fourth quarter—one by Ham and another by J. T. Thomas—helped put the game away, and Pittsburgh won, 24–13.

"They beat our butts," said Madden after the game.

The reception at the Pittsburgh International Airport was unprecedented and chaotic, even for the Steelers faithful. As the plane touched down, at 12:56 a.m., more than ten thousand Steelers supporters had crowded into the terminal to greet the team.

The challenge awaiting Chuck the next morning was what, if anything, he wanted to do differently than the Colts had done after the 1968 season. When the team gathered Tuesday, he did not tell any cautionary tales about Super Bowl III or the nightmare of recriminations that followed it. But he did warn his players to not invest the game with more importance than it already carried. It was another football game, and the Steelers would treat it as such.

When the Steelers flew to chilly New Orleans on Sunday a week before the game, Chuck brought the players into a banquet room at the Fontainebleu Hotel.

"So the meeting goes, 'Here is the schedule for the week,'" said Bleier. "There is no curfew tonight or tomorrow night, and Tuesday is media day. We will go to our normal week's practice as we have done all season long, then we will have Wednesday offense, Thursday defense, combination on Friday as we have done. Nothing will be different. This game isn't any more important than last week's game or the game before that. It is just another game.'"

The team reveled in the lack of a curfew that Sunday and Monday night—Andy Russell somehow managed to *lose* a rental car somewhere in Fat City. Joe Greene didn't even unpack, just dropped his luggage in the room and headed out with his line mates, L. C. Greenwood, Dwight White, and Fats Holmes. They wound up sitting by the sidewalk in an open-air restaurant along Bourbon Street. "We had you-peel-it shrimp," said Greene. "And we drank Heineken until they had no more." The night left Dwight White with a case of food poisoning and, eventually, admitted to the hospital with pneumonia, which seemed certain to rule him out of the game. Everyone but White reported for meetings Tuesday morning and prepared as usual.

There was a sense that freedom on the first nights in New Orleans, along with the innate confidence that the team had gained, left them looser for the game itself. That week, Radakovich showed the offensive line old game footage of him playing for Penn State against Jim Brown and Syracuse in the '50s. Chuck even allowed the players' wives to stay with them the night before the game.

On the eve of the Super Bowl, Chuck and Marianne and Dan and Pat

Rooney dined at a Mexican restaurant in the French Quarter. That Saturday night meal was marked by an impassioned conversation, Chuck evincing annoyance with all the league-mandated activities that took him, the staff, and the Steelers out of their weekly routines. "Chuck and I got into this big discussion, 'What's more important: the package or the product?,'" said Pat Rooney. "The league handled everything. You didn't have much say about it. But you know, just back and forth."

Bud Grant's Vikings had been mauled twice—in Super Bowl IV against Kansas City and in Super Bowl VIII against Miami—but they returned to New Orleans intent on running the football against as formidable a defense as they'd ever faced.

It poured down rain in the gray New Orleans morning, and the wind chill made it feel like it was in the low 20s. Prior to the game, equipment manager Tony Parisi was fitting the players for new shoes that he'd gotten from Canada, with spiral cleats. When Dwight White barged into the door of the locker room, his Steelers teammates let out a rousing cheer. He'd lost nearly twenty pounds in the hospital, but he was determined to play.

The players weren't expecting a rousing speech from their coach, and they didn't get one. "Play the way you've been coached," Chuck said. "You're going to have a good time." After the build-up and the preparation, he had the team's attention and could have said more. But there was nothing left to say, so he turned and the Steelers headed out for the field.

In the tunnel, before pregame introductions—starters on the Vikings' offense and the Steelers' defense were being introduced individually— Glen Edwards spied his old Florida A&M teammate, Vikings' tackle Charles Goodrum, and shouted a greeting. Goodrum looked nervously over to Edwards and didn't respond. Finally Edwards went over to slap hands and wish Goodrum good luck. But Vikings' coach Bud Grant had forbade his players to even speak to the Steelers. Agitated and emboldened, Edwards said, loud enough for everyone in the tunnel to hear, "Okay, I'll tell you what. Y'all better strap it on, motherfuckers, 'cause you're about to get your asses whipped!" Once again, the Steelers' defense would deliver on a guarantee from a member of their defense.

The Vikings had gained 164 yards on the ground against the Rams in the NFC Championship Game, and they'd seen the film of the Steelers using the Stunt 4–3 against Oakland. But as in the earlier Super Bowls, they never adapted. Aging center Mick Tinglehoff was overmatched against Greene to begin with, but he had no chance with Greene tilted at an angle, knifing forward at the snap. "The way [Greene] played, he basically charged into the 'V' in the neck of the center in such manner so the center could not reach him if it was a strong-side play," said Bud Carson. "If you weren't prepared for it, it made the guard totally ineffective."

The first half had a stultifying feel, to match the cold. The Steelers drove across the 50 twice, close enough for two field-goal attempts, but the elfin Gerela pulled one field goal wide, and then Walden, his holder, bobbled the snap on another attempt. When Fran Tarkenton mishandled a handoff to the Vikings Dave Osborn, the ball squirted free, was accidentally kicked back toward the end zone, where the Vikings' quarterback scrambled on top of it, just in time to be touched down for a safety.

In the final two minutes of the half, Pittsburgh leading 2–0, Edwards' pregame words would prove prophetic. The Vikings were driving, nearing the end zone, when Tarkenton threw to John Gilliam, coming across the middle. Edwards hit Gilliam high with a nasty shot—a pair of forearms to Gilliam's facemask—sending the Vikings' receiver backward and the football squirting back into the air, where Blount made the interception. The teams got to halftime with the score still 2–0.

Bradshaw was unabashed at halftime. "We're whipping their asses off and still ain't got but two points!," he said. Mansfield allowed that two points just might be enough. Chuck spoke to Bradshaw about finding tight end Larry Brown more often.

The second half began with more special teams calamities, Gerela slipping on the wet turf during the kickoff, which squibbed in and out of the hands of the Vikings' fullback Bill Brown, before the Steelers' Marv Kellum recovered. Harris's outside run to the left, behind a stellar block from pulling right guard Gerry Mullins, put the Steelers up 9–0.

The Vikings were completely toothless, their vanilla offensive schemes easily stifled by the defense. Russell had studied their tendencies so well—and could see that they were stubbornly sticking with them—that he would yell up to Holmes and White, "Hey, it's gonna be 17 straight! Play it . . . left hand, left shoulder, Fats."

That's where the score stayed until another special teams miscue, Minnesota's Matt Blair breaking free to block Walden's punt, resulting in the Vikings' Terry Brown recovering in the end zone to make the score 9–6 (though the Vikings then failed to convert the extra point). With ten minutes left in the fourth quarter, and the entire season on the line, the ball was in the hands of the Steelers and Terry Bradshaw.

He'd grown a bristly playoff beard, and the facial hair gave him an aspect of maturity. Five years of playing under Chuck had given him a toughness; if he was not quite assured, he possessed a deeper understanding of his role. Now, he expertly mixed the runs to Harris and Bleier with key passes—including third-down throws to Larry Brown for 30 yards and a 6-yard toss to Bleier on third-and-five. On third and goal from the 4, the Steelers called time out. A touchdown would nearly seal the game. Being held to a field goal would leave Pittsburgh vulnerable to a late Vikings' drive.

On the sidelines, Bradshaw deferred to his coach. "What do you want to run?," he asked.

"Goal line three thirty-three," said Chuck. It was a run-pass option, meant to give Bradshaw time to make his decision and punish the Vikings if they bunched up for another inside run.

Chuck watched quietly as Bradshaw returned to the field, called the play, rolled out to elude the rush, and found Larry Brown open in the end zone. The pass was sharp and accurate and gave the Steelers a 10-point lead that, with the way the defense was playing, seemed insurmountable. Wagner intercepted Fran Tarkenton on the Vikings' next play, and the celebration on the sidelines soon began.

Joe Greene had dominated the game, made an interception and recovered a fumble, but Franco Harris won the MVP for his then-record 158 rushing yards. Now Greene and Harris lifted Chuck up in their arms—not quite to their shoulders—and carried him off the field. Roy Blount Jr. had returned to spend time with the Steelers for the game and later wrote about "the winning smile on Noll's face. I had never seen Noll's mouth so wide open. It was as though the Dragon Lady had gone all soft around the eyes and said, 'Oh, baby.'"

In the commotion of the locker room after the game, the team and the commissioner celebrated Art Rooney, as the Chief—his ever-present cigar lodged firmly in his jaw—accepted the Super Bowl trophy. Chuck mostly stayed out of camera range. "Chuck never wanted to be in the front row," said Jack Ham.

Then came the congratulations, the press interviews, the return to the hotel room, and the handshake with Marianne.

All through the scenes of celebration, Chuck's smile was genuine. Only the words were forced. Even that night, at the Steelers' victory party, he was still not able to articulate the emotional weight of the accomplishment. "I remember going into his room that night," said Andy Russell. "I don't know if a number of us decided to congratulate him. And he was like, 'Okay, guys. This is why we work. This is why we pay the price, blah, blah, blah.' He wasn't one of those guys who was gonna run around the hallways, all excited."

"It was one of my early lessons," said Chris Noll. "My father liked a good party, a small one, at home. But Super Bowls, he was always kind of . . . he cares about the doing and once the doing is over it is a huge letdown. Even though you won."

Chuck wasn't totally oblivious to the emotion. Of the last drive, he said of his team, "You could see it in their eyes; we were going to be number one."

On NBC's Super Bowl postgame broadcast, Curt Gowdy was attempting to put the win in perspective. "They're still a very young team," said Gowdy. "I would say their best years are still ahead of them. A team that may not have reached its peak, and their future opponents are going to have some trouble."

With several decades of hindsight, the chaotic circumstances in which the Steelers won the Super Bowl in the 1974 season remain unprecedented. There have been a scattered few instances in which a future Super Bowl champ changed quarterbacks during the season (Washington in 1987; Baltimore in 2000). For the state of constant flux, the closest analog may have been the 1969 Kansas City Chiefs, who began the year with Len Dawson, replaced him with Jacky Lee when he was injured, replaced him with Mike Livingston when Lee was injured, then went back to Dawson—then Livingston again after Dawson was reinjured—then back to Dawson for the end of the regular season and the playoffs. But that shuffling was all based on the future Hall of Famer Dawson's gimpy knee. The '74 Steelers were in a different realm with three different quarterbacks starting, and all three being benched for poor performance at one time or another during the season. The tinkering, if it had ended in anything other than a Super Bowl title, would have left Chuck exposed to charges of indecisiveness or over-coaching.

Perhaps the re-jiggering really did scar Bradshaw for the rest of his career, as he would argue in later years. But it's equally likely that the insistence on accountability—that no quarterback would keep the job if he didn't perform—revealed the true character of each quarterback. Hanratty, though well-liked by his teammates, didn't have the arm for the job. Gilliam, brilliant, mercurial, in a difficult role with unseen pressures, ultimately buckled (and may have started to buckle before he lost the starting job). Bradshaw—the eternal insecure child, the headstrong, naive country boy who'd spent too many Sundays after awful performances with his head on the steering wheel of his car in the parking lot, sobbing in frustration—kept with it, kept trying, kept studying. He worked to become the quarterback Chuck wanted him to be. Eventually, in 1974, he found the form to lead the Steelers to the title.

The day after the game, back in Pittsburgh, 120,000 revelers gathered in the Golden Triangle despite 26-degree temperatures and twelve-mile-per-hour winds—to toast the champions. In the glow of their victory, it was the team leader Greene who made the definitive statement about the Steelers' collective mind-set going into the game. "The Man handled it so perfectly, just like he always does," he said of Chuck. "He told us to stay cool and enjoy it. Almost everybody took the whole week in just that mood, and we had a great time."

✦　✦　✦

A few weeks after the Super Bowl, the phone rang at the Noll home. After Marianne answered, Chuck said, "Hi!" Rather than his usual businesslike tone on the phone, he sounded playful, mischievous.

She knew instantly something was afoot.

"Lord . . . what have you done?"

"If I buy this plane, this man says he'll teach me how to fly it."

It was a Beechcraft Bonanza, known colloquially in the flying community as "The Doctor-Killer," due to its unusual controls (doctors had the means to afford the plane but often not the time to learn how to handle its peculiar flying style).

Chuck loved it. He started building up hours in the midst of the miserable winter weather of 1975. ("Some people fly only when it's nice," said Marianne. "But then you never learn how to deal with difficulties.") Soon he was taking Marianne and Chris out for touch-and-goes and practiced stalls. Others were more circumspect. Lionel Taylor soon refused to ride with Chuck ("No small planes for me," he said; "if I'm going down, I want it to be on TWA").

Chuck had rewarded himself and spent that off-season—and several to follow—lost in his new passion. Flying was both a practical and an artistic pursuit. But on a more pragmatic level, it was one of the dwindling few places where he could truly get away.

The month of June became the getaway, the re-set. At their condo on Sanibel Island, the Nolls would unwind, usually with one or more of the Deininger nephews.

It was also when Chuck spent the most time with Chris. They would snorkel off the coast of Sanibel, but soon Chuck took Chris and Kenny down to the Florida Keys for scuba diving, going eighty feet down to augment Chris's seashell collection.

"He did a lot of scuba diving when I was in high school, but that was my passion and he just did it to be with us," said Chris. "We all learned and became certified. He would fly me down in his plane just because I loved it. He got excited by it, too. Diving, birds, those were all kind of family things that weren't his passion, but was a way for the family to do things."

That summer, on vacation in Florida, the Nolls were walking into a morning Mass when a stranger walked up and said, "Chuck, you look great, you lost some weight!"

Marianne's thin smile matched Chuck's, while the seventeen-year-old Chris stood in shock.

"I was just kind of like, *Oh, God,*" Chris said. "I remember thinking, 'We are public now.' I was offended, but at the same time stunned. And then you started seeing how people recognized him all the time. It was harder to go to the store. But in terms of him and what we did—it didn't change anything."

Or perhaps it did. Even the most rudimentary errands—trips to the barbershop and to fill the car with gas—were now obstacle courses of adoring fans. People remained polite, but they were more invasive, more insistent, and there were a lot more of them.

For his part, Chuck strived to stay out of the public eye. He hadn't done a TV show in years, and for the most part avoided any endorsement offers. "He did one, for Pittsburgh National Bank," said Chris. "He did it as a personal favor for a guy. The ad said, 'Save $500, get this free shirt, and you'll look good, too.' It showed him wearing the shirt, smiling, with his arms folded in front of a blackboard that had C-15T diagramed on it, a tackle trap. He thought it was going to be a one-shot deal, a newspaper ad, but they put it on billboards all over town, one of them just as you enter the Fort Pitt tunnel. He had to see it every day when he drove to work, and every time he passed it he groaned."

Even going out became a problem. "In the first couple of years, there wasn't an issue there," said Marianne. "People weren't that interested in the Steelers. And then it got crazy. But the funny thing is, everybody will know he is in the room or at the airport or something. But nobody comes over until one person does. Then you are descended upon." Chuck was unvaryingly gracious, but uncomfortable, with the constant public attention.

"Pittsburgh has this mentality of ownership," said Pat Rooney. "You're the head coach and you won and now you're *ours*. I think they enjoyed it but I think they were a very reserved, very quiet couple. I think up to a point it was okay. But they sure were not prepared for it."

fourteen

REPEAT

✦　✦　✦

By the time of the 1974 Super Bowl win, Chuck and Marianne's social life in Pittsburgh was well established. They had already developed a small, close-knit circle of friends, with whom they would remain close for decades.

Sunday nights in the fall usually involved dinner with Dan and Pat Rooney, occasionally at a restaurant up on Mount Washington, but usually back in Upper St. Clair, with Marianne cooking at home. Beyond that, it was very rare that the Steelers' world intruded on Warwick Drive. Even when the Rooneys did come over, the talk was rarely about football. Chuck and Dan intentionally dwelled on other topics.

"It was very interesting to me," said Pat Rooney, "because to me it was like someone was trying to fool the other guy. They *never* talked football, maybe for two seconds, then went right into whatever. So you just never ever got the feeling that, 'Hey, we just lost last week and we lost again this week.' We would go to their house after each game. He was a wine connoisseur, so we always had wine. He'd give the whole history of the wine and the whole process. They would always have something." One week, it might be Chuck showing off his new speakers. Another, it might be his indoor orchid garden.

Others on the team who stopped by Warwick Drive quickly noticed the complete absence of evidence that the people who lived there were in any way involved in football. "When you went up to Chuck's house," said John Brown, "all you saw when you walked through the front door was a whole wall of family pictures, which told me that meant a lot to him. As soon as you walked through the door, boom, all family pictures."

By 1974, Chuck and Marianne's closest friends—next to each other, of course—were Red and Patricia "Pat" Manning. Red Manning was the basketball coach (and later the athletic director) at Duquesne. The friendship began with the wives. "We met them playing tennis, we went to the same church—it was inevitable that we would meet," said Marianne. "We just hit it off. Everybody thought we were sisters. We didn't look that much alike; it was probably body language." Marianne and Pat Manning seemed cut from the same cloth—both lanky, athletic, and attractive, both assured, both warmly shepherding their essentially shy husbands through social situations. Their sensibilities and tastes were perfectly aligned. When they met, they realized they even owned some of the same dresses and outfits.

"They even looked somewhat alike," said Fr. Tom Kredel, the young, motorcycle-driving priest from St. Thomas More, who knew both couples and was a regular attendee of games. "They were both striking, with dark hair—and they were their own people." (This was true, though by the mid-seventies, Marianne's dark hair started graying.)

Pat Manning became the sister Marianne had never had. As coaches' wives, they'd both learned to subjugate their personality in service to their husbands. They were both secure enough about themselves to not feel resentful because of it. Red Manning, raised in a male world, wasn't comfortable with many women. But he found Marianne approachable, and they shared a love for art. Chuck had few female friends, but he responded to Pat Manning's intellectual bent, and they often talked about education and education studies.

And their husbands found a calm sense of common ground. Both Chuck and Red Manning had been raised as Catholics, had cerebral views toward their respective games, and were working in a town starved for success. But they rarely discussed coaching philosophy. Even their temperaments and world view were aligned. Red Manning had been seven years old, living in the mill town of Homestead, Pennsylvania, when his father died. His mother worked as a housemaid, while Red, in his late teens, took a leadership position within the family. "I don't even know if he was so disciplined not to have time for nonsense," said his son Patrick Manning. "He just didn't *get* nonsense."

Golfing, the two couples would go out as a foursome (though after Marianne drove a golf cart into a tree, she ceased piloting any vehicles anywhere under any circumstances). In tennis, where Red and Pat were both accomplished players, they'd play mixed doubles, Red and Marianne against Pat and Chuck. After tennis, they would often go for beers and pizza at Bimbo's Pizza joint in the South Hills area. In these situations, completely relaxed, Chuck was more animated. Before his first swig of beer, he'd announce, "Time to replace some bodily fluids."

At dinners in the off-season, Chuck would be fully relaxed. He would go from convivial to, with an evening full of spirits, "effervescent," in the words of John Manning, Red and Pat's oldest son. Chuck would play the guitar or ukulele. He might invite Marianne to dance the Charleston. She'd comply, but she also remained vigilant. Before too long, she would smile at him and say, "Charles, it's time to go."

In the professional sphere, Marianne had become more than the first lady of the Steelers. She was the socially gracious one, keeping a hand on Chuck's arm at formal dinners, reminding him who a certain businessman was. But she had also fashioned her own life. With Pat Manning, she took continuing education classes and played tennis. At Thomas More Parish, she taught the Confraternity of Christian Doctrine (CCD) classes. She developed an artist's eye and began painting more seriously during the '70s. And at home, she continued making dinners throughout the season (in the off-season, Chuck often cooked on the weekends).

At Steelers' games, they were frequently joined by the Manning family, sitting in the poured concrete open-air box (John Manning compared it to "a German machine-gun nest on the beach at Normandy"), seated on chairs with heavy casters, with a couple of space heaters above them for colder days, and a formica table top upon which to set their drinks and binoculars.

There, they would watch, and Marianne—the most passionate of the group, and the most likely to swear during the game—would pace. She was vociferous and opinionated.

Starting with the 1972 season, Chris was on the field, working as a ball boy. So at 11:30, after Mass at Thomas More, Red and Pat and their boys would pick Marianne up at the house. The older Manning boys, John and Patrick, were used to riding to Duquesne games with their taciturn father, and they knew well enough to be quiet in the backseat. Fr. Tom Kredel, rushing over after the late Mass, often arrived late in the first quarter.

For Red Manning, watching a game didn't involve fandom so much as intense empathy. He would sit with his arms crossed, rarely speaking. "You went down to watch and support," said John Manning. "My dad never said a word; my mom was a little more rambunctious."

Through the week, Marianne would comb the opinion columns in the sports pages and listen to the talk radio discussions of the Steelers. Chuck was loath to spend the time himself focused on distractions, but she would tell him what she knew he needed to know. In truth, publicity men Joe Gordon and Ed Kiely could highlight the same things. But Chuck wouldn't ask them. Nor would he ask Marianne—but she'd often tell him anyway.

Beyond those handful of social outings, the Noll family circle was mostly a self-contained one. Chuck, Marianne, and Chris at home. Quiet nights, reading books, watching old movies, listening to tasteful jazz and classical music on the stereo, for which Chuck always seemed to be buying high-end speakers.

This was the world Chris Noll grew up in. His father was perhaps the single most famous man in the city, yet this was barely acknowledged in the home. There was a dutiful quality to Chris.

In the late '60s, his cousin Ken Deininger, about Chris's age, though much more outgoing, started spending each summer with the Nolls. When the cousins were practicing, whatever the sport may be, their solemn agreement was that they would have to stop before Chuck came home. He would get out of the car and, unbidden, offer pointers on extending their arm during the throw or following through.

"He was the constant coach, the constant teacher," said Ken.

Chris went out for the football team at Upper St. Clair High School and wound up as a reserve.

"I remember thinking, 'Boy, what a disappointment—everybody must be thinking, *The coach's son*,'" said Ken. "During the summers we never played football. We would always play basketball and baseball. I would say, 'Let's throw the football around,' and he would say, 'No, lets run bases or pitch.'" (Chris would recall it differently. "I remember us playing football all the time," he said.)

It was a way to connect with his son, but it sometimes drove Chris to distraction. Chuck tried to teach Chris how to drive, but they were too alike. One time, Chris became so angry, he got out of the car at a stoplight and shouted to his father that he was walking home. But Chris got his driver's license on his sixteenth birthday, December 22, 1973. Chuck wouldn't have to drive Marianne to the grocery store any longer.

As the social revolution of the '60s led to the inevitable backlash of the '70s, neighbors all around them on Warwick Drive were splitting. The nasty divorce of their next-door neighbors, Don and Arlene Connelly, spilled over to their house, with some of the Connelly's seven children staying at 81 Warwick for a spell. The parents of one of Chris's friends, David Land, were also getting divorced. But for Chuck and Marianne, there were no arguments—only the occasionally animated discussion, usually about politics.

"They are best friends, and they are private," said Chris. "They rely on each other. I can never remember them having a fight in front of me. They would have disagreements, or discussions, but they were always under control. That was about as far as I had ever seen them argue; that is the extent of their discord."

Marianne listened to rock 'n' roll on the radio when Chuck was at work, but turned it to something more low-key before he came home.

"For entertainment, he loved music," said Chris. "But his music never went beyond the '50s. If I wanted to make him angry, I would play some rock 'n' roll."

One day in the summer of 1972, Chuck was driving with Chris and Ken and a song came on the radio. As the boys hummed, Chuck looked perplexed.

"What are those words?," Chuck asked. "I don't get it. Brand X?"

Chris and Ken laughed, before Ken cleared up the title of the Looking Glass hit single.

"No, Uncle Chuck, it's *Brandy*," Ken said. "It's a girl's name."

One would never see Chuck in repose. His was a purposeful, achievement-driven lifestyle. "He never read fiction," said Chris. "He read magazines relentlessly, because he wanted to learn so he would get interested in something, whether it was photography or flying or boating, and he would become an expert on it by reading information on a topic, and he would ask lots of questions from people who he knew." That led to the love of wines—by the late '70s, he would start making his own version of dandelion wine.

Even when they were on the same sideline, father and son didn't bond directly over football. Chris was an avid fan and a ball boy. But his father gave him no inside scoop. "I learned to stop asking after a while," Chris said. "I would ask a question once in a while, but not very often because it was clear that he didn't want to talk about it. They were all short answers—the same thing that he would give sportswriters. There was never a long answer, so I gave up. Because I would ask questions like a fan would."

The work week during the season was set and unwavering—Chuck home at 8 o'clock on Monday nights, after 10 p.m. Tuesdays (the one long night, preparing the game plan for the following Sunday), 8 p.m. Wednesdays, 7 o'clock on Thursdays, 6 or 6:30 on Fridays, and early afternoon on the Saturdays before home games—though he then would drive down to the Sheraton South Hills, where the team stayed on the eve of home games, by 6 p.m. On most nights, save Tuesday, Chris would wait and dine with his parents. Eventually, Chris started cooking some of his own meals, mastering frozen and canned foods, then a wok.

Chuck was hypersensitive to his son being spoiled. If Chris wanted a new bike, they would work out a deal whereby he would pay half of the cost. But there were moments. "I can remember early in high school," said Chris, "and I was really into fish and aquariums. One day he said, 'Come on,' and we got in the car, and he drove to the store and bought two huge aquariums. It was clear to me at that point that it was kind of his 'I love you,' you know? Because it was just such a shock."

The discussions of drugs and alcohol—even the sex talk—became the province of Marianne. "All those conversations were left to my mother," Chris said, "probably because he wasn't around all of the time."

Chris was shy, self-conscious, and particularly sensitive to those who wanted to befriend him because of his father. Growing up in Pittsburgh, he virtually never mentioned the connection, unless he absolutely had to.

His father's job meant that some of the traditional parental rites—coming to school plays, cheering for the child at games—were complicated. "I knew so I had no expectation," Chris said. "He is going to miss this; okay, that's part of the job; that comes with the territory." Chuck would miss Chris's high school football games, but he would occasionally come to soccer games. Often, Chuck and Marianne would watch from the car, so the father wouldn't be a distraction from the son.

Chris, loyal but also willful, asserted himself whenever he could. The more Chuck strived to reach out to his son, the braver Chris became about insisting those times be on his terms.

"He was big into photography, and he wanted to develop some film, and he wanted me to come with him," Chris said. "I had no interest, because he liked it. Well, I made a deal with him. If I could play my music while he was developing it, I would hang out with him. So we were both tolerating each other to spend time together."

The scene played itself out more than once that summer: Chuck and Chris would stand in the infrared light of the improvised darkroom on Warwick Drive, Chuck carefully dipping photo paper into developing solution, while in the background, Chris stared dutifully and intently and tapped a sneakered foot to the sounds of *Led Zeppelin IV* playing in the darkroom.

✦   ✦   ✦

At the first meeting with the team at training camp in 1975, Chuck gave another of his rare speeches to remember.

"You know, you can take those Super Bowl rings you've got," he said, "and you can put them up on a shelf right now. There is not a damn thing you did last year that will win you a spot on this football team this year. You have an opportunity—and you are the only team in football that has it—to repeat as champions. But you have to realize that every team is going to play their best football game against you. You will see film of them the week before the game and you will say, 'Boy, this team is crap.' Well, they are not going to play like that against you. You can either accept that challenge and win it again, or we will be like the other Super Bowl teams and just fall by the wayside."

The 1975 season began as the last one had, with the Steelers obliterating their opening day opponents, and the starting quarterback looking stellar and assured. Bradshaw, in this instance, completed 21 of 28 passes for 227 yards and two touchdowns. Chuck would have been permitted a note of satisfaction that his quarterback had found the consistency to continually perform at a high level.

It didn't last long. A week later, at home against the Bills, O. J. Simpson gashed the Steelers for 227 yards, and the game was lost on five turnovers. Bradshaw threw an interception and fumbled and was essentially dreadful, before Chuck lifted him for Joe Gilliam, who was competent. It wasn't enough, as Buffalo won, 30–21.

It was nearly the last blip on the season. They went into Cleveland and humiliated the Browns, 42–6 (though Greene was ejected for a late-game brawl in which he kicked the Browns' offensive lineman Bob McKay in the groin). The Steelers' defense was better than ever, and Bradshaw had matured. He had his best season yet as a pro, both Harris and Bleier posted what were then career-high rushing totals, and the Steelers ran off eleven straight victories. They'd clinched home-field advantage throughout the AFC playoffs even before they took the field for the season finale, at the Los Angeles Rams.

It had been an excruciating season for Gilliam, still bedeviled by drugs and alcohol. Frenchy Fuqua remembered being at one of the city's black nightclubs and seeing Gilliam doing heroin—the street name was "boy"—at the bar. He also swore he saw Joe Greene slap the drug out of Gilliam's hand and ask, "What are you doing? I thought we had a talk about that." (Greene doesn't recall the incident.)

"A lot of the guys, especially the black guys, would talk to the guys at the bars that we hung at and the pushers backed off," said Fuqua. "So guess where he got his dope at? Baltimore. Sunday nights he would leave and drive down to Baltimore and get boy. Then he got beat up down there. You'll not find that many of the teammates who were feeling sorry for him."

"He had been late at least thirty times for quarterback meetings during the 1975 season," said Dan Radakovich, "and I'm not exaggerating."

With the division title and their playoff seeding clinched, Chuck viewed the game as a chance to rest some of his regulars and give backups some key playing time against a quality opponent. By the time of this game, though, Gilliam was barely functional. Rocky Bleier and Terry Bradshaw, among others, had seen Gilliam sniffing a white powder in his locker before the game.

Chuck hadn't seen that, but he was vexed by Gilliam's flighty behavior during the pregame meeting. At one point, he walked over to Lionel Taylor and speculated, "Gilliam's drunk."

Taylor went over and sat with Gilliam for a few minutes, before returning to Chuck's office in the visiting team's locker room with his verdict: "Chuck . . . he's not *drunk*."

Gilliam's first pass bounced on the turf. He had a abysmal day, completing 2 of 11 passes for 29 yards and two interceptions. Lynn Swann, playing in front of his family and friends at his old home stadium, was furious with Gilliam for playing so poorly.

Gilliam continued behaving erratically on the flight home, which led to a confrontation with Greene. "He was just cursing and just acting up, saying derogatory things," said Greene. "I just told him, 'That is beneath you and beneath all of us for you to be acting like that. Joe—I will kick your ass right here on this plane.'"

The next day, Chuck reluctantly demoted Gilliam to third string.

"Terry Hanratty and I would laugh about it, and we always wondered why Chuck didn't do anything," said Bradshaw. "Gilly was constantly late for practice, and each time he was tardy he'd have a new excuse. If it wasn't a sick relative, Gilly would fabricate a story about taking a cab and the driver not knowing how to find the stadium. One time Gilly said somebody had thrown a bucket of paint on his brand-new Mercedes and he'd been out trying to clean it off. Chuck even went out the parking lot and examined Joe's car but found no traces of paint."

Mystery remained about why it took Chuck so long to act.

"Chuck's background might have made him more lenient, because Chuck put up with it for a long time," said Lionel Taylor. "But Chuck was not street smart."

Gilliam was late for warm-ups during the opening game of the playoffs the following week, when the Steelers hosted the Colts. It was the final indignity. "Get dressed," Chuck snapped when Gilliam finally appeared. "You're not going to make the rest of the team suffer for your mistakes, but after this season, you're gone."

The Gilliam saga would hurt Chuck deeply, and it would mark the

Steelers for the rest of Chuck's tenure. In the end, all the staff felt they had missed an opportunity. "Boy, Joey," said Artie. "It was like a movie with a bad ending."

As the 1975 playoffs began, the pressure to repeat was profound, but Chuck exuded an air of calm. Before the first playoff game, at home against the Colts, he stopped by PR man Joe Gordon's office and found him wrestling with a balky drawer in his filing cabinet. And there, less than an hour before kickoff, Chuck repaired the casters in Gordon's filing cabinet.

The Steelers beat the Colts 28–10, despite five turnovers, two of them Bradshaw interceptions. Bradshaw had to be helped off the field by Jackie Hart and Ralph Berlin at halftime, but he came back into the game in the second half. The defense stood firm and Mel Blount—voted the team's MVP in 1975—made two interceptions. "Our offense could have stayed home and we still would have won," said Chuck after the game.

The next week was the inevitable playoff rematch against the Raiders, the fourth in as many years, with the AFC Championship at stake. The conditions in Three Rivers were windy and raw, temperatures in the low teens, and the sides of the field virtually frozen (a circumstance that, the Raiders were convinced, was allowed to occur so as to deter their speedster, Cliff Branch). "It was the most brutal game I ever played in," said the Raiders' John Vella. "You had twenty-two guys on a 30-yard-wide field. So the defenses knew what was going on."

The game had an epic quality—at times remorseless in its intensity. Bradshaw inadvertently kneed Raiders' linebacker Monte Johnson in the head, knocking him out. The Raiders' George Atkinson laid a heavy blow on Lynn Swann, knocking him out of the game and into the hospital with a concussion.

Afterward, reflecting on the "viciously played game . . . between two great football teams," Chuck endorsed Bradshaw's play, despite his three interceptions. "Terry throws well in windy weather," he said. "He throws a perfect spiral almost every time. If you get the nose up or down in the wind, it will take off on you, or if you flutter the ball at all it will fall like a ruptured duck. It has to leave your hand just right. Terry does that and he's not affected by the wind as a lot of passers."

They enjoyed it all the more the second time around. The team all met at Jack and Joanne Ham's for a victory party. Almost all of the assistants came, along with Ralph Berlin and Tony Parisi. Virtually all of the players came. The only person of note on the team who *didn't* come was Chuck. "And the thing is," said Ham, "I knew that he knew about it. And yet I never *expected* he'd come." Chuck and Marianne shared a bottle of wine when he finally got home.

The next morning, he started getting ready for the Dallas Cowboys.

+ + +

The build-up to Super Bowl X was different than the year before. The Steelers were by now familiar to the national media. And the opponent wasn't the dour Bud Grant and the Vikings but Tom Landry—already a renowned figure of stern corporate control—and the Cowboys, who with their shiny, space-age helmets and famously computerized draft process had established themselves as the NFL's great innovators. This reputation was encouraged by the crusty architect of the team, Tex Schramm, who was by turns brilliant and egotistical and who had established himself— from his close friendship with Rozelle and his position as chairman of the NFL's vastly influential Competition Committee—as the league's most influential club executive.

The Cowboys had been saddled with the tag "Next Year's Champions" after playoff setbacks in 1966, 1967, 1968, 1969, losing the Super Bowl in 1970, finally winning it in 1971, then falling short in the playoffs in 1972, 1973, and missing the playoffs for the first time in nearly a decade in 1974. Retooled with ten rookies, and with Roger Staubach having matured into a dynamic leader, the Cowboys had upset the Vikings in Minnesota on Staubach's Hail Mary pass to Drew Pearson, then steamrolled the favored Rams, 37–7, in the NFC Championship Game at the Los Angeles Memorial Coliseum.

It was a more experimental Cowboys' offense, one that had begun using Red Hickey's old shotgun formation, the quarterback taking the snap 5–7 yards behind the line of scrimmage. The Cowboys pass rush, and their base flex defense—which found one lineman offset a yard off the line of scrimmage—was equally problematic for offenses not accustomed to facing it.

"We talked a lot about that, how they had a great pass rush, and then getting ready for them was not easy," said Chuck. "They tried to fool you as much as beat you physically. We needed the two weeks to get ready and we used all of it. That sort of worked on our people, too."

Chuck had felt the team was getting a little bit tight, preoccupied with defending their last title rather than going out to grab the next one. At the team meeting two days before the game, he brought the team together and shared a story about focus.

"This reminds me of the two Tibetan monks who are walking in the mountains," Chuck said. "They come to a swift stream. On the bank they find a damsel in distress. She doesn't know how to cross the stream without hiking up her skirt. The monks see her problem and agree to help her. The first monk picks her up in his arms, wades across the stream, sets her back down on the shore, and continues on the journey. The monks walk in silence for another mile or so when the second monk says to the first, 'You know, the rules of our order prohibit physical contact with members of the opposite sex.' They walk on in silence until the first monk responds, 'That is right. But I put the lady down on the other side of the stream. You're still carrying her.'"

Then Chuck smiled and left.

In the mostly bewildered silence that followed, Russell, Ham, and Bleier slowly started chuckling. Others, like Ernie Holmes, looked around in befuddlement. It was not uncommon for Chuck's story to leave some players grasping at air. "Andy or Ray would have to come into the locker room after some of these meetings and explain to the team what he was talking about," said Joe Greene. "Rocky got that one. I couldn't get it."

The stylistic contrasts between the two teams were marked, and the Cowboys seemed eager to prove that they would not be intimidated. Tom Landry told a Dallas writer, "The Steelers are an arrogant team. They haven't learned humility, but they will." The Cowboys' Cliff Harris made some disparaging remarks questioning Swann's toughness, in light of the concussion he suffered in the AFC title game.

But Chuck brought none of this up in his pregame speech. It offended his sensibilities to appeal to emotion. Instead he was spare, focused, matter-of-fact. It would be just another game. "Guys, this is what we played for all year," he said to the Steelers. "Let's go out and play."

From the opening kickoff, the Cowboys attempted to outsmart Pittsburgh, with Preston Pearson—who'd signed with the Cowboys after his preseason release from Pittsburgh—handing to rookie linebacker

Thomas Henderson on a reverse. He ran it out to the Steelers' 44, where he was upended by kicker Roy Gerela, who bruised his ribs on the tackle and was erratic the rest of the game.

Dallas went up early, 7–0, on a touchdown pass where Wagner didn't make an adjustment in time—on the sidelines, he told Carson, "It's my fault, I saw it."

But Pittsburgh came back and tied the game on 333—the same play that Bradshaw had connected with Larry Brown on in Super Bowl IX. This time it was Randy Grossman catching the pass. But Dallas led 10–7 at halftime, and the Steelers seemed strangely listless.

The momentum swung, all parties agreed, after Gerela's second missed field goal in the third quarter. Following the play, Dallas safety Cliff Harris tauntingly patted Gerela on the top of the helmet and pantomimed a congratulatory hug. Lambert, who'd been a wing blocker in the field goal formation, was trudging off the field when he noticed Harris's act. He stepped back to where Harris was still taunting Gerela and grabbed the Cowboy by the back of his shoulder pads and threw him to the turf. Pittsburgh had been subdued all day—Greene had aggravated his neck injury and was already out for the remainder of the game—but this was the moment that galvanized the Steelers.

Pittsburgh took control of the game, then won it on a big play by Bradshaw. He was knocked unconscious on a touchdown pass—a 64-yard bomb to Swann that he got off just as Larry Cole's helmet hit his chin—to put Pittsburgh up 21–10.

But Dallas wasn't finished, as Staubach hit Percy Howard for a 34-yard touchdown pass to cut the lead to 21–17. Pittsburgh was at the Dallas 42-yard line after recovering an onside kick.

On the Steelers' ensuing drive, Chuck wanted to run out as much clock as possible, keeping the ball on the ground. He ran three times, with the Cowboys using their three timeouts after each down. That left the Steelers at fourth-and-nine on the Cowboys' 41, as the Cowboys called their last timeout and the Steelers' offense came off the field.

Terry Hanratty, subbing for the concussed Bradshaw, came to the bench after the third-down play, in which Bleier gained one yard to leave it at fourth-and-nine. But Chuck told him to go back out to the huddle and ordered Walden to stay on the sideline. Walden had mishandled one punt, and the Cowboys had nearly blocked two others.

George Perles, next to Chuck, frantically pointed out that it was fourth down, and the Steelers needed to punt. But Chuck had made up his mind. "If we don't stop them," Chuck said, "we don't *deserve* to win."

He sent Hanratty back into the huddle with a basic run to call—84 Trap—and the hopes that it would succeed. When Hanratty went back out on the field, an alarmed Radakovich, who'd been out of earshot, moved to chase Hanratty down and pull him back. But Chuck grabbed Radakovich and said, "We're not going to punt. We're running the ball."

Bleier would be tackled after a 2-yard gain, giving Dallas the ball on its own 39-yard line.

Even some of the Steelers were disbelieving. "We all walked off the field shaking our heads, thinking, 'What kind of play was that?,'" said Rocky Bleier. "It was the stupidest play ever, ever called in history."

But the calculation was clear in Chuck's mind—the special teams had been poor that day, Walden had been inconsistent—and he didn't want to risk a disastrous block or a big return. But it was simpler even than that: Chuck had immense faith in his defense.

"We had a little problem with a punt earlier, and Dallas had put a pretty good rush on," Chuck said. "We'd rather give them the football there with no timeouts when they had to score a touchdown. I figured our defense would hold them."

Most of the players on the defense understood ("Yeah, well, Bobby Walden was knocking the ball sideways and stuff," said Glen Edwards). And in this Chuck was, once again, proved correct. Staubach marched Dallas to the Pittsburgh 37, but there were no more Hail Marys to be answered, as Edwards intercepted the final pass.

The Steelers were two-time champions. Chuck joined Vince Lombardi and Don Shula as the only coaches to win back-to-back Super Bowls. And in the locker room, he was the same. A big smile, lots of handshakes, but always composed.

In the postgame euphoria of the locker room, it was Lambert who provided the perspective that was eerily similar to what Chuck had told the team in the preseason. "Everybody gives us their best shot," Lambert said. "We have to give everybody else our best shot. They might only have to do it once or twice a season, but we have to do it every week, and that's what we proved this year—that we can do it."

By the end of their second Super Bowl run, the Steelers were more than the best team in football. They had the ability, like the Browns of the '50s or the Packers of the '60s, to win games with their persona. And they had the confidence, borne of Chuck's disciplined steadfastness, to focus only on the matter at hand. "When we went out to play, you could just tell that we were going to win the football game," said L. C. Greenwood. "You could see it during the week leading up to the game. It was all about attitude. We were physically fit to do it, and we were prepared for it. So, when you have that and the right attitude, you are going to be successful. And our opponents knew there was nothing they could do about it."

fifteen

THE PRICE OF SUCCESS

✦   ✦   ✦

On the first day of training camp in 1976, the cars were lined up, backing up out past St. Vincent Drive, for miles up the road on the choked State Highway 30. Pittsburghers, western Pennsylvanians, and dislocated Steelers fans who'd come back to take a look had all congregated to watch the two-time world champions.

The fundamentals of training camp, which had been performed in 1969 in front of a crowd of a handful of civilians, and had grown to dozens and then hundreds over the previous years, now reached to new realms, with more than ten thousand in attendance on the first day of camp.

They had come for something more than to bear witness to the amplified smack of helmets clashing in the muggy summer air. At a time when the city's industrial base was on its knees (foreign imports of steel—often sold below cost in the States—increased nearly 50 percent between 1975 and 1977), the people of Pittsburgh wanted to feel good about themselves and their hometown again.

To have reached the pinnacle twice was to feel a sense of both satisfaction in the achievement, as well as a bedrock conviction in the way the achievement was accomplished. Chuck was never boastful, but he did allow himself a certain measure of satisfaction in the ensuing year after the second Super Bowl triumph.

After the Super Bowl, the Cowboys' Tex Schramm and Tom Landry had been very public in their complaints about the officiating. Perhaps still mindful of Landry's pregame comment that the Steelers were arrogant, Chuck made his most pointed swipe to date. Showing reporters his new Super Bowl ring during the off-season, he said, "It has a little button on the side. Push it and the top flips up. Inside is a miniature tape recorder. . . . You can hear Tom Landry crying."

Chuck had reached the end of his rope with Joe Gilliam, who was released, and Hanratty was left unprotected and subsequently selected by Tampa Bay in the expansion draft. The new backup quarterback would be a rookie, Boston College quarterback Mike Kruczek, drafted in the second round in 1976.

Meanwhile, Chuck's now-entrenched starting quarterback was madly in love. Bradshaw had fallen for the ice skater Jo Jo Starbuck ("Not only is she pretty and talented and a celebrity, but she's a super Christian," he said. "She read the Bible, prayed, wore a cross around her neck, and was loaded with religious tracts. I just couldn't be with her enough.") In the '75 season, he had taken to flying to see her on his off days.

In the off-season, after Super Bowl X, he and Starbuck were married. Over that summer, Bradshaw had decided to follow her in pursuing a show business career. He started playing music gigs at the Palamino Club in Los Angeles and got a bit part in the Burt Reynolds movie *Hooper*. During the filming, he hurt his elbow, doing a stunt in which he jumped through a window. Bradshaw later said he didn't tell the team about it, "but I'm sure Chuck would have gone absolutely crazy if he'd have known."

✦   ✦   ✦

Though Chuck was busier and more prominent than ever before, his familial role hadn't changed. In June 1976, the Nolls took a week's vacation in Sanibel, along with Chuck's nephew, Ken Deininger, whose easy affability made him the most extroverted of Chuck's nieces and nephews. Ken had been undecided not only on where he wanted to attend college but whether he wanted to do so at all. Out in the Atlantic, bobbing on inner tubes, Chuck finally brought the subject up with him.

"Well, what are you going to do?"

"I don't know," said Ken. "I was going to try to apply to some colleges."

"Why don't you come to St. Vincent with us when we go to training camp? Let's see if we can get you in there. If you don't like it, you can transfer."

Ken was noncommittal. He'd also been considering a stint in the Navy, and he was less than thrilled about the prospect of an all-male campus. But he agreed to consider it.

"So I was thinking he was not going to get me in St. Vincent," said Ken. "So we go down there for the first day. We are setting up training camp. He says, 'Let's go over to the admissions.' We walk into admissions and all of a sudden here comes Chuck Noll, who had just won two Super Bowls. Everybody falls. And he talks to the admission guy and he goes, 'Hey I got a kid here that didn't apply for any schools. I was wondering if you have any positions.' The guy goes, 'Did you take any college credits?' I go, 'Oh yeah, everything was college-bound.' He goes, 'All right, if your grades are good we will get you in.' I said, 'My grades were fine.' He goes, 'You're in.' I almost died. I was like, 'What did I just do?' The whole time, Uncle Chuck is just snickering."

At the 1976 training camp, Chuck tabbed Ken—along with Chris—to help with the filming of practices. Eventually, Ken would be hired to help the young film man Bob McCartney, the former ball boy.

"I remember the first day of training camp," said Ken. "We are all in the cafeteria eating. I remember him standing up on a chair, giving this whistle of power and authority, and saying, 'Guys, meeting at 7. Don't be late.' And I am just, like, 'Holy shit, that's my uncle.' I had no idea."

✦　✦　✦

As he strode on the field for the first game of the 1976 season, Chuck was at the height of his profession. The team he'd coached had won twenty-eight of its previous thirty-four regular-season and postseason games. He had successfully secured his pilot's license, his son was beginning college at Rhode Island University, his wife was flourishing both personally and in the community. In short, he was becoming—in the words of Steelers' radio broadcaster Myron Cope—"The Emperor" of Pittsburgh.

Then the Oakland Raiders came out, intent on settling scores. Though they were in different divisions, the two teams had played each other seven times over the previous four seasons. "When we practiced before Oakland games," said Dick Hoak, "Chuck was always looking around because he, I guess, knew Al had done that before, you know, tried to sneak people up to watch the practice and stuff like that. That is when I realized what was going on."

Jack Ham had already sorted out that, though Chuck never looked beyond the next game, never demonized another team, the preparation for Raiders week felt different. "I think he had a little disdain for the Cowboys, the whole America's Team kind of thing," said Ham. "But I think if you had to rank them, the Raiders were enemy number one for him. He never said anything or stuff like that, but you kind of sensed it. Plus, they were always big games. They were always in our way to get to the Super Bowl and, conversely, we were in their way, too."

The mind games never ended. During pregame calisthenics, when the Steelers divided up into units, Al Davis—slicked-back pompadour, leather jacket, black slacks—would routinely walk over to the Steelers' side of the field, stand on the sidelines with his arms crossed, and simply stare at Ham, Lambert, Russell, and their linebacker mates. "I don't know why he always did that," said Ham.

As the 1976 season began, there were still hard feelings between both teams. The Raiders were convinced that the Steelers had neglected the field at Three Rivers for the 1975 AFC Championship Game. The Steelers were still furious about George Atkinson's brutal hit on Lynn Swann in the same game, which had knocked Swann out and landed him in a hospital for the next two days.

The old grudges were resurrected quickly. Late in the first half of the '76 opener, on a play in which Bradshaw dumped a screen pass to Franco Harris, Atkinson ranged across the field and did the very same thing, clubbing Swann from behind, at the base of the skull, with a vicious forearm shiver, knocking him unconscious again.

Pittsburgh was up 28–14 and driving in the fourth quarter when a crucial Harris fumble opened the door. The Raiders eventually tied, before a tipped Bradshaw pass was intercepted, allowing Oakland to drive for a last-minute field goal to win 31–28. They scored 17 points in the final four minutes of the game.

Chuck was already frustrated entering his postgame press conference, and his temper flared when someone mentioned Atkinson's hit on Swann. "There was a lot of discussion about putting a rule in against it this year," he said. "It wasn't done and the reason given was that, although it was illegal, no special rule was needed. There should've been a rule against slapping receivers years ago. Maybe they're waiting for somebody to get killed." He went on, never mentioning Atkinson by name, but focusing on the incident: "They went after Swann again. People that sick shouldn't be allowed to play this game. Watching something like that clouds the hell out of what their offense did. It seems to come only from their defensive unit. Maybe that's a reflection on their coaching."

He stewed on the loss, and the hit, during the long flight home to Pittsburgh. He awoke the next day, to confirmation of Swann's latest concussion, more agitated than ever at Al Davis, John Madden, and the Raiders. At his weekly Monday press conference inside Three Rivers, the anger spilled over. "People like that should be kicked out of the game or out of football," he said of Atkinson. "There is a certain criminal element in every aspect of society. Apparently, we have it in the NFL, too.'" Asked to compare his team's tactics to the Raiders, Chuck replied, "We usually hit people straight on, nose-to-nose. There's nothing wrong with hard-hitting football, but not when your back is turned. It's something that has to be straightened out. I don't think that's football. . . . We play football. We don't want to get involved with criminal actions."

Dan Rooney had been out of town in meetings most of the day. Late in the afternoon, he phoned publicity director Joe Gordon, to ask how the press conference went; Gordon told him it had gone fine. But that night, when Rooney returned to Pittsburgh, the airwaves were full of talk about Chuck's comments. Dan phoned Gordon at home.

"Joe, did Chuck really say this?!"

"Yeah, he said it," said Gordon.

"Well, why didn't you tell me?"

"I agreed with him—and I didn't think it was that serious."

"We are going to get sued on this."

That would come later. In the meantime, Atkinson would be fined $1,500 by the Commissioner's office for the hit. But Pete Rozelle pointedly fined Chuck an identical amount for being publicly critical of the officiating and of Atkinson.

The Steelers seemed to suffer a hangover from the dispiriting loss. A week later, they shook off a 14–0 halftime deficit at home against the Browns, coasting to a 31–14 win. But then they lost at home to a young Patriots team, and again on the road on *Monday Night Football* to the Vikings, despite holding Minnesota to just 26 yards passing. Sitting at 1–3, and traveling to Cleveland for a big divisional game, the team spoke of taking them one game at a time. But every single team on their schedule played at an inspired level against the two-time champions, and Cleveland Municipal Stadium was a cauldron of noise and hostility. Cleveland lost its first two quarterbacks—Brian Sipe to a concussion and Mike Phipps to a separated shoulder—while the Steelers lost Bradshaw when defensive lineman Joe "Turkey" Jones recklessly spiked him head-first into the field on a sack. Bradshaw was diagnosed with a concussion and a sprained neck.

Behind third-string quarterback Dave Mays, the Browns prevailed 18–16, dropping the champions to an unthinkable 1–4.

"We're about as good as a grade school team right now," said Chuck.

In the locker room, it was left for Joe Greene again to set the tone. "If we have to be in this position, all I can tell you is I'd rather be in it with this team, with these people, and particularly with the man running it."

Meeting with the staff preparing for the trip home, Chuck only said, "Let's go to work." The rookie quarterback Mike Kruczek was tabbed to take over.

To the team, Chuck's message was simple. "Terry is hurt. We're putting Kruczek in. We're not throwing the ball. We might have to win 2–0. Whatever it takes." The defense redoubled its efforts

The next week, against Cincinnati, the magnificent Steel Curtain banner that had graced the stands for years was turned backward. Kruczek was in at quarterback. "Nice guy," said Lionel Taylor. "He couldn't throw the ball 25 yards."

In the event, he didn't need to. Kruczek would win six starts during the season, even though the Steelers' passing game was reduced to a rumor. At one point during the season, following the November 21 game against Houston, when Kruczek had completed just eight passes (only one to a wide receiver), the offense was looking at game film and, during one of the Steelers' rare passing plays, Stallworth and Swann stood up in mock applause.

But the formula worked. Pittsburgh beat Cincinnati, 23–6, before three consecutive shutouts—of the Giants, Chargers, and Chiefs. Bradshaw was back starting again when they beat Miami, 14–3. They finally surrendered a couple touchdowns, the first in six games, in a blowout win over the Oilers. Then they closed the season with a hard-fought win over Cincinnati, 7–3, before shutting out Tampa Bay and Houston.

By the end of the regular season, it was clear to even the Steelers' players that the defense was playing at a rarefied level unsurpassed in football history. "We could have taken everyone on that defense, every starter, to the Pro Bowl," said Mel Blount, "and it would have been very fair."

It was after the 42–0 shutout win over the expansion Buccaneers (they held their old teammate Hanratty to 1 of 4 passing for –1 yard), that the news hit out of Oakland. George Atkinson was filing a lawsuit for $3 million against Chuck, the Steelers, and a local Oakland newspaper, whose columnist had speculated that Atkinson's hit might have killed Swann. Chuck preached about the avoidance of distractions. But as the Steelers entered the playoffs, vying for their third straight title, his own remarks had become a distraction.

The first playoff game was at Baltimore in front of 60,020 fans primed for revenge from the tough playoff loss a year before. Instead, Pittsburgh scored on a long touchdown pass from Bradshaw to Frank Lewis on the third play of the game and leapt to a 26–7 lead on the way to a 40–14 rout. But the win came at a price. Both Franco Harris and Rocky Bleier were injured, as was Roy Gerela (Ray Mansfield kicked the final point after touchdown) during the 40–14 win. The surreal footnote came fifteen minutes after the game, while Chuck still doing postgame interviews, when a man flying a single-engine plane crashed it into the upper deck of the stadium.

A week later, the Steelers traveled to face the Raiders once again, and the Atkinson lawsuit moved back on the front pages. Chuck took it in stride. His most expansive comment on the suit came in the days before the playoff game at Oakland, when he was being interviewed by Tim Ryan of CBS Sports.

"You know I don't really give much thought to those things, because I have no control over what another team does," said Chuck. "And to waste energy worrying about what someone else does, maybe in your business that's what you do, but in my business, there's not enough left over—

we have to worry about our football team, get our football team ready. That's why we have very little patience for speculation and the other kind of things. Because what we have to do takes the concentration to get it done." In conclusion, he added, "Some people crash into stadiums for attention, and other people do other things."

But with Harris and Bleier out, and running back Frenchy Fuqua already banged up, the game would be a mismatch. Chuck had decided to go primarily with one-back sets featuring Reggie Harrison. Bradshaw threw thirty-five times, but Pittsburgh ran for just 72 yards. The Steelers fell behind early, and lost 24–7. The kings were dead—"we got our asses kicked," said Radakovich—and the loss was particularly galling as it came at the hands of their bitterest rival.

"We played without 50 percent of our offense," said Chuck afterward, noting the absence of Harris and Bleier. "I'm sorry we didn't have more weapons."

He was also frustrated that the Raiders had been prepared for the Steelers' one-back sets—Chuck suspected the Pittsburgh media had been too forthcoming in its portrayal of the Pittsburgh practices, and that Davis wouldn't have needed to send spies.

And as the season ended, Chuck knew he'd be spending much of the next several months dealing with the lawsuit.

"It would be one thing for Al to stand up and complain and take shots at the Steelers and at Noll in a league meeting," said NFL executive Joe Browne. "But he was in the public courts, so it elevated the discussion and leveled the issue, which is never a pleasant issue for us, and that is violence in our sport. But Al was being Al. His defenders would say he is so competitive, but other than those four people, everyone else would say he wasn't trying to be constructive; he is always trying to be destructive and that is the spirit in which we believe the lawsuit was filed."

That was the tone that marked the off-season in 1977.

✦ ✦ ✦

The NFL's annual league meetings, held each spring, were another chance for Chuck and Marianne to get away, especially now that Chris was off to college. The meetings were usually held in Maui, spilling over more than a week in March. Chuck would occasionally get together with the Packers' Bart Starr, with whom he'd developed a friendship, or sit down with his old boss Sid Gillman. But the coach from another team with whom he was closest remained Shula.

Marianne was more social. The Chiefs' owner Lamar Hunt managed a tennis tournament for the owners and coaches and their wives, and Marianne would participate in that.

Coaches, invariably, worried about the machinations of the league's influential Competition Committee. The league's rulemaking body had grown increasingly important in the television age and, since the merger, it had been chaired by Rozelle's close friend (and former boss, back in the '50s when he was general manager of the Rams), Cowboys' president Tex Schramm. Schramm had been joined on the committee by Paul Brown, Al Davis, and Don Shula, whom Schramm had tabbed to join the committee after the death of Vince Lombardi in 1970.

"Tex would come staggering out about 10 or 11 o'clock in the morning with a Bull Shot to start the meeting," said Shula. "Marianne and I used to play tennis, so we would be up playing tennis at 8 o'clock in the morning, and then I'd come back and shower and get ready for the meeting, and Tex would come out." The group would meet, usually on the beach itself, which allowed for both a beautiful view and the freedom of movement—when discussing blocking rules, it was not at all uncommon for Schramm and Shula to get down in three-point stances to illustrate the pros and cons of a possible rule change. "Then at 5 o'clock," said Shula, "Paul Brown would say, 'Okay, the drinking lamp is lit.' So he would get his Chivas, and he would always have like two Chivases, and then he would leave. He wouldn't go to dinner with us."

One of the issues that preoccupied the committee in the spring of 1977 was the way the Steelers played bump-and-run defense. "I call it the bump-grab-hit-roll block-catch-funnel and run," said Brown. That spring, the Competition Committee plotted the course of football's future and recommended a rule change that would, when approved by the owners, change the game, change the way it was strategized and contested, and effectively remove one of the key components of the Steelers' defense. Starting in 1977, defenders would get just a single point of contact with a receiver while he was running his route. It effectively killed the bump-and-run technique popularized by the Raiders and, later, perfected by Mel Blount and the Steelers.

"If you look at the old film of the NFL in the '50s, nobody held anyone up," said Mike Brown, Paul's son, by then taking an increasingly influential role with the Bengals in the '70s. "If you came across at any depth, a linebacker would kill you, and receivers were very wary of crossing, but the outside guys didn't grab you. But the Steelers did, and we thought it was pass interference."

Greeted with the news of the change—some around the league were calling it "the Mel Blount rule"—Chuck was sanguine. It was only later, in 1978 and 1979, that Schramm and Brown and Shula and Davis would realize what they had wrought.

✦ ✦ ✦

In addition to the lawsuit, Chuck begun the off-season dealing with his trusted aide, Lionel Taylor, leaving for Los Angeles to join the Rams. Taylor's exit would remain something of a mystery. Some suspected he'd simply got an offer for more money. If this was the case, Taylor was not forthright about it. He would in his later years joke about wanting to find out if he could "really coach," without the benefit of the immensely skilled Swann and Stallworth. (Some suggested a personality conflict with fellow assistant Widenhofer, but both men denied it.)

To replace Taylor, Perles recommended the raspy-voiced, prematurely white-haired assistant Tom Moore as receivers coach. Moore had coached at Dayton in the past and Perles knew his keen understanding of the passing game would be an asset. "Hire him, and if you don't like him in a year, you can fire us both."

It was a tempting offer, partly because Chuck had already grown weary of the interview process. He wasn't comfortable getting to know a coach well enough to decide whether he'd hire him, then having to inform someone he'd chosen a different candidate. He relented, and Moore came in to fill Taylor's shoes. (There was a limit to the utility of hiring any and all teachers. Another Chuck hire, the former Dayton assistant John Spezaferro—a Marine with a manic air of macho—fit less well, though the players originally got a kick out of his outsized personality. He came in '76, as a high school coach who would work as an offensive assistant, and was gone by the end of the season.)

Steeler rookies were due to report to camp on July 14, 1977. Chuck was still on trial in a San Francisco district courthouse then. Much of the off-season had been spent with depositions and meetings in lawyers' offices, as a player from the team that had won the previous Super Bowl prepared to litigate against the coach of the team that had won the two Super Bowls before that.

"That is something Chuck should never have said," said Don Shula. "There were hits like that before, and there have been hits like that after. It is just the game of football, you know. Pretty violent game, pretty tough game. You get a lot of hits, some that aren't what they should be."

It was concern about that mind-set—that Chuck really did go too far—that informed the worry heading into the suit.

Two days before the lawsuit was to begin, Chuck and Dan received a letter from the Steelers' insurance company, urging them to accept a settlement deal with Atkinson for $50,000. "It is our opinion that while the monetary demand of $50,000 maybe [*sic*] negotiable to some degree, settlement of this lawsuit on the basis of that demand would not be unreasonable to eliminate the hazards attached to a trial of the issues involved. We recommend such a settlement." The company went on to assert that, if Chuck and Dan didn't want to settle, they would be liable for any verdict beyond the $50,000.

But there was never a chance of a settlement.

"It was just 'No,'" said Marianne, of Chuck's reaction. "He and Dan both felt very strongly. There wasn't ever a real discussion about settling."

"We felt we had to go to court to save the game," said Dan.

The case began in San Francisco district court on July 11. Chuck would be required to take the stand, as the sixth witness to do so, but then would be allowed to return to training camp in Pittsburgh, in time for the veterans to report on July 17, provided Dan stayed in San Francisco throughout the trial. They were put up at the St. Francis Hotel.

For players like Bleier, Bradshaw, Swann, and Harris, called out as witnesses, it was a chance to see Chuck in another element. Bleier and Harris flew out to California together for their testimony. "We were up in their suite," Bleier said, "and we had a beer or two with Marianne, who loved beer, and Chuck and Franco. I don't even know who else was there. But it was kind of a relaxed time. Because he normally didn't socialize with the players at all."

Over the course of examination, Chuck tangled with Daniel S. Mason, an attorney for Atkinson, who was accompanied by a blackboard on which he wrote the headline "NOLL'S NFL CRIMINALS." Through the interrogation for most of the day, Chuck wound up conceding that other players were guilty of similar violent hits. At one point, later in the questioning, he even conceded that Mel Blount and other Steelers had been guilty of the same sort of hits that Atkinson routinely engaged in. Mason turned that back on Chuck, and soon enough the headlines wrote themselves ("Noll: 3 Steelers Among NFL's 'Criminal Element'"; "Trial Brings Out Blount Sins"; "Noll Rips Steelers").

Back home in Georgia, fuming over his own stalled contract negotiations, Blount—jokingly called "Little Chuck" by some of his teammates, who knew how much Chuck valued the cornerback—announced that he would sue Chuck for $5 million and wouldn't play for him again.

The trial lasted for another week. Chuck was back in Latrobe when the jury, after four hours of deliberation, returned a verdict of not guilty on Friday, July 22. A UPI press report noted Chuck's reserve: "'We're very happy,' he said without emotion while eating dinner at his team's Pennsylvania training camp." Outside of the courthouse, Dan Rooney said, "I'm pleased. It has been the most depressing experience of my life, but I'm happy."

Summarizing the trial in *Sports Illustrated*, William Oscar Jonson wrote, "the ugliness of it had stained everything and everyone involved, and may well continue to smear the NFL for a long time to come."

For the league, the impact was clear, though less sudden. "I know what [Pete Rozelle's] ultimate reaction was," said Joe Browne. "He got Al off the Competition Committee. That was the straw that broke the camel's back."

The more tangible result of the aftermath of Atkinson's hit was that, in another year, the league would add a seventh official, a side judge, who would be responsible for surveying the field for infractions away from the ball. As Art McNally was huddling with Rozelle and other league officials, it became clear that none of the six officials on the field had done their job incorrectly.

Though Chuck was exonerated by the court, his troubles were far from over.

Jack Lambert was holding out, Blount was vowing never to play for Chuck again, and Glen Edwards continued to spar with the Steelers' prime negotiator, business manager Jim "Buff" Boston, over his contract.

"I would tell him, 'Man, this ain't *your* money. Not 'we,' not 'our,'—this ain't your money," said Edwards, who was angered by a deal considerably less than what fellow safety Mike Wagner had signed for.

While Blount was furious about Chuck's comment, he was even more riled about his own negotiations with Buff Boston, who flew down to Georgia during the off-season and offered him a $5,000 raise. When Blount declined, Boston replied, "Well, you'll starve then."

Blount took it as the affront it was. "So now I'm pissed," Blount said. "It's an insult. In today's world, it would be a racial slur." (Of Buff Boston, Joe Gordon would say, "He was a good friend of mine, but his negotiating style was from the Neanderthal days.")

Blount held out for eight weeks, finally reporting on September 15, just days before the season opener. In doing so, he consented to play for Chuck again.

"We never was enemies," Blount said of his coach. "Anytime you're in a war, you have a tendency to say things. Some things, they're meant. Some things, they're not. I've always said I felt Chuck was a fine coach and a fine gentleman."

The day Blount came back, Chuck reinstalled him at his starting spot at cornerback. Bud Carson, who'd been critical of Blount over the years, had considered starting cornerback Jimmy Allen, a fourth-rounder in the 1974 draft, but Allen had been injured. Blount, by now a seasoned vet at a crucial position, soon proved he didn't need a training camp. During the season he'd be joined in the secondary by a rookie who'd never played the position before—and who would eventually find, through Chuck, a path to his own life's work.

The second day of the 1977 draft, Tony Dungy was in Minneapolis, waiting to receive one call earlier in the day, telling him he'd been drafted. Instead he received several calls later in the day, after he'd gone undrafted, from teams hoping to sign him to a free-agent contract and bring him into camp.

Dungy had choices. Montreal owned his rights in the Canadian Football League, and GM Bill Polian and coach Marv Levy were urging him to come north and be a star quarterback. But Dungy wanted to play in the NFL. He was leaning toward signing with the Buffalo Bills when he got a call from his old college coach Tom Moore, who'd been at Minnesota before coming to the Steelers.

"I will fly out there with a contract tomorrow," said Moore. "You are the type of guy Chuck would like." Dungy was persuaded and signed with the Steelers the next day.

In July, he reported to training camp in Latrobe. The first full practice with veterans and rookies would remain with Dungy for the rest of his life. "Number one is your stance, and every single player got in his stance," said Dungy. "And Chuck looked at every single player, and he is adjusting people, and I am thinking, *Wait a minute now; Joe Greene has been to eight Pro Bowls*, and Chuck is moving his foot and getting him in the right spot. It was a lecture taught by a senior professor on how to block and how to tackle."

The Steelers had signed Dungy with a guarantee that he could try on offense, but after three days in camp—and a closer look at Swann, Stallworth, and the other receivers—they convinced him to try it as a defensive back. Moore told him later, "We knew we would have a tough time selling you if we said you were gonna be on defense right way, but we knew that would be the best place for you, so we had to kind of let it play out."

It played out as Chuck would have hoped. Dungy traded in the black and white offensive practice jerseys for the gold defensive practice jerseys, started hounding the film man Bob McCartney daily for cut-ups to learn the techniques of safety play, and the intricacies of the coverage schemes, and by the second preseason game had shown a deep enough understanding of the defense that Carson felt free to put him in the game.

Edwards gave him the best advice: "All you got to do is look at the quarterback and where he is looking, and that is where you go, because that sucker ain't going to have time to reload. So don't hesitate—just go."

That training camp, players on both sides of the ball looked with fascination upon the preternaturally mature rookie. "I saw Dungy and I said, 'There is no way that this *average* human being is gonna make this team,'" said Fuqua. But Dungy adapted, began playing nickel back before the next-to-last preseason game. Moore had been right—he was precisely Chuck's kind of player.

For the rookie Dungy, thrilled to have made the team at a position he'd played for less than six weeks, it was a continual learning curve. He was, like every marginal player on the team, assigned special teams duties. One day, he was put in as the wide man on the punt return team, squaring off against the punting team's "gunner" one of two outside men who could release downfield before the ball was punted.

Chuck was coaching special teams and walked Dungy through it. "You and another guy are here, you're 2-on-1, and you're just holding this guy up, so he cannot get off the line scrimmage and downfield. You've got to just eliminate him, and make him a total nonfactor in the play, and here is how we do it."

Dungy responded to Chuck's clean, elegant teaching style—the what and how, clarified by the why—and internalized the reasoning.

The next day, Dungy was on the punting team and put out at the gunner position. Chuck came to him again, to explain the salient points.

"Okay, now they've got two guys on you," he explained. "No way they can hold you up. You've got to pick out one guy, beat him first, then take on the second guy and beat him. You've got to get down there—"

"But, Coach," said Dungy, "you just told me yesterday there is no way this guy can get down there. Now you're telling me there is no way these two guys can block him." Dungy didn't mean it disrespectfully, and Chuck didn't take it as such. The hint of a smile creased the corners of his mouth, and he fixed Dungy with a steady gaze.

"You know what it is?," Chuck said. "It is who is going the hardest, and what state of mind they are in. That is going to determine who gets the job done. The whole game is a state of mind."

It was in that moment, in which Chuck brought together technique, strategy, philosophy, and the added ingredient of will, that Dungy fully bought in. After the practice, spotting Dungy in the locker room, Chuck came over and added, "Tony—if it was easy, there would be 80,000 people doing it, and 47 people watching. There are no easy jobs down here. It is hard. It is a state of mind, and who has the toughest mentality."

Dungy, jug-eared, wide-eyed, sat at his locker, transformed. "He made you think, 'Yeah, this might be an impossible job. But if I do it the way he says to do it, I can do it.' That is what his genius was, to me."

For most of the veterans, the 1977 season—barring the bizarre sideshow of the Atkinson lawsuit—was business as usual under Chuck. Though the lawsuit was a distraction, their coach didn't *seem* distracted.

"Chuck had the most incredible ability to put things where they belong—this goes in here—and he always had that," said Marianne. So

Chuck compartmentalized the lawsuit, never mentioned it to the team, and focused his energies on the season.

Yet the season still began with the team in flux. Andy Russell and Ray Mansfield had both retired following fourteen-year NFL careers. Gordon Gravelle had been traded, so there were changes at linebacker and along the offensive line.

Defensively, Chuck and Bud Carson, along with Widenhofer and Perles, had spent much of the off-season discussing how the new rule changes—which would prohibit defenders from touching a receiver more than once on his route—would affect the defense. "We are not going to let them legislate our aggressiveness away from us," said Chuck.

In Houston, in the third game of the season, Bradshaw broke his wrist and his backup Kruczek was injured as well. After Ralph Berlin gave him the news that Kruczek was also out for the game, Chuck walked over to find the former college quarterback Dungy on the sidelines. "Tony, what do you remember from those first three days at camp?"

Dungy blinked and looked up at Chuck. "I know 19 Straight, Flow 36, some running plays, a few passes." Dungy went in at quarterback, and the Steelers ran those handful of plays for the remainder of the game, during which Dungy threw an interception, earning him the distinction of being the only player in the two-platoon era to intercept a pass and throw an interception in the same game.

It was a season of stops and starts. The Steelers could look superb, as in a 28–13 thrashing of the Cowboys in the middle of the season. And they could look hapless, as they did in a 21–7 loss to the ascendant Broncos—in the full bloom of their "Orange Crush" mania—during the season.

They were good in 1977, but they weren't lucky. On December 9, on his way to a restaurant on the eve of a Saturday game in Cincinnati, Chuck slipped on the ice and fractured his elbow. He went ahead and went to dinner, not going to the hospital until later that night. (What George Perles remembered best was on Saturday, when the team boarded the bus for the ride to Riverfront Stadium, Chuck insisted on carrying his own bags.)

The next day would find the game played in a testing freeze. The field was covered with urea pellets, made from cow urine, to melt the ice on the artificial turf of Riverfront Stadium. Ernie Holmes knocked Bengals' quarterback Ken Anderson out of the game in the third quarter, but

Anderson came back, throwing the game-winning pass to Pat McInally. The final score, 17–10, meant that Cincinnati owned the tiebreaker over Pittsburgh if both teams won their games the following week.

But the Oilers, showing signs of life under the homespun Bum Phillips, beat Cincinnati, to open the door for Pittsburgh. Pittsburgh trailed San Diego 9–0 at halftime before rallying for a 10–9 win, intercepting Dan Fouts three times in the process. "We ought to give Bum Phillips the game ball," said an ebullient Bradshaw after the Steelers' win.

Joe Greene, weighing Pittsburgh's chances in the playoffs, tried to put the team's strengths in their Super Bowl–winning seasons in perspective. "We won it the first time on defense," he said. "The second time it was 50–50. This time, I think the offense will have to go about 60–40 with us. Sure, the defense can still come up with the big play, but I don't think we can dominate anymore."

The playoff game in Denver was a microcosm of the season. The offense outplayed the Broncos in the first half, outgaining them 183–44, but the teams entered halftime tied, thanks to a blocked punt and a Franco Harris fumble. Greene, growing frustrated with the holding tactics of Paul Howard, punched the Broncos lineman after one play late in the first half, and the two teams nearly brawled heading to the locker room at halftime.

Broncos' coach Red Miller and Babe Parilli, the former Steelers' assistant, were both shouting at Greene, and Perles was shouting back at them. Chuck and the Broncos' head coach, Red Miller, had to be separated in the tunnel.

The missed opportunities of the first half were compounded by two Bradshaw interceptions in the fourth quarter. And as the clock ran out, there was an air of finality to the defeat.

In the locker room afterward, Greene wouldn't apologize for the punch to Howard, Bradshaw put on a brave face ("I'm not going to hold my head down," he said), while Chuck simply refused to talk about the scuffle or the punch that precipitated it.

"I remember the ride home," said Ken Deininger, then in his first year of working as a game assistant to Bob McCartney on the Steelers' film crew. "Because Aunt Marianne came with us. We are riding in the car and this is one of the few times where I was riding home with them, because usually I would get off the plane and have to go develop the film, so I would go with Mac. Because it was the end of the season, we didn't have to develop the film right away, so I just came home with them. I remember the car just being somber. My gut feeling was that there was Uncle Chuck, just going over the game in his head again and again."

For new players like Dungy, the result was mystifying. "We had all that great talent," he said, "but there were lots of problems. Players unhappy over money mostly. Teams we were better than just simply beat us."

To Chuck, there was the painful end of the season, the loss due to self-inflicted wounds, a team behaving in a way that was largely uncharacteristic. To others, viewing the defense's decline and a team two seasons removed from Super Bowl glory, the game marked more than the end of a season.

Vito Stellino, writing in the *Post-Gazette,* was emphatic in his conclusion to his game story: "They rang down the Steel Curtain on the end of an era this weekend."

sixteen

A DIFFERENT WAY

✦ ✦ ✦

It was midway through the 1977 season, during one of the informal weightlifting sessions after a midweek practice. In the cramped weight room deep inside Three Rivers, Terry Bradshaw spotted Art Rooney Jr. and motioned him over. The two weren't close, but both had tangled with Chuck. That was common ground enough for Bradshaw.

Speaking conspiratorially, rattling his weight equipment to keep from being overheard by others, Bradshaw launched into an extended critique of his head coach. The litany of complaints—Chuck was too serious, he never laughed, he made you feel foolish, and you were never sure of yourself—were familiar to both men. Artie stood there, nodding in acknowledgment but still circumspect. Bradshaw, seeking encouragement, pointed out the obvious: "You're always getting into it with him, too."

This much was true, but the personnel man raised his palms in a conciliatory gesture. "Look, he's made me a genius," said Artie. "And you may have gone somewhere and struggled, and played for years and then got traded somewhere else, or been somewhere they brought a new coach in.

Both of us, he made us look like we're something special. You actually *are* special."

Bradshaw pondered that for a moment, then said, "Aw, dammit, you're probably right."

A week later, being interviewed by a TV broadcaster, Bradshaw parroted back Artie's words, almost verbatim, without attribution. Even after two Super Bowl rings, the quarterback was a work in progress, as both a player and a person. He would cloak himself in attitudes, submerge himself into a new mind-set—the devout Christian, the country hayseed, the introspective artist. Beneath the serial facades, by all accounts, Bradshaw continued to feel insecure, unappreciated, and unloved. He had few close friends on the team or, to put a finer point on it, he had one or two close friends for a while and then would switch to others.

"Terry never stayed close to anyone very long," said one longtime Steeler.

But he was forced to stay close to his coach.

By 1977, Hanratty and Gilliam were gone. Mike Kruczek remained the backup and, starting in 1977, the new third quarterback was a strong-armed project out of Youngstown State named Cliff Stoudt, whose talents had shown through the triple-option offense his team ran in college. (Knowing the Packers were interested in Stoudt as well, Chuck had executed a draft-day trade to acquire the pick one spot before Green Bay's and selected Stoudt in the fifth round.) Every day, after practice, Chuck would bring the three quarterbacks in for film review.

"We were normally there until 7 p.m. every night," said Stoudt. "We would watch practice film, then we would go down to the little kitchen at the end of the hallway and make sandwiches, and then we would go back and watch more film. The film was constantly breaking, and instead of taking a break while Chuck fixed it, he would bring out his little kit and meticulously put the tape back together and rethread it. It was the longest, most silent, most boring time of my life. But we learned a *lot*. We watched film so much it was unbelievable. Our whole life was spent with Chuck."

The daily meetings often evolved into an unspoken battle of the wills between Chuck and his starting quarterback. Bradshaw would bring a cup in which to spit his tobacco, though his aim was less than perfect. Tobacco stains dotted the carpet of Chuck's office. "Chuck put up with

it," said Stoudt. "If it was me, I think I probably would have had to sham-
poo the carpet every night. Bradshaw got away with it." Chuck's patience
wasn't endless. On the occasions where Bradshaw brought one of Art
Rooney's mammoth cigars into the office, Chuck placed a fan right on his
desk, blowing the cigar smoke back into Bradshaw's face.

For Chuck, it went beyond a question of temperament. Bradshaw's
casual methods and lack of conviction were unseemly to him, bespeaking
a lack of dedication or commitment. It annoyed Chuck that the leader of
his team spent so much of his free time traveling out of town to see his
wife, Jo Jo Starbuck. It vexed him that Bradshaw wore a Red Man chewing tobacco cap on the sidelines. It had annoyed Chuck when Bradshaw
repeatedly called Joe Gilliam "Sweet Nigger" (it was meant, by Bradshaw,
as a term of endearment) during the '73 season. In the spring of 1978,
Chuck and Bradshaw tried to play a round of golf together. They only
lasted nine holes.

While some Steelers players felt Chuck drove Bradshaw too hard, most
felt that the coach made many allowances to protect his quarterback.

"I never saw the supposed hatred or animosity between these two
guys, and I didn't have my head in the sand for twelve years here," said
Jack Ham. "I always felt that Chuck tended to be a little bit more lenient
with Terry on issues, versus everybody else, where if it was me or Jack
Lambert or Andy Russell, it would have been cut and dry. I just think
Chuck was trying to deflect a lot of that stuff away from Terry."

"I don't ever remember Chuck yelling at him at practice," said Stoudt.
"He would almost call him close and whisper things to him, so that
nobody else did hear it. But I think he knew exactly how he had to treat
Terry Bradshaw, and it certainly worked for Terry Bradshaw."

Many players remembered Bradshaw's horrifically bad performance
against Buffalo early in the 1975 season—at times, he seemed to be
throwing to no one in particular or, if anyone, then perhaps a Bills player.
"Chuck somehow went home and read that you need to eat an X amount
of pasta because if you don't, something with your vision suffers," said
defensive lineman Gary Dunn. "We come into our Tuesday meeting and
Chuck gets up and he starts talking this whole speech on nutrition and
pasta. And we are ready to get chewed out, and we are talking about nutrition and pasta, and people's vision. He didn't mention it but we knew it
was about Bradshaw. Saying that it helps your vision and you need a bet-

ter diet and all this stuff. You know what, he hardly talked about the game. We all walk out going, *What the heck was that? It was all about pasta.* And, 'Brad, you've got to eat some more pasta.' He goes, 'Okay, I will eat some pasta.' So the next day, Lynn Swann threw like fifty boxes of spaghetti in Bradshaw's locker."

By the start of the 1978 season, the two men had made an uneasy truce, each aware of the other's idiosyncrasies, both accepting of the fact that the team's fate was tied in large part to how well they worked together.

The memory of the two game-killing fourth-quarter interceptions at the playoff game in Denver the previous year was still fresh. What Chuck concentrated on heading into the '78 season, with receivers coach Tom Moore, was a way to keep Bradshaw's aggressiveness, while minimizing the mistakes.

Accompanying this was the recognition that the Steelers' receivers were going to be freer than ever before in '78, after the league further liberalized the passing rules—defenders still could hit a wide receiver just once before the ball was thrown, and now that contact would have to be within five yards of the line of scrimmage. Tex Schramm and Paul Brown had pushed the rule through the Competition Committee, at least partially with an eye toward further neutralizing the physical tactics of the Steelers' secondary.

The rule was a detriment to the Steelers' defense but a boon for the Steelers' offense. Pittsburgh passed for less than 2,000 yards and twelve touchdowns in 1974. In 1978, the offense would throw for nearly 2,700 yards and twenty-eight touchdowns. Chuck and Moore had devised a new offensive wrinkle, taking out a tight end on some plays to bring in a third wide receiver, usually the fleet second-year man Jim Smith from Michigan. They would stick with two backs, so they'd still have a running threat, as well as the ability to pick up blitzes.

"It was a combination of the rules changing and those guys having been together for a period of time, and it all kind of fell into place," said Moore. "But to Chuck's credit, it was his greatness to realize, 'Hey, here's what we've got. Let's utilize it and take advantage of it.'"

✦ ✦ ✦

On June 1, the *Pittsburgh Press* reporter John Clayton reported that that the Steelers were working out in pads during some of their off-season workouts, in violation of the league rules prohibiting pads for off-season activities. An embarrassment to the team, it revealed a glimpse of how insular Chuck had become, and it was clear how much it rankled him that he was perceived as skirting the rules in the same way his nemesis Al Davis had. Chuck exacerbated the situation when speaking to the *Press's* columnist Glenn Sheeley a few days later. "That story had no news value whatsoever," Chuck said. "The thing that made it very bad was that the story was of no news to the people of Pittsburgh. So I have to assume that [Clayton] is working for the competition. He certainly wasn't working in the interest of the paper or the fans. As far as I'm concerned he was working for the other people. The only way I can read it is espionage. I know for a fact that other people use other media for their interests, to spy."

During the interview, Chuck stormed out of his own office. Even later, his handling of the controversy was disingenuous at best. "I made no attempt to hide that practice session," he said. "It was a silly rule and the league knew how I felt about it. Anytime you've got people going full speed on a football field, they've got to wear pads—for their own protection. My views weren't any secret. But it was written as if I'd tried to put something over. The writer didn't call me about it to hear my explanation. He simply called the league and said, 'What are you going to do about it?' Then he asked [NFLPA executive director] Ed Garvey the same thing. That's why I got upset." (Of course, this explanation ignored the fact that the rule was in place precisely so players weren't going full speed in off-season workouts.)

Despite the controversy over practicing in full pads, the team seemed more harmonious and focused entering training camp in 1978. Bud Carson had decided that he would never be elevated from Chuck's shadow, and therefore he needed to go somewhere else to improve his chances. The Rams' Carroll Rosenbloom, who'd hired Lionel Taylor a year earlier, broadly hinted to Carson that he'd be in line for the next head-coaching job with the Rams. "Chuck was a victim of his own success," said Dan Rooney. "The assistants thought, 'Chuck is getting all the credit here.' They weren't mad about it, exactly." Dan Radakovich also left for the Rams' staff, making it three former assistants of Chuck's in L.A.

Carson's exit was a loss, but it did eliminate the persistent tension between him and George Perles; both men had waited impatiently for head-coaching offers that hadn't come. In the absence of Carson, Chuck promoted Perles and Woody Widenhofer. Initially, he'd suggested they be co-defensive coordinators, but eventually Perles received the title, while Widenhofer performed the tasks the title conferred, sitting in the booth above the stadium and calling the defensive coverages.

Widenhofer was going through a divorce at the time. "He found out I was staying in a hotel, and I was looking for a place to live," said Widenhofer. "He invited me to live with him and Marianne. I mean, I didn't do it, but that guy is unbelievable. He treated me like a son."

Even among the players, the fractiousness and distractions of the 1977 season had dissipated. Three weeks into camp, Tony Dungy called his mother in Michigan and told her to save her money—she would need it to travel to Miami for the Super Bowl the following January. "We basically had all the same players," said Dungy, "but the money problems had been taken care of. Everyone was happy."

Well, not everyone. Later in the season, Chuck made the decision to trade Glen Edwards—Donnie Shell was overdue for a starting job anyway, and he could be moved to strong safety. The discussion between Chuck and Edwards was typically short, with Chuck informing Edwards he'd been traded to the Chargers, thanking him for his hard work, and wishing him good luck in the future. ("He put his head down, and couldn't look me in the eyes," said Edwards.)

"It was almost like a funeral that day, the atmosphere, when Glen Edwards left," said the rookie cornerback Ron Johnson. "He's been a family member, he's been a warrior with these guys, and they traded him to San Diego."

But the defense took on a younger cast. The unit had been rejuvenated by Robin Cole at linebacker, John Banaszak, and Gary Dunn on the defensive line, the rookie Johnson starting at cornerback, and Dungy as the nickel back.

What Johnson and the rest of the defensive backs had to deal with were the repercussions of the new rule changes.

For years, under Carson, the Steelers' cornerbacks disguised their intentions by lining up eight or nine yards from the line of scrimmage. They could move forward into man coverage, or back into a zone, but either way, they'd still be able to engage the wide receiver and push him off his route.

Now, with the new rule mandating that any contact had to be within five yards of the line of scrimmage, the flexibility was lost. In the new environment, there were things that were surrendered. "You'd get some balls in behind the corners in the Cover Two, in the side pockets," said Tony Dungy. Normally the corners were 12 to 15 yards deep, and maybe now they are only 8 to 12, because they had to be up closer to get that jam. People started trying to find the tight ends with great speed to get down the middle and threaten you, and it all depended on the pass rush. We thought we could handle it if we got good enough rush, but if you've got time to protect and time do things because you could get some separation between the corners and the deep safeties, now you had a bigger hole in the zone."

"We don't care about disguise," Chuck told the secondary. "Disguise used to be important for us. It is not now. We don't care if they know where we are at."

✦   ✦   ✦

Though they had been left for dead just nine months earlier, the Steelers began the '78 campaign superbly. Bradshaw threw for two touchdowns and more than 200 yards in each of the team's first three games, then the Steelers gutted out a tough 15–9 win at home over Cleveland, before storming on to three more easy victories en route to a 7–0 start.

The streak ended at home, against the steadily improving Houston Oilers and their rookie sensation, Earl Campbell. While he was held to just 89 yards on 21 carries, he scored three touchdowns in the 24–17 win.

The defense was back to its old dominant self, holding Los Angeles to just 10 points (though in a losing effort, as Bradshaw threw three interceptions) and Cincinnati to two field goals, in a 7–6 win. From there, the Steelers stormed to the end of the NFL's first sixteen-game regular season, holding their last five opponents below 100 yards rushing, and putting up a league best 14–2 record.

Bradshaw could still be maddeningly erratic. But by this point, the coach and the quarterback had reached an understanding. He led the league with twenty-eight touchdown passes and won the MVP award, though Chuck still blanched at the carelessness with the football that led to twenty interceptions.

"Chuck was just, that wasn't the way you played the game," said Dungy.

"I mean, 'We've got this set up, we're doing this, here is what the defense is doing, and now we are ready to go.' It was a constant battle, and by the end they had kind of grown used to each other, and it had become very efficient. We kind of knew Terry would have some of those, but the defense was good enough, and he was good enough that, if he threw an interception, he is going to come back and make plays so it was just kind of an unspoken, 'That's the way it is.' But I know Chuck would have preferred it the other way."

Seeded number one in the AFC, with home-field advantage throughout the playoffs, the Steelers returned to Three Rivers for their first home playoff game in three seasons—to play the Broncos, whom they'd beaten in Denver in the regular-season finale. The game was still in doubt, Pittsburgh leading 19–10, when Joe Greene blocked a field goal attempt in the third quarter. Bradshaw found Stallworth on a 45-yard touchdown pass and Swann on a 38-yard score within a minute of the fourth quarter (the Steelers special teams recovered a fumble on the intervening kickoff). What had happened over the course of the season was a subtle shift that would have broad implications. The strong, steady Stallworth had emerged as, at least, the equal to the flashy Super Bowl MVP Swann.

The next week featured frigid, wet weather, and the build-up of the game focused on how the indoor Oilers would be able to adapt to the extreme conditions. The temperature was 27 degrees, with freezing rain, at kickoff.

The Steelers took an early 14–3 lead, then scored 17 points in the final minute of the first half, on the back of two Houston turnovers.

"Tell the defense to stop getting the ball back to us so fast," Bradshaw told Chuck before heading out onto the field again. "I haven't had time to think what I'm going to call."

He had the presence of mind to send Stallworth into the end zone, giving the Steelers a 31–3 halftime lead. The final score was 34–5, and the Steelers—less than a year after even hometown reporters were pronouncing it the end of an era—were heading back to the Super Bowl.

"Weather is a state of mind," said Ham after the game. "We didn't care what the weather was going to be. Nothing bothers this team. That's something that comes down from Chuck. He doesn't let anything bother him, and it rubs off."

There was another party at Jack and Joanne Ham's that night. Players, staff, even most of the coaches were there. Chuck stayed home. "He encouraged all of that," said Dungy. "But, no, it is just not something he would have done."

The Super Bowl would again be in Miami, and would again be against the Cowboys, the defending Super Bowl champions. Two nights before the game, Chuck and Marianne went out to dinner with Don and Dorothy Shula and John and Ruth Sandusky. "He knew all the good wines," said Shula. "He was ordering wine that they thought that they had, and they would bring it up and there was dust on the bottles, from being down in the basement for a long period of time. And Chuck would say, 'That's the one.'"

The game itself was billed as a battle of contrasts, the Steelers' work-manlike power game against the snap and dazzle of the Cowboys' multiple offense and Flex defense. The two most successful football teams of the decade, each with a pair of Super Bowl wins to their credit. Even *Newsweek* put the coming game on its cover.

Many in the NFL resented Schramm's bluster and the conscious positioning of the Cowboys as "America's Team." Chuck and the Steelers obviously had less to be jealous of, but there was an edge there nonetheless. When Chuck and Marianne hosted his assistant coaches and their wives for a dinner each off-season, he often brought out the ukulele to sing "Mama Don't Let Your Babies Grow Up to Be Cowboys."

Added to that was the pregame controversy sparked by Cowboy linebacker Thomas "Hollywood" Henderson's remarks, that Bradshaw "couldn't spell 'cat' if you spotted him the C and the A." At his Super Bowl week press conference, Chuck defended Bradshaw's intelligence and delivered a casual swipe at Henderson. "Empty barrels make the most noise," he said, echoing the maxim that his grandmother Steigerwald often used.

In fact, Chuck had grown weary with the Cowboys' reputation as the innovative darlings of the league. Though the Steelers were one of the first teams to use a dedicated flexibility program (hiring Paul Uram in 1973), the Cowboys earned the title of innovators. Though the Steelers had drafted as well as anyone since 1969, the Cowboys were viewed as cutting-edge with their computerized system (which, in truth, was used by many teams in the NFL by that point).

"None of that stuff impressed him," agreed George Perles. "He thought it was all bullshit."

"Chuck did not like the Cowboys," said Gary Dunn. "We used to play the last preseason game every year down in Dallas [from 1974–81], hot as heck. And Chuck would be up there, and you would think it was the Super Bowl. I mean he wanted to beat those guys. He didn't tell us but he was definitely extra enthused to play the Cowboys down in Miami. I would have to say he still had a pretty relaxed demeanor the whole time, but we knew that was a big rivalry there."

Even visually, Chuck and Landry provided a noticeable contrast. Landry in his inevitable fedora, suit, and tie, looking every bit the banker on the way to an important meeting. Chuck, not exactly relaxed, but *composed*, in a white-collared Steelers shirt and a black Steelers windbreaker.

In the locker room beforehand, his speech to the team was customarily succinct. "Fellas, what is it?," Chuck asked. "What turns you on? Is it the ring? You get to wear that ring the rest of your life? Is it the money? Is it the extra paycheck you're going to get? Something has got to excite you." That was it. He then repeated an earlier maxim—*Sunday is fun day*—and led the team out to the field.

On the field during warm-ups, Bradshaw spoke for a few moments with Staubach, but spent more time scanning the stands for his wife, Jo Jo Starbuck, whom he'd invited to the game. "She didn't care about football and didn't particularly want to come to the game. . . . I'm coming off my greatest year, playing the biggest game of my career, having spent most of the year alone because my wife was traveling around the world ice skating, and on top of this I've got this clown Henderson insulting my intelligence."

After taking a 7–0 lead on a strong opening drive, Bradshaw spent the next fifteen minutes looking like the inept quarterback of the early '70s. He threw a bad interception, fumbled the ball twice, the second time having it stripped from him and returned for a touchdown by the Cowboys' Mike Hegman, to give Dallas a 14–7 lead.

Earlier in his career, he might have pouted or panicked, but the veteran Bradshaw was more resilient. He found Stallworth on the sideline, on one of the Steelers' 70 Basic routes, and the receiver broke one tackle and ran diagonally across the field for a 75-yard touchdown. Near the end of the half, Bradshaw drove Pittsburgh down again, finding Bleier in the end zone on a rollout run-pass option, similar to what Pittsburgh had scored on in Super Bowls IX and X, to go into halftime with a 21–14 lead.

Forged in the crucible of Chuck's intense coaching, Bradshaw had emerged to have what Tom Moore described as "the greatest demeanor of any guy I have ever seen in calling plays. Because he kind of thought every play was first and ten, you are always on the 50, the score was always nothing to nothing. Don't worry about it, just play smart, not scared."

The old edginess in the huddle never entirely disappeared. Others would jabber, the cantankerous Webster still would call his quarterback "Turdshaw" to his face—men expressing affection through hostility—but the rest of the offense had come to believe in him, in ways they hadn't during the first pair of Super Bowls. "That was the key—his confidence," said Gerry Mullins. "He was lacking that before '74. But then he finally took control of the team."

The Cowboys were driving to tie the game with a touchdown when Jackie Smith dropped Staubach's pass in the end zone, leading to a Dallas field goal. Pittsburgh started the fourth quarter up, 21–17. When Bradshaw's deep pass to Swann elicited an interference call against Dallas cornerback Bennie Barnes, the Steelers had the break they needed. Up in the Cowboys' luxury box on the Orange Bowl mezzanine, right next to the commissioner's box, the Cowboys' Tex Schramm became unhinged. Pounding on the clear window separating his box from Rozelle's, he hurled epithets at Rozelle and gave the whole box—including Pete's elegant wife Carrie—the finger. Three plays later, Harris scored on a 22-yard run to give Pittsburgh a 28–17 lead. As in Super Bowl X, Dallas rallied late, but Pittsburgh prevailed by 4 points, this time 35–31.

The Steelers had become the first team to win three Super Bowls. They'd won their third title in the span of five years. (Back in Cleveland, as the relatives watched the game, it was Chuck's aunt Helen Steigerwald who, in the midst of the celebration at the final score, piped up and said, "Somebody go tell Chuckie to quit winning Super Bowls and let somebody else win.")

After the win, Chuck, in his white polo with the black windbreaker over it, smiling broadly, stood up on the podium between Pete Rozelle and Art Rooney. As Rozelle was presenting the Lombardi Trophy, Chuck stepped back and put an arm around Mr. Rooney's waist, moving him closer to the center of the podium.

After Rooney thanked his coach, his sons, and his team, broadcaster Mike Adamle put the microphone in front of Chuck. He wasn't even asked a question, but just began speaking: "I said one thing to our football team after the game, and I sincerely believe it. I don't think we've peaked yet. And we're looking forward to even bigger and better things."

From the players in the locker room, shouts of "Four!" could be heard. The gauntlet was thrown down. And Chuck stepped off the podium.

"I remember in the locker room, him just smiling like I'd never seen him smile before," said Gary Dunn.

"Hey, this is what we are in it for," Chuck told Tony Dungy. "This is what all of this work from July on has been for."

As Tom Moore sat in the locker room, having won his first Super Bowl, Chuck came over to shake his hand, and he said, "Congratulations. It's been a great ride. Let's do it again."

Dungy noticed the satisfaction but also what Chuck had said on the podium. "That was his way," said Dungy, "of saying, 'Hey, this is great—but don't rest on your laurels.'"

seventeen

LAST STAND

✦　✦　✦

After the third Super Bowl win, Chuck took his coaches and their wives to Acapulco, for another weeklong getaway. When he returned, he had a letter waiting from Blanton Collier, who'd coached him as an assistant with the Browns, and who'd later succeeded Paul Brown in Cleveland. Collier was considered by many to be among the great pure teachers in football history, and he was writing to congratulate Chuck on both the Super Bowl win and his more nuanced coaching and strategic efforts. "Your work in helping Bradshaw develop the use of his tremendous talent has been outstanding," wrote Collier. "The soft floating pass technique, a la Graham, has given him another dimension. . . . Finally that draw trap on [Cowboys' defensive tackle Randy] White was a work of art. I suppose the umpire helped a little by getting in the way but still the play design, execution and not to mention the strategy were all great." Chuck did not save much of his personal correspondence, but he saved the cherished Collier missive for the rest of his life.

Having returned to the summit of pro football, Chuck again threw himself with particular zest into his other interests during the off-season. He was shopping for high-end speakers again and fascinated with screen quality of new laser disc players. He'd upgraded his plane, selling the Bonanza to Dan Rooney, who'd caught the flying bug, and getting into a bigger, faster twin-engine plane, a Beechcraft Baron. By the time the coaches and their wives visited for his annual cookout in the summer, Chuck had made his first batch of dandelion wine. He was at the height of his powers, both on and off the field. But his life was about to get complicated in a different way.

Back in Cleveland, his sister Rita had reached her limit in trying to influence her second-youngest daughter, the vivacious and irrepressible twenty-year-old Joanne.

The Deiningers had escaped the neighborhood on 141st Street, to move west out to suburban Lakewood. They left a neighborhood with petty crime and empty lots and wound up in a middle-class environment with rampant drug use and widespread disaffection. Against that backdrop, Joanne was surviving, if not flourishing. Rather than attend college, she'd started working at the Cleveland department store Halle's and had advanced to a manager's job, working days and spending many of her nights drinking beer in Cleveland's eighteen-year-old clubs.

Marianne talked it over with Chuck, then consulted with Rita, then made the offer to Joanne by phone: "Okay, you need to go to school, you need to get a degree. Why don't you come here and go to Wheeler [Business School], and you can live with us for a while?"

It would be an adjustment on both sides. "I was in the bars," Joanne said. "My friends were in bands. You know, we did things. When I first came to Pittsburgh, there was none of that."

The Nolls had kept a loose rein on Chris, but he'd seemingly been born conscientious and inherited much of his father's preternatural maturity. Chuck knew how to deal with boys—there was Chris, of course, and the Manning boys—but raising a girl, even a twenty-year-old one, was new territory. Before Joanne arrived, Chuck cancelled his subscription to HBO.

"My mom didn't have cable, so I didn't even know what HBO was," said Joanne. "My uncle was very protective of me."

Joanne liked being there. She liked the cloth napkins, the fine china, the gourmet food, the enlightened conversation, and that they'd let her drink wine with them at the table.

"I realized they were human beings," said Joanne. "I mean, they were on pedestals. They were just the greatest people, and then all of a sudden I realized, *Okay, they're human.* They eat. They drink. They have fun. They argue. Well, they don't argue; they never argued."

Joanne quickly recognized the topics of discussion at Warwick Drive. "He never talked about football when we were together, at least when I was present," said Joanne. "He talked about everything *but* football—nature, whatever the political goings-on were, what was going on in the church, things like that, anything but football."

Joanne would witness the daily rhythms of Chuck and Marianne's life together, as well as the numerous ways they accommodated one another's tastes and idiosyncrasies. "Our kitchen was on the second floor in the back," said Marianne, "so I could see him when he drove in, and I would be playing all of this rock music, and he would be listening to public radio on the way home. So when he would pull in, I would switch the radio. Well, I didn't see him come in one time, and he walks in the door and he said, 'What the hell is this music?' And Joanne says, 'She listens to that all the time when you're not here.'"

By the time Joanne turned twenty-one in January, and started going out with friends, she'd internalized the family code. "I realized I can't really go drinking and come home drunk," Joanne said. "There is no way I could ever walk in that house drunk, you know. It was a big, big adjustment."

✦ ✦ ✦

The company that manufactured the Steelers' Super Bowl rings, Josten's, was under strict instructions to deliver the rings to the team no later than June 1. "We wanted that to be in the past by the time training camp started," said Dan Rooney. "Chuck made it very clear to the team each year that last year was over, in the past."

As Chuck returned for his eleventh training camp, the expectations were impossibly high.

Bradshaw, coming off his MVP year, had been very pointed about taking the off-season to decide whether he wanted to come back. Few of his teammates took him seriously. When he spoke to the press after the first day of training camp, he made a point of having agonized over a decision. "They gave me lots of space, and I made my own decision," Bradshaw said, before adding, "Of course, if they had called and said they needed me, I'd have come back, too."

As he came back to camp, though, Chuck got word that Bradshaw and his wife, Jo Jo Starbuck, were separating. The quarterback was miserable, and though Starbuck still spent most of the year touring, she'd insisted on taking possession of their Pittsburgh house.

Chuck called him into his office and made him the same offer he'd made a year earlier with Widenhofer, when he was going through a divorce.

"Terry, if you need a place to stay, you're welcome to stay with us."

Abashed, Bradshaw thanked him, but said he'd be okay.

What was clear to Chuck, and even clearer to his staff, was that many of the veterans on whom he'd counted for much of the past decade were no longer dominant. On the defensive line, Dwight White was being pressured by a young draftee from North Carolina A&T named Dwaine Board. Perles and Widenhofer believed Board had outplayed White in the pre-season. But Chuck insisted they keep White. For all his talk about players needing to prove themselves each season, and his vows that he couldn't get close to them, his quiet loyalty was a factor. Chuck didn't discuss it with his assistants, but he'd never forgotten White's superhuman effort to leave the hospital to play in Super Bowl IX.

"People thought Chuck didn't care," said trainer Ralph Berlin. "Chuck cared. Chuck cared very deeply about the players."

But even in those instances, even when it was one of his favorite players, he often couldn't or wouldn't express it. He summoned Tony Dungy to his office in the middle of training camp in 1979. The words were brief and to the point. "You have really played well for us for two years," Chuck said. "We have traded you to San Francisco. I think it is going to be a good opportunity for you. Thank you for your hard work." It could end that quickly.

At times, even some of the players wondered about Chuck. And in the absence of his praise, they could take even perceived slights to heart. The day before opening the '79 season, the Steelers flew to Boston, where they would open on *Monday Night Football* against the Patriots.

The team gathered for a meeting Sunday before practice. Several of the veterans were in the back of the large conference room.

"First game of the year tomorrow night," Chuck said. "I want to welcome all the new members to the team. We're going to go through short-yardage today. But before we do that, I want to introduce the captains for this coming year. Offensive captain, has been for some time, is number 57, Sam Davis. Sam, stand up and say hi."

Davis stood up to his teammates' cheers.

"For defense, we have two captains this year. First is number 75, Joe Greene. Joe, stand up. And our other captain is . . ."

The pause that followed lasted a beat too long. Jack Lambert, in the back, with a newspaper still partially raised over his face, whispered out of the corner of his mouth to Bleier and Wagner, and said, "He forgot my *name*. Jesus Christ, the fucker forgot my name."

Chuck finally resumed, ". . . and our other captain will be—that playboy back there." And he pointed toward Lambert, and the team applauded again.

"Mother*fucker*," hissed Lambert under the applause, and then Chuck picked up with the schedule for the special teams practice.

As the team dispersed to practice, Lambert waited outside the door and heard Chuck telling Hoak, on the way out, that he'd simply forgotten Lambert's name for the moment.

An hour or so later, in the visitors' locker room at Schaefer Stadium, as the team was preparing to go out for drills, Lambert fell in step with Hoak and lodged his complaint.

"He doesn't care about us," Lambert said. "Can't even remember my fucking name. Doesn't give us the time of day."

Hoak, serious and earnest, insisted, "Jack, Chuck *does* care. Maybe he forgot your name one minute, but he really does care. I know him. I've seen it."

Halfway down the field, Chuck was conferring with punter Craig Colquitt.

"Yeah, there's Chuck," said Lambert. "He's got his arm around those assholes over there, who can't play worth a shit. He never talks to Rock or me."

"He doesn't *have* to talk to you guys," said Hoak. "You give 110 percent all the time. You guys do a lot of work. There are some guys who put a tenth of what he needs them to, and he needs to prop them up."

By this time, Colquitt had started punting, and just as Lambert was responding to Hoak, saying, "But that's not fair—," an errant Colquitt punt drifted over to the sidelines and smacked into Lambert.

Rocky Bleier, standing nearby, froze.

"It hits Jack right in the face, and he doesn't have his helmet on," said Bleier. "He turns and, if looks could kill, Colquitt is *vaporized*. Jack's face is red."

From up the field, near Colquitt, Chuck called, "Well, if you weren't just standing there, you wouldn't have been hit."

Lambert turned to Hoak and said, "See what I mean!?"

✦ ✦ ✦

The next night, on *Monday Night Football*, the Steelers began their title defense with an overtime win at New England, Chuck's one hundreth victory as a head coach.

Pittsburgh's defense was still strong but, as Greene had hinted earlier, was no longer the dominant force of the mid-'70s. There were small factors, barely noticeable at first. The linemen weren't shedding blockers at first contact as adroitly as they once had. In the mid-'70s, outside rushers rarely turned the corner on the Steelers' defense, but now Greenwood wasn't always able to seal the edge. The pass rush, which had reliably harried quarterbacks with just the front four rushing for years, had slowly become less dominant. "Guys were starting to throw the football on first down against us," said Ham. "We are not getting a pass rush." Widenhofer called more blitzes, which helped create more sacks, but also led to longer gains.

The offense noticed the change as well. "We were getting older and things were not as easy," said Stallworth. "Those first few years, we'd say that nobody is going to drive the ball. If we kick off and we tackled the guy on the 20, nobody is going to score. Nobody is going to drive the ball 80 yards on us. We started to see some 80-yard drives."

There were more shootouts. Brian Sipe threw eight touchdown passes in two games against the Steelers in 1979, but Pittsburgh won both. The first was a 51–35 win in Cleveland. In that game, Bradshaw came off the field following the seventh touchdown drive of the day, to put Pittsburgh back up by 16, barking to Greene and Ham and the other defenders, "You think you guys can fuckin' hold 'em now?"

The defense did stand up during the marquee regular-season game, the Cowboys' visit to Pittsburgh. Staubach was knocked out of the game with a concussion, and the Steelers won 14–3. (Cowboys' president Tex Schramm, still arguing that Dallas not Pittsburgh should be considered for the amorphous title "Team of the Decade," was particularly disappointed.)

The defense, aging and battered—Greene was never fully healthy, Wagner broke his neck, Ham was out for much of the year—soldiered on. "Now, we are outscoring people," said Jack Ham. "Defensively, like I said, there wasn't—it was kind of like a putt that drops in the hole on the last half-revolution. There wasn't another revolution in it."

But offensively, the new rules were allowing more room for receivers, and in this environment, the Steelers were among the most dangerous teams in pro football. Other teams had a receiver who might have been the equal of Swann or Stallworth. But nobody else had two receivers of that caliber.

Bradshaw professed no preference, though in the next breath could express his skepticism about Swann's dedication. "When Lynn became a perennial All-Pro, however, it seemed his dedication slipped," he said. "He began working for ABC-TV and had so many outside interests. I questioned whether football was really that important to him anymore. Some games he didn't get open when I thought he should have, so I began looking for Stallworth."

Bradshaw's own outside interests were substantial as well—he also had his singing career, a burgeoning acting career, a stable of horses, and his own line of Terry Bradshaw Peanut Butter. But by now, Bradshaw and the nearly two dozen Steelers who'd been around since 1974 were accustomed to the attention. Despite a late-season loss on *Monday Night Football* to the upstart Oilers, Pittsburgh ended the season 12–4, and won the AFC Central again.

That gave the Steelers two weeks off before their first playoff game, and with Chris home for the holidays, they had their most conventional Christmas in years. On December 22, Chris's twenty-second birthday, Chuck had opened a bottle of 1966 Chateau Margaux. Chris only found out later that his father was so congested, he couldn't even taste a bottle of the most valuable wine he owned.

A night or two later, with snow gently falling among the tasteful, softly lit brick homes in the sanctuary of Upper St. Clair, the Nolls would have some surprise visitors. A group of Steelers had met at Swann's house that evening for a Christmas tree decorating party. Eventually they headed out to Art Rooney Sr.'s house and were invited in for drinks. The next stop was Dan Rooney's home, and then Artie's house (no one answered the door). Finally, someone said, "Let's go to Chaz's!" And soon enough, there were Mullins and Swann and Harris and Ham and some of their wives, knocking on the door at 81 Warwick Drive.

"I opened the door," said Chris, "and they were singing, and he said, 'Come on in.' They came in the living room and they sang songs. He got the guitar out and did the whole entertaining thing. I think it was just Christmas carols and silly stuff, and they had drinks. I was like, 'Oh, my God—this is so cool!' And that was the only time, because he tried to keep them at a distance."

The players themselves were prepared for almost anything—but none of them particularly expected to be charmed. Chuck eventually brought out the guitar and started playing songs. Marianne spoke about the framed photographs of wildlife, part of Chuck's penchant for photography. Mullins recognized one of the birds. "There was just so much warmth in that house," said Swann.

Leaving Warwick Drive that night, Swann said he felt like they had finally "pierced the veil. We have broken through. We kind of pushed ourselves on him, but he invited us in and treated us with respect, like regular folks. It was great. So a whole new era in our relationship with Chuck Noll had begun. And then the next day—it was the same thing. He was back to being Chuck."

Swann was in the training room, being taped, when Chuck walked by.

"I said, 'Hey, Chuck, how are you doing?' He just kind of nodded his head. I expected a more friendly response, and I didn't get it. That's just the way it was."

✦ ✦ ✦

Pittsburgh's first playoff game was the Sunday after Christmas, with a rematch of the '72 AFC title game at Three Rivers against the Dolphins. But while a few faces were the same—it would be Larry Csonka's last pro game—the outcome was far different. The Steelers scored on three long first-quarter drives to take a 20–0 lead, both Stallworth and Swann catching touchdown passes, then coasted to a 34–14 victory.

After the perfectly executed thrashing of the Dolphins, Joe Greene was asked what it was that set the Steelers apart from the rest of the NFL.

"Singleness of purpose," he said. "That just about covers it all."

Someone asked a follow-up—where did that come from?

"Chuck Noll," said Greene. "It all starts with him."

The next week was a rematch against the Oilers, who had defeated San Diego on the road the previous week. While the weather was marginally better than the year before—it was just cold, not wet this time—the results were the same. Pittsburgh held Earl Campbell to just 17 yards on 15 carries, and weathered an early error by Bradshaw (an interception returned 75 yards by Vernon Perry for the opening score) to take a 17–10 lead into the second half.

Late in the third quarter, with the Oilers driving, Mike Renfro made an acrobatic catch in the end zone, barely getting two feet down, but he was ruled out of bounds by the back judge. The Oilers, furious at the ruling, had to settle for a field goal. Pittsburgh continued to pound, scoring twice more in the final quarter to win 27–13. A day after Chuck's forty-eighth birthday, the Steelers had clinched their fourth Super Bowl trip in six seasons.

But the build-up to Super Bowl XIV would be different than any that Chuck had previously experienced. In addition to trying to become the first team to win four Super Bowls and the first to repeat back-to-back wins, they would be matched against the Rams, whose coaching staff was populated by three former Steelers' assistants, Bud Carson, Lionel Taylor, and Dan Radakovich.

"The whole thing with the papers and the TVs," said Dick Hoak, "was, 'Well, the Rams have an advantage. They have three ex-coaches from the Steelers so they know what the Steelers are going to do.' And my argument was always, well, we coached with those three guys, so we know what the hell *they're* going to do, so it evens out."

The defense threw in a few wrinkles, courtesy of Widenhofer, for blitzes that the Rams hadn't seen before. On offense, Chuck and Tom Moore agreed to change the live color—which had been "brown" virtually throughout the Noll years—that Bradshaw would call at the line if he wanted to change the play. They added a few new plays.

There was an extra note of gravity in the matchup between old friends.

"I know how to beat Bud," Chuck told Marianne in the week before the game.

By now, Super Bowl trips were becoming common for Chuck's friends and family. The Mannings made the trip, along with Rudy and Marilyn Regalado. Chris flew in from Rhode Island; Ken was there; Joanne celebrated her twenty-first birthday at the commissioner's party on the Friday before the game. As always, Chuck remained impervious, detached from it all, hermetically sealed in the process leading up to the game.

When the game started, at the Rose Bowl in Pasadena, under a brilliant southern California sky, a few things were apparent. The Rams' defense was inspired, formidable, and, as Chuck would put it later, "there was no question they knew everything we would do."

During the first half, Chuck became perturbed with all the fans who were using the reflective cards for the halftime spectacle to shine the reflection in players' eyes. He got word to Don Weiss, who was the NFL's game coordinator, and instructed the PA announcer to tell people to refrain.

All throughout the contest, there was a sense that the Steelers were on borrowed time. In the huddle, a more nervous than usual Bradshaw kept calling trap plays into the teeth of Fred Dryer. ("Brad, no," said Bleier in the huddle, when Bradshaw first called it.) The first play went for a two-yard loss, and it wouldn't soon get better. At the time, Bleier grew worried, thinking "He is really uptight about this game, for whatever reason. I mean, he is not listening. He is not loose."

The Rams, judiciously mixing the passing game while running successfully against the vaunted Steelers' front line, wouldn't be cowed, taking a 13–10 lead in the first half.

The Steelers' locker room was sober.

"I was concerned," was how Lambert put it. There was little emotion from Chuck, only a calm recitation of areas that need to improve and points of emphasis for Bradshaw.

There had been one brief, anomalous vignette. As Chuck started walking toward the locker room at the start of halftime, he noticed a CBS cameraman striding backward to hold a tight shot on him. The old self-consciousness returned, this time with a hint of playfulness. He took a first tentative step then swung his arms and pumped his legs as though to break into a dead sprint. Panicked, the alarmed cameraman rushed to keep up. And in that whisper of a moment it was over, Chuck slowed back down to a leisurely trot and smiled back at the cameraman.

Up in the stands, Chris was beaming. "I said, '*That* is the dad I know,'" he said. "He never shows anything funny. You never saw that, but all of a sudden one day, for some reason, he just kind of jumped at the guy."

The third quarter found the two teams trading touchdowns and then, with Bradshaw driving the Steelers toward the lead, two drives in a row ending on Bradshaw interceptions.

When the fourth quarter started, Pittsburgh still trailed 19–17, the running game was stalled, and Swann was out for the rest of the game with blurred vision. "We couldn't run the football," said Stallworth. "So we ended up going 60 Prevent Slot Hook and Go, because we knew that's what Bud likes to do—we knew he was going to double the wides."

Chuck told Bradshaw to call the play. "They're not going to give us anything short, so we have to go deep to beat these guys," he said. And then, before Bradshaw returned to the huddle, Chuck added, "You can do it!"

From the Rams' sideline, Carson had sent in a call in which his nickel back, Eddie Brown, was supposed to remain mindful of his deep responsibility. "I blew it," Brown said. "I should have gone to the inside but I took the outside receiver instead."

From the slot, Stallworth eluded Rod Perry, who had man-to-man responsibility on him, and knifed between safeties Dave Elmendorf and Brown. The pass hit Stallworth in stride and went for a 75-yard touchdown. The Steelers were back in front, 24–19.

But not, it appeared, for long. The Rams had outrushed the Steelers all day and drove back down the field. With the game hanging in the balance, they were in Pittsburgh territory again, driving for the lead. Lambert ducked his head into the huddle and looked at his teammates. "What the hell is the matter with you guys?! It's the fucking Super Bowl!" Two plays later, he intercepted a Vince Ferragamo pass, setting the stage for Bradshaw's dagger, another deep pass to Stallworth.

From the sidelines, Chuck watched Bradshaw launch a majestic throw that arched in a precise parabola (exactly the sort of throw he hadn't been able to make during the early years of his pro career) before settling into Stallworth's arms—he'd adjusted marvelously on the fly, switched shoulders, and came down with the ball behind Perry, for a 45-yard gain.

"Greatest catch I ever saw," said Lionel Taylor, watching from the other sideline. "I almost died."

Five plays later, Harris would bring it over to put Pittsburgh up, 31–19. A few minutes later, the Pittsburgh Steelers won their fourth Super Bowl in six seasons.

The team that walked off the field was comprised of forty-five players. Every one had played his entire professional career as a Steeler. Twenty-one of those Steelers had been on all four Super Bowl teams.

In the locker room, an interviewer asked Chuck if this was the Steelers' best team. "I don't think I have to say this is the best team we've ever had," Chuck said. "I think the facts speak for themselves."

Bradshaw, having won his fourth Super Bowl in ten seasons, speculated that he might retire now, while Lambert treated that statement with the same seriousness as most of Bradshaw's proclamations: "I don't know what he's talking about. I'll *make* him come back."

"It's tougher to win every year," said L. C. Greenwood. "The new season seems to start a couple of days after the old one ends."

To a man, the former Steelers' assistants on the Rams' sideline thought they should have won the game. When they gathered at the Rams' postgame party, the feelings of frustration deepened.

"It was like death," said Linda Carson, Bud's wife. "It was dead. Nobody was talking. I was dancing with Dan Radakovich's fourteen-year-old son, and Bud came up, drinking a lot of course, and grabbed me by the shoulder and said, 'Stop flirting with all of the guys here; stop flirting with this guy.' This is a fourteen-year-old kid of one of our best friends.

"So I am so mad at him, and he is so mad at the entire world, so we go upstairs to our room, which has a floor-to-ceiling window, and he sits down on the bed, and we are having this really big argument, and I say, 'Well, I'm just leaving you. It's over! I'm leaving you!' And I hear this noise and I think, *Oh, he's crying.* So I turn around, and—he's snoring! He went sound asleep during my big speech. So I decide—I had been drinking, too—okay, I'm going to push him out the window. So I start trying to push that bed across the room, and I'm going to throw him out of that floor-to-ceiling window. Fortunately, that window didn't open and I couldn't move the bed, but that was the kind of night it was."

By the time their old friends were arguing across town, Chuck and

Marianne were with family, friends, and the Steelers family at the Steelers' victory party. The festivities had a different feel—more relief than jubilation.

They were still in Pasadena when Chuck, the next morning, sat down with Marianne and gave her a message that resonated with dark gravity: "Get ready," he said. "We're old. And we're tired. The drafts haven't been very good. We've got some tough years ahead."

And Marianne knew, at once, something that forty-five players and thousands of Steelers fans wouldn't find out until the following fall. This time, an era really was ending.

eighteen

"ONE FOR THE THUMB"

✦　✦　✦

Chuck and Marianne were out to dinner one Thursday night. They had, typically, chosen a tasteful, quiet place, with a small dining room. Not an "in" place, but somewhere they knew the chef and the owner, where they could get a quick table, not in the center of the dining room. They wanted fine cuisine without a lavish fuss.

But sometimes people still stopped by. By now they had seen it all. Drunken fans wanting to relive entire seasons. Men with multiple pieces of memorabilia for Chuck to sign. A woman ogling Chuck from across the room, despite his being completely focused on Marianne, puckering her lips at him and, finally, walking by their table and sliding a napkin with her lipstick print by his elbow.

On this night, though, a man from a nearby table kept staring at them. Chuck and Marianne went on with their night, ate their food, sampled each other's dishes, discussed the wine, talked about the world.

At the end of the dinner, the man finished his meal and walked over to their table. Marianne girded herself. Chuck was always gracious, but drunks could hold forth for a much longer period of time.

The man approached. "I know who you are," he said to Chuck.

"Okay," said Chuck evenly.

"I just want to let you know," he continued, and then looked at both of them, "that I've never seen two people so in love in my entire life."

Chuck and Marianne laughed, exchanged a look, and thanked the man. He nodded and turned to go, but then caught himself. Touching Marianne on the shoulder, he blurted, "You . . . you *are* his wife, right?"

Marianne confirmed that she was Mrs. Noll, and the man retreated.

Chuck and Marianne laughed about that all the way home.

There was truth in the man's observation. The relationship wasn't merely symbiotic—Chuck providing the structure and security that Marianne needed, and Marianne providing the support and social graces that Chuck needed. They completed each other's sentences, they basked in each other's attention.

Early into his adulthood, Chris told them, only half-jokingly, "I'm never going to get married. I'm never going to find a relationship like you have."

It had been years since Chuck went to the mall or any traditional stores. Marianne would go shopping for his clothes, then bring them to him. He'd try them on, keep what he liked, and she'd return the rest.

In the mornings, Marianne would have coffee ready, and Chuck would eat a light breakfast—often cereal.

"They were a couple that communicated without talking," said Joanne. "I mean, they knew each other so well, and I am convinced that my uncle is as great as he is because she was there. Whatever needed done, she always did it. They were just perfect; they were made for each other."

At first glance, the division of labor couldn't have been any clearer or more traditional: The father went out, made the money, and came home. The mother kept the house, cooked the meals, and raised the child.

What didn't fit the conventional mold is the degree to which Chuck and Marianne continued growing together even after she stopped working traditional jobs. Marianne handled the checkbook but also the taxes, the real estate, the investments, virtually all of the long-term planning.

"She managed all the finances," said Chris. "She did all the investing; she did everything. He spent his whole life worrying about it, so now he didn't have to worry about it."

For all that, Chuck remained introverted with other people around. In the mornings, Joanne would hear him walk out the door, and Marianne tell Chuck she loved him.

"Okay . . . same," he would reply.

"He was always proper," said Joanne, "especially with me when I'm around. He didn't show affection. He didn't show any of that stuff. But I knew that they loved each other. It was obvious in just their everyday activities; just the way they dealt with each other."

✦   ✦   ✦

To his Dayton friends and old Brown teammates, Chuck was still the Pope. But in Pittsburgh, he was now "The Emperor," an equally infallible figure whose presence was reassuring to the Steelers' fan base. He had meant so much to the Steelers, who in turn had meant so much to the city.

After four Super Bowls, he finally consented to an in-depth profile. *Sports Illustrated*'s prickly, intense Paul "Dr. Z" Zimmerman spent time with Chuck out in wine country, for a lengthy two-part profile that ran in the summer of 1980. It was the most complete piece ever written about Chuck, as they bonded over both wine and old friends (Zimmerman had set up Marilyn Hall and Rudy Regalado).

The story touched on Chuck's nebulous politics, in which Chris intimated that his father supported John Connelly in 1980 but probably had voted for Carter in 1976 (Chuck hedged: "Chris said I voted for Carter? I'm not so sure.") The staunch liberal Joe Gordon viewed Chuck as one of his own: "I think Chuck was, at that time, a liberal. Civil rights and stuff like that, because he is very fair-minded."

Talking to Zimmerman, Chuck simply reiterated the belief that he'd been raised with: "In the first place, politicians deal in words, in leadership through rhetoric," he said. "I'm not in that business. But if you want to know what I'm against, it's handouts—getting too much in front."

"I would say he is more middle of the road," said Joanne. "Not too far right or too far left. He believed that everyone should earn what they get."

He had earned what he'd gotten. The summers were now being spent at Hilton Head (nearer to fly to than Florida), a world removed from the one that Chuck grew up in. Though adamant about never flaunting it in his personal appearance—there were no Rolexes, no tailored suits—the gadgets were a different matter: the first laser disc players, some of the finest high-end stereo systems ("he handed his old ones down to me," said Chris, "so he could get new ones"), planes, a player piano that went into the great room on Warwick Drive.

At dinner one night in Hilton Head, he was interrupted by a group of beatific Steelers fans, who hung around for autographs longer than usual.

When they finally left, as the family returned to their meal, his niece Marilyn—visiting from Cleveland—piped up, "Uncle Chuck, why don't you just tell them to go away?"

"Those fans pay my paycheck," Chuck said. "They're the reason why I'm here—they're the reason we get to do all this."

While Chuck reveled in the vacations, it was also true that the whole family could sense him growing more purposeful, more active—more in football mode—by the end of every month.

One summer, a couple of weeks before training camp, Chuck sat Marianne down one day and said, "Dear, I think it's time you started to run."

"Chuck, I play golf, I play tennis, I play racquetball . . ."

But he persuaded her, and late each afternoon, they would go down to the beach at Hilton Head and run in tandem. By late June, they were up to two miles a day. One afternoon, after they arrived on the beach, he turned to her and said, "Okay, I want you to start running backward."

Marianne smiled but was firm. "There's no way I'm ever going to be a DB."

Even he laughed. And two days later, he left for Latrobe.

✦ ✦ ✦

Expectations were impossibly high for 1980, as the Steelers attempted to match the Packers' accomplishment of winning five NFL titles in seven seasons. Joe Greene had announced that the team needed to win "one for the thumb."

On the first day of training camp, the Steelers were again greeted by over ten thousand fans lining the hills and sidewalks at St. Vincent. The rookie Tunch Ilkin, fresh out of Indiana State, looked around awestruck, thinking that there hadn't been that many people in attendance for the Sycamores' homecoming games.

In Bonaventure Hall, Chuck gave the same speech he'd given for years. Twelve-year veteran Jon Kolb, sitting near the back, had committed much of the talk to memory and softly mouthed the words along with Chuck.

"Leave the girls on campus alone," said Chuck, before adding, "We have already checked them out, you know."

It fell flat, like most of Chuck's jokes. ("He wasn't a good joke-teller," said George Perles. "He wanted to, but they always came out corny when he did them.")

"I remember the joke, and I remember Chuck did not tell jokes," said Ilkin, the son of a Turkish immigrant who'd been spotted on one of Artie Rooney's circuitous scouting trips through Big Ten country. "But I remember his presence. That is the one thing you just couldn't help but see; Chuck always had this presence about him."

The staff was back virtually intact. Even after four Super Bowl titles in six years, Perles and Widenhofer and Hoak had not found head-coaching offers. "They started getting upset that they weren't getting offers as head coaches, and I can see why," said Dan Rooney of the assistants. "Because everybody had so much respect for Chuck, they said, 'He does the whole thing. What am I going to hire this other guy for?'"

Stability was a virtue, though not when it came to players. The recent drafts hadn't been particularly fruitful, though both of the rookies Ilkin and Craig Wolfley looked like comers on the offensive line. But the age of the Steelers' core was an issue.

In the coaches' meetings at night during that preseason, Chuck seemed particularly pained. Rather than sitting at the head of the long table during the nightly meetings, he paced back and forth behind it. It was Mullins. The brash, likable lineman from Southern Cal had been a reliable mainstay on all four Steelers' Super Bowl teams. But Chuck sensed that at thirty-one, he had lost a step. What made the cut difficult was that it was a harbinger of others.

At a quarterback meeting in August, there was a knock on the door. A sheriff asked to speak with Bradshaw.

When Bradshaw stood up, the man said, "Sorry, Terry, but I need to personally hand you these papers."

Bradshaw thanked the man, took the envelope and placed it down, unopened. He then turned his attention back to the meeting.

Chuck continued, but noticed that Bradshaw was drifting.

"Don't you need to read that?," he asked Bradshaw.

Finally, Bradshaw opened the envelope and read the inevitable—his wife, Starbuck, was filing for divorce.

"Man, I started bawling," Bradshaw recalled. "I hadn't known I was getting divorced until I opened that envelope. I was devastated."

Despite losing twice to the resurgent Bengals (by a total of three points), the Steelers were 4–2 going into a Monday night home game against the Raiders. Bradshaw was sharp early, leading the Steelers to 10–0 and 17–7 leads, but Pittsburgh couldn't mount a pass rush, and the Raiders were expertly picking up Widenhofer's blitzes.

In the second half, Jim Plunkett threw three touchdown passes over the Steelers' defense, of 54, 45, and 36 yards.

"Man, it was Pearl Harbor out there," said Banaszak afterward. "It was just bombs away."

The Steelers trudged off the field, having lost 45–34, and as they reached the tunnel, some of the Steelers were still buzzing about what was at that point the highest-scoring game in *Monday Night Football* history.

"We came back into the locker room," said Wolfley. "I remember pulling my shoulder pads up, and everything else, trying to get undone. Everyone is talking and it is loud. All of a sudden, there was this *BOOM!* I remember I was kind of caught looking like a groundhog out of my shoulder pads, you know. I looked and I saw this helmet rattling around the locker where the source emanated from. I looked up and I see 'Greene' above it. Then I scoped back over, and it was Joe standing in the doorway. He just growled."

Bradshaw had bruised his right thumb during the game and had to sit out the next week. Stoudt stepped up and threw for 310 yards against the Browns, but Sipe riddled the Steelers, and suddenly Pittsburgh was 4–4, and sitting in third place in the AFC Central.

But they weren't done, winning two straight then playing host to the Browns at Three Rivers. Near the end of the game, Cleveland leading 13–9, Pittsburgh drove down the field. On second and then third and goal, the Steelers tried a quarterback option play called Sprint Right Pick.

"I remember the signal came in," said Wolfley. "Chuck wanted to run it again. I remember Bradshaw signaling time out, going over to the sidelines, and they are standing on the sidelines discussing it. Terry was making his plea to, at least, I don't know, run Sprint *Left* Pick, you know, something like that. And I remember Chuck nodding his head, and then another conversation. Finally, I saw that bulldog look come over him, and

I saw him mouth the words, 'Run it again.' And Bradshaw came back out, and everybody *knew*. And it scored and we won the game."

As the days shortened, and the games dwindled, the Steelers players bore down. Tempers got short. On the field, the Steelers were fighting among themselves. In a win over Miami in late November, Greene and Lambert nearly came to blows. Lambert had grabbed Greene by the waistband of his pants to move him into position at one point, and by the time they got to the sidelines, the argument threatened to spill over into a fistfight. (They went into a separate room after the game and emerged with the issue settled.)

A road loss to Buffalo had hurt, but the killing blow came a week following the Miami game, in an inept offensive performance—three Bradshaw interceptions and two Franco Harris fumbles—that sealed a 6–0 road defeat to the Oilers. It all but mathematically eliminated the Steelers, even after a win over Kansas City the following week. It wouldn't be enough.

Through the season, the team began to get a sense of its own mortality.

As age and injuries took their toll, the components of the Steel Curtain were disintegrating. Holmes was already gone, and now his old line mates were diminished as well. "Dwight White was gradually losing his place to John Banaszak," said John Stallworth. "John's a good player, and Dwight's losing that place. Joe is going through the injury that he has. L. C.'s out of the lineup and nursing his thumb. Ham is hurt and so he's not playing well. Franco's ankle is bothering him. Rocky is gone now and so guys are starting to come in and they are trying to take that role, and nobody seems to fit."

The 1980 regular season ended with a road game in San Diego, just as it had in 1972 when the Steelers began their string of eight consecutive playoff appearances, but this season would end without a postseason trip. For the first time in the professional careers of almost all the players, the football season was over by Christmas.

Bradshaw was furious during and after the finale, claiming some of his cohorts had stopped trying ("When I saw some of my teammates giving a half-assed effort, I was so appalled that I almost wanted to quit right after the game"). To the press, though, he was resolute. "Next year, everyone will write us off, and we'll come back and blow them out."

✦ ✦ ✦

The other footnote of the season was that it spelled the end to Chuck's flying career.

The circumstances were odd. In 1978, the writer Tom Callahan—who knew Chuck from the pick-up basketball games at the Towson Y during Chuck's years with the Colts—was working at the *Cincinnati Enquirer.*

During one of Callahan's off-the-record interviews with Paul Brown, Brown revealed that Chuck had been an epileptic. Callahan's memory of the conversation is that Brown told him the he cut Chuck in 1959 because he couldn't risk Chuck having an epileptic seizure on the field. Brown was prone to fits of pique with former players and assistants who'd crossed him, but this comment seemed more careless than malign. ("My father admired Chuck Noll," said Mike Brown. "He liked him. He wouldn't have tried to hurt him.")

When Callahan pitched the story to the Steelers, Joe Gordon confirmed that it was true (though he himself hadn't known about Chuck's condition until he asked Dan Rooney about it), but he asked Callahan not to report it. Callahan sat on the story and then, in the summer of 1979, wrote a column in the *Inquirer* about a sports figure "who presides over great events," and was a licensed pilot, and yet suffered from epilepsy. He didn't mention Chuck by name, but there were precious few figures in sports who were as well known as Chuck for being licensed pilots.

Several weeks later, the Federal Aviation Administration contacted the Steelers and asked Chuck to submit to a battery of tests to prove his fitness to fly.

Chuck considered the possibility and ultimately decided against it. He didn't want the distractions.

"All I know was his disappointment," said Joanne, "that he could no longer fly."

It necessitated a switch. Chuck had been out on boats before . . . he'd even bought a small craft with an outboard motor when they were married. Now, having to give up the plane, he considered a yacht. "He wanted a sailboat," said Joanne, "and my aunt said no, because she knew she was going to be the crew."

"It didn't take long," said Patrick Manning. "We're not talking a matter of months—we're talking weeks, and then he had the new boat."

When anyone would ask Chuck why he wasn't flying anymore, he was terse and oblique. He told them his plane had been hijacked.

✦   ✦   ✦

He had traded him for a draft choice two years earlier, but in 1981, Chuck hired Tony Dungy to be his secondary coach. He felt Dungy, though just twenty-five, had the patience and intellect to be a good coach.

Dungy was bright and serene and devoutly religious—he neither drank nor smoked, and his teammates had respected him for the degree to which he followed his own path. Chuck saw something more—an aspect of teaching that was similar to his own.

Dungy accepted the offer and arrived ready to immerse himself in the Noll system. Seeking more specifics from Chuck one day, Dungy asked, "What do you want me to do? Am I going to be taking off tape? Am I going to assist the defensive backfield coach?"

There was a moment of silence.

"Well, you're a coach now," Chuck said. "Your job is to help your players play better."

On the first day of training camp in 1981, Dungy arrived a half-hour before the scheduled coaches meeting. Perles was reading the newspaper, Widenhofer was shaving.

"I'm like, 'Okay, I've got my notebook, what are we going to do?,'" said Dungy. "Then I realized: You *know* what we are going to do. It is not going to change. Here is what we have to cover. The same thing we covered the first day last year. The same thing we covered the first day when I was a player. There is no meeting. This is it. That is when I understood. That was the beauty of it. There wasn't a lot of wasted time or wasted energy."

Walking through the front of the room at Bonaventure Hall, with eighty sets of eyes on him, Chuck asked his players, "You remember all of those reporters that were out here last year, when we had ten thousand people show up the first day of camp? They went somewhere else, because we didn't win, and now we're not the expert. They went to where the expert is."

For his part, Bradshaw had spent the off-season vowing to retire if the television pilot he did with Mel Tillis—a sitcom called *Stockers*—wound up being picked up. It did not, and he reported to camp on time.

The great debate during camp, between Chuck and Perles, was whether

Joe Greene continued to be the unquestioned starter at defensive tackle. It was one of dozens of discrete personnel decisions discussed in training camp. But this one had larger implications, because of Greene's stature on the team and his relationship with Chuck.

Tom Beasley was a young lineman, drafted from Virginia Tech in the third round of the 1977 draft. Chuck was aware of Beasley's limitations. But Perles was frank and uncompromising: "Chuck, I know it's tough, but Joe just doesn't have it anymore."

Chuck, slumped at his desk, considered the new players that had replaced his Super Bowl mainstays, and then exhaled. "Well," he said, "at least he *had* it."

And in that sense, an analysis could be made of the Steelers of the '80s. The players who'd arrived in the late '70s—Dunn and Beasley and Banaszak—were all useful players within the realm of a great defense, but none of them could be the linchpins of a great defense.

It was a sputtering year. Pittsburgh was at 5–3 when they lost to the 49ers, ascendant under Bill Walsh and Joe Montana. They lost again the next week, to fall to 5–5, before beginning a three-game winning streak, leaving them at 8–5.

It fell apart the next week in Oakland, where the Steelers lost to the Raiders for the fifth straight time, as Bradshaw broke his throwing hand on the helmet of the Raiders' Rod Martin while following through on a pass. A week later, at Three Rivers, second-year quarterback Mark Malone started as the Steelers lost the division—and any playoff hopes—to Cincinnati, 17–10. The season ended the next week with a 21–20 loss to Houston.

A day later Joe Greene returned to Chuck's office, for the conversation both knew was coming.

"Chuck," Greene said. "It's time. I've decided to retire."

"Well," said Chuck, "I guess it's time for you to get into your life's work."

Chuck shook his hand and thanked him for all the hard work. But he did not reminisce.

(Down the hall a few minutes later, Greene told Dan Rooney, who said, "Joe, do you remember that day in Philadelphia when you threw the football into the stands? You know what? I feel that same way.")

At the press conference, Chuck was not expansive but was emphatic. "There will never be another Joe Greene," he said.

✦ ✦ ✦

Over the summer of 1982, George Perles finally got a head-coaching job he'd long coveted, having been hired by the Philadelphia Stars of the upstart United States Football League, which would play its first season in the spring of 1983. (Just weeks later, Perles left the Stars to coach his alma mater, Michigan State.)

Jon Kolb, who'd retired after the 1981 season, had applied to be the Steelers full-time strength coach. But now Chuck had other ideas. Kolb was barbecuing in the backyard of his vacation cottage with his friend, Jets' defensive tackle Joe Klecko, when the phone rang. It was Ralph Berlin, calling from the Steelers' offices. He put Chuck on the phone.

"George Perles left," said Chuck.

"Yeah, I saw that," said Kolb.

"Well, I was trying to think of somebody to take his place . . ."

"Gee, Chuck, I don't know any defensive line coaches."

There was an extended silence.

Finally, Chuck said, "I thought maybe you would want to work with the defensive line."

Kolb paused a moment to comprehend what Chuck was asking, before replying, "Sure, that would be great."

"Okay, be at the stadium Monday at 9."

Kolb went back outside and explained to his family and Klecko about the call. The next day, he and Klecko flew to Pittsburgh and started watching game film, so Kolb could better understand the nuances of the defensive line play that he'd spent his entire playing career trying to parry.

In some ways, the hire was absurd. Kolb had never coached the position. Yet as a career offensive lineman, he was uniquely qualified to recognize how effective the defensive line could be. One of Kolb's earliest conclusions was that the Steelers had some of the speed but not enough of the firepower to continue to play the Stunt 4–3. At the meeting that Monday, Kolb and Chuck got into an intricate, animated discussion about the strengths and weaknesses of moving to a different base front.

They spent several minutes debating, before Chuck became irritated and, finally, convinced. "Fine, do that then," he said. It would characterize many of their discussions—spirited, at times heated, but never personal.

"I call it 'Last Chalk,'" said Kolb. "Whoever has the chalk last, wins."

In the weeks ahead, Kolb became aware of the invisible dividing line that Chuck always observed, the fact that even longtime players belonged in the other camp once they started coaching. "I walked in the dressing room," said Kolb, "and Mike Webster and a couple other guys were sitting there talking and they did exactly what we used to do when a coach walks in. You are talking and then you sit back and the conversation stops, and your conversation goes to some generic topic that the coaches are okay to hear. I walked in and that happened, and I thought, *Ten minutes ago, I was a player.* That was one of the things that was really a struggle for me and Mike. Tunch Ilkin and I remained good friends, and Craig Wolfley and I are really good friends. But Mike and I never connected again after that."

Chuck kept Woody Widenhofer as defensive coordinator, and brought in Dennis Fitzgerald to coach the linebackers. With Paul Uram leaving as conditioning coach, he hired Walt Evans, a consultant for General Nutrition Corp., who had befriended Kolb. The shake-up of the coaching staff continued into the training camp, when offensive line coach Rollie Dotsch was hired by the Birmingham Stallions of the USFL. Chuck hired Ron Blackledge, the father of Penn State's senior quarterback Todd, to be his new line coach.

When Walt Evans arrived, he'd cut out all the fats and grease from the players' diet. White bread and mayonnaise were off the training table— in fact, away from the cafeteria all together—as a morose Lambert was informed by a polite but dutiful nun in the kitchen.

It finally came to a head a few days after the Steelers broke camp.

The players took their lunch up at the Allegheny Club, and Evans's draconian dietary restrictions were on the menu up there as well. Grabbing some pumpkin seeds and berries in a plastic cup, Lambert got on the elevator and marched, past secretary Pam Morocco, and into Chuck's office.

Lambert strode up to Chuck's desk, where he was meeting with some assistants, placed the cup on it. "Here, I just wanted to bring you down a lunch," he said. "I can't play like this." And then he turned and walked out.

Chuck looked into the cup for a moment, then back at his coaches, before evincing the shadow of a smile. Later that day, with the team gathered around him, Chuck asked, "How many people are sick and tired of all the healthy food we've been eating?" A cheer went up among the players and, the next day, white bread and mayonnaise returned to the Steelers' training table.

While Lambert was comfortable enough to communicate with Chuck,

Bradshaw still often felt and behaved like a recalcitrant teen. When his elbow was aching the day before the Steelers' exhibition game against the Patriots in Knoxville, Tennessee, he asked the team physician, Dr. Paul Steele, to give him a painkilling shot but insisted that he do it without Chuck's knowledge. "The two of us sneaked away from the field and hid inside the men's room, like a couple of junkies," said Bradshaw. "What I didn't know was that it would deaden my ulna nerve, as the novocaine went all the way down my forearm and into my fingers."

Bradshaw hadn't even told Chuck his elbow was hurting; now he came to him a half hour before the game to tell him that his arm was hurt, he'd had it shot with painkiller, and now he couldn't grip a football.

"Chuck was . . . let's say exasperated," said an assistant. "That's a good word. Terry was doing all this stuff off the reservation. There was a trust issue."

✦　✦　✦

While Chuck had been a charter member of the NFL Players Association in 1957—it was a professional association at the time, not a trade union—he had come to believe that modern players were too spoiled. This was not uncommon among former players who had moved to coaching in the '70s and '80s. It wasn't just that the money being paid to athletes by the '80s was exponentially larger than anything Chuck made. It was that there were sincere doubts among coaches that a free-agency system similar to baseball could work in pro football.

During the preseason, Chuck spoke with Gary Dunn and asked, "Do you really care about the players that play for the Cleveland Browns?"

Dunn considered for a moment, then said, "Well, yeah, I care about them, Chuck."

"You do?"

"Well, yeah. I mean, I still want to beat them, but . . ."

"I'm just trying to figure out what your strike is about."

They would have to agree to disagree, but as the strike date neared—the NFLPA was calling for a strike following the second game—Chuck spoke to the team and said, "You can't play this game for money. You guys thinking that it is all about money. You have to play for pride. Money should not enter into why you are here and what you doing as a man on this football team."

(Of course, one of the stated motivations for Chuck when he got out of college was that a pro football career would earn him almost double the money he would have made as a young teacher.)

The economic downturn that had coincided with the Steelers' rise had struck with a savage effectiveness in western Pennsylvania. Unemployment in the state was up to 12 percent. That made it a particularly inopportune time for the NFLPA to threaten a strike, but the players were bargaining for free agency and a 55 percent share of the league's gross revenues.

In Pittsburgh, some of the veterans didn't want to go out. While the NFL required teams to lock players out of the facilities, the Steelers opened the grass practice field down the street from Three Rivers to the striking players, and Tony Parisi moved their equipment to the visiting locker room and gave player rep Tunch Ilkin a key.

A few veterans—Swann and Stallworth and Donnie Shell—were loyalists. The day after the strike was called, they reported to Three Rivers at the normal time for practice. They dressed out in shorts and went into the meeting room.

Chuck walked in and saw the players.

"You can't be here," he said.

"Chuck," said Swann. "We don't agree with it. We want to be here."

"You can't be here," Chuck repeated. "You can't cross the line. You've got to leave."

They spoke for a couple more minutes, then got up to leave.

The strike lasted longer than anyone could have anticipated. It was still going on in October, when the Steelers had planned a dinner to honor the fiftieth season of the franchise. It brought together a black-tie, high-society Pittsburgh crowd, the franchise's greatest players, many of whom had just retired, and was hosted by Howard Cosell (with his standard needling shtick, asking Marianne, "My dear Marianne, what are you doing with Chuck? You could've had such a wonderful life with me").

Chuck gave a brief speech, looking around at the combination of active and now-retired greats ("I feel like we could put together a pretty good team right here"). But something felt off. He was unusually restless.

"At the end of the ceremony," said John Stallworth, "people are looking around and, 'Where is Chuck?' He's not there. Marianne is there. I don't think she knows where Chuck is. So we leave in two busses. And the first bus gets back to the stadium, and he is standing outside the door. It's kind of chilly, but he's outside the door and just standing there. He left and I don't know how he got back to Three Rivers, but he got back, and I think he's just standing there because he was uncomfortable being there. The journey of the season had been interrupted, for whatever reason, and we were not doing what we were supposed to be doing. So I felt like he was not comfortable, because we're not preparing for a game—so he just left."

The season lost seven full games before the two sides settled. When the players returned, there were significant financial concessions. Super Bowl money was doubled, from $18,000 to $36,000 for the winners. A team working its way through the four rounds of the playoffs stood to make $70,000 per man.

"I don't know about you guys," said Chuck, "but $70,000 is a lot of money to me. Let's go kick some ass."

"And we were all going, 'Wait, didn't he say back in September you can't play for money?,'" said Gary Dunn. "Yeah, but he didn't like any of that. You definitely got a feeling Chuck was not sympathetic to that type of stuff."

Pittsburgh finished the truncated regular season 6–3; in the expanded playoffs (with sixteen teams, eight from each conference), the Steelers played host to the San Diego Chargers. For much of the day, Bradshaw was at his best, completing 28 of 39 passes for 339 yards and two touchdowns. But on third down, with an 11-point lead four minutes into the final quarter, he scrambled and made a poor throw that was intercepted, swinging the momentum in the game. "If I hadn't been so hot, maybe I wouldn't have tried it," Bradshaw said of the key interception. "Maybe I would have run with the ball, like I should have. Only God knows why I threw the thing, and I think even He was telling me not to."

"If we had the momentum until then," said Chuck, "we gave it back right there. It shocked us all."

After the Chargers closed to within four, the Steelers' drive stalled and their barefoot punter, John Goodson, shanked a 20-yarder that gave San Diego the ball on its own 36. Dan Fouts hit Kellen Winslow for the winning score.

Another season ended in disappointment, and as Chuck's staff started breaking down film to review the season, a few things were clear: Bradshaw was thirty-four, still robust, and, in many ways, better now than he'd been when the Steelers were winning Super Bowls.

The defense, though, was found wanting. Ham retired after the season, and only Lambert, Blount, and Shell remained from the original Steel Curtain defense. The pass rush remained the big problem. A year earlier, Chuck had said there would never be another Joe Greene. But now, as he started preparing for the 1983 draft and beyond—started imagining a Steeler team for the decade ahead—he couldn't resist looking for a logical successor.

nineteen

THE ONE THAT GOT AWAY

✦ ✦ ✦

The Steelers had the twenty-fourth selection in the 1983 draft. They had many needs, but with Bradshaw's strong performance in 1982, quarter-back didn't appear to be one of them. In what looked like a historically deep class of quarterbacks, it seemed unlikely that any of the top-rated ones—John Elway, Jim Kelly, Dan Marino, or Todd Blackledge—would still be around when their pick was taken.

"We're hoping as many quarterbacks as possible go before us, because that leaves more players available at the positions we're looking for," said Artie on the eve of the draft.

The Steelers were enamored of Gabe Rivera, "Señor Sack," the behemoth defensive tackle from Texas Tech. Chuck envisioned Rivera as the cornerstone to the Steelers' move to a 3–4 front. In his dominating line play and quick first step, there were flashes of the player that Greene had been.

There was one detail that nagged in the back of Chuck's mind. It was Bradshaw again. In early March, he'd undergone elbow surgery from Dr.

Bill Bundrick, a bone-and-joint specialist in Shreveport. Though Bradshaw would later insist the Steelers knew about it ("We sent them a Mailgram stating that I was to be operated on by Dr. Bundrick, unless the Steelers organization objected, in which case I would fly to Pittsburgh and be operated on by Dr. Steele," he said), but neither Chuck nor the Steelers' executives were aware that he was having the surgery, nor of the seriousness of the procedure. Bundrick said that Bradshaw probably wouldn't be able to participate fully in off-season conditioning but that his arm should be "at full strength" in time for training camp.

So on April 26, as the first round began, four quarterbacks were indeed selected before the Steelers' choice, but Marino—the local boy who'd led Pitt to the brink of a national title his junior year before having a disappointing senior season—wasn't one of them.

His draft stock had been hurt by Pitt's shortcomings; the rise of Todd Blackledge (the son of Chuck's offensive line coach, Ron Blackledge), who'd led Penn State to a national title 1982; and rumors that Marino had used recreational drugs.

"We knew a little bit too much about Marino," said Tony Dungy. "You heard all the rumors and everything." Yet Dungy also recalled Marino's workout for the Steelers at Three Rivers, when Pitt teammates Julius Dawkins and Dwight Collins ran routes on a windy day. "Marino threw the ball right on the money," said Dungy, "and these guys dropped every ball. I remember thinking to myself, *I know why this guy had a bad year. These guys can't catch.*"

Chuck was an admirer of Marino. He liked his toughness and strong arm. But the Steelers had an All-Pro quarterback they trusted, and for Chuck, there were two considerations. First, the team needed a pass rush and an anchor on the defensive line. Second, still haunted by the Joe Gilliam experience, he didn't want to bring in another quarterback with question marks about character. Fair or not, some had those questions about Marino.

That day, as the Steelers' first choice drew closer, Dan Rooney entered the draft room and said he'd heard a suggestion he wanted to share. What if, asked Dan, the Steelers traded Cliff Stoudt (who in three years as a little-used backup had completed less than 50 percent of his passes and thrown two touchdowns and seven interceptions) to a team with a pick early in the second round, then used their first-round pick to draft Marino?

Someone asked Dan who suggested it. When he answered, "John Clayton," he was greeted with a chorus of groans and heckles. Clayton was the *Pittsburgh Press's* smart, opinionated young beat writer whose meek countenance camouflaged a tenacious reporting style. Clayton was still earning the respect of the men he was writing about, but Chuck remained miffed about Clayton blowing the whistle on the Steelers for using pads during their off-season workouts, which cost them a third-round draft choice in 1979.

(While drafting Marino was a prescient suggestion, it's doubtful that the scenario Clayton described would have been possible. "I do not think we could have gotten a number two for Stoudt," said Artie Rooney. "And Rivera had to go in round one.")

"We built this team on defense, and we should do it again now," Chuck said in the Steelers' draft room. And no one disagreed with him.

"In Chuck's mind, it was still what we talked about," said Dungy. "This was going to be a throwing league even more, so there was more of a premium on putting pressure on the passer, and he saw Gabe Rivera as someone able to do some of the things that Joe Greene had done."

There was one other factor. "It was a weird time," added Dungy. "And Chuck was very loyal to those guys. Drafting Marino, as much as Bradshaw says he didn't care about his feelings and stuff, that would have *killed* Bradshaw, and he still thought he was going to play a couple more years. There was a lot to that. It changed the course of the franchise, for sure."

The Steelers assistants and scouts cheered in unison when the pick was announced.

In the background, the Chief was circumspect. He'd met Marino and was extremely fond of him. More than once that weekend, Art Sr. would sidle up to Artie and say, "You took the wrong guy."

Six picks later, when the Dolphins took Marino, Chuck got on the phone with Don Shula and congratulated him. "You probably got the best guy in the draft."

✦   ✦   ✦

Three months later, the Steelers' training camp began with the astonishing news that Bradshaw wasn't yet cleared for throwing. "We had words," said Bradshaw. "Serious words." The elbow wasn't responding and wasn't healing. And so the Steelers approached the new season without their quarterback.

Bradshaw would remember a time later in camp when Chuck stopped by his dorm room and played the guitar with him. "Chuck would say, 'Why did you get this thing operated on? You threw the ball great last year.' And I'd say, 'Chuck, I know I threw it great, but my elbow hurt constantly.'"

For all of Bradshaw's progress under Chuck, he still didn't feel comfortable enough with him to level with his coach about his own physical condition.

So the season began full of doubt, Chuck starting Cliff Stoudt, who beat out Mark Malone for the job. With Tom Moore calling most of the plays for him, Stoudt excelled. The Steelers started the season 5–2, with a terrific pass rush, and the young Rivera had shown hints of promise despite some nagging injuries.

On Thursday evening, October 20, Chuck and Marianne were just back from dinner when the call came in from Dan Rooney—earlier that evening, Rivera had been critically injured in a car accident. It would, as it turned out, end his football career and leave him paralyzed. Shaken by the news, Chuck closed the locker room from the press the next day.

But the Steelers kept winning, defeating Seattle and eventually extending the streak to seven games. How they accomplished it was a mystery. The aging Franco Harris was averaging just 3.6 yards per carry, Swann had retired, and the injured Stallworth caught only eight passes all year.

After the loss to the Vikings—when Stoudt had completed just 13 of 30 passes—Chuck was asked in the Monday press conference what he thought of Bradshaw's chances of returning. "I don't know if he can throw or not," Chuck said. "Maybe he's ready for his life's work."

To Bradshaw and his fragile psyche, the words stung. "Until that moment," he said, "I hadn't realized that playing quarterback for the Steelers was simply preparation for my real job. Man, that was a head slap. For something that wasn't personal, that sure sounded personal."

But to Ilkin and the rest of the team, it was nothing out of the ordinary. "Chuck would say that all the time. 'If you're thinking about retiring, you need to get on with your life's work.' 'If you can't get excited about this game, you need to get on with your life's work.' He believed that if you weren't completely focused on football, that you needed to think about getting on with your life's work. And so that was just like saying, 'Same foot, same shoulder,' which he said a million times. 'Strike a rising blow,' which he said a million times. 'They can't pay you enough to play this game.' He would say that. He just had all these sayings that he would say over and over and over. 'You don't have to be the biggest and the strongest and the fastest to make plays.' So to say, 'Maybe Terry ought to get on with his life's work,' I understand that might have been quite personal to Terry. To me, it was just what he would always say. He would say that about everybody."

As the season wore on, the Steelers' offense bogged down. On Thanksgiving Day, Pittsburgh suffered a 45–3 blowout loss to the Lions, the worst of the Noll era. Stoudt completed 9 of 25 passes and was lifted for Malone, who went 2 of 8. Next came a 23–10 loss to the Bengals, in which Stoudt completed 8 of 19 passes for just 88 yards, and the team gained only nine first downs, leading to more questions about when Bradshaw might return.

"Look, he's getting close," Chuck said. "But so is Christmas."

But the week of the game at Shea Stadium against the Jets, with the Steelers on a three-game losing skid and their playoff prospects in peril, Chuck announced Bradshaw would play.

Typical of their relationship by this point, Bradshaw concealed the fact that his troublesome elbow was already sore by Friday. ("If I went to Chuck and told him I couldn't play, it would make Chuck look bad and put me in a terribly embarrassing position," Bradshaw reasoned. "It would have made the Steelers look like fools.")

On Saturday afternoon, December 10, the last football game ever played at Shea, Bradshaw led the Steelers onto the field, and engineered two first-half drives ending in touchdowns. Bradshaw later recalled he'd "felt something snap" in his elbow after the first scoring pass, and he took himself out of the game after the second scoring pass. But the win clinched the Steelers' first AFC Central title since 1979, and put them into the playoffs for the second year in a row.

It was another short visit, this time to Los Angeles, where the Raiders had relocated. The Raiders were a far better team, on their way to a second Super Bowl title in four seasons. Lester Hayes intercepted a Stoudt pass and returned it for a touchdown in the first quarter, and the Raiders won, 38–10.

The Steelers faced an off-season of uncertainty about their quarterback. Meanwhile, Dan Marino had taken over the starting quarterback job in Miami during the regular season, gone 7–2, thrown twenty touch-down passes to just six interceptions, and led the Dolphins to the AFC East title.

The coda to Bradshaw's story came in the 1984 off-season. That winter Pittsburgh lost both Stoudt and wide receiver Jim Smith to the USFL—a product of the Steelers' hard line on contracts. The team reported for minicamp on May 30, 1984, and there was more than the usual inter-est, to see how Bradshaw's balky elbow had progressed. He'd been doing weight work, at the behest of Dr. Frank Jobe.

But on the first day of the minicamp, throwing casually, Bradshaw said he felt the elbow pain once again, and in that moment, decided he'd reached the end. He left the practice field and walked into the weight room. Chuck eventually followed him in there and asked if he was okay.

"Chuck, that's it," said Bradshaw. "I can't play anymore. It's over."

Chuck surveyed Bradshaw and nodded. Then he shook his hand and thanked him for the effort. By the end of the day, Bradshaw was on a flight back to Louisiana. A month later, he announced his retirement. (Years later, Bradshaw would recall walking away and Chuck "staring at me with those cold, unfeeling eyes, not saying a word.")

At the end of the 1983 season, while Chuck was casting about looking for a linebackers coach to replace Widenhofer (who'd left for a head-coaching job in the USFL)—eventually settling on former Vikings' assis-tant Jed Hughes, who'd been recommended by Bud Carson—he also needed to name a new defensive coordinator.

The best candidate was Dungy—young, cerebral, and soft-spoken—already being viewed as a protégé of Chuck by other assistants, who noticed how close the two were in demeanor. Dungy's wife, Lauren, had pushed him to be less soft-spoken, a more decisive advocate for himself. An opportunity arose when Chuck and Dungy traveled together to the 1984 scouting combine.

"So Lauren keeps asking me, 'Are you going to be the defensive coor-dinator?,'" said Dungy. "I haven't heard. I don't know what he is going to do. So the combine is in New Orleans that year. Chuck says, 'Hey, I would like you to go to dinner with me.' So, I figure we are going to go to dinner, and he is going to tell me that I am the defensive coordinator. So I called Lauren and said, 'Hey, Chuck invited me to dinner.' So we go. We go out someplace that he picks out, and then we go to Preservation Hall. And we see this guy play jazz and everything, and I am kind of hanging out, and I am waiting for him to say what he's got to say. And at the end of the night, we go back to the hotel, and that's it. He says, 'Wasn't that great? Did you enjoy that?' And I said, 'Yeah!' So I get back to the room and I call and tell Lauren, 'He didn't say anything, so he must be hiring someone else.' So she says, 'Well, you need to ask him.' So I wait until the combine is over. We get back, and another week has gone by, and we get back to Pittsburgh, and I say, 'Coach, can I ask you a question? Do you know what you are going to do about the coordinator?' He said, 'You are the coordinator. Who else would it be?' And I said, 'Well, yeah, I kind of hoped that you felt that way, but I just hadn't heard it.' And he kind of gave me one of those looks like, *Why would I need to tell you? Who else would it be?*"

The team and the assistants grew so used to that unemotional approach, it could be disconcerting on those occasions Chuck varied from it. During a preseason game in '83 against the Cowboys, Kolb had the young, hungry defensive line in midseason form, with exotic spacing on the 50 defense and a dizzying series of stunts and twists. Keith Willis and Keith Gary were both exerting pressure on the quarterback, and the Cowboys' Tom Landry was growing increasingly perturbed on the sideline. After the game, a 24–7 win, Chuck and Kolb fell in step walking to the locker room in Texas Stadium.

"Good job," Chuck said.

Kolb was startled. His eyes widened, and he looked stunned. It was perhaps the first on-field compliment Chuck had given him in fifteen years. Chuck saw Kolb's look of surprise and—partly abashed, partly annoyed—said, "Well if you weren't doing a good job, you wouldn't be here." Then he picked up the pace and went on ahead.

The encounter lingered with Kolb. "I am sitting there in the shower going, *I think I wished I wouldn't have walked by him.* Because what started out as a compliment, ended up being . . . I still don't know what it was."

It was Chuck being Chuck.

✦ ✦ ✦

The Steelers hadn't won a playoff game since the last Super Bowl. They arrived at training camp without Bradshaw, Greene, Greenwood, Blount, Swann, or Franco Harris, the latter of whom was holding out for a better contract.

The '84 training camp took on an aspect of ruthlessness that had not previously been associated with Chuck's coaching. The Oklahoma drill—the ritual hand-to-hand combat that tested the mettle of the players—opened with the annual battle of Webster vs. Lambert. Unlike previous years, the intensity never subsided. "There was some criticism that he had carried the Super Bowl players too long," said Wolfley. "I remember that year as being a brutal training camp. As a matter of fact, we called it 'The Purge of '84.' The theme was *You can't make the club in the tub.*"

More than fifteen years after seeing Alvin Roy bring weight training to the Chargers, Chuck remained a skeptic. The '70s had featured an increase in the use of anabolic steroids—there was still no formal NFL policy against their use—but Chuck continued to rail against them. Which is not to say that steroids weren't as prevalent in the Steelers' locker room as they were in the rest of the NFL.

"At that time, it was a 'don't ask, don't tell' thing," said assistant coach Bill Meyers. "I remember Webby telling me one time he would take a little during the season to help him maintain his strength."

There were whispers about all the Steelers' offensive linemen, none more so than Steve Courson. He'd adopted the machismo so common in heavy steroids users, coming to training camp dressed in military fatigues. While Courson scored well on strength testing, he lacked the technique to consistently stay on his feet. The fundamentals—"strike a rising blow," "same foot, same shoulder"—continued to elude him. And fighting tendinitis in that '84 preseason, Courson sat out of practices, though he'd been cleared by the team doctors. In July, Chuck decided to trade him, to Tampa Bay. The news didn't sit well.

"Courson was crazy," said Meyers. "Shit, I hid in my closet. I thought that son of a bitch was going to get a gun and shoot me. I literally did. He was yelling though the door looking for me."

When the trade was announced, the *Pittsburgh Post-Gazette*'s John Adams asked Chuck about Courson's statement that his injury was "career-threatening."

"Life is career-threatening," said Chuck. "Most people are their own worst enemies. The mind is career-threatening."

But the bigger story in training camp was Harris's protracted holdout. Slated to make $385,000 for the season, he was holding out for a raise and a two-year deal.

Chuck maintained his long stance of not commenting about contract negotiations, but the Harris holdout—for a thirty-four-year-old running back and team leader—vexed him.

"I need somebody," Chuck told Dan Rooney. "It's not about money. It's about team, and basically what you have illustrated is that contract is more important than this team. And I need senior leadership that cares about this team."

Questioned about Harris's whereabouts in a press conference, Chuck responded, "Franco who?"

Harris, always prideful, was insulted by the comment. As with the comment about Bradshaw a year earlier, the player in question took umbrage, while most teammates took the comment in stride.

"Face value," said John Stallworth, "you have to think, *How could you?* But the deeper meaning in my mind at least, and certainly Chuck could have chosen his words better, but in my mind at least is that he was saying, 'I've got to concentrate on the people that are here. Franco's not here.' If you've got a coaching philosophy that says everybody is important, and that everybody has value, and that you are participating in this team sport, and that we've all got to do our thing—and then you've got a bunch of guys and a bunch of egos that you got to somehow keep in line, in check. Those things are in conflict all the time."

On the day the Steelers waived Harris, he stopped by the house on Warwick Drive, and he and Chuck talked. "I went over to his house just to tell Chuck I'd like to come back on the team," Harris said. It was not a long conversation. Both men had their code, and they'd followed it too far to turn back. After a short talk, less than ten minutes, they shook hands and Harris left.

(Though hurt at the time, Harris felt the controversy over the "Franco who?" comment was overplayed. "Chuck is not a mean man in that particular way," he said.)

"I remember when I got the news that Franco had been released, there was this feeling that, you know what—nobody's job is safe," said Wolfley. The corollary message was also clear: No one, not even a future Hall of Famer, was bigger than the team.

Joe Greene, watching from afar, understood. "You want them there, but if they're not there, you have to move on."

With Bradshaw's retirement and Stoudt's defection to the USFL leaving the unproven Mark Malone at quarterback, Stallworth aging, and Harris cut, the Steelers looked like a much different team.

"Chuck never made it a distraction," said Tom Moore. "You play the hand that's dealt you, and you work, and you coach, and you teach, and you go from there."

Somehow it worked. Despite the bleak predictions, the Steelers remained competitive. The first month of the season saw rookie wideout Louis Lipps, who'd taken over for Swann, give a standout performance, catching six passes for 183 yards in an opening-day loss to Kansas City. By week four, Lipps had fumbled six times, and linebackers coach Dennis Fitzgerald, overseeing the special teams, pulled him off of punt return duty. But Chuck ordered him back in, and Lipps almost took the next punt all the way for a touchdown.

Chuck was waiting for him on the sidelines, with a brief message —"Squeeze the fucking ball!"—that Lipps took as both an admonition and a vote of confidence.

In October, the Steelers went to San Francisco and knocked off the 49ers (San Francisco's only loss of the season, as it turned out). "If Chuck doesn't like something, there is no point in trying to talk him into it," said Bill Meyers. "He just thought Bill Walsh was a blowhard."

The criticism of Mark Malone had been that he was a film room guy, someone who took impeccable notes in team meetings ("you could put his notes in the Hall of Fame," said one assistant), but who was too mechanical on the field. Malone found reliable weapons (the ageless Stallworth caught 80 passes for 1,395 yards and eleven touchdowns, and running backs Frank Pollard and Walter Abercrombie—splitting time in Harris's absence—combined for nearly 1,500 yards) and blossomed under the tutelage of Moore, who had been elevated to offensive coordinator.

At a time when most coaches were calling plays for their quarterbacks, Chuck finally relented. Moore's stoic, throaty croak was tempered with a gambler's glint for the odd trick play.

Occasionally, talking to Chuck on the headset, he would say, "We've got this halfback pass, Chuck. What do you think?"

"No guts, no blue chips."

After a two-game losing streak dropped them to 6–6, the Steelers won three of their last four, including a crucial regular-season finale win over the Raiders in Los Angeles, which they needed to win to qualify for the playoffs and win the AFC Central.

They went to Denver to play the AFC West champion Broncos. Some of the Steelers went out to dinner on Saturday night and heard Broncos fans loudly speculating about how their team would do the following week against Miami in the AFC Championship Game.

Instead, what the Denver fans saw the next day was a vintage Steelers' performance, with Pittsburgh sacking John Elway four times, intercepting him twice, and, as Chuck often preached, wearing the other team down and winning the battle of hitting by the fourth quarter. Frank Pollard's 2-yard touchdown run gave the Steelers a 24–17 win.

They were back in the AFC Championship Game for the first time in five years, though this time it was in Miami, where they'd have to meet the high-scoring Dolphins and second-year quarterback sensation Marino.

They couldn't keep up with Miami's passing game—and couldn't survive Malone's three interceptions (though he also threw for 312 yards and three touchdowns)—and fell, 45–28. As Marino jogged off the field to go to the Super Bowl, more than one member of the Steelers' entourage might have reflected on how things might have been different if the Dolphins' quarterback had been wearing black and gold.

Lambert's dislocated toe wasn't healing and finally, after the end of the 1984 season, he decided to retire. He phoned Dan Rooney and gave him the news. Rooney asked if he'd spoken to Chuck.

"No, and I, uh, hadn't really planned on it."

"Well, I think that is something you should do."

So Lambert called and reached the Noll home on one of the rare occasions where Chuck answered.

"Coach, this is Jack Lambert. This toe is just not gonna work. I can't play. I can't push off. I can't tackle. I'm going to retire."

"Well," said Chuck. "Thank you very much for your contribution over the years. And good luck to you."

"Thanks, Coach. Good luck to you."

What that 1984 season was marked by, in the end, was a team that didn't have playoff talent, advancing deep into the playoffs. People like Kolb, who'd been around when the Steelers were physically and emotionally dominant, were all the more impressed with Chuck's job in 1984.

"Chuck would talk about the essentials," said Jon Kolb. "Those other things were going to take care of themselves. People that are brilliant are not brilliant on thirty things. They're brilliant on one or two things and they don't lose track of them. And he was perfectly content to just continue to hone in on, 'You've got to know that to do; you've got to know how to do it.' My memories are in meeting rooms when I started coaching, in broken chairs. Because we would set chairs up to represent the T [formation] and chairs to represent the linemen, and we would be talking about how you need to do something. Particularly Chuck and Woody, they broke chairs—not over each other's head, but they would be arguing what the technique was, what this was about. And one of the big life lessons for me was, Chuck never said, 'You dumb ass.' And Woody never said, 'You dumb ass.' It was always the about the chair, or the T, or the circle. They were mad at the circles. They were arguing about the circles, and how do we beat out the circles, and the chairs. All people are equal. All ideas are not equal. So let's get in here and talk about ideas. That was the thing that always amazed me."

All that was left was the Pro Bowl, traditionally coached by the staffs that had lost the conference championship game. Chuck had coached the game twice before, following the '72 and '76 seasons, and won both times.

Now, at the beginning of the week, he told the AFC players, "It's $15,000 for the winners, and $7,500 for the losers. That may not be a lot of money to you, but it is a lot of money to me and my coaches. We are going to win this game."

They were in full pads on that Tuesday, prompting some of the AFC's stars to press the assistants for an explanation. "They are coming up to me and saying, 'Hey, man, *what's* with your coach?,'" said Tom Moore. "I said, 'Go tell him, he is right over there.' They said, 'No, no, I ain't going over there.' I said, 'Go see him.' Then after practice, we ran. He wasn't trying to punish them, but he said some of these guys haven't had pads on in five weeks."

The practices in pads continued throughout the week. By Thursday, Raiders' cornerback Lester Hayes approached Tony Dungy and asked, "Is there something wrong here?"

"Lester," Dungy said with a smile. "This is how we do things."

Hayes's teammate, Howie Long, was more amazed than annoyed. "Do you guys *always* practice like this?," he asked Bill Meyers.

"Every day, buddy," said Meyers. "Full pack and rifle. Every single day."

"You guys are nuts," said Long.

The AFC won again, 33–28.

✦   ✦   ✦

All the things that had fallen right in 1984 took a negative turn in 1985.

The season was marked by difficulty from the start. Malone began the season and soon played himself out of a job. He was replaced by David Woodley, who threw fourteen interceptions and just six touchdowns.

It wasn't just the performance; some of the team's mind-set felt different as well. The Thursday before the Dolphins game in early October, Woodley came up to John Stallworth and confided, "John, we can't beat these guys."

For the hypercompetitive veteran Stallworth, those were fighting words. He snapped at Woodley and later told Tony Dungy about it. Dungy urged him to tell Chuck.

"I told him I chose not to tell Chuck," said Stallworth, "because even with that attitude, Woodley was better than the option we had."

The other option was Malone. Tall, strong, and smart, he was a keen student of the game. But he lacked the improvisational genius that Bradshaw brought to the game.

"If you didn't do it the way it was drawn up, Mark could not adjust to it," said another teammate.

"If he didn't have it written down," said Dick Hoak. "He was a heck of an athlete. But he did not have the arm that Terry had. You know, Terry could go back and throw the ball, and somebody is covering, Terry is going to get it there, and they're going to catch it. Mark couldn't do that. His ball couldn't do that."

The past intersected with the present in Miami, where Bradshaw was working on the CBS crew. "Before the game, Chuck passed me on the field and walked right by, completely ignoring me," said Bradshaw. "I know that he saw me; it was devastating to have your coach of more than fourteen years act as though you were invisible. I looked him right in the eyes—as always, they were empty—hoping that he'd come over and shake my hand. He didn't."

"Yeah, well, Terry also could have gone over and shook *his* hand," said one assistant. "It goes both ways. Also, the idea of Chuck standing around and shooting the shit with former players before a game? If you think that's happening, then you don't know Chuck."

They fell 24–20 to Miami and, a week later, lost 27–13 to the Cowboys in Dallas, to drop to 2–4. But they fought back and, after beating Houston, 30–7, at the Astrodome on November 17, they moved into first place in the AFC Central at 6–5. But then Pittsburgh gave up 115 points in the next three games—losses to Washington, Denver, and San Diego—to stumble home. The team still had its characteristic resilience, rallying from a 21–0 deficit to beat the Bills 30–24 in the last home game of the season. But only 35,953 fans attended, the smallest crowd for a Steelers home game since the Pitt Stadium days in 1969. After losing to the Giants, 28–10, in the finale, the Steelers finished the year 7–9, their first losing season since 1971.

Asked in the postseason press conference how long he would remain with the Steelers, Chuck said, "I'm locked in. I don't know anything else."

The acerbic columnist Bruce Keidan asked him to evaluate his own job that season.

"Well, it's pretty much already evaluated," Chuck said. "I'm a 7–9 coach. Nothing more, nothing less."

Chuck's teams had gone to the playoffs eleven of the previous fourteen seasons. But in Pittsburgh, expectations were now set at a different level, perhaps unrealistically so, in the hypercompetitive, parity-producing, zero-sum world of the NFL.

"People start expecting a championship every year," said Dick Hoak.

twenty

PALACE INTRIGUE

✦ ✦ ✦

On the first day of the 1986 draft, the Steelers' scouts and coaches were sitting around the conference table, waiting for their pick in the third round.

Everyone was in agreement that the team needed some help in the secondary, and when Chuck asked defensive coordinator Tony Dungy who could help them most, Dungy didn't waver. "I like Patrick Hunter," he said, of the aggressive Nevada cornerback.

Shortly thereafter, the linebackers coach Jed Hughes spoke up and volunteered that he felt differently—that Kansas safety Alvin Walton was the player the secondary most needed.

Around the room, eyebrows were raised. It was a small disagreement, but not an insignificant one. Coaching staffs were built on emerging consensus: position coaches would confer with the unit coordinator, and then after finding agreement, would take their case to the head coach. All differences among the coaching staff would be settled well before the selecting began—so the coaches could present a unified front when considering the scouting department's recommendations. But now on the day of the draft, with a decision hanging in the balance, Hughes directly contradicted Dungy.

Faced with that division, Chuck took neither player, instead sticking with the scouting staff's recommendation to select Bubby Brister, the raw, talented rookie quarterback from Northeast Louisiana.

There had been some doubts whether the soft-spoken Dungy would be tough enough to be a coordinator, but he had learned quickly on the job, developed a good rapport with the players, and had earned their respect. Instead, his bigger problem was with Hughes. And it wasn't merely Dungy—Jon Kolb had been angered by Hughes's freelancing during practices (often going away from the practice routine they'd worked out beforehand), and many of the other assistants grew weary of him. More than anything, Hughes took greater liberties than any position coach ever had, not only in seeking out Chuck for one-on-one conversations but also in suggesting developments that contradicted coordinator Dungy's defensive philosophy or circumvented his authority.

"All I remember is that no one liked Jed," said Marianne Noll.

The animosity wasn't a secret. "He was known as Jed the Snake," said one writer who covered the team.

But what Chuck saw, at least at first, was a protégé with a formidable intellect and an active imagination. Hughes soon took to accompanying Chuck on post-meeting walks up to the abbey at St. Vincent during training camp evenings.

"Jed was a self-promoter and not a team player," said one longtime Steelers executive. "Bright guy. But he didn't get the team part of it."

By the time the '86 season began, this had become an annoyance to Dungy and the other assistants. It would soon get worse.

The third-round pick Brister was, at first glance, a copy of Bradshaw: raw, talented rookie from a small Louisiana college whose bluster covered up a bit of insecurity.

He was also a product of the modern age, holding out for a better contract. As camp started without his rookie quarterback, Chuck had asked Tom Moore, more than once, "How can a guy in the *third round* hold out?"

When the deal was finally signed after a two-week holdout, Moore drove in from Latrobe to pick up Brister at the Pittsburgh International Airport.

Moore knew Chuck's patience had already worn thin. "Goddamn, if you would have waited another day . . . ," said Moore.

On the first play from scrimmage of his first practice, Brister turned the wrong way on a simple handoff and earned Chuck's anger.

"That is the first damn play we put in at camp, and you don't even know that!," Chuck barked. "Get out of the huddle."

Chastened, Brister strode to the sidelines, but he remained resolute and gradually picked up the offense. Later in camp, one of the players complained that he couldn't understand Brister's Southern drawl in the huddle. "Well, you better learn to understand him," Moore said. "Because he is staying, so if we have to, we'll get somebody else who *can* understand him."

Pittsburgh lost the first three games of the 1986 season by a combined score of 82–17. After the season-opening loss to the Seahawks, Chuck vowed—to both the team and the press—to get back to the basics. In the visiting locker room at the Kingdome, the coaches and players shared the same shower. Wolfley, lathering up, animatedly mocked his coach to Ilkin. "'Back to basics! Back to basics!,'" said Wolfley. "I can hear him now, all week long, 'back to fucking basics.' I'd like to see Chuck go back to fucking basics."

Ilkin didn't know how to tell his friend that Chuck had just entered the shower area and had heard it all.

Just then, Chuck spoke up and said, "Oh—that'll be a great idea. We'll do that."

Ilkin hurried out of the shower area, to avoid laughing.

After the third loss, at Minnesota, Chuck reiterated that the team would have to get "back to basics," always an ominous phrase to the veterans. "He believed that you practice like you play, or you play like you practice," said Craig Wolfley. "He was a true believer in that. If you ever heard postgame interviews where he said, 'We were out-physicaled,' or 'It's back to basics,' you know that was going to be a heck of a bad week coming up. It's not punitive; it's what he truly believed was a correctional tool at his disposal. That meant one-on-ones, extra conditioning, extra reps, what have you, because he was a true believer in 'Whatever It Takes.'"

Bradshaw, serving as an expert commentator for the Pittsburgh television station KDKA, began regularly criticizing the team, as well as Chuck's coaching methods.

On the sidelines, Chuck's calm demeanor was increasingly laced with a look of consternation. He had the aspect of a celebrated conductor, hearing understudies mangling a piece of beautiful music.

After breaking the skid by beating Houston, the Steelers lost by three points to Cleveland (their first loss at home to the Browns since 1970), during which Malone was injured. Chuck elevated the rookie Brister to a starting role, and he showed flashes in a two-point loss to Cincinnati, but then the Steelers were shut out again, 34–0, in a home loss to the Patriots, their worst loss in the history of Three Rivers. With the team's record at 1–6, the front page of the next morning's *Pittsburgh Post-Gazette* asked, "The Steelers—Can It Get Any Worse?"

In the midst of the season, the tension between coaches and scouts continued, with the former disappointed in the new class of rookies, while the scouts—just as predictably—were disappointed in the lack of opportunities offered the rookies and the inability of coaches to harness what they viewed as self-evident talent.

By the mid-'80s, the rest of the league had largely caught up with the Steelers' drafting methods. It didn't mean the scouting staff didn't make strong selections, or unearth sleepers, but they didn't do so as often as before. And because the team was almost always competitive, it was rare that the Steelers would get a top-ten pick.

The first-round choice in 1985, Darryl Sims, looked like the first certifiable first-round bust of the Noll era (or, to put a finer point on it, the Art Rooney Jr. era). And the third-round pick in '85, cornerback Liffort Hobley of LSU, couldn't even make the team as a rookie. In '86, Sims still wasn't playing much, and the scouts were grousing about it. Finally, Chuck went to defensive line coach Jon Kolb and asked him if he was going to put Sims in. Kolb had adhered for more than two decades to Chuck's mantra that nothing was going to be given to newcomers, no matter how highly touted they were.

"You've always said you've got to earn the right to play," Kolb said, adding that Sims hadn't been focused in practice. "Have we changed our philosophy?"

Kolb had struck a nerve. Chuck silently conceded the point, turned and walked out.

"Sims was indeed a mistake when we needed to make no mistakes," said Artie Rooney. "I recall Chuck telling me that he was a flashy player, inconsistent, and made some big plays and a lot of ordinary bad plays."

The tension between the scouts and the coaching staff—as well as the internal friction among assistant coaches—was beginning to have an effect. By this time, Hughes's undermining of Dungy was an open secret, apparent even to those on the personnel side of the Steelers. "I told Jed to stop going behind Tony's back," said Artie. "Jed got pissed at me and walked away, but then came back to work with me. I think Noll and I were the only two guys that liked and respected Jed. The more time Jed and I spent together watching film and talking football and scouting, the more I got to respect Jed, and later like him. He was impossible, maybe a bit of a jerk, but otherwise okay."

He counseled Hughes to stop being so grandiose. "Eisenhower did not have Patton take our fleet across the channel," Artie explained. "He used Bradley. Jed, you have to be Omar Bradley and not General Patton."

Chuck and Artie's relationship had always been nebulous ("I was in charge, but Chuck had the final say," was how Artie put it), and now as the disagreements festered, and the team continued its early season slump, Dan Rooney felt as though he'd seen enough. He called his brother into his office and explained to Artie that he was moving him out of the football end of the club operations. "We have to make a change," Dan said. "It has to be this way. It won't work."

Dan and Artie then went to their father's office and hashed it out further. Art Rooney Sr. had long given Dan the latitude to make decisions at the club, and now he supported one son who was essentially firing the other.

"He was reassigned," said Dan. "I never told him he had to get out of the office, that he didn't have a job. I never told him that he was not going to get his pay." What Dan did, that struck his brother more deeply, was take away Artie's title and authority. After a life spent in football, Artie was cast aside from the job he loved. He still owned a piece of the team, but lacked a shred of influence.

"Dan felt I was an obstacle to him running the entire team," said Artie. "Maybe that was correct."

"He did a very good job," said Dan. "He did the job well. It was the other things that created a problem."

Years later, Dan would maintain that if he didn't reassign his brother,

Chuck would have left, wearied by the infighting. "Chuck Noll," he said, "didn't like those kinds of confrontations."

And Chuck and Marianne maintained that no such thing was the case. "I think Artie wanted credit, you know?," said Marianne. "And Chuck always said when you win there is enough to go around. It wasn't an issue with Chuck, but it was for Artie. I think we both felt badly about that, but that's his whole life."

Despite all the staff in-fighting, Chuck held the team together. From a 1–6 start, the team rallied, winning five of its next eight games, behind the healed Malone. Yet the season ended with one of the least disciplined Steelers' performances in memory, a 24–19 loss to a punchless Chiefs team vying for its first playoff berth in fifteen years. While the Steelers' offense moved the ball consistently that day, it was crippled by an inability to score touchdowns. Three tries on first and goal at the 1 gained no yards. The Chiefs' first touchdown came when the Steelers fumbled in their own end zone; the second on a kickoff return; the third on a Steelers' field goal attempt, blocked by by Bill Maas and returned 78 yards by Lloyd Burruss. The special teams mishaps were particularly painful, as Chuck continued to insist—at a time when every other NFL team had an assistant coach dedicated to special teams—to handle the majority of the special teams coaching duties himself.

Back in Dallas, retirement hadn't particularly suited Joe Greene. Facing the challenge of all great athletes at the end of their playing careers, he had taken his shot at being a game broadcaster for CBS during the 1982 season and hadn't enjoyed the experience. He and retired basketball player Cincy Powell had ventured into the restaurant business in 1982 and soon expanded to three locations. But by the time the phone call came in early 1987, Greene was ready for a change. It was Joe Gordon, calling on behalf of Chuck, who needed a new defensive line coach in the wake of Jon Kolb's moving to a full-time strength coach position after Lou Riecke's exit.

Though he was financially well-off, Greene remained unfulfilled. The summons from Chuck was an offer he couldn't refuse. That summer, Chuck presented Greene for induction at the Pro Football Hall of Fame, and cited him as "one of the great football players, who had his antenna out and was really sensitive to the people around him and as a result, I think we played together as a football team."

For Greene, the job was a sense of purpose renewed, and a triumphant return to Pittsburgh. For Chuck, it was a reconnection with the glories of the past, and the arrival of an ally with significant institutional memory in a more complicated present.

But even Greene, Chuck's first draft choice, and the linchpin of the Steelers dynasty, found it somewhat uncomfortable to work with his mentor.

"Every day, he would come by the office and we would watch tape, and he would talk," said Greene. "It was not like he was teaching me, but he was."

The time was valuable but also somewhat awkward. And Greene didn't know how to get out of it.

"Then I found out," said Greene, "that Chuck really didn't like cigar smoke. At that time, because the Chief was walking around smoking, anybody could smoke. And the Chief would give me cigars. When I started smoking the cigars, Chuck walked by the door and he wouldn't come in."

Greene was glad to be back with his old coach. But also started smoking a lot of cigars that spring.

Though Artie was gone, the system he'd built for the Steelers remained in place, with Dick Haley heading up the personnel department, aided by the onetime Steelers' ball boy and longtime high school coach Tom Donahoe. The 1987 draft class was a strong one. Taking Purdue's Rod Woodson in the first round, and two other defensive backs by round four, the Steelers fortified their depleted secondary.

In the fifth and sixth rounds, they found two unheralded linebackers, Hardy Nickerson from California and Greg Lloyd of Fort Valley State. In the tenth round, they landed a tough, deceptively elusive running back named Merril Hoge from Idaho State.

Like a lot of the players from that era, Hoge was intimidated by Chuck. In the fifth week of camp, when he ran a wrong route during a practice, Hoge became concerned.

"Merril, gosh dang it," barked Dick Hoak. "That's a flat, not a flare."

As he walked back to the huddle, he saw Chuck looking over at Hoak and heard him saying, "I thought you said this guy was smart."

Only with hindsight would Hoge conclude, "It was his way of saying, *I'm watching you*. It didn't stop there. He was always doing stuff like that." Hoge made the team.

The 1987 preseason began ignominiously. On the first play from scrimmage, on the road at Washington, the Steelers had to call timeout because they had too many men on the field.

"What are we doing!?," asked Chuck. "Who is out there who's not supposed to be?"

It was the rookie, Greg Lloyd, who came to the sidelines apologetic. "I'm sorry, coach," he said to Dungy. "I've never been in a game where I didn't start, so I just got caught up in it and ran out on the field."

Dungy, as if speaking to a child, said, "The fact that you were practicing on the second team all week, and when we announced the starting lineup, it didn't have your name in it, did that tip you off that maybe you weren't starting?"

"I know, I know, coach, but . . ."

It promised to be a long season, and it was. After the second week of the regular season, the NFL players union went on strike. For the second time in five years, the work stoppage would gut a season.

Chuck's public pronouncements were pro forma—"nothing I can do about it"—but behind the scenes, he was more active. He wrote a letter to Bubby Brister, encouraging him to cross the picket lines to continue his maturation at quarterback. "It would be a great opportunity for you to get some experience, and get to where we want you to go."

"I didn't write him back," said Brister. "I just didn't cross. I couldn't do it. You know, it was just a steel town and all the guys. It hurt me a little bit, and it would have been a great year for me to play and get experience, but you know there is so much tradition there with the players and the union and all that in Pittsburgh. I mean, if I was going to be there, and if I did that, I knew it was going to hurt me more than if I didn't do it."

Brister sent word back through Tom Moore that he just couldn't cross.

Five years earlier, Chuck had told John Stallworth and others not to cross the picket line. Now, in 1987, he was urging his future team leader to do so. Even on a team where relations with management were more harmonious ("We weren't striking against the Rooneys," said Tunch Ilkin, "we were striking against the NFL"), Chuck had put Brister in an impossible position.

As the strike wore on, Chuck grew more disenchanted.

"Free agency?," he said. "I'll give them all free agency."

"He empathized with the players who wanted to get as much as they could," said Dungy, "but to him striking and work stoppage just didn't make sense. No one did that. If you really loved football, you didn't do that. We had a ton of guys in '87, who started coming in before the strike was settled. A lot of them said, 'I will give you one game check, symbolically, to show some unity, but I am coming back the second week, so I hope it is settled.'"

The strike of 1982 had left both sides embittered, but by 1987, NFL owners were determined that the league wouldn't shut down. The executive committee of the NFL's Management Council, led by the Cowboys' Tex Schramm and Buccaneers' owner Hugh Culverhouse, had convinced the owners to hire replacement players and carry on with games.

So less than two weeks after the strike started, the NFL resumed their games, with "scab" players dominating the rosters. To avoid any ugly scenes, the Steelers set up camp about an hour southeast, in Johnstown, Pennsylvania. The replacement players were bussed there and billeted at the Holiday Inn.

The three weeks spent in a Johnstown Holiday Inn were, in some ways, a return to the purer aspects of teaching. The Steelers' scouting department had found a group of credible ballplayers.

"We will get some good players out of this," Chuck told his staff. "There will be some guys that maybe should have made the team before that have four more weeks to prove us wrong. We are going to evaluate by production, like we always do."

Pittsburgh went 2–1 during the strike, and when it ended, Chuck seemed less relieved than annoyed. "I remember in a walk-through, the week we all came back, he got a little pissed off," said Hoge. "Things weren't happening smoothly, and he got pissed off about how unorganized everything was, and how disheveled people were. As a coaching staff, they were kind of cold."

But soon enough, Chuck's philosophical nature kicked in. At one of the early practices back after the strike was settled, he said to the team, "Look, a couple of guys who weren't on this team are now going to be on this team. We are still one team; we are the Pittsburgh Steelers. Let's remember that."

The Steelers' competition in the AFC Central had grown formidable. In Cleveland, the Browns were being coached by the earnest, intense Marty

Schottenheimer, who'd played under Chuck for a week of training camp in 1970. ("He was a brilliant communicator," said Schottenheimer. "It wasn't just direction; it was reason informing it.") Schottenheimer was cut from the same cloth as Chuck.

Not so for the other two coaches in the AFC Central Division—Houston's Jerry Glanville and Cincinnati's Sam Wyche. In both '84 and '85, Chuck had refused to shake Wyche's hand after games. "I'm not very friendly," Chuck said. Those close to him said he found Wyche glib and vacuous. "Harry High School," was his description; he viewed some of the Bengals' strategic flourishes, like the no-huddle offense and the shotgun, as gimmicky, a borderline dishonest way to run a football team.

But if there was an antithesis to Chuck in the coaching ranks in the late '80s, it could only have been the Oilers' Jerry Glanville. Voluble and acerbic, he seemed at times like a character in a one-man play about a homespun football coach with equal reserves of self-regard and sarcasm.

"He is just an arrogant little twerp," said Marianne, reflecting Chuck's opinion.

Glanville's personality grated less than the football philosophy he instilled in the Oilers. "They were the cheapest bunch," said Tunch Ilkin. "You know Glanville promoted that stuff; I knew a bunch of guys on the Oilers, and they told me that. So when we played them, all bets were off, man. We didn't care about penalties. I mean, it was real; that was no show. Those guys played it that way, so we played it that way. I can remember running behind guys on the field and drilling them in the middle of the back, you know, just hitting guys for the sake of hitting them. That was the kind of game it was when we played them."

Before the December 20 game at Houston, Chuck had counseled his team to avoid being goaded into penalties. But once the contest started, and the Oilers engaged in a symphony of late hits and piling on, Chuck grew irate.

"I precipitated it," said Tom Moore. "I had coached with Jerry Glanville at Georgia Tech, so I knew Glanville. I knew that he used to give this award called the 'Riddell Enema' award that he gave the guy who took his helmet and knocked the shit out of a player. And it was just punishing, so I was telling Chuck, 'The guy is doing it on purpose—he is *teaching* them to injure people.'"

When the Steelers' Earnest Jackson gained two yards on a run, a group of Oilers stood him up and battered him further.

"Chuck, when are you going to do something about that son of a bitch?!," asked Moore via the headset. "He is doing it on *purpose*, and somewhere along the line, you have got to do something."

On the sidelines, Chuck had been barking at the referees, and his anger escalated from there. At one point, he spoke to the Oilers' cornerback Steve Brown and said, "Hey, why don't you tell your coach to meet me out in the middle of the field, and we will go at it one on one? Who are you going to bet on?"

"Um, I bet on you, coach," said Brown.

After the game, Chuck met Glanville on the field for the traditional postgame handshake. Glanville breezily stuck out his hand, but Chuck wouldn't let go of the grip, and eventually shoved a finger at Glanville's chest. "If you keep having your guys jumping people like that, it's gonna get *your* ass in trouble." Glanville finally broke away and trotted away, but he surely overheard Chuck's closing salvo, "Just know that—I'm serious!"

In the moment, Glanville seemed stunned and then cowed. But by the end of the week, he had regained his poise. "He was a perfect gentleman when they were beating us every year," Glanville said. "Last year they beat us twice, and he said I was doing a great coaching job. When you get beat, different frustrations come into play. He's a very intense coach."

The two losses to end the season—to the Oilers and in the finale to Cleveland—cost the Steelers a playoff spot. In the last two games, Mark Malone threw five interceptions but no touchdown passes, adding to the criticism of his performance at the end of the season. It was clear that the Steelers still hadn't found a suitable successor to Bradshaw.

The end of the season also marked another milestone, as both John Stallworth and Donnie Shell—two of the last three players who had been on all four Super Bowl champions—announced their retirement.

Stallworth had, over the years, become exactly the sort of player Chuck valued most. He'd had talent to begin with, then maximized it by treating the game with utmost seriousness (he'd begun, in the late '70s, bringing a briefcase to Three Rivers each day).

One day in 1987, when Chuck was in the locker room, engaging in small talk with some of the rookies, he delivered his setup line, "Do you know the difference between a bad haircut and a good one?"

Stallworth, sitting alongside the younger players, had heard the joke multiple times, and piped up, "Two weeks, coach."

"John," said Chuck, smiling. "You've been here too long."

Later in the season, Dan Rooney called Stallworth—Chuck couldn't bear to do it—to confirm his retirement and make plans for a press conference and ceremony.

The morning of the retirement reception, Chuck walked up to Stallworth and said, "John, I feel like crying. But that probably wouldn't be a good thing, would it?"

"No, Chuck, it probably wouldn't."

Of Stallworth and Shell, Chuck spoke in his typically matter-of-fact style, but he also added a note of gratitude and admiration. "They were good for the Pittsburgh Steelers. And they also were good for the National Football League, and good for the human race."

As Chuck prepared for his twentieth season, there would be only one holdover who had played on all four Super Bowl champions—the grizzled center Mike Webster.

✦　　✦　　✦

In the 1988 draft, Dick Haley pushed hard to select Aaron Jones, a lanky defensive end out of Eastern Kentucky. Only later did the Steelers' coaches spot the setup. "Aaron was strong, he was fast and quick, and you know, the Eastern Kentucky coach, when we asked him about Aaron, he kept talking about John Jackson [the Pro Bowl lineman whom the Steelers would take in the tenth round]," said Tony Dungy. "Now, if I had been a seasoned coach, I would have picked up on that. And I think Chuck knew better, but he drafted him in the first round."

But it was more than just one miss. While they respected one another, Chuck and Haley never found the rough understanding that Chuck and Artie had reached. "Chuck was, 'I looked a little bit on this guy and I like him,' you know," said Dick Haley. "That's not enough. We spent days and weeks and months trying to figure this guy out, and you just can't do that—now you might be right but you've got a good chance of being wrong, too. That was the whole thing. Art just struggled with that—we were spending so much time and money to get as much information to make the decision we could, and to have someone just take a tape and run down to the other end to look at it, and come back and say, 'I don't like this guy.' That wasn't the way you do it. And so Art fought that and his last name being right, he could fight it. My last name wasn't right so I couldn't fight it."

Over the off-season, the Steelers had traded Malone to San Diego and signed Todd Blackledge, the 1983 first-round pick (drafted ahead of both Jim Kelly and Marino) who'd fallen out of favor in Kansas City, to compete for the starting quarterback job.

Bubby Brister, just off his second season, came in to Chuck's office before training camp to make his case. "Coach, *I'm* your guy," Brister said. "I am going to get this done for you. I want you to know that, and I'll work hard. If there is something else you think that I need to do more of, just tell me; I'm the guy."

On August 20, 1988, the morning of a preseason game at the Giants, Chuck joined Tunch Ilkin and Craig Wolfley in a meeting with Joe Browne of the NFL office, at the Steelers' hotel near Giants Stadium, so that he could appeal the fines they'd received in the previous season's game against the Oilers. "So Chuck shows the film," said Ilkin. "And I will never forget this, because I think this was the first time I ever heard this word. He said, 'If you don't let these guys take up for their teammates, you will have emasculated them.' Wolf and I look at each other and go, 'Whoa—*emasculated!*' So, I just remember him sticking up for us."

Chuck finished making his case, turned off the film showing the late hits, and waited for Browne to reach his verdict.

"Yeah, good argument," said Browne. "But no. Appeal is denied."

Just a few days later, on August 25, 1988, Art Rooney died. It cast a pall over the team, and the season would only deepen that sense of disappointment. Pittsburgh beat the Cowboys to open the season, then lost six straight, including a 34–14 loss to the Oilers, that was so bitterly fought that the loyal soldiers Wolfley and Ilkin followed Chuck out to the middle of the field after the game. "We went out to kind of see what was happening, and also to watch Chuck's back," said Wolfley. "You don't know what is going to happen in a situation like that, and whatever you want to say, we loved our man. So we went out there to check that out." The handshake, this time, was terse. Chuck had bigger problems.

The frustration escalated. Chuck, always a nervous eater, was exercising less and eating more. "We never saw the food," said his secretary, Pam Morocco. "He just gained weight when things were going bad."

On October 19, with the Steelers sitting at 1–6, Brister went in front of a beer distributor crowd in a Days Inn in New Kensington and told some after-dinner banquet jokes, saying at one point that the Steelers' offense was so predictable, "we might as well just punt on first down." In the same talk, Brister stated that the Steelers should use a shotgun offense, but that Chuck was "too stubborn" to do so. He also recounted a Ralph Berlin anecdote, that when Bradshaw was dealing with a dislocated finger and a broken wrist, Chuck refused to even consider the shotgun. "Don't even try" to talk Chuck into it, Berlin told Brister.

That and more was on page A-1 of the *Post-Gazette* two mornings later, though Chuck remained outwardly unruffled. "I just hear he went out to entertain some people and committed a few indiscretions," Chuck said. "When you're not going good—and we aren't now—those things happen. Does it bother me? It's part of weathering it and being tough enough to stay with it and be firm of purpose, and have a mind-set to get the thing going, which we will do."

What Chuck still wouldn't do, as Berlin had predicted, was consider using the shotgun. "In the shotgun, you have to take your eye off the coverage to see the ball when it's snapped," said Dungy. "And Chuck just never was going to believe that trade-off of being back a little farther would offset having to look at the ball. And it also took a lot of your running game away. You could argue until you were blue in the face about that, and it didn't make sense to him."

They snapped the six-game losing skid with a win over the Broncos, but a week later, in an October 30 game against the Jets, the promising young running back Hoge bobbled a catch in the flat that was scooped up by Robin Cole (playing his first game against his old team), who returned it for a touchdown. Later in the game, Hoge—the short man on the punt team—bungled an assignment, picking up the wrong rusher on a punt that was blocked.

Coming off the sidelines, Hoge could tell that Chuck was livid. This error was costly and embarrassing but, even worse, it was a mental mistake.

"You are the *dumbest* football player I've ever seen," yelled Chuck. "Get your ass on the bench!"

At the end of the game, walking to the locker room, Chuck saw that Hoge was downcast. "Merril, if you learn how to catch the ball and count, we don't lose this game. Get dressed. We are out of here."

To the press, Chuck was unusually pointed in his critique of Hoge. "He's the key guy back there," he said. "We tried to make it simpler. All he had to do was block outside. I don't know what happened. I can't explain it. We can't make it any simpler."

It had been nine years since the Steelers had won a Super Bowl, but each of their division rivals had built teams to respond to that Steeler monolith, and the increased level of competition only underscored Pittsburgh's struggles. "The Oilers were unbelievable, Cincinnati was awesome, and Cleveland had probably the best defense around," said Brister. "So just in our little division, we were lucky to go .500." In the 1988 season, each of the other three teams would qualify for the NFL playoffs. "Those other teams had better talent than we had right then. We were close. We needed a few more pieces. Our defense was getting better, and we had Woodson, and we had Louis Lipps. We just needed some more pieces to the puzzle, I thought. We tried hard and we played hard and Chuck was a great motivator, but it was just hard to get over the hump with those three teams in our division."

As the '88 season unraveled, Dan Rooney fended off calls for Chuck to be fired. Yet even at that point, Chuck somehow kept his players together. The message he gave to the team was, "Find out how good of a football player you can be."

That, at its base, was Chuck's message and his process. Traveling to Houston for a Sunday night game, Chuck got the most rousing performance of the season, a riveting, back-and-forth 37–34 win over the Oilers, which knocked Houston out of contention for the division title.

But the following week, they were hapless again, losing 20–14 to Mark Malone and the Chargers.

"That was the season that you expected to go right over the edge," said Wolfley. "Everybody said the message is not being received, he has lost the team, that sort of thing."

What he definitely lost was a semblance of coherence among his coaching staff. Jed Hughes continued undermining Tony Dungy in a ploy that the other assistants viewed as a bid for Dungy's defensive coordinator job. For his part, Hughes was complaining to Chuck that Dungy and Greene seemed to be "ganging up" on him.

"In the mornings, he would go to see Chuck before Tony, who was the coordinator, had a chance to get in there," said Dan Rooney. "He would go in, and Chuck would let him. That's where Chuck was wrong. He should have said, 'Hey I'm waiting.'"

"He was an intelligent guy," said another assistant. "And I think he got in Chuck's ear. And Chuck knew that he was an intelligent person, and so he would listen to some of these things, and I think it hurt the defense.

That's what got Tony, I think. I don't know how he got in Chuck's ear, but he did, and a lot of the things he suggested, Chuck would do."

During the dark final weeks of the season, after the latest example of Hughes's subterfuge, Dan Rooney took action. He didn't want to talk in the office, fearing for the privacy of the conversation, but instead invited Chuck out to the Chief's old house on the North Side (where Dan Rooney himself would move a few months later).

The old friends sat down in the library, over a glass of wine, and Rooney got to the point.

"You've got to get rid of Hughes," he said.

"I'm not going to get rid of him," said Chuck.

"You *have* to get rid of him. He is not our kind of guy."

"Yes, he is; he's all right."

"No, he isn't—the stuff with Tony, the stuff with Joe. Chuck, why can't you see this?"

"Well, this is going to break us up," Chuck warned.

"Look, I want you to be our coach as long as you can be the coach, but I can't stand by and watch this."

"Well, you said I had the right to hire my staff."

"Yes," said Dan, "but I also added this caveat, and you will remember this: I said you have the right to hire the staff unless there is a reason for getting rid of the person. We have to fire him."

Chuck allowed that the stipulation had been mentioned. That night, they agreed to disagree. But Dan had made himself clear: Hughes was going to be fired. It was up to Chuck whether he wanted to stay.

So the two men were on a collision course. And the season finale, at home game against Shula and the Dolphins, carried a little more gravity. "I remember, we got ready," said Merril Hoge. "And he didn't even go over to the chalkboard. He didn't go over our first three plays, punting. He didn't say any of that. He walked in and said, 'Guys, I want to win this one.' We were like caged animals man, when he said that, because he wanted to whip [Shula's] ass. You just saw forty-five guys go out of the locker room slobbering." The result was a 42–20 rout of the Dolphins; after a 2–10 start, Pittsburgh had won three of its last four games. Chuck had, once again, kept his team, though at 5–11, it was the Steelers' worst performance since 1970.

Joe Greene, standing in the locker room, was sure that he had seen

Chuck coach his last game. At Three Rivers the next day, Greene stopped by Dan's office. "I just want to thank you for everything you've done for me. I grew up here."

"What do you mean?," asked Dan. "This shouldn't be, Joe. I am not running Chuck out of here. I want him to stay. We've got a problem with this one guy, and you know about that."

It's not clear what happened in the intervening day. Chuck did not discuss the matter at length with any of his assistants, but made clear to Marianne that he wasn't ready to stop coaching just yet. The next morning, Chuck walked into Dan's office and said, "Okay, we'll do it."

Though agreeing to the firing, Chuck never really fully acknowledged Hughes's treachery, and in so doing, he committed the error of assuming that the soft-spoken Dungy wasn't ready to be a defensive coordinator. He decided to bring in Rod Rust as the new defensive coordinator, and he offered Dungy his old secondary job back.

"Chuck, if that's your decision, then I'm going to go look for a new job," said Dungy, who knew that he wouldn't move forward in the profession by taking a demotion in Pittsburgh.

When the announcement was made, two days before Chuck's fifty-seventh birthday, it was revealed that Hughes, Dennis Fitzgerald, Hal Hunter, and Walt Evans had all been fired but that Dungy had resigned "to go to a new spot or have a new opportunity."

At the same time, Chuck had signed what the Steelers described as a "lifetime contract," guaranteeing him an annual income of $100,000 per year for at least ten years after he finally retired as a head coach. It meant that when the time came, Chuck could leave on his own terms, with financial stability.

Hughes, tearful, showed up at Warwick Drive the day of the announcement, but Chuck wasn't there. Days later, Chuck tried to help Hughes, making a rare call to Al Davis to recommend Hughes for the vacant defensive coordinator's job with the Raiders (he eventually wound up on the staff of former Steelers' assistant Bud Carson, hired to take over in Cleveland).

But mostly, the event served to hint that Chuck was susceptible. He had a blind spot. And in the late '80s, Jed Hughes was it. Hughes was surely smart and thoughtful. Just as clearly, his scheming had a poisonous effect on the coaching staff.

"Chuck would be oblivious to anything that was external to the football operation," said a longtime Steelers' executive. "Say if he was a philanderer or a drug addict or something like that, as long as Chuck did not see any problem with his performance as an assistant coach."

Between the losses on the field, and the dissension among the coaches, it had been arguably Chuck's toughest season. At the end of it, a reporter asked him if the difficult circumstances of the season made it tougher to evaluate his team.

"No," said Chuck. "This is one of the easiest teams I have ever evaluated. Because now I already know who will quit on me, and they will no longer be a part of me building this team. They will not be here."

Though he forged ahead, the environment was different. With no more reliable pipelines to the college ranks, Chuck began surrounding himself with different sorts of coaches: Both Rod Rust, hired to replace Dungy, and Dave Brazil, brought in to replace Hughes, had extensive previous pro experience.

And by this time, something else became clear. There was a growing distance between Chuck and Dan.

The Rooneys always stopped by the Nolls' around the Christmas season, but the 1988 holiday came with the rest of Dan's family keenly aware of the awkwardness. Dan's son Jim wound up being drafted to go, and while the night was cordial, it was less than comfortable.

By the time that 1988 season ended, Chuck and Marianne and Dan and Pat weren't having regular Sunday night dinners anymore. There were other considerations—the Rooneys were about to move into Dan's father's house on the North Side, so a trip to the St. Clair Country Club was more out of the way.

But those closest to Chuck and Dan doubted if that was the only reason. "It eventually did stop," said Joanne. "I don't know why. I just remember in the beginning they used to do that. It very well could be it changed when they started to lose; I don't know."

Two young men in a hurry: Dan Rooney, left, prepares to introduce Chuck at the 1969 press conference announcing his hiring as the new head coach of the Steelers. *Courtesy of the Pittsburgh Steelers.*

The foundation. Chuck, during his first training camp, in 1969, with the first pick of the Noll era, Joe Greene of North Texas State. *Courtesy of the Pittsburgh Steelers.*

Chuck during a 1969 preseason game against Cincinnati, where his old coach, Paul Brown, was on the opposing sideline. *Courtesy of the Pittsburgh Steelers.*

The project. Terry Bradshaw, selected first overall in the 1970 draft, was determined to live up to his reputation as a can't-miss prospect. He would become, in many ways, Chuck's greatest coaching challenge. *Courtesy of the Pittsburgh Steelers.*

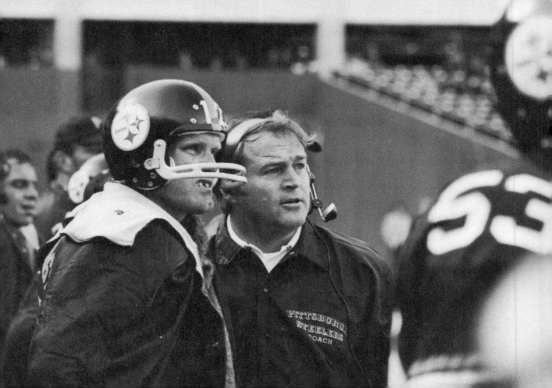

Chuck carried off the sidelines by Jim Clack and Ray Mansfield, after the Steelers clinched their first divisional title ever, on the regular season's final day in San Diego, 1972. *Courtesy of the Pittsburgh Steelers.*

By 1973, Chuck's coaching staff—heavy on assistants with little or no previous pro coaching experience—was coming into place. First row, from left, Paul Uram, Bud Carson, Chuck, and Dick Hoak; second row, Bob Fry, Lionel Taylor, Babe Parilli, Woody Widenhofer, and George Perles. *Courtesy of the Pittsburgh Steelers.*

Coaching them up: Though initially reluctant to draft him, Chuck grew to appreciate Franco Harris, right; throughout the 1974 season, he vacillated between starting Joe Gilliam (below left) and Bradshaw (below right).
Courtesy of the Pittsburgh Steelers.

As the seconds tick off, Chuck concedes a smile before the Steelers win Super Bowl IX in New Orleans.
Courtesy of the Pittsburgh Steelers.

Franco Harris and Joe Greene carry Chuck off the field following the Super Bowl IX win.
Courtesy of the Pittsburgh Steelers.

Chuck congratulates Joe Greene after the brutal 16–10 win over the Oakland Raiders in the 1975 AFC Championship Game, sending the Steelers to their second straight Super Bowl.
Courtesy of the Pittsburgh Steelers.

On top of the world (from left): Dan Rooney, Chuck, Art Rooney, Jr., Art Rooney, Sr., with the Steelers' four Super Bowl trophies.
Courtesy of the Pittsburgh Steelers.

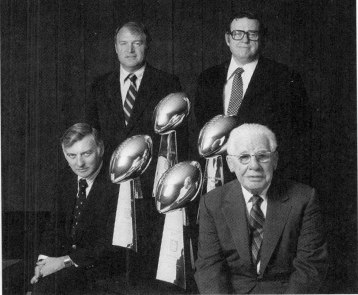

Through much of the '80s, Chuck promoted and worked closely with defensive coordinator Tony Dungy (right) and offensive coordinator Tom Moore. When Dungy left after the '88 season, and Moore a year later, Chuck became an increasingly isolated figure, losing not only their football expertise but also two crucial conduits to his players.

Courtesy of the Pittsburgh Steelers and Tom Moore.

After a draining game, the family—from left, Linda Churchill Noll, Chris Noll, and Marianne—gather in Chuck's office.
Courtesy of the Noll Family.

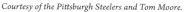

Chuck escorts his niece, Joanne Deininger, down the aisle for her wedding with Glenn Mikut. Joanne lived with Chuck and Marianne for eleven years, from 1979 to 1990. *Courtesy of Jerry Deininger.*

Chuck in his final season. He retired after going 7–9 in 1991, completing a twenty-three-year tenure as the head coach of the Steelers. *Courtesy of the Pittsburgh Steelers.*

Chuck in the parade on the occasion of his induction into the Pro Football Hall of Fame. *Courtesy of the Pittsburgh Steelers.*

The inner circle in robust retirement: Chuck and Marianne with their closest friends, Pat and Red Manning. *Courtesy of John Manning.*

The final meeting. Rita rode over to Pittsburgh to visit Chuck in the spring of 2010. It would be the last time that the siblings would see each other. *Courtesy of the Noll Family.*

The soul mates. As his condition deteriorated, Chuck and Marianne's world grew smaller. Together at a party in 2010. *Courtesy of the Noll Family.*

twenty-one

TWO WEDDINGS AND
A (PREMATURE) FUNERAL

✦ ✦ ✦

On June 17, 1989, Chuck and Marianne attended their son's wedding at the chapel at Phillips Exeter Academy in Exeter, New Hampshire, the hometown of his bride, Linda Churchill. Chris had met her in the master's program at the Bread Loaf School of English at Middlebury College. Vibrant and smart, Linda drew out Chris in much the same way that Marianne had complemented Chuck, a similarity that both women (and, for that matter, both men) noticed quickly.

Chris Noll had grown up thoughtful and reticent, wry when he was comfortable with people, which wasn't very often, and steadfastly resistant to articulating his feelings. In other words, very much his father's son. (Linda was the one who called Chuck and Marianne to give them the news: "We're getting married—save the date.")

Later, Linda observed to her mother-in-law that Chris didn't talk much about his feelings. Marianne rolled her eyes and gave a commiserative laugh. The Noll men.

Neither Chuck nor his son were prone to public displays of affection or speeches. The wedding toast was perfunctory—Chuck was always more comfortable one-on-one. He did pass on some unsolicited advice to his daughter-in-law. "I can't remember why we started talking about it," said Linda, "but Chuck said to me, 'Relationships are never 50-50. Sometimes they're 30-70, and sometimes they're 90-10, and you just adjust to what you need to do.'"

Marianne's advice to her was more pointed—"Always work on your own relationship first, because your children grow up and move away."

The Nolls' HNS *Seascape* (the initials stood for "Hanes Noll Ship"), a forty-two-foot Grand Banks trawler—"Essentially a condo on water," in Linda's description—was docked in nearby Portsmouth, New Hampshire. Chris and Linda spent their honeymoon on the HNS *Seascape* with his parents.

"It was an interesting honeymoon," said Linda. "We got married and the next day we got on the boat, and just went up the coast of Maine. We had about a week together."

Shortly after their return, Chuck left for Latrobe. His team hadn't been to the playoffs since their AFC Championship Game loss at the end of the 1984 season. Change was in the air.

✦   ✦   ✦

The great experiment began with a bobbled snap. The first shotgun snap of Chuck's twenty-one years as the head coach of the Steelers was high and outside and pulled in by Bubby Brister. Chuck had finally relented, after some subtle persuasion from Tom Moore ("Tom was the one who got that done," said Brister), who urged Chuck to give the shotgun a chance, since it would help neutralize some of the blitz-heavy schemes that the Steelers' division foes were fond of using.

There were also several new faces in the coaching staff. Replacing Dungy, the old pro Rod Rust had taken the job as the defensive coordinator. He brought in Dave Brazil as the linebackers coach and a young, ambitious Pitt assistant named John Fox to coach the secondary. The veteran offensive line coach Jack Henry had come in to spell Ron Blackledge, who spent much of the summer battling cancer.

Among the new acquisitions was veteran tight end Mike Mularkey, who'd played seven years for the Vikings, mostly under Bud Grant, who often were the last team to report to camp, and then spent much of their practices in shorts. Early in camp, Mularkey was still adapting to the full-contact practices, in full pads, at full speed. Walking back to the huddle after one particularly jarring encounter, assistant coach Jon Kolb fell into step with Mularkey and said, "You're not in Minnesota anymore."

Brister was the unquestioned starter, and Moore was allowed to open up the offense. So there was a sense of fresh promise and possibility surrounding the team as the 1989 season opened, on September 10, under warm, cloudy skies, at a sold-out Three Rivers. The Steelers were playing host to the Cleveland Browns, whose new head coach was Chuck's old assistant Bud Carson—after fifteen seasons as a defensive coordinator with the Steelers, Rams, Colts, Chiefs, and Jets, he had finally landed his first head-coaching job.

As Gary Anderson's opening kickoff hung in the air to begin the new season, Chuck intoned, over his headset to Tom Moore up in the booth, "Let the second-guessing begin."

There would be plenty.

The opener would quickly devolve into one of those phantasmagorical incidents in which virtually every conceivable thing that could go awry did. Tim Worley fumbled the ball, deep in Steelers' territory, and the Browns' Clay Matthews returned it for a touchdown. Worley fumbled again on the next possession, and the Browns recovered, eventually settling for a field goal. Down 10–0, the Steelers ran a reverse to Louis Lipps, but the ball was snatched out of his hands by the Browns' David Grayson, who returned it for a touchdown. Cleveland led 30–0 at halftime. On the first play from scrimmage in the second half, Worley fumbled again. Four plays later, the Browns scored. On the next possession, Brister's pass was intercepted and returned for a touchdown. It was an auspicious NFL head-coaching debut for Carson, but even he suffered looking across the field at Chuck absorbing the record-breaking defeat. Carson let the Browns throw just a single pass in the second half. The final score, of 51–0, was as shocking as it was convincing.

"It was the worst I've ever seen as a coach," Chuck said afterward.

"Bud could not stop the scoring," said Carson's wife, Linda. "He did not mean to humiliate Chuck. He would have been happy with 7–6. But that felt to him like he had done a horrible thing to his friend by winning like that, because you never run up the score. He walked over to put his arm around Chuck, and Chuck just walked the other way."

The next week, the Steelers went to Cincinnati and were equally inept, falling behind 20–3 at the half, and losing the game 41–10 to a Bengals team that seemed faster, smarter, and better prepared.

That left the Steelers at 0–2, having been outscored 92–10. To the press, Chuck was wryly philosophical. "Either the Super Bowl champ comes out of the Central Division," he said, "or we're pretty bad." After fielding postgame questions, Chuck showered and changed, but he didn't immediately pack up his belongings to leave. Instead, he sat in his slim, coaches' locker at Riverfront Stadium, metal slats on either side of his shoulders.

Head down, thumbs pressed into his forehead, he stared at the floor. Joe Greene was within earshot, but he knew that Chuck was talking to himself, when he said, in a hushed rasp, "We're not sound. We're just . . . *unsound.*"

The flight home was quiet. But before the players dispersed at the Pittsburgh airport, Chuck pulled aside co-captain Tunch Ilkin and urged him, "Keep 'em up, Tunch. Keep your head up, keep them smiling." Ilkin assured Chuck he would.

In the papers and on the airwaves, the team was being mocked. "You sense a trend here," wrote *Post-Gazette* columnist Bruce Kiedan after the second loss. "By October, they may hold some hapless opponent to a single-figure margin of victory."

But most of the enmity was directed at the coach who was beginning his twenty-first season with the Steelers. Monday, at Chuck's weekly press conference, one reporter told Chuck that "some people say coaches coach too long."

"Let them say whatever they want," said Chuck.

Under the circumstances, Chuck's talk to the team on Tuesday was something of an understated work of art. The gist of his speech was direct and realistic: "Nobody is coming riding in from the East. Nobody is coming in from the West. There is not some grandiose trade. We are not about to change the offense. This is what works. I know it works, and it will get done. All the answers to all your questions are in this locker room."

Instead of his go-to metaphor ("Your brain is like a computer"), Chuck had a new analogy on this day. "Your brain," he said to the players, "is also like a swimming pool. What do you have in a swimming pool? You've got water. You've got chlorine, you've got muriatic acid to lower the pH . . ."

Wolfley, sitting among his teammates, felt the collective comprehension in the room sinking to dangerously low levels. "You could just see him as he is explaining it to us," said Wolfley, "because there is not a lot of rocket scientists in the room. We are all sitting there and he is trying to explain all the elements of chlorine and all this and that. He is getting frustrated, because he can see the glaze coming over our eyes."

Chuck paused and looked out at his players, and he must have realized that he had lost some of his crowd. His fingers curled into fists at his side. "In other words," Chuck said, "what I'm trying to say is: Don't let anybody piss in your pool." Then he walked out, leaving a roomful of football players recognizing that their coach had given them something to think about.

"Everyone went, 'Did we just hear what we heard?,'" said Wolfley. "But it made absolute sense. It cut through everything, and we realized what he was saying."

Later in the week, he made a more positive point to the team. "Guys, everybody thinks you are the laughingstock of the league," he said. "Everybody is making jokes about you. It is everywhere. But I want you to know something. I believe in you. I don't care if you lost 91–0. I know we have been bad, and they have every right to say what they're saying. But I believe in you. Now here is what we need to do: We've got to do it better. It doesn't matter what they do. It's how *we* play. We are going to turn this thing around."

The following game against the Vikings was aided by a scouting find, Moore and the offensive coaches deduced an airtight response to a look that Minnesota showed on defense. Pittsburgh exploited it to take a 21–14 lead at halftime, and added two more field goals in the second half to upset the previously unbeaten Vikings.

It was the foothold the team needed and, from there, the Steelers fought back to respectability. They weren't immediately transformed—the defense was still too young, Brister still too inexperienced—but they stuck together, and, Chuck never stopped teaching. The entire season was an uphill struggle. Having fought back from 0–2 to 2–2, they then lost to Cincinnati to go 2–3, with Brister suffering a knee injury that would knock him out for three weeks.

At 2–3, going on the road to Cleveland without their starting quarterback, to face the Browns team that had embarrassed them in the opener,

Chuck posted a note on the Steelers' bulletin board at the beginning of the week. It read:

TEAMWORK

When geese fly in formation, they travel 70 percent faster than when they fly alone.

Geese share leadership. When the lead goose tires, he goes back into the "V" and another flies forward to become the leader.

Geese keep company with the fallen. When a sick or weak goose drops out of flight formation, at least one other goose joins to help and protect.

By being part of a team, we too can accomplish much more, much faster. Words of encouragement and support (honking from behind) help energize and inspire those on the front lines, helping them to keep pace in spite of the day-to-day pressures and fatigue.

The next time you see a formation of geese, remember that it is a reward, a challenge and a privilege to be a contributing member of a team.

In a defensive slugfest, the Steelers took a 3–0 halftime lead. Back-up Todd Blackledge found Rodney Carter for a 14-yard touchdown pass to take a 10–0 lead, and Pittsburgh held on for a 17–7 win. From there, they fell to 3–4, then fought back to 4–4 with Brister making a triumphant return against Kansas City. But then they lost two straight games, at Denver and Chicago, to fall to 4–6.

"There's an astronomically small chance for us to make the playoffs, with all the teams in front of us," said Chuck to the team the week before its next game. "But if we can win five of our last six games, we will put ourselves in position to do that."

It was a big ask, but the players responded—"He said it, and we believed it," said Mularkey. Then, they went out and did it. They beat San Diego and Miami (after trailing 14–0 in a torrential downpour) to stand at 6–6.

For Brister, who was growing into the job, the formidable Moore proved to be a vital resource, not only a talented coordinator but also a man who helped him relate to Chuck.

A key coaching point with Brister was to calm him down and help him focus. "Because my motor was running fast all the time," said Brister. "Tom helped me out a lot with how Chuck was, and what to expect, because he'd already seen it. Tom would tell me, 'Why don't you just go in there and talk to him about it.' You know, because we would have issues, and he would understand but he didn't want it to be his deal." Moore also moved down from the press box to the sidelines, so he could be there to intercede as necessary between the two.

While the offense was adapting to the shotgun and the first full season of Brister as the undisputed starter, there was an undercurrent of criticism within the building. Some pegged it to Donahoe's criticism of Moore's play-calling, others felt that there was tension between Donahoe and Chuck. While Chuck was unperturbed by the in-house critique, the proud Moore was not. "I came home and told my wife that the '89 season might be my last year," he said. "I felt bad if Chuck was being pushed because of me, because Chuck didn't deserve that. He didn't deserve to have to come in and defend me."

After an agonizing early December loss to Houston, to drop to 6–7, the Steelers needed three wins and help from other teams to qualify for the playoffs. They beat the Jets, 13–0, and easily topped New England, at home, 28–10. Next, they flew to Tampa Bay for the regular-season finale, in need of a win and four other results to earn a playoff spot.

Chuck arrived in Tampa on Saturday afternoon and took his brother Bob out to dinner, along with his nephew, Bob Jr. They went down to Bern's Steak House for the meal, where Bob and Bob Jr. regaled Chuck with news of the two hundred gallons of wine that they made down in Bob Noll's basement. It ran in the family.

The next day, the Steelers throttled Tampa Bay, 31–22, and as they came to the locker room in Tampa Stadium, they received the other results— the Raiders had lost to the Giants, the Dolphins had lost to Kansas City, and the Colts had lost to New Orleans. What they still needed, after all that, was the Bengals to lose to Minnesota on Monday night. Talking to the team after the Steelers' win, Chuck was positive: "Go home, enjoy your Christmas, and come to work on Tuesday." Minnesota beat the Bengals on Monday night, and so Pittsburgh—outscored 92–10 and left for dead after its first two games—found itself in the playoffs.

On Tuesday morning, when not all of the players made it back in time, Chuck remarked, "It looks like we've got a few non-believers."

Many of his assistants were convinced it had been Chuck's finest coaching job. "I remember when we were 0–2, and of course the media world wanted to change everything," said Tom Moore. "And Chuck said, 'We are just going to get better. We are not changing anything.'"

✦ ✦ ✦

They would face their division foe, the Oilers, in the wild-card round of the playoffs. Houston had defeated them twice on the season, but the Steelers were a different team by the end of the season.

Ninety minutes before the kickoff at the Astrodome, Chuck was sitting behind the desk in the visiting coach's room adjacent to the locker room. Tom Moore, tense and restless, walked in and saw Chuck relaxed and intent, reading a book.

But it wasn't a playbook or a scouting report.

"Chuck, what are you reading?," he asked.

Chuck looked over and lifted the book so Moore could see the cover. It was titled *Celestial Navigation for the Yachtsmen,* a guide to how one could navigate a boat by the stars.

Even for a longtime Noll protégé, Moore was awestruck. "Chuck, how can you . . . ?" His voice trailed off.

"Tom," said Chuck, "you've got to be able to relax."

That week, Chuck's message to the team was defiantly confident—despite the fact the Oilers had swept the Steelers that season. "They are going to move the ball, it is hard to stop," he said. "That's what they are good at—the 20 to the 20. The second they get to the 20-yard-line, and the field tightens up, it's a different game."

The game went largely as Chuck had predicted. The Oilers threw for 315 yards and took the lead in the fourth quarter on a pair of Warren Moon to Ernest Givins touchdown passes, but Pittsburgh fought back to tie the game and send it to overtime. Early in the overtime period, the Steelers drove to the Oilers 33 before the drive stalled, at the very edge of veteran kicker Gary Anderson's range. Chuck's instincts were to pin the Oilers deep in their territory, but Rod Rust had surveyed his troops and gave Chuck a dose of honesty. "I don't think we can hold them one more time," he said. "We've got to go for the field goal."

Chuck agreed, and sent Anderson out to attempt the 50-yard game-winner. As Anderson's kick cleared the bar, the raucous "House of Pain" was instantly transformed into a somber mass of stunned disappointment.

Ilkin was racing around the field, shouting "House of Pain!" to the Oilers' players. "How's the House of Pain feel now?! House of Pain, boys!"

"Tunch was never one to rub it in too much," said Wolfley. "I just remember, there was a great deal of satisfaction."

It was augmented, perhaps, by the knowledge that the loss would likely cost Glanville his job, which it did.

"I don't like to see anybody get fired," said Merril Hoge. "But to know, it was like he had been gut-shot when that game was over. Jerry Glanville was standing there paralyzed at what had just taken place. We knew he was getting fired. That was the greatest moment I ever had."

Chuck took it in stride, even as some of the Steelers' younger players were overjoyed by the upset. "Chuck was walking off to shake hands after the game," said rookie Carnell Lake, "and Delton Hall went up and he wanted to try to put Chuck on his shoulders so he grabbed one of Chuck's legs and Chuck said, 'Put me down. What the hell are you doing?' Now it is really funny because you're trying to pick up a guy who already won four Super Bowls. This was a long way away. But we were young, and we were excited."

The following week back in Pittsburgh, during what was already a brutal winter, the team practiced in the Pittsburgh Convention Center, whose low ceilings prevented Brister from practicing his deep throws. Then they flew to Denver, where they'd visit John Elway and the heavily favored Broncos. The game plan was classic Chuck—batter the undersized Broncos line with the Steelers' running game.

The Broncos had scouted Pittsburgh thoroughly and knew what was coming. And, as Chuck had predicted, it didn't make much difference.

"They were barking out about half the things we were doing before we did them," said Hoge. "And the more they barked, the more we gashed them."

It was Chuck's vision being realized. The game wasn't about trickery or scheme. It was about execution.

"There is always a time, from a player's perspective, that a coach has to earn that trust," said Hoge. "Like, 'Oh my gosh, he is right.' Sometimes it's just natural to go, 'I don't know if I believe this.' Then they do something and you think, 'I guess he *does* know a little bit. I guess he has been around a while for a reason.'"

With Mile High Stadium shaking—even people watching on TV back in Pittsburgh saw the vibration—Hoge had the game of his life, and the Steelers pushed Denver to the very limit. Hoge and Worley combined for more than 200 yards rushing, though three of the offense's long drives ended in short Gary Anderson field goals. Dermontti Dawson went down with an injury, and Hoge was playing with what turned out to be a fractured jaw. Pittsburgh led 10–0, 17–7, and 23–17, but the defense couldn't stop Elway on a long drive and with 2:27 left, the Broncos took a 24–23 lead.

It was one of those raucous endings in which everything around the game is cacophonous, but on the field, and on the sideline, where Chuck and Tom Moore were conversing, there was utter calmness. A perfect play call by Moore, smartly executed by Brister, found him hitting rookie tight end Mark Stock (in for the injured Mularkey), wide open in the middle of the field, only to have Stock drop the pass. On the next play, center Chuck Lanza (in for the injured Dawson) rifled a low snap to the right of Brister's ankles, and the loose football was pounced on by Denver. The Broncos would escape.

"There's not a helluva lot to say, except that I'm proud of our football team," said Chuck afterward. "This group has all the heart and all the good stuff to be a champ. I'm just proud as hell of them."

On the bus heading to Denver's Stapleton Airport, he walked to the back and found rookies Jerry Olsavsky and Tim Worley talking. Chuck and Worley were soon discussing jazz and the best places to see music in Pittsburgh.

"Worley had this big boom box, okay?," said Olsavsky. "A Bose boom box. And Chuck said, 'Oh, that's a nice system you've got there. That sound is engineered, it's not just a massive speaker that goes boom, boom, boom.' And he is telling him exactly how the Bose systems work. And I had been shopping for a stereo at the time, and I'm thinking to myself, 'What *doesn't* he know?' It was surreal."

Before heading back to the front, Chuck paused by where Hoge was seated and asked, "I've got one question for you. If we had won . . . could you play Sunday?"

Hoge did not know yet that his jaw was fractured, that his rib was cracked, and that the head of his fibula had been broken in the pile-up for the last-minute fumble. He simply answered, "Yes."

"That's all I needed to know," said Chuck, who headed back to the front of the plane.

"It was the only time I felt worthy," said Hoge. "That I was at peace that

I played the way he expected me to play. So it wasn't like I was uneasy or nervous."

✦　✦　✦

Back home after a long but ultimately encouraging season, Chuck soon had another wedding to tend to. Joanne—who'd by then been living with Chuck and Marianne for eleven years—was getting married.

Joanne had been three years old the day her father died. As she grew up, her lone memory of him was Clarence bringing candy to his children. "I think psychologically, Joanne was crushed when her daddy died," said her sister Marilyn. "I was one. The bond wasn't strong. With her, I think it was really strong, and I think she needed a daddy with her personality."

She had found that in Chuck.

Pixieish and winsome, she had plenty of suitors—Marianne understood this aspect and also that her niece didn't have the same freedoms she'd had. There was a boyfriend for a while, who picked her up a few times on Warwick Drive, but there had been little beyond a polite introduction of her aunt and uncle.

Among Joanne's group of racquetball friends, it became obvious that—even in Pittsburgh, in the age of the Steelers—she knew a great deal about the sport. But it wasn't until someone in the group asked, "How do you know so much about football?," that Joanne told her friends who her uncle was.

One of the men in Joanne's circle of friends was an Upper St. Clair native—a couple of years younger than Chris—named Glenn Mikut, who was paying his way through college by working at a gas station.

One night, after having parked across the street at Eisenhower Elementary (to avoid getting the car stuck in the snow), Chuck's tires were slashed, another editorial comment from a fan base that had grown obsessive and insistent and, at times, intrusive.

Joanne called Glenn and explained the situation. "Can you change some tires for us?"

He came in and dutifully fixed the tires. Chuck and Marianne invited him to join them later for dinner. Glenn was tall and casually handsome, self-effacing but with a teasing sense of humor that was easily concealed at times.

"When he ran home to clean up, my uncle made lasagna rolls, ravioli, and sausage, and cooked it all up," Joanne said. "Then the four of us had dinner together." (Before he returned, Glenn grabbed his sister for help—"I'm like very intimidated about going over for dinner with this huge celebrity," he said. "I don't know what to wear, so I asked my sister to take me to the mall to buy some clothes.")

Upon arriving back at Warwick Drive, Glenn Mikut soon recognized the prevailing ethos. Away from Three Rivers, Chuck seemed transformed, a genial, confident presence, eager to talk about a wide array of subjects, provided football wasn't one of them.

Afterward, Marianne waited until the dishes were cleaned, then she said to her niece, "Keep him. He's worth it."

It was months later before they started dating, another two years before Glenn proposed, and then came the reality of planning a wedding around the football calendar.

"It was very important that they were involved," said Joanne, "and it was very important that I did it non-season, so we had to work it in at a good time because, at that point, in the month of June, they went away—that was their vacation. So it couldn't be in June, it couldn't be July through February."

Joanne had suggested she could wear a regular off-white dress, but here Marianne intervened—and they wound up selecting a grander, ivory silk gown with puffy sleeves and a scoop neckline.

Chuck's marital advice derived directly from the "Whatever It Takes" mindset. "Give 80 percent of yourself and expect 10 percent back, and your marriage will survive," he said.

On May 12, 1990, Chuck took her arm and walked her down the aisle, with a proud parent's joy and the confidence that Joanne had wound up with the right man.

At the reception, after the wedding, the guests congregated at Warwick Drive. Chuck, dashing and elegantly handsome in a tux, led his nieces and nephews in a sing-along by the player piano, his sturdy tenor singing "Sweet Georgia Brown," "La Bamba," and "I'd Like to Teach the World to Sing."

There were no long speeches from the uncle of the bride to the groom. "Just 'Treat her right,'" said Glenn. "That was the common theme. I remember talking to him in the kitchen, during the reception, and he was pouring me a glass of wine, and he is kind of giving me an overview of how to conduct myself. Just 'treat her well.'"

Glenn and Joanne went on a honeymoon for eight days. When they returned to Pittsburgh and visited Warwick Drive, Marianne had already turned Joanne's bedroom of eleven years into a workout room.

"Wow," said Joanne. "I've only been gone a week!"

Marianne smiled. "Marriage is forever, dear."

twenty-two

A MAN ALONE

✦ ✦ ✦

As the 1990 training camp began, Chuck was becoming an increasingly solitary figure. Dungy had been gone for a year, and Tom Moore left following the '89 season, having taken the title assistant head coach/offensive coordinator in Minnesota, to work for his old coach, Jerry Burns, who'd recruited him to play at Iowa.

Both Dungy's and Moore's football credentials were solid—as would become even more apparent in later years. But the greatest loss to Chuck wasn't merely strategic. He'd lost two allies but also two important liaisons to the players. Dungy was young (he'd been retired from playing for less than a decade) but preternaturally able to find common ground with players. Moore was in his fifties and had looked grizzled and worn for more than a decade. But he had served as a crucial conduit for Chuck to the offensive players, especially the quarterbacks.

The men who succeeded Dungy and Moore—Rod Rust (in 1989) and now Dave Brazil on defense, Joe Walton on offense—were capable. But they couldn't match the rapport with the players or with Chuck that their predecessors possessed. Chuck had always been his own man. But he was becoming a man alone.

In the spring of 1990, Rust left to take the head coach's job in New England, and Chuck moved Dave Brazil up to the defensive coordinator position. To replace Brazil at linebackers coach, Chuck went with the coach who'd been pressing hardest for an opportunity, a Cal-Berkeley assistant named Dennis Creehan, whom Chuck had considered for a special teams coaching position a year earlier. The face-to-face interview was short. Chuck flew him in, watched some film, and asked him to explain his defensive philosophies, then offered him the job.

The press release was sent out a day later.

It was Joe Gordon who'd first gotten word that something was amiss. Creehan *had* been at Cal the previous season, but since January he'd been the head coach at the Division II school San Francisco State, working on recruiting, installing a new offense, and meeting with boosters. He either never told Chuck that he'd taken the new job or, as Creehan later claimed, mentioned it in passing at a meeting with Chuck in January. He didn't mention it in March when he interviewed with Chuck in Pittsburgh. And he didn't mention it when he sent Chuck a note on Cal stationery a few weeks earlier. But those who knew Chuck best, and knew how much he disliked the interviewing process, correctly inferred that Chuck had never spoken to anyone at Cal to check Creehan's references.

"He really didn't like interviewing new guys," said one of his assistants.

It was embarrassing for Chuck and the Steelers, who fired Creehan the next day, and of course to Creehan—"You've ruined my career and completely humiliated my family," Creehan told the *Pittsburgh Post-Gazette*'s Ed Bouchette. But the reason for the misunderstanding, in the end, was that Chuck hadn't done due diligence.

In the wake of Creehan's quick exit, Chuck hired Pitt linebackers coach Bob Valesente.

There was a growing sense that Chuck was no longer invulnerable. Dan Rooney still supported him, but they didn't dine every Sunday night as they once had. Maybe that had nothing to do with the increased amount of criticism of Chuck inside and outside Three Rivers, but the increased criticism came nonetheless.

"There was a lot of second-guessing that went on after the games," said one assistant. "'You should have done this,' or 'you should have done that,' which there never was until then. There was pressure being applied from the outside; I don't want to say it was [Dick] Haley and it was Tom Donahoe, whoever it was—there was pressure."

That tension would define Chuck's last years with the Steelers.

✦ ✦ ✦

Training camp remained the same. Forty-five minutes of blocking and tackling. Approach, contact, fit, follow through. "I would see him go from position to position," said the offensive line coach Jack Henry. "He would never take over a drill or anything. He wouldn't demean the coaches that way, but he would say things that would be so intrinsic to what was being done that it was obvious that he had studied their playbook, he had been to the meetings, he had been a part of the decisions that have been made in terms of how we do things."

By then, Chuck was more distant, more befitting an eminence, "The Emperor," as Steelers' radio broadcaster Myron Cope had dubbed him. The players knew him less intimately than the players in the '70s had— there were more of them, more coaches between them, and more support staff throughout the game—but still enough to get a sense of his intellect.

"He was the smartest guy in the room," said Tunch Ilkin. "No matter what you conversed about, you thought Chuck knew more about it than you did. He was a walking textbook. He loved to teach. We were getting ready to play the Raiders on Monday night, and I forgot exactly how the story went but it was something like, 'The Spartans were so committed to victory that when they got to Corinth, they burned their own ships, so the only way they could return home was victorious, on Corinthian ships.' And he said, 'That's how committed we have to be.' I remember, we were all just sitting there. We had a guy, I forget his name, but he says, 'Does that mean we're going to blow up our plane when we get to Oakland?'"

Yet there were still moments when he dazzled the people around him.

In the preseason of 1990, dining at the William Penn Hotel before a home game, assistants Joe Greene and John Fox were talking about the new movie *Total Recall*, the futuristic thriller in which a special formula is invented that allows scientists to inject specific memories and impressions into the brain.

Greene and Fox were musing about the amazing possibilities of injecting into the mind an entirely new and different point of view. At which point Chuck, who'd seemed wholly oblivious to their conversation, leaned over toward them and said, "They've had that around for hundreds of years."

Greene and Fox looked at each other and then back at Chuck.

"It's called reading books."

✦   ✦   ✦

In Tom Moore's place would come Joe Walton, the gruff, opinionated former head coach of the Jets, who was raised in Pittsburgh and whose father, Frank "Tiger" Walton, had played in the NFL for the Redskins. Joe Walton had ridden his success as offensive coordinator of the Redskins to a head-coaching job, and while he was fired after seven seasons coaching the Jets at the end of 1989, he still was regarded as one of the game's bright offensive minds.

Chuck, embattled for his stodgy offense—even as the Steelers were employing the shotgun and moving to within one step of the AFC Championship Game, they gained fewer yards offensively than any team in the NFL—was willing to turn the reins over to Walton, in much the same way he'd turned the defense over to Carson, Perles, Widenhofer, and Dungy through the years.

This led to a difficult transition period for the offensive players. The Walton offensive playbook was a compendium of beautiful vectors and angles, a series of carefully drawn route trees and progressions. But while the photocopies were crisp and clean, the language was completely different, and the logic of the system was not intuitive.

In the modern nomenclature of football, the playbook featured an X receiver (the split end), a Y receiver (the tight end), and a Z receiver (the flanker). In Walton's system, any pre-snap shift or motion that found one receiver crossing the other had the identity of the receivers changing.

"All of a sudden, you went from being the Z to being the Y, and you had to know what the Y was doing now, even though you were normally a Z," said one assistant. "It was very confusing to them."

"Listen, if he would call zoom motion, there is probably four or five guys that shit their pants in the huddle," said Merril Hoge, "because that means that one guy starts on one side of the field and goes all the way across, so every time somebody crosses your face, you are changing, but now you also have got to know the other guy. It was too gosh dang complicated."

"Joe Walton comes in and it is a totally different offense, and the players were not buying into it," said Jack Henry. "Chuck was phenomenal. He was much more open to Joe's system than what the players were, because they had known this system forever."

Chuck's offensive philosophy, distilled into one of his own mantras, was "wear down the opponent's will to win by outhitting your opponent over the first three quarters, and in the fourth quarter, impose your will on the opponent." Contrasting that elemental outlook, Walton relied on misdirection and complexity, then hoped to capitalize on a defense's confusion. (In truth, the best offenses combined both physical play and misdirection, but Chuck's view strongly tended toward the former, Walton's the latter.)

There was a near mutiny in training camp, as the players resisted the entirely new nomenclature of the Walton system.

The Steelers did not score an offensive touchdown in any of their first four games in the regular season.

"The only thing our offense led the league in that year was delay of game penalties," said one coach.

"I felt sorry for Joe," said Brister.

After a play called by Walton and relayed by Louis Lipps was garbled upon reaching Brister in the huddle, the confusion prompted Brister's immortal line: "By the time it got from Joe, to Louie, to me down on the field, it was just a damn lie."

"Players were literally reciting the alphabet as they were going in motion," said Mularkey, as they tried to keep their assignments straight. Chuck defended Walton and his methods, and the team did eventually integrate the elements of Walton's system (although the terminology and the playbook were simplified by the end of the season).

At times, Brister would get so frustrated in the huddle, he'd just tell his teammates, "Screw it—let's call a Tom Moore play."

Against New Orleans in December, Brister called a play that Merril Hoge didn't immediately recognize. As they were coming up to the line of scrimmage, Hoge asked for his assignment. Brister, in his cajun drawl, ordered him into the slot.

Tim Worley, taking a step up from behind Brister, said, "Hey, Bub—what's it on?"

Brister turned around and loudly proclaimed, "It's *two*, motherfucker!"

As the Saints All-Pro linebacker trio of Sam Mills, Pat Swilling, and Rickey Jackson looked on in wonder, Hoge improvised a play where he ran out into the flat. Brister found him for a 22-yard gain.

Two days later, when the Steelers' offense reported to watch the game films, they came to the play, and Walton barked, "Turn the lights on."

Someone turned on the lights.

"What the hell is this?," said Walton. "This isn't my offense! What are you guys doing out there?"

Later on, with running back coach Dick Hoak, Hoge protested, "Dick, that was the *best play* of the game."

"Just ignore him," said Hoak. "Forget it."

For all the dissension, the Steelers wound up improving slightly (from twenty-fourth to twentieth in scoring, and from twenty-eighth to twenty-fourth in total yards), and Brister had arguably his best season, throwing a career-high twenty touchdown passes.

Pittsburgh was 9–6 and still alive for a playoff berth heading into the final game at Houston, but this time the magic couldn't be summoned, and they couldn't contain Moon and the Oilers' receivers. After the 34–14 loss, Chuck was very matter-of-fact.

"Guys," he said to a quiet locker room. "It ends very quickly, and that is what we are all feeling right now. It's over."

✦   ✦   ✦

In the following months, little in the way of specifics about his coaching future was discussed between Chuck and Marianne. Nothing was formally decided. But sometimes, couples reach an understanding wordlessly. At some point in the 1991 off-season, Marianne allowed herself to hope that this might be the last combine, the last draft, the last minicamp, the last training camp.

The off-season was marked by a project that Chuck had first explored during the 1990 season, after Brister was sidelined with a concussion. Chuck spoke to the Steelers' staff neurosurgeon, Dr. Joe Maroon, a diminutive, wiry triathlete who'd played football at Indiana, and who advised him that Brister should sit out two weeks.

Chuck was nonplussed, but also curious, to know the rationale for the two-week recovery period. It was from a set of guidelines devised by a panel of experts, Maroon among them.

"He looks good to me," said Chuck. "He knows his plays. He's very active and has no complaints. If you want me to keep an athlete from playing football, you have to give me objective data, not your opinion or some specious guidelines."

The conversation would stick with Maroon, who subsequently asked a colleague to find the objective data that Chuck was seeking, only to discover that hardly any such data existed. Little formal research had been done on the recovery time of football players suffering concussions.

Maroon told Chuck—and Dan Rooney—that if they wanted to have objective data, they needed to spend time doing baseline tests for all the players. Chuck spent part of the off-season in meetings with Maroon, devising the baseline protocol for head injuries. (Later, Maroon and his colleague, Dr. Michael Lovell, would develop the IMPACT—Immediate Post-Concussion Assessment and Cognitive Testing—protocol for head injuries, which would become standard operating procedure throughout professional and collegiate football.)

The 1991 preseason began with plenty of ugliness. Terry Long, the stalwart offensive lineman, tested positive for steroids. Upset with the revelation, he later attempted suicide. Tim Worley, the first-round draft choice who was viewed by some in Pittsburgh as the second coming of Franco Harris, tested positive for cocaine and, like Long, was suspended by the NFL.

The season itself was a cascade of injuries and disappointment. Brister could only start eight games (Pittsburgh won five of them), due to injury, with second-year quarterback Neil O'Donnell starting the other eight.

As the losses mounted, the criticism intensified. With the team standing at 3–6, Donahoe, newly named Director of Football Operations, said, "This is not a team with mediocre talent," a comment that could only be read as a criticism of the coaching.

At home, Chuck seemed increasingly alienated. Not by the players' dress or manner or effort but by their priorities. "He said he couldn't motivate them," said Joanne. "Their reasons for being there were different than what he could handle."

One gray October evening in the midst of the losing streak, Chuck came home earlier than usual, and walked up the stairs into the kitchen. Marianne was cooking, but dinner was not quite ready. Chuck put his briefcase down. There, sitting in the kitchen, in a quiet, level voice, he told her, "We have a Super Bowl team. I'm just too tired."

They had broached the topic before. He knew exactly how much Marianne wanted him to leave it behind. And she knew it was going to have to be his idea. The new deal, signed after the '88 season, called for a lifetime contract with the Steelers, so the financial security that he'd always wanted was there. Nothing more was said. But from that point, Marianne felt certain that Chuck was coaching his last season.

In the final months of the '91 season, there were noticeably fewer "back to basics" speeches, and fewer instances of Chuck dropping into position meetings to deliver a coaching point. "You know, maybe those were signs that he was getting tired and losing some of his energy, or maybe he found out the assistant coaches didn't like it," said Joe Greene. "I don't know. But he *always* seemed so within himself. He was always, to me, the same. He would tell a joke that you couldn't find the punch line. But he was famous for that."

Some of the younger players—used to coaches who were less remote, more involved—found Chuck not only intimidating but also at times unfeeling. They had to adjust to all the hitting during regular-season practices. By the early '90s, most teams tapered off their physical practices through the course of the season. But the Steelers still practiced in full pads three days a week throughout the season.

"He seemed distant to me because, the guys in the locker room, we felt like Chuck didn't care for us because we felt like he was just a businessman," said second-year running back Barry Foster. "There was a lot of talk about Chuck not caring about the players."

Dick Hoak had played for Chuck for one season and coached for him for twenty-one seasons. The quiet, loyal assistant wasn't particularly close to Chuck—they'd never been out alone socially. But he saw Chuck's demeanor changing. Hoak left Three Rivers one night, made the long drive to his home in Greenburg, and told his wife, Lynn, "He's not coming back next year."

"He wasn't paying attention," said Hoak. "He wasn't getting upset over things he used to get upset over. Like somebody making a mistake. At one time, he would have been, 'Why did this happen?' But by then, you might start telling him and he'd just go, 'Ah, okay.' He still recognized it, but he wasn't as strict about what you do about it. He just let some of it go, whereas when we were doing all of this, none of that was let go, you know."

By December, some of the veterans got a sense that Chuck was different in a *different* way.

"I can't tell you that there was anything that actually happened," said Merril Hoge. "I could sense it in his body language with things. How he walked down the hall, the things he used to say. Or he would come in and see somebody doing something, and Chuck would look at them, and then they would start working. And those things stopped."

There were rumors heading into the final game of the season—at home against the Browns—that Chuck was retiring, but nothing solid to go on.

On the big scoreboard screen above the Three Rivers Field, the Steelers had been flashing Christmas greetings from players and team personnel. Early in the fourth quarter, a picture of Chuck and Marianne appeared, with the message, "Happy Holidays from Chuck and Marianne Noll."

The cheering started slowly, among the 47,070 in attendance, then built to a standing ovation and a crescendo of noise. Chuck glanced up at the scoreboard and must have understood what the roars meant, but he didn't acknowledge it—just another distraction from the game.

After the 17–10 win on December 22, Ilkin met with the other co-captains, Bryan Hinkle and David Little. "I am going to give this one to Chuck," Ilkin said.

Raising the football in the middle of the locker room, Ilkin said, "This one is for our coach."

Chuck had suggested giving it to Ricky Shelton, who'd returned an interception for a touchdown. But Ilkin and the players were adamant.

"Thank you," said Chuck at last. "It means a lot." There was sustained applause in the locker room, but no word on Chuck's plans.

The following days took on a surreal tone at the Noll household. Chuck had not said the words out loud, but Marianne, Chris and Linda, Joanne and Glenn all expected him to retire. They were all wearing their Steelers gear over the holidays, but there was a pregnant silence over his pending decision.

Finally, on Thursday morning, December 26, he got up and headed to Three Rivers. Chuck went in that morning and sat down with Dan Rooney.

"I think it's time," he said, "for me to get on with my life's work."

Rooney had been preparing to discuss staff changes with Chuck. But now, faced with the news, he could only express sorrow and gratitude. There was little reminiscing, only a quick discussion of the logistics, mutual thank yous, and a handshake.

Chuck went back to his office, and called Pam Morocco, his secretary, at home, to give her the news. Chuck placed calls to the members of his coaching staff, each of them short and direct.

Interviewed later that day by the *Post-Gazette*'s columnist Ron Cook, Morocco said, "You don't have any idea how hard this is for him. People seem to think he's some cold piece of stone with no feelings. But he cares. He's a very emotional man. He has feelings. Believe me, he has feelings."

Composing himself after sharing the news with Morocco, the pressure seemed to break. As he walked out to inform the rest of his colleagues, he was calmer. He went to the trainer's room. Ralph Berlin started to brief him on injured tight end Bennie Cunningham's condition, but Chuck looked at him, then walked up and put his arm around Berlin. "I am going to retire," he said. "Thank you."

There was nothing else. "He turned around," said Berlin, "and walked out and had the press conference and he retired. That was as close I had to having a conversation with him."

In the minutes before the press conference, Chuck walked down the hallway again, past the receptionist, over to the administrative side to get a cup of coffee. The veteran writer Ed Bouchette of the *Post-Gazette* was there, along with Bob Labriola of the house organ *Steelers Digest,* the wizened exec Buff Boston, maybe one or two others. They discussed holiday plans and the likely outcome of the upcoming New Hampshire primary, by then just five weeks away. Finally, after a few minutes, Joe Gordon emerged in the hallway.

"Chuck," he said. "It's time."

Dan Rooney, looking stricken, opened the press conference by relating his wife's statement that if they ever needed someone to raise their children, they'd choose Chuck Noll.

Surrounded by the sentimentality of the occasion, Chuck strained to remain matter of fact. Asked how he wanted to be remembered, he quoted Emerson: "Your actions speak so loudly that I cannot hear what you say." Then he added, "And I'd like to keep it that way."

As the word filtered in—phone calls, radio broadcasts, all of Pittsburgh's TV stations cutting into the press conference—the players and the city absorbed the news. "It wasn't a surprise, yet it was a shock, if that makes any sense," said Ilkin.

Chuck had just completed his thirty-ninth consecutive fall in professional football. Many had tried to leave and been dragged back, a few others crawled back. But when Chuck packed up his few belongings from his office at Three Rivers, he knew that his work was done.

He wasn't simply retiring. He was ready to get away from it all. Thirty-five years into his marriage, he was finally going to enjoy an extended spell with his wife, the timing of which would not be defined by the rhythms of the football season. Marianne, calm and reserved through the final weeks of the season, had been beaming by Christmas. The hard part was over.

Or so it seemed.

twenty-three

ON THE BOAT

✦ ✦ ✦

A few weeks after the retirement, Chuck and Marianne were sitting on the Steelers' private charter jet out of Pittsburgh headed down to Hilton Head. There was one other passenger—Bill Cowher, who'd recently been named to succeed Chuck as head coach. Cowher's face was an open book: nose broken by too many tackles, thick mustache giving the appearance of a new cop on the beat, an energized conversationalist who occasionally emitted clouds of spittle when he was particularly excited. In personality and demeanor, he was the polar opposite of Chuck.

But Cowher also had a deep respect for football history and the tradition he was inheriting in Pittsburgh. Leaning over before takeoff, he said to Chuck, "I would appreciate your input. Is there anything you think I should know?"

"You'll be fine," Chuck said. "Be yourself, do your best, and I am sure you're going to be fine."

That was all he offered. Chuck made allowances for neither sentimentality nor mentoring—Dan Rooney had arranged for Chuck to have an office in Three Rivers, but Chuck never went there. He didn't want to get in the way or have his presence be a distraction.

Of course, Cowher getting the coaching job meant that Joe Greene hadn't. On the day of Chuck's retirement press conference, Bill Nunn had brought Greene into his office and counseled him that, while he might be a head coach one day, he was not ready for the job yet. But Greene, as the player most responsible for the Steelers dynasty, and the first—and most important—player Chuck ever drafted, had to be considered for the job.

When it was offered to Cowher, Greene didn't resent the choice, but he also knew that it might be uncomfortable for him coaching under Cowher (and it might be uncomfortable for Cowher to have him doing so). Within days of Cowher's hiring, Don Shula offered Greene a job as the defensive line coach on the Dolphins' staff. Chuck had made one phone call. (Though, unsurprisingly, he never told Greene he'd acted on his behalf.)

Within weeks of the retirement announcement, Chuck bought a boot-sized early forerunner to the modern cellular telephones and headed off with Marianne on the boat—"He wanted to be sure he could be reached, so he could help his coaches get jobs," said Marianne.

Meanwhile, Cowher in his first year coaching the Steelers had to acclimate to what his new team understood to be the norm. "We were practicing once and we were going at it pretty good," said John Jackson. "Cowher brings the team together and he says, 'Listen—we're not play-ing the Steelers this week! You guys are hitting way too hard.' Somebody stood up and goes, 'Coach, this is how we practice. We don't know any other way.' We would go back to practicing and he would stop practice again. He'd say, 'Stop. Take off all your equipment and just leave your hel-met on.' You could *hear* us hitting. We had to hit somebody. He finally understood, I think, later. But when you raise somebody a certain way, that's how they're raised."

✦ ✦ ✦

Chuck and Marianne reveled in their freedom, traveling up and down the intercostal waterway, scouting out possible locations before deciding to stay on Hilton Head (they soon sold the house on Warwick Drive, down-sizing and making a clean break from the Steelers' years).

There was always someplace to go, always something to see. There was good wine, unlimited seafood, and the never-ending conversation of soul mates. "We lived on the boat for months and I loved it," said Marianne. "I would have stayed there forever." They journeyed, they fished, they came ashore for a while and explored, then returned to the sea, freshly stocked with wine and provisions, and set out again.

"That was the big joke," said Chris Noll. "When I was in college, they could never find me. And when they retired, I could never find them. Turn the tables."

Later in the spring of '92, Joanne and Glenn flew down to spend time on the boat. They went out to deep water, but as soon as they couldn't see land, Joanne got seasick. It wasn't until they went back to the intercostal waterway that her stomach calmed. It meant that their route down the coast was less direct, and that there was more traffic.

"That was my first encounter with Chuck's intensity," said Glenn Mikut. "So we are coming upon this one drawbridge and they show the height of the water, he knows the height of the boat and everybody is waiting for the drawbridge to go up, which is every half hour or whatever it is or whenever they have enough boats to go under, right? So Chuck decides through this calculation that we can make it. So he starts going. Everybody else is staying back. There's Chuck, full speed ahead. And Marianne and I are up on the top. The mast is up there. We are like eyeing it, and Chuck is screaming, "Are we gonna make it or not!?" All of these expletives and everything. And I'm like, "I *think* we can make it," which is not good enough with Chuck. There is no gray area there. It's like, 'Yeah!' You are better off saying yes and breaking the mast off because then you have made a decision. We made it. Thank God. I'm still here. I would have been fish bait."

Chuck and Marianne became a formidable team in the board game *Trivial Pursuit*. Chris and Linda, two teachers with advanced degrees in literature, were no slouches, but they were routinely victimized. "This isn't even fair," muttered Chris one night.

In the all-star *Trivial Pursuit* pairing, Marianne was the most accomplished. Among the Dayton chums that got together for an annual golf outing in Tennessee, the husbands routinely defeated the wives in the battle of wits. "Until the year Marianne came down with Chuck," remembered Jim Currin. "That ended that. She was unstoppable."

When Chris visited his parents in Pittsburgh, he found his father exquisitely at home in the kitchen, working on one gourmet dish or another, eagerly lifting the burden that Marianne had assumed during the season for so many decades.

Chuck—with memories of jelly sandwiches, and his mother overcooking all manner of meats—liked to get choice cuts from the butcher's. He enjoyed whipping up elaborate coq au vin or beef Wellington.

"Sounds great," said Chris one night. "What's the vegetable?"

"Vegetable?!," asked Chuck, as though the question itself was absurd.

People who know football coaches often can't imagine them doing anything else. So there had been murmurs, and others thinking that he might one day consider a return. But a year into his retirement, Jack Henry—Chuck's last offensive line coach—phoned the house on Warwick Drive. The Giants had just fired head coach Ray Handley, and general manager George Young (who'd worked with Chuck in Baltimore) was looking for a veteran coach.

Henry was getting ready to take an assistant's job with Pitt, but he first wanted to see if his old boss might consider returning. But Chuck had never wavered.

"No, it's over for me," he said. "I'm done."

Another call came, two weeks later, informing Chuck that he'd been elected to the Pro Football Hall of Fame. There were many letters of congratulations in the weeks to follow, perhaps the most eloquent written by Artie Rooney, who'd mellowed in the nearly seven years since his brother had pushed him out of the personnel spot.

"You more than anyone I know deserve this honor," Artie wrote to Chuck. "You were like Moses leading us through the Red Sea and across the desert to the 'Promised Land.'"

That spring, on an annual golf outing at a resort in Tennessee, Chuck casually invited many of his Dayton friends to come to the late summer induction ceremony.

Later that summer, they all converged on Canton—sixty miles south of Cleveland on Interstate 77—for the induction ceremonies, while thousands of Steelers fans made the two-hour drive to be there for the enshrinement.

On the embankment near the front entrance of the Hall of Fame, the cramped amphitheater where the ceremonies were held, the Pittsburgh faithful did something they'd never done during twenty-three seasons at Three Rivers. They began a chant just for the coach. "We Want Chuck! We Want Chuck!" they thundered, and all he could do was bashfully smile.

Chuck's speech was filled with platitudes, but it was also heartfelt. As he strode to the podium, he said, "[fellow inductee] Dan Fouts is holding the money for the guy who cries the longest . . . and I'm gonna win it."

But he remained composed throughout the ten-minute speech, which emphasized the importance of teamwork and decried the way—in his view—modern society seemed to naturally embrace conflict ("male vs. female, black vs. white, labor vs. management").

"Right now, you hear about teamwork," he said, "and it's defined as 50–50, and that is a falsehood. There's no such thing as 50–50. You know, you do whatever you have to do as part of the team."

There were two things about the speech that only seemed noteworthy many years later. In citing the example of teamwork, he mentioned the day against the Oilers when the offensive line was decimated by flu and the quarterback was injured, and he described the defense rising to the occasion—"Joe Greene was in the running lane, and Jack Lambert was hammering on them." Later, Chuck mentioned the first game at Three Rivers, as a preseason game in 1970 against the Jets—"That was the team we lost to in Super Bowl III." And only someone who was intimately familiar with the history of the franchise, or was being scrupulously literal, would have quibbled with Chuck by pointing out that the game he mentioned against the Oilers was played in 1972—two seasons before Lambert arrived in Pittsburgh—and that the preseason game was actually against the New York Giants, not the New York Jets. They seemed small oversights at the time, simple lapses in memory. Only later would people look back and wonder, *Was it a sign?*

That entire day, there was a crush of friends and family. The Dayton teammates had been reveling in their friend's great moment, drinking and celebrating. Jim Reiff, wheeling Jerry Von Mohr around, came up on a hill and the legless Von Mohr slipped out of his wheelchair. "What's the matter with you!?," protested Reiff. "Can't you even hold on?" Somewhere, Marianne rolled her eyes.

After the ceremony, there was a party back at a local hotel. But even in his moment of glory, he was mindful of family commitments. Chuck waited for his cousin, Pete Schreiber, and Schreiber's daughter, to get back from a softball championship game she had to play that day in Cleveland. "I'm not leaving until Pete comes with his daughter," Chuck said.

✦   ✦   ✦

In 1995, the Steelers returned to the Super Bowl for the first time in fifteen seasons. Chuck wanted to be there; some of his old players—Rod Woodson, Dermontti Dawson, Carnell Lake, Greg Lloyd, Neil O'Donnell—formed the nucleus of the team that Cowher had built into a perennial contender.

That week in Phoenix, Chuck did a series of commentary pieces for KDKA in the week leading up to the game, mostly remembrances of his experiences in the previous Super Bowls.

Just as Chuck had so often done, Cowher got the Steelers to play their best game—hanging with a superior Dallas team for much of the game, before Neil O'Donnell made an ill-timed pass, intercepted by the Cowboys' Larry Brown and returned for a touchdown. The Cowboys won, 27–17.

After the game, Chuck and Marianne drove to the Doubletree Hotel in Paradise Valley for the postgame party, a muted affair in which the Steelers' administrators and players were gathered. As they were walking toward the front door of the banquet hall, Chuck stopped.

"I don't want to do this," he said to Marianne. And they turned around and left.

"It broke his heart when they lost," said Marianne. "Those were his guys."

They tried to spend most of their time on Hilton Head, where the boat was docked, and where Chuck had planted a full herb garden, but the thirteen-hour commute to and from Pittsburgh eventually became too much. Chuck and Marianne had gone to a golf outing in Williamsburg, Virginia, with Pat and Red Manning, and they enjoyed the area. Eventually, they'd build a house in Williamsburg—a more manageable six-hour drive from Pittsburgh—and got a condo in Sewickley, twenty minutes northwest of downtown, just above the Ohio River, with a charming downtown of shops and artisans, where they were close to the Pittsburgh airport and where Marianne could walk.

As Chris and Linda, and then Glenn and Joanne, became parents, the Noll family gatherings grew richer and more relaxed. Chris and Linda's daughter Katie, the first grandchild, was born in 1993. Glenn and Joanne had their son, Christopher, just a few months later.

The time with his grandson and his grand-nephews and grand-nieces softened Chuck—"I don't think I hugged him until I had my own kids," said Chris.

Chris and Linda brought Katie with them to Williamsburg. As the young girl became more mobile, Chuck and Marianne were faced with the question of how they should properly be addressed.

"What do you want her to call you?," Linda asked Marianne.

"Mimi is fine," said Marianne. "That was my nickname as a kid."

Linda then turned to Chuck. "What about you?"

He gave a bemused smile. He'd not given the subject much thought.

"Oh, I don't know," he said. "Call me Bubba."

They all laughed. To Katie—and eventually her younger brother Connor, born in 1999—Chuck would be "Bubba" for the rest of his days.

"It never stopped," said Chris. "*He* was being a smart-ass. It was pretty funny. I'm not sure why he chose that."

In the fall of 1997, Chris and Linda Noll had moved to Farmington, Connecticut, to work on the faculty of Miss Porter's School. Jim Currin, Chuck's friend from Dayton, thought that Chris was leading the life that Chuck had always dreamed of—being a teacher.

Armed with eleven years of experience with Joanne, and freed of the constraints of the head coach's life, Chuck moved seamlessly into the role of a doting grandfather. He and Katie would spend hours fishing in the ocean.

Eventually, Katie began to get a sense of her grandfather's special place in society when they would travel. "I have a lot of memories of stopping at McDonald's or Burger King on road trips," Katie Noll said, "and having random people come up to us and say, 'Oh, Mr. Noll, thank you so much for everything you've done.' That's really when I realized he wasn't like most grandpas."

✦　✦　✦

It was January 1999, less than a week after Chuck's sixty-seventh birthday, when he traveled to Orlando with many of his old coaches—

George Perles came, as did Woody Widenhofer, Rollie Dotsch, and Joe Walton.

Chuck had been invited to coach one of the teams in something called the First All-Star Gridiron Classic, which matched a team of college seniors who'd played high school or college ball in Florida against Team USA, of players from around the country.

On Thursday, January 14, two days before the game, he was instructing one of his players in a backpedal technique when he collapsed to the ground. His Achilles tendon—the same one that had troubled him on and off since at least his days at Dayton—finally snapped. When Marianne returned from her outing that day, she found Chuck in a full leg cast in the hotel. They left before the game—"I certainly wasn't going to spend two months in Disney World," she said—and Joe Walton took over Team USA.

It seemed like a blip at the time, but the recovery from the injury took nine months. Convalescing from his torn Achilles, Chuck took longer than expected to get back to his old self. Moving around awkwardly with a scooter, gaining weight, he seemed unusually sluggish and struggled to regain his old mastery.

"They were kind of living the life on the boat, and having a blast doing that, and he was doing some stuff with the NFL," said Chris. "But then it kind of started with the torn Achilles, and from then on it was just one thing after another."

Looking back, all those closest to Chuck agreed that his larger health troubles began with the injury and lengthy recovery. "It was the anesthesia that started to accelerate stuff," said Chris.

One night, a few months later, Marianne and Chuck were having a quiet night at home. They'd turned in and were in bed, her head resting on Chuck's chest, when she realized something was amiss.

His heartbeat was irregular. They went in to have it looked at the next day and discovered a defective heart valve, which they hoped could be managed with medication. By then, they both agreed than another operation was out of the question.

He had not been particularly close to the players while he was coaching, and he wasn't particularly close in retirement. But there were interactions. He'd run into Jack Ham and his wife in Sewickley, or he'd see Lynn

Swann, who had an office there. At the final game at Three Rivers Stadium, in December 2000, he saw Merril Hoge on the sidelines and told him, "I left at the right time. Because I am not going to recruit."

The few reunions he attended found Chuck friendly with his former players, though not prone to linger. They all shared stories of physical maladies, and he inquired as to how each of them were doing pursuing their life's work.

None of the Steelers' stories were sadder than Mike Webster. The irascible Hall of Fame center's body was wracked with the effects of his career-long steroid abuse and countless concussions. Fuqua saw him a few hours before he died, loaning him $50. By then—September 24, 2002, Webster was divorced and living out of a car. "Man, things are bad," Webster told Fuqua.

A day later, Webster was dead of a heart attack at fifty.

"It's not the natural order," said Chuck. "It's like losing a son or daughter. It's not supposed to be that way."

Bradshaw—who'd skipped the funerals of Art Rooney Sr. and former teammate Steve Furness—returned for Webster's funeral.

Throughout the years of Chuck's retirement, the issue that kept coming up repeatedly was Bradshaw. Virtually every other Steeler of significance seemed to have reconciled his relationship with Chuck. Bradshaw had written two autobiographies—*Looking Deep* (1989) and *It's Only A Game* (2001)—the unifying theme of both being his own searing insecurity, bracing self-disclosure, and the degree to which he still felt done wrong by Chuck—even as he reluctantly acknowledged that Chuck was vital to his development. "I played for a coach, Chuck Noll, whom I never understood and who never really understood me; I loved him but we parted badly, and haven't really spoken since," he wrote in the preface to *It's Only A Game.*

Later in the book, Bradshaw wrote, "I'd like to be able to say Coach Noll helped me. I really would like to be able to make that claim—but it wouldn't be true. Chuck Noll took to me like a duck takes to an oil spill . . . the scars he inflicted on me those first few seasons never went away."

For his part, Chuck never rose to the bait, and so the cold war was largely one-sided.

At the 2002 Daytona 500, Cliff Stoudt was there as a guest of the driver Michael Waltrip, and on pit row, he ran into Bradshaw, who'd had a team that raced in a preliminary event on Saturday.

The publication of *It's Only A Game* had brought Bradshaw's complaints back to light.

"When are you going to give it up, Terry?," Stoudt asked. "I mean, damn—the man treated you exactly how you needed to be treated, and that is why you did everything you did. He never was harder on you than anybody else. He gave you the reins to go ad lib with whatever you wanted to do, and he sat on you when he needed to."

Bradshaw still carried a grievance over Chuck speculating that it might be time to get on with his life's work and mentioned that to Stoudt.

"Terry, that wasn't a slam at you—that was protecting *me*," Stoudt said. "I had to go out there and replace you after winning four Super Bowls. Chuck was just trying to say, 'Let's not bring up Terry Bradshaw every day.'"

Bradshaw conceded the point, but still felt aggrieved. In 2003, Bradshaw was slated to be the guest of honor at the Dapper Dan Dinner in Pittsburgh. In an attempt at reconciliation, Bradshaw asked the event organizers if Chuck would be willing to introduce him. When asked, Chuck readily accepted. The day of the event, February 9, 2003, the *Post-Gazette's* Ed Bouchette wrote a story about the significance of the reconciliation. The headline told much of the story: "One-Way Feud Finally Ends as Bradshaw Shows Appreciation, Love for Noll."

The men's contrasting personalities—when uncomfortable, Bradshaw was all emotion, and Chuck was all intellect—made it unlikely that they would find an easy sense of closure. Chuck remained cordial throughout the evening's dinner. Bradshaw was polite and deferential behind the scenes that evening, then gushed once he got up on the podium.

Alternately abashed and tearful during his talk to the banquet, Bradshaw apologized "for every unkind word and thought I ever had," and claimed that he and Chuck were now close. "If we lived in San Francisco, we'd be married now," he said, the tasteless joke falling mostly flat. A year later, when Bradshaw was roasted at the Mel Blount Youth Home annual dinner, he told Chuck they'd play golf. But he never called.

For other players, who didn't have the issues Bradshaw had, it was still odd—even surreal—to see their old coach. Later in 2004, at a card show, Chuck saw Gary Dunn—whom he hadn't spoken to since Dunn's playing career ended in 1987. It was an event at the Pittsburgh Convention Center. "It was kind of weird because everybody is getting paid to be there, and Chuck is right next to me signing autographs," said Dunn. "And Chuck is being paid to be there; I know he is not doing it for nothing. And it was just a weird, different thing, because now he is not my boss, and we just talked. And you know, we talked about things back then. And we laughed. He couldn't be nicer. A different guy, totally different. There was so much to him. When I had him in that situation, I couldn't believe it was Chuck just talking on. But see, I wasn't as scared either. I was saying whatever I wanted. It was very good."

At the same show, Ron Johnson walked over and asked Chuck to sign an autograph for a client of his. "Ron, if it will help you make a sale, I'll sign it."

John Stallworth also visited with Chuck at the same event. "He asked a little about my business," said Stallworth, "and we were doing well, and he had heard about how well we were doing in the business. He asked me about that and that probably was the longest conversation I had with him. I don't know that I was ever totally at ease talking to him, and so in that sense, the brief conversations were okay."

On his good days, even those who loved him couldn't tell much of a difference in Chuck's demeanor. But there were more off days, each of which provided glimpses that something wasn't right.

The litany of health setbacks diminished him and made traveling more of an effort. When his older brother, Bob, died in the summer of 2002, some relatives noticed that Chuck seemed different at the funeral, more distant than usual, slower to recognize them. Pat Manning died of cancer the same year, and though Chuck and Marianne attended the funeral, he was clearly laboring, his extended health troubles leaving him visibly weakened.

In Pittsburgh, they began spending even more time with Glenn and Joanne, and Chuck would often show Glenn his latest photography. "So we would go on the computer and we'd go through the pictures," said Glenn, "but we kept going through the pictures more than once, and he wasn't sure if he looked at them yet. So I thought that it was just him getting old and just forgetful."

Marianne had noticed a loss in sharpness ever since the torn Achilles.

After going under for the surgery, Chuck seemed less mentally nimble for a long time afterward. And now she wondered, *Had he ever fully recovered? Is this him? Or is this the new normal?*

No one wanted to say it, but they couldn't help but notice. The man with the formidable intellect and voracious thirst for knowledge had slowed, he seemed less sharp, less focused, less mentally acquisitive.

On April 24, 2004, the family gathered in Cleveland for Jerry Deininger's wedding to his girlfriend, Maria. The youngest boy of the seven siblings, and the last to marry, Jerry had missed out on some of the time that the others had enjoyed.

It was a festive weekend, with Rita surrounded by her brood, and Chuck and Marianne in for the weekend. That was the weekend that the nieces and nephews first sensed something was wrong.

"He walked into the room, and as soon as I saw him, I went up and hugged him," said Margie, "and he was real stiff and cold. I didn't know how to interpret that."

Nothing was said to Chuck and Marianne. Joanne fretted to herself and later to Glenn.

"Forever, the two of them worked so well together," she said. "He couldn't think of a name, and my aunt would tell him."

That summer, with the extended family at the vacation home in Williamsburg, Chuck kept losing his way back from a restaurant, prompting Chris to lose his patience.

"I was getting angry and getting angry, and then finally I realized something was wrong," said Chris. "I wasn't around him that often. So we would be on vacation, and we were together for two weeks, and it was really clear because he covers it so well."

He continued to do so, often quite successfully. That same year, Chris, Linda, Katie, and Connor came down for Thanksgiving, to see the new condo Chuck and Marianne bought, on the main street in Sewickley. The four-year-old Connor was sporting a form-fitting Spiderman costume and mask that day. Chuck walked through the supermarket in Sewickley, holding hands with his tiny Spiderman. On Thanksgiving day, Chuck and Chris tried to smoke the Thanksgiving turkey and wound up setting off the fire alarm, bringing a fire truck (to Connor's delight) to the condo. It was, if one didn't look too closely, a typical Noll holiday gathering.

But for all of them—Marianne, Chris and Linda, Glenn and Joanne—

a nameless disquiet hung in the air. The heart troubles worsened, as did the bulging disc in Chuck's back. A visit to the hospital only exacerbated things, leaving Chuck with a staph infection and in critical condition in an intensive care unit. The recovery time for each malady was slower than usual. On the streets of Sewickley, late in the summer of 2005, when Marianne saw the Steelers' Dr. Joe Maroon, he asked about Chuck's back.

"We have the X-rays at home," Marianne said.

"Well, let me stop by and take a look at them," said Maroon.

"Sure," Marianne said, then paused, before continuing. "But we're dealing with something else now. It's worse than the damn back . . ."

✦ ✦ ✦

The connection between boxers and dementia was a clear and understood reality for decades in American sports. The connection between football players and Alzheimer's was more tenuous but no less a factor. The results of the landmark study of 3,439 ex-professional football players—which revealed that players were four times more likely to suffer ALS and Alzheimer's disease as the general public—were not yet conclusive.

Chuck had heard in 2001 about his old teammate Otto Graham, who'd been diagnosed with early stage Alzheimer's. Across pro football, the disease took root. The vacant eyes, the repeated anecdotes, the slurred speech. He'd begun to see some of those traits in his own players.

At Maroon's behest, Marianne took Chuck for a battery of tests, during which he maintained an imperturbable good cheer. "Here, hold my watch and ring," he said to her before the MRI.

After the tests were completed, they went to the University of Pittsburgh Medical Center to see Dr. Steven DeKosky, the head of neurology. The CT scan results were clear enough—there was damage. DeKosky showed them both the pictures, then asked Chuck to step outside for a moment.

After Chuck stepped into the hallway, DeKosky leveled with Marianne, uttering the inevitable, dreaded word.

"He has it," DeKosky said. "He has Alzheimer's."

Marianne listened numbly, as he continued.

"Now you have to call your family," DeKosky said. "Call the people you think it is important to know this. Call your attorney. And Marianne —you *have* to tell Chuck."

A few moments later, she left. Chuck and Marianne drove back to Sewickley mostly in silence, NPR playing over the car stereo. They parked and headed up the stairs. She had Chuck sit in his favorite chair, in the corner of the living room, close to the window, where he could see out to the patio and the street, just across from the television set that was off.

"Okay, we have to talk," she said.

She went to the kitchen and collected herself and then returned and sat down opposite Chuck on the footstool.

She took his hands in hers and delivered the news: "The doctor says you have Alzheimer's disease."

Chuck looked back at her. There was a long moment of silence. And she could see him weighing the reality, and the implications, and a lifetime of things that had been left unsaid.

Then he squeezed her hands tightly and looked back into Marianne's eyes, with the steady, determined gaze she's seen so many times before. He had just one thing he had to tell her.

"I will . . . *never* . . . forget who you are," he said.

Then they embraced and dissolved into tears.

twenty-four

BRAVE AND HONEST DEEDS

✦   ✦   ✦

In the glory of this hour, may your heart rest undisturbed
In the care of the one who loves you best
In a story filled with wonder, brave and honest deeds
May you wind up with the one who loves you best
—Jon Dee Graham, "Best"

The picture deteriorates first around the edges, like a Polaroid in reverse, growing dimmer on the periphery, the fog enveloping the outer realms of the consciousness, moving toward the center. The moment is fixed and then it slips. Primary people and places remain, for the most part, but the threads of connection that were built up over a lifetime of memory start to fray.

Marianne would tell Chuck something, and he would focus on the piece of information, attempt to incorporate it, then often look up and ask her, "Please say that again."

Or he would nod his head and repeat a name he'd spoken hundreds of times, and then he would search his memory to discover whether he retained any associations with that name.

This was the battle he waged on two fronts for the rest of his days: the universal physical deterioration of aging (in his case exacerbated by the punishment he took during his playing career), as well as the slow, inexorable loss of his memory, his ability to concentrate, and his analytical agility.

Those in the inner circle—Marianne, Chris and Linda, Joanne and Glenn, Joe Gordon and his wife Babe—saw Chuck's days run together in a slow downward ebb, with fits and starts. Some days were better than others. Family and friends would visit, and Marianne would meet them at the door, with a purposeful, "We're having a good day."

Other days, when the pain in his back prevented him from sleeping, or the medicine he was taking left him disoriented, Marianne adopted a gaunt look. She'd mastered the stoicism of the Germans. "We're okay," she'd say. "We had a tough night."

He'd been diagnosed with spinal stenosis. Surgery might have been an option for some patients, but not for those with Alzheimer's, not after what had happened following the Achilles surgery.

He wouldn't speak directly about the affliction, but occasionally he would reference it. Searching his memory for a detail that he couldn't summon, he would look at Glenn ruefully and say, "Short-term memory sucks."

With the rest of the world, he developed a mask of familiar joviality. The best way to not let down the people in your life is to act like everyone you see must be familiar to you.

They went out less—his back made it hard to move, and standard restaurant chairs were just too uncomfortable—but still entertained regularly, with family and close friends. Dinner was served, everyone around the table, Marianne leading the conversation. She poured wine, then poured seconds. When Chuck would raise his glass for more, she would gently mention, "Chuck, you've had enough."

"Well, our guest needs more," he'd say mischievously.

Then, after Marianne had filled a guest's glass, Chuck would slyly raise his own glass and say, "While you're pouring . . ."

In the weeks after the diagnosis, Chuck and Marianne were faced with a decision.

They could tell the world—through a brief, sober press release via the Steelers—explaining Chuck's diagnosis and asking the public to respect their privacy. His friends, his players, his former assistants would all know. They could all steel themselves for what to expect, and they could visit him on occasion, realizing that almost everyone—no matter how dear or important—can be a stranger to a person afflicted with Alzheimer's.

The alternative was to tell virtually no one, and leave Marianne to protect that secret and their privacy, keeping even some of his longtime friends at arm's length and providing vague and increasingly implausible explanations for why they couldn't together or why Chuck couldn't come to the phone.

They chose the latter course.

This decision would define the rest of Chuck's life. And, of course, Marianne's.

✦　✦　✦

Not far from Chuck, Tony Dungy was following in his old coach's footsteps.

When he got his first head-coaching job, for the downtrodden Tampa Bay Buccaneers in 1996, he ran into Chuck on the banquet circuit, and his old boss was proud. "Just do what you believe in," Chuck told him, "stick to your guns, do things the right way, and you are going to be fine."

Were they platitudes or was it a real message? There was still the lingering awkwardness over the job demotion after 1988, but Chuck recognized Tony as the obvious inheritor of his tradition. And for Dungy, "95 percent of what I learned about coaching, I learned from Chuck." Dungy built Tampa Bay into a perennial playoff team, then was fired when he couldn't get them to the Super Bowl after the 2001 season. He took the head-coaching job in Indianapolis, where he retained Tom Moore as offensive coordinator, and suddenly two of Chuck's most loyal assistants were working together again.

Of all the branches on the Noll coaching tree, it was Dungy who had the greatest similarity to Chuck's style, from his cool demeanor to the involved, almost intellectual way he would respond to the game at hand.

"You can see it, see it in the way he was on the sidelines, see it in the way he holds his arms," said Joe Greene. "He doesn't do it intentionally, but that is just who he is, and his mannerisms, all of that. He doesn't holler or scream at his players. He gets upset, but you have to watch real closely to see it or notice."

As Dungy was winning in Tampa, and then Indianapolis, he found himself wanting to check in with his old coach on occasions. He knew that those connections could only be initiated in one direction. "He is just not that way," said Dungy. "He is not going to come by. He is not going to call you in those situations, and I would have to call him. And by the time we are really rolling pretty good here, I would have a chance to go . . . I might get Marianne, but I wouldn't get him after '99 or 2000."

In the 2006 season, after starting out 9–0, the Colts lost four of their next six games, culminating in a pair of punishing division losses to Jacksonville and Houston, during which they gave up 375 and 191 yards rushing.

The owner, Jim Irsay, was apoplectic. And Dungy drew strength from one of the lessons he'd learned. *Stay the course. Be yourself, because you're going to be second-guessed anyway.*

"Jim Irsay thought the world had come to an end," said Tom Moore. "'What are you going to do?!' Tony says, 'Relax. We don't change anything. We are just going to get better.' And that is the persona he carried with the players, and the players, they feasted off Tony's demeanor."

It was less a matter of scheme than personnel and execution. The Colts went back to basics in practice, and safety Bob Sanders recovered from an injury in time for the postseason. In their opening playoff game, they dominated the line of scrimmage, holding Kansas City without a first down until 3:11 remained in the third quarter, and coasted to a 23–8 win. A week later, on the road at Baltimore, the Colts' defense held the Ravens to 83 yards rushing, prevailing 15–6 in a defensive slugfest.

Back in Indianapolis, on January 21, with the AFC title on the line, Dungy was unflappable, despite his team falling behind 21–3 to their nemesis, the New England Patriots. They kept fighting, kept rising above, and came back to beat New England in one of the most compelling games of the decade.

It earned Indianapolis a berth in the Super Bowl in Miami, where they'd play the Chicago Bears. Dungy and Moore went through Super Bowl week, with reminders of Chuck everywhere.

On Friday, two days before the biggest game of his coaching life, Dungy called Chuck. Marianne answered. He explained that he just wanted to tell his coach how much he appreciated all that he'd passed on.

Marianne, still protecting the secret, was warm but firm.

"He's not having a good day," she said. "The back is really a problem. He's sleeping right now, but I know he'll be so glad you called."

"I can call back later, if that would be easier"

"No, let me just tell him you called."

Two days later, the Colts won the Super Bowl title—and Dungy became the first African American to coach a Super Bowl champion. There was jubilation in the locker room, and Dungy remained composed and happy but not quite jubilant.

"A carbon copy of Chuck," in Moore's words.

In the bus on the way back to the hotel for the party, Moore said to Dungy, "I hope Chuck understands how much he has given us to get to this point. Tony, we are both forever indebted to Chuck Noll."

Dungy agreed. But he'd also gotten the message that Chuck wasn't available and wouldn't *be* available. He wouldn't try again.

✦ ✦ ✦

The late 2000s were a time of almost constant physical anguish for Chuck. One day he fainted at Mass, and he had to be hospitalized. While he was in the hospital, he developed a staph infection, which further damaged his back. For a time, Chuck was entirely immobilized. Doctors were concerned that he would never walk again. For the better part of a year, he wore a constricting molded fiberglass brace, enveloping his torso, a rounded rectangular breastplate pushing his chest back. He was able to take it off at night, but even when he got up to go to the bathroom in the middle of the night, he had to put it back on. He wore it without complaint, and soldiered on, the stoic German throughout. Finally, around 2010, at the age of seventy-eight, Chuck conceded and allowed himself to be wheeled through the long airport corridors at Pittsburgh and Fort Myers.

The scenes would play themselves out in the years ahead. The strong jaw line was softening, the broad cheeks growing paunchy. He was less certain but also less guarded, possessed of a guileless good cheer in the presence of strangers. He labored mightily to carry on a conversation, to follow a thread. Sometimes, when Marianne was explaining something to him, he'd pause, focus intently, then calmly but firmly ask her to repeat it. Everything was an effort. The blue eyes remained alive and clear, darting, dancing, open to the possibilities, still searching for that moment when the gears would click into place.

He would sit, lost in thought, captured in a permanent present, with only wispy fragments of his own past at his disposal. His cheeks billowed as he let out a distracted whistle, over and over and over. The loop he'd been caught in was that of an active, productive man, just about to shift his attention to another task, if he could only remember what that might be.

Marianne was always close, doing a needlepoint, reading a book— she'd resumed their old custom of reading out loud—or simply being there to provide reassurance.

What Chuck would say, most often, is "Ba-Room-Bah."

It was his way of self-soothing.

"Do you know what Ba-Room-Bah is?," he'd ask a guest. "That's the sound an elephant makes."

For Marianne and Joanne and Glenn, this was an increasingly common part of daily life with Chuck. But for those who hadn't seen him in a while, it could come as a shock. After seeing Chuck for the first time in many years, Ken Deininger, despaired to one of his siblings, "That's not the Chuck I know!"

Marianne and Chuck did what they always did, what the Nolls were seemingly born to do. They carried on. Doctors had pointed out the importance of retaining as many of the mental capacities as possible. Marianne bought jigsaw puzzle boxes by the armful. Anything to keep his mind agile. He couldn't follow an extended thread, but he could summon his mastery of special relations to find a spot to fit each piece.

He'd still noodle at the piano, or strum on the ukulele, or sometimes just sing softly to himself while on the exercise bicycle. At the table, someone would mention alcohol, and someone else would mention whiskey, and he'd be off again, breaking into song.

> Whiskey, rye whiskey, rye whiskey I cry
> If I don't get my whiskey
> If the ocean were rye whiskey, and I were a duck
> I'd dive to the bottom and never come up

At the end of a verse, Chuck would often look around at his audience, emit a small, wry smile and say, absently, "Something like that."

In that diminished state, he still exhibited flashes of awareness. At the condo in Sewickley, Marianne would explain when she was going grocery shopping, but she would also leave notes before leaving, "It's 1:23 . . . I'm going shopping . . . I'll be back by 1:57." Chuck would read the notes over and over again, fixing the information in his mind. Setting the note down. Picking it up and studying it again.

Marianne would come through the door near the appointed time, and Chuck would be prepared: "You're two minutes late."

Not long after the diagnosis, Chris and Linda gave the news to their children, Katie and Connor. Chuck's granddaughter, by now a teenager, was erudite, cheerful, and engaging, taking closely after her mother. Connor, six years younger, was trim, reserved, and serious, already another Noll male.

His passion was skateboards.

On vacations, Chuck would ask Connor about his T-shirts.

"Woodward Skate Camp—what's that?"

"I really love skateboarding, Bubba," Connor would patiently explain. "And this is where I go every summer."

Fifteen minutes later, Connor would return to the living room. Chuck would greet him and cheerfully ask, "Woodward Skate Camp—what's that?"

Others, on the outside, had less to go on. Merril Hoge wrote a book about surviving his fight with cancer, and cited Chuck as an inspiration, but when he went to visit him in Sewickley in 2009, Chuck was genial but distant.

"I brought one of my books and I gave it to him, and just thanked him for his impact in my life," said Hoge. "He was happy and he was very nice, but I don't know if he remembered me being there. He didn't say anything about me, so I don't think that—but he was smiling. It was nice to sit there."

There was a card and signing show late in the 2000s. Stallworth went because he knew Chuck was going. "We were signing at different times, so when I got there, he was actually in the middle of his signing," said Stallworth. "I went over to him, and he was signing, and I tapped him on the shoulder and he turned and I did not get the sense that he knew who I was, but he smiled and kind of recovered from that. Later on, he was still there and he and Marianne were about to leave, and Mel [Blount] was there, so we were staying there talking a little bit, and I told him I wanted to tell him thank you—'I wanted to say thank you for all that you've done for me.' I wanted in the dearest way for him to understand that, and appreciate the depth of that from me. I'm not sure he did."

The pattern was set. Chuck and Marianne stuck mostly with close friends and family. When others would call, she would talk about Chuck's back, but she would rarely bring him to the phone to talk to even his oldest friends and colleagues.

"I went to see Chuck when I was in Florida," said Lionel Taylor. "The reason I don't go more often is I think Marianne is very protective. *Extremely* protective. And I call. I never talk to Chuck."

But for her, reflexively used to protecting him, the potential encounters felt like a fruitless exercise in damage control. She despaired that Chuck would be disoriented and that his visitors would be hurt, disillusioned. So the inner circle, already small, grew smaller. Joe Gordon— longtime PR man of the Steelers—would stop by regularly for dinner or to check on things. But for the most part, Chuck stuck with family and the Mannings.

Back in the '90s, Andy Russell and Ray Mansfield persuaded Chuck to be part of an auctioned dinner to benefit the Pittsburgh Children's Hospital. Russell was the most forthright of Chuck's former players in asking about events of the past, but even then Chuck remained discreet. Asked why he cut a particular player, Chuck might say, "Well, Andy, that is what we had to do at the time."

But by 2012, they weren't having the dinner. "He hasn't done that dinner in the last two years," he said, "because Marianne says they're too busy, or they can't do it, or whatever. She may just not want me to know how he is doing."

Russell would find out one day at the Pittsburgh International Airport, where a life-size wax figure of Franco Harris making the Immaculate Reception was one of two VIPs (the other was George Washington) that greeted travelers heading to and from the terminals. In the concourse one day, Russell saw Chuck, getting ready to board a flight to Florida. Russell rushed down and gave Chuck a big hug. "I'm not sure he even remembered who I was," said Russell. "No, I think he did. I didn't see anything obvious, and he did get on the plane right away."

Mostly, among former players, there was a sense of Chuck's absence. "My wife communicates with Marianne," said Mel Blount. "She'll call and ask how he is doing. You know, women chat, and every time we need something, like we have a big dinner coming up, they get him to sign stuff. But it's sad, man."

✦   ✦   ✦

On January 5, 2012, Chuck turned eighty. The Steelers had solicited former players for cards and well-wishing. The notes came from all over. Warren Bankston, who played for the Steelers for just two years, wrote, "You had probably more influence in my life than any other coach, mentor, family, or friend. I never played well for you, and I have deep regrets for that. However, you developed a work ethic and mental toughness in me that carried over to the Raiders and extended an extra six years to my career." Rocky Bleier wrote, simply, "You changed our lives and we are better for it."

"Chuck, sorry I am late (don't fine me)," wrote Terry Hanratty. From Moon Mullins came, "I have taken your direction on into my life's work. In reflecting back, your ability to motivate and judge character provided the backbone for one of the greatest teams ever." Gordon Gravelle wrote, "You instilled in me many values and life lessons that I have tried to carry with me throughout my life and pass on to my children and others. I can't begin to name them all but some are: work hard, be humble, treat all equally, never rest on your laurels, earn respect, never quit, never back down, be honest with yourself and others, have pride in yourself and your efforts, and be the best you can be." Ron Johnson took the team picture of the 1979 Super Bowl team—which he dubbed "the greatest team that this football world has ever seen."

Andy Russell felt the need to express his gratitude in capitals: "You taught us the importance of PERSEVERENCE, CONCENTRATION, INTENSITY, FOCUS, PATIENCE, ATTITUDE, MOTIVATION, INTEGRITY, NEVER QUIT, ACCOUNTABILITY AND LEADERSHIP (and much more)—thank you, Sir—you are still my hero."

But there were no big reunions. Chuck had stopped doing card shows. Soon, he and Marianne stopped going to watch games at Heinz Field.

And eventually their world was reduced to the essential elements. Glenn and Joanne over each week for dinner. Chris and Linda and the grandchildren visiting every two or three months. Joe Gordon, and his wife Babe, swinging by for an occasional meal or to have Chuck sign a football or a helmet for charity. The weekly visits from Chuck's physical therapist. They spent part of the year in Pittsburgh and their winters in their condo in Estero, Florida. Chuck seemed more comfortable in Florida. He would stand on the back patio and watch the golfers go by. But for Marianne, Sewickley offered the neighborhood and the chance to walk.

A few close friends still managed to get through. Marianne could tell most everyone no, but it was hard to say no to George Perles, Chuck's longtime "social director." So he visited from Michigan, and they went out to a dinner, and Perles soon realized how bad it had gotten. They ordered wine and dinner, and a few minutes later, Chuck asked when they were going to order dinner.

The Dayton teammate Jim Currin had faithfully stayed in touch through the decades—impervious to Chuck's long absences, still able to get a rise out of him, still able to make him laugh. One day early in 2013, Jim and his wife Judy drove down from their winter home in Venice, Florida, to visit. Chuck was sitting in his easy chair, not even feeling energetic enough to work a jigsaw puzzle.

Chuck didn't say much; he was mostly quiet during the visit, but he would perk up a bit when Jim mentioned one of the old Dayton buddies. He moved with the help of two canes but mostly sat.

Sitting in the occasional awkward silences, Currin would wince at the sight of Chuck's arms. Marianne struggled to control Chuck's aimless scratching. The medications left his skin itchy, and he'd absently claw at his forearms, first the right hand on the left arm, then the left hand on the right. Eventually, he'd draw blood, but he would keep scratching. It was one of those days.

"It just seemed like he was out of it for a while," said Currin. "He would just look around and then repeat himself."

As the Currins were getting ready to leave, Chuck roused himself. He used his canes to deftly walk down the stairs, onto the landing of the condo by the front door. There, in the vestibule, something clicked. Chuck fixed Currin a look. And recognized the longtime pal he'd once dubbed Dennis the Menace. He reached out and put an arm around Currin and hugged on him. As Chuck patted him on the back, he said, slowly and clearly, "Good old friend."

✦　✦　✦

On a bright October afternoon in Sewickley in 2013, sun shining through the windows, Chuck did his strength and flexibility exercises with his physical therapist, Renee, while Marianne was up on the roof, tending to the flowers. The stretching was painful, but he didn't curse, simply remained stoic. After ten minutes, Renee walked him into the office and study, where the walls were covered with plaques and awards from his football career. He was comfortable here, and as she steadied him on the stationary bicycle, she left him to go speak with Marianne. And there, just three months shy of his eighty-second birthday, Chuck Noll began pedaling.

Soon, he found a thread of a memory and grabbed hold of it. No one would have heard it at first, but eventually as he set a pace on the stationary bike, his breathy tenor picked up as well. Looking off into the middle distance, his mind found his way to some well-worn synapses, and he began singing, softly and sweetly.

> The preacher walked by with a tear in his eye
> Said his wife had been down with the flu
> He said that I ought to give him a quart
> Of that good ol' mountain dew

Pedaling then leaning into the song, the edges of his lips turning up at the end of each verse, he seemed happy, transported, perhaps imagining himself strumming the ukulele and entertaining guests. Or, maybe envisioning a younger day, watching his father surrounded by sisters, brothers, cousins, in-laws.

> My uncle Mort, he was sawed-off and short,
> He measures about four-foot-two
> But he thinks he's a giant when you give him a pint
> Of that good old mountain dew
>
> They call it that good old mountain dew
> Them that refuse it are few
> I'll hush up my mug if you'll fill up my jug
> With that good old mountain dew.

Chuck finished and exhaled, breathing more heavily now. Then he said, to himself, "Something like that."

✦ ✦ ✦

Chuck and Marianne had taken care of each other for more than fifty years. Another generation noticed the deep connection.

"They still act like teenagers sometimes," said their granddaughter, Katie. "It's very evident that they're still in love, and very much so. I don't remember what they said, if it's like Eskimo kissing . . . I look away, but it is very, very touching."

But her family and friends worried about Marianne.

"The thing that defines their relationship, and the thing that makes life difficult now—she has always been the center of his world," said Linda Noll. "Not football, not coaching, not Chris. Marianne is the center of his world, and she loved being the center of his world, and that's why it always worked. He would defer to her. If she really wanted something, they would do it her way. And it never was a power struggle, and it never was her being more assertive or more domineering. That was what worked for them, and it worked really well. That's why now it's hard, because while she remains the center of his world, he can't give to her the things that she loved. The conversations. They would have just great conversations all the time about all sorts of topics, and now, without the short-term memory, it is really hard to carry on a conversation. They enjoyed so many things together that now they can't enjoy as much, which makes it hard. But she laughingly always talks about being the queen, and being very happy being the queen.

"I think what has been so hard for her these last few years is that he just doesn't have that capacity any more. I mean, he still makes her laugh, but there is not as much give and take. That is what there always was in the relationship, and now it is out of balance."

"She will say, 'My world has become so small,'" said Chris. "The reality is, it wouldn't be a whole lot bigger if he was healthy, in terms of they are always very private, and didn't have a whole lot of friends."

Glenn and Joanne offered to give her a break for a night or two. Chris and Linda offered to come up and let her get away for a few days. She politely but firmly declined all such offers. "She won't leave him," said Chris.

Awkwardly, and with great care, the relatives would take turns suggesting that perhaps the time had come to get help.

"She won't have it," said Chris. "We have a little more conversation all the time, or at least admitting things. She spent her whole life protecting him, so she is going to continue to do that."

But there was also a sense that Marianne had let the matter go on too long. They were all grateful that Chuck still responded—still seemed to know who they all were. "It hasn't happened yet, and the doctors say in part it is because of the medicine, and in part it is because how she interacts with him daily, and forces him to exercise his brain, and in part it is because he is such a smart man," said Linda. "I haven't always agreed with Marianne. I think she should have said, maybe about a year ago, 'Chuck has Alzheimer's.' It is a disease; there is no need to be ashamed of it, you know, but this is her protective nature."

In the end, what remained for them was the nightly ritual of dinner, which continued to be the centerpiece of their life together.

Her tastes continued to be adventuresome, and once the stock pot was on, or the dish was in the oven, Chuck would get up from watching TV or working a jigsaw puzzle and ask, "What can I do to help?" He would still chop tomatoes or onions, while she poured the wine.

She missed the talks. The epic, careening, give-and-takes over politics, art, culture, society, religion—any topic, really, save for football—that used to enliven the dinner table. They still ate dinner, and they still talked during dinner. But the crackle and sure through line of the talk had vanished.

They'd sit down in the dining room. And as it had been for so long, they'd share the details of their day. Only now, Chuck couldn't remember any of them, and Marianne was left to guide him through it.

"It's a lonely conversation," said Chris.

✦ ✦ ✦

The spring of 2014 in Florida was pleasant enough. They all visited—Glenn and Joanne down from Pittsburgh for an extended stay, Joe and Babe Gordon on their annual Florida getaway, Chris and Linda made a couple of trips.

"Chris was down in Florida with his son in February, and Marianne said to me, 'I just had to deal with three male Nolls—they're all alike,'" said Joanne. "I just laughed. That's what happens. You learn from your parents, and that's how you're taught. They don't have to say things. You still learn how they are. Like my mom never said she loved us, but we knew she did. It's just the way they were brought up. They just did not tell you; you just knew it."

They got back to Pittsburgh in May, and Glenn and Joanne were there, helping with things around the house. In June, Joe Gordon called, to see when he and Babe would stop by. Marianne and he settled on the following week.

A rash Chuck had developed on his arm seemed to be getting worse, so Marianne called the Steelers' team physician, Dr. Tony Yates. He stopped by on Wednesday, June 11, examined the rash and said it wasn't infected, though Chuck was still in a lot of pain.

On that Friday, Chuck got up late, received a visit from a nurse to check on his rash, did his physical therapy with Renee, and then he and Marianne spent the afternoon working on another jigsaw puzzle, while listening to Rod Stewart singing the American songbook. Later, he helped chop the tomatoes for their dinner. That night, over a bottle of red, they ate, and he asked for seconds.

He was moving slowly by the end of the meal and mentioned he didn't feel well. She helped him to bed, told him she loved him, and went in the kitchen to clean up. When she returned to the bedroom later to check on him, he had stopped breathing. Marianne rushed across the hall to her friend, Betty Pomeroy, a registered nurse. Paramedics were called and made an effort to revive him, then pronounced him dead. She then called Chris, Joanne, and Joe Gordon with the news.

That very same night, in suburban Cleveland, Rita's children were gathering at Rick Deininger's house on the eve of Rita's ninetieth birthday celebration. They were sitting on the back porch, discussing old times and logistics for the next day's party at Light of Hearts Villa, the retirement home where Rita had lived for years, when Marilyn's cell phone rang. There was good-natured banter and crosstalk, discussions of the posters that they had printed out for the event, showing the most popular things in 1924, the year their mother was born.

But then Marilyn snapped, "Everybody quiet! Uncle Chuck just died."

What followed the initial response was the inevitable trajectory, from concern for Chuck to concern for their mother to concern for their Aunt Marianne.

"We just kind of sat around and talked quietly and said a few things, and just said, 'Wow. How do we do this?,'" said Jerry Deininger. "As we spoke, we all did a little brainstorming and tossed ideas out. Does the party still go on tomorrow? Yeah, it has to. It's 10:30 at night . . . it's too late to call mom."

Rita's children hoped that she would fall asleep without listening to talk radio and decided to wait to call her until the next morning. It was Joanne who wished her mother a happy ninetieth the next morning, and also conveyed the sad news. Hearing of her younger brother's death, Rita sobbed. But later that day, the party went on—everyone agreed that Chuck would surely have wanted it to—and they all ate the white cake with the thick frosting and watched Bill's slide show of the life of Rita Noll Deininger.

Everyone who came—and there were nearly a hundred people in all—wished her happy birthday and passed along condolences in the same breath.

"I feel like I'm at a birthday party and a funeral at the same time," Rita said.

That day, Chris and Linda—three days away from their twenty-fifth wedding anniversary—flew down to Pittsburgh with their children; Joanne drove the two hours to Cleveland, so all seven children could be with Rita.

Dan Rooney and Joe Gordon drove to Sewickley that Saturday morning to help a distraught Marianne plan for the memorial services. Dan was from the Catholic tradition of moving quickly to the grieving. There was a viewing scheduled for Sunday night, two on Monday, and the funeral service scheduled for Tuesday.

And on that bittersweet Saturday, as the news spread, the city of Pittsburgh began to mourn. By coincidence, that same night in Pittsburgh, at the Meadows Racetrack and Casino, Terry Bradshaw was back in the city, touring with his one-man show. He said a few words about Chuck at the beginning of his performance. Bradshaw, pointedly, did not stay for the viewing or the funeral.

The day after Rita's ninetieth birthday, all the nephews and nieces drove to Pittsburgh to be with the Nolls. "When Chris laughed at the funeral home," said Bill Deininger, "he sounded exactly like Uncle Chuck. It was spooky."

The funeral was just what one would have expected the Chuck Noll funeral to be. No eulogies. No gushing. Marianne sat with Chris on one side of her. Later, Glenn Mikut stood a few feet from the casket, eyes fixed on the procession of people coming by, ready to roust anyone who tried to furtively snap a picture with their cell phone (there were three who did so).

Bishop David Zubik told the story about Chuck agreeing, in the spring of 1979, to give a speech the following winter to a group of high school athletes with whom Zubik was working. As it turned out, the speech was scheduled only two days after the Steelers' fourth Super Bowl win. Zubik assumed Chuck would cancel, but Chuck showed up as promised and spoke to hundreds of youths. His only precondition was that no one knew about it, that no media be alerted.

The pallbearers included Red and Pat Manning's three boys—John, Patrick, and Michael—and Glenn and Joanne's son, Chris Mikut, along with Joe Gordon, Art Rooney II, Joe Greene, and Andy Russell. They carried the casket out of St. Paul Cathedral and loaded it into the hearse that transported the casket to the mausoleum at Northside Catholic cemetery.

The former players had returned by the dozens. "And I think what came to fruition for a lot of us today, as we sat here," said J.T. Thomas, "was the idea that 'Wow, if it hadn't been for Chuck, where would we all be? What would have happened to us?' So this was a celebration of him, what he meant to us and the fact that we loved him."

After the burial, there was a reception at Heinz Field, Chuck's family and players and assistants gathering one more time. Marianne returned home that evening, understandably exhausted; Chris stayed in town for a while, to provide her some company. Three days later, he left to return to Connecticut.

That night, Marianne Noll hugged her son and closed the door. Later that evening, she turned out the lights out and headed back into the darkness of her bedroom. For the first time in fifty-seven years, there was no one to take care of, no chest to rest her head on, no breathing to align with hers. Through that lonesome night, she was consoled by one thought: Somehow, through the faded memories of that final decade, Chuck had answered her devotion with one last brave and honest deed of his own.

He had kept his promise. He never forgot.

EPILOGUE

✦ ✦ ✦

"I don't concern myself with eventualities. I just competed the best way I knew, and let the chips fall. I did it the only way I knew how. There's nothing else."

—Chuck Noll

It was the first game of the 2014 season for the Pittsburgh Steelers, at home against the Cleveland Browns.

And less than three months after the death of their patriarch, the Noll family—Marianne and her son Chris, his wife Linda, and their children Katie and Connor—stood in their Sunday best, awaiting the pregame ceremony at Heinz Field.

It was the quiet skateboarder Connor, fifteen, who most visibly bristled at the circumstances. Before the ceremony began, he leaned to his mother and said, "I don't want to be here."

Linda calmly reminded him of the occasion. "We're doing this for Bubba."

Connor remained unconvinced. "Bubba *definitely* wouldn't want to be here," he said.

"Okay, well, we're doing it for Mimi," said Linda. "She *has* to be here."

Placated, Connor joined the rest of his family for the ceremony, accompanied by Dan Rooney and Art Rooney II. Greeted with hearty, extended applause, they squinted into the midday sun, three generations of Nolls smiling their rather-be-elsewhere smiles.

They were, of course, deeply appreciative. Glad that Chuck was remembered by the Steelers' faithful, glad that the Steelers' helmets would be adorned in 2014 with a decal honoring his memory (a suitably understated black oval with the initials CHN in gold), and yet firm in their belief that the Chuck Noll that the older Steelers fans remembered and revered was only a partial facet of the husband, father, and grandfather they knew.

✦ ✦ ✦

It wasn't for lack of effort on the part of the players. In June 1999, at the groundbreaking for Heinz Field (which would replace Three Rivers Stadium by the beginning of the 2001 season), Joe Greene summoned up the courage to tell Chuck what he'd meant to his life.

"Chuck, I just want to say that you had great bearing on whatever success that I had and, as a football player, I know I brought something to the table being a determined athlete, but you helped mold my character, and I think about you once or twice a week, still."

Chuck smiled, but he couldn't find the corresponding words to say what Greene had meant to him. "Joe, you were important to this football team. You were important to the organization, and I appreciate it."

That space between what Chuck could articulate and what the experience meant to him was significant. But Chuck's inability to articulate it didn't mean it wasn't there.

Most of his players were able to reconcile that distance.

"You cannot decipher and understand people all the time," said Frenchy Fuqua. "But you can take the points. Chuck, to me, was not a father or brother, but sometimes football coaches are *more* respected than fathers. Not only was he a football coach, but he was also a coach of life. He taught football, which I understood very well, but even more so, he taught me a lot of things about life, small things that were instrumental in my life ten, fifteen, twenty years after I retired. Those lessons made my life just a little bit more comfortable, a little bit more easy, and a little bit better in passing on some of those traits to my kids."

When Paul Zimmerman wrote the two-part piece on Chuck in *Sports Illustrated* in 1980, he mentioned asking several coaches how they want to be remembered. Chuck's response was predictable: "A teacher," he said. "A person who could adapt to a world of constant change. A person who could adapt to the situation. But most of all a teacher. Put down that I was a teacher."

"I think he knew that he had to be a certain way," said John Stallworth. "He had to be aloof. He had to be not too close to us, but deep down inside, I don't think that was his nature. I think he liked relationships, but he did what he thought he needed to do to make the kind of decisions that he eventually would have to make. But I think he got a lot closer to us than . . . well, certainly, some of those decisions were a lot harder than others."

In those bonds—with Joe Greene or Jack Ham or John Stallworth or Andy Russell or Mel Blount or Tunch Ilkin—the connection was deep and the effect was profound. More than thirty years after his last football game, Jack Lambert's watch was still set five minutes fast, to what he described as "Chuck Noll time."

Yet the nature of all those relationships implied a distance, and words left unsaid.

"I'm not sure I was ever entirely comfortable," said Craig Wolfley of his relationship with his head coach. "I mean, if we really come down to it . . . I've got to tell you he had this way of creating unease in you. He could look at you—he was a nice man, he was a friendly man—but he could give you this withering glare that, as Tunch likes to say, could make you want to pee down your leg. Joe Greene said the same thing, so it was not just us, as rookies back in 1980, that suffered that. It was the great ones, too. He just had that ability to mind meld you. He was a Jedi before *Star Wars*."

The effect could last long after players were outside his sphere of daily influence. For Cliff Stoudt, who spent five seasons with the Steelers, the realization came a decade later. His young daughter had been lazing around the house, in his view, and he gave her a speech about constant striving—how it wasn't enough to do her best for a while, but that she had to keep trying to be her best. When his chastened daughter left the room, Stoudt noticed his wife, Laura, standing in the doorway, having surveyed the scene.

"What's wrong?" he said. "Do you disagree with anything I said?"

"No, not at all," said Laura. "It's just that . . . every word out of your mouth right now to your six-year-old daughter was vintage Chuck Noll."

When she pointed it out, Stoudt recognized as much. Later, he sat down and wrote a letter to Chuck. "I can't believe it has been so many years now," he wrote. "It has been ten years since I left Pittsburgh and I never got a chance to talk to you. I should have taken that time because you stood by me the year I broke my arm; you stood by me when I was a player rep during the strike, and you did everything you ever could have possibly done for me, and I wish I had to chance to go back and do it all again now that I think I understand you a little bit better. I never did until I was gone from Pittsburgh. And I never really did understand you until I became a parent and I realized that some of the stuff you were teaching us we didn't get, because it was more about being a man than a football player. And it would make you a better football player if you became a better man. Ninety percent of what I teach my kids comes right out of your office, and if I never get a chance to see you again I would at least like to be able to thank you for how you stuck by me and believed in me and the chance that you gave me."

Stoudt never got a response. But a couple years later, at a small benefit golf tournament in Beaufort, South Carolina, he ran into Chuck, who greeted him pleasantly. Still intimidated by his coach, Stoudt hesitantly worked up the courage to ask about the letter.

"Hey, coach, that letter I sent you a couple years ago, did you ever get that?"

Chuck nodded and smiled, "Yes, I did."

And then there was silence.

"Okay, great," said Stoudt. "Guess I better get on the tee."

But the true coda to the story came later, in 2001, when Stoudt and his wife were at a black-tie event for the opening of Heinz Field. On the way out he caught Marianne's eye—she was talking to someone else—and waved a greeting. Marianne paused her conversation and said, "Cliff, stay here—I want to talk to you."

Standing and waiting for Marianne, alongside his wife, Stoudt felt his anxiety level rising: *"I feel like I'm in trouble. I haven't seen the Nolls for seventeen years, and here I am in trouble again."*

When she broke free, Marianne came to where Stoudt was standing and took his hands into hers and confided, "That letter you sent to Chuck—you have no idea how much that touched him."

"Oh, yeah," said Stoudt, "like I got through to the great Chuck Noll."

She blinked her eyes and two tears ran down her face. "He really liked you," she said, "and coming from you, that really touched him."

"You just made my whole career," Stoudt said. "Because I wanted to please Chuck Noll. When I went to practice, I wanted to please Chuck Noll and Jack Lambert. Because Chuck controlled my job, and Jack could kick my ass."

So many other stories were similar. Chuck taught and imparted wisdom. Players, sooner or later, came back to express gratitude. When it came to emotions, Marianne acted as the go-between and the translator. And then Chuck got ill, and the illness was a secret, and there was so much more for her to go between, so much more for her to translate.

✦ ✦ ✦

From the time of the diagnosis, the people around him all grappled with the nagging and unknowable question, one increasingly asked by the families of retired football players everywhere: Did football lead to Chuck's condition?

"You have to wonder," Chris had said earlier. "He will claim that he never had a concussion, but they are also showing now it's multiple, micro-concussions, or whatever. If you open up the Cleveland Browns alumni magazine, and see that ten guys have passed, and eight of them had Alzheimer's, it's hard to say no."

The question had a corollary that also begged to be asked: If the punishment he took on the football field contributed to his condition, was it still worth it?

Marianne had thought about it, agonized in the early days, but made her peace.

Chris, ever the pragmatist, reasoned that Chuck's journey justified the cost. "Part of me says yes," said Chris. "Not because of what he did for us, but it got him out of Cleveland, it got him out of the neighborhood. It got him into college. It got him into what he was passionate about, so it is hard to say it wasn't worth it. He was almost seventy [before the effects became noticeable]. It's not like he was fifty years old when he started having problems like some of these guys now. So I'm not going to play that game of saying was it worth it or not, because it's done. I can't do that to myself because I am Catholic. I know we like guilt."

"He could have become a lawyer or he could have become a teacher," said Linda Churchill Noll. "And he might have loved teaching, but his intensity and his passion and his competitive edge really thrives in the world of football. And we will never know if it was football that caused the Alzheimer's. We will never know that. It could have happened anyway."

It was the conclusion that a great majority of football players—and a great majority of football players' families—reach.

✦　✦　✦

His legacy in football seems clear. The boy who'd played in the vacant lot next to a Nabisco factory as a ten-year-old now has a street named in his honor close to the Steelers' new stadium. The field where the Steelers train in Latrobe also carries his name. More than forty years after their dynasty begin, the Steelers of the '70s are still considered by many to be the greatest football team ever.

For those looking for it, the power of Chuck's influence can still be seen in the game in the twenty-first century.

"I see Chuck with the athletic defenders; that was his thing," said Tony Dungy, shortly after Seattle won the Super Bowl in 2014. "When you look at the Seattle Seahawks, that was vintage Chuck. I don't know who is going to get the credit for that, or where Pete [Carroll] goes back to but that is athletic front people, big physical defensive backs. Play simple, sound zone defense and knock the heck out of them, run the ball effectively and make a couple of big plays in the passing game. That was Steeler football."

Yet another way, Chuck's influence has been lost. He was one of the last of hugely successful NFL coaches to have an identifiable life outside of football, to be such a well-rounded person. In so many realms of American life—sports, politics, business, the arts—the public was animated by the notion of the Renaissance man. And yet modern American life often awarded those with a monomaniacal focus. By the twenty-first century, a Super Bowl–winning coach (Jon Gruden) was famous for setting his alarm for 3:17 in the morning, so as to be awake and working before his competition. (Another Super Bowl–winning coach, Brian Billick, when asked when he got up in the morning, drily replied, "An hour before whenever Gruden says he gets up.") There was a dark heart at the end of such obsession, and many people who've succeeded in coaching have felt lost when they no longer had a game to prepare for or a team to lead. In this sense, as well, Chuck remained a notable exception. The game compelled, but it never consumed him. "Chuck had an off switch," as Art Rooney II once put it.

In 2015, the Patriots' Bill Belichick became the second coach to win four Super Bowls. But Chuck's perfect 4–0 record in the games remains unmatched. After his death, more people had come to recognize the value of the coach in the Steelers' dynasty.

"I always tell people, 'Yeah, we had Bradshaw, we had Joe Greene, we had Franco Harris, and all of these guys," said Jack Ham. "But we don't win four Super Bowls without Chuck Noll. There are a bunch of teams that could win this every year. Why were we able to win four, and back-to-back twice? I mean, that chemistry—and I'm sure he was in his own office, making sure that personnel, how it fits together and so forth. But we don't win four without him. You could win without Jack Ham, or you could win without—maybe not without Bradshaw—but Chuck was the glue that put this thing together and built it like this."

Only the most prominent member of the team remained unconvinced. "He didn't understand me," insisted Terry Bradshaw. This may have been true. But Noll did understand how to make Bradshaw the best football player he could be. That is a different thing but, in the context, still an important thing.

The best player Chuck ever coached had the final say.

"He's the most consistent man I've ever known," said Joe Greene.

✦   ✦   ✦

Of course, it wasn't just the players for whom things were left unsaid. Though she lived with Chuck and Marianne for eleven years, though he walked her down the aisle on the occasion of her wedding, Chuck never told Joanne he loved her.

"Germans don't do that," Joanne said. "Those are words that the Germans don't give out very easily. I don't think until maybe five or ten years ago that my mom ever said it, or I ever said it to my mom. It was just something that—it's there, we know it. We don't need to say it. With my family, we never did those things until my brothers got girlfriends. Then they would come home and give my mom a hug, and I would laugh hysterically. 'Well, you never gave her a hug before—what's changed?

Oh—you've got a girlfriend now!' We just, in public, don't show our emotions."

Both Chuck and his sister Rita were a product of their times and upbringing, but those who saw them together over the years never doubted the strength of their connection. In the end, they remained there for each other like they'd always been.

"If one of us would come up with a problem," Rita said, "the other one would help out. It wasn't like something that you felt obligated to do—it was just something that you did. It was something that was instilled in us from very early on. That's what you do. That's family."

For Rita's seven children, the effect of Chuck in their lives was immense. Rick and Bill went to Case Western, Margie and Marilyn to Dayton, Jerry to Ohio U., Ken to St. Vincent, Joanne to Robert Morris. Their family was transformed by his presence.

"We idolized him," said Margie.

"But it was always at a distance," said Rick

"He was a human being to me," said Joanne. "He was my uncle. You know, he was someone I looked up to. He was not a superstar to me. I mean, all they did for us, you know, helping my mom out financially, encouraging us to go to college, taking care of us. He was like the father we never had."

For Chris Noll, Chuck was the father he *did* have. The son, like the father, became expert at the art of nonverbal communication. How did he know when his dad was pleased? "By the look," said Chris. "It wasn't communicated directly, that's for sure."

Up until the effects of the disease made it impossible, Chuck strived to impart knowledge—about photography, biology, wine, food, stereophonic sound—to his son. But there were never any lectures. "He never gave me any advice," said Chris, "other than what he exuded, which is significant."

They had grown comfortable, in the way that proud fathers and grateful sons can become. And, toward the end, Chris bridged the distance. "I would get in his face the last five years, and say 'I love you,' and hug him, and he would respond," Chris said. "But it took me to initiate it, which wasn't easy, either."

In the end, the person who missed Chuck Noll the most was the one person to whom he was able to most easily express his love. Back home in Sewickley, in the months following Chuck's death, Marianne was still adjusting to his absence. She took all the jigsaw puzzles downstairs to the basement of her condo and left them out, "for everybody to use." She reluctantly returned to her artwork and craft projects. It was months before she could bear to listen to one of their CDs again; all of it—Sinatra, jazz, Rod Stewart—reminded her of Chuck.

That Christmas, she wrote a friend: "I'm doing okay. I take walks every day; sometimes it helps."

✦ ✦ ✦

In the end, Chuck did more than bring four Super Bowl titles to Pittsburgh. He helped crystallize the city's vision of itself—tough and dedicated, resilient and indefatigable. And that self-belief and identification would resonate across the decades, and around the country, as the members of Steelers nation filled the sports bars and far-flung stadiums whenever and wherever their team played.

This complex alchemy of human action and response created an ineffable connection between the team and its fans. Chuck wasn't comfortable with the ineffable, though even he might have appreciated what he and his players set in motion. But he never would have felt the need to describe it or comment upon it.

Those who wanted more from Chuck Noll—self-analysis or confession or words of gratitude—perhaps didn't appreciate how much he was a product of his time and his code.

In the world he grew up in, a man was judged by his actions and not his words. Those were the terms by which Chuck Noll lived his life. He overcame his difficulties, he made his way, he remained loyal to his family. In time, he found his life's work, and did it well. In time, he found his life's love, and they lived a happy life together. For Chuck, and those closest to him, nothing more needed to be said.

ACKNOWLEDGMENTS

✦ ✦ ✦

I first met the Steelers' owner Dan Rooney in 2000, when I interviewed him for my book *America's Game*. A few weeks after the book was published in 2004, I received a note from Mr. Rooney, telling me that he'd read the book and enjoyed it—but that there wasn't enough in it about the Steelers.

By the time he contacted me in the summer of 2012, he was U.S. Ambassador (to Ireland) Rooney. In the midst of his busy schedule, he told me that someone should write a biography of Chuck Noll. He felt so strongly about this that he helped commission this book even though I retained complete editorial control over the finished product. I appreciate him reaching out to me in the first place, and I am grateful for his cooperation through the time it took to write. (I'm hoping that this book has enough in it about the Steelers to suit him.)

The people I pestered the most over the three-plus years of writing were Chuck's family: Chuck and Marianne Noll hosted me for several dinners in Pittsburgh—and their winter home in Estero, Florida—while he was still living, and Marianne did the hard work of recollecting key events when Chuck's memory faltered. Later, even as she was grieving his passing, she remained gracious, open, honest, and cooperative. "I can't believe I'm being so accommodating," she said at one point—and neither could I. The Noll family is very private; one reason that public families choose to be private is so they don't have to answer a battery of questions from people like me. But Chuck, when he was alive, and Marianne and their son Chris, his wife Linda, Chuck's sister, Rita, and her seven children—especially Joanne Deininger Mikut and her husband Glenn— were all patient and helpful. Joanne continued to take my calls and field my questions even as she was undergoing a round of chemotherapy and beating cancer. The family is made of strong stuff.

Peter Kracht, director and acquiring editor at the University of Pittsburgh Press, ensured that this book enjoyed a home-field advantage. I'm grateful to him for his guidance throughout and to editorial and production manager Alex Wolfe for his patience and sharp, lucid editing skills. The errors that made it through are my own. (If you find any, please contact me at maccambridge@mac.com.) Marketing director David Baumann and publicist Maria Sticco helped get the word out. The University of Pittsburgh Press went the extra yard to acquire the rights to my favorite photograph of Chuck—from the legendary Walter Iooss Jr.—to grace the cover of the book, and University of Pittsburgh Press's Joel W. Coggins created the compelling jacket design.

My conduit to the Steelers and the city was Joe Gordon, who, near as I can tell, is the de facto mayor of Pittsburgh. He knows everybody and gets things done. He and his wife Babe are good company at dinner (and have the best seats in the house for Independence Day celebrations in Pittsburgh). I was also grateful to several others in the Steelers family for their help and guidance, most especially Burt Lauten, Diane Lowe, Colleen Kimmel, Bob Tyler, Lynne Molyneaux, and Rebecca Mihalcik.

In getting up to speed on the Steelers' history, the collected works of Hall of Fame honoree Ed Bouchette of the *Pittsburgh Post-Gazette* was the logical place to start. Bouchette has seen it all, and written about it all, for more than three decades covering the Steelers, and he was a valuable resource for explaining Chuck Noll's often complicated relationship with the media. I'm also indebted to the work of Bob Labriola of *Steelers Digest*, whose accounts of the Steelers' playoff history, available on the internet, should be between hard covers somewhere. Friend, scholar, and Steeler lifer Ed Krzemienski was also an important early resource.

Fans like to think that their favorite team is made up of not only special football players but also special people. This is a defensible position in Pittsburgh. I shall not soon forget visiting Joe Greene and John Stallworth, Franco Harris and Jack Ham, Frenchy Fuqua and Rocky Bleier, Mike Wagner and Dick Hoak, Lynn Swann and Andy Russell, Tunch Ilkin and Craig Wolfley, Jon Kolb and Louis Lipps, Bubby Brister and Merril Hoge, and many others.

Terry Bradshaw, pointedly, chose not to talk to me for this book, despite numerous interview requests, from both myself and intermediaries, including Dan Rooney and Joe Greene. "There's two things Terry doesn't like to talk about," confided his assistant over the phone. "One of them, I'm not going to say. The other one is Chuck Noll." Lots of quarterbacks harbor resentments against their micromanaging head coaches. Not many of them have four Super Bowl rings to show for their aggravation. With Bradshaw refusing to speak to me, I was left with his previously published (and sometimes conflicting) account of events from his books and interviews, as well as the recollections of his coaches and teammates.

It's safe to say that most of Chuck's coaches revered him, and Tony Dungy, Tom Moore, Dick Hoak, Lionel Taylor, Woody Widenhofer, Ron Blackledge, George Perles, and Jack Henry, among others, spent many hours talking about Chuck as a teacher and as a leader. When they weren't around, I could always turn to Larry Kindbom, longtime head football coach at Washington University in St. Louis. He continued guiding me through my my football education, especially with the Steelers' trap game and the obscure roots of the football jargon "Oskie."

One of the most fascinating figures in Chuck's story was Art Rooney Jr., who was forced out as the head of the Steelers' personnel department in 1986. Though he frequently clashed with Chuck, he remained extraordinarily fond of him and was pin-sharp in his recollections of the key events of their time together.

All of the interviews were faithfully and accurately transcribed by Shannon McCormack, my longtime transcriptionist, whose patient and unerring ear captured the distinctive rhythms and vernacular of football players and coaches.

Along the way, I received assistance from Roy Blount Jr., who found a file of research he compiled while writing the classic *About Three Bricks Shy of a Load*. He wasn't the only one. Bruce Weber, former radio announcer, carefully preserved many of his interviews with Noll and the Steelers and shared those with me. I'm grateful for the insights they offered into the players, especially, in the moments following games. Longtime KDKA-TV videographer Michael Challik unearthed his footage of Chuck's infamous handshake with Jerry Glanville. I'm also grateful to Dave Plaut and Chris Willis and the team at NFL Films, who opened the vaults to all manner of Steelers- and Noll-related material. Joel Bussert, the NFL's unofficial historian, still knows more than anyone alive about the league's Competition Committee; he was, once again, a great resource. And the wise heads Joe Browne and Greg Aiello, at the League office, both provided important context for understanding the history of the NFL. Saleem Choudhry again guided me through the massive library at the Pro Football Hall of Fame.

In the early stages of the project, I was aided by Pittsburgh native (and former student) Jen Cozen, as well as Ashley Carpenter and Scott Allen, all of whom did yeoman research work on my behalf.

In going back over Chuck's life, I received invaluable assistance from his childhood friend, Ralph Yanky, who showed me the old neighborhood. Chuck's grandniece, Maggie Deininger, pointed me in the direction of John J. Grabowski, the Krieger Mueller Associate Professor of Applied History at Case Western. Grabowksi patiently helped me understand the migration patterns into Cleveland in the early part of the twentieth century and opened the door to further research. Ann K. Sindelar, reference supervisor at the Western Reserve Historical Society, was a vital resource in finding information about Chuck's family. William Barrow and his staff at Cleveland State University allowed me access to their rich clip files from the old *Cleveland Press*. The late Elsie Lyttle vividly recalled details about growing up Catholic in Depression-era Cleveland.

Benedictine and Dayton were two important chapters in Chuck's life. Fr. Gerard Gonda, president of Benedictine, shared the school's history, and the late Joe Hornack, Benedictine class of 1951, came back to give me a tour of the place and helped show me what it was like when Chuck attended. At Dayton, Sports Information Director Doug Hauschild was extremely helpful and still had the hand-written athlete's publicity questionnaire that Chuck filled out more than sixty years ago. Two of Chuck's

Dayton teammates, Jim Currin and Pat Maloney, were vital to my reconstruction of Chuck's college days.

Thanks also to Tony Dick of the Cleveland Browns, Todd Tobias (who has written extensively on the history of the San Diego Chargers), and Upton Bell, who has commendable recall of Chuck's years as an assistant with the Colts.

In tracing the arc of Chuck's life, I'm also thankful to Jo Ferrazza, who shared a family video of Chuck's Hall of Fame induction weekend. The sons of Red and Pat Manning—John, Patrick, and Michael—grew up with the Nolls and provided insightful details on Chuck and Marianne's life away from the public eye.

Much of this book was written while I was in single-parent mode. And, in the event, it really *does* take a village. My village people during this time included dear friends Rich and Suzanne Moffitt, Akin and Manju Owoso, Col. Pat and Marilyn Breitling, Jim and Susan Craig, Brent and Paivi Tetri, Michael and Lin Sutter, Rebecca Tominack and Glenn Hachey, Anne Rodgers, Danielle Frost, Kevin Lyttle, and my mother, Lois MacCambridge (who also helpfully reminded me I was behind schedule— again). I am grateful to all of them for harboring my teenagers at various times over the past three years. In addition, vital help and companionship was provided by Rosie Roegner, Tom and Amy Seat, Chris and Jenny Bosworth, Avery and Christine Archer, Trey Gratwick, Andy Lovins, Arika Cannon, Sophia Lopez, and Lana Ponce. Thanks also to Jennifer Harrison for her optimism and support throughout the writing of this book.

Kudos to the great Jon Dee Graham for words of inspiration and wisdom, as well as the title of chapter 24.

Writing is a solitary existence and that can drive writers crazy. My dear friend Rob Minter kept me sane by taking my daily calls. Thanks also for friendship and support along the way from Hal Cox, Larry Johnson, Loren Watt, Stan Webb, Chris Brown, Michael Hurd, Doug Miller, Tony Owens, Steve Bosky, John Bridges, Russell Smith, Rindy Weatherly, Brian Shanley, Tim Shanley, Jeff Zivan, Doug Allen, George McMahon, Lesley McCullough McCallister, Eric Pils, Gerald Early, Barbara Morgan, Greg Emas, Peter Blackstock, Kirk Bohls, Cedric Golden, Mark Rosner, and Bob Moore. Thank you as well to Pat Porter, Laura Pfeifauf, Susan Lillard Reckers, Ross and Betty Lillard, Katherine and Jay

Rivard, Dr. Reggie Givens, Denise Lieberman, Don McLaughlin, Scott Granneman, Brad Garrett, Ryan Marquez, Kristin Elizondo, Victoria Fikes, Heather Diamani, Neal Richardson, Brian Hay, Joe Posnanski and Vahe Gregorian, as well as Nicole and James Stubbe, John and Lois Stob, Howard Potratz, Michael Korein, Jim Ross, Jim Murphy, Teri McCarthy, Riza Raffi, and Earl Summers. I wouldn't be in a position to write books for a living without the guidance and wisdom of Sloan Harris and Rick Pappas.

I'm also grateful to Angie Russo for the many data points at the end of the project.

A special thank you to my sister and brother-in-law, Angie and Tom Szentgyorgyi—who provided invaluable support during my move to Austin in the last year of writing this book.

Finally, I owe a debt of gratitude to my children, Miles and Ella, who have spent more time inside stadiums and sports bars—and in the back seat of cars, driving to same—than would be strictly necessary for any teenagers. They have endured all this (mostly) without complaint, and they are fun to hang out with at the end of a day.

NOTES

✦   ✦   ✦

Unless otherwise noted, all interviews are with author.

Epigraph

ix   Joan Didion, "John Wayne: A Love Song," *Saturday Evening Post*, August 14, 1965.

Prologue

xi   **From the sidelines . . . :** Super Bowl IX broadcast, NBC Sports, January 12, 1975, https://www.youtube.com/watch?v=hv5GX08M404; NFL Films, *NFL: America's Game—Pittsburgh Steelers: The Story of Six Championships* (Mount Laurel, NJ: NFL Films, 2009).

xi   **It was in . . . :** Chris Noll interview, June 6, 2013; Marianne Noll interview, February 8, 2015.

xi   **All the shared . . . :** Chris Noll interview, June 6, 2013; Dick Hoak interview, March 28, 2013.

xii   **Yet even in . . . :** NFL Films, *NFL: America's Game—Pittsburgh Steelers: The Story of Six Championships*; John Quinn, "Super Bowl IX, Steelers vs. Vikings," YouTube, November 22, 2015, https://www.youtube.com/watch?v=hv5 GX08M404.

xiii **In the midst . . . :** Dick Hoak interview, March 28, 2013; John Quinn, "Super Bowl IX Steelers vs. Vikings," YouTube, November 22, 2015, https://www .youtube.com/watch?v=hv5GX08M404.

xiii **"Congratulations, Andy," he . . . :** Andy Russell interview, March 25, 2013.

xiii **Then he shook . . . :** Frenchy Fuqua interview, August 24, 2013

xiii **NFL Commissioner Pete . . . :** NFL Films, *NFL: America's Game—Pittsburgh Steelers: The Story of Six Championships*; John Quinn, "Super Bowl IX, Steelers vs. Vikings," YouTube, November 22, 2015, https://www.youtube.com/ watch?v=hv5GX08M404.

xiii **More than two . . . :** Marianne Noll interview, February 23, 2014; Mike Wagner interview, October 07, 2014.

xiv **And, just as . . . :** Marianne Noll interview, February 23, 2014.

xiv **Part of it . . . :** Roy Blount Jr. interview, May 13, 2015; Roy Blount Jr., *About Three Bricks Shy . . . and the Load Filled Up: The Story of the Greatest Football Team Ever* (Pittsburgh: University of Pittsburgh Press, 2004); Dave Brady, "Steelers' Chuck Noll Is an Unspectacular Genius," *Washington Post*, from *Sarasota Herald-Tribune*, August 15, 1976.

xv **"I worked there . . ." :** John Clayton, "Doing It His Way: Noll Goes by the Playbook, but It Is Missing a Chapter on Socializing with Players," *Pittsburgh Press*, December 25, 1983.

xv **But the measure . . . :** NFL, *2014 Official NFL Record & Fact Book* (New York: Time Home Entertainment, 2014).

xv **"Losing," he said . . . :** Jack Sell, "Noll Gets Three Years to Build Steelers," *Pittsburgh Post-Gazette*, January 28, 1969.

xv **Jack Ham, the . . . :** Peter King, *The Season After: Are Sports Dynasties Dead?* (New York: Warner, 1989), 55.

xvi **Noll was "square" . . . :** Joe Greene interview, January 26, 2015.

xvi **His press conferences . . . :** Phil Musick, "Noll Sticks to Same Old 'Game Plan' for Buffalo," *Pittsburgh Press*, December 17, 1974; Paul Zimmerman, "The Teacher," *Sports Illustrated*, July 28, 1980.

xvii **For Noll, the . . . :** Brady, "Steelers' Chuck Noll Is an Unspectacular Genius"; Roy Blount Jr., *About Three Bricks Shy . . . and the Load Filled Up: The Story of the Greatest Football Team Ever* (Pittsburgh: University of Pittsburgh Press, 2004), Kindle edition, location 2808.

xvii **The view then . . . :** Pat Maloney interview, November 3, 2012.

xvii **Part of the . . . :** Ted W. Engstrom, *The Making of a Christian Leader* (Grand Rapids: Zondervan, 1978), 206.

xvii **He also had . . . :** Peter King interview, April 10, 2015.

xviii   **There were, in . . . :** Ed Bouchette, "The Curtain Falls: Steelers Noll Decides to Get on with His Life's Work," *Pittsburgh Post-Gazette*, December 27, 1991.

xviii   **Because of this . . . :** John Stallworth interview, March 31, 2014.

xviii   **"The bottom line . . ."** Frenchy Fuqua interview, August 24, 2013.

xix   **"I heard this . . ."** Ron Johnson interview, August 24, 2013.

Chapter 1

1   **On the morning . . . :** Rita Deininger interviews, October 11, 2012; June 18, 2014; and September 9, 2014; Pete Schreiber interview, November 2, 2014; Five-Generation Pedigree Chart for Charles H. Noll, Western Reserve Historical Society, Cleveland, OH; William V. Noll birth certificate, Western Reserve Historical Society, Cleveland, OH; "Ohio, County Marriages, 1789–2013," Database with images, Family Search (https://familysearch.org /ark:/51903/1:1:XDGQ-LP1:), William Noll and Catherine [*sic*] Steigerwald, 27 June 1917; citing Cuyahoga, Ohio, United States, reference 27628; county courthouses, Ohio; FHL microfilm 1,888.790.

2   **It wasn't easy . . . :** *1900 United States Federal Census*, Ancestry.com. Original data via the United States of America, Bureau of the Census, *Twelfth Census of the United States, 1900* (Washington, DC: National Archives and Records Administration, 1900), T623, 1854 rolls; *1900 United States Federal Census*, Census Place: Dover, Cuyahoga, Ohio, roll 1260, page 17B, Enumeration District: 0213, FHL microfilm: 1241260; Frank Stewart, "Clevelanders Play Leading Parts in History of Old Avon Parish," *Cleveland Press*, April 4, 1953; Rita Deininger interview, October 11, 2012; Five-Generation Pedigree Chart for Charles H. Noll, Western Reserve Historical Society, Cleveland, OH.

2   **But it was . . . :** Eleanor Prech, "Black and White Mix Enriches City Church," *Cleveland Press*, August 6, 1980; Rita Deininger interview, October 11, 2012 and June 18, 2014; Case Western Reserve University and Western Reserve Historical Society, "Encyclopedia of Cleveland History: HOLY TRINITY PARISH," http://ech.case.edu/cgi/article.pl?id=HTP1; Five-Generation Pedigree Chart for Charles H. Noll, Western Reserve Historical Society, Cleveland, OH.

3   **Over the long . . . :** Rita Deininger interview, August 14, 2014.

3   **Henry and Mary . . . :** Rita Deininger interview, August 14, 2014; Five-Generation Pedigree Chart for Charles H. Noll, Western Reserve Historical Society, Cleveland, OH; *1910 United States Federal Census*, Census Place: Cleveland Ward 20, Cuyahoga, Ohio, roll t624_1171, page 2.1, Enumeration District: 0310, FHL microfilm: 1375184.

3   **William Noll was . . . :** Rita Deininger interview, August 14, 2014, and September 8, 2014.

3   **William had registered . . . :** *Ohio Military Men, 1917–18*, Ancestry.com. Original data via *Official Roster of Ohio Soldiers, Sailors and Marines in the World War, 1917–1918*, vols. 1–23 (Columbus, OH: F. J. Heer Printing Co., 1926).

4   **"She was strict . . .":** Rita Deininger interview, September 11, 2013.

4   **As the homemaker . . . :** Rita Deininger interviews, September 11, 2013; June 29, 2014.

4   **But the love . . . :** Rita Deininger interview, June 29, 2014.

4   **"No, I mean . . .":** Rita Deininger interview, June 29, 2014.

5   **William and Kate . . . :** *1940 United States Federal Census*, Ancestry.com. Original data via United States of America, Bureau of the Census, *Sixteenth Census of the United States, 1940* (Washington, DC: National Archives and Records Administration, 1940), T627, 4,643 rolls; Rita Deininger interview, October 11, 2012, and June 29, 2014.

5   **From there . . . :** Rita Deininger interview, June 29, 2014.

6   **This was the . . . :** Rita Deininger interview, May 20, 2013.

6   **Kate had been . . . :** Rita Deininger interview, May 20, 2013, and June 29, 2014.

7   **The church was . . . :** Rita Deininger interview, May 20, 2013; Prech, "Black and White Mix Enriches City Church."

7   **The boxy school . . . :** Ralph Yanky interview, August 20, 2013; Rita Deininger interview, May 20, 2013; Joseph Devera interview, August 28, 2013.

7   **It was an . . . :** Ed Steigerwald interview, November 2, 2014.

7   **The Nolls celebrated . . . :** Ed Steigerwald interview, November 2, 2014; Pete Schreiber interview, November 2, 2014.

8   **By 1940, they . . . :** Paul Zimmerman, "The Teacher," *Sports Illustrated*, July 28, 1980.

8   **At the time . . . :** Rita Deininger interview, April 14, 2014; Ralph Yanky interview, April 15, 2014; Ed Steigerwald interview, November 2, 2014; Pete Schreiber interview, November 2, 2014.

8   **As the war . . . :** Rita Deininger interview, April 14, 2014.

8   **Robinson in 1941 . . . :** Rita Deininger interview, April 14, 2014.

10   **Back in Cleveland . . . :** Rita Deininger interview, April 14, 2014; Ralph Yanky interview, June 28, 2014.

10   **It was still . . . :** Ralph Yanky interview, June 28, 2014.

10   **The school day . . . :** Ralph Yanky, June 28, 2014.

10   **But he was . . . :** Ralph Yanky interview, June 28, 2014.

10   **He played football . . . :** Rita Deininger interview, April 14, 2014.

10   **"Chuck only wanted . . .":** Joseph Devera interview, August 28, 2013.

11   **There was a . . . :** Ralph's cousin, Phyllis Koenig, lived with the Yanky family for a while, while her parents were divorcing. Chuck related the sad story to

his mother, and every holiday Kate Noll would make a special corsage that she'd send with Chuck to present to Phyllis. Ralph Yanky interview, June 28, 2014.

11 **Once a basketball . . . :** Joseph Devera interview, August 28, 2013; Ralph Yanky interview, June 28, 2014.

11 **At Holy Trinity . . . :** Ralph Yanky interviews, June 28, 2014; July 15, 2014.

12 **While the ethnic . . . :** John Grabowski interview, November 4, 2014.

12 **For Chuck and . . . :** Rita Deininger interview, September 8, 2014.

12 **The white flight . . . :** Joe Hornack interview, April 5, 2014.

12 **One day, Chuck . . . :** Ralph Yanky interviews, April 14, 2014; June 28, 2014.

13 **The integrated nature . . . :** Ralph Yanky interview, April 14, 2014.

13 **"We were lucky . . ."**: Ralph Yanky interview, June 28, 2014.

14 **Kate Noll worried. . . . :** Ed Steigerwald interview, November 2, 2014; Pete Schreiber interview, November 2, 2014.

14 **He wondered occasionally . . . :** Rita Deininger interview, May 20, 2013; Robert Noll interview, February 24, 2014.

15 **"I remember Chuck's . . ."**: Ralph Yanky interview, June 28, 2014.

15 **"He had no . . ."**: Rita Deininger interview, May 20, 2013.

15 **"My favorite dish . . ."**: Chuck Noll interview, July 24, 2013.

15 **"My mother never . . ."**: Rita Deininger interview, May 20, 2013.

15 **"I wouldn't say . . ."**: Zimmerman, "The Teacher."

16 **On June 3, . . . :** Program, Graduation Exercise, Holy Trinity School, June 3, 1945, from Noll family private papers.

16 **The public school . . . :** Chuck had watched (along with some friends) Benedictine play for the East Senate championship in basketball, losing in the end to Catholic powerhouse Cathedral Latin. He and Ralph were pretty sure that the Bengals' big center—Mike Medich, who scored more than 20 points per game—had gotten a raw deal. Ralph Yanky interview, June 28, 2014; Joe Hornack interview, June 7, 2013.

Chapter 2

17 **Throughout that summer . . . :** Paul Zimmerman, "The Teacher," *Sports Illustrated*, July 28, 1980.

17 **Chuck began his . . . :** *Cleveland Press*, September 4, 1945; Joe Hornack interview, June 7, 2013.

18 **The school had . . . :** Joe Hornack interview, June 7, 2013; Fr. Gerard Gonda interview, May 21, 2013.

18 **The previous March . . . :** Benedictine High School academic transcript for Chuck Noll, 1945–49; Jodie Valade, "The Super Man of Steel," *Cleveland Plain Dealer*, December 28, 2008.

18   **Chuck didn't go . . . :** Fr. Placid Piatek interview, May 21, 2013.

18   **"Chuck was never . . .":** Ralph Yanky interview, July 15, 2014.

18   **There were other . . . :** Leonard Schreiber was married to William's sister Margaret; Tony Ferente interview, July 29, 2015; Rita Deininger interviews, April 14, 2014; June 18, 2014; May 6, 2015; Ralph Yanky interview, July 15, 2014.

19   **He soon looked . . . :** Rita Deininger interview, May 6, 2014.

19   **At other times . . . :** Rudy Lawrenchik interview, April 6, 2014.

19   **The conditions that . . . :** Ralph Yanky interview, September 10, 2013.

19   **During the Benedictine . . . :** Rita Deininger interview, May 20, 2013.

20   **By the fall . . . :** Rita Deininger interview, May 20, 2013; Joe Hornack interview, April 15, 2014.

20   **In Cleveland that . . . :** Michael MacCambridge, *America's Game: The Epic Story of How Pro Football Captured a Nation* (New York: Random House, 2004), 21–37.

21   **In 1936, the . . . :** Case Western Reserve University and Western Reserve Historical Society, "Encyclopedia of Cleveland History: CHARITY FOOTBALL GAME," accessed June 13, 2016, http://ech.case.edu/cgi/article.pl?id=CFG.

21   **By the fall . . . :** Ralph Yanky interview, September 10, 2013; Joe Hornack interview, June 7, 2013; Fr. Gerard Gonda interview, November 4, 2014.

21   **At home, Chuck's . . . :** Ralph Yanky interview, September 10, 2013; Rita Deininger, June 18, 2014

22   **"I remember one . . .":** Rita Deininger interview, May 6, 2014.

22   **By then, Chuck . . . :** Rita Deininger interviews, May 20, 2013; September 11, 2013; May 6, 2014; Ralph Yanky interviews, April 14, 2014; June 28, 2014; July 15, 2014; Marianne Noll interviews, February 8, 2013; February 8, 2015.

22   **The men carried . . . :** Fr. Placid Piatek interview, May 21, 2013.

22   **He'd had a . . . :** Rita Deininger interviews, September 11, 2013; May 6, 2014.

23   **The stigma of . . . :** Ralph Yanky interview, April 14, 2014.

23   **Within the family . . . :** Rita Deininger interview, May 6, 2014.

24   **Though embarrassed by . . . :** Chuck Noll interview, February 22, 2014.

24   **Chuck was an . . . :** Rita Deininger interviews, October 11, 2012; August 14, 2014; Bill Veeck and Ed Linn, *Veeck—as in Wreck: The Autobiography of Bill Veeck* (Chicago: University Of Chicago Press, 2001); National Baseball Hall of Fame and Museum, "Bill Veeck," accessed June 13, 2016, http://baseballhall.org/hof/veeck-bill.

24   **On their junior . . . :** Ralph Yanky interview, July 15, 2014.

24   **The summer and . . . :** Ralph Yanky interview, July 15, 2014; Elsie Lyttle interview, December 26, 2014.

25   **By the start . . . :** Ralph Yanky interview, September 10, 2013; Joe Hornack

interview, June 7, 2013; Fr. Placid Piatek interview, May 21, 2013; the Bengals had the makings of a great line: center Ray Gembarski and right tackle and team captain Eddie Powell were already being courted by Notre Dame. Ed Stakolich and Ray Borovich were gifted ends who could block and catch passes efficiently. Eventually, Chuck earned a starting job on the line.

25   **Strosnider had been . . . :** Ed Steigerwald interview, November 2, 2014.

25   **"He was a . . .":** Not for attribution interview, Cleveland, Ohio, 2014.

25   **For his part . . . :** Bob August, "Brown Knew All the Time about Noll," *Cleveland Press*, December 15, 1955.

26   **On October 3 . . . :** Benedictine High School, *Benedictine 49'er* (Cleveland, Ohio, 1949).

26   **The 1948 Charity . . . :** Marlo Termini interview, June 20, 2014; Ralph Yanky interview, July 15, 2014; *Benedictine Alumni Homecoming Game Program*, Benedictine vs. Cathedral Latin, November 5, 1948.

27   **"I learned very . . .":** Roy Blount Jr., *About Three Bricks Shy . . . and the Load Filled Up: The Story of the Greatest Football Team Ever* (Pittsburgh: University of Pittsburgh Press, 2004), Kindle edition, location 1248.

27   **The spring of . . . :** Ralph Yanky interview, September 10, 2013; Rita Deininger interview, June 18, 2014; Ed Steigerwald interview, November 2, 2014.

27   **He had always . . . :** Ralph Yanky interview, September 10, 2013.

27   **Chuck was still . . . :** Ralph Yanky interview, April 14, 2014; Joan Bulger Yanky interview, April 14, 2014.

28   **By that spring . . . :** That spring, Chuck went out on more dates, often doubling with Ralph and his girlfriend, Joan Bulger. Chuck took a date to the senior prom—Rita paid for the corsage, because, in her words, "I was the only one working in the family at the time." Rita Deininger interviews, May 20, 2013; June 29, 2014; Marianne Noll interview, February 8, 2015; Len Kestner interview, June 29, 2014.

28   **"To be honest . . .":** Ralph Yanky interview, April 14, 2014.

28   **But he'd developed . . . :** *The Benedictine 49'er*, described by Benedictine president Gerard Gonda as "neither a conventional yearbook or a school newspaper, but actually a chronological review of the school year in the format of newspapers—a substitute for the traditional yearbook . . . published in May 1949."

Chapter 3

29   **When Chuck arrived . . . :** Leonard Wolniak interview, June 5, 2015; William Whiteside interview, June 9, 2015; Albert Kohanowich interview, June 5, 2015; Charles "Chuck" Doud interview, June 9, 2015.

29   **The Fighting Irish . . . :** Arch Ward, *Frank Leahy and the Fighting Irish: The Story of Notre Dame Football* (New York: G. P. Putnam's Sons, 1944), 40–46.

29   **All Chuck had . . . :** Jim Currin interview, February 16, 2013; Pat Maloney interview, March 24, 2014; Marianne Noll interview, February 9, 2015; Rita Deininger interview, April 14, 2014.

30   **There was little . . . :** Ralph Yanky interview, September 10, 2013; Fr. Placid Piatek interview, May 21, 2013.

32   **It had already . . . :** Jim Currin interview, February 16, 2013; Pat Maloney interview, March 24, 2014.

32   **Many of the . . . :** Doug Hauschild interview, February 1, 2013; Paul Cassidy, March 26, 2014; Len Kestner interview, June 29, 2014; Dan Ferrazza interview, June 28, 2014; Jo Ferrazza interview, March 24, 2014.

33   **So, on September . . . :** Len Kestner interview, June 29, 2014.

33   **Dayton, which sat . . . :** Michael Barone and Grant Ujifusa, *The Almanac of American Politics 2000* (New York: Times Books, 1999), 1256–57.

34   **The wave of . . . :** Jim Currin interview, February 16, 2013; Pat Maloney interview, March 24, 2014.

34   **Before they'd even . . . :** Pat Maloney interview, November 3, 2012; Jim Currin interview, February 16, 2013.

34   **Sometimes the freshmen . . . :** Doug Hauschild interview, February 1, 2013; Pat Maloney interview, November 3, 2012.

35   **Eventually, though, by . . . :** Dan Ferrazza interview, June 28, 2014; Jim Currin interview, February 16, 2013.

35   **Chuck's life centered . . . :** Don Donoher interview, December 13, 2013.

35   **The thin walls . . . :** A rough-hewn New Yorker named Paul Cassidy once put a beer sign in his dorm window. A freshman named Dick Bertrand used to run toward the window of his third-floor dorm room, hop through feet first, and then grab the windowsill, while his feet landed on an arch just below the window. "He would kind of stand on that," said Jim Currin, "and then he would pop his head up over the edge and scare the hell out of people. But he would actually jump out the window." Don Donoher interview, December 13, 2013; Jim Currin interview, February 16, 2013.

35   **Another frequent member . . . :** Jim Currin interview, February 16, 2013; Pat Maloney interview, March 24, 2014.

36   **In a room . . . :** That spring break, Chuck tagged along with Maloney and Currin on a trip down to Florida, only to suffer another seizure. Maloney and Currin were rattled, as well as curious. But Chuck clearly didn't want to talk about it. Jim Akau interview, April 10, 2014; Len Kestner interview, June 24, 2014.

36   **That summer, Chuck . . . :** Jim Currin interviews, February 9, 2013; September 15, 2013; Fort Scott Camps Website, http://www.fortscottcamps.com/.

37   **As sophomores, Chuck . . . :** Paul Cassidy interview, March 26, 2014; Pat Maloney interview, March 24, 2014.

37   **"He had the . . .":** Jim Currin interview, February 9, 2013.

38   **"Charlie ate up . . .":** Tom Carroll interview, July 2, 2014.

38   **Even that first . . . :** Pat Maloney interview, June 27, 2015; Jack T. Clary, with illustrations by Dick Oden, *The Gamemakers* (Chicago: Follett, 1976), 133–61.

38   **Chuck's roommate was . . . :** Pat Siggins interview, December 6, 2013; Frank Siggins Jr. interview, September 6, 2013.

38   **"When you'd walk . . .":** Tom Carroll interview, July 2, 2014.

38   **Both were strong . . . :** Don Donoher interview, December 13, 2013.

39   **"We would go . . .":** Jim Currin interview, February 9, 2013.

39   **At St. Joe's . . . :** Chris Harris interview, December 12, 2013; letter from Kate Noll to Chuck Noll, undated, Noll family private collection.

40   **Chuck's first meaningful . . . :** Pat Maloney interview, March 24, 2014.

40   **That fall, Chuck . . . :** Rita Deininger interview, June 18, 2014.

40   **Rita was drawn . . . :** Rita Deininger interview, June 18, 2014; Sr. Geraldine Deininger interview, May 20, 2013; Don Shula interview, April 15, 2013.

41   **Back in Dayton . . . :** Jim Currin interview, February 9, 2013.

41   **At the end . . . :** Rita Deininger interview, June 18, 2014; Jim Currin interview, February 9, 2013.

41   **One day, Chuck . . . :** Pat Maloney interview, March 24, 2014.

Chapter 4

43   **They had spent . . . :** Chris Harris interview, December 12, 2013; Paul Cassidy interview, March 26, 2014; Pat Maloney interview, March 24, 2014; Jim Currin interview, February 9, 2013.

44   **Chuck's nickname was . . . :** Jim Currin interview, February 9, 2013.

44   **"The Pope." It . . . :** Pat Maloney interview, March 24, 2014; Jim Currin interview, February 9, 2013; Len Kestner interview, June 29, 2014.

44   **The nickname poked . . . :** Don Donoher interview, December 12, 2013.

44   **"They built a . . .":** Chuck Spatafore interview, March 25, 2013.

44   **"He was incredible."** Chris Harris interview, December 12, 2013.

45   **For the rest . . . :** Jim Currin interview, February 9, 2013.

45   **And so it . . . :** Chuck Spatafore interview, March 25, 2013.

45   **During one season . . . :** Pat Maloney interview, March 24, 2014.

45   **One day that . . . :** Tom Carroll interview, October 10, 2013.

46   **Throughout the time . . . :** Jim Currin interview, December 9, 2013; Chuck Spatafore interview, March 25, 2013.

46   **One day on . . . :** Tom Carroll interview, October 10, 2013; Pat Maloney interview, March 24, 2014.

46   **Dayton's 1951 training . . . :** Jim Currin interview, December 9, 2013; Chuck Spatafore interview, March 25, 2013.

47   **Others noticed that . . . :** Tom Carroll interview, October 10, 2013.

47   **With Siggins . . . :** Jim Currin interview, December 9, 2013; Tom Carroll interview, October 10, 2013.

48   **On the morning . . . :** Jim Currin interview, December 9, 2013; *Dayton Flyers, University of Dayton Football Media Guide 2012.*

48   **There were real . . . :** Pat Maloney interview, March 24, 2013; Tom Carroll interview, October 10, 2013; Jim Currin interview, December 9, 2013.

49   **It would be . . . :** *Salad Bowl Souvenir Official Football Program*, January 1, 1952.

49   **The game itself . . . :** Michael MacCambridge, ed., *ESPN College Football Encyclopedia: The Complete History of the Game*, with introduction by Dan Jenkins (New York: ESPN, 2005), 1611.

49   **They still returned . . . :** *University of Dayton Football 1952 Media Guide.*

49   **Training camp for . . . :** Pat Maloney interview, March 24, 2013.

50   **"I don't want . . .":** Jim Currin interview, December 9, 2013.

50   **The players understood . . . :** Dan Ferrazza interview, March 24, 2013; Pat Maloney interview, March 24, 2013.

51   **"No, the Browns . . .":** Paul Zimmerman, "Man Not Myth," *Sports Illustrated*, July 21, 1980.

51   **After William Noll . . . :** Rita Deininger interview, September 18, 2014.

51   **The standard contract . . . :** Chuck Noll interview, July 5, 2012.

52   **"Well, you're big . . .":** Zimmerman, "Man Not Myth."

52   **In his meeting . . . :** John Vukelich interview, October 17, 2013.

52   **"I remember we . . .":** Tom Carroll interview, October 10, 2013.

52   **By the end . . . :** Pat Maloney interview, March 24, 2013; Tom Carroll interview, October 10, 2013; Jim Currin interview, December 9, 2013.

53   **At Kramer's, they . . . :** Tom Carroll interview, October 10, 2013.

53   **For many of . . . :** Shirley Stemley McIntosh interview, April 16, 2014.

53   **"They were really . . .":** Pat Maloney interview, March 24, 2013; Shirley Stemley McIntosh interview, April 16, 2014.

53   **Decades later, Chuck . . . :** Zimmerman, "Man Not Myth."

54   **With Stemley, Chuck . . . :** Shirley Stemley McIntosh interview, April 16, 2014.

54   **That summer of . . . :** Chris Harris interview, December 12, 2013.

54   **They'd found work . . . :** Tom Carroll interview, October 10, 2013; Shirley Stemley McIntosh interview, April 16, 2014.

54   **When they returned . . . :** Tom Carroll interview, October 10, 2013; Chris Harris interview, December 12, 2013.

55   **Friday, July 3 . . . :** Pat Maloney interview, March 24, 2013; Jim Currin interview, December 9, 2013.

Chapter 5

57   **Rookies did not . . . :** Herman Goldstein, "Brown's Call Me Paul Set Pattern," *Cleveland Press*, January 25, 1956.

58   **"I am Paul . . .":** Adapted from Herman Goldstein, "Some Little Things That Made Browns Big," *Cleveland News*, December 16, 1946; and Paul Brown's preseason speech. His players said the speech was remarkably unchanged in content every year, though in later years Brown spent more time on things he was against—agents, unions, drugs, long hair, loud music, and new attitudes about authority.

58   **He warned against . . . :** Don Colo interview, May 13, 2013; Curly Morrison interview, March 10, 2014.

59   **By 1953, Paul . . . :** Michael MacCambridge, *America's Game: The Epic Story of How Pro Football Captured a Nation* (New York: Random House, 2004), 21–37.

59   **Brown wasn't outwardly . . . :** Howard Preston, "Pro Title Completes the Grid Cycle for Paul Brown," *Cleveland News*, December 23, 1946.

59   **Unlike the Rams . . . :** Mike Brown interview, November 11, 2013.

60   **The son of . . . :** Don Colo interview, May 13, 2013; Bob Gain interview, April 15, 2014.

61   **For fringe players . . . :** Don Colo interview, May 13, 2013.

61   **Chuck had not . . . :** Jim Currin interview, February 16, 2013.

62   **But Chuck remained . . . :** Years later, in 1959, a young Len Dawson was at training camp, sitting next to the Browns' veteran kicker Lou Groza. "Lou—you're taking this test?," Dawson asked. "Oh, yeah," said Groza. "Doesn't he know what type of individual you are?—you have been here thirteen years or whatever." "It doesn't make any difference," said Groza. "Everybody does it."

62   **Over the years . . . :** In Terry Pluto's *When All the World Was Browns Town* (New York: Simon and Schuster, 1997), the player Bernie Parrish said "everyone cheated like crazy on those tests. They used crib sheets with all the answers. Hell, I remember seeing Chuck Noll do it, and Paul would brag about how smart Chuck was" (26). This claim is refuted by several teammates. Don Colo noted that the only players who took it seriously were the quarterbacks and defensive backs, but that the questions were the sort of thing that Chuck already knew. Don Colo interview, May 13, 2013; Bob Gain interview, April 15, 2014; Curly Morrison interview, March 10, 2014.

62   **"We used to . . .":** Don Colo interview, May 13, 2013.

62   **Brown had long . . . :** Bud Volzer, "Paul Brown to Stress Speed on His Cleveland Pro Eleven," *Canton Repository*, June 25, 1946.

62   **By the middle . . . :** Harold Sauerbrei, "Noll Prefers to Perform on Line," *Cleveland Plain Dealer*, August 13, 1953.

63   **On August 23 . . .** : Kate Cassidy, "A Class Act," *University of Dayton Quarterly* (summer 1993): 40.

63   **"You were right" . . .** : Shirley Stemley McIntosh interview, April 16, 2014.

63   **The area where . . .** : Murray Olderman, "All You Got To Do Is Ask," *Victoria Advocate*, October 1, 1976.

63   **At training camp . . .** : Hal Lebovitz, "'Sorry, Gals!' Handsome Chuck Noll's Heart Belongs to Cleveland Browns," *Cleveland News*, November 26, 1953.

64   **To Chuck, the . . .** : Roy Blount Jr., *About Three Bricks Shy of a Load: A Highly Irregular Lowdown on the Year the Pittsburgh Steelers Were Super but Missed the Bowl* (Boston: Little, Brown, 1974), Kindle edition, location 4257.

64   **It was also . . .** : Lebovitz, "'Sorry, Gals!'"

64   **Two old Dayton . . .** : Jim Currin interview, February 16, 2013; Paul Cassidy interview, March 26, 2014.

64   **But he was . . .** : Lebovitz, "'Sorry, Gals!'"

65   **Chuck had broken . . .** : Shirley Stemley McIntosh interview, April 16, 2014; Pat Maloney interview, March 24, 2014.

65   **The Saturday after . . .** : Ralph Yanky interview, April 15, 2014; Curly Morrison interview, January 6, 2014.

66   **Including 1951's loss . . .** : Shelby Strother, "Life in the Fast Layne," *NFL Top 40: The Greatest Pro Football Games Ever Played* (New York: Viking, 1988).

66   **While the ending . . .** : Marianne Noll interview, February 9, 2015; Rita Deininger interview, June 29, 2014; Ralph Yanky, April 15, 2014.

66   **There was still . . .** : Cleveland Directory Co., *Cleveland City Directory 1954* (Cleveland, OH, 1954), 742.

66   **While many of . . .** : Dan Ferrazza interview, June 28, 2014; Jo Ferrazza interview, June 27, 2014.

67   **Now they were . . .** : Jack T. Clary, with illustrations by Dick Oden, *The Gamemakers* (Chicago: Follett, 1976), 136.

67   **"Chuck came in . . ."** : Pat Maloney interview, June 27, 2014.

67   **There was a . . .** : Shirley Stemley McIntosh interview, April 16, 2014.

68   **At the beginning . . .** : Leo Murphy interview, May 21, 2013.

68   **NFL Commissioner Bert . . .** : Upton Bell interview, April 30, 2014.

68   **Before the next . . .** : NFL Films, *75 Seasons: 1920 to 1995, the Story of the NFL* (New York: PolyGram, 1994), VHS.

69   **Chuck had wanted . . .** : Rita Deininger interview, September 11, 2013.

70   **Throughout the first . . .** : Marlo Termini interview, June 29, 2014.

70   **To make some . . .** : Don Colo interview, May 13, 2013; Curly Morrison interview, January 6, 2014.

71   **"He's big enough . . ."** : Bob August, "Brown Knew All the Time about Noll," *Cleveland Press*, December 15, 1955.

71   **"All of a . . .":** Curly Morrison interview, January 6, 2014.

71   **In fact, it . . . :** Don Colo interview, May 13, 2013.

72   **It was just . . . :** Herschel Forester interview, May 15, 2013.

72   **Hall had a . . . :** Marilyn Hall Regalado interviews, April 24, 2013; March 9, 2014; July 1, 2015; Marianne Noll interviews, June 2, 2014; September 30, 2015.

Chapter 6

74   **By that point . . . :** Marianne Noll interviews, August 29, 2012; February 23, 2014; October 4, 2014.

74   **The pretty, willful . . . :** *Portsmouth High School Yearbook*, 1951.

76   **All the while . . . :** D. E. Newman letters to Marianne Hanes, Noll family private collection, undated.

77   **Cleveland, 1953. Marianne's . . . :** Marilyn Hall Regalado interviews, April 24, 2013; March 9, 2014; Alice Bowman Nye interview, April 12, 2014; Ed Nye interview, April 12, 2014.

78   **Marianne's combination of . . . :** Marilyn Hall Regalado interview, April 24, 2013; Rudy Regalado interview, March 9, 2014.

80   **They often began . . . :** Marianne Noll interviews, October 4, 2014; February 8, 2015.

80   **In those early . . . :** Jeanne Ippilito DiSanto interview, June 28, 2014; Dan Ferrazza interview, March 28, 2013.

81   **Earlier, Chuck brought . . . :** Marilyn Hall Regalado interview, April 24, 2013; Marianne Noll interview, October 4, 2014.

81   **Chuck was slower . . . :** Pat Maloney interview, June 27, 2014.

81   **At the Wagon . . . :** Dan Ferrazza interview, March 28, 2013.

82   **By early 1957 . . . :** Marilyn Hall Regalado interview, April 24, 2013.

83   **Then, in April . . . :** Marilyn Hall Regalado interview, April 24, 2013; Alice Bowman Nye interview, April 12, 2014; Marianne Noll interviews, February 8, 2015; February 9, 2015.

83   **"I didn't know . . .":** Don Colo interview, February 10, 2014.

83   **But Chuck's family . . . :** Rita Deininger interview, June 18, 2014.

83   **There was little . . . :** Marianne Noll interviews, February 6, 2014; February 8, 2015; Rita Deininger interview, June 18, 2014.

84   **The ceremony was . . . :** Marianne Noll interview, February 6, 2014.

84   **For Chuck's old . . . :** Jim Currin interview, February 16, 2013.

84   **As the wedding . . . :** Don Colo interview, February 10, 2014; postcard from Deluxe Motel, Mentor, OH, Noll family private collection.

84   **"We borrowed $3,000 . . .":** Marianne Noll interview, February 6, 2014.

86   **Coming off the . . . :** Don Colo interview, February 10, 2014; Curly Morrison interview, January 6, 2014.

86   **On the plane . . . :** Chuck Noll letter to Marianne Noll, Noll family private collection, undated.

87   **On October 27 . . . :** Leo Murphy helped him off the field, but it was the policy of NFL telecasts in the '50s that images of injured players weren't shown to the television audience. Marianne had been watching the used black-and-white TV that they'd bought for $40, and when she returned she noticed Chuck wasn't in the game anymore. "And so I waited and waited," she said, "and finally a neighbor came over after the game and said, 'How badly do you think he is hurt?' I'm thinking, 'I have no idea, because I don't know what happened.'" Leo Murphy interview, May 21, 2013.

87   **When he arrived . . . :** Marianne Noll interview, February 6, 2014.

88   **On Christmas Day . . . :** Rita Deininger interview, June 18, 2014; Dan Ferrazza interview, March 28, 2013.

88   **Dissatisfied with selling . . . :** Marianne Noll interview, February 6, 2014; Don Colo interview, February 10, 2014.

89   **Over the summer . . . :** Chuck Noll letter to Marianne Noll, Noll family private collection, undated.

89   **Their biggest challenge . . . :** Marianne Noll interview, February 6, 2014.

90   **The '58 season . . . :** Chuck Heaton, "Hickerson, Smith, Noll Give Browns Zip," *Cleveland Plain Dealer*, December 1958.

90   **"Stop the film" . . . :** Don Colo interview, May 13, 2013; Bobby Mitchell interview, circa 2000, for Michael MacCambridge, *America's Game: The Epic Story of How Pro Football Captured a Nation* (New York: Random House, 2004).

91   **The team's strong . . . :** MacCambridge, *America's Game*, Kindle edition, location 2360.

91   **During the 1959 . . . :** Chuck Noll letter to Marianne Noll, August 31, 1959, Noll family private collection.

92   **Chuck's old roommate . . . :** Jim Currin interview, December 9, 2013.

93   **He called Paul . . . :** Marianne Noll interview, February 6, 2014; Mike Brown interview, November 11, 2013.

Chapter 7

94   **Chuck had made . . . :** Michael MacCambridge, *Lamar Hunt: A Life in Sports* (Kansas City: Andrews McMeel, 2012), 88–107.

94   **So Chuck reached . . . :** Marianne Noll interview, June 2, 2014.

95   **Gillman was a . . . :** Michael MacCambridge, *America's Game: The Epic Story of How Pro Football Captured a Nation* (New York: Random House, 2004), Kindle edition, location 1838.

96   **After the phone . . . :** Chuck Noll interview, February 22, 2014.

96   **To his players . . . :** MacCambridge, *America's Game*, Kindle edition, location

4038; Don Colo interview, May 13, 2013; Marilyn Hall Regalado interview, April 24, 2013.

97   **Chuck's old friend . . . :** John Vukelich interview, October 17, 2013.

97   **Back in Cleveland . . . :** Marianne Noll letter to Chuck Noll, 1960, Noll family private collection.

97   **As they waited . . . :** Chuck Noll letter to Marianne Noll, Noll family private collection, undated.

98   **He found a . . . :** Marianne Noll interview, February 9, 2015; Chris Noll interview, June 16, 2013.

98   **Down at the . . . :** Jack Faulkner interview, circa 2001, for MacCambridge, *America's Game*; Al Davis interview, circa 2003, for MacCambridge, *America's Game*.

99   **But Chuck made . . . :** John Clayton, "Doing It His Way: Noll Goes by the Playbook, but It Is Missing a Chapter on Socializing with Players," *Pittsburgh Press*, December 25, 1983. Elsewhere in the story, Faulkner says he recommended Noll to Gillman. But all other accounts of the hiring have Noll calling Gillman. More likely, after Gillman mentioned the call, Faulkner gave Noll an endorsement.

99   **Chuck's friend Vukelich . . . :** John Vukelich interview, October 17, 2013.

99   **The first Chargers . . . :** Three USC players, who had been extras in the movie *Spartacus*, got a tryout. "I had nine roommates," said Paul Maguire, the Citadel receiver and punter who was moved to tight end and, eventually, linebacker. "One guy, they brought him in after breakfast, timed him, and sent him home before lunch. Hell, I never met the guy." Gillman's preoccupation with an extra edge remained. The Chargers were fined by the league office, before training camp began, for beginning workouts prior to the agreed-upon start date. Paul Maguire interview, February 20, 2014; Todd Tobias, *Charging through the AFL: Los Angeles and San Diego Chargers' Football in the 1960s* (Paducah: Turner, 2004); Ed Gruver, *The American Football League a Year-by-Year History, 1960–1969* (Jefferson: McFarland, 1997).

100   **The Gillman passing . . . :** Sid Gillman interview, circa 2001, for MacCambridge, *America's Game*.

100   **"A meeting was . . .":** Paul Maguire interview, February 20, 2014.

101   **The Chargers' opening . . . :** MacCambridge, *Lamar Hunt*; Sid Gillman interview, circa 2001, for MacCambridge, *America's Game*; Jack Kemp interview, circa 2000, for MacCambridge, *America's Game*; Richard Crawford, "Hilton's Chargers Left L.A. after Whirlwind Courtship," *San Diego Union-Tribune*, October 1, 2009.

101   **They packed up . . . :** John Vukelich interview, October 17, 2013; Marianne Noll interview, February 9, 2015.

102   **"My only memory . . ."**: Chris Noll interview, June 16, 2013.

102   **At the earliest . . .** : "I was a fan then," Chris Noll said. "I could name all the players on the Chargers, Lance Alworth and Paul Lowe and Keith Lincoln, and go through the whole mix. I can remember meeting them"; Bob Petrich interview, February 5, 2014.

103   **A tougher sell . . .** : Al Davis interview, circa 2003, for MacCambridge, *America's Game*; John Brown interview, March 25, 2013.

104   **On the field . . .** : Chuck Allen interview, July 18, 2013; Bob Petrich interview, February 5, 2014.

104   **"Sid was a . . ."**: Bill Chastain, *Steel Dynasty: The Team That Changed the NFL* (Chicago: Triumph, 2005), Kindle edition, location 302.

105   **On Saturday evening . . .** : Margie Deininger Ervin interview, November 2, 2012; Ken Deininger interview, November 2, 2013; Rita Deininger interview, September 11, 2013. Margie, eight years old, had been gone for twenty minutes and was just coming back from the store. "I remember coming home and seeing the ambulance in the yard," said Margie. "We were walking down the street, and I started running. We just assumed it was grandpa or grandma. We got in and we couldn't believe it was our dad."

106   **Three days later . . .** : Marianne Noll interview, Oct 5, 2014.

Chapter 8

107   **In the midst . . .** : Marianne Noll interview, Oct 5, 2014.

107   **What Rita's children . . .** : Margie Deininger Ervin interview, November 2, 2012.

108   **It wasn't all . . .** : Rick Deininger interview, January 13, 2014; Robert Noll interview, February 24, 2014.

108   **By then, William . . .** : Rick Deininger interview, January 13, 2014; Ken Deininger interview, November 2, 2013.

109   **Back in San . . .** : Marilyn Hall Regalado interview, March 9, 2014; Marianne Noll interviews, February 23, 2014; September 30, 2015; when Rudy and Marilyn Regalado's first son Perry was born in 1962, they asked Chuck and Marianne to be the godparents. "When I called, and asked the priest if we could do the baptism on Monday morning, because that was Chuck's day off, he said, 'You can't do a baptism on Monday. We're not doing that; this is the regulation,'" said Marilyn. "I started to explain to him, and then he said, 'Oh, *Chuck?! Chuck Noll?*' I said, 'Yes, Chuck and Marianne are the godparents.' He said, 'You come on over Monday morning and I'll be here.'"

109   **A few times . . .** : Paul Maguire interview, February 20, 2014; Bob Petrich interview, February 5, 2014.

109   **They were also . . .** : Marianne Noll interview, February 9, 2015.

110   **"If you said . . ."**: Paul Maguire interview, February 20, 2014.

110   **On a trip . . . :** Paul Zimmerman, "The Teacher," *Sports Illustrated*, July 28, 1980.

110   **While they relished . . . :** Marianne Noll interview, February 9, 2015; Chris Noll interview, May 12, 2015.

110   **There was a . . . :** Sid Gillman interview, circa 2001, for MacCambridge, *America's Game*; Jack Faulkner interview, circa 2001, for MacCambridge, *America's Game*; Dale Grdnic, *Tales from the Pittsburgh Steelers Sideline: A Collection of the Greatest Steelers Stories Ever Told* (New York: Sports, 2013), 99.

111   **Chuck would help . . . :** Marianne Noll interview, February 9, 2015.

111   **The solution, as . . . :** Bob Petrich interview, February 5, 2014.

111   **"Sometimes you ate . . .":** Todd Tobias, *Charging through the AFL: Los Angeles and San Diego Chargers' Football in the 1960s* (Paducah: Turner, 2004), 56.

111   **"I'd never been . . .":** Bob Petrich interview, February 5, 2014; Chuck Allen interview, July 18, 2013.

112   **From the location . . . :** Millard Baker, "The Amazing History of Anabolic Steroids in Sports," MESO-Rx.com, April 11, 2001, https://thinksteroids.com/articles/history-anabolic-steroids-sports/.

113   **By the second . . . :** Tobias, *Charging through the AFL*, 73–74.

113   **Chuck didn't resort . . . :** Bob Petrich interview, February 5, 2014.

114   **"I will tell . . .":** Paul Maguire interview, February 20, 2014.

114   **"He would tell . . .":** Dick Westmoreland interview, March 9, 2014.

114   **"None of us . . .":** Paul Maguire interview, February 20, 2014.

115   **One day, after . . . :** Marianne Noll interview, February 9, 2015; Mike Brown interview, November 11, 2013.

115   **"The Chargers' practice . . .":** Paul Zimmerman, "Screen Gem," *Sports Illustrated*, September 2, 1991.

115   **Over the course . . . :** Dick Westmoreland interview, March 9, 2014; Larry Kindbom interview, March 5, 2015.

116   **The season's jarring . . . :** Chris Noll interview, May 12, 2015; Marianne Noll interview, February 9, 2015.

116   **The Chargers went . . . :** Bob Petrich interview, February 5, 2014; Paul Maguire interview, February 20, 2014.

116   **Gillman was boldly . . . :** Gruver, *The American Football League a Year-by-Year History*.

116   **"With Chuck, I . . .":** Bob Petrich interview, February 5, 2014.

117   **But 1963 was . . . :** MacCambridge, *America's Game*, Kindle version, location 4465.

117   **While the personnel . . . :** Chuck Allen interview, July 18, 2013.

118   **Chuck took a . . . :** Upton Bell interview, April 30, 2014.

118   **"I told them . . .":** Chris Noll interview, August 28, 2012.

118   **The news was . . . :** Margie Deininger Ervin interview, November 2, 2012.

Chapter 9

120   "I knew the . . .": Don Shula interview, April 15, 2013.

120   "Don was so . . .": [Get citation].

120   "I hired him . . .": Don Shula interview, April 15, 2013.

121   Earlier that spring . . . : Rita Deininger interview, April 14, 2014.

121   On the same . . . : Rick Deininger interview, January 13, 2014.

121   On one of . . . : Margie Deininger Ervin interview, November 2, 2012.

122   The Nolls' move . . . : Rita Deininger interview, April 14, 2014; Marianne Noll interview, February 9, 2015; Margie Deininger Ervin interview, November 2, 2012; "So he came, and I remember all the fighting, 'Who is gonna go with Uncle Chuck?,'" said Margie. "But he came and he drove, and that was an eight-hour [round-trip] drive. We went to Washington, DC. Only vacation we'd ever had in our lives."

122   "What's everybody doing . . .": Marianne Noll interview, February 9, 2015.

123   On defense, Chuck . . . : Don Shula interview, April 14, 2013.

123   It was the . . . : Chuck Noll interview transcript with Roy Blount Jr., circa 1973, for Blount's book About Three Bricks Shy of a Load: A Highly Irregular Lowdown on the Year the Pittsburgh Steelers Were Super but Missed the Bowl (Boston: Little, Brown, 1974).

123   "When I first . . .": Bill Chastain, Steel Dynasty: The Team That Changed the NFL (Chicago: Triumph, 2005), Kindle edition, location 340.

124   "If you got . . .": Dennis Gaubatz interview, October 3, 2014.

124   The Colts finished . . . : Richard Sandomir, "Little Consolation in Third-Place Game," New York Times, February 6, 2011.

124   Chuck's two biggest . . . : Bill Deininger interview, May 20, 2013.

124   "My grandmother was . . .": Rick Deiniger interview, May 19, 2013.

125   By 1967, he . . . : Rita Deininger interview, June 29, 2014; Joanne Deininger Mikut interview, October 7, 2014.

125   Rita, hewing to . . . : Rita Deininger interview, June 29, 2014; Marilyn Deininger Lopez, January 8, 2014.

125   From Baltimore, it . . . : Chris Noll interview, May 18, 2014.

125   The visit in . . . : Margie Deininger Ervin interview, June 24, 2015; Marilyn Deininger Lopez, January 8, 2014; Joanne Deininger Mikut interview, October 7, 2014.

126   "I absolutely love . . .": Ken Deininger interview, May 13, 2015.

127   With the 1967 . . . : Larry Harris, "Noll Back on Job," Baltimore Sun, October 31, 1967.

127   The following spring . . . : Frenchy Fuqua interview, August 24, 2013; Marianne Noll interview, February 18, 2013.

128   **The summer of . . . :** Rita Deininger interview, June 29, 2014; Marianne Noll interview, February 9, 2015.

128   **By the beginning . . . :** Gerry Sandusky interview, October 10, 2014; Upton Bell interview, April 30, 2014.

130   **Marianne and Chris . . . :** Chris Noll interview, May 12, 2015.

130   **There were worrisome . . . :** Marianne Noll interview, February 9, 2015.

131   **In the week . . . :** Tex Schramm, "Baltimore Lowers the Boom," *Sports Illustrated*, January 6, 1969.

132   **"I remember clearly . . .":** Chris Noll interview, May 12, 2015; Marianne Noll interview, February 18, 2013; Don Shula interview, April 15, 2013.

132   **By the weekend . . . :** Michael MacCambridge, *America's Game: The Epic Story of How Pro Football Captured a Nation* (New York: Random House, 2004), Kindle edition, location 5220.

132   **There was no . . . :** Dave Anderson, *Countdown to Super Bowl* (New York: Random House, 1969).

133   **By kickoff . . . :** Preston Pearson interview, April 8, 2013.

133   **Back at the . . . :** Marianne Noll interview, February 9, 2015.

134   **And when it . . . :** Dennis Gaubatz interview, October 3, 2014.

134   **When the team . . . :** Marianne Noll interview, February 9, 2015; Upton Bell interview, April 30, 2014.

134   **Volk, Chuck's prized . . . :** Rick Volk interview, July 11, 2013.

134   **Later, Chuck made . . . :** Upton Bell interview, April 30, 2014.

Chapter 10

135   **In 1933, the . . . :** Ray Didinger, *Pittsburgh Steelers* (New York: MacMillan, 1974), 10–13; Roy Blount Jr., *About Three Bricks Shy . . . and the Load Filled Up: The Story of the Greatest Football Team Ever* (Pittsburgh: University of Pittsburgh Press, 2004); Art Rooney Jr., *Ruanaidh: The Story of Art Rooney and His Clan* (Pittsburgh, 2008), 33–35; Dan Rooney, *Dan Rooney: My 75 Years with the Pittsburgh Steelers and the NFL* (New York: Da Capo, 2007), 7–37; Dan Rooney interview, March 27, 2013.

136   **For the first . . . :** Josh Katzowitz, "Remember When: Philly and Pittsburgh Merged to Form Steagles," CBSSports.com, October 11, 2013.

136   **The team's first . . . :** Michael MacCambridge, *America's Game: The Epic Story of How Pro Football Captured a Nation* (New York: Random House, 2004), Kindle edition, location 1947.

137   **Even when they . . . :** Dan Rooney interview, October 6, 2014.

137   **"I got very . . .":** Len Dawson interview, December 2, 2013; "Lions Trade Bobby Layne to Steelers," *Chicago Tribune* (special), October 7, 1958.

138   **There were further . . . :** Dick Hoak interview, July 5, 2012.

138   **Inevitably, he would . . . :** Dan Rooney interview, April 8, 2014.

139   **They made the . . . :** Dan Rooney interview, July 22, 2013.

139   **Austin's attempts to . . . :** Dick Hoak interviews, July 5, 2012; March 28, 2013.

139   **One day at . . . :** Dan Rooney interview, July 22, 2013.

140   **Nowhere was the . . . :** Ralph Berlin interview, October 21, 2013.

140   **By 1968, Bill . . . :** Rocky Bleier interview, July 2, 2012.

141   **Bill Nunn, the . . . :** Bill Nunn interview, April 7, 2014.

141   **As the losses . . . :** Ralph Berlin interview, October 21, 2013.

142   **"It was like . . .":** Andy Russell interview, September 22, 2012.

142   **Austin and Dan . . . :** Dan Rooney interview, July 22, 2013.

142   **By the time . . . :** Dan Rooney interview, July 22, 2013; Upton Bell interview, April 30, 2014.

143   **The Rooneys had . . . :** Dan Rooney interview, July 22, 2013; Marianne Noll interview, July 4, 2012.

143   **"A city of . . .":** Pat Livingston, "Noll Laughs Off Claim You Can't Win in Pittsburgh," *Pittsburgh Press*, January 28, 1968.

143   **Later that day . . . :** *Pittsburgh Steelers 1969 Media Guide.*

144   **Nunn, hoping to . . . :** Bill Nunn interview, April 7, 2014.

144   **In the draft . . . :** Bill Nunn interview, April 7, 2014; Art Rooney Jr. interview, May 19, 2014; Steve Halvonik, "Peers, Ex-Players, Praise Noll's Control," *Pittsburgh Post-Gazette*, December 27, 1991.

145   **Pitt coach Carl . . . :** Carl DePasqua, BLESTO Scouting report on Joe Greene, Pro Football Hall of Fame; Joe Greene interview, August 17, 2012.

145   **After the draft . . . :** Chris Noll interviews, December 12, 2013; May 11, 2015; Marianne Noll interview, February 8, 2015.

145   **Marianne was sold . . . :** Dan Rooney interview, April 8, 2014.

146   **By now, William . . . :** Marianne Noll interview, February 8, 2015; Rita Deininger interview, May 20, 2013.

146   **Rita found a . . . :** The agreed closing date was July 5. On July 4, a tornado swept through Lakewood, felling over 100 trees in ten minutes. An oak tree on what would be Rita's lot fell on a neighbor's Volkswagen and knocked out all of the electricity on the block, but left only a hole in one window of the house. "But we didn't own the house until the next day," said her daughter, Marilyn. "So we had nothing to do with it. It was the previous owners' responsibility. God's hand has been on my mother all of her life"; Marilyn Deininger Lopez interview, January 8, 2014; Rita Deininger interview, May 20, 2013.

147   **Lombardi's approach was . . . :** MacCambridge, *America's Game*, Kindle edition, location 4802.

147   **Many made note . . . :** Richard Whittingham, *Sunday's Heroes: NFL Legends Talk about the Times of Their Lives* (Chicago: Triumph, 2003).

148 **He would never . . . :** Andy Russell interview, September 22, 2012; Rocky Bleir interview, July 2, 2012.

148 **"Quiet," he snapped. . . . :** Andy Russell interview, September 22, 2012.

149 **"There was no . . .":** Dick Hoak interview, April 8, 2014.

149 **Chuck introduced him . . . :** Joe Greene interview, April 8, 2013.

149 **"I remember Don . . .":** Joe Greene interview, April 8, 2013; one of the choices acquired from the Saints, the fifth rounder in 1971, was used to draft longtime Steelers tight end and tackle Larry Brown.

149 **"I knew what . . .":** Bill Chastain, *Steel Dynasty: The Team That Changed the NFL* (Chicago: Triumph, 2005), Kindle edition, location 423.

150 **Before the end . . . :** Dan Rooney interview, April 8, 2014; Chuck Spatafore interview, March 25, 2013.

150 **"Roy was not . . .":** Dan Rooney interview, April 8, 2014; Roy Jefferson interview, July 13, 2013.

151 **When she was . . . :** Mariane Noll interview, October 4, 2014.

151 **"The offices were . . .":** Robert Markus, "Pittsburgh's Noll Is a Connoisseur, Too," *Chicago Tribune*, July 13, 1975.

151 **The Steelers won . . . :** Chris Noll interview, June 16, 2013.

151 **Chuck's training camp . . . :** Andy Russell interview, September 22, 2012; Tony Parisi interview, October 21, 2013.

152 **Against the Cardinals . . . :** Andy Russell interview, March 25, 2013.

152 **At home, he . . . :** Chris Noll interview, June 16, 2013.

153 **The afternoon of . . . :** Dan Rooney interview, April 8, 2014; Marianne Noll, February 8, 2015.

Chapter 11

154 **Dan Rooney offered . . . :** Bill Chastain, *Steel Dynasty: The Team That Changed the NFL* (Chicago: Triumph, 2005), Kindle edition, location 698.

154 **There was no . . . :** Scouting report on Terry Bradshaw by John Bridgers, Pro Football Hall of Fame.

155 **The offers came . . . :** Dan Rooney interview, October 6, 2014.

155 **Like many of . . . :** Mel Blount interview, March 29, 2013.

155 **"Where's my mama? . . .":** Terry Bradshaw with Buddy Martin, *Looking Deep* (Chicago: Contemporary Books, 1989), 48.

156 **In the AFC . . . :** Art Rooney II interview, April 14, 2015; Dan Rooney interview, April 8, 2014.

157 **In the off-season . . . :** Lionel Taylor interview, February 8, 2014.

157 **Chuck also hired . . . :** Lou Riecke interview, July 31, 2013.

157 **At St. Vincent . . . :** Joe Greene interview, November 18, 2013; Roy Jefferson interview, July 13, 2013; "Colts Trade Willie Richardson," *Chicago Tribune*, August 21, 1970.

158   **The whole team . . . :** Dan Rooney interview, April 8, 2014.

158   **Two days later . . . :** Ralph Berlin interview, October 21, 2013; that week, the Steelers played the Boston Patriots in Shreveport, Louisiana (it was Bradshaw's homecoming), and before going on to the field, Chuck sidled up to trainer Ralph Berlin and said, "Don't let Jefferson get hurt." The flummoxed Berlin ("I am thinking to myself, *What am I going to do? Go out on the field and protect him?*") just nodded his head.

158   **"You haven't reached . . .":** "The Steelers considered me good riddance," Jefferson said. "They felt they couldn't control me. They felt I was a menace to the team's morale. They felt I might alienate the players against the coaches. I was the team player representative. Maybe that influenced them. I don't know for sure" (Marty Rabolvsky, *Super Bowl: Of Men, Myths, and Moments* [New York: Hawthorne, 1971], 167).

158   **For Jefferson's teammates . . . :** Frenchy Fuqua interview, August 24, 2013; Andy Russell interview, June 11, 2015; "Coach Noll would say, 'Look, if any of you break my rules, I will fire you, you will be gone,'" said Andy Russell. "So my reaction when I heard about the trade was, 'Well, Roy just didn't follow the rules.'"

158   **The first football . . . :** NFL Films, 1970 Pittsburgh Steelers Highlight Films (Mt. Laurel, NJ: NFL Films Archives).

158   **That afternoon, Chuck . . . :** [citation needed]

159   **"Terry always revved . . .":** Not for attribution interview, circa 2013.

159   **The maturity didn't . . . :** Joe Greene interview, April 8, 2013; Tony Parisi interview, October 21, 2013.

160   **At a time . . . :** Frenchy Fuqua interview, August 24, 2013.

161   **"Bradshaw needed help . . .":** Ralph Berlin interview, October 21, 2013.

161   **After the Steelers . . . :** Terry Bradshaw with Buddy Martin, *Looking Deep* (Chicago: Contemporary Books, 1989), 22.

161   **By the middle . . . :** Preston Pearson interview, April 8, 2013.

161   **Of his rookie . . . :** Terry Bradshaw with David Fisher, *It's Only a Game* (New York: Pocket Books, 2001), Kindle edition, location 56.

162   **On the bus . . . :** Ralph Berlin interview, October 21, 2013.

162   **The last game . . . :** Andy Russell interview, March 25, 2013; Joe Greene interview, April 8, 2013.

163   **On January 21 . . . :** Art Rooney Jr. interview, May 19, 2014; Marianne Noll interview, June 2, 2014.

163   **The funeral a . . . :** Ken Deininger interview, November 2, 2013; Margie Deininger Ervin interview, November 2, 2012; Rita Deininger interview, August 14, 2014.

163   **The loss of . . . :** Ken Deininger interview, November 2, 2013.

163   **"When he came . . .":** Marilyn Deininger Lopez, January 8, 2014.

163   **It would be . . . :** "Walt Hacktt Dies, Steeler Line Coach," *Pittsburgh Press*, April 25, 1971.

164   **Chuck had already . . . :** Babe Parilli interview, August 27, 2014.

164   **The coach remained . . . :** Rocky Bleier interview, July 2, 2012.

164   **The humor was . . . :** Warren Bankston interview, February 4, 2014.

165   **Another morning at . . . :** Jon Kolb interview, October 21, 2013.

166   **By this point . . . :** Dan Rooney, *Dan Rooney: My 75 Years with the Pittsburgh Steelers and the NFL* (New York: Da Capo, 2007), Kindle edition, location 4732.

166   **But it went . . . :** [find citation—Myslenski]

167   **"I thought, I . . .":** Jack Ham interview, March 26, 2013.

167   **In the third . . . :** Chastain, *Steel Dynasty*, Kindle edition, location 942; Tex Maule, "No Paralysis Is the Analysis," *Sports Illustrated*, October 11, 1971.

167   **They hadn't entirely . . . :** Len Dawson interview, December 2, 2013.

167   **Back home in . . . :** Chris Noll interview, May 12, 2015.

167   **"Now that, in . . .":** Rocky Bleier interview, March 28, 2013.

168   **There was some . . . :** Dan Radakovich interview, March 28, 2013.

168   **White was sensitive . . . :** Lionel Taylor interview, February 8, 2014.

169   **Artie, though, was . . . :** Art Rooney Jr., Pittsburgh Steelers Senior Scouting Report Form on Franco Harris, October 20, 1971, Pro Football Hall of Fame, Canton, OH.

169   **"Artie did not . . .":** Dan Rooney interview, October 6, 2014.

169   **So Chuck and . . . :** Art Rooney Jr. interview, May 19, 2014.

170   **Through BLESTO, the . . . :** Dick Haley interview, February 25, 2014.

170   **"Tell Chuck that . . .":** Art Rooney Jr. interview, May 19, 2014.

170   **As the '72 . . . :** Bill Nunn interview, April 7, 2014; Dan Rooney interview, October 6, 2014.

171   **"He's gonna be . . .":** Dan Rooney interview, October 6, 2014; Art Rooney Jr. interview, May 19, 2014.

171   **After the draft . . . :** Robert Markus, "Pittsbugh's Noll Is a Connoisseur, Too," *Chicago Tribune*, July 13, 1975.

171   **"Chuck said he . . . :** Marianne Noll interview, September 30, 2015.

Chapter 12

172   **At Eisenhower Middle . . . :** Chris Noll interview, August 28, 2012.

172   **Before training camp . . . :** Chris Noll interview, November 3, 2013; Marianne Noll interview, September 30, 2014.

173   **Chris didn't complain . . . :** Chris Noll interview, November 3, 2013; Bob McCartney interview, May 19, 2014. McCartney would later become the Steelers' video coordinator. Bill Nunn's son, Bill Nunn Jr., would pursue act-

ing. In 1989 he played the pivotal role of Radio Raheem in Spike Lee's *Do the Right Thing.*

173   **The biggest change . . . :** Linda Carson interview, April 25, 2014; Bill Chastain, *Steel Dynasty: The Team That Changed the NFL* (Chicago: Triumph, 2005), Kindle edition, location 1022.

174   **"The day of . . .":** Linda Carson interview, April 25, 2014.

174   **Chuck also hired . . . :** George Perles interview, July 25, 2012.

175   **"All I know . . .":** George Perles interview, August 25, 2013.

175   **That preseason, Chuck . . . :** Dick Hoak interview, April 8, 2014.

176   **The 1972 campaign . . . :** Jack Ham interview, March 26, 2013.

176   **From the sidelines . . . :** Joe Greene interview, November 18, 2013.

176   **The statement victory . . . :** Dick Hoak interview, April 8, 2014; there were extenuating circumstances (decades later, some of the retired Chiefs were still angry that a Steelers' groupie had infiltrated the hotel and managed to seduce more than one of the Chiefs' offensive players the night before the game).

177   **After a narrow . . . :** Chastain, *Steel Dynasty*, location 1075.

177   **As the Steelers . . . :** Chastain, *Steel Dynasty*, location 1183.

177   **They routed Cleveland . . . :** John Husar, "Joe Greene Is Really Not Mean . . . Just Ornery," *Chicago Tribune*, November 14, 1975.

178   **"I've never seen . . .":** Skip Myslenski, "Steelers Noll Doesn't Want Sour Apples," *Philadelphia Inquirer*, August 14, 1973.

178   **There was elation . . . :** "Steelers Win 1st Title in 40 Years," *Pittsburgh Post-Gazette*, December 18, 1972; Myslenski, "Steelers Noll Doesn't Want Sour Apples."

178   **On the field . . . :** Claudine McGee interview, July 30, 2013.

179   **The two defenses . . . :** Andy Russell interview, June 11, 2015; Michael K. Bohn, "Forty Years Later, Immaculate Reception Still a Source of Debate," *Miami Herald*, December 21, 2012.

179   **Among the Steelers' . . . :** Glen Edwards interview, February 19, 2013.

179   **"I remember standing . . .":** Andy Russell interview, June 11, 2015.

179   **Terry Hanratty, standing . . . :** Roy Blount Jr., *About Three Bricks Shy of a Load: A Highly Irregular Lowdown on the Year the Pittsburgh Steelers Were Super but Missed the Bowl* (Boston: Little, Brown, 1974), Kindle edition, location 1253; Terry Hanratty interview, June 18, 2013.

179   **Chuck sent in . . . :** Paul Zeise, "Steelers Receiver Barry Pearson Came Away from 'The Play' with a Great Story to Tell," *Pittsburgh Post-Gazette*, October 12, 2014.

180   **Chris Noll was . . . :** Chris Noll interview, May 18, 2014.

180   **Afterward, other Steelers . . . :** John Dockery interview, January 22, 2014.

180 (**The NFL remained** . . . : Chastain, *Steel Dynasty*, Kindle edition, location 1354.

181 **Pittsburgh was in** . . . : Mike Freeman, *Undefeated: Inside the 1972 Dolphins' Perfect Season* (New York: It Books, 2012), 184.

181 **As the game** . . . : Freeman, *Undefeated*, 184.

181 **Less a product** . . . : Don Shula interview, April 15, 2013.

181 **"That fake punt** . . ."**: Glen Edwards interview, February 19, 2013.

182 **"Walking off that** . . ."**: Chastain, *Steel Dynasty*, Kindle edition, location 1551.

182 **But over the** . . . : Joe Greene interview, November 18, 2013.

182 **A few days** . . . : Not for attribution interview, circa 2013.

183 **It was six** . . . : [Blount]; Marianne Noll interview, February 8, 2015.

183 **Chuck had begun** . . . : Woody Widenhofer interview, January 24, 2015.

184 **"You know, what** . . ."**: John Brown interview, March 25, 2013.

184 **By the third** . . . : John Dockery interview, January 22, 2014.

185 **Parilli still loved** . . . : Dick Hoak interview, March 28, 2013.

185 **The good cop** . . . : Babe Parilli interview, August 27, 2014.

185 **"You could just** . . ."**: Mike Wagner interview, March 27, 2013.

185 **"I don't think** . . ."**: Gerry Mullins interview, April 7, 2014.

185 **One of Chuck's** . . . : Terry Bradshaw with Buddy Martin, *Looking Deep* (Chicago: Contemporary Books, 1989), 19.

185 **Others viewed it** . . . : Jack Ham interview, October 22, 2013.

186 **"Terry, why do** . . ."**: Andy Russell interview, June 11, 2015.

186 **Receivers would have** . . . : Chastain, *Steel Dynasty*, Kindle edition, location 1608.

186 **Bradshaw knew Chuck** . . . : Myslenski, "Steelers Noll Doesn't Want Sour Apples."

186 **Privately, he often** . . . : Mike Wagner interview, March 27, 2013.

186 **"He put up** . . ."**: Andy Russell interview, June 11, 2015.

187 **"Chuck was carrot** . . ."**: Mike Wagner interview, March 27, 2013.

187 **"Joe was the** . . ."**: Ralph Berlin interview, October 21, 2013.

187 **The most surprising** . . . : Roy Blount Jr. interview, May 13, 2015.

187 **"Chuck was against** . . ."**: Dan Rooney interview, November 17, 2015.

187 **"I never heard** . . ."**: John Dockery interview, January 22, 2014; Woody Widenhofer interview, January 24, 2015.

188 **Some other writers** . . . : Jack Ham interview, October 22, 2013.

188 **For Blount, who** . . . : Roy Blount Jr. interview, March 27, 2013.

189 **The season began** . . . : Myslenski, "Steelers Noll Doesn't Want Sour Apples."

189 **Throwing against the** . . . : Roy Blount Jr., *About Three Bricks Shy . . . : and the Load Filled Up: The Story of the Greatest Football Team Ever* (Pittsburgh: University of Pittsburgh Press, 2004), 179.

190   **"It took getting . . .":** Blount Jr., *About Three Bricks Shy . . . : and the Load Filled Up*, 230.

190   **The dynamic in . . . :** Terry Hanratty interview, June 18, 2013; John Clayton, "Doing It His Way: Noll Goes by the Playbook, but It Is Missing a Chapter on Socializing with Players," *Pittsburgh Press*, December 25, 1983.

190   **"It was funny . . .":** Paul Zimmerman, "The Teacher," *Sports Illustrated*, July 28, 1980.

191   **"We're too good . . .":** Blount Jr., *About Three Bricks Shy . . . : and the Load Filled Up*, 256.

Chapter 13

192   **As they prepared . . . :** Art Rooney Jr. interviews, July 5, 2012; May 19, 2014.

192   **But other times . . . :** Roy Blount Jr., *About Three Bricks Shy . . . : and the Load Filled Up: The Story of the Greatest Football Team Ever* (Pittsburgh: University of Pittsburgh Press, 2004), 266.

193   **Chuck was churlish . . . :** Art Rooney Jr. interview, May 19, 2014; Dick Haley interview, February 25, 2014.

193   **In so doing . . . :** Gary Pomerantz, *Their Life's Work: The Brotherhood of the 1970s Pittsburgh Steelers, Then and Now* (New York: Simon and Schuster, 2013), Kindle edition, location 1799.

194   **In the second . . . :** Woody Widenhofer interview, January 27, 2015.

195   **"People—including a . . .":** Roy Blount Jr., *About Three Bricks Shy of a Load: A Highly Irregular Lowdown on the Year the Pittsburgh Steelers Were Super but Missed the Bowl* (Boston: Little, Brown, 1974), Kindle edition, location 307.

197   **"We heard that . . .":** Ray Didinger, *The Super Bowl: Celebrating a Quarter Century of America's Greatest Game* (New York: Simon and Schuster, 1990), 161.

197   **The 1973 season . . . :** John Brown interview, March 25, 2013.

197   **"Elvin Bethea of . . .":** Jon Kolb interview, April 7, 2013.

198   **The coaching staff . . . :** Joe Greene interview, November 18, 2013.

198   **When Pearson entered . . . :** Preston Pearson interview, April 8, 2013.

199   **The rookies reported . . . :** Bob Whitley, "Walden Crosses Picket Line, Mum on Why," *Pittsburgh Post-Gazette*, July 17, 1974.

199   **As a rule . . . :** Bill Nunn interview, July 3, 2012; Chris Noll interview, November 3, 2013.

200   **"You're going to . . .":** Paul Zimmerman, "The Teacher," *Sports Illustrated*, July 28, 1980; Terry Bradshaw with Buddy Martin, *Looking Deep* (Chicago: Contemporary Books, 1989), 37.

200   **The decision reverberated . . . :** J. T. Thomas interview, October 22, 2013.

200   **The season opened . . . :** *Sports Illustrated*, September 23, 1974.

200 **A week later . . . :** Jon Kolb interview, April 7, 2013.

201 **"Most quarterbacks are . . .":** J. T. Thomas interview, October 22, 2013; Jon Kolb interview, April 7, 2013.

201 **"Most teams, if . . .":** Rocky Bleier interview, July 2, 2012.

202 **It wasn't until . . . :** John Stallworth interview, March 31, 2014.

202 **"So the stories . . .":** Rocky Bleier interview, July 2, 2012.

202 **With Bradshaw, Pittsburgh . . . :** Vito Stellino, "Quarter-Bucks Stop at Noll," *Pittsburgh Post-Gazette*, October 30, 1974.

202 **A week later . . . :** Dave Fink, "Bengals Lance Steelers, 17–10, to Tighten Race," *Pittsburgh Post-Gazette*, November 11, 1974.

203 **Chuck refused to . . . :** Dan Rooney interview, April 8, 2014; Joe Greene interview, July 28, 2014.

203 **"If we are . . .":** George Perles interview, July 25, 2012; Woody Widenhofer interview, March 4, 2013.

203 **To the press . . . :** David Fink, "Silence Is Golden as Noll Picks QB," *Pittsburgh Post-Gazette*, November 23, 1974.

204 **While the quarterback . . . :** "SpOilers Stun Pittsburgh 13–10," *Chicago Tribune*, December 2, 1974.

204 **The frustration had . . . :** Joe Greene interviews, August 17, 2012; July 28, 2014; January 26, 2015.

204 **"The first thing . . .":** Lionel Taylor interview, October 9, 2015.

205 **The crucial moment . . . :** Glen Edwards interview, February 19, 2013.

205 **The next week . . . :** Dan Jenkins, "For Openers, Super Bowl VIII 1/2," *Sports Illustrated*, December 23, 1974.

205 **Chuck spent some . . . :** Rocky Bleier interview, July 2, 2012.

206 **The playoffs began . . . :** Joe Greene interview, August 27, 2012; George Perles interviews, July 25, 2012; August 25, 2013; Dan Rooney, *Dan Rooney: My 75 Years with the Pittsburgh Steelers and the NFL* (New York: Da Capo, 2007), Kindle edition, location 2597.

207 **"We're happy to . . .":** Ed Bouchette, "Pittsburgh Runs Herd over Buffalo Bills," *Indiana* (PA) *Gazette*, December 23, 1974.

207 **By Monday morning . . . :** Roy Blount Jr., *About Three Bricks Shy . . . : and the Load Filled Up*, 266; George Perles interview, July 25, 2012; Marianne Noll interview, July 4, 2012; Joe Greene interview, July 28, 2014.

207 **"It wasn't long" . . . :** Jack Ham interview, July 6, 2012.

208 **On Christmas Day . . . :** Associated Press, "Mrs. Chuck Noll—Wife, Mother, Fan," *Cleveland Plain Dealer*, January 11, 1975; Marianne Noll interview, February 9, 2015; Chris Noll interview, June 6, 2016.

208 **In the build-up . . . :** "Steelers Ready for 'Hostility,'" *New York Times*, December 29, 1974.

208   **That Sunday afternoon . . . :** Joe Greene interview, July 28, 2014; J. T. Thomas interview, October 22, 2013; Glen Edwards interview, February 19, 2013.

208   **The reception at . . . :** Regis Stefanik, "Celebrating Fans Crowd Triangle," *Pittsburgh Post-Gazette*, December 30, 1974.

209   **"So the meeting goes . . .":** Rocky Bleier interview, July 2, 2012; Joe Greene interview, April 8, 2013; Andy Russell interview, March 25, 2013.

209   **There was a . . . :** Dick Hoak interview, March 28, 2013; Dan Radakovich interview, January 23, 2014.

209   **On the eve . . . :** Patricia Rooney interview, April 8, 2014; Marianne Noll interview, October 5, 2014.

210   **It poured down . . . :** Tony Parisi interview, October 21, 2013; Joe Greene interview, April 8, 2013.

210   **"Play the way . . .":** Jack Ham interview, March 26, 2013; Joe Greene interview, April 8, 2013.

210   **In the tunnel . . . :** . Glen Edwards interview, February 19, 2013.

210   **The Vikings had . . . :** Bob McGinn, *The Ultimate Super Bowl Book: A Complete Reference to the Stats, Stars, and Stories behind Football's Biggest Game—and Why the Best Team Won*, 2nd ed. (Minneapolis: MVP Books, 2012), 70.

211   **Bradshaw was unabashed . . . :** Pomerantz, *Their Life's Work*, Kindle edition, location 2909.

211   **The Vikings were . . . :** Andy Russell interview, June 11, 2015; Joe Greene interview, April 8, 2013.

212   **On the sidelines . . . :** Bradshaw, *Looking Deep*, 128.

212   **Joe Greene had . . . :** Blount Jr., *About Three Bricks Shy . . . and the Load Filled Up*, 262.

212   **In the commotion . . . :** Jack Ham interview, March 26, 2013.

213   **All through the . . . :** Andy Russell interview, June 11, 2015.

213   **"It was one . . .":** Chris Noll interview, May 12, 2015.

213   **Chuck wasn't totally . . . :** Didinger, *The Super Bowl*, 164.

213   **On NBC's Super . . . :** NFL Films and NFL Network, *America's Game: The Super Bowl Champions. Pittsburgh Steelers Collection, Super Bowl IX* (Burbank: Warner Home Video, 2007).

214   **The day after . . . :** David Fink, "Steelers Calmly Accept Plaudits," *Pittsburgh Post-Gazette*, January 14, 1975.

214   **A few weeks . . . :** Mariannne Noll interview, February 9, 2015; Dan Rooney interview, October 6, 2014.

214   **Chuck loved it. . . . :** Mariannne Noll interview, February 9, 2015; Lionel Taylor interview, August 30, 2012.

215   **It was also . . . :** Robert Markus, "Pittsburgh's Noll Is a Connoisseur, Too," *Chicago Tribune*, July 13, 1975.

215   **That summer, on . . . :** Chris Noll interview, May 12, 2015.

215   **For his part . . . :** Zimmerman, "The Teacher."

216   **Even going out . . . :** Marianne Noll interview, February 23, 2014.

216   **"Pittsburgh has this . . .":** Patricia Rooney interview, April 8, 2014.

Chapter 14

217   **Sunday nights in . . . :** Dan Rooney interview, April 8, 2014; Patrick Manning interview, April 12, 2015; Marianne Noll interview, October 5, 2014; Joanne Deininger Mikut interview, April 5, 2014.

217   **"It was very . . .":** Patricia Rooney interview, April 8, 2014.

218   **Others on the . . . :** John Brown interview, March 25, 2013.

218   **By 1974, Chuck . . . :** John Manning interview, April 12, 2015; Patrick Manning interview, April 12, 2015; Marianne Noll interview, October 5, 2014.

218   **"They even looked . . .":** Fr. Tom Kredel interview, April 13, 2015.

218   **And their husbands . . . :** Patrick Manning interview, April 12, 2015.

219   **Golfing, the two . . . :** John Manning interview, November 18, 2015; Patrick Manning interview, November 18, 2015; Marianne Noll interview, October 5, 2014.

220   **For Red Manning . . . :** John Manning interview, November 18, 2015.

220   **In the late . . . :** Ken Deininger interview, November 2, 2103; Chris Noll interview, May 12, 2015.

221   **"They are best . . .":** Chris Noll interview, June 16, 2013.

221   **"For entertainment, he . . .":** Chris Noll interview, June 16, 2013; television was rarely on in the Nolls' household and almost never on football. "PBS or a nature series, that kind of stuff," said Chris. "I used to tease him about it, because he was so straitlaced. I would ask what dirty movie he was watching —you know, wildlife."

221   **One day in . . . :** Ken Deininger interview, June 16, 2013.

222   **"He never read . . .":** Chris Noll interview, June 16, 2013.

222   **The work week . . . :** Marianne Noll interview, October 5, 2014; Chris Noll interview, May 12, 2015.

222   **The discussions of . . . :** Marianne Noll, February 9, 2015; Chris Noll interview, June 16, 2016.

223   **His father's job . . . :** Chris Noll interview, August 28, 2012.

223   **Chris, loyal but . . . :** Chris Noll interview, June 16, 2016.

223   **"You know, you . . .":** Andy Russell interview, June 11, 2015; Mike Wagner interview, October 7, 2014; Jack Ham interview, March 26, 2013.

224   **It had been . . . :** Frenchy Fuqua interview, August 24, 2013.

224   **With the division . . . :** Rocky Bleier interview, July 2, 2012; Terry Bradshaw with Buddy Martin, *Looking Deep* (Chicago: Contemporary Books, 1989), 104–5.

225 **Chuck hadn't seen . . . :** Lionel Taylor interviews, February 8, 2014; October 9, 2015.

225 **Gilliam continued behaving . . . :** Joe Greene interview, April 8, 2013.

225 **"Terry Hanratty and . . .":** Bradshaw, *Looking Deep*, 104–5.

225 **"Chuck's background might . . .":** Lionel Taylor interview, February 8, 2014.

225 **Gilliam was late . . . :** Frenchy Fuqua interview, August 24, 2013.

225 **The Gilliam saga . . . :** Art Rooney Jr. interview, May 19, 2014.

226 **As the 1975 . . . :** Joe Gordon interview, October 5, 2014.

226 **The Steelers beat . . . :** Robert Markus, "Pittsburgh Defense 'Wins,' 28–10," *Chicago Tribune*, December 28, 1975.

226 **The next week . . . :** Peter Richmond, *Badasses: The Legend of Snake, Foo, Dr. Death, and John Madden's Oakland Raiders* (New York: Harper, 2010), 257.

226 **Afterward, reflecting on . . . :** Richmond, *Badasses*, 262; Robert Markus, "Bradshaw, Up from the Ashes, Gets Zapped Again," *Chicago Tribune*, January 5, 1976.

226 **They enjoyed it . . . :** Jack Ham interview, July 6, 2012.

227 **The Cowboys pass . . . :** Phil Musick, "A Classic Shootout for Men Only," in *The Super Bowl: Celebrating a Quarter-Century of America's Greatest Game*, ed. Ray Didinger (New York: Simon and Schuster, 1990), 172.

228 **"This reminds me . . .":** Joe Greene interview, July 28, 2014; Jack Ham interview, March 26, 2013; Andy Russell interview, April 14, 2014.

228 **The stylistic contrasts . . . :** Musick, "A Classic Shootout for Men Only," 173.

228 **But Chuck brought . . . :** Jack Ham interview, March 26, 2013; Andy Russell interview, April 14, 2014.

229 **Dallas went up . . . :** Mike Wagner interview, March 27, 2013.

229 **George Perles, next . . . :** Bob McGinn, *The Ultimate Super Bowl Book: A Complete Reference to the Stats, Stars, and Stories behind Football's Biggest Game— and Why the Best Team Won*, 2nd ed. (Minneapolis: MVP Books, 2012), 78.

230 **He sent Hanratty . . . :** Dan Radakovich, *Bad Rad* (Moon Township: Touchdown Books, 2012), 75.

230 **Bleier would be . . . :** McGinn, *The Ultimate Super Bowl Book*, 78.

230 **"We had a . . .":** Leonard Shapiro, "Steelers Retain Super Bowl Crown," *Washington Post*, January 19, 1976.

230 **Most of the . . . :** Glen Edwards interview, February 19, 2013.

230 **In the postgame . . . :** David Fink, "Cowboy Mistake: Riling Lambert," *Pittsburgh Post-Gazette*, January 19, 1976.

231 **By the end . . . :** Dale Grdnic, *Tales from the Pittsburgh Steelers Sideline: A Collection of the Greatest Steelers Stories Ever Told* (New York: Sports Pub., 2013), 102.

Chapter 15

232 **On the first . . . :** Dan Rooney interview, July 22, 2013.

232 **They had come . . . :** Harold Meyerson, "The State of Work in the Age of Anxiety: The Forty-Year Slump," *American Prospect*, November 12, 2013.

233 **After the Super . . . :** Phil Musick, "A Classic Shootout-for Men Only," in *The Super Bowl: Celebrating a Quarter Century of America's Greatest Game*, ed. Ray Didinger (New York: Simon and Schuster, 1990), 171.

233 **Chuck had reached . . . :** Dan Radakovich interview, March 28, 2013; Jack Ham interviews, March 26, 2013; November 17, 2015; Mike Wagner interviews, October 7, 2014; November 17, 2015; Joe Greene interview, November 17, 2015; Joe Gordon interview, November 18, 2015; Dan Rooney interview, November 17, 2015. In his rambling memoir *Bad Rad*, Radakovich said that in the weeks after Super Bowl X, he was summoned to a meeting with Jack Ham and Mike Wagner at Station Square—they had pointedly wanted to meet "away from the office." At the meeting, Radakovich said that Ham and Wagner asked him to prevail upon Chuck to keep the erratic Joe Gilliam. Concerned about Bradshaw's frequent injuries, they felt that Gilliam could be essential to winning a third Super Bowl. A few days later, in Chuck's office, Radakovich conveyed the message. "Chuck said it didn't matter what those guys thought," said Radakovich. "Joe Gilliam had to go. He said a group of black players had come to him and told him that they wanted Joe out of here." Dan Radakovich, *Bad Rad* (Moon Township: Touchdown Books, 2012), 80. (Later, Wagner and Ham didn't recall meeting with Radakovich, and neither Greene nor any other defensive starters recalled a meeting in which they insisted on Gilliam's ouster. Radakovich remained adamant that the meeting took place.)

233 **Meanwhile, Chuck's now-entrenched . . . :** Terry Bradshaw with Buddy Martin, *Looking Deep* (Chicago: Contemporary Books, 1989), 199.

233 **In the off-season . . . :** Bradshaw, *Looking Deep*, 194.

233 **Though Chuck was . . . :** Ken Deininger interview, November 2, 2013; Chris Noll interview, June 6, 2015.

235 **Then the Oakland . . . :** Dick Hoak interview, April 8, 2014.

235 **Jack Ham had . . . :** Jack Ham interview, March 26, 2013.

235 **Chuck was already . . . :** Bob Labriola, "Trial Was Theater of the Absurd," *Steelers Digest*, June 5, 2011.

236 **Dan Rooney had . . . :** Joe Gordon interview, October 5, 2014; Dan Rooney interview, April 8, 2014.

237 **In the locker . . . :** Dan Rooney, *Dan Rooney: My 75 Years with the Pittsburgh Steelers and the NFL* (New York: Da Capo, 2007), Kindle edition, location 3041.

237   **Meeting with the . . . :** George Perles interview, August 25, 2013; Dick Hoak interview, November 18, 2015.

237   **The next week . . . :** Lionel Taylor interview, February 8, 2014.

238   **By the end . . . :** Peter King, *The Season After: Are Sports Dynasties Dead?* (New York: Warner, 1989), 57.

238   **It was after . . . :** Labriola, "Trial Was Theater of the Absurd."

238   **"You know I . . .":** Raw footage from interview conducted with Chuck Noll, NFL Films Archive, Mount Laurel, NJ.

239   **"It would be . . .":** Joe Browne interview, June 17, 2013.

239   **The NFL's annual . . . :** Dick Hoak interview, March 28, 2013.

240   **"Tex would come . . .":** Don Shula interview, April 15, 2013.

240   **"If you look . . .":** Mike Brown interview, November 11, 2013.

241   **In addition to . . . :** Woody Widenhofer interview, September 30, 2015; Dan Rooney interview, November 17, 2015; Lionel Taylor interview, October 9, 2015; not for attribution interview, circa 2015.

241   **To replace Taylor . . . :** George Perles interview, August 25, 2013.

241   **It was a . . . :** Joe Greene interview, July 28, 2014.

242   **"That is something . . .":** Don Shula interview, April 15, 2013.

242   **Two days before . . . :** Charles A. Kerr letter to Chuck Noll, July 6, 1977, Noll family private collection.

242   **"It was just . . .":** Marianne Noll interview, February 9, 2015.

242   **"We felt we . . .":** William Oscar Johnson, "A Walk on the Sordid Side," *Sports Illustrated*, August 1, 1977.

242   **For players like . . . :** Rocky Bleier interview, October 7, 2014; Franco Harris interview, July 23, 2013.

242   **Over the course . . . :** Vito Stellino, "Noll: 3 Steelers among NFL's 'Criminal Element,'" *Pittsburgh Post-Gazette*, July 14, 1977; Ron Rosen, "Trial Brings Out Blount Sins," *Washington Post*, July 14, 1977; Associated Press, "Noll Rips Steelers," *Uniontown* (PA) *Morning Herald*, July 14, 1977.

243   **Back home in . . . :** Joe Greene interview, July 28, 2014; Mel Blount interview, March 29, 2013.

243   **The trial lasted . . . :** Rooney, *Dan Rooney*, Kindle edition, location 3146.

243   **Summarizing the trial . . . :** Johnson, "A Walk on the Sordid Side."

243   **"I would tell . . .":** Glen Edwards interview, February 19, 2013.

244   **While Blount was . . . :** Mel Blount interview, March 29, 2013; Joe Gordon interview, October 5, 2014.

244   **"We never was . . .":** Associated Press, "Blount Ends Holdout," *Spokane Spokesman-Review*, September 16, 1977.

244   **The second day . . . :** Tony Dungy interview, August 21, 2012; Tom Moore interview, February 10, 2014.

245 **In July, he . . . :** Tony Dungy interview, August 21, 2012.
245 **The Steelers had . . . :** Tom Moore Interview, February 10, 2014.
245 **Edwards gave him . . . :** Glen Edwards interview, February 19, 2013.
245 **That training camp . . . :** Frenchy Fuqua interview, August 24, 2013.
245 **For the rookie . . . :** Tony Dungy interviews, February 24, 2014; February 10, 2014.
246 **For most of . . . :** Marianne Noll interview, October 5, 2014.
247 **Defensively, Chuck . . . :** Tony Dungy interview, February 10, 2015; Woody Widenhofer interview, January 24, 2015.
247 **In Houston, in . . . :** Tony Dungy interview, February 24, 2014; Tom Moore interview, February 10, 2014.
247 **They were good . . . :** George Perles interview, August 25, 2013.
248 **Joe Greene, weighing . . . :** Phil Musick, "A Unique Victory Message," *Pittsburgh Post-Gazette*, December 19, 1977.
248 **Broncos' coach Red . . . :** Woody Widenhofer interview, January 24, 2015; Dick Hoak interview, March 28, 2013.
248 **"I remember the . . .":** Ken Deininger interview, May 13, 2015.
249 **For new players . . . :** Sam Topperoff, *Lost Sundays: A Season in the Life of Pittsburgh and the Steelers* (New York: Random House, 1989), 99.
249 **Vito Stellino, writing . . . :** Vito Stellino, "The End of an Era for Fading Steelers," *Pittsburgh Post-Gazette*, December 26, 1977.

Chapter 16

250 **It was midway . . . :** Art Rooney Jr. interview, May 19, 2014.
251 **"Terry never stayed . . .":** Not for attribution interview, circa 2014.
251 **"We were normally . . .":** Cliff Stoudt interview, August 18, 2013.
252 **For Chuck, it . . . :** Marianne Noll interview, February 9, 2015; John Clayton, "Doing It His Way: Noll Goes by the Playbook, but It Is Missing a Chapter on Socializing with Players," *Pittsburgh Press*, December 25, 1983; not for attribution interview, circa 2014.
252 **"I never saw . . .":** Jack Ham interview, March 26, 2013.
252 **"I don't ever . . .":** Cliff Stoudt interview, August 18, 2013.
252 **Many players remembered . . . :** Gary Dunn interview, April 15, 2013.
253 **The rule was . . . :** Tom Moore interview, July 7, 2014.
253 **On June 1 . . . :** John Clayton, "Steelers Secret Slips Out," *Pittsburgh Press*, June 1, 1978.
254 **During the interview . . . :** Paul Zimmerman, "The Teacher," *Sports Illustrated*, July 28, 1980.
254 **Despite the controversy . . . :** Dan Rooney interview, October 6, 2014.
255 **Widenhofer was going . . . :** Woody Widenhofer interview, January 24,

2015; Tony Dungy interview, February 10, 2015; Sam Toperoff, *Lost Sundays: A Season in the Life of Pittsburgh and the Steelers* (New York: Random House, 1989), 99.

255   **Well, not everyone. . . . :** Glen Edwards interview February 19, 2013.

255   **"It was almost . . .":** Ron Johnson interview, August 24, 2013.

256   **Now, with the . . . :** Tony Dungy interview, February 10, 2015.

256   **"We don't care . . .":** Tony Dungy interview, February 10, 2015.

256   **"Chuck was just . . .":** Tony Dungy interview, February 24, 2014.

257   **"Tell the defense . . .":** Tom Moore interview, August 21, 2012.

257   **"Weather is a . . .":** Ritter Collett, "Steelers Reflect Noll's Personality," *Dayton Journal-Herald*, January 9, 1979.

257   **There was a . . . :** Tony Dungy interview, February 24, 2014.

258   **The Super Bowl . . . :** Don Shula interview, April 15, 2013; Gerry Sandusky interview, October 10, 2014.

258   **Many in the . . . :** George Perles interview, August 25, 2012; Dick Hoak interview, March 28, 2013; Chris Noll interview, May 12, 2015.

258   **Added to that . . . :** Ed Steigerwald interview, November 2, 2014; Pete Schreiber interview, November 2, 2014.

259   **"None of that . . .":** George Perles interview, August 25, 2012.

259   **"Chuck did not . . .":** Gary Dunn interview, April 15, 2013.

259   **In the locker . . . :** Gary Dunn interview, April 15, 2013; Tom Moore interview, August 21, 2012; Jack Ham interview, March 26, 2013.

259   **On the field . . . :** Terry Bradshaw with Buddy Martin, *Looking Deep* (Chicago: Contemporary Books, 1989), 139.

260   **Forged in the . . . :** Tom Moore interview, August 21, 2012; Gerry Mullins interview, October 7, 2015.

260   **The Cowboys were . . . :** Greg Aiello interview, June 17, 2013.

260   **The Steelers had . . . :** Marilyn Lopez Deininger interview, November 2, 2014; Ed Steigerwald interview, November 2, 2014; Pete Schreiber interview, November 2, 2014.

261   **After Rooney thanked . . . :** NFL Films and NFL Network, *America's Game: The Super Bowl Champions. Pittsburgh Steelers Collection, Super Bowl XIII* (Burbank: Warner Home Video, 2007).

261   **"I remember in . . .":** Gary Dunn interview, April 15, 2013.

261   **"Hey, this is . . .":** Tony Dungy interview, February 24, 2014.

Chapter 17

262   **After the third . . . :** Blanton Collier letter to Chuck Noll, January 22, 1978. The letter was actually sent on January 22, 1979, as it referred to events in Super Bowl XIII, played January 21, 1979.

263   **Having returned to . . . :** Marianne Noll interview, October 4, 2014; Dan Rooney interview, April 8, 2014; Chris Noll interview, June 6, 2016.

263   **Back in Cleveland . . . :** Rita Deininger interview, September 11, 2013; Marianne Noll interviews, June 2, 2014; September 30, 2015; Joanne Deininger Mikut interviews, August 23, 2012; October 7, 2014; November 17, 2015.

263   **Marianne talked it . . . :** Marianne Noll interview, June 2, 2014; Joanne Deininger Mikut interview, August 23, 2012.

263   **Joanne liked being . . . :** Joanne Deininger Mikut interview, August 23, 2012.

264   **Joanne would witness . . . :** Marianne Noll interview, June 2, 2014.

264   **By the time . . . :** Joanne Deininger Mikut interview, August 23, 2012.

264   **The company that . . . :** Actually, the second Super Bowl ring was manufactured by LG Balfour Jewelry company, owing at least in part to the fact that former Steeler Jack Wiley was an executive for the company; Peter King, *The Season After: Are Sports Dynasties Dead?* (New York: Warner, 1989), 55.

264   **As Chuck returned . . . :** Mike Herney in *St. Petersburg Times*, January 21, 1980.

265   **As he came . . . :** Marianne Noll interview, June 2, 2014.

265   **What was clear . . . :** George Perles interview, August 25, 2013; Woody Widenhofer interview, March 4, 2013.

265   **"People thought Chuck . . .":** Ralph Berlin interview, October 21, 2013.

265   **But even in . . . :** Tony Dungy interview, August 21, 2012.

266   **"First game of . . .":** Not for attribution interview, circa 2013; Rocky Bleier interview, October 7, 2014; Dick Hoak interview, April 8, 2014; Mike Wagner interview, October 7, 2014; Jack Lambert interview, May 15, 2014.

267   **The offense noticed . . . :** John Stallworth interview, March 31, 2014; Jack Ham interview, March 26, 2013; Joe Greene interview, January 26, 2015.

267   **The defense did . . . :** Jack Ham interview, March 26, 2013.

268   **Bradshaw professed no . . . :** Terry Bradshaw with Buddy Martin, *Looking Deep* (Chicago: Contemporary Books, 1989), 88–89.

268   **A night or . . . :** Lynn Swann interview, April 14, 2015; Gerry Mullins interview, April 7, 2014; Franco Harris interview, July 23, 2013; Mike Wagner interview, October 7, 2014; Chris Noll interview, May 17, 2014.

269   **The players themselves . . . :** Paul Zimmerman, "The Teacher," *Sports Illustrated*, July 28, 1980.

269   **Leaving Warwick Drive . . . :** Lynn Swann interview, April 14, 2015.

270   **"Chuck Noll," said . . . :** Phil Axelrod, "Greene Praises Noll for Steelers' Playoff Success," *Pittsburgh Post-Gazette*, December 31, 1979.

270   **"The whole thing . . .":** Dick Hoak interview, April 8, 2014.

270   **The defense threw . . . :** Woody Wienhofer interview, January 27, 2015; Tom Moore interview, December 11, 2014.

271 **"I know how . . .":** Marianne Noll interview, February 8, 2014; Tom Moore interview, June 10, 2016.

271 **When the game . . . :** Bob McGinn, *The Ultimate Super Bowl Book: A Complete Reference to the Stats, Stars, and Stories behind Football's Biggest Game—and Why the Best Team Won,* 2nd ed. (Minneapolis: MVP Books, 2012), 109.

271 **During the first . . . :** Don Weiss interview, circa 2000, for Michael Mac-Cambridge, *America's Game: The Epic Story of How Pro Football Captured a Nation* (New York: Random House, 2004).

271 **All throughout the . . . :** Rocky Bleier interview, October 7, 2014.

271 **"I was concerned," . . . :** Jack Lambert interview, May 15, 2014.

271 **There had been . . . :** NFL Films and NFL Network, *America's Game: The Super Bowl Champions. Pittsburgh Steelers Collection, Super Bowl XIV* (Burbank: Warner Home Video, 2007); Chris Noll interview, May 12, 2015.

272 **Chuck told Bradshaw . . . :** Bradshaw, *Looking Deep,* 148.

272 **From the slot . . . :** McGinn, *The Ultimate Super Bowl Book,* 107.

272 **But not, it . . . :** Jack Lambert interview, May 15, 2014; Ron Johnson interview, August 24, 2013.

272 **From the sidelines . . . :** Lionel Taylor interview, October 9, 2015.

273 **In the locker . . . :** Mike Herney in *St. Petersburg Times,* January 21, 1980.

273 **Bradshaw, having won . . . :** Mike Herney in *St. Petersburg Times,* January 21, 1980.

273 **"It was like . . ."** Linda Carson interview, April 25, 2014.

274 **They were still . . . :** Marianne Noll interview, February 8, 2014.

Chapter 18

275 **Chuck and Marianne . . . :** Marianne Noll interview, February 18, 2013.

276 **Early into his . . . :** Marianne Noll interview, February 9, 2015; Joanne Deininger Mikut interview, October 7, 2014; Chris Noll interview, May 18, 2014.

276 **"They were a . . .":** Joanne Deininger Mikut interview, October 7, 2014.

276 **"She managed the . . .":** Chris Noll interview, May 18, 2014.

277 **"He was always . . .":** Joanne Deininger Mikut interview, October 7, 2014.

277 **After four Super . . . :** That same summer, Pittsburgh writer Phil Musick interviewed Chuck for a long piece in the NFL's house organ, *Pro!* magazine, but that was informed by Musick's years on the Steelers' beat for the *Pittsburgh Post-Gazette.*

277 **Talking to Zimmerman . . . :** Paul Zimmerman, "The Teacher," *Sports Illustrated,* July 28, 1980.

278 **When they finally . . . :** Marilyn Deininger Lopez interview, October 8, 2014; Joanne Deininger Mikut interview, October 7, 2014.

278 **One summer, a . . . :** Marianne Noll interview, February 9, 2015.

278   **On the first . . . :** Tunch Ilkin interview, July 23, 2013.

279   **It fell flat . . . :** George Perles interview, August 25, 2013.

279   **"I remember the . . .":** Tunch Ilkin interview, July 23, 2013.

279   **The staff was . . . :** Dan Rooney interview, July 22, 2013.

279   **In the coaches' . . . :** Woody Widnehofer interview, January 24, 2015; Dick Hoak interview, March 28, 2013.

279   **When Bradshaw . . . :** Terry Bradshaw with Buddy Martin, *Looking Deep* (Chicago: Contemporary Books, 1989), Kindle edition, location 1823.

280   **"Man it was . . .":** John Banaszak interview, November 11, 2015.

280   **"We came into . . .":** Craig Wolfley interview, October 6, 2014.

281   **As the days . . . :** Gary Dunn interview, April 15, 2013; Jack Ham interview, March 26, 2013; Jack Lambert interview, May 15, 2014; Joe Greene interview, January 26, 2015; "The two of them were nose to nose," said Craig Wolfley. "I am on the offensive end of the bench. I started coming down to see what was going on. I thought, 'Oh, my goodness, these guys are going to fight.' Mike Wagner got in the middle of them, and then Mike got out. I saw Coach Noll coming down. He saw, and he looked, and he just turned around and went the other way. He let them deal with it. I thought that was interesting, the way it was handled. They went into the equipment room after the game was over, and I remember they emerged after a period of time, and they had settled it in whatever way was done."

281   **As age and . . . :** John Stallworth interview, March 31, 2014.

281   **Bradshaw was furious . . . :** Bradshaw, *Looking Deep*, 151; David Israel, "Chargers Replace Dash with Muscle to Beat Steelers," *Chicago Tribune*, December 23, 1980.

282   **The other footnote . . . :** Tom Callahan interview, November 20, 2015; Joe Gordon interview, November 18, 2015; Mike Brown interview; November 21, 2015.

282   **Several weeks later . . . :** Joe Gordon interview, November 18, 2015; Marianne Noll interview, October 5, 2014; Joanne Deininger Mikut interview, October 7, 2014.

282   **"It didn't take . . .":** Patrick Manning interview, July 23, 2013.

283   **Dungy accepted the . . . :** Tony Dungy interview, February 10, 2015.

283   **Walking through the . . . :** Tony Dungy interview, February 10, 2015; Dick Hoak interview, April 8, 2014; Jon Kolb interview, April 7, 2014.

283   **For his part . . . :** Bradshaw, *Looking Deep*, 154.

283   **The great debate . . . :** George Perles interview, August 25, 2013; Woody Widnehofer interview, January 24, 2015; Dick Hoak interview, March 28, 2013.

284   **A day later . . . :** Joe Greene interview, January 26, 2015.

285   **Jon Kolb, who'd . . . :** Jon Kolb interview, April 7, 2014.

286   **When Walt Evans . . . :** Jack Lambert interview, May 15, 2014; Dick Hoak interview, March 28, 2013; Tony Dungy interview, February 19, 2013.

286   **While Lambert was . . . :** Bradshaw, *Looking Deep*, 158.

287   **"Chuck was . . . let's . . .":** Not for attribution interview, circa 2014.

287   **During the preseason . . . :** Gary Dunn interview, April 15, 2013.

287   **They would have . . . :** Tunch Ilkin interview, July 23, 2013; Gary Dunn interview, April 15, 2013.

288   **In Pittsburgh, some . . . :** Dan Rooney interview, April 14, 2015; Tunch Ilkin interview, July 23, 2013.

288   **A few veterans . . . :** John Stallworth interview, March 31, 2014.

288   **Chuck gave a . . . :** John Stallworth interview, March 31, 2014.

288   **"At the end . . .":** John Stallworth interview, March 31, 2014.

289   **"I don't know . . .":** Gary Dunn interview, April 15, 2013.

289   **"If I hadn't . . .":** Israel, "Chargers Replace Dash"; Bradshaw, *Looking Deep*, 154; Bob Verdi, "Charged-Up Fouts Fires Final Shot," *Chicago Tribune*, January 10, 1983.

Chapter 19

291   **We're hoping as . . . :** Gary Tuma, "Steelers Seek Receivers Far and Wide," *Pittsburgh Post-Gazette*, April 26, 1983.

291   **There was one . . . :** Terry Bradshaw with Buddy Martin, *Looking Deep* (Chicago: Contemporary Books, 1989), 160

292   **"We knew a . . .":** Tony Dungy interview, February 10, 2015.

292   **That day, as . . . :** Dan Rooney interview, October 6, 2014; John Clayton interview, January 13, 2016.

293   **(While drafting Marino . . .):** Art Rooney Jr. interview, May 19, 2014.

293   **"We built this . . .":** Tony Dungy interview, February 10, 2015; Woody Widenhofer interview, January 27, 2015.

293   **"In Chuck's mind . . .":** Tony Dungy interview, Feb 10, 2015.

293   **Six picks later . . . :** Don Shula interview, April 15, 2013.

293   **Three months later . . . :** Bradshaw, *Looking Deep*, 160.

294   **On Thursday evening . . . :** Dan Rooney interview, April 14, 2015; Dick Hoak interview, April 8, 2014; Marianne Noll interview, February 9, 2015.

294   **After the loss . . . :** Tunch Ilkin interview, July 23, 2013.

295   **Typical of their . . . :** Bradshaw, *Looking Deep*, 162.

296   **But on the . . . :** Bradshaw, *Looking Deep*, 160–62.

296   **At the end . . . :** Tony Dungy interview, February 24, 2014.

297   **"Good job," Chuck . . . :** Jon Kolb interview, October 21, 2013.

298   **The '84 training . . . :** Craig Wolfley interview, October 6, 2014.

298   **"At that time . . .":** Bill Meyers interview, November 15, 2013.

298   **"Courson was crazy . . ."**: Bill Meyers interview, November 15, 2013.

298   **When the trade . . .** : John Adams, "Steelers Deal Courson to Tampa," *Pittsburgh Post-Gazette,* July 31, 1984.

299   **"I need somebody . . ."**: Dan Rooney interview, July 22, 2013; Franco Harris interview, July 23, 2013; John Stallworth interview, March 31, 2014.

299   **On the day . . .** : Marianne Noll interview, February 8, 2015; Franco Harris interview, July 23, 2013; John Stallworth interview, March 31, 2014.

299   **"I remember when . . ."**: Craig Wolfely interview, October 6, 2014.

299   **Joe Greene, watching . . .** : Joe Grene interview, April 8, 2013.

300   **"Chuck never made . . ."**: Tom Moore interview, December 11, 2014.

300   **Chuck was waiting . . .** : Louis Lipps interview, July 24, 2013.

300   **In October, the . . .** : Bill Meyers interview, November 15, 2013.

300   **The criticism of . . .** : Not for attribution interview, circa 2014.

300   **Occasionally, talking to . . .** : Tom Moore interview, December 11, 2014.

301   **Lambert's dislocated toe . . .** : Jack Lambert interview, May 15, 2014.

302   **"Chuck would talk . . ."**: Jon Kolb interview, October 21, 2013.

302   **All that was . . .** : Tom Moore interview, December 11, 2014.

302   **The practices in . . .** : Tony Dungy interview, February 24, 2014.

303   **Hayes's teammate, Howie . . .** : Bill Myers interview, November 15, 2013.

303   **It wasn't just . . .** : John Stallworth interview, March 31, 2014.

303   **"If you didn't . . ."**: Not for attribution interview, circa 2014.

303   **"If he didn't . . ."**: Dick Hoak, April 8, 2014.

303   **The past intersected . . .** : Bradshaw, *Looking Deep,* 21.

304   **"Yeah, well, Terry . . ."**: Not for attribution interview, circa 2014.

304   **"Well, it's pretty . . ."**: Bruce Keidan, "Autopsy: Dr. Noll Examines the Late, Lamented," *Pittsburgh Post-Gazette,* December 24, 1985.

304   **"People start expecting . . ."**: Dick Hoak interview, April 8, 2014.

Chapter 20

305   **On the first . . .** : Tony Dungy interview, February 19, 2013; Jed Hughes interview, February 4, 2015; Dick Hoak interview, March 28, 2013; Art Rooney Jr. interview, May 19, 2014.

306   **"All I remember . . ."**: Marianne Noll interview, February 9, 2015.

306   **The animosity wasn't . . .** : Not for attribution interview, circa 2016.

306   **"Jed was a . . ."**: Not for attribution interview, circa 2014.

306   **The third-round . . .** : Tom Moore interview, December 11, 2014.

307   **On the first . . .** : Bubby Brister interview, August 1, 2013.

307   **Chastened, Brister strode . . .** : Tom Moore interview, December 11, 2014.

307   **Pittsburgh lost the . . .** : Craig Wolfley interviews, October 6, 2014; April 13, 2015; Tunch Ilkin interviews, July 23, 2013; April 13, 2015.

307   **After the third . . .** : Craig Wolfley interview, October 6, 2014.

308 **After breaking the . . . :** "The Steelers—Can It Get Any Worse?," *Pittsburgh Post-Gazette*, October 20, 1986.

308 **"You've always said . . .":** Jon Kolb interview, April 7, 2014.

309 **"Sims was indeed . . .":** Art Rooney Jr. interview, April 13, 2015.

309 **The tension between . . . :** Art Rooney Jr. interview, May 19, 2014.

309 **Chuck and Artie's . . . :** Art Rooney Jr. interview, April 13, 2015; Dan Rooney interview, October 6, 2014.

309 **"He was reassigned . . ."** Dan Rooney interview, October 6, 2014.

309 **"Dan felt I . . .":** Art Rooney Jr. interview, April 13, 2015.

309 **"He did a . . .":** Dan Rooney interview, October 6, 2014.

309 **Years later, Dan . . . :** Dan Rooney interview, October 6, 2014; Marianne Noll interview, February 9, 2015.

310 **Back in Dallas . . . :** Joe Greene interview, January 26, 2015; Joe Gordon interview, October 5, 2014.

310 **Though he was . . . :** Pro Football Hall of Fame, "Defensive Tackle 'Mean Joe' Joe Greene," http://www.profootballhof.com/players/joe-greene/#sthash .d3vniR2a.dpuf.

311 **"Every day, he . . .":** Joe Greene interview, January 26, 2015.

311 **Though Artie was . . . :** Tom Donahoe interview, May 20, 2014; Dick Haley interview, February 25, 2014.

311 **Like a lot . . . :** Merril Hoge interview, February 17, 2014; Dick Hoak interview, November 18, 2015.

312 **The 1987 preseason . . . :** Tony Dungy interview, February 10, 2015.

312 **Chuck's public pronouncement . . . :** Tom Moore interview, December 11, 2014; Bubby Brister interview, August 1, 2013.

312 **Five years earlier . . . :** Tunch Ilkin interview, July 23, 2013.

312 **"He empathized with . . .":** Tony Dungy interview, February 10, 2015.

313 **The three weeks . . . :** Dan Rooney interview, November 17, 2015; Tony Parisi interview, October 21, 2013; "The food was too good," said Tony Parisi. "Everybody got fat."

313 **"We will get . . .":** Tony Dungy interview, February 10, 2015; Dick Hoak interview, March 28, 2013.

313 **Pittsburgh went 2–1 . . . :** Merril Hoge interview, February 17, 2014.

313 **But soon enough . . . :** Tony Dungy interview, February 10, 2015; Dick Hoak interview, March 28, 2013; Tunch Ilkin interview, July 23, 2013.

313 **The Steelers' competition . . . :** Marty Schottenheimer interview, May 12, 2014.

314 **Not so for . . . :** Ed Bouchette, "No Shake: Noll Snubs Wyche Again," *Pittsburgh Post-Gazette*, October 29, 1985.

314 **"He is just . . .":** Marianne Noll interview, February 9, 2015.

314 **"They were the . . .":** Tunch Ilkin interview, July 23, 2013.

314   **"I precipitated it,"** . . . : Tom Moore interview, December 11, 2014.

315   **On the sidelines** . . . : Associated Press, "Glanville Defends Oilers, Shows Film of Steelers' Late Hits," *Pittsburgh Post-Gazette*, December 22, 1987.

315   **"After the game . . ."**: Jerry Glanville feature on *Outside the Lines* (https:// www.youtube.com/watch?v=2hAwTf6_EKk), ESPN, July 2, 2007.

315   **In the moment** . . . : Associated Press, "Glanville Defends Oilers."

315   **One day in** . . . : John Stallworth interview, March 31, 2014.

316   **Of Stallworth and** . . . : Paul Meyer, "Time Out: Steeler Greats Shell, Stallworth Are Ready for Life after Football," *Pittsburgh Post-Gazette*, January 23, 1988.

316   **In the 1988** . . . : John Jackson interview, September 15, 2013; Tony Dungy interview, February 10, 2015.

316   **But it was** . . . : Dick Haley interview, February 25, 2014.

317   **Bubby Brister, just** . . . : Bubby Brister interview, August 1, 2013.

317   **On August 20** . . . : Joe Browne interview, June 17, 2013; Craig Wolfley interview, October 6, 2014; Tunc Ilkin interview, April 13, 2015.

317   **Just a few** . . . : Craig Wolfley interview, October 6, 2014; Tunc Ilkin interview, April 13, 2015.

317   **The frustration escalated** . . . : Pam Morocco interview, October 21, 2013.

317   **On October 19** . . . : Bubby Brister interview, August 1, 2013; Tom Moore interview, December 11, 2014.

318   **That and more** . . . : Ed Bouchette and David Fink, "Brister Blisters Steelers," *Pittsburgh-Post Gazette*, October 20, 1988.

318   **What Chuck still** . . . : Tony Dungy interview, February 19, 2013.

318   **They snapped the** . . . : Merril Hoge interview, February 17, 2014.

319   **It had been** . . . : Bubby Brister interview, August 1, 2013.

319   **As the '88 season** . . . : Jon Kolb interview, April 7, 2014; Tunch Ilkin interview, April 13, 2015.

319   **"That was the . . ."**: Craig Wolfley interview, October 6, 2014.

319   **What he definitely** . . . : Jed Hughes interview, February 4, 2015; Tony Dungy interview, February 10, 2015; Joe Greene interview, January 26, 2015.

319   **"In the mornings . . ."**: Dan Rooney interview, April 14, 2015.

319   **"He was an intelligent . . ."**: Not for attribution interview, circa 2014.

320   **During the dark** . . . : Dan Rooney interview, April 14, 2015.

320   **So the two** . . . : Merril Hoge interview, February 17, 2014.

320   **Joe Greene, standing** . . . : Joe Greene interview, January 26, 2015; Dan Rooney interview, April 14, 2015.

321   **When the announcement** . . . : Associated Press, "The Steelers Keep Noll, Fire Aides," *Philadelphia Inquirer*, January 4, 1989.

321   **Hughes, tearful, showed** . . . : Jed Hughes interview, February 4, 2015; Marianne Noll interview, Feb 8, 2015.

322   **"Chuck would be . . .":** Not for attribution interview, circa 2014.

322   **"No," said Chuck . . . :** Tom Moore interview, December 11, 2014.

322   **The Rooneys always . . . :** Dan Rooney interview, April 14, 2015; Patricia Rooney interview, April 8, 2014; Marianne Noll interview, June 2, 2014.

322   **But those closest. .** Joanne Deininger Mikut interview, April 11, 2015.

Chapter 21

323   **On June 17 . . . :** Marianne Noll interview, February 8, 2015; Chris Noll interviews, May 17, 2014; May 11, 2015; Linda Churchill Noll interview, May 17, 2014.

323   **Later, Linda observed . . . :** Linda Churchill Noll interview, May 17, 2014.

324   **Marianne's advice was . . . :** Marianne Noll interview, October 5, 2014.

324   **The Nolls' HNS . . . :** Marianne Noll interview, October 5, 2014.

324   **"It was an . . .":** Linda Churchill Noll interview, May 17, 2014.

324   **The great experiment . . . :** Tom Moore interview, December 11, 2014; Bubby Brister interview, August 1, 2013.

324   **Among the new . . . :** Mike Mularkey interview, March 18, 2016.

325   **As Gary Anderson's . . . :** Tom Moore interview, July 7, 2014.

325   **The opener would . . . :** Tom Moore interview, December 11, 2014; Tunch Ilkin interview, April 13, 2015.

325   **"It was the . . .":** Abby Mendelson and David Aretha, *The Steelers Experience: A Year-by-Year Chronicle of the Pittsburgh Steelers* (Minneapolis: MVP Books, 2014), 132.

325   **"Bud could not . . .":** Linda Carson interview, April 25, 2014.

326   **Head down, thumbs . . . :** Joe Greene interview, November 18, 2013.

326   **The flight home . . . :** Tunch Ilkin interview, April 13, 2015.

326   **In the papers . . . :** Bruce Kiedan, "An Ugly Trend Is Developing," *Pittsburgh Post-Gazette*, September 18, 1989.

326   **But most of . . . :** Ed Bouchette, "Steelers Suffer Another Loss—Hinkle," *Pittsburgh Post-Gazette*, September 19, 1989.

326   **Instead of his . . . :** Craig Wolfley interview, October 6, 2014; Tunch Ilkin interview, April 13, 2015.

327   **Later in the . . . :** Dick Hoak interview, April 8, 2014; Craig Wolfley interview, October 6, 2014.

327   **At 2–3, going . . . :** Bob Labriola, "Magic Runs Out in Denver," Steelers Digest.com, July 20, 2011.

328   **There's an astronomically . . . :** Dick Hoak interview, April 8, 2014; Tom Moore interview, December 11, 2014.

328   **It was a . . . :** Mike Mularkey interview, March 18, 2016.

328   **For Brister, who . . . :** Bubby Brister interview, August 1, 2013.

329   **While the offense . . . :** Tom Moore interview, December 11, 2014.

329   **Chuck arrived in . . . :** Robert Noll interview, February 24, 2014.

329   **The next day . . . :** Tom Moore interview, December 11, 2014; Dick Hoak interview, April 8, 2014; Carnell Lake interview, May 20, 2014.

330   **Ninety minutes before . . . :** Tom Moore interview, December 11, 2014.

330   **The game went . . . :** Tom Moore interview, December 11, 2014; Rod Rust interview, May 15, 2015.

330   **Ilkin was racing . . . :** Craig Wolfley interview, October 6, 2014; Tunch Ilkin interview, April 13, 2015.

331   **"I don't like . . .":** Merril Hoge interview, February 17, 2014.

331   **Chuck took it . . . :** Carnell Lake interview, May 20, 2014.

331   **"They were barking . . .":** Merril Hoge interview, February 17, 2014.

332   **"There's not a . . .":** Labriola, "Magic Runs Out in Denver."

332   **On the bus . . . :** Jerry Olsavsky interview, March 27, 2013.

332   **Before heading back . . . :** Merril Hoge interview, February 17, 2014.

333   **Joanne had been . . . :** Marilyn Deininger Lopez interview, October 8, 2014.

333   **Among Joanne's groups . . . :** Joanne Deininger Mikut interview, October 7, 2014; Glenn Mikut interview, October 7, 2014.

334   **Afterward, Marianne waited . . . :** Joanne Deininger Mikut interview, October 7, 2014; Marianne Noll interview, February 9, 2015.

334   **"It was very . . .":** Joanne Deininger Mikut interview, October 7, 2014.

334   **At the reception . . . :** Joanne Deininger and Glenn Mikut wedding video, Noll family private collection.

334   **There were no . . . :** Glenn Mikut interview, October 7, 2014.

335   **Glenn and Joanne . . . :** Joanne Deininger Mikut interview, October 7, 2014; Marianne Noll interview, February 9, 2015.

Chapter 22

336   **As the 1990 . . . :** Tom Moore interview, December 11, 2014; Rod Rust interview, May 15, 2015.

337   **It was Joe . . . :** Joe Gordon interview, October 5, 2014.

337   **"He really didn't . . .":** Not for attribution interview, circa 2014.

337   **It was embarrassing . . . :** Ed Bouchette, "Creehan: Newspapers Ruined Me," *Pittsburgh Post-Gazette*, March 14, 1990.

337   **"There was a . . .":** Not for attribution interview, circa 2014.

338   **Training camp remained . . . :** Jack Henry interview, October 22, 2013.

338   **By then, Chuck . . . :** Tunch Ilkin interview, July 23, 2013.

338   **Yet there were . . . :** John Fox interview, April 24, 2015; Joe Greene interview, January 26, 2015.

339   **Chuck, embattled for . . . :** Joe Walton interview, November 18, 2015.

339   **"All of a . . .":** Not for attribution interview, circa 2015.

339   **"Listen, if he . . .":** Merril Hoge interview, February 17, 2014.

340 **"Joe Walton comes . . .":** Jack Henry interview, October 22, 2013.

340 **"The only thing . . .":** Not for attribution interview, circa 2015.

340 **"I felt sorry . . .":** Bubby Brister interview, August 1, 2013.

340 **"Players were literally . . .":** Mike Mularkey interview, March 18, 2016.

340 **At times, Brister . . . :** Bubby Brister interview, August 1, 2013.

340 **Tim Worley, taking . . . :** Barry Foster interview, April 6, 2013; Tunch Ilkin interview, July 23, 2013.

341 **In the following . . . :** Marianne Noll interview, February 8, 2015.

341 **Chuck was nonplussed . . . :** Dr. Joe Maroon interview, September 25, 2015; interview transcript with Dr. Joe Maroon, *The Frontline Interviews*, "League of Denial: The NFL's Concussion Crisis," http://www.pbs.org/wgbh/pages /frontline/sports/league-of-denial/the-frontline-interview-dr-joseph -maroon/.

342 **Maroon told Chuck . . . :** Dan Rooney interview, November 15, 2015.

342 **As the losses . . . :** Ed Bouchette, "Coach's Call Comes True after 7–9 Season," *Pittsburgh Post-Gazette*, December 27, 1991.

342 **At home, Chuck . . . :** Joanne Deininger Mikut interview, April 4, 2014.

342 **One gray October . . . :** Marianne Noll interview, September 30, 2015.

343 **In the final . . . :** Joe Greene interview, January 26, 2015.

343 **"He seemed distant . . .":** Barry Foster interview, April 6, 2013.

343 **Dick Hoak had . . . :** Dick Hoak interview, March 28, 2013.

344 **By December, some . . . :** Tunch Ilkin interview, April 13, 2015.

344 **The following days . . . :** Marianne Noll interview, September 30, 2015; Joanne Deininger Mikut interview, April 4, 2014; Chris Noll interview, June 16, 2013; Patrick Manning interview, July 23, 2013.

344 **Finally on Thursday . . . :** Dan Rooney interview, October 6, 2014.

345 **Interviewed later that . . . :** Ron Cook, "Noll May Have Checked Out Earlier Than He Wanted To," *Pittsburgh Post-Gazette*, December 27, 1991.

345 **Composing himself after . . . :** Ralph Berlin interview, October 21, 2013.

345 **In the minutes . . . :** Ed Bouchette interview, April 8, 2014; Joe Gordon interview, October 5, 2014.

345 **Dan Rooney, looking . . . :** Dan Rooney interview, October 6, 2014; Tunch Ilkin interview, July 23, 2013.

346 **Chuck had just . . . :** Marianne Noll interview, September 30, 2015; Joanne Deininger Mikut interview, April 4, 2014; Chris Noll interview, June 16, 2013.

Chapter 23

347 **A few weeks . . . :** Joe Gordon interview, October 5, 2014; Dan Rooney interview, July 22, 2013; Marianne Noll interview, February 8, 2015.

348 **Of course, Cowher . . . :** Bill Nunn interview, April 7, 2014; Joe Greene interview, July 28, 2014.

348   **When it was . . . :** Joe Greene interview, July 28, 2014; Don Shula interview, April 15, 2013.

348   **Meanwhile, Cowher in . . . :** John Jackson interview, September 15, 2013.

348   **There was always . . . :** Marianne Noll interview, February 9, 2015.

349   **"That was the . . .":** Chris Noll interview, May 18, 2014.

349   **"That was my . . .":** Glenn Mikut interview, April 5, 2014.

349   **Chuck and Marianne . . . :** Chris Noll interview, May 18, 2014; Jim Currin interview, December 9, 2013.

350   **Chuck—with memories . . . :** Chris Noll interview, May 18, 2014.

350   **People who know . . . :** Jack Henry interview, October 22, 2013.

350   **Another call came . . . :** Marianne Noll interview, February 9, 2014.

350   **"You more than . . .":** Art Rooney Jr. letter to Chuck Noll, Noll family private collection, undated.

350   **That spring, on . . . :** Jim Currin interview, December 9, 2013; Pat Maloney interview, September 15, 2013. His old roommate Frank Siggins, who wasn't along on the outing and never got a call, was reportedly miffed that Chuck had overlooked him. Chuck had been the godfather of one of Siggins's daughters.

350   **On the embankment . . . :** Home videotape of Hall of Fame induction ceremonies, from Hank and Jo Ferrazza; Chris Noll interview, June 16, 2013; Marianne Noll interview, February 9, 2015.

351   **That entire day . . . :** Jo Ferrazza interview, June 27, 2014; Jim Currin interview, September 15, 2013; Pat Maloney interview, September 15, 2013.

351   **After the ceremony . . . :** Marianne Noll interview, February 9, 2015; Pete Schreiber interview, November 2, 2014.

352   **That week in . . . :** Merril Hoge interview, February 7, 2014; in the stands in Tempe, sitting near Merril Hoge, he told his former player that he'd make a good coach.
       "Okay, I can coach," said Hoge. "But tell me what it is I need to be a good coach, to do it like you did it." Chuck became serious and turned around in his chair to fully face Hoge. "Here is what you need: passion. You need—" "Okay, stop right there," said Hoge. "I don't have that." Hoge was in the midst of transitioning to a broadcasting career, and the prospect of keeping coach's hours—even the relatively civilized, reasonable sort of hours that Chuck's coaches kept—didn't appeal to him.

352   **After the game . . . :** Marianne Noll interview, February 9, 2015.

353   **As Chris and . . . :** Chris Noll interview, May 11, 2015; Linda Churchill Noll interview, May 11, 2015.

353   **In the fall . . . :** Chris Noll interview, May 11, 2015; Jim Currin interview, September 15, 2013.

353   **It was January . . . :** Marianne Noll interview, October 4, 2014.

354   **Chuck had been . . . :** Jerry Greene, "Freak Injury Sidelines Team USA Coach

Noll," *Orlando Sentinel*, January 16, 1999; Woody Widenhofer interview, September 30, 2015; Joe Walton interview, November 18, 2015.

354 **They left before . . . :** Marianne Noll interview, October 4, 2014.

354 **"They were kind . . .":** Chris Noll interview, May 11, 2015.

354 **One night, a . . . :** Marianne Noll interview, October 4, 2014.

354 **He had not . . . :** Merril Hoge interview, February 17, 2014.

355 **September 24, 2000 . . . :** Frenchy Fuqua interview, August 24, 2013.

355 **Throughout the years . . . :** Terry Bradshaw with David Fisher, *It's Only a Game* (New York: Pocket Books, 2001), Kindle edition, location 56.

355 **Later in the . . . :** Bradshaw, *It's Only a Game*, Kindle edition, location 783.

356 **The publication of . . . :** Cliff Stoudt interview, August 18, 2013.

356 **Bradshaw conceded the . . . :** Ed Bouchette, "One-Way Feud Finally Ends as Bradshaw Shows Appreciation, Love for Noll," *Pittsburgh Post-Gazette*, February 9, 2003.

356 **Alternately abashed and . . . :** Gary Pomerantz, *Their Life's Work: The Brotherhood of the 1970s Pittsburgh Steelers, Then and Now* (New York: Simon and Schuster, 2013), Kindle edition, location 4390.

356 **For other players . . . :** Gary Dunn interview, April 15, 2013.

357 **At the same . . . :** Ron Johnson, August 24, 2013.

357 **John Stallworth also . . . :** John Stallworth interview, March 31, 2014.

357 **The litany of . . . :** Marianne Noll interviews, August 29, 2012; October 4, 2014; September 30, 2015.

357 **In Pittsburgh, they . . . :** Glenn Mikut interview, April 5, 2014.

358 **On April 24 . . . :** Jerry Deininger interview, August 19, 2014; Maria Deininger interview, August 19, 2014.

358 **"He walked into . . .":** Margie Deininger Ervin interview, June 28, 2014.

358 **"Forever, the two . . .":** Joanne Deininger Mikut interview, April 5, 2014.

358 **"I was getting . . .":** Chris Noll interview, May 11, 2015.

358 **But for all . . . :** Marianne Noll interviews, August 29, 2012; October 4, 2014; Dr. Joe Maroon interview, September 25, 2015.

359 **After Chuck stepped . . . :** Marianne Noll interviews, August 29, 2012; October 4, 2014; September 30, 2015.

Chapter 24

361 **In the glory . . . :** Jon Dee Graham, "Best," written by Jon Dee Graham, JonDeeGrahamMusic BMI/admin. By Bug Music.

361 **Marianne would tell . . . :** Marianne Noll interviews, August 29, 2012; October 4, 2014; February 8, 2015.

362 **Some days . . . :** Marianne Noll interviews, August 29, 2012; June 2, 2014; Linda Churchill Noll interview, May 11, 2015; Chris Noll interview, May 11,

2015; Joanne Deininger Mikut, March 24, 2013; Glenn Mikut interview, April 5, 2014.

362   **Other days, when . . . :** Joanne Deininger Mikut, March 24, 2013; Glenn Mikut interview, April 5, 2014; Joe Gordon interview, October 5, 2014.

362   **He wouldn't speak . . . :** Glenn Mikut interview, April 5, 2014.

362   **They went out . . . :** Marianne Noll interview, February 22, 2014; Chuck Noll interview, February 22, 2014; Marianne Noll interview, May 20, 2014; Chuck Noll interview, May 20, 2014.

363   **Not far from . . . :** Marianne Noll interview, June 2, 2014; Tony Dungy interview, February 24, 2014; Tom Moore interview, December 11, 2014.

363   **"You can see . . .":** Joe Greene interview, November 18, 2013.

363   **As Dungy was . . . :** Tony Dungy interview, February 24, 2014.

364   **"Jim Irsay thought . . .":** Tom Moore interview, December 11, 2014; Tony Dungy interview, February 24, 2014.

364   **On Friday, two . . . :** Marianne Noll interview, February 22, 2014; Tony Dungy interview, February 24, 2014.

365   **"A carbon copy . . .":** Tom Moore interview, February 10, 2014.

365   **The scenes would . . . :** Chuck Noll interviews, July 4, 2012; July 24, 2013.

366   **For Marianne and . . . :** Marianne Noll interviews, August 29, 2012; June 2, 2014; Linda Churchill Noll interview, May 11, 2015; Chris Noll interview, May 11, 2015; Joanne Deininger Mikut, March 24, 2013; Glenn Mikut interview, April 5, 2014; Ken Deininger interview, November 2, 2013; Margie Deininger Ervin interview, June 28, 2014.

366   **"Whiskey, rye whiskey . . .":** "Rye whiskey," adapted by Scottish folk song "Up on Clinch Mountain," by Tex Ritter.

366   **At the end . . . :** Chuck Noll interviews, July 4, 2012; July 24, 2013.

366   **In the diminished . . . :** Marianne Noll interview, August 29, 2012; Chuck Noll interview, July 24, 2013.

367   **Not long after . . . :** Connor Noll interview, May 17, 2014; Linda Churchill Noll interview, May 17, 2014.

367   **Others, on the . . . :** Merril Hoge interview, February 17, 2014.

367   **There was a . . . :** John Stallworth interview, March 31, 2014.

368   **"I went to . . .":** Lionel Taylor interview, October 9, 2015.

368   **Back in the . . . :** Andy Russell interview, June 11, 2015.

368   **Mostly, among former. .** Mel Blount interview, March 29, 2013.

369   **On January 5 . . . :** Letter to Chuck Noll from Warren Bankston; letter to Chuck Noll from Rocky Bleier; letter to Chuck Noll from Terry Hanratty; letter to Chuck Noll from Gerry Mullins; letter to Chuck Noll from Gordon Gravelle; letter to Chuck Noll from Ron Johnson; letter to Chuck Noll from Andy Russell; all from Noll family private collection.

370   **A few close . . . :** Marianne Noll interview, October 4, 2014; George Perles interview, August 25, 2013.

370   **The Dayton teammate . . . :** Marianne Noll interview, October 4, 2014; Jim Currin interview, September 15, 2013.

371   **"The preacher walked . . .":** "Good Ol' Mountain Dew," written by Bascom Lamar Lunsford and Scotty Wiseman.

372   **"They still act . . .":** Katie Noll interview, May 17, 2014.

372   **"The thing that . . .":** Linda Churchill Noll interview, May 17, 2014.

372   **"She will say . . .":** Chris Noll interview, May 17, 2014. The relatives were worried because Marianne looked haggard at times, but also because of the largely unspoken fear—what if Marianne, exhausted by the around the clock care, were to die first? On a trip to Virginia, the topic was broached. "You guys will have to figure that out," Marianne told Linda. "I can't figure that part out." Eventually, her strong will would hold sway. After rebuking the efforts, she would say—by way of reassurance—"I'm not a martyr. If I need help, I will ask for it. I'm not a martyr."

373   **"It's a lonely . . .":** Chris Noll interview, May 17, 2014.

373   **"Chris was down . . .":** Joanne Deininger Mikut interview, March 24, 2013.

374   **They got back . . . :** Marianne Noll interview, October 4, 2014; Joe Gordon interview, October 5, 2014.

374   **That very same . . . :** Rick Deininger interview, June 24, 2014; Margie Deininger Ervin interview, June 24, 2012; Marilyn Deininger Lopez interview, June 24, 2012; Bill Deininger interview, June 24, 2012.

374   **"We just kind . . .":** Jerry Deininger interview, August 19, 2014.

375   **"I feel like . . .":** Rita Deininger interview, August 14, 2014.

375   **Dan Rooney and . . . :** Joe Gordon interview, October 5, 2014; Dan Rooney interview, October 6, 2014: Marianne Noll interview, October 4, 2014.

375   **The day after . . . :** Bill Deininger interview, June 24, 2012.

375   **The funeral was . . . :** Glenn Mikut interview, October 7, 2014.

376   **The pallbearers included. .** Paul Zeise, "Noll's Funeral a Lesson on Greatness," *Pittsburgh Post-Gazette*, June 18, 2014.

Epilogue

377   **"I don't concern . . .":** Jack T. Clary, with illustrations by Dick Oden, *The Gamemakers* (Chicago: Follett, 1976), 159.

377   **And less than . . . :** Linda Churchill Noll interview, May 11, 2015.

378   **It wasn't for . . . :** Joe Greene interview, January 26, 2015.

378   **"You cannot decipher . . .":** Frenchy Fuqua interview, August 24, 2013.

378   **When Paul Zimmerman . . . :** Paul Zimmerman, "The Teacher," *Sports Illustrated*, July 28, 1980.

379 **"I think he . . .":** John Stallworth interview, March 31, 2014.

379 **In those bonds . . . :** Joe Greene interview, January 26, 2015; Jack Ham interview, March 26, 2013; Jack Lambert interview, May 15, 2014.

379 **"I'm not sure . . .":** Craig Wolfley interview, October 6, 2014.

379 **The effect could . . . :** Cliff Stoudt interview, August 18, 2013.

380 **Stoudt never got . . . :** Cliff Stoudt interview, August 18, 2013; Marianne Noll interview, February 9, 2015.

381 **From the time . . . :** Joanne Deininger Mikut interview, July 22, 2013.

382 **"You have to . . .":** Chris Noll interview, May 11, 2015.

382 **"He could have . . .":** Linda Churchill Noll interview, May 11, 2015.

382 **"I see Chuck . . .":** Tony Dungy interview, February 10, 2015.

382 **Yet another way . . . :** Brian Billick interview, circa 2001, for Michael Mac-Cambridge, *America's Game: The Epic Story of How Pro Football Captured a Nation* (New York: Random House, 2004); Art Rooney II interview, April 14, 2015.

383 **"I always tell . . .":** Jack Ham interview, March 26, 2013.

383 **Only the most . . . :** Terry Bradshaw with David Fisher, *It's Only a Game* (New York: Pocket Books, 2001), Kindle edition, location 40.

383 **"He's the most . . .":** Joe Greene interview, July 28, 2014.

383 **"Germans don't do . . .":** Joanne Deininger Mikut, July 22, 2013.

384 **"If one of . . .":** Rita Deininger interview, May 15, 2016.

384 **"We idolized . . .":** Margie Deininger Ervin interview, June 24, 2014.

384 **"But it was . . .":** Rick Deininger interview, June 24, 2014.

384 **"He was a . . .":** Joanne Deininger Mikut, July 22, 2013.

384 **For Chris Noll . . . :** Chris Noll interview, May 12, 2015.

385 **That Christmas, she . . . :** Marianne Noll interview, February 9, 2015.

385 **In the end . . . :** But for those of a certain age and a certain mind-set, the connection ran deeper. "I had a great life as a Steeler," said Artie Rooney. "People still think I'm the man who shot Liberty Valance. We all know it was John Wayne—but in my case, it's Chuck Noll."

AUTHOR INTERVIEWS

✦ ✦ ✦

Dr. Bernard Abrams, Ernie Accorsi, Greg Aiello, Jim Akau, Chuck Allen, Mike Arata, Steve August, John Banaszak, Warren Bankston, Upton Bell, Ralph Berlin, Ron Blackledge, George Blair, Rocky Bleier, Mel Blount, Roy Blount Jr., Bucky Bockhorn, Ed Bouchette, Bobby Boyd, Dave Brazil, Bubby Brister, John Brown, Larry Brown, Mike Brown, Joe Browne, Joel Bussert, Barry Carlin, Tom Carroll, Paul Cassidy, Michael Challik, Linda Carson, John Clayton, Don Colo, Diane Connelly, Don Connelly, Dick Coury, Jim Currin, Judy Currin, Dermontti Dawson, Len Dawson, Bill Deininger, Sr. Geraldine Deininger, Jean Deininger, Jerry Deininger, Jim Deininger, Ken Deininger, Maria Deininger, Rick Deininger, Rita Deininger, Joseph Devera, Jeanne Ippilito DiSanto, John Dockery, Tom Donahoe, Don Donoher, Charles "Chuck" Doud, Tony Dungy, Gary Dunn, Glen Edwards, Margie Deininger Ervin, Tony Ferenti, Dan Ferrazza, Jo Ferrazza, David Flynn, Herschel Forester, Barry Foster, John Fox, John "Frenchy" Fuqua, Bob Gain, Dennis Gaubatz, Charlie Getty, Fr. Gerard Gonda, Joe Gordon, John Grabowski, Joe Greene, Bishop Roger Gries, Randy Grossman, Dick Haley, Todd Haley, Jack Ham, Pat Hanlon, Terry Hanratty, Chris Harris, Dick Harris, Franco Harris, Doug Hauschild, Jack Henry, Dick Hoak,

Merrill Hoge, Joe Hornack, Jed Hughes, Tunch Ilkin, John Jackson, Roy Jefferson, Ron Johnson, Larry Kindbom, Len Kestner, Peter King, Albert Kohanowich, Jon Kolb, Fr. Tom Kredel, Linda Kulzer, Bob Labriola, Carnell Lake, Jack Lambert, Willie Lanier, Rudy Lawrenchik, Marv Levy, Frank Lewis, Louis Lipps, Jerry Logan, Marilyn Deininger Lopez, Elsie Lyttle, Jerry Magee, Paul Maguire, Pat Maloney, John Manning, Michael Manning, Patrick Manning, Dr. Joe Maroon, Bob McCartney, Claudine McGee, Shirley Stemley McIntosh, Bill Meyers, Glenn Mikut, Joanne Deininger Mikut, Tom Moore, Pam Morocco, Curly Morrison, Jay Moyer, Mike Mularkey, Gerry "Moon" Mullins, Jerry Mulvahill, Leo Murphy, Zoltan Nadasdy, Chris Noll, Chuck Noll, Connor Noll, Katie Noll, Linda Churchill Noll, Marianne Noll, Robert Noll, Bill Nunn, Alice Bowman Nye, Ed Nye, Jerry Olsavsky, Babe Parilli, Tony Parisi, Preston Pearson, George Perles, Bob Petrich, Fr. Placid Pientek, Dan Radakovich, Marilyn Hall Regalado, Rudy Regalado, Lou Riecke, Art Rooney II, Art Rooney Jr., Dan Rooney, Patricia Rooney, Andy Russell, Rod Rust, Gerry Sandusky, Marty Schottenheimer, Donnie Shell, Don Shula, Frank Siggins Jr., Patricia "Pat" Siggins, Chuck Spatafore, John Stallworth, John Sterling, Cliff Stoudt, Lynn Swann, Lionel Taylor, Marlo Termini, J. T. Thomas, A. Michael Turco, Bruce Van Dyke, Bob Valesente, Rick Volk, John Vukelich, Rose Vukelich, Mike Wagner, Joe Walton, Dick Westmoreland, William Whiteside, Woody Widenhofer, Craig Wolfley, Leonard Wolniak, Joan Yanky, and Ralph Yanky.

BIBLIOGRAPHY

✦ ✦ ✦

Adler, Brad. *Coaching Matters: Leadership and Tactics of the NFL's Ten Greatest Coaches.* Washington, DC: Brassey's, 2003.

Anderson, Dave. *Countdown to Super Bowl.* New York: Random House, 1969.

Barone, Michael, and Grant Ujifusa. *The Almanac of American Politics, 2000.* Washington, DC: National Journal, 1999.

Blount, Roy, Jr. *About Three Bricks Shy . . . and the Load Filled Up: The Story of the Greatest Football Team Ever.* Pittsburgh: University of Pittsburgh Press, 2004.

Blount, Roy, Jr. *About Three Bricks Shy of a Load: A Highly Irregular Lowdown on the Year the Pittsburgh Steelers Were Super but Missed the Bowl.* Boston: Little, Brown, 1974.

Bradshaw, Terry, with David Fisher. *It's Only a Game.* New York: Pocket Books, 2001.

Bradshaw, Terry, with Buddy Martin. *Looking Deep.* Chicago: Contemporary Books, 1989.

Chastain, Bill. *Steel Dynasty: The Team That Changed the NFL.* Chicago: Triumph, 2005.

Clary, Jack T., with illustrations by Dick Oden. *The Gamemakers.* Chicago: Follett, 1976.

Daly, Dan. *The Pro Football Chronicle: The Complete (Well, Almost) Record of the Best Players, the Greatest Photos, the Hardest Hits, the Biggest Scandals, and the Funniest Stories in Pro Football.* New York: Macmillan, 1990.

Didinger, Ray. *Pittsburgh Steelers.* New York: Macmillan, 1974.

Didinger, Ray. *The Super Bowl: Celebrating A Quarter Century of America's Greatest Game.* New York: Simon and Schuster, 1990.

Engstrom, Ted W. *The Making of a Christian Leader.* Grand Rapids: Zondervan, 1978.

Finks, Jim. *Colors: Pro Football Uniforms of the Past and Present.* Edina, MN: Beavers Pond Press, 2009.

Freeman, Mike. *Undefeated: Inside the 1972 Dolphins' Perfect Season.* New York: It Books, 2012.

Grdnic, Dale. *Tales from the Pittsburgh Steelers Sideline: A Collection of the Greatest Steelers Stories Ever Told.* New York: Sports, 2013.

Green, Jerry. *Super Bowl Chronicles: A Sportswriter Reflects on the First 30 Years of America's Game.* 2nd ed. Indianapolis: Masters Press, 1995.

Gruver, Ed. *The American Football League a Year-by-Year History, 1960–1969.* Jefferson, NC: McFarland, 1997.

Katzowitz, Josh. *Sid Gillman: The Father of the Passing Game.* New York: Clerisy Press, 2012.

King, Peter. *The Season After: Are Sports Dynasties Dead?* New York: Warner, 1989.

Lorant, Stefan, and others. *Pittsburgh: The Story of an American City.* Garden City, NY: Esselmont, 2003.

MacCambridge, Michael. *America's Game: The Epic Story of How Pro Football Captured a Nation.* New York: Random House, 2004.

MacCambridge, Michael. *Lamar Hunt: A Life in Sports.* Kansas City: Andrews McMeel, 2012.

MacCambridge, Michael, ed. *ESPN College Football Encyclopedia: The Complete History of the Game.* New York: ESPN, 2005.

McGinn, Bob. *The Ultimate Super Bowl Book: A Complete Reference to the Stats, Stars, and Stories Behind Football's Biggest Game—and Why the Best Team Won.* 2nd ed. Minneapolis: MVP Books, 2012.

Mendelson, Abby. *The Pittsburgh Steelers: The Official Team History.* Dallas: Taylor, 1996.

Mendelson, Abby, and David Aretha. *The Steelers Experience: A Year-by-Year Chronicle of the Pittsburgh Steelers.* Minneapolis: MVP Books, 2014.

Millman, Chad, and Shawn Coyne. *The Ones Who Hit the Hardest: The Steelers, the Cowboys, the '70s, and the Fight for America's Soul.* New York: Gotham, 2010.

Natali, Alan. *Brown's Town: 20 Famous Browns Talk amongst Themselves.* Wilmington: Orange Frazer, 2001.

NFL. *2014 Official NFL Record & Fact Book*. New York: Time Home Entertainment, 2014.

NFL Films. *NFL: America's Game—Pittsburgh Steelers: The Story of Six Championships*. Mount Laurel, NJ: NFL Films, 2009.

NFL Films. *75 Seasons: 1920 to 1995, the Story of the NFL*. New York: PolyGram, 1994, VHS.

NFL Films, NFL Films Archives. *Alive & Kicking (1986)*. Highlight film. Mount Laurel, NJ: NFL Films Archives, 1986.

NFL Films, NFL Films Archives. *A Blueprint for Victory (1975)*. Highlight film. Mount Laurel, NJ: NFL Films Archives, 1975.

NFL Films, NFL Films Archives. *A Cut Above (1979)*. Highlight film. Mount Laurel, NJ: NFL Films Archives, 1979.

NFL Films, NFL Films Archives. *Defending Champions (1973)*. Highlight film. Mount Laurel, NJ: NFL Films Archives, 1973.

NFL Films, NFL Films Archives. *Forging a Future (1988)*. Highlight film. Mount Laurel, NJ: NFL Films Archives, 1988.

NFL Films, NFL Films Archives. *Getting Down to Business (1990)*. Highlight film. Mount Laurel, NJ: NFL Films Archives, 1990.

NFL Films, NFL Films Archives. *Growing Pains (1985)*. Highlight film. Mount Laurel, NJ: NFL Films Archives, 1985.

NFL Films, NFL Films Archives. *The Measure of a Champion (1976)*. Highlight film. Mount Laurel, NJ: NFL Films Archives, 1976.

NFL Films, NFL Films Archives. *A New Beginning (1984)*. Highlight film. Mount Laurel, NJ: NFL Films Archives, 1984.

NFL Films, NFL Films Archives. *A New Beginning (1992)*. Highlight film. Mount Laurel, NJ: NFL Films Archives, 1992.

NFL Films, NFL Films Archives. *A New Era (1991)*. Highlight film. Mount Laurel, NJ: NFL Films Archives, 1991.

NFL Films, NFL Films Archives. *1968 Pittsburgh Steelers*. Highlight film. Mount Laurel, NJ: NFL Films Archives, 1968.

NFL Films, NFL Films Archives. *Pride of the Steel City (1980)*. Highlight film. Mount Laurel, NJ: NFL Films Archives, 1980.

NFL Films, NFL Films Archives. *Return of the Champions (1978)*. Highlight film. Mount Laurel, NJ: NFL Films Archives, 1978.

NFL Films, NFL Films Archives. *The Right Stuff (1983)*. Highlight film. Mount Laurel, NJ: NFL Films Archives, 1983.

NFL Films, NFL Films Archives. *Six Straight Playoffs (1977)*. Highlight film. Mount Laurel, NJ: NFL Films Archives, 1977.

NFL Films, NFL Films Archives. *Steelers Seventy-One (1971)*. Highlight film. Mount Laurel, NJ: NFL Films Archives, 1971.

NFL Films, NFL Films Archives. *The Steelers Year (1972)*. Highlight film. Mount Laurel, NJ: NFL Films Archives, 1972.

NFL Films, NFL Films Archives. *Steel Town Tough (1982)*. Highlight film. Mount Laurel, NJ: NFL Films Archives, 1982.

NFL Films, NFL Films Archives. *Super Steelers (1974)*. Highlight film. Mount Laurel, NJ: NFL Films Archives, 1974.

NFL Films, NFL Films Archives. *Unfinished Business (1981)*. Highlight film. Mount Laurel, NJ: NFL Films Archives, 1981.

NFL Films, NFL Films Archives. *Wait Till Next Year (1969)*. Highlight film. Mount Laurel, NJ: NFL Films Archives, 1969.

NFL Films, NFL Films Archives. *Winners (1970)*. Highlight film. Mount Laurel, NJ: NFL Films Archives, 1970.

NFL Films, NFL Films Archives. *Winning Ways (1987)*. Highlight film. Mount Laurel, NJ: NFL Films Archives, 1987.

NFL Films, NFL Films Archives. *Yes We Can! (1989)*. Highlight film. Mount Laurel, NJ: NFL Films Archives, 1989.

NFL Films, and NFL Network. *America's Game: The Super Bowl Champions. Pittsburgh Steelers Collection, Super Bowl IX*. Burbank: Warner Home Video, 2007.

NFL Films, and NFL Network. *America's Game: The Super Bowl Champions. Pittsburgh Steelers Collection, Super Bowl XIII*. Burbank: Warner Home Video, 2007.

NFL Films, and NFL Network. *America's Game: The Super Bowl Champions. Pittsburgh Steelers Collection, Super Bowl XIV*. Burbank: Warner Home Video, 2007.

Palmer, Pete, Ken Pullis, Sean Lahman, Tod Maher, Matthew Silverman, and Gary Gillette, eds. *The ESPN Pro Football Encyclopedia*. 2nd ed. New York: Sterling Publishing, 2007.

Piascik, Andy. *The Best Show in Football: The 1946–1955 Cleveland Browns, Pro Football's Greatest Dynasty*. Lanham: Taylor, 2010.

Pluto, Terry. *When All the World Was Browns Town*. New York: Simon and Schuster, 1997.

Pomerantz, Gary. *Their Life's Work: The Brotherhood of the 1970s Pittsburgh Steelers, Then and Now*. New York: Simon and Schuster, 2013.

Rabolvsky, Marty. *Super Bowl: Of Men, Myths, and Moments*. New York: Hawthorne, 1971.

Radakovich, Dan, and Lou Prato. *Bad Rad*. Pittsburgh: Moon Township, 2012.

Rhoden, William C. *Third and a Mile: The Trials and Triumphs of the Black Quarterback*. New York: ESPN, 2007.

Richmond, Peter. *Badasses: The Legend of Snake, Foo, Dr. Death, and John Madden's Oakland Raiders*. New York: Harper, 2010.

Rooney, Art, with Roy McHugh. *Ruanaidh: The Story of Art Rooney and His Clan*. Pittsburgh, 2008.

Rooney, Dan. *Allegheny City: A History of Pittsburgh's North Side*. Pittsburgh: University of Pittsburgh Press, 2013.

Rooney, Dan, as told to Andrew E. Masich and David F. Halaas. *Dan Rooney: My 75 Years with the Pittsburgh Steelers and the NFL*. New York: Da Capo, 2007.

Sports Illustrated Books. *Super Bowl Gold: 50 Years of the Big Game*. New York: Sports Illustrated Books, 2015.

Sporting News. *Complete Pro Football Draft Encyclopedia 2006: Best Picks, Biggest Busts, All 70 Years of the NFL Draft*. Sporting News, 2006.

Strother, Shelby. *NFL Top 40: The Greatest Pro Football Games Ever Played*. New York: Viking, 1988.

Tobias, Todd. *Charging through the AFL: Los Angeles and San Diego Chargers' Football in the 1960s*. Paducah: Turner, 2004.

Toker, Franklin. *Pittsburgh: A New Portrait*. Pittsburgh: University of Pittsburgh Press, 2009.

Toperoff, Sam. *Lost Sundays: A Season in the Life of Pittsburgh and the Steelers*. New York: Random House, 1989.

Veeck, Bill, and Ed Linn. *Veeck—as in Wreck: The Autobiography of Bill Veeck*. Chicago: University of Chicago Press, 2001.

Ward, Arch. *Frank Leahy and the Fighting Irish: The Story of Notre Dame Football*. New York: G. P. Putnam's Sons, 1944.

Whittingham, Richard. *Sunday's Heroes: NFL Legends Talk about the Times of Their Lives*. Chicago: Triumph, 2003.

INDEX

✦ ✦ ✦